THE GREAT WAR GENERALS

THE
GREAT WAR GENERALS

ON THE WESTERN FRONT
1914–18

ROBIN NEILLANDS

Robinson
LONDON

Robinson Publishing Ltd
7 Kensington Church Court
London W8 4SP

First published in the UK
by Robinson Publishing Ltd 1999

This paperback edition 1999

A copy of the British Library Cataloguing in Publication
Data for this title is available from the British Library

ISBN 1-84119-063-2

Printed and bound in the EC

10 9 8 7 6 5 4 3 2 1

CONTENTS

LIST OF MAPS

ACKNOWLEDGEMENTS

In an attempt to base the opinions in this book on a bedrock of fact I consulted a large number of Great War experts before starting on the first draft. I would therefore like to say 'thank you' to the many historians of that war who have read the text and made helpful suggestions. As far as I have been able to discover, there is no book like this one, which considers the Great War generals *as a group* and analyses the war on the Western Front through the eyes of the officers who had command there. The subject is exceedingly complex and I would not have been able to write about it without the generous help of the people listed below.

Thanks, therefore, to Colin Fox and my fellow students on Colin's Great War Studies course at Windsor in 1996–7. They ranged from a librarian at the Staff College to a man from the Commonwealth War Graves Commission – who gave us a fascinating lecture on the history and development of the war cemeteries – but all of them were interested in Great War studies and their enthusiasm fired mine. Thanks to Colin Lyle for his comments on the 'Easterners'. For their company on a ten-day walk down the Old Front Line from Dixmude to the Somme my thanks to John Gorringe, Peter and Terence Knee – whose father fought in many of the Great War battles we discussed on the way – Peter Chambers, Keith Howell and David Elliott. Keith kindly read the drafts of the book from the 'interested layman' angle and saved me from many errors. So too did Toby Buchan, my editor and stout supporter throughout the two years of this project. Thanks also to Terry Brown, my Royal Marine 'oppo' for over forty years, for his excellent maps.

A considerable debt of thanks is due to Jeffery Williams, author of *Byng of Vimy*. Also to Colonel Terry Cave of the Western Front Association, who read every chapter in draft and made suggestions I have not hesitated to adopt. John Hussey, that peerless expert on the Great War, and Colonel Mike Crawshaw of the *British Army Review*, read the early drafts, picked up a quantity of errors and pointed them out without knocking me down. Any factual errors remaining are my fault, not theirs, and I am entirely responsible for the opinions this book contains.

Thanks also to Richard Timmins and Robin Prewett who, like Keith Howell, read the drafts from the 'interested layman' point of view, and helped me to keep it clear and simple, and relevant to the task in hand. When writing about the Great War it is all too easy to wander off the point into some arcane field of Great War studies; they kept me focused on the allegations concerning the generals, which is what this book is really about. Thanks also to Major-General Julian Thompson, CB, OBE, formerly of the Royal Marines and now of King's College, London, who read the penultimate draft and picked up errors that had crept back in.

Among historians, I am grateful to Peter Liddle of the Liddle Collection at the University of Leeds; to Dr John Bourne of the University of Birmingham; to Peter Simkins, Simon Robbins and Laurie Milner at the Imperial War Museum, London, especially for help with the Maxse Papers; and to Gary Sheffield of the Royal Military Academy, Sandhurst, who gave me much good advice. Thanks to Andrew Robertshaw of the National Army Museum, London, for his help with the Rawlinson Papers and for inviting me to lecture on the Great War generals at the National Army Museum, an offer that concentrated my mind most wonderfully. Thanks also to Dr A. J. Peacock, editor of *Gunfire*, for sending me back issues of his excellent magazine and permitting me to use them, and to Lieutenant-Colonel Sir John Baynes, Bt, for his views on General Sir Ivor Maxse.

In Canada my thanks go to Jack Jensen, an old friend and fellow history buff, who died of cancer before this book was completed but stopped the car on the way to hospital to post me some Canadian books I had asked him to find. Thanks to Canadian historian Donald Graves, who disagreed with most of my conclusions but helped me anyway and who, with his wife Diane, late of Holts' Tours, was tireless in checking out facts about the splendid Canadian Corps, and in finding photos of General Sir Arthur Currie. We also had a tremendous time in Ottawa, but that is another story. Thanks must also go to one of my regular helpers in that delightful country, Don Bowden of Daysland, Alberta, for his help in finding more information about Currie.

In the United States my thanks go to writer and military historian Byron Farwell, whose new book on the American Expeditionary Force, *Over There*, should appear at the same time as this one; I intend to be at the head of the queue to buy it. Thanks also to Jack Capell, for his views on infantry training, and to the staff at the Library of the US Military Academy, West Point.

In Australia, thanks to my old Royal Marine Commando 'oppo', Derek Lou Lucas of Chakola, New South Wales, and to Annie Yamasaki, who carried out some valuable research at the Australian War Memorial in Canberra and dug up some useful books and works of reference. In South Africa yet another Royal Marine, Joe Cartwright, did similar service, and for this and many years of friendship I am grateful.

Apart from their assistance and advice, the most encouraging contribution from all these people was their enthusiasm for the project itself. Clearly there is a need to set the record straight in the public mind, and get the truth about the Great War generals more widely understood. Why the various myths about their conduct and the war still persist is baffling, for many excellent writers and historians – Gary Sheffield, Paddy Griffiths, Robin Prior and Trevor Wilson, Shane Schreiber, Bill Rawling, and Peter Simkins, but most notably John Terraine – have been hammering away at these legends for years, yet still the notion that the generals were useless remains imprinted on people's imagination.

Whether reading this book will change their minds is hard to tell; I can only say that writing it changed mine. I have attempted to set the reasons for what happened on the Western Front into a relevant order, have written about them in a way I believe the general public, now largely untrained in military affairs, will be able to understand, and have asked them to relate the problems faced by the generals to their own experience – and to use their common sense.

I do believe that getting it right is important. The historian Lawrence James has said that 'History is to a nation what memory is to an individual. Just as an individual can suffer from 'false memory' syndrome, so there is a danger of the British nation being fed a false version of its recent past.' That sage comment was made about the British Empire, but it would apply with equal force to the events of the Great War. The people listed above know that much of what the public believe about the Great War generals is simply not true. I hope that our efforts to point that out will dent this popular perception.

Robin Neillands
1998

'Show me a general who has made no mistakes and you speak of a general who has seldom waged war.'

Marshal Turenne, 1641

THIS BOOK IS DEDICATED TO
JACK JENSEN
1933–1996
A MAN WHO LOVED BOOKS AND HISTORY

INTRODUCTION

*'To throw good money after bad is foolish. But to throw
away men's lives where there is no reasonable chance of
advantage is criminal. In the heat of battle mistakes in
command are inevitable and amply excusable. But the real
indictment of leadership arises when attacks that are
inherently vain are ordered merely because if they could
succeed they would be useful. For such manslaughter, whether
it springs from ignorance, a false conception of war, or a
want of moral courage, commanders should be held
accountable to the nation.'*

B. H. Liddell Hart, *History of the First World War* (1970)

To tell any story, a writer needs a point of view. This rule is especially relevant to a writer who, to mix a metaphor, is leaning over backwards to keep an open mind, and is vital when writing of an event of historical significance and considerable contention, like the Great War of 1914–1918. Thousands of books have been written about that war, and before producing another one a writer needs something to say.

This book is not an attempt to whitewash the Great War generals, or quarrel with other opinions, or write yet another 'mud-and-blood' account of the battles. The shelves groan under the weight of such books, many reaching, by whatever route, the same conclusion. The simple purpose of this book is to examine certain allegations levelled against the British* generals in the war of 1914–1918 and widely believed by the public at large.

The popular allegation made against these generals can be broadly summarised as follows:

---

* 'British' in this context should be taken to include commanders from the forces of the British Empire and Dominions, and not just British-born commanders of British troops. Currie, for instance, was a Canadian, and Monash an Australian.

'The British field commanders in the Great War were all incompetent and callous cavalry officers, living in châteaux well behind the
lines and speeding millions of hapless soldiers up to the front, there
to perish in fruitless attacks which were constantly repeated until the
end of the war.'

Put simply, this allegation maintains that *everything* that went wrong on the
Western Front during the Great War was entirely the fault of the generals.
To confirm that this is the widespread, popular opinion it is only necessary
to ask around among one's neighbours and friends or consult that popular
expert, the man or woman in the street. The question that then arises is, is it
true? Well, you, the reading public, are the jury and when the evidence has
been presented, you must decide.

The *only* purpose of this book is to examine that allegation. This is a rare
venture, though John Terraine should have demolished this accusation once
and for all with his excellent book *The Smoke and the Fire*, which appeared
in 1980. In general though, Great War histories fall into two broad schools.
There is the 'mud, rats and shellfire, view-from-the-trenches' kind, often
with lots of 'oral' personal accounts, and the academic overview variety,
which covers the entire war, takes in every theatre and delves deeply into the
archives. Both tell the reader *what* happened, often in considerable detail,
but not many explain *why* it happened, though Peter Simkins, Gary
Sheffield and many more have illuminated various aspects of the war in
great detail: even so, the general public remain unconvinced. This book
inches down the duckboards in the centre, to explain why a battle was
fought in a particular way or at a particular time and place, and to describe
the factors which influenced or inhibited the decisions and actions of the
generals.

My own opinion is that such decisions and actions are determined by two
main factors: the circumstances of the time, and the character of the
protagonist. Examining these two factors takes up much of this book.
The circumstances of the time dictate what must be done, the character of
the protagonist dictates how it is done. The bold man pushes on, the timid
man pulls back, the cautious man hesitates, and so on; in the end, much of
what happens comes down to character, something we know from our own
experience. I do not ask readers to accept my conclusions on this point, or
indeed on any point; I do ask them to use their common sense. I ask them to
accept that the facts set down here are accurate and as detailed as a general
work of this nature can permit. They have been carefully checked by people
in a position to know, and they tell a tale which I believe is true. But don't
take my word for it; study the facts and make up your own minds.

Great War studies, as a subject, is a battlefield of conflicting opinions,
where experts and academics and a multitude of buffs war to the knife over
the most arcane aspects of the struggle, and form their own armies to fight
those of a conflicting opinion. I have declined to join any such army, and I

do not ask the readers to join mine or take my word for what happened on the Western Front in the Great War. Just study the facts, and that should lead to a certain conclusion.

The first step was to set a standard, a level of expertise – a point of view, if you like – to establish the point at which culpability begins. After a great deal of thought, I settled on Liddell Hart's dictum, which seems to lay down the acceptable standard of performance citizens should demand from any general, though it must be recognised that war is not *easy* and errors are inevitable. A course of action that seems obvious to an academic historian writing seventy years later in the calm of his Oxbridge study may not have been so clear to a tired and worried officer amidst the frantic atmosphere of his headquarters in the middle of a Great War battle. Careful study of the detail in Liddell Hart's dictum will make what follows easier to understand, if not necessarily easier to accept.

Liddell Hart's general views on the war and the senior British commanders are not universally accepted, and it therefore seemed necessary to use a source of basic facts that was generally regarded as accurate, at least as far as the *facts* are concerned. The general consensus among military historians is that the relevant volumes of the British *History of the Great War: Military Operations France and Belgium*, a fourteen-volume work usually referred to as the Official History (OH), has its *facts* right in the majority of cases but is perhaps less sound in its *opinions*. I have therefore relied heavily on the OH, as well as on the Official Histories of the Australian, Canadian, and South African contingents, for my *facts*, but the *opinions* expressed here, unless attributed to someone else, can be put down to me.

The relevant facts have then been mustered in what I believe is a logical order. The contention that the Great War losses were entirely due to the stupidity of the generals is an easy one to make and an easy one to sustain, given a long succession of disasters. It becomes especially easy if the writer wishes to be economical with the facts, or chooses to present only those that sustain the argument. Those who go a little deeper soon discover that it is necessary to go deeper still, and it is difficult to prevent any analysis of the Great War descending from the few stark and well-known facts into a confusing welter of conflicting opinions.

It is therefore hardly surprising that objective views on the generals who fought the Great War are somewhat hard to come by. When, in the course of researching this work, I came across books entitled *British Butchers and Bunglers of the Great War*, or *The Life of Field Marshal Sir John French, First Earl of Ypres, KP, GCB, OM, GCVO, KCMG*, with every honour crammed on to the spine of the book – which was written by the Field Marshal's son – it was not hard to guess that whatever other merits these books might possess, objectivity was not among them.

There was also the matter of bias not simply in choosing to present a critical point of view, but in presenting facts and then drawing conclusions quite the opposite to those the evidence presented. In his *Haig's Command*,

Dennis Winter concludes his brief biography of Lientenant-General Sir Launcelot Kiggell, which lists his pre-Great War appointments as Commandant of the Staff College and Deputy Chief of the Imperial General Staff – a total of ten years on staff duties at the highest level – with the comment, 'It is hard to see why Haig chose such an inexperienced officer as his Chief of Staff,' which in turn leaves one wondering if some people ever read what they write. Kiggell may have been useless – that is a matter of *opinion* – but the *facts* suggest he was highly experienced. The argument that 'Those who can, do, and those who can't, teach' is one I can accept, but not one I expected to hear from a teacher.

The Great War is a complex subject, and I do not claim that the generals are blameless for what happened on the Western Front; I only suggest that they were not *entirely* to blame. But before I start to recount this tale readers might like to know what brought me to this subject and the point of view from which I am attempting to write this story . . . or 'where I am coming from', as my children put it.

I am not an academic nor a professional military historian. I claim no particular military expertise. My service career peaked at the dizzy heights of sergeant – though that *was* in the Royal Marines, and when writing this book I found my military experience useful since I served in the Commandos as a Vickers machine-gunner and mortarman, using weapons that a Great War soldier would have found familiar. In addition, having served in the ranks, I have, as we used to say, 'been buggered about by experts'. The fact that some officers, even some senior officers, are not all that bright, did not therefore come as a revelation.

I earn the bulk of my living as a journalist and travel writer, but for as long as I can remember I have read history. I have been reading military history for more than fifty years, and over the last fifteen years I have also written about it. The kind of history I write is usually described as 'popular', covering subjects as diverse as the Hundred Years War and D-Day, generals like Wellington and Gordon, and the stories of men in the Commandos, the Special Air Service or Special Forces, or in the 7th Armoured Division, and their battles, these last being mainly oral histories.

When asked to give a definition of 'popular history' I usually reply that it is the kind that attempts to entertain as well as inform, or is the kind written by people who are not professional historians, or – if provoked – that popular history is academic history with the boring bits left out. I would also define it as the kind of history which takes a popular belief and examines it carefully to see if that belief is valid. That the Great War generals were a group of callous, incompetent clowns is just such a popular belief.

Before embarking on this book, I had not made a close study of the Great War. My interest and knowledge was roughly the same as that of the bulk of the people who will read this book, and it is to that audience, interested, curious but not greatly informed, that I have addressed myself. This book is not aimed at the Great War buffs, or that group of people for whom the

Great War is an obsession, but squarely at the general public. Its target audience, therefore, are those people who, like myself, love history and enjoy finding out more about it. Like them, I have been on battlefield tours, and spent days roving the battlefields and cemeteries, from Dixmude to Verdun and the Argonne. I calculate that I have visited the Western Front more than a hundred times in the last thirty years, six times for this book alone, including a ten-day walk down the Old Front Line, from the North Sea to the Somme in the company of a group of potential readers – and most active critics.

Like them, I have read most of the popular books, from Macdonald and Middlebrook to Graves and Sassoon, from Terraine and Barnett to Henry Williamson and Sebastian Faulks. I have read the works of Alan Clark and Dennis Winter; books by people who side with the generals and by a rather greater number who loathe them. Like my intended readers, I have seen the videos and the films, watched the Great War documentaries, attended performances of *Journey's End* and *Oh What a Lovely War* – the play and the film – fallen about watching *Blackadder Goes Forth* and flinched at the executions in *Paths of Glory*. Like most of the public. I came out feeling that the Great War generals were useless.

Then, some years ago, it occurred to me that this could not be true. Not only is it highly unlikely that *all* the generals were useless – for there were thousands of them – but Britain and her allies did win the war. So I started to read a little more, and to delve somewhat deeper. I ransacked the shelves of the London Library, spent days at the Imperial War Museum and attended a symposium there, prowled the archives at the National Army Museum, toured half a hundred military museums, took a course in Great War studies with the splendid Colin Fox, consulted experts and historians in Britain, Canada, Newfoundland, Australia and the United States, and collected a vast catalogue of papers, which now spill from a dozen drawers and a stack of filing boxes. Eventually, I started to write this book.

Over the last three years the Great War has been fought out in my office. Now I too, need an armistice. I do not claim to have read every book, studied every paper and consulted every authority on the Great War, but I have done a great deal and I know a great deal more about it than I did three years ago. As a result, I do not believe that the popular view of the Great War generals is either right or fair.

Accusations should be proved, not just asserted. It seems to me now, as it did when the idea of this book first came to me, that to lay the bulk of the blame on the generals is at best simplistic. It may be that there were other reasons for the tragedies, débâcles and disasters of the Western Front; that the one-line reason for half a million British deaths and one and a half million wounded – *because the generals were incompetent and uncaring* – is not the entire story. Perhaps the cause was more complex, and perhaps a lot of what the public – people like me – have come to believe about the Great War and the senior British generals is simply myth. If so, it should be challenged, for some of these myths do great harm. It cannot, for instance, be a good thing that generations of children in Australia or Canada have been brought up to believe that their grandparents or great-grandparents were duped into dying for the British Empire while the British Tommies swilled tea in safety and the British generals drank champagne in their châteaux. It cannot be a good thing that a whole period in British history has become so distorted, and that the distortion goes on, repeating malignant accusations about honourable men, accusations that go uncontested or unexamined by the public at large.

This is a subject with few absolutes; it is possible to refute any example with another example, but I believe that the overall picture that comes out of this book differs from that which the general public currently believes, and is a much more accurate one. As a member of that general public, and neither a battlefield buff nor an academic, I am in a position to state that much with some confidence. To make this book accurate I have drawn fully and freely on the knowledge – and patience – of a large number of Great War historians and experts, whose help I have acknowledged elsewhere. I hope the result will justify their confidence, their belief that what this book says needed saying, and their kindness to me over the past three years. If not, the fault is entirely mine.

CHAPTER 1

THE BACKGROUND
TO THE WAR, 1871–1914

*'The Spring and Summer of 1914 were marked
in Europe by an exceptional tranquillity . . .'*

Winston S. Churchill, 1922

This is the story of twenty-four men who held high command during the Great War of 1914–18. These men were the generals who commanded corps and armies along the Western Front during those years, and were therefore largely responsible for the conduct and management of the battles that took place there. The majority of the commanders who feature in this story are British.

Over the last half-century these generals – and especially the British generals – have come to be regarded by the public at large – and especially by the British public – as a group of aristocratic, incompetent, callous cavalry officers, who spent the war in châteaux well behind the lines and sped millions of brave young men 'up the line to death', causing a loss from which the British nation has never fully recovered.

This book is not a history of the Great War or a biography of the general officers who fought it, though it contains strong elements from both disciplines. The only purpose of this book is *to examine the notion that the generals were incompetent and callous, and see if it has any validity*. It does not seek to whitewash the generals, prove a point, or grind an axe, but instead attempts to look at the war through the eyes of the men who were responsible for fighting it and see if posterity has treated them honestly, or even fairly. It is not an attempt to re-fight the First World War in detail or to provide an account of every engagement, though a good deal of detail is necessary in order to clarify what the generals were up against.

At this point it is important to add that among military historians and military experts – the two are not always the same – the popular view that the generals were both incompetent and callous is not widely held. John Terraine spoke up for the generals some years ago – and got a hostile reception – but over the years his views have achieved a wider acceptance while informed historical opinion has mellowed somewhat. A fair summation of present-day opinion, at least among those who have studied the Great War in detail, is that while some generals were incompetent and a large number mediocre, some were extremely good. It is generally conceded that the bulk of the generals were at least adequate, and that all of them faced a situation on the Western Front which made a war of attrition and its consequent heavy casualties inevitable.

It is only fair to add that not all informed opinion subscribes to that view. The generals are still under attack from many quarters and modern historians from countries of the old British Empire, especially in Australia and Canada, are particularly prone to taking a highly critical view of British generalship, comparing it unfavourably with that offered by their own commanders. Why they do this with such relish is open to question, but Donald Graves, for ten years a staff historian with the Directorate of History, Department of National Defence in Ottawa, puts the argument like this:

> As for what you term 'pommie-bashing' it all depends on your point of view. The fact is that we lost a lot of good men on the Western Front because of the incompetence of the British leadership and this is the reason why Currie and Monash were determined that if their men were to go into action they would do their utmost to give them a chance. This does not seem to have been the attitude of the British generals . . . particularly Haig. If despising incompetence and wishing to avoid needless sacrifice is 'pommie-bashing', so be it. (Letter to the author, May 1997.)

Donald Graves has been immensely helpful with this book, and his views deserve careful consideration. Nevertheless, as I said to him in Ottawa, I find it hard to accept that any general, even a British general, actually woke up in the morning and wrote, 'Memo to Self: Get 20,000 of our chaps killed today' on the message pad beside his bed.

Even in the former Dominions, however, a growing body of opinion inclines to the view that the British commanders, as a group, have been misjudged. It is now eighty years since the guns fell silent on the Western Front; perhaps it is time this group was treated with a little charity and a certain understanding.

'The point you make about the generals as a group seems to me to be fundamental. It is no good acquitting one or two generals of incompetence, since popular belief has always done this anyway, regarding Plumer, Monash, Currie or Rawlinson for example. The charge of incompetence stands against them *as a group* and it is as a group that they are in need of reassessment.' (Dr John Bourne, Department of History, University of Birmingham, in correspondence with the author.) It might be said that concentrating on the British generals is taking the narrow view, but the same is true for the British Army on the Western Front as a whole. Until the middle of 1916 the British were not 'major players' in the Great War, and that conflict 'should not be regarded as the Cavalry Club fighting on an 80–90 mile front from Picardy to Flanders'. (John Hussey, letter to the author, June 1997.) There is a tendency for the British, in particular, to regard the actions of the British generals as uniquely culpable, when in fact the same problems affected all the generals in all the armies, and produced similar, often equally costly, results.

If those who have studied the subject in detail are now less inclined to think the generals incompetent, public opinion in Britain, Australia, Canada and elsewhere, as I have said, still thinks otherwise. The public are encouraged in their views by writers who genuinely believe that these generals were both incompetent *and* callous, or persuaded to that opinion by a regular stream of articles, television documentaries, films and books written by the less well-informed – or the totally ignorant – or by jingoistic 'pommie-bashers' in the old Dominions, who are happy to profit by spreading this fiction, often in the cause of present-day national politics or in response to republican political pressure. Clearly, a great deal went wrong on the Western Front, and went wrong far too often. There is no smoke without fire, but laying *all* the blame on the generals to the exclusion of all other factors seems, at best, simplistic. No war has ever been fought without mistakes, and the particular fury with which the Great War generals have been savaged in the years since 1918 goes beyond the point of reason when all the motives for their actions have been taken into account.

There are also a few hard truths about war that ought to be grasped by the general reader at the start. The first and most important of these has been summed up succinctly by Major-General Eric Sixsmith: 'There can be no greater fallacy than to suppose that battles can be won painlessly. However brilliant the plan, in the end the soldier must advance, cost what it may, and destroy the enemy. When the enemy is prepared to fight, as the Germans always were, this means bloody battle and heavy casualties.' (*British Generalship in the Twentieth Century*, p. 176.)

This book will attempt to find out *why* things went awry on the Western Front, by examining the actions of the commanding generals in the battles for which they were responsible. It will also examine the background to their battles, the situation in which they found themselves, the orders they were given by their political masters and the problems with which they were faced as a result. These problems did not only lie across no man's land. The generals who fought on the Western Front were affected by actions taken behind their backs in the corridors of Westminster, or among the ranks of their allies, or in other theatres of war. The Great War – which did not become the 'First World War' until another conflict broke out in 1939 – was still a world war. This book's concentration on a small group of generals on a ninety-mile front should not obscure that fact, but to tell the tale such concentration is necessary. But the broader picture should still be borne in mind, and will be referred to from time to time.

The situation faced by the Great War generals was nothing if not complicated. Two things should not be forgotten, however. Firstly, by 1917, the British armies had become a formidable military machine, and swept all before them in the last months of 1918. Secondly, the British and French armies, with their allies *did win the war* . . . and largely under the command of those same generals the public and many historians are happy, or even eager, to denigrate today.

The British generals featured in this book are Lord Kitchener, who as Secretary of State for War and a field marshal on the active list, occupied a most unusual position in the first years of the war. Then comes Robertson, the Chief of the Imperial General Staff (CIGS) for much of the war and a stout supporter of Haig. Robertson never commanded an army, but did his best work fighting for the army against the politicians in Britain. There follow Field Marshal French, the first Commander-in-Chief of the British Expeditionary Force (BEF), Haig, his successor, then Smith-Dorrien, Allenby, Rawlinson, Byng, Plumer, Gough, Horne and Birdwood, all of whom commanded armies on the Western Front, and the devious Wilson, who did not command an army, but took over from Robertson as CIGS. To these are added two Dominion generals, Currie and Monash. These operated at a slightly lower level, commanding the Canadian and Australian Corps respectively, and have to be included not just for their considerable skills but because, as leaders of Dominion contingents, they held slightly unusual positions *vis-à-vis* the British High Command. It is worth pointing out that for much of the war these two splendid corps were ably commanded by British generals.

Since their actions or decisions bore heavily on the British Western Front commanders, four French generals, Foch, Joffre, Nivelle, and Pétain have also been included. To add some transatlantic balance, the American Expeditionary Force commander, General 'Black Jack' Pershing, appears in the latter stages of the book. Finally, since it seemed impossible to ignore the German generals who opposed the Allied armies on the Western Front, four of the German commanders, Moltke, Falkenhayn, Hindenburg and Ludendorff, have also been included.

These are the 'principal characters', or main players, the ones who exercised higher command, but there are many other generals who appeared at corps or divisional level, or who flared briefly across the front, men like the British general and master of tactics Sir Ivor Maxse, and the German artillery expert, Colonel Bruchmüller, or tank commanders, then relatively junior, like Fuller and Elles. All these will have parts to play, as will a number of politicians, among them Asquith and Winston Churchill (who commanded a battalion on the Western Front for some months, but did his best war work as Minister of Munitions in 1917–18), President Woodrow Wilson of the USA, Prime Minister Clemenceau of France and – above all –

David Lloyd George, Prime Minister of Great Britain from 1916. Then too there were 'political generals' like Sir Henry Wilson, who is one of the most interesting characters in the whole Great War saga. The concentration, however, remains on the British front-line generals who served on the Western Front.

A great deal of the background for this book has been culled from the various biographies of these generals and the autobiographies they left behind, but quite early in the research phase it became clear that these memoirs should be viewed with a certain amount of caution. One such indication came from a note from Brigadier-General Sir James Edmonds pasted inside a copy of Major General Sir Charles Callwell's biography of Field Marshal Sir Henry Wilson in the library of the Staff College at Camberley:

> There are many misleading statements and important omissions from this book which is based on Wilson's diaries. Wilson was not tempted away from the Intelligence Division in 1897 by the offer of a brigade-majorship. He was 'fired' by the DMI [Director of Military Intelligence] General Sir John Ardagh for being below the standard of education desirable in a staff officer.
>
> The story of how Wilson left GHQ to become liaison officer at French Grand HQ suppresses the truth. I happened to witness his dismissal. At St Omer in 1914 I was billeted – with Earl Percy and Sir Ernest Swinton, the Father of Tanks – in the house next door to the C-in-C's in the Rue St Bertin. Just before Christmas as I came out I found Sir John French and Wilson in altercation on the pavement; Henry was begging not to be sent home and French, purple in the face with rage shouted 'You have done me down every time, you impostor, and you shall not stay here; you can go and live with the d——d French you are so fond of.'
>
> In 1917 when Wilson was liaison officer with the French, the French Government requested that he might be removed as a persona non grata, and he went home . . .

Attached to this pretty tale was a handwritten letter from Brigadier-General Sir James Edmonds – the Official Historian of the Great War on the Western Front – addressed to the librarian and suggesting that a copy of this missive should be pasted into every copy of Callwell's book. 'You may or may not like to paste the enclosed note into Callwell's life of Wilson, I have sent a copy to the War Office library. Wilson's death makes me think that the punishments for ill doing are awarded on this earth.'

The letter is dated 13 May 1955. The events it alleges happened *forty years* before and Henry Wilson had been murdered by the IRA in 1922 . . . yet Edmonds was still bearing some kind of grudge. While this may be an extreme example of animosity among the generals, too much can be made of what they said about the events of the Great War, and what they said about each other.

To concentrate on just twenty-four men in a war which involved, for Britain alone, the actions of millions and the deaths of hundreds of thousands may seem strange, but there are good reasons for focusing on such a small number. Just to begin with, no book on these Great War generals *as a group* has yet been written, yet it is *as a group* that they are condemned. Biographies and autobiographies abound, but their subjects' individual skills and merits are concealed in the general condemnation. It is worth adding that even those writers who condemn the generals *as a group* will admit that some of them – Byng, Plumer, Currie, Monash, Rawlinson (after the Somme, at least) – were at least much better than the rest . . . and so the complications begin. These men were a 'group' in another sense, for many, though not all of them, shared similar military backgrounds and a great deal of common campaign experience, in South Africa, the Sudan, India and on the North-West Frontier, and followed each other into the Staff College and thence to the command of brigades, divisions and the various Home Commands, the military organisations in the United Kingdom. They were an elite group in a small army and they knew each other well – which is not to say that they were all bosom friends.

The second reason for concentration on the High Command is because the Great War is nothing if not complicated. The wise writer therefore states a case at the beginning of the book, defines the limits of the enquiry and the objectives of the task, and sticks to that aim until the case is proved – or at least presented. At the risk of labouring the point, this book aims to take an objective look at the actions of the generals *in the context of their times* and see if their present odious reputation is justified. It would be equally possible to follow that well-worn track which condemns them out of hand as callous and incompetent. The evidence for such a verdict is there, if selectivity with the facts and economy with the truth are permitted, but is that fair? I think not, and if the writing of history is not fair it is not history but propaganda or polemic. The first step towards a fair summation is to put the relevant facts – all the relevant facts – in context, though there is endless scope for argument as to what facts are relevant and what facts are not.

The third reason for concentrating on a small group of generals is because this book seeks to explain not just *what* happened – which all the histories do in their various ways – but *why*, which most books neglect to cover at all, or do so only in the most superficial manner. To understand and explain *why* takes a great deal of time and a certain amount of detail, a point that can best be illustrated by a well-known example.

It is generally agreed by all the histories that at 07.30 hours on 1 July 1916, the British infantry rose from their trenches and, having formed up in long lines, advanced across no man's land towards the German front line on the Somme. Within minutes, the soldiers were brought under heavy enemy machine-gun, mortar and artillery fire and the attack was halted along most of the Somme front. By the end of that day the British Army had suffered 57,470 casualties, of which nearly 20,000 were killed, the greatest disaster to British arms since Hastings. Most of the histories add that the 'extended-line' formation adopted by the British infantry on that fateful day contributed in no small measure to the disaster which followed.

Why did this happen? The extended-line formation, generally though by no means universally adopted by the British infantry on 1 July, certainly contributed to the casualty list by providing a wonderful target for the German machine-gunners, so why was it used? That troops advancing in the open were vulnerable to aimed fire from modern weapons had been obvious for years, most recently from the dreadful slaughter inflicted on the German troops assaulting the British infantry at Mons or Langemarck in 1914, or British troops attacking across open ground at Aubers Ridge or Loos in 1915, or against French troops attacking almost anywhere since the war began. Advancing against entrenched troops equipped with machine-guns was an invitation to disaster, so *why* did the British attempt it in July 1916?

An examination of the records reveals that it was hoped that the seven-day bombardment which preceded the infantry assault on the Somme would have destroyed the German defences and wiped out the defenders. There was also a theory, advanced in a pamphlet (*Training of Divisions for Offensive Action GHQ May 1916*), which held that when advancing to capture a trench 'a single line of men has usually failed, two lines of men have sometimes succeeded but usually failed, three lines of men have generally succeeded but sometimes failed and four lines of men have usually succeeded,' a statement that makes this author – a Vickers machine-gunner in his service days – tremble for the men so instructed. It was also generally believed by those in the High Command that the infantry of Field Marshal Kitchener's 'New Army' which were employed in quantity here for the first time, were not well-enough trained to cope with more sophisticated 'fire-and-movement' tactics over open ground.

If they were not well-enough trained, *why not*? These were the men – hundreds of thousands of them – who had volunteered in response to Kitchener's famous appeal in August 1914. By the time they went 'over the top' on 1 July 1916, most of them had been in the Army for almost two years. What had they been doing in all that time, if they had not learned the basics of infantry tactics? Surely it cannot be seriously maintained that they were incapable of absorbing such training? They were all volunteers, the pick of the nation: many were artisans, clerks, professional men, adequately or even well educated; all were keen to learn. Their leaders, the junior officers, were middle-class, public-school men, often with university educations – these men were not ignorant fools.

Besides, it is not necessary to be a rocket scientist to learn the basics of 'fire and movement', a tactic which consists of one part of the attacking force firing on the objective to keep the enemy's head down while the other rushes towards it. Then that part of the force – the 'movement' group – goes to ground and provides covering fire while the 'fire' group comes up. This process is repeated until the attackers are close enough to the enemy position to form an assault line and carry the enemy position with the bayonet. Anyone who has understood the last three sentences already has a grasp of 'fire and movement.' All that is then required is practice, and such refinements as left- and right-flanking attacks can be added in the process. In fairness, however, it has to be pointed out that the fire-and-movement tactics of 1914 depended on bolt-action rifles for the 'fire' part, and the tactic did not become fully effective until the Lewis light machine-gun was brought into service as a platoon weapon later in the war.

Fire and movement was the basic infantry tactic of the British Army in 1914 (see the Official History, Volume I, p. 9), and remains the basic tactic of the British Army in 1998, so *why* was it abandoned for the Somme assault in 1916? The ground the British troops had to cross to reach the German line is undulating, and had been torn up by a week of constant bombardment. If the enemy defences had not been quelled by the artillery, if even one machine-gun remained in action, then fire and movement was the way to advance. Adequate cover existed for an attack by fire and movement on 1 July, but that method was not generally employed. *Why not*?

Well, we shall see why not when we come to the relevant chapter, discovering in the process that by no means every battalion advanced in extended line, and also that the casualty figures were not so heavily affected by the formation adopted as is generally supposed. There were many other reasons for the tragedy that took place on 1 July, but this example indicates that even examining the simple question of the tactical assault formation in just one battle soon leads the writer to a deeper analysis.

The same holds true for most other aspects of the war, and it is therefore very necessary to beware of absolutes when studying or writing about any aspect of this conflict. For every rule there is an exception, for every example proving one point it is possible to find another proving the contrary. The situation on the Western Front was nothing if not complicated, and asking the question 'Why?' after each action has been 'explained' often only adds to the mystery.

For all these reasons, therefore, and for others which will become apparent, this book elects to stick within the narrow parameters described above. There is little unanimity about the Great War among historians, and the opportunities for debate and disagreement are endless, but when the entire situation is laid before them the public at large may realise that the generals were not all, and not entirely, to blame for what happened on the Western Front.

To describe the story in full is not easy. The research for this book revealed the existence of a great many shuttered minds in people who will not believe anything other than their current notion, that most of the Great War senior commanders were butchers and the British generals were the worst of the lot. It might therefore be as well to ventilate some of the most common accusations levelled against the generals in the hope that that those people whose minds are already made up will take time to consider another possibility – that they might just be mistaken. An airing of these accusations will also allow the story to progress to more important matters.

As an example, let us take the ever-popular belief that the generals were all aristocratic cavalry officers, who lived in châteaux well behind the lines and sent millions of young men, either duped working-class heroes or sensitive middle-class poets, to their deaths.

Military historian Dr John Bourne makes several good points about this deep-seated cavalry officer accusation:

> First of all, it seems to me that the supposed connection between being a cavalry officer and being stupid or anti-technology needs to be proved rather than simply asserted and there seems to be no foundation for either charge.
>
> During the Great War, below the level of Army Commander there was no domination by the Cavalry. Haig did not favour cavalrymen for his closest appointments; his closest appointments, Kiggell, Davidson, Butler, were all infantrymen and Charteris was a Sapper. At Corps level he favoured Gunners. Of the 47 men who commanded divisions on the Western Front only nine began their careers in the cavalry and the majority of these commanded cavalry divisions. Of the eighteen men commanding Corps on the Western Front on 11 November 1918 only one, Kavanagh, was unambiguously a cavalryman and he was commanding the Cavalry Corps! The others, with one exception, were all infantrymen, and the exception was an ambiguous cavalryman, De Lisle, who began his military career in the Durham Light Infantry and spent ten years with them before transferring to the 5th Dragoon Guards. (Correspondence with the author.)

Quite apart from being generally untrue, as Dr Bourne demonstrates, this 'aristocratic-cavalry-officer' accusation reveals a great deal of ignorance about the British Army. If a general is competent in command his birth or antecedents, or his arm of service, have nothing to do with his ability to exercise that function, though having connections in high or influential places has never been a bar to progress, in any walk of life, at any time. Lord Louis Mountbatten, head of Combined Operations in the Second World War, then Supreme Commander, South-East Asia, later the last Viceroy of India, and later still First Sea Lord, was a grandson of Queen Victoria and a cousin of Queen Elizabeth II – a true-blue aristocrat, and he did not care who knew it. But no one denies that he was competent, or threw his birth in his face. That said, social connections were certainly useful at the start of the century. They are still useful in the present day.

None of the Great War generals was as well-connected as Mountbatten.

Most of them were professional soldiers, of limited means: indeed Field Marshal Sir William, Robertson's father was a village postmaster and Wully, as he was invariably known, began life in the ranks, making his way to the top by sheer ability. Haig's family was originally 'in trade' and sold whisky, but had long since joined the squirearchy . . . And so on . . . for the truth is that the 'aristocrat' *canard*, though totally unimportant, can easily be dismissed. These men were mainly middle-class, professional soldiers, not the idle rich or the effete aristocracy. Byng was the younger son of an earl, it is true, and Rawlinson a baronet, but it is generally admitted that both were good soldiers.

Then there is the 'cavalry' accusation. Quite why it was wrong to have served in a cavalry regiment is never made clear, except by a vague indication that the horse-obsessed cavalry officer could not handle infantry, and again there is a whiff of inverted snobbery in the charge. This allegation is not generally true either, for the Western Front commanders were *not* all cavalrymen. French, Haig, Robertson, Allenby, Byng and Gough had originally served in the cavalry, but Smith-Dorrien, Plumer and Rawlinson were infantrymen, Horne was a Gunner and Kitchener a Sapper. Monash and Currie were not professional soldiers at all; Monash had been a lawyer before the war and Currie was an estate agent – a realtor.

Colonel Terry Cave of the Western Front Association has rightly described this cavalry-generals allegation as another 'hoary old myth', and backs up Dr Bourne's point with some statistics for the entire war:

> Out of a total of 223 British divisional commanders (major-generals) during the Great War, 148 were from the infantry, 35 from the cavalry, 29 from the artillery and 11 were Sappers. Of the 52 corps commanders (lieutenant-generals) 29 were infantry, 13 cavalry, 8 artillery and 2 Sappers.
>
> On the eve of the war in 1914 in the 8 Home Commands 6 of the GOCs [General Officers Commanding] were infantry, 1 artillery and 1 cavalry (Lieutenant-General Haig, at Aldershot). The 6 Regular divisions of the BEF were commanded by 5 infantry officers and one artillery officer – Allenby's cavalry division was only formed on mobilisation. Of the 14 Territorial Force divisions 10 of the commanders were infantry, 3 came from the artillery and 1 from the cavalry. Finally the Army Council posts – CIGS, Adjutant-General, Quartermaster-General and MGO [Master-General of the Ordnance] were filled by 2 infantry officers, an artillery officer and a Sapper.

These are the facts, willingly provided by two people in a position to know, but open to any careful enquiry, and yet many writers and historians *still* maintain that the bulk of the senior officers in the British Army at the time came from the cavalry, implying that this in some way contributed to the tragedy. The first point is simply not true. Even if it were, the allegation is at best contentious.

A number of writers have attempted to blur these facts by stating that, given the relatively small size of the cavalry arm, the number of corps and army commanders from the cavalry was disproportionate. It so happens that different parts of the British Army tend to provide the senior officers at different times. In the late nineteenth century it was the Sappers – men like Gordon and Kitchener. In more recent years the Gunners and the Green-jackets have made it to the top, and at the end of the twentieth century service in the SAS appears to be the path to high command. In the early 1900s it was the cavalry's turn, but the main catalyst for progression to high command was ability . . . and passing the Staff College course.

As for living in châteaux behind the lines, where else would a commanding general of the time have had his headquarters? Can it be seriously maintained that an officer commanding half a million or a million men should scribble out his orders on a notebook while kneeling in a front-line trench? Does the chief executive of any large peacetime enterprise operate on the factory floor or in the typing pool? What a wealth of ignorance, wilful stupidity and class hatred lies behind that accusation!

The business of a general is command and control, and the two are interlinked. Without control – and we shall hear more of this – the general is unable to command. He therefore needs access to telephones and radios, to roads and airfields, to up-to-date, reliable information. He needs space, somewhere he can plan and work, brief his officers, consider the enemy's reactions and command his troops. To help him in that command function he needs a trained staff – and there will be more on this as well – Intelligence officers, Gunners, Sappers and logistical experts, communications people, a map room, plus the usual clerks and signallers, drivers, cooks and batmen. As the war progressed, the problems of the staff and of command became more complicated and a large staff became a necessity.

A general had to meet his subordinate commanders and allies and cope with a constant stream of visitors ranging from politicians to journalists. In the case of Field Marshal Haig, who was frequently hauled back to London by his political or military masters, his headquarters had to be close to the Channel ports. All these requirements called for a suitably sited headquarters, well beyond the range of the enemy guns, handy for touring the front and with first-class communication facilities. Anyone who has been part of a large organisation, military or civilian, will understand why this was so; will understand, too, why that particular accusation falls before the considerations brought on by using common sense.

The army commanders did *not* spend all their time in their main headquarters. They and their staff officers were out every day, visiting the front, and all of them used an advanced HQ, closer to the front, when a battle was in progress. Haig, having several armies to command, made good use of a headquarters train. Moreover, generals could be killed as easily as other men. Seventy-eight British generals were lost their lives during the War either in action, or as a result of wounds or on active service; a further one hundred and forty-six were wounded. As for strife between the front-line soldier and the staff, that has been going on for centuries – an encounter between Harry Hotspur and a staff officer makes a telling scene in Shakespeare's *Henry IV* – but most of the Great War staff officers had served in battalions at the front, or had fought other battles in their time.

In 1917, the wife of the much-maligned Brigadier-General John Charteris, Haig's Chief of Intelligence, asked him to describe his day. His account began with meeting Haig at 0900 hours – having been up for two hours already – and went on until 2200 that night. This thirteen-hour stint, he told her is, 'A fairly typical day when I am not out to see one or other of the armies . . .' and when there was no battle in progress Charteris and the other staff officers worked twelve hours, or longer, day after day, often for weeks on end without weekend breaks or Sundays off. Just consider what a general and his staff had to do, and living behind the lines will be seen as highly sensible; no amount of sneering from the ill-informed should obscure that fact.

Commanders also shared the dangers of the men at the front. The notion that the generals stayed well out of artillery range has been refuted by Frank Davies and Graham Maddox in their excellent and well-documented book *Bloody Red Tabs*, which records the fate of 224 British general officers who were killed or wounded during the Great War. Ten were killed or wounded in the first five months of the war and no fewer than seventy-six in 1918; eight generals were wounded twice. Three died in one day during the Battle of Loos in 1915. The idea that the generals lurked in safety well behind the lines is refuted by these figures.

One final slander that might be nailed here is that these generals sent 'millions' of men to their deaths on the Western Front. This lie is due either to a wilful distortion of the facts or an inability to distinguish between 'casualty' figures and figures giving the number of men killed. One reasonably accurate total for the number of British soldiers killed while serving in the British Army on the Western Front between 1914 and 1918 is 510,821 (*General Annual Reports of the British Army, 1913–1919*, 1921), though Great War statistics have to be treated with care for they seem to vary with the source, and are in any case subject to revision and speculation. Charles Carrington, for example, gives a figure of 611, 654 British and Empire dead on the Western Front, with 488,000 of the dead coming from the UK. These figures are quoted in his book and are culled from official statistics (*Soldier From the Wars Returning*, p. 306), but the Official History gives the following figures for war dead:

British Isles (Army): 704,803 (Western Front 564,715)
Dominion of Canada: 56,639
Commonwealth of Australia: 59,330

Dominion of New Zealand: 16,302
Union of South Africa: 6,606
Newfoundland: 1,204
Colonies: 49,763
India: 62,056

The variations probably arise from the fact that the final 'killed' figure includes those who died of wounds, many of them weeks or months after being hit. Since the figures were compiled at different times and used different datum points, the cumulative totals vary. However, the point being made is that none of the Western Front figures given approach even 1 million dead. Critics are asked to note that I do not say 'only' 510,821 or 'only' 488,000, or 'only' 564,715 – I am not dismissing these totals; every death is one too many and a great sadness to comrades, family and friends.

However, since 'millions' must imply at least 2 million, the accepted figure of 'millions' of British dead on the Western Front amounts to an error of 300 per cent, yet 'millions' is the figure frequently quoted and therefore widely believed by the general public. When I gave the true figures to a group of educated, well-travelled people on a walk down the Western Front in 1997, they flatly refused to believe me. This popular error probably arises from the fact that a further 1,523,332 British soldiers were wounded on the Western Front, and these two figures have been added together to produce the general belief that *millions* of British soldiers were killed in France and Belgium. The same applies to other nations. Canada's *casualty* figure, for instance, is 207,000, but the actual number *killed* is much lower, and in any case seems to vary. The number of war dead recorded on the Canadian War Memorial on Vimy Ridge is 66,655, a figure quite literally written in stone and given in the supporting documentation . . . but the Canadian Official History (p. 548) gives a total figure of 59,544 . . . And so the confusion continues.

Percentages are another source of argument, not least in casualty figures for the Empire countries, where the number of killed and wounded may be related to the total population, or the total male population, or the number of men who enlisted, or who served overseas, or any other denominator that can inflate the percentage to suit a writer's argument. I do not intend to go down that road. If a woman loses her husband, or a mother her only son, or a child its father, the loss is 100 per cent, and the grief is the same in every home, whatever the nation concerned.

Regarding the generals, the figures are revealing. According to Dr Bourne, 1,193 British generals served on the Western Front during the Great War (letter to the author 1997), and in *Bloody Red Tabs* Davies and Maddocks record that a total of 232 general officers were killed, wounded or captured during the Great War. Not all of these were lost on the Western Front, but most of them were, and even if those lost at Gallipoli, in the Middle East and elsewhere are excluded from the total, the number of general officer casualties on the Western Front still exceeds 200. Exact figures are difficult to arrive at, for a general might be wounded at the front and die of his wounds in Britain much later; others died in training or, like Lord Kitchener, from enemy action at sea; nevertheless, some 200, say about 17 per cent of the generals serving on the Western Front, became casualties there – an average of one general lost to enemy action every week of the war. At the Battle of Loos in 1915, eight generals were lost in nine days: Major-Generals Capper, Thesiger and Wing, and Brigadier-Generals Nickells and Wormald were killed. Brigadier-Generals Pollard and Pereira were wounded and Brigadier-General Bruce was captured. These facts tend to refute the allegation that the generals stayed in safety at châteaux well behind the lines.

The preceding paragraphs should not, however, lead anyone to assume that this book refutes all the accusations against the generals. They had part of the responsibility for the conduct of the war and they must share part of the blame, but it is necessary to remove the meretricious claptrap before looking closely at what actually went wrong, and *why*.

Even in a book restricted to the relatively narrow study of the commanding generals on the Western Front, it is necessary to explain some of the background to the war, to describe how and why it began and what steps, political, military and technological, led to the way it in which was conducted. This will help to explain why the war could not be ended, as it otherwise should have been, when overall victory on the battlefield became too costly. Much of this pre-1914 background to the conflict serves as a historical constant throughout the war, and from time to time the reader will be reminded of some background factor that affects the situation on the battlefield under discussion. The choice of where to start explaining the background to the Great War is wide, but the obvious place to begin is with the politics.

The spark which ignited the conflagration of the Great War was the assassination of the Archduke Franz Ferdinand, heir to the Austro–Hungarian Empire, at Sarajevo in the Balkans on 28 June 1914, but the fuel for the conflict was provided by the defeat of France by Prussia in the war of 1870–1, which altered the balance of power and the political geography of Western Europe. The defeat of France enabled Prince Otto von Bismarck, the Prussian Chancellor, by uniting Prussia with the other Germanic states, to form the first German Empire, a creation fuelled by a growing and well-educated population, proud of, even arrogant about, its military prowess, advancing towards European primacy in science, industrial power (especially in the new industries of steel and chemicals), and chafing at its confinement within Europe. The defeat of 1871 cost France a colossal sum in reparations and the provinces of Alsace and Lorraine. It also fired the French with the desire for *revanche* – revenge – and a determination to get these two provinces back.

It is one of the tragic ironies of the Great War that one of the prime causes of its rapid escalation into a Continentwide struggle was a system of alliances designed to prevent a European war occurring at all. With the exception of France, which hoped to regain Alsace and Lorraine, and Austria-Hungary, which wanted to crush the Serbs, no nation went to war in 1914 seeking territorial gains – though such aims did come later. Bismarck had no wish to expand the German Empire outside Europe and after 1871 he devoted his life to consolidating the territories already gained, while surrounding his creation with a network of alliances. The first of these came as early as 1872, a year after the Franco-Prussian War, when he linked Germany with Austria-Hungary and Russia in what became known as the 'League of the Three Emperors'. This alliance was fragile, for Austria-Hungary and Russia were in dispute over the Balkans where both hoped for territorial gains when the Ottoman (Turkish) Empire, the 'Sick Man of Europe', finally died. In 1882 Bismarck negotiated another pact with Austria-Hungary and Italy, in what became known as the Triple Alliance. This was renewed in 1887, so that by the time he left office in 1890, Bismarck believed that he had constructed a firm basis for German security.

This belief proved false. After the war broke out, Italy first declared herself neutral and then joined the other major European power block, the Triple Entente, a group consisting of France, Russia and Great Britain, though the latter had made no firm commitment to any alliance until after the war began. Germany and Austria-Hungary were then joined by Turkey – the Ottoman Empire – in a group which became known collectively as the Central Powers. The origin of all these alliances can be traced back to fear of Imperial Germany, or Germany's fear of 'encirclement', a hemming-in of her frontiers by the alliance of France and Russia.

Germany remained peaceful, if wary of France, until 1888, when a new Kaiser, Wilhelm II, succeeded his father to the Imperial throne. Wilhelm dismissed Bismarck and swiftly managed to upset the fragile political equilibrium of Europe. An erratic, unstable man, his sabre-rattling unnerved a number of the surrounding nations, with the result that in 1891 republican France formed an alliance with Tsarist Russia, an alliance concluded by the Franco-Russian Pact of 1893, which in turn developed into a military 'Convention' by which each nation promised to aid the other if attacked. This convention stated quite openly that the potential aggressor was Imperial Germany.

These alliances, pacts and conventions, all of which aimed to establish a 'balance of power' and so keep the peace, were to escalate a small Balkan crisis into a major war in the summer of 1914. The Great War involved a number of nations which entered the fight without 'war aims' or any particular national reason, except to honour their commitment to an alliance. This lack of 'war aims' was to bedevil the search for peace later on in the war, a fact which has to be noted now, for it will affect the situation later.

If one man is to be blamed for bringing that war about, however, then that man is Kaiser Wilhem II. Wilhelm was not a particularly bad man, but his personal faults were magnified by his position. Half the things he said he did not mean, and most of his actions were eventually regretted, but not everyone appreciated that the Kaiser's bite was almost all bark. His high-handedness and conceit, his suspicion, jealousy and arrogance, his bluster-ing speeches, his threats, kept tension high on the Continent of Europe and fuelled other nations' moves to arm and form alliances. A typical example of the Kaiser's behaviour is provided by his remarks during a visit to the King of the Belgians in 1904:

> I told him I could not be played with. In the case of a European War, whoever was not for me, was against me. As a soldier I belonged to the school of Frederick the Great, to the school of Napoleon. As the Seven Years War began with the invasion of Saxony, and the latter had always, with lightning speed, forestalled his enemies, so should I, in the event of Belgium not being on my side, be actuated by strategical considerations only. (Paul M. Kennedy [ed.], *The War Plans of the Great Powers, 1979*.)

Such delusions of grandeur apart, the Kaiser's conviction that Germany had a divine right to paramountcy in Europe and to what his Chancellor Bülow called 'a place in the sun', was shared by many of the ruling Prussian class. The Germans were not content with dominance in Europe, with having the greatest army in the world and a growing industrial base, and they made the mistake of upsetting everyone at once. The Kaiser upset France by his interference in Morocco in 1905, a country then under French control. He did it again with the 'Agadir Incident' in 1911, when the German gunboat *Panther* was dispatched to Morocco on his orders in yet another attempt to intervene in French affairs. In 1896 he sent what became known as the 'Kruger Telegram' to President Paul Kruger of the Transvaal, congratulat-ing him on repelling the Jameson Raid and assuring the Boers of German support in the event of a war with Great Britain. When that war came he supported the Boer republics – as did many other European nations – and he expanded and modernised the High Seas Fleet, in spite of warnings that the British regarded this as a hostile act. All this, with the accompanying bluster, made the Kaiser an embarrassment to his politicians and a constant worry to the rest of Europe.

If Wilhelm II was aware of the disquiet he caused, he did not care, and though he was occasionally contrite he was never apologetic. 'We Hohen-zollerns [the Imperial House of Prussia] are the bailiffs of God,' he told his fellow European sovereigns, and with this conviction in his mind, any action taken by other countries to protect themselves from his loudly declared ambitions only fed his paranoia. The problem was that even those who regarded the Kaiser as a buffoon had to face the fact that Germany was the greatest and most modern military power in Europe, a nation of 66 million people, a major industrial power that was also a militaristic, Prussian-Junker-dominated society, perpetually preparing for war.

In such circumstances smaller countries like France – with a population in 1914 of 37 million – clearly needed allies. Some bilateral treaties seemed only sensible, but the Franco-Russian Pact was regarded by the Kaiser not as a legitimate response to his provocation but as 'encirclement', a deliberate threat to the security of Germany. The German generals, who occupied high positions in the government and in German society, agreed with the Kaiser on this point. They were convinced that the French would one day attempt to take back Alsace and Lorraine while their Russian allies stabbed Germany in the back; in 1912 the German Chief of Staff (effectively the Army C-in-C), General Helmuth von Moltke, declared that 'War is inevitable, and the sooner the better.' So the tensions mounted and the prospect of war grew nearer.

The Kaiser's conviction that a conspiracy was being prepared against Germany grew stronger when his detested uncle, King Edward VII of Great Britain, made a state visit to France in 1904 and, by sheer charm, defused several hundred years of Anglo-French rivalry and the more recent upset caused by the clash of the two countries' interests at Fashoda in the Sudan. This visit sparked off the talks that led to the 'Entente Cordiale' of 1904. Three years later, in 1907, the British Foreign Secretary, Sir Edward Grey, negotiated the Anglo-Russian Convention, which ended decades of dispute between the two countries over India. Both of these agreements were actually concluded to resolve issues raised by Britain's imperial expansion, and the latter did not in fact become a full member of the Franco-Russian alliance, but these moves were watched with apprehension by the Kaiser and added to his conviction that Germany was threatened with 'encirclement'.

German apprehension was further increased in 1906, when the French and British began 'conversations' on military matters, which among other things discussed the possibility of Britain coming to the aid of France in the event of a European war. These meetings had been fuelled on the British side by the Kaiser's declared intention of enlarging the German High Seas Fleet into a world-wide striking force, an intention which the British regarded, correctly, as a direct threat to the position of the Royal Navy as the world's leading naval power.

Britain needed a large navy to protect her huge merchant fleet and defend her maritime empire; Germany had very few colonies – another source of German envy – so why should the Kaiser expand his fleet unless with the aim of challenging the Royal Navy? This worrying belief was confirmed when the Germans began to widen the Kiel Canal so that it could be used to move the largest German Dreadnoughts – the new breed of heavy-gunned iron clad battleships – from the Baltic to the North Sea. The British promptly began to modernise and expand their fleet, and came to an agreement with the French whereby the latter took charge of naval security in the

Mediterranean while the Royal Navy guaranteed the security of the French Channel ports. Again, the Kaiser saw this not as a response to his own actions, but as another unprovoked threat to Germany.

Britain was also concerned to maintain the 'balance of power' in Europe, and in particular to maintain the neutrality of Belgium, something which had been guaranteed by all the major European powers – France, Prussia, Austria, Russia and Britain – by the Treaty of London in 1839. Germany, the heir to Prussia, had accepted that neutrality after 1871 and maintained the guarantee. There were, inevitably, other reasons for the British support of Belgium. Nations are not so altruistic that they fight wars only over matters of principle or to guarantee the territory of other nations. Quite apart from the demands upon national honour made by this commitment to Belgian neutrality, Britain would not permit a large, hostile, and expansionist power like Germany to gain possession of ports on the Channel coast, close to the English shore.

This was undoubtedly a possibility, for Belgian neutrality was under threat. While these various alliances were being established at the end of the nineteenth century, Germany was preparing a war plan to combat the problems of 'encirclement', a scheme masterminded by the then Chief of the German Imperial Staff, General Count Alfred von Schlieffen. Schlieffen believed that in the event of war – and he regarded war as inevitable – Germany would have to fight on two fronts, in the west against France and in the east against Russia.

His plan was based on the theory that, thanks to her well-developed network of modern rail communications and the fact that she possessed the strategic advantage of interior lines of communication, it would be possible for Germany to fall on France in great force and defeat her *before* the vast but obsolescent Russian Army could be mobilised and move to help. With France defeated, the full might of the German Army would then turn on Russia to win a second victory. Given the size and professional skill of the German Army, which stood at around 850,000 men by 1914 and could be rapidly expanded by the recall of reserves, and the construction of railways, which spanned Germany from the Ardennes to the Oder, this plan was feasible.

The Schlieffen Plan required that the bulk of the German Army should be massed in the west and on the right wing, to sweep into France from the north-east – through Luxembourg and *Belgium* – and, hooking round west of Paris would hustle the French Army up against its own fixed defences along the Franco-German border. The French had their own plan, the well-honed Plan XVII, which dictated a thrust east into Germany immediately on the outbreak of war with every man, horse and gun. The effect of the Schlieffen Plan, however, would be like that of a swinging door, catching the French from behind as they surged east to the Rhine. This strategy would require great speed and mobility – as well as the violation of Belgian neutrality – and contained two snags. The first was that speed and mobility were not adequately available in the marching armies of 1914 with their largely horse-drawn transport. The second snag was that invading Belgium would bring Great Britain and her empire into the war.

The Schlieffen Plan passed through various drafts but was finally adopted in 1905. The French Plan XVII will be discussed later, but it was the Schlieffen Plan which escalated the war, for it dictated that Germany must mobilise and strike *first*, to defeat France *in six weeks*, before the Russian armies could take the field. Within a few years the broad details of the Schlieffen Plan were known abroad, not least when Schlieffen published an article criticising his successor, Moltke, for tinkering with the plan, mainly by reducing slightly the forces committed to the right wing. When Schlieffen died in 1912, his dying words were said to be, 'Remember, keep the right wing strong.'

With matters so delicately poised in the west and east, it is time to look at the situation developing in Germany's principal European ally, Austria-Hungary. By the start of the twentieth century, the Austro–Hungarian Empire was beginning to crumble, but although the cracks were there the structure generally appeared solid. The exception lay in the ever-turbulent Balkans, and in particular with Serbia, an independent state outside the Austro–Hungarian Balkan hegemony.

However, a large number of ethnic Serbs lived within the Austro–Hungarian Empire, especially in the newly annexed provinces of Bosnia and Herzegovina which Austria-Hungary had taken over in 1908. These 'ethnic Serbs' wished to join those provinces with Serbia to create a 'Greater Serbia' – an aim that is still being energetically pursued at the end of the twentieth century – and were agitating for their freedom with demonstrations and acts of terrorism inside Austria-Hungary. A further complication was that Tsarist Russia, which always regarded herself as the ultimate protector of Slav interests in the Balkans, had offered guarantees of support to Serbia in the event of Austro-Hungarian intervention. If, for any reason, Serbia and the Austro-Hungarian Empire came to blows, Russia would not stay on the sidelines.

That reason was supplied on 28 June 1914, by a young Bosnian Serb student, Gavrilo Princip, when he fired two shots at the Austrian heir, the Archduke Franz Ferdinand, who was making a state visit to Sarajevo, the capital of Bosnia. The shots killed the Archduke and his morganatic wife and started a war that would kill over 9, 000,000 people (some estimates say 13,000,000) in the next four years. The majority of these people died a long way from the battlefields of the Western Front, but from the moment those shots were fired in Sarajevo, that interlocking network of Continental pacts and alliances began to exert its deadly effect.

It has been claimed that if Austria-Hungary had simply invaded Serbia on the day after the assassination, the conflict would never have spread outside the Balkans. However, weeks were to pass before any military action was taken, weeks in which each side mustered allies and spread the war. The process conjures up the mental image of locks on some great, iron-bound chest, the tumblers of each lock turning, one after the other, to unleash the full force of total war. The process began slowly, then speeded up as more agreements, treaties, pacts and 'conversations' were recalled and invoked and the armies began to mobilise. No one really wanted war, and a few of the more far-sighted statesmen could visualise just how traumatic a European conflict would be, but the tensions of the last decades were forcing the nations on to a path that led directly to the battlefield. Among the public, however, the prospect of war was popular. In Berlin and Paris, Vienna and London, cheering crowds took to the streets, applauding the first columns of marching troops, encouraging the reservists hurrying to the depots.

Austria-Hungary began the process, by issuing demands to Serbia for the prompt investigation of the assassination and punishment of the assassins, demands couched in language that no sovereign nation could accept. This was the entire purpose of the Austrian note, to make demands that Serbia was sure to reject and so provide the excuse for a war in which Austria-Hungary could absorb Serbia and thereby stamp out nascent Balkan independence once and for all. The Serbs duly appealed to the Tsar, and Russia murmured warningly that she would protect Serbia's interests if Austria's demands went too far. This threat in turn required Austria to call in her mighty German ally, and on 5 July, a week after the assassination, Germany assured Austria of her 'faithful support' in the event of war . . . a 'blank cheque' of assistance if Austria found herself drawn into a war with Russia.

Thus encouraged, on 23 July, Austria-Hungary issued her final ultimatum to Serbia, ordering the latter to stamp on the people demanding independence for the Austrian Serbs and requiring Serbia to admit Austrian officials to supervise the investigations into the murder of the Archduke. Serbia's reply, even according to Kaiser Wilhelm, was so conciliatory that it 'dissipated any cause for war', and the German Emperor then departed on his yacht, the *Hohenzollern*, for his annual summer cruise in the North Sea, leaving peace in his wake. His departure was premature. On 26 July the Austrians rejected the Serb response. On 28 July Austria-Hungary declared war on Serbia and sent ships up the Danube to bombard Belgrade.

On that day Russia took the next step in the escalation by mobilising her forces on the Austrian frontier, which was then on Russia's southern border. This order to mobilise had the effect of both alerting and alarming the German General Staff, whose entire strategy was based on the theory that Russia would still be mobilising her forces while her western ally, France, was crushed. If the Schlieffen Plan was to be implemented successfully, the Russians must not be given time to mobilise. Austria then mobilised her forces along the Russian frontier, and on 31 July both she and Russia ordered total mobilisation. On that day also Germany entered the fray. The Kaiser had hurried back from his cruise and the German government, their eyes on the clock and the calendar, ordered Russia to halt the drift to war and demobilise again, within twelve hours This ultimatum was ignored by the Russians. On 1 August, therefore, Germany ordered general mobilisation with the intention of declaring war on Russia at 1700 hours that afternoon and implementing the Schlieffen Plan.

At this moment the Kaiser got cold feet. He knew that if he declared war on Russia, France would strike at Germany's western frontiers. Plan XVII, the French plan for an attack on Germany, where it was well known, required that the bulk of the French Army be flung across the German frontier at once. The Franco-Russian Pact and France's own interests obliged her to follow that strategy. If the war began, therefore, the Kaiser would be faced with a war on two fronts, the ultimate result of 'encirclement'.

There was, however, a possible way out. In a telegram from London, the German Ambassador to Britain declared that the British Foreign Secretary, Sir Edward Grey, was offering to mediate in the Balkan dispute and keep France out of the war . . . or so it seemed. Hours ticked away while the German government attempted to find out what Sir Edward was actually proposing and General von Moltke paced his office, waiting for the order to implement the Schlieffen Plan.

Snatching at any way to avoid the war he had done so much to bring about, Kaiser Wilhelm told Moltke that since the British could keep France out of the fighting, Germany could turn all her might against Russia. 'All we have to do,' he told his Army Chief of Staff, 'is march the whole of our forces against Russia.' Moltke was aghast and rejected this proposal forthwith. 'It cannot be done,' he told the Kaiser bluntly. 'A plan prepared and rehearsed over many years cannot be dismantled in a few hours and if we do as Your Majesty proposes we will send nothing more than an armed mob against Russia.'

General von Moltke was being economical with the truth. Germany could have used her interior lines and her first-rate railway network to move her armies east, but the Schlieffen Plan dictated that France was the main enemy and that the vital railway junctions in Luxembourg must be seized within hours of a declaration of war. Moltke pleaded with the Kaiser for permission to proceed, but Wilhelm clung on frantically to what shreds remained of a peaceful solution. Europe held its breath as the hours ticked away.

Then, at 2300 hours that night, 1 August, a telegram from the German Ambassador in London revealed exactly what Sir Edward Grey was proposing. It transpired that the Foreign Secretary had offered to keep France neutral if Germany promised not to go to war with *either France or Russia*, while a solution was sought to the conflict between Austria and Serbia. It was, however, too late for that. The Russians were already mobilising and refused to stop. The Kaiser read the telegram several times before showing it to Moltke; then, with the words 'Now you can do what you like,' he walked from the room. Moltke went to the telephone and, within a few minutes, the telegrams ordering the German Army to advance on Luxembourg and Belgium were going out, and the troops were starting to march. Slowly, but with gathering speed, the peace of Europe began to unravel.

On Saturday, 1 August, Germany declared war on Russia, and Belgium mobilised her army. At 0800 hours on 1 August the French Commander-in-Chief, General Joffre, went to the Minister of War and asked permission to begin a general mobilisation of France's reserves at midnight. The order for 'general mobilisation' was handed over at 1530 hours and sent out to post offices all over France by the 1600 hours post. France also replied to a telegram which Britain had sent to France and Germany, asking if they would respect the neutrality of Belgium in the event of hostilities. The French replied that they would; Germany prevaricated, knowing that by then her advance brigades were already in Luxembourg and on or over the Belgian frontier.

Britain had not yet declared her intentions, and the French were frantic for some sign of British commitment, believing, or rather choosing to believe, that those military 'conversations' between the two staffs amounted to a firm commitment on the part of Britain to deploy a 160,000-strong British Expeditionary Force on the French left flank, immediately on the outbreak of war. Britain had made *plans* for such a deployment but had made no *commitment* to do so, but the French were masters at stretching any agreement as far, or further, than it would willingly go. They were to demonstrate that capability frequently over the next few years.

On Sunday, 2 August, Herr von Below-Saleske, the German Ambassador in Brussels presented an ultimatum to the Belgian Government, demanding unopposed passage through Belgium for the German Army. On Monday Belgium rejected this ultimatum, declaring that she would defend every foot of her territory against any invader. All eyes now turned to Britain, which was still deliberating on a course of action, and by now under considerable pressure from both France and Germany. The former wanted Britain to enter the war on the side of France. Germany wanted Britain to stay neutral, declaring that she should not intervene in a Continental quarrel over 'a scrap of paper' – their term for the treaty which guaranteed Belgian neutrality.

Britain had already assured the French that the Royal Navy would protect France's shipping and her Channel ports against aggression, but the French wanted the *immediate* commitment of a British Expeditionary Force, and muttered about British perfidy when the troops did not arrive. Rather more pressing on Britain's honour was the neutrality of Belgium, to which France and Germany also stood guarantee. Albert I, King of the Belgians, sent an appeal to King George V, begging for assistance in the event of a German invasion, and Sir Edward Grey stated plainly that 'The preservation of the neutrality of Belgium might be an important factor in determining our attitude,' advising the German Ambassador that his country could not count on Britain standing aside 'in all circumstances', a plain hint that German actions in Belgium would be crucial. For the moment, however, Grey did not request any movement towards France by troops of the British Army.

In declining to support the immediate dispatch of the BEF, Sir Edward was simply reflecting the fact that many people in Britain – and in the British Government – could see no reason why their country should become involved in a Continental war when her own interests were not directly threatened. The French chose to regard this hesitation as perfidious; many British people regarded it as common sense. There remained the matter of Belgium, for what happened there would be decisive.

On 3 August, the day on which Belgium rejected the German ultimatum, Germany declared war on France. On the following day Germany informed the Belgian Government that her troops would march through Belgium, using force if necessary, to carry out a move they considered essential to their security, further declaring, falsely, that French troops had already violated Belgian neutrality and her aircraft had bombed German towns. The German move into Belgium had in fact already begun, and within hours German troops were shooting Belgian civilians for allegedly barring their progress through that country. The British Government therefore ordered general mobilisation and recalled all reservists to the Colours before sending an ultimatum to Germany, requiring an assurance that the latter would respect Belgian neutrality. Germany refused to give such an assurance and accordingly, at 2300 hours on 4 August 1914, Britain declared war on Germany.

The Prime Minister, Herbert Asquith, explained Britain's reasons for entering the war in a conversation with the American Ambassador, W.H. Page, on the afternoon of 4 August.

> The neutrality of Belgium is assured by Treaty. Germany is a signatory power to that Treaty and it is upon such compacts as this that civilisation rests. If we give them up or permit them to be violated what becomes of civilisation? Ordered society differs from mere force only by such solemn agreements or compacts. But now Germany has violated the neutrality of Belgium. That means bad faith. It means the end of Belgian independence and it will not stop with Belgium. Next will come Holland and after Holland, Denmark. This very morning the Swedish Minister informed me that Germany had made overtures to Sweden to come in on Germany's side. The whole plan is thus clear; this one great military power means to annex Belgium, Holland and the Scandinavian States and to subjugate France.
>
> Britain would be for ever contemptible if it should sit by and see this Treaty violated, and its position would be gone if Germany were

thus permitted to dominate Europe. If Germany's position on Belgian neutrality is not reversed, Britain will declare war.

'I came away,' said the American Ambassador later, 'with a stunned sense of the impending ruin of half the world.'

CHAPTER 2

THE WESTERN ARMIES,
AUGUST 1914

*'Did they remember, when they went headlong into a War
like this, that they were without an Army, and without any
preparation to equip one?'*

Field Marshal the Earl Kitchener of Khartoum,
address to Members of Parliament, 2 June 1916

The first volume of the British *History of the Great War: Military
Operations, France and Belgium*, sums up the British Expeditionary
Force – or BEF – that went to France in August 1914, with two lines of
ringing praise, instantly followed by a significant qualification. 'In every
respect,' it says 'the Expeditionary Force of 1914 was the best-trained, best-
organised and best-equipped British Army that ever went forth to war.'
Except, this entry continues,

> In the matter of co-operation between aeroplanes and artillery and
> the use of machine-guns . . . in heavy guns and howitzers, high-
> explosive shells, trench mortars, hand grenades, and much of the
> subsidiary material required for trench warfare it was almost totally
> deficient. Further, no steps had been taken to instruct the Army in
> knowledge of the probable theatre of war or of the German
> Army . . .

When all those qualifications are taken into account it is hard to justify the
opening sentence, let alone the conclusion that, these details apart, the
British Army would stand comparison with the German Army, and was
certainly no worse than any other army. In reality, the first statement is only
partly true. The British Army was superbly trained and was an excellent
army *for its size*, but it was not equipped or prepared in any way for a large-
scale Continental war, let alone for the trench warfare that followed the
initial engagements along the Belgian frontier with France and on the Aisne.

It was also very small, certainly when compared with the large armies being deployed on the Continent, and this factor alone was to influence British actions, and British relations with the French, in the months and years ahead. The Empire forces, from Canada, Australia, India, New Zealand and South Africa, that came to join the BEF in France, though very welcome and of superb quality, were likewise small and unprepared for modern war. Nor did the problems stop there. The arms and munitions industry necessary to support a large army in a worldwide struggle was also non-existent; in the event it took years to develop an armaments industry large enough to cope with the growing demands from the front line and to equip the new divisions being hurriedly raised at home.

None of this was the fault of the British generals or the Army High Command. The British Government of the day were simply not prepared to spend the money or recruit the numbers that would produce a large army equipped for a major Continental campaign, or to develop a munitions industry that could support the expenditure of ammunition in the quantities that a European war would demand. In this the Government had the support of the British electorate, which would not then – as it will not now – willingly spend large sums on armaments for the services in time of peace. It may be alleged that there is no reason why any British Government, pre-1914, should have catered for a large army equipped for a Continental war, when defence of the Empire was the prime consideration for Britain's armed forces – hence the emphasis on the Royal Navy. That allegation neglects the political activity and increasing tension in Continental Europe, the growing threat from Germany to almost all the European nations, including Britain, and the 'conversations' which took place between Britain and France. The danger to the British Empire no longer lay along the North-West Frontier of India, but just to the east of the Rhine.

The Official History makes the point that, because the British Army was very small, the British contribution in the early months of the war was not of military significance, at least from the point of view of numbers, and that the BEF could only maintain itself in the field by close co-operation with the French. Here, buried in that official text, lie some of the major problems that were to inhibit the actions of the British generals in the first years of the Great War: small numbers: a shortage of heavy guns: a shortage of ammunition for guns of every calibre; and the need, indeed the order, to co-operate fully with the French.

Where the BEF made its mark was by being committed to the fight at all, and through the fact that its initial deployment on the western flank of the French Fifth Army in 1914 placed it directly in the path of General Alexander von Kluck's army as it swept round the French left wing. To this we might add the fighting ability of the British soldier, of every arm, in the early engagements at Mons and Le Cateau. Useful though those actions were, the BEF only played a small, albeit useful, part in the early fighting – notably at First and Second Ypres in 1914 and 1915 – and was not able to do more until its numbers and artillery been substantially increased. For the first two years of the war, Britain's contribution to the war against Germany was extremely small.

Before proceeding any further it would be as well to look at the four principal armies that fought on the Western Front from the outset – British, French, Belgian and German – as well as the Russian Army, to examine the main elements of these armies, the infantry, cavalry, artillery, command and logistics, and to see how they compared in size and combat effectiveness. There is no need to do this in any great detail, for the discrepancies and differences are obvious, but it is necessary to appreciate some of the deep-seated problems – such as the lack of reliable communications – which were to handicap the actions of the battlefield commanders.

To put the British Expeditionary Force of 1914 in perspective, we have go back a few decades to the Cardwell reforms of the 1870s, when the British Army made a final break with the army that had been formed during the Napoleonic Wars and which had suffered so much in the Crimea in the 1850s. Until the 1860s the British Army was trapped in a Wellingtonian time-warp, but technology, in the shape of heavy guns and rifled weapons, was changing all that. An influential and far-sighted British officer, General Sir Garnet Wolseley, saw as much when he visited the Union forces during the American Civil War. Wolseley joined the Union Army during the Antietam campaign of 1862 and was immediately struck by the sheer size of the volunteer Union armies, in which more than 3 million men took the field, and by the vast logistical and communications network such large armies required.

A few years later, another British officer, Herbert Kitchener, spent time with the French Army during the Franco-Prussian War of 1870–1. During that brief campaign he saw large European armies in the field, and observed how the Prussian Army was able to call back its reserves for service and soar in weeks to a strength of nearly a million men. In 1870, the British Army had a ration strength of around 200,000, no reserves at all . . . and an empire to protect.

Change, however, was already in hand. In 1868, Sir Edward Cardwell became Secretary of State for War. Although a Liberal and a pacifist, Cardwell saw that Britain needed a modern army, and above all a good one. In his efforts to achieve this end Cardwell found a few allies, like Wolseley, but was otherwise resisted every step of the way by the British military establishment and in particular by the Commander-in-Chief of the Army, Field Marshal HRH the Duke of Cambridge, a cousin of Her Majesty Queen Victoria. He met equally strong opposition from the army rank and file.

Cardwell abolished the purchase of commissions and promotion, and introduced a policy of 'get on or get out' under which officers could only spend a certain number of years in one rank; then they must either gain promotion or leave the service. He also began to abolish the numbered regiment system and established instead the concept of two-battalion, territorially linked infantry regiments which his successor as Secretary for War, Hugh Childers, had in place by 1881. To create reserves Cardwell introduced 'short service', a twelve-year term of enlistment under which most men served seven years with the Colours and then spent five on the Reserve, where they were liable to instant recall to their regiments in the event of mobilisation. This improved the number and quality of the recruits – since volunteers could now see that they need not serve in the army for life – and provided the country with a small reserve of trained soldiers. Cardwell also improved pay, education, weaponry, especially artillery, and barrack facilities. Between 1868 and 1874 Cardwell – and Childers in the 1880s – dragged the British Regular Army into a shape that it still retained in 1914.

However, the army still needed a general staff to plan and direct strategic military operations, though further reform had to await another hand. The next major leap forward came after the South African War of 1899–1902. A committee chaired by Lord Esher in 1903 proposed a new War Office structure and a general staff. The implementation and development of these proposals took a good deal of time and effort, however, and was mainly due to the efforts of Esher and, from 1905, of R.B. (later Lord) Haldane, a Scots lawyer who became Secretary of State for War in December 1905, and who had the help of a rising cavalry officer, Major-General Douglas Haig, then Director of Military Training at the War Office.

The British Army had learned some harsh lessons at the hands of the Boers, and put some of them, like marksmanship and a grasp of fieldcraft and minor tactics, into immediate effect. British soldiers spent a great deal of time on the rifle range and became good shots, capable of developing a heavy weight of accurate rifle fire. However, the generals had not done well in South Africa, the staff work was frequently deplorable, and the Reserve system had not provided enough troops to contain the situation on the veld. The army needed a complete overhaul at the higher level and Haldane set out to provide one.

The post of Commander-in-Chief of the British Army had been abolished in 1904 and replaced by an Army Council, composed of four senior army officers and two civilians, the Financial Member and the Civil Member, and chaired by another civilian, the Secretary of State for War. The C-in-C's former function of overseeing the efficiency of troops was vested in a new post, the Inspector-General of the Forces, and the officer holding that post became directly responsible to the Army Council.

The next step was to set up a general staff. The Army already had a Staff College at Camberley, where officers of field rank (that is, from major upwards) were trained in staff duties – organisation, transport, intelligence, logistics – but the 'General Staff' to command and control the army was a new function, established by an Army Order on 12 September 1906. Haldane charged the General Staff with organising the land forces of the Empire into a form that could cater adequately for emergencies anywhere in the Empire, as in South Africa, but could also, if need be, fight a European war. The head of the General Staff, later the 'Chief of the Imperial General Staff' (CIGS), after the Dominion governments became involved in the Empire's defence, became the head of the army and principal adviser to the Secretary of State for War.

Haldane built on the Cardwell system and created a United Kingdom army based around an 'Expeditionary Force' of six regular infantry divisions and a cavalry division. Each infantry division consisted of three brigades and each brigade contained four infantry battalions, as well as brigade and divisional troops. By 1914, each infantry battalion also contained two Maxim machine-guns but was currently re-equipping with the excellent Vickers medium machine-gun (MMG) which the British Army would retain for the next fifty years. Each infantry division had a ration strength of 18,000 men, made up of 12,000 infantry and 4,000 artillerymen, the latter manning 54 18-pounder field guns, 18 4.5-inch howitzers and 4 60-pounders, on a scale of 76 guns per division. The 60-pounders were withdrawn into the heavy artillery reserve in 1915. The other 2,000 men were signallers, Sappers, Royal Army Medical Corps (RAMC) doctors and orderlies, wagon drivers and transport staff, farriers, clerks and storemen. A cavalry division comprised four brigades, each of three regiments (a cavalry regiment is roughly the same as an infantry battalion), plus transport and Royal Horse Artillery (RHA) elements. Cavalry divisions were much smaller than infantry divisions, mustering around 9,000 men, armed with rifles, swords and lances as well as two medium machine-guns per regiment; the RHA batteries were equipped with 13-pounder field guns.

The units, infantry and cavalry, were drawn from 'First Line' troops, and at full strength the 'Expeditionary Force' mustered around 100,000 men. A further 60,000 men formed the supporting elements – signals, pioneers, gunners, medical services, engineers. This amounted to the bulk of the army in the United Kingdom, eighty-one battalions in 1914. There were another seventy-six infantry battalions, plus artillery and cavalry units, stationed in British bases abroad, but in 1914 the entire British Army worldwide did not amount to more than eleven Regular divisions, about the same as the army of Serbia.

It will be seen that, even after all the changes and improvements of the late nineteenth and early twentieth centuries, the British Army, by its size alone, was not ready to fight a European war, but this fact concealed another problem. The age-old conflict between *teeth* – fighting troops – and *tail* – support and supply – has never been resolved, and was as strongly fought as ever in the years before 1914. An army cannot function or fight for very long unless it has a continuous supply of ammunition, food, equipment and reinforcements. In so far as the British Army had these assets in 1914, it had them only in relation to its size at that date.

It has to be stressed, yet again, that the British Army was *small*. In 1914 the French and German Armies could be numbered in millions, for each had over *4 million* soldiers, Regular or Reservist, trained, equipped, and ready for battle. On the day war broke out Britain's Regular Army comprised 247, 432 men of all ranks, of which 79,000 were in India. The number of ex-Regular Reservists totalled 145,350. The 'Second Line', Territorials and Special Reserve, totalled 270,859. The Territorial Force (TF), which, apart from infantry, provided fourteen yeomanry brigades, was not fully equipped with the latest weapons, and there was no capacity in the munitions industry of 1914 for those immediate increases in production that could swiftly re-equip them and still provide for the hundreds of thousands of civilians now flocking to the Colours. This shortage of military supplies applied at every level and to every item, boots, clothing, webbing, barracks, even buttons, as well as to rifles and bayonets. The facilities – indeed, the factories – needed to remedy these deficits simply did not exist. In September 1914 men able to turn up for training with their own boots and greatcoat were paid 10 shillings by a grateful government.

Quality, not quantity, was the hallmark of the British Army. The men were all volunteers for, unlike the Continental powers, Britain did not have conscription; the bulk of the British population had no knowledge of arms and had no wish to learn. The Army, if admired, was not a popular way of life. Private soldiers enlisted for a twelve-year engagement and although many signed on for a further term, the majority went on to the Reserve list after seven years and hoped they would not be called out again. Some 60 per cent of the men who went to France with the BEF in 1914 were ex-Regulars, recalled to the Colours from the Reserve . . . and when the call came they went willingly.

Having organised his Expeditionary Force, Haldane then turned his attention to forming that 'Second Line' reserve, a Territorial Force of infantry, cavalry and artillery units, organised into fourteen divisions, each commanded by a Regular Army general. This 'Territorial Army' was designed for home defence, but it was capable, if the men volunteered and after perhaps six months of training, of deployment overseas in support of the Expeditionary Force. Haldane did not envisage the Expeditionary Force simply in terms of a European war; his idea was to create a highly professional army that could be shipped to any part of the world where British interests were threatened, not just across the Channel.

And so we move on to 1914. The cream of the British Army on the outbreak of war was its infantry, well-trained, adequately equipped profes-sional soldiers, men skilled in the use of their much-loved Short Magazine Lee-Enfield .303 rifle, the famous SMLE. Each battalion also contained a Maxim or Vickers medium machine-gun section of two guns (in 1914 most of them were Maxims), but the task of manning the weapons was not popular; the gun was heavy, the tripod alone weighing 50 pounds, the task of setting up the barrel inside the water-jacket before firing was time-consum-ing, and the job of cleaning the weapon after use was not a task the men looked for. (The author recalls many weary hours spent servicing and cleaning the Vickers MMG.) Among the military, views on the usefulness of MMGs varied. A substantial number of officers considered that a scale of two per battalion was adequate, and while many officers saw how useful machine-guns might be, it was not until the outbreak of war that the Army grasped just how deadly this complicated weapon could be in the defensive role. The British troops also lacked hand grenades and a mortar to provide high-angle fire and close support. Mortars were useful for trench warfare and assaulting an enemy in prepared positions; neither situation had yet appeared before a British army in the field with sufficient frequency to require the acquisition of such weapons.

Many of the soldiers had gained battle experience in Britain's colonial wars, in South Africa or on the North-West Frontier, where they had been shot at and had become used to the sound of guns. The infantry were mustered into territorially based regiments, and bore famous names like the Royal Sussex, the Cameron Highlanders, the Royal Dublin Fusiliers, units drawn from every corner and county of the kingdom. Most of these regiments, following the Haldane reforms, had two Regular battalions and a linked Territorial Force battalion of part-time volunteers. Even the cavalry, though their regimental names tended not to reflect territorial links, were generally affiliated to specific areas of Great Britain, as were the yeomanry, the Territorial cavalry units.

The artillery was well-trained and efficient, but small and short of shells and it lacked heavy howitzers and heavy guns. The Royal Regiment of Artillery was divided into field artillery, which supported the infantry, horse artillery to support the cavalry, and garrison artillery, which served heavy guns set in forts and for coastal defence in peacetime, but was soon deployed in France manning the heavier guns and howitzers. Royal Field Artillery batteries were an integral part of each infantry division, and although the machine-gun has captured the popular imagination as the main weapon on the Western Front battlefields, the Great War was primarily an artillery war. It is a fact that far the greater proportion of casualties on that front were caused by shellfire.

Cavalry was a declining arm in 1914, though many senior officers, and especially those with a cavalry background, were most reluctant to admit that fact. Cavalry had dominated battlefields for nine centuries, but its day was over, killed off by the aeroplane, which rapidly took over the cavalry reconnaissance role, and by the magazine rifle and the machine-gun which could produce, at a considerable range, a volume of fire sufficient to chop down any *arme blanche* cavalry charge made in the good old style, knee-to-knee with lance and sabre. The plain truth was that since the 1850s, with the introduction of the reliable, rifled percussion musket, the role of the cavalry had been reduced to that of mounted infantry, and would remain that way until some geneticist invented a bullet-proof horse.

The British cavalry carried the standard Short Magazine Lee-Enfield

(SMLE) .303 rifle, were proficient in its use and were ready and willing to dismount and go into action on foot, a skill they owed largely, though not entirely, to General Sir Horace Smith-Dorrien who, following the experiences in South Africa during the Boer War, had insisted on cavalry units learning infantry tactics during his time in command at Aldershot. The cavalry regiments were not entirely obsolescent by 1914, however. They were useful for scouting and in harrying a retreating enemy, and horses still provided the only form of rapid off-road deployment. Cavalry came in useful during the 'open warfare' period at the start and end of the war and enjoyed a brief renaissance on other fronts. During General Allenby's campaigns against the Turks in 1917–18, cavalry units like the Australian Light Horse were deployed with useful effect, but on the Western Front it is fair to describe the cavalry role as 'limited' for much of the war.

The troopers were armed with lance, sword and the standard infantry rifle, with Vickers supplied on the infantry battalion scale of two machine-guns per regiment – a cavalry regiment being the equivalent of an infantry battalion – while the Royal Horse Artillery attached to each cavalry division to provide support manned twenty-four 13-pounder field guns per division. Garrison artillery had heavier guns of 60-pounder calibre and above, guns which were soon in action in France. Their high-explosive shells and plunging trajectory were to prove far more effective against trenches and fixed positions than the shrapnel shells and direct fire of the lighter guns deployed by the field and horse artillery. A battery of 60-pounders was attached to each infantry division. It soon became clear, however, that the British artillery needed more guns, of larger calibre, and with reliable fuses for the shells. It will also transpire that for at least the first eighteen months of the war, the Royal Artillery was chronically short of ammunition.

The two significant differences between the BEF and the French and German Armies were recruitment and size. France introduced peacetime conscription in 1871, after the débâcle of the Franco-Prussian War, and by 1914 was calling up her young men for three years' military training, after which they spent twenty years in various reserve classes. By mobilising front-line reservists, France could rapidly produce an army numbering in excess of 1 million men, and further reserve categories were available which could raise the number of soldiers to 3½ million or more. In 1914, the front-line forces of the French Republic and its colonies could muster sixty-two infantry divisions and ten cavalry divisions, roughly seven times that of the British Army in the United Kingdom.

There were, however, a number of snags with this vast army. The first was the matter of doctrine. After the defeat of 1871 the French Army had pondered long and hard upon the problem of finding a method which would guarantee success on the battlefield when the struggle with Germany began again. These studies went on for years and led to the abandonment of any thought of defence, or any training in defensive fighting. The offensive was the thing, as in the glory days of the Emperor Napoleon, and all-out attack, *l'attaque à outrance*, dominated military thinking throughout the French officer corps in the years before 1914. The principal advocate of the *attaque à outrance* was Colonel de Grandmaison, Chief of the Troisième Bureau (Operations Branch) of the French General Staff, aided by the Chief of the École de Guerre, Colonel Ferdinand Foch.

The French soldiers of 1914 wore clothing which reflected this 'First Empire' doctrine, from the red pantaloons worn by many of the infantry to the helmets, breastplates and plumes of the cavalry, who carried a short-range carbine as well as sword and lance. A more serious anomaly was the matter of artillery. With the exception of the famous 75-mm field gun, the 'Soixante-Quinze', most of the French artillery was obsolete and, as with the BEF, there was a shortage of heavy guns and high-explosive shells. On the other hand the French had plenty of the Soixante-Quinze, an adequate supply of shrapnel shells, and such useful trench-fighting tools as the hand grenade. Having a large army, France also had a large armaments and munitions industry, but otherwise the logistical back-up was small. Horses provided all the armies with mobility for much of the war, and died in tremendous numbers, but the internal-combustion engine was already in general use and motor transport became ever more important and effective as the war continued. However, in 1914 the French Army, like all the other armies, was a marching and horse-powered army, slow and ponderous in movement.

The Belgian Army was very small indeed, mustering no more than six infantry and a cavalry division in 1914, a force which, after a gallant defence of the frontier forts and Antwerp, spent much of the war on the extreme left of the Allied line, defending that small portion of Belgium which had not fallen into German hands.

There was also the Russian Army, the largest of all, with 114 infantry divisions and 36 cavalry divisions in 1914, an army counted in millions. Apart from being a drain on Britain's slender stock of artillery ammunition, Russian actions did not directly affect the BEF to any marked degree until March 1918, so apart from noting its vast size, the Tsar Nicholas II's Imperial Army can be put aside, at least for the moment. The Russian Army fought both Austrians and Germans on the Eastern Front where, as was not true of the west, the war was marked by movement, with advances and retreats of hundreds of miles. Mobile warfare was never absent in the east, and the German armies that fought there had a good grasp of open-warfare tactics when they came west in 1918 after Russia was forced out of the war.

And so to the enemy. The German Army of 1914 was a formidable, professional, fighting force, and remained so until almost the end of the war. In their eagerness to blame the failures of Allied attacks on the incompetence of the British High Command, many critics fail to give due credit to the fact that the generals were fighting the *German* Army, the product of a nation which had elevated militarism into a creed.

The effective combination of numbers, professionalism, equipment, the skill of its staff and senior officers, the quality of its NCOs and the fighting ability of the ordinary German soldier, gave this fighting force a great advantage on the battlefield. It is fair to say that the German Army outclassed every other army on the Western Front for much of the war . . . but at a price. For this was the kind of army that only a society dedicated to militarism and conquest can produce. Countries like Britain, which maintain small armies and go to war ill prepared, suffering great losses in consequence, tend to be pleasanter places to live in, more interested in democratic institutions and civilised values – and less of a threat to their neighbours. Neither the general public nor latter-day critics can have it both ways, and not least because that lack of military preparedness for a European war was to cost the British Empire a quantity of lives. As Rudyard Kipling, who lost his only son at Loos in 1915, was to note in 1922, the British Army's unpreparedness in 1914 'has been extolled as proof of the purity of this country's ideals, which must be a great consolation to all concerned'. By contrast, the path of the German Army through Belgium was marked by atrocities from the first day, from the shooting of civilians and the destruction of towns and villages, to the imposing of punishments and fines on the citizens of captured cities. This conduct destroys much of the argument against the Allies' determination to fight the war, for the German military machine and the political will that drove it was a clear threat to democracy and civilised rule in Western Europe.

The German Army was huge, numbering at full strength over four million men mustered into twenty-five regular corps, each of two divisions, and each corps and division equipped with a full range of artillery. By recalling reserves German could muster a further sixteen corps, and ten more reserve corps were raised later in the war. In 1914 the German Army had 3,500 heavy guns, the French 300 heavy guns, and the BEF just 480 guns of every calibre. In addition to a 1.5 million-strong field army ready for immediate use, Germany had a mass of well-trained, instantly available reserves. Most of her army consisted of infantry, and 'man for man' this infantry was as good as any in Europe – with the possible exception of the BEF.

This vast force – which was formed from the armies of Prussia, Bavaria, Saxony and the other states after the Empire was established in 1871 – had 4,500 Maxim machine-guns in 1914, the French Army had 2,500 of the obsolescent St-Étienne machine-gun, and the British Army 1,963 Vickers or Maxim machine-guns. Since the German Army was so large, this quantity of machine-guns only provided their front-line infantry with the same scale of weapons, two per battalion, as the British infantry, but the number available was rapidly increased, and German machine-gun fire was to add considerably to the strength of their defences. German cavalry, though the Kaiser's favourite arm, was no more effective on the Western Front than the cavalry of the Allied nations, but German cavalry divisions also contained light infantry (Jäger), battalions, often deployed with great effect. Like the British and French, the German cavalry had its own artillery and machine-gun detachments.

The German artillery is mentioned with awe in most books on the Great War, although the focus of popular attention is usually on their siege artillery, those large-calibre 210-mm and 150-mm guns and the super-heavy 280-mm and 420-mm guns which smashed the defences of Liège and Namur and destroyed the French fortresses around Verdun. Their field and horse artillery was less remarkable, though there was plenty of it, and the German 150-mm (5.9-inch) howitzer was to become the most fearsome artillery weapon of the war. This artillery was also blessed with an armaments industry, geared to support such a large force, which had little difficulty in raising production to keep pace with Western Front demands.

The Germans had had a general staff since the time of the Franco-Prussian War; indeed, there had been the embryo of a general staff as early as 1817. The effectiveness of the German General Staff of 1914 had, however, been compromised in recent years by the actions and attitude of the Kaiser – or the 'Supreme War Lord', as he liked to be called – who interfered constantly with the higher command, and had to be prevented from taking command at pre-war manoeuvres since he insisted that whichever side he commanded must win. It is fair to add that once the war started he left the command of his armies to his generals, though orders were issued in his name.

The German generals and the General Staff were highly efficient, but this does not mean that they never made mistakes, or constantly ran rings round their French and British opponents, or always handled their men in a fashion that minimised casualties. German doctrine in 1914 was that objectives must be taken and held at any cost; if lost, they must be retaken by immediate counter-attack. Their basic field instructions, issued in 1906, make this very clear: 'The actions of the infantry must be dominated by this one thought; forward on the enemy, cost what it may . . . an uninterrupted forward movement and the desire to get ahead of its neighbours should animate all units in the attack.' (*Felddienstordnung* 1906, paras 265–327.)

There will be plenty of examples later to disprove the popular fiction that the German commanders conserved their infantry, but the idea that the German generals were universally intelligent and invincible can be dismissed now. In 1914–15, the Kaiser's generals threw their men into exactly the same kind of frontal attacks for which the British commanders have been so severely criticised by posterity. The German Army was also saddled with the Austro-Hungarian Army – a situation which one German general described as like 'being chained to a corpse' – but the latter made no impact on the British sector of the Western Front and can therefore, like the Russian Army, be excluded from much of this book.

Although their armies differed in many ways, the commanders fighting on the Western Front shared many of the same problems and handled them in similar, though not identical, ways. The German generals had the advantage that for much of the war they were fighting on the defensive and behind fixed positions, which gave them the inestimable benefit of good communications. Essentially, however, the Great War confronted all the commanders with some entirely new situations, especially trench warfare, with which they were hard-pressed to cope.

Of no army is this more true than that of Great Britain, but when the BEF went to war in 1914 no one, let alone the generals or the politicians, fully realised how different this war would be. At least to begin with, much went as planned, as prior arrangements proved their worth. In the years before 1914 the British Government had prepared a detailed 'War Book', a precise, detailed plan covering every aspect of national activity in the event of a European war. The War Book covered such matters as the requisitioning of naval transport, the organisation of trains, and the movement of the BEF, with its supplies of food, heavy weapons, ammunition, transports, fodder and equipment, from its barracks in the UK to the assembly areas in France. Telegrams were prepared for the recall of Reservists, proclamations awaited only the King's signature, ships and trains were ordered to stand by. Everyone involved in the mobilisation knew what had to be done, and who would do it.

This preparation paid off. The nation went to war in 1914 with considerable enthusiasm and without great difficulty as the War Book plans and decisions were implemented. One of the most efficient procedures was the one governing army transport. Although motor transport was making an appearance, the British Army had only sixty motor vehicles in service. It was still a horse-drawn army in 1914, and it remained so for much of the war. More horses were needed urgently and in the first week of war some 120,000 were requisitioned from the public for military use. Motor transport was also requisitioned, and the railway systems of Britain and France were soon heavily engaged transporting troops and supplies to embarkation points or onwards to the assembly area. These modern developments, railways and the internal-combustion engine, were later to prove invaluable in solving the army's logistical problems.

Stores, everything from socks and boots to food and ammunition, were shipped out by the train- and ship-load, and depots were set up in the French ports and railheads from which the British divisions at the front would be supplied. It is hard to find any cause for complaint in the way the BEF went to war, at least from the logistical and administrative point of view, and the generals and staff officers deserve full credit for the way this sudden and complicated task was handled. However, no significant benefit accrued to the commanders from recent technological developments in the field of communications.

The problems the army commanders were to face in France lay deeper than the complications of transport and logistics, and among the first and most enduring of these problems was the matter of battlefield communications. It has been said – and it is probably true – that if the British commanders of the Great War had enjoyed the use of battlefield radios and 'walkie-talkies' casualties in their actions might well have been halved. Examples showing where and how a lack of good communications caused or exacerbated a problem abound in any Great War history, and will be covered in detail later in this book when particular battles are analysed, but the overall communications picture should be described now and borne in mind hereafter.

There was no Royal Corps of Signals in 1914. The Army's communications were in the hands of the Corps of Royal Engineers, the Sappers, who were responsible for laying telephone lines up to the front line and establishing telephone exchanges, and of regimental signallers, often the brighter members of the battalion, who had been trained in telephone procedure, Morse code and flag-semaphore, and who could repair and maintain telephone lines in the battalion area and back to brigade HQ. Radio existed but was not yet reliable, and in any case the early radio sets were too big – the size of an ammunition limber – for deployment on the battlefield. Radio was not in general use on the ground until 1917, and then only as far forward as brigade. Before that the various corps and army HQs used the existing civilian telephone network, which was not particularly widespread in the countryside of France and Belgium in 1914, or set up their own land lines, or used motorcycle dispatch riders, or sent staff officers to carry orders about in cars or on horseback. Carrier pigeons were also widely used. Behind the front line the communications network functioned after a fashion, but for much of the war communication, even at the higher level, was frequently unreliable and always slow.

At the 'sharp end', in the front-line trenches and beyond, the situation was much worse; for beyond those trenches *there was no reliable means of communication at all*. Methods used during an attack might involve dogs or carrier pigeons or messages flashed in Morse code by lamps, but the main way of getting messages between the commanders and the troops, once the shooting started, was by runner . . . and on a shell-swept, machine-gun- and sniper-infested Great War battlefield, a runner making his way to and fro across the open ground was not likely to live long. Communications problems did not affect the German Army to the same degree. After early 1915 that army stood mainly on the defensive, and was thus able to multiply its communication systems and protect them carefully in deep dugouts or trenches.

The underlying task of battlefield communications was *control* not conversation: control of the attack, or the gunfire support; communication to order the deployment of reserves, the calling-off of a fruitless attack, the calling-down of artillery fire to help a company or battalion in trouble, to observe and report enemy movements or counter-attacks. Communication was vital, but the army that went to France in 1914 was sorely underequipped with means of communication, and remained so for the greater part of the war. This was not due to any inefficiency or carelessness by the commanders; the necessary equipment had either not yet been invented or had not yet reached that point in its development where it could be deployed on the battlefield.

This point will come up again and again in later chapters, but should be kept in mind throughout. The Great War generals are often blamed for preparing rigid plans of attack and then failing to control their battles after they had started, or when things went wrong, but much of the blame heaped upon them is due to the communications factor, over which they had little or no practical control. As the war progressed communications improved and increasing use was made of reports sent in by radio – or 'wireless', as it was then called – from reconnaissance or artillery-spotting aircraft of the Royal Flying Corps -- but this was WT (wireless telegraphy) using Morse code, not RT (radio telegraphy) using voice.

The Royal Air Force had not yet been formed and in 1914 the embryo Royal Flying Corps (RFC) was an Army formation, staffed by soldiers and using Army ranks. (The Royal Navy also had its own air force – the Royal Naval Air Service [RNAS], a number of whose squadrons were to be deployed on the Western Front.) The aircraft were fairly basic machines, which looked flimsy, and were rather slow and prone to crashing, but war has its own dynamic and no area of invention saw such rapid progress during the Great War as did those of aircraft development and air-to-ground communications. In 1914 the Royal Flying Corps had aircraft which could manage a top speed of 60 mph and had to be tied down when a strong wind blew across the airfield to prevent them blowing away; by 1918 the Royal Air Force (formed on 1 April that year by amalgamating the RFC and RNAS) had the Vickers Vimy bomber which was later to make the first flight across the Atlantic. That is the measure of technological progress in four years of a conflict in which the aeroplane was to make an immense and growing contribution to the art of war, both on the battlefield and in terms of military strategy. This growing power and efficiency was spurred on by far-sighted RFC officers like Trenchard who later became a Marshal of the Royal Air Force.

When the BEF crossed the Channel in August 1914 an Aircraft Park went with it, somewhat to the consternation of the transport and billeting officers who did not know what an 'Aircraft Park' was, let alone what do with it. Within days, however, the RFC squadrons had set up their machines and were flying out over the Belgian countryside, seeking the enemy columns. Four RFC squadrons, mustering a total of 63 aircraft, went to France with the BEF. The pilots flew well-established types like the BE2 biplane, and before long their reports came to be greatly valued by the field commanders as the most reliable and up-to-date intelligence data available.

Rapid strides in the development and use of air power is one indication that the British generals were not determined to stick to tried and tested – though far from effective – methods. If something useful was available in 1914, the generals would use it. Within days, air reconnaissance was being used to track German units. Within weeks, RFC observers were taking aerial photographs,* which were soon found to be far more reliable than the existing small-scale military maps. Then artillery-spotting by two-seaters was added to this role, and the RFC soon moved on to air combat, to prevent the enemy enjoying such advantages or to protect their own two-seaters, followed later in the war by the bombing and strafing of German transport and trenches.

The RFC and the British Army learned many of these techniques from the Germans, who had 30 Zeppelin airships and more than 300 military aircraft in service when the war broke out. Some of the best aircraft brought into service during the war were designed by the French, who began the war with just over 100 aircraft and a few airships, but in the use of aircraft in battle and the development of air power as a strategic weapon, the British learned fast and were soon the equal of any other combatant.

The BEF of 1914, though small and desperately short of heavy guns, was in many respects as good an army as any, but its success in battle depended on the intelligence and training of the officer corps. The skills of the French and German officers have already been touched on, and will be looked at again later, but a closer examination of the British officer corps now seems necessary.

In 1914, the British officer corps, drawn largely from the upper middle class, was small, clannish and idiosyncratic. The officers came mainly from the well-educated professional classes, many from families that had been providing officers to the British Army or the Royal Navy for generations. Their ranks contained many aristocrats, although at least one general, Sir William Robinson, had risen from the ranks and was prone to drop his aitches. Older or more senior officers had usually seen action in Zululand, India and on the Frontier, in the Sudan, and in a score of colonial conflicts like the First Boer War – and most especially in that graveyard of military reputations, the South African War of 1899–1902. None of this experience, useful though it was, had prepared them in any way for handling the vast numbers of men, the new conditions of warfare, or the changes in battlefield techniques required, indeed demanded, by advances in technology. No one on either side envisaged the development of trench warfare on the Western Front. The British officers had learned their trade in open warfare and had therefore trained their soldiers to fight that sort of war. Unfortunately for all concerned, the war that broke out in 1914 was to be unlike any other war in history.

There is also the matter of the Staff – the managers of the Army. 'The Staff get a bad press,' writes Major-General Julian Thompson (letter to the author, 1997).

* There were no specialist 'fighter' aircraft in 1914. Most machines were two-seaters, with an NCO as pilot and an officer as observer and aircraft commander. Single-seat – or sometimes two-seater fighters, or 'scouts', as they were then called, were developed to protect the vital two-seaters from enemy air attacks.

What needs to be pointed out is that in 1914 there were only 908 officers in the British Army who could put the letters 'psc' (passed Staff College) after their names or were otherwise qualified for Staff duties; I have these figures from John Hussey, who is sound on such matters. Some of these were [field] commanders anyway, and not on the Staff. When the army was hugely expanded, to five full armies, staff officers had to be found for all the new formations, and where were they to be found? Good staff officers do not grow on trees. Some of the staff in the original BEF formations became casualties and some were promoted. New staff officers were found among the talent available and trained on short courses at Hesdin in France. Many had spent at least a year or more in battalions or regiments in action and indeed were selected because they had front-line experience. They were good at their jobs or they would have been sacked.

The staff work involved in just ministering to the hundreds of thousands of men – and animals – in an army or corps was prodigious; food, ammo, water, defence stores, casualty evacuation, mail, etc., etc. On top of that were operations, with all that entailed, mache timetables, fire plans and so on. One finds very few serious complaints about poor administration among the troops, other than the usual grumbles one would expect anyway and the British Army was well administered when compared with say, the French Army. Of the three Western Powers, France had the highest rate of deaths from wounds, for their medical services were hopelessly inadequate; French wounded were evacuated from the Front in cattle trucks, many catching tetanus as a result. Most of the British wounded, well over 80 per cent, eventually recovered and returned to duty. Poor administration was one of the causes of the French Army mutinies of 1917. Personally, I find it a source of wonder that there were so few 'cock-ups' by the Great War staff and there were certainly none on the Crimean scale.*

It is one of the tragedies of war that the tactics often lag behind the technology. Many officers had also studied the Franco-Prussian War – from which most of them drew the erroneous lesson that any European war would be short. A more useful study, given the increasing range and power of weapons, was the Russo-Japanese War of 1904–5, in which machine-guns and howitzers were deployed with terrible effect and the defence made much use of entrenchments. Another useful subject for study would have been the US Civil War of 1861–65, on which the American historian Bruce Catton makes a pertinent point. Writing of the Union generals, Catton says:

* The supply and administration of the British Army during the Crimean War of 1854–5 had been a national scandal of epic proportions.

In many ways, the Generals had been brought up wrong. Close order fighting in open country where men with bayonets charged men with smooth-bore muskets used to work well enough because the range at which the killing began was very short. Given a proper advantage in numbers a charging line could get to close quarters provided the men could just stand the gaff during the last hundred yards of their advance. Then the rifle came in and changed all that. The trench and the rifle put together made the old tradition as dead as Hannibal. The hard fact was that by 1864 good troops using rifles and standing in well-built trenches, and provided with suitable artillery support could not be dislodged by any frontal assault whatever. (*A Stillness at Appomattox*, New American Library, 1955.)

That observation, so true of the fighting between 1861–65, was equally true of the fighting in France fifty years later. Yet until 1918 most of the generals, French and German as well as British, still sent their men over open ground to attack an entrenched or invisible enemy – and this when the killing power of military technology, especially in the much greater range of all weapons after the introduction of smokeless propellants towards the end of the nineteenth century, the rate of fire of automatic weapons and the power and accuracy of artillery had increased tenfold over that employed in the American Civil War. The lessons of Gettysburg and Antietam and a score of battles in the 'War Between the States' had not been learned, and many men died because of it, not just British soldiers at Loos and on the Somme, but French soldiers in Champagne and on the Chemin des Dames, and German soldiers in half a hundred battles on the Western Front. Technology killed them in their hundreds of thousands, and would continue to do so until further advances in technology found a way to restore open warfare to the battlefield. This is not to say that a great saving in lives could not have been made by the employment of sensible battlefield tactics, and these too were gradually developed. By 1918 the effectiveness of 'all-arms' offensives combining tanks, artillery, infantry and air support in a co-ordinated fashion was clear, but the casualties continued. It was the *war*, not just the way it was fought, that caused the losses, a fact amply demonstrated by the losses suffered during open warfare in the Second World War, in North-West Europe in 1945 and in Russia in 1941–4. To give just one example, in France in June and July 1944 the 3rd Infantry Division lost some 6,000 men as casualties; at Arras in April 1917 the 3rd Infantry Division suffered 5,400 casualties. As General Thompson remarks: 'This is a very important point, and one often missed by the "antis", that losses in North-Western Europe in 1944–5 reached Great War levels, yet no one accuses Monty, Dempsey, O'Connor, Ritchie, Bucknall, Horrocks, or any of the Second World War divisional commanders, of being callous. If you are fighting the German Army of 1914–1918, or 1939–1945, you take casualties; sometimes very heavy ones indeed.' (Major-General Julian Thompson, letter to the author, 1998).

This chapter has provided the background to the armies and covered some of the problems that were to inhibit the generals' actions from the day the war began, until the day it ended. The officers commanding on the Western Front were faced with a conflict on a scale they could never have imagined and, certainly in the case of the BEF commanders, they had to fight it at first with totally inadequate means. When the BEF met the enemy on the battlefield, these pre-war deficiencies had to be made good with blood and guts . . . but can it be seriously maintained that this was *entirely* the generals' fault? The blame for the lack of adequate preparation must be laid at the door of the British Government, but since Great Britain is a democracy some blame must also fall upon the electorate. In short, if censure is called for, there is enough blame to go around.

As time went by, matters improved; the armies, especially the British and French Armies, became better at staying alive while killing larger numbers of the enemy which, though hardly a matter for satisfaction in human terms, is what well-trained armies are supposed to do. How matters improved for the British commanders and their soldiers is one of the themes of this book. Before this story continues, however, one final point needs to be remembered.

Warfare is not *easy*, and battles are immensely complicated. Matters will go wrong from the moment the first shot is fired, and frequently much earlier. Many histories give the impression that a commander's plans are set in stone, and that if they go wrong it is entirely his fault and a matter for outrage and condemnation. Soldiers with experience of battle know not only that things will always go wrong, but that problems on the battlefield are inevitable. Men will be frightened, and rightly so; communications will break down; the enemy will do the unexpected. War is not *easy*.

It is not necessary to command armies to appreciate this fact. Anyone who has spent a field day with a school Combined Cadet Force will realise within half an hour that military affairs are more than usually prone to failure or confusion. Fighting battles is not a normal activity and when men are scared or confused, matters go awry. Many historians, as well as the general public, ought to realise this, for most accounts of war from men engaged at the sharp end tell the same kind of story, whatever war they are describing.

'Gentlemen,' said Brigadier James Hill, addressing 3 Parachute Brigade before D-Day, June 1944, 'Do not be daunted if chaos reigns; it undoubtedly will.'

'Describe a typical operation?' said Brigadier Peter Young, DSO, MC and two Bars.

> Well, it would be dark, half the blokes would be seasick and there would be a sea running. It would take twice as long as we thought to get into the landing craft and then half the craft would vanish. Eventually the cox'n would put us ashore on what then turned out to be the wrong beach, and while we were trying to work out where we were, we would be shelled by the Royal Navy . . . and that was on a good day.

Major Philip Neame commanded A Company of the 2nd Battalion, the Parachute Regiment, during the fighting for Darwin and Goose Green in the Falklands War of 1982:

> The plan was for a six-phase attack but since that never happened we need not waste much time on it. Things started to go awry when we were driven off the track on to a minefield and if what happened after that sounds confusing, well, battle is confusing.
>
> We came under [Argentine] fire from the right flank and we attacked that position, though we had no idea how big it was. Heavy machine-guns fired on us from the flank and it got pretty chaotic. We did not know where B Company was, we had a platoon pinned down and another one had vanished into the dark to attack some enemy position. We eventually took the position, losing two men killed and another two wounded, but it is fair to say that one hour after leaving the start line, chaos was reigning.

Chaos was reigning, confusion abounding, but as Major-General Maurice Tugwell has pointed out, 'confusion in battle is like pain in childbirth, the natural order of things.' *That is what war is like*, and it cannot be avoided. These brief statements from experienced front-line officers, flash-forwards to later wars, illustrate what war is like, even with the advantages of modern communications. High-toned accounts from academic historians 'playing general' in their studies, far from the battlefield and long after the war is over, often seem to overlook the fact that fighting a battle – any battle – is very difficult indeed. As we go on to read of what happened on the Western Front, and attempt to analyse why matters went right or wrong, it would be as well to remember what these experienced front-line officers are saying. War is difficult, chaos inevitable, and no one who knows anything about war should expect it to be any different. With that much established, this story can follow the BEF to France.

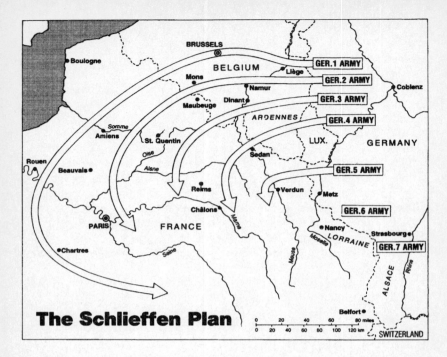

The Schlieffen Plan

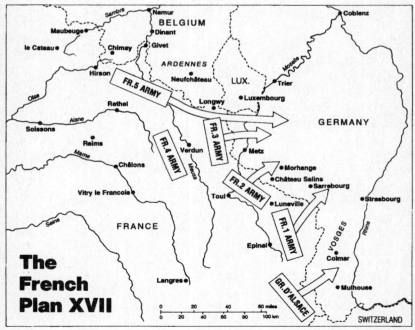

The French Plan XVII

CHAPTER 3

ENTER THE GENERALS, AUGUST 1914

*'The position of a general will depend a great deal
on the size of force he commands.'*

Field Service Regulations 1909, Part 1, Chapter VII

On 4 August 1914, Great Britain declared war on Imperial Germany and Austria-Hungary and began to muster her military strength for the coming struggle. Some steps towards meeting the threat of war had already been taken. The First Sea Lord, Admiral Prince Louis of Battenberg, had stopped the Home Fleet dispersing after the review at Spithead during which *forty miles* of British warships were inspected by the King. The newly appointed First Lord of the Admiralty, Winston Churchill, had then ordered the Royal Navy to its war stations, ready to repulse any incursion by the German High Seas Fleet into the Channel.

The Army was soon on the move, though few people in Europe thought that this sudden, unexpected war would last very long. The British public confidently expected that it would 'all be over by Christmas', and the Kaiser had already assured his departing legions that they would be 'home again before the leaves fall'. The war was generally regarded as a brief explosion caused by the tensions that had been accumulating in Continental Europe over the last few years; after a short campaign the nations would arrive at some suitable compromise and peace would be restored.

The important thing for most young men in Europe that August was to take part in this great adventure before it was all over. Such hopeful estimates were to fall woefully short of the actual time it would take to end this war, and some politicians and senior army officers were fully aware that the course on which the European nations were now embarking could only have a painful end. Such thoughts could, however, be put on one side for the moment, while the British and French Armies strove to bring their forces together on the Belgian frontier.

In London, the various measures listed in the War Book were implemented with great efficiency, and discussed at two meetings of the Army Council on 5 and 6 August attended by the Cabinet, Field Marshal Lord Kitchener, Field Marshal Sir John French, Lieutenant-General Sir Douglas Haig, Major-General Henry Wilson and members of the General Staff. The purpose of these meetings was to decide what to do and there was considerable discussion of the various options, including a proposal by French that the BEF should go, not to France, but to Antwerp. The structure of the BEF was established and orders issued for its march to war. The first decision was to send the entire Expeditionary Force to France at once, six infantry divisions and a cavalry division, but this decision was soon overturned by the newly appointed Secretary of State for War, Kitchener, who felt that Britain should keep some units of the Regular Army back for home defence. The proposal to reduce the Expeditionary Force infuriated that strongly francophile General Henry Wilson, but it was finally decided that just four infantry divisions, plus the cavalry division, should be sent to France, with more to follow later as required.

These first four infantry divisions were formed into two Corps; I Corps, consisting of the 1st and 2nd Divisions, would be commanded by General Haig. II Corps, consisting of the 3rd and 5th Divisions, would be commanded by Lieutenant-General Sir, J.M. Grierson. The Cavalry Division would be commanded by Major-General E.H.H. Allenby, and the entire force would be under the command of Field Marshal Sir John French, with Lieutenant-General A.J. Murray as his Chief of Staff, Major-General Wilson as Major-General, General Staff (MGGS) or Sub-Chief of Staff, and Major-General Sir William Robertson as Quartermaster-General. The total force under French's command amounted to around 100,000 men, a puny force when compared to the vast armies of France and Germany, but an efficient and completely professional one, even though some 60 per cent of the private soldiers were Reservists recalled to the Colours.

A plan for shipping the BEF to France, and its concentration in the area Maubeuge–Le Cateau–Hirson, on the left flank of the French Army, close to the Belgian frontier, had been worked out by the British and French staffs as long ago as 1911, though this plan had never been seen – at least by the British Government – as any form of commitment. Now, however, it could be put into effect, and at least one officer, Henry Wilson, was ecstatic, though annoyed that the full seven divisions envisaged in the original discussions were not sent to France at once . . . and placed under the command of the French Army. Nevertheless, the commitment of even this reduced force had not taken place without some discussion.

The Prime Minister, Herbert Asquith, had already lost two members of his Cabinet who, declining to support the war, had advised that Britain should stay out of this Continental quarrel and had resigned when their advice was rejected. Asquith had been acting as Secretary for War since that spring, when Colonel John Seely had resigned over the 'Curragh Incident', but on 5 August he recalled Field Marshal Earl Kitchener of Khartoum to

London and offered him the job of Secretary of State for War. Kitchener was then at Dover, in the process of returning to his post as British Resident in Egypt, but he came back at once and took up his new position on 6 August.

Although the appointment of Secretary of State for War was a political one, Kitchener was on the active Army List, the most senior officer of the British Army on that list after Field Marshal Lord Roberts, VC, and as a result Asquith's choice was to cause problems. Kitchener was an autocrat, a man used to getting his own way, a soldier rather than a civil administrator and conciliator, yet he was faced with a huge administrative and logistical problem, and one which would involve working closely with politicians in Britain and France. By his temperament alone, Kitchener was ill-suited to this task, but he took up his new duties at once and flung himself into the task of expanding the British Army and the munitions industry that supported it.

Horatio Herbert Kitchener, first Earl Kitchener of Khartoum, or 'K of K', as he was often called, was widely regarded as Britain's most distinguished soldier. Commissioned into the Royal Engineers, he had served as an intelligence officer behind the Dervish lines during the unsuccessful expedition to relieve General Gordon in Khartoum, of 1884, and had achieved great success in the Sudan campaigns of 1898–9 with his victories over the Dervish armies at the Atbara and Omdurman. His role as Commander-in-Chief in South Africa during the latter stages of the war against the Boers had been less distinguished – though that could be said of many British officers, including his predecessor there, Lord Roberts – but he had at least seen what steps were necessary first to contain, and then to defeat, the Boer commandos, and so eventually brought the South African War to a successful conclusion.

Following that war, Kitchener had gone to India in 1902, where he had been C-in-C of the Indian Army until 1909, a time largely spent battling with the Viceroy, Lord Curzon, over the control of the Indian Army, a battle which Kitchener had won. He had then presided over the reorganisation of that army, a task which included setting up the Indian Army Staff College at Quetta, before leaving to take up his present post in Egypt. He had been on leave in England when the war broke, and the Government considered him too good a man to waste on Egypt when bigger matters were brewing on the Continent.

Herbert Kitchener was a complex character. His most dominant personal characteristic was a driving ambition, and he let no one stand in the way of his relentless climb to the top of the military tree. He was also a thoroughgoing snob and took great care to shine in the eyes of the royal family and any member of the aristocracy, the Government, or the military Establishment who might be useful to him. His inferiors, or those who could not further his ambitions, he simply ignored. He had few interests outside his own career, and never married. He enjoyed the exotic social life of Cairo and spent a lot of time in the company of handsome young officers, who were allowed liberties with 'K of K' that less well-favoured officers would not have dared to take. He also collected porcelain and *objets d'art*, and was devoted to a small poodle. None of this, however, is to imply that Kitchener was homosexual; he had been disappointed in love early in life and after that rebuff had devoted himself entirely to the service. This dedication to his Army career had proved profitable, for his path been strewn with regular promotion and some splendid appointments. Kitchener was a competent officer, and one marked for the highest rank from an early stage, in spite of certain doubts about his abilities as a battlefield commander.

Though his courage was undoubted – he bore the scars of battlefield wounds to prove it – Kitchener tended to become unsure of himself in the presence of the enemy. On the eve of the Atbara battle in the Sudan in 1898, he caused consternation in Cairo and Downing Street when, having received conflicting advice from his subordinate generals, he telegraphed to the then British Resident in Cairo, Lord Cromer, and the Government in London, asking if he should attack the Dervishes or not. It was not usual for a British general, in command of an army and in the presence of the enemy, to ask his political masters, thousands of miles away, for military advice. In the end Kitchener decided to attack and the battle was duly won, but his superiors had endured some anxious moments. He tended towards caution at the beginning of the Battle of Omdurman, before slaughtering the dervishes in quantity, and showed similar hesitation in his early days in South Africa. Although caution in a commander is not always a bad thing, Kitchener was clearly more effective at some distance from the front line.

Kitchener's confidence improved as his rank increased, though his performance was inhibited by his deep reluctance to delegate any task, even to a trusted subordinate. Although he had founded the Indian Army Staff College at Quetta, he had no staff training himself and was not interested in staff functions. He was, in modern terms, a 'one-man band'; moreover, he expected everyone to dance to his tune. On the other hand, he could be charming, and he had demonstrated an ability to handle delicate, even dangerous, political situations.

Shortly after the victory at Omdurman in 1898, Kitchener had to take a small force up the Nile to head off a French military expedition that had appeared on the river at Fashoda and was about to lay claim to parts of the Southern Sudan. His masterly and tactful handling of the 'Fashoda Incident' may well have prevented France and Britain going to war; certainly less competent handling of the confrontation would have inhibited the establishment of the Entente Cordiale in 1904. Kitchener always had a grasp of the broad picture, and possessed an almost intuitive ability to judge what should be done at any particular time. His first decisions as Secretary for War reflected a judgement that was, on balance, broadly correct, and would serve his country well in the months and years ahead.

His initial proposal, which the Government accepted, was to keep two

Regular divisions in Britain, though this decision infuriated the French and their warm supporter, Henry Wilson. Kitchener was also one of the few people in Britain to realise that this war would be a long one – Haig was another – and that the country would need to raise, equip and train armies running into millions, and to prepare for a conflict that might last years. In both these conclusions he was quite correct. His next decision, however, that the Territorial Force was not a suitable medium for the raising of these vast new armies, is at best debatable, and probably wrong.

It is alleged that Kitchener's decision to overlook the development and expansion of the Territorial Force and opt instead for a newly recruited army was due to his experience of French territorial troops in 1870, when he served as a volunteer during the Franco-Prussian War. The fact that Britain's Territorial Force of young and enthusiastic part-time soldiers was a vastly different organisation from the French territorial body of ageing, poorly armed, post-regular-servicemen he had seen in 1870, was not a view Lord Kitchener cared to entertain. Since Britain did not have conscription and was not prepared to introduce it on the outbreak of war, he set out to raise his own army of volunteers, drawing on the enthusiasm of the general public and relying on the high reputation he had acquired with the retired officers and NCOs of the Regular Army, who would be recalled to train the new force.

Kitchener's popularity with the common soldiers was surprising, for he never went out of his way to court their admiration. As far as is known, he never spoke to a private soldier if he could help it, but he did take care not to squander their lives and, according to his friend and admirer General Sir Ian Hamilton, later to command the Gallipoli fiasco of 1915, 'It was as hard to get troops out of him as to get butter out of a dog's mouth.'

Hamilton's admiration was the exception, however. Kitchener was much less popular with the majority of the officer corps, and was not widely admired by the generals and other senior officers in the British Army. They regarded him as a 'colonial soldier', since the bulk of his experience was drawn from service with the Indian and Egyptian Armies. Many may also have been jealous of his rank and reputation, but his lack of experience in the British Army and of British life in general was to prove a drawback in his new appointment, and soon brought him into conflict with the Commander-in-Chief of the BEF, Field Marshal Sir John French.

Nor was Kitchener successful in Cabinet. Like many soldiers, he disliked and distrusted politicians, and not being a 'team player', could not grasp the notion of collective Cabinet responsibility. He also believed, correctly, that the Cabinet talked and talked and rarely reached a conclusion, a luxury for which there was no time in war, and that it leaked details of Army plans like a sieve. His greatest public success in 1914–15 was in recruiting the men for the New Armies – the force that was proud to be known as 'Kitchener's Army' – and the poster depicting his face and pointing finger, with the message 'Your Country Needs You', remains the most famous and effective recruiting poster in history.

Opinions vary both about the wisdom of appointing Kitchener to the post of Secretary for War, and about the way he executed his duties. On balance, however, he was right more often than not, and – with the exception of his views on the Territorial Force – proved to be the right man in the right place at this time. He served his country well in 1914–16, and possessed the experience and the personal influence to press his views home upon those generals, like French, who had little time for politicians – the much-despised 'frocks' – but who found it difficult, though not impossible, to defy a man who was both their political master and the nation's most revered soldier.

Kitchener's first task as Secretary for War was to frame the orders for the Commander-in-Chief of the BEF. These summarise many of the difficulties Field Marshal Sir John French was to face in the field, and underline the fact that, *at least until the end of 1916*, the BEF was a comparatively small force that needed to work with the French Army in order to fight at all:

> The force under your control [French was informed] is to support and co-operate with the French Army . . . in repelling the invasion by Germany of French and Belgian territory and eventually to restore the neutrality of Belgium . . .
>
> The numerical strength of the British Force and its contingent reinforcement is strictly limited . . . and it will be obvious that the greatest care must be taken towards a minimum of losses . . . and while every effort must be made to coincide with the plans and wishes of our Ally . . . the gravest consideration will devolve upon you as to participation in forward movements where large French bodies are not involved and where your Force may be unduly exposed . . .

Finally, there came a reminder: 'I wish you to distinctly understand that your command is an entirely independent one and that you will in no case come in any sense under the orders of any Allied General.'

Kitchener's orders did not, however, extend to advising Field Marshal French as to how these points were to be handled in practice. To co-operate sympathetically without becoming involved, to be independent when your bases and lines of communication depended entirely on your allies – it would have taken a general far more gifted than French to comply with such orders in a sensible fashion. Nevertheless, French bore these instructions in mind and, on most occasions at least, tried to follow them, often at considerable cost to his own troops. The Secretary for War's orders were understandable in the circumstances, for the BEF was too small to operate as a separate force, but they placed an intolerable burden on French and on his successor, Haig, when it came to the matter of planning the timing, location and length of their battles. Those vital elements depended to a very large degree on the wishes of the French, who could be relied on to press the point about 'support and co-operation' as far as it would go, if not further. In this, as it turned out, they were aided by the volatile character of the BEF's commander.

Like a number of other senior British officers, Field Marshal Sir John French was an Ulsterman, a product of that embattled province which, in the words of the historian Correlli Barnett, 'has given the British Army the closest thing it has to a Junker class'. French was sixty-two in 1914. He had begun his military career in the Royal Navy but life at sea did not suit him and in 1874 he left the Navy and was gazetted to the 8th Hussars, leaving that regiment after a few weeks to join the 19th Hussars.

The family was not wealthy and French had some difficulty maintaining the lifestyle required of an officer in a fashionable cavalry regiment. This eventually got him into debt and later in his career, having speculated unwisely in South African gold shares, he only avoided having to resign his commission when a wealthy brother officer, Douglas Haig, loaned him £2,000 (well over £100,000 in today's money). He was also extremely fond of women, another expensive hobby, and apart from marrying twice, had a string of mistresses. As a young man, French was a keen point-to-point rider and polo player, but he took care not to let either of his sporting enthusiasms divert him from studying his profession. He developed an interest in military history and was a great admirer of Napoleon Bonaparte, acquiring, among other souvenirs, Napoleon's Légion d'honneur and a dinner plate used by the Emperor during his final exile on St Helena. Physically, French was a small, slender man, at least in his youth, which is no bad thing for a cavalry officer, but by 1914, he had filled out. Photographs of the time show a plump, jowly man with a heavy white moustache, the archetype of the pompous cavalry officer.

The problem with Field Marshal French lay not with his habits or his experience, but with his character. Hot-tempered and argumentative, he was a man who tended to bear grudges, but the most dominant of his natural characteristics was his volatility. He could and did change his mind within minutes, and was always liable to pay most heed to the last person he had spoken to, especially if that person was Wilson or Wilson's much-admired ally that silver-tongued French commander, General Ferdinand Foch. French's manner in conversation with his colleagues was at times excitable, even verging on the hysterical. Haig once remarked that a conversation with French was 'like opening a soda-water bottle, all froth and bubble, without the ability to think clearly and come to a reasoned decision,' but since Haig was notably taciturn – and was angling for French's job at the time – this remark cannot be regarded as completely unbiased. Even so, this volatility was to surface time and again in France, and would prove a sore trial to French's allies and subordinates.

Like Kitchener, French had learned his trade in India and the Sudan, and latterly in the South African War. He had missed the campaign against

Colonel Arabi in Egypt in 1882, but served in the Desert Column during the Gordon relief expedition up the Nile in 1884–5, seeing action for the first time, aged thirty-two, at Abu Klea, where the 19th Hussars formed part of the British square and, fighting dismounted, helped to beat off heavy dervish attacks in a desperate hand-to-hand struggle. He took command of the 19th Hussars in 1888, served in India from 1891 to 1893, and after his return to England was appointed Assistant Adjutant-General at the War Office in 1895, with the rank of full colonel.

Then, in 1899, came the South African War. French made his name at the battle of Elandslaagte in October of that year, an engagement which culminated in a charge against the retreating Boers by two cavalry squadrons, one each from the 5th Lancers and the 5th Dragoon Guards, who did some execution with lance and sabre. French was to command the cavalry for most of the war and, after escaping from the siege of Ladysmith, he led the cavalry in harassing the Boers around Colesburg, and once the Boers had been forced to adopt guerrilla tactics, during the campaigns that led up to the end of the war in May 1902.

French was one of the few commanders who returned from South Africa with an enhanced reputation, and his services were recognised by promotion to lieutenant-general and the award of the KCB and the KCMG. He was also offered the important and prestigious appointment of the Aldershot Command . . . and it is at this point that some doubts begin to emerge about his fitness for higher command. French was a cavalry general, and he returned from South Africa convinced that the cavalry still had a role to play in modern warfare. He was not alone in this; horsed cavalry remained an important part of many armies, including the German and Soviet Armies, and in 1914 all the armies went to war with strong cavalry contingents. Senior officers of the time could not visualise a war without cavalry; senior officers with vision, however, could see that the day of the horse soldier armed with sword and lance was already ending.

The 'cavalry' role in South Africa had largely been supplanted by that of 'mounted infantry' – which is what the Boers were, soldiers who rode to battle but fought on foot with infantry weapons. French was fully aware that mounted infantry were useful, but saw them as auxiliary to a traditional cavalry force. According to French, the cavalry should be equipped with sword and lance, rather than the rifle, and settle the outcome of a battle by the traditional *arme blanche* cavalry charge. He maintained this view and, in October 1902, stressed it in a letter to Lord Roberts when commenting on a disastrous action against the Boers fought by the 17th Lancers, a regiment commanded by his good friend, the then Lieutenant-Colonel Douglas Haig:

> Personally, I think it a very great pity that the 17th had no swords on this occasion – I feel quite sure they would then have charged – and even had they lost a few men they would certainly have thrown back the enemy instead of drawing him on . . . this is not the first

instance of Cavalry feeling the want of a weapon for mounted offence since I have been operating in this Colony.

What men with swords could do that men with magazine rifles could not (other than, perhaps, the shock effect of a full charge against a surprised or demoralised enemy force) remains a mystery, but French remained a convinced devotee of the *arme blanche* during his term as C-in-C at Aldershot. He seems to have ignored the rapid developments in military technology that were then taking place and devoted himself to practising and promoting a mode of warfare that was clearly out of date. In this he showed himself blinkered and outmoded, for while junior officers may yearn for the glory of the past, senior officers are supposed to display foresight, and to train their soldiers for the wars to come. French was also at odds with his superiors over their directive that officers who had passed the Staff College course should receive preference in promotion. French had not taken the course, and took his own experience and advance to high rank as indications that an officer could handle a senior command very well without staff training.

An even more significant argument came over the training of cavalry. In his *Life of Field Marshal Sir John French*, his son, Major the Hon. Gerald French, refers to this argument, which exercised higher minds in the Army in the years before the Great War:

> Ever since the South African War there had been a lively controversy regarding the future training of cavalry. One side . . . held that firearms were of greater value than steel weapons . . . and that training in the use of the rifle should in future form the principal part of the cavalry soldier's training. The other side remained faithful to sword and lance and believed in the devastating effect of shock tactics, whilst agreeing that rifle work should not be neglected.
>
> My father was a stout upholder of the latter doctrine . . . and worked hard against any campaign to convert the cavalry into mounted infantry.

Then follow pages of letters from French to his superiors at the War Office, spread over his years at Aldershot, all praising the use of sword and lance and the knee-to-knee cavalry charge, and disparaging the practice of dismounting the cavalry for action on foot with the rifle – ignoring the painful lessons learned in the South African War.

This stubborn reluctance to face obvious facts indicates that French was not the right soldier to entrust with the high command in a war which, whatever else it might be was certain to be unlike any war the British had experienced since the Crimea, or even the Napoleonic Wars of a century earlier. His commitment to the traditional cavalry role was to affect his attitude to one of his subordinate commanders in the first weeks of the coming campaign.

That said, it is possible to feel a certain sympathy for Field Marshal French. He was sent to fight a war in a country of which he knew nothing, with allies and against an enemy who had at their command armies much larger than anything in his experience; nor had he any background in handling a force even the size of the BEF, small as it was compared to the French and German Armies. His situation can be compared to that of a man competent to run a small concern, who finds himself suddenly propelled by fate into managing a vast international company. In truth, no officer in the British Army had the relevant experience for such a task, but French's successors, at army and GHQ level, had time to learn and work their way up to senior posts. French, however, was pitched headlong into the role, and it is hardly surprising that the task was beyond him.

French left Aldershot in 1907 – when his post was taken over by Lieutenant-General Sir Horace Smith-Dorrien – and became Inspector-General of the Forces. In this capacity he visited Canada to inspect the Canadian forces in 1910, and in 1911 he became ADC-General to the new King, George V, who had succeeded his father, Edward VII, that year. In that year, too, French was invited to visit the summer manoeuvres of the German Army as a guest of the Kaiser, Wilhelm II, and in 1912, now a full general, he became Chief of the Imperial General Staff – the effective head of the British Army,* the military adviser to the Cabinet. French was clearly destined for all the glories his profession could bestow, and in 1913 he became a field marshal. Then, in March 1914, came the 'Curragh Incident' . . . and professional disaster.

In the spring of 1914, Ireland was finally moving towards 'Home Rule' – self-government – and that independence from Britain which most of her Catholic inhabitants had wanted for so long. There was, however, a problem. The Protestants of the northern province, ulster, led by Sir Edward Carson, were determined to resist Home Rule and, organised as the Ulster Volunteers, had smuggled in rifles and ammunition to contest the takeover by the Catholic majority in the South, by force if need be. The British Government were determined to push the Home Rule Bill through, and in March 1914 a cable was sent to Brigadier-General Hubert Gough, VC, commanding 3 Cavalry Brigade at the Curragh camp near Dublin, ordering him to issue live ammunition to his troops and be prepared to march on Belfast to restrain Carson's Volunteers and to quell any disturbances – in short, to see that Home Rule was imposed.

On the following day, 21 March, at an Army conference in Dublin, it was stated that any officer who came from Ulster and who did not wish to take part in this attempt to coerce the Protestants, could go on leave until the

---

* The titular head of the British Army – indeed, of all the armed services – then as now, was the monarch. The CIGS would now be called the 'service chief', for – again then as now – he was subject to Parliament and to the War Office.

crisis was over, while any other officer who opposed this action should inform his commanding officer and resign his commission. As a result, practically all the officers of 3 Cavalry Brigade sent in their papers. It suddenly became abundantly clear to the British Government that the Army would not take up arms against the Protestants or support any attempt to bully them. In this the officers were quite right. Soldiers must obey all lawful orders, but an order to coerce their fellow citizens into the arms of another country – for the Home Rule Bill would effectively have established Ireland as such – is not one that they are obliged to comply with.

There followed a good deal of discussion, which culminated in the Government directing the Secretary of State for War, Colonel John Seely, himself an Army officer but also a Member of Parliament, to assure the cavalry that 'while the Government retained the absolute right to use all the forces of the Crown anywhere in the Kingdom, including Ireland, the Government did not intend to take advantage of this right to crush political opposition to the policy or principles of the Home Rule Bill.'

Brigadier-General Gough, himself an Ulsterman, regarded this assurance as a fudge, and wrote out a clarification, which he added to the Government declaration, in which he stated that 'I understand the meaning of the last paragraph to mean that the troops under our command will not be called upon to enforce the Home Rule Bill on Ulster and that we can so assure our officers.' The Brigadier showed this to his fellow Ulsterman, French, who concurred with his interpretation and signed the paper 'This is how I read it, (Sd) J.F., CIGS,' and this opinion was confirmed by Colonel Seely. The officers then withdrew their resignations. The Government, however, promptly repudiated both Gough's amendment and French's concession. Sir John and his political master, Seely, as well as the Adjutant-General of the Army, Sir John Ewart, felt that they had to resign, while Gough became vastly unpopular with certain Westminster politicians. The Curragh Incident also worried the French, and, naturally, delighted the Germans.

There was a great public outcry over the Curragh Incident. Moreover, it seemed that now, in March 1914, five months before the outbreak of the Great War, French's career was over. However, British field marshals are appointed for life and when war loomed at the end of July, French was recalled to duty and told that in the event of war, he would be appointed Commander-in-Chief of the British Expeditionary Force.

All this duly came to pass. On 14 August 1914, Field Marshal Sir John French and his staff embarked on the cruiser HMS *Sentinel* at Dover, and at 1730 hours that evening the Field Marshal arrived in Boulogne to meet the greatest challenge of his long and distinguished career.

After declaring war on Germany, the British Government needed to know what their allies the French were doing. In response, the French therefore sent to England a Military Mission, headed by Colonel Huguet, an officer who had previously been Military Attaché at the French Embassy in

London. Huguet knew all the senior British commanders and spoke English well, but was no great admirer of the British military establishment. Colonel Huguet flits about many of the memoirs of 1914–15, not least because his visit to England provoked a major row between Lord Kitchener and Major-General Henry Wilson, Field Marshal French's Sub-Chief of Staff.

If Henry Wilson had not been such a colourful character, it might be accurate to call him French's *éminence grise*. John Terraine has written that while French was prepared to leave great responsibility and a huge volume of work to Lieutenant-General Sir A.J. Murray, his Chief of Staff, he leaned much more on Wilson for ideas. Certainly the latter was never short of ideas, but he had one fixation: that Britain's military efforts should be closely linked, if not entirely subordinate, to those of France.

Henry Wilson was the archetypal francophile, and a very interesting man. Born in Ireland in 1864, he was one of the 'Protestant Ascendancy', descended from an English family 'planted' in Ireland during the reign of Charles II. His family employed a succession of French governesses and they imparted to the infant Henry a love of all things French and a good command of the French language. Other aspects of his education were less successful, however, for though he attended two good public schools, Marlborough and Wellington, and intended to make his career in the Army, he failed the entrance exams for Sandhurst and Woolwich* no fewer than five times and finally entered the Army 'by the back door', taking a commission in the Irish Militia (the Militia then performed roughly the role of Territorial troops).

Eventually, in 1884, he was gazetted into the Rifle Brigade and sent to join the 1st Battalion in India. He served in the Burma campaign of 1887, during which he was attacked by a dacoit (armed robber) and received a wound in the face that scarred him for life . . . and Wilson was not handsome to begin with. A joking telegram sent by a brother officer to 'The Ugliest Officer in the British Army, Victoria Barracks, Belfast' found him without difficulty. Henry Wilson had an immense Irish charm, was full of life (as evinced by his fondness for practical jokes) and, being no mean soldier, was popular with his colleagues and his men. It was not his ability, however, but his character, that caused problems in his career.

After a slow start, he made steady progress in the Army. He attended the Staff College in 1892 – the other students on his course included future Great War generals like Rawlinson, Snow and Hamilton – where he studied military history and tactics under Major G.R. Henderson, a well-regarded officer, and took part in 'staff tours', an early form of TEWT (Tactical Exercise Without Troops), in which various forms of warfare and tactics can be tried out in theory. While at the Staff College he also made the first of many visits to the battlefields of the Franco-Prussian War.

* The then Royal Military College, Sandhurst, trained officers for the cavalry and infantry; the Royal Military Academy, Woolwich, trained them for the artillery, engineers, and other arms of service.

After graduation he went with Rawlinson, who became a close friend, on yet another battlefield tour, and was then posted to the intelligence Department of the Army, a job which took him back to France for discussions with French commanders. On some of these missions he was accompanied by Captain a'Court, a man who later, under the byline 'Colonel Repington', became the Military Correspondent of *The Times* and another of his close friends. Wilson was then appointed Brigade Major to 2 Infantry Brigade and went with it to the South African War in 1899.

Wilson saw a good deal of action in South Africa. He served at Colenso, the Modder River and Spion Kop, and his observations on the conduct of those battles and that campaign are both accurate and telling. He soon realised that General Sir Redvers Buller, the commanding general, until his replacement by Lord Roberts in 1900, was not up to the task – a fact that Buller himself had pointed out – but noted that many other British generals were equally outmatched by the Boer commanders. A diary entry in 1900, during Buller's slow but repeated attempts to relieve besieged Ladysmith, records:

> It is exactly two months since we came here and in that time we have lost heavily, fought heavily, marched heavily and are no nearer Ladysmith. And through no fault of the troops. Our entire failure is due to two causes. The first is that we have only a quarter of the number of troops necessary and the second is bad generalship. Not that Napoleon could have got through without more troops, but our losses have been much greater than they ought to have been, owing to bad generalship and this on the part of several generals.

Wilson's commanding officer, Lieutenant-General The Hon. Sir Neville Lyttelton, recalls him at this time;

> The high opinion I formed of him at Aldershot was more than borne out in the much more trying experiences in the field in South Africa. I think the most remarkable trait in his character was his unfailing cheerfulness in the arduous conditions that prevailed in Natal. Nothing affected his spirits, he had a joke for everyone, but he was far from being a 'farceur'. He was equally good at his duties in the camp and field . . . and in fact the 'little green tent on the hill' as my Headquarters was called, was the only cheerful spot in that gloomy seat of War.

Lyttelton's personal assessment may have been accurate at the time, but as the years passed the most dominant trait in Wilson's character became a passion for intrigue – or 'mischief', as he himself was to call it. A man who earned such tributes and showed such good sense and practical ability should have 'got on' and attained not only promotion but high command as well, but though Wilson eventually became a field marshal and CIGS, the top field commands in the Great War were to elude him. His capacity for intrigue made him enemies, and even his friends were wary of him. Wilson was the sort of man who had to be kept busy, for if he had time to spare he would use it to foment trouble or stir things up. For the moment, though, all was going well. He became Military Secretary to Lord Roberts, who replaced Buller in South Africa, and on his return to Britain in 1901 was appointed to the DSO and raised to brevet lieutenant-colonel, a man marked for promotion.

After South Africa, Wilson's career flourished and he achieved regular promotion. He took a prominent part in the shake-up in the Army that followed the South African War and supported the changes and reforms introduced by successive War Ministers, including Haldane's creation of a General Staff. From 1907 to 1910 he was Commandant of the Staff College and during this time he went to France, where he paid a courtesy call on his opposite number at the École Supérieur de la Guerre Général, General Ferdinand Foch.

This was a fateful meeting. It is fair to say that Wilson was smitten with Foch, fell completely under his spell, and remained that way for the rest of his life. Invited for a chat before lunch, Wilson returned in the afternoon for further discussions and yet again on the following day, later declaring that these encounters had been a meeting of minds. 'Foch's appreciation of German moves through Belgium are completely the same as mine,' he recorded, 'the important line being between Verdun and Namur.'

These first meetings took place in December 1909; in mid-January 1910, Wilson was back in Paris again. In May of that year Foch came to visit Wilson at Camberley, and in June the latter went with Foch on the École de la Guerre staff tour. From then on the relationship flourished, with visits to and fro and constant communication, but there is no doubt that Foch was the master and Wilson the disciple in this warm and developing relationship. Wilson openly declared around the War Office that 'this fellow – Foch – is going to command the Allied armies when the big war comes on,' and did all he could to introduce Foch to the British military and political Establishment and stress Foch's undoubted abilities to his British colleagues.

Ferdinand Foch was born in 1851. As a student in 1871 he had seen his Emperor, Napoleon III, ride in defeat through Metz, but Foch spent most of his service career as a military thinker and theorist rather than as a regimental officer or a commander. He was a man of strong views, who believed that the most important element in any battle was the character and will of the commanders, that victory would go to the man who did not recognise the possibility of defeat. Foch believed in the 'Will to Conquer'. Given that, plus the bayonet and a battery of quick-firing 75-mm guns, anything was possible. He wrote books on military theory – his *Principes de la guerre* laid out his beliefs in detail – and his views had a profound influence on French military thinking before the Great War, especially after he found a platform for indoctrination during his stint at the École de la Guerre, first as Professor of Strategy from 1894, then as its Commandant from 1907–11.

Fortunately, there was more to Foch than theories. He had a good grasp of strategy and he thoroughly understood the business of war, the importance of logistics and the need to integrate all arms in successful combination. He had his blind spots, however. In 1910 he said that the aeroplane was 'all very well for sport but for the Army it is useless,' and, like the rest of the French High Command with the possible exception of Pétain, he was a devotee of the Grandmaison *attaque à outrance* philosophy, and played a major part in formulating Plan XVII, the French scheme for an all-out assault on Germany on the outbreak of war, a war which Foch confidently believed would be a short one. When war came Foch was commanding the XX Corps, the famous 'Iron Corps' of the French Army, at Nancy, where he proved a tough, hard-fighting battlefield commander, though he was soon to leave that position to take command of the Ninth Army. He also kept in close contact with his old friend, Henry Wilson.

After Wilson left the Staff College he became Director of Military Operations at the War Office, a post directly concerned with operations overseas. He made no secret of the fact that his main aim was to prepare plans to link the BEF with the French when war came, drawing up programmes and timetables under which the BEF would be rapidly transported from Britain to its post on the left of the French line. To the British Government, Wilson's talks with the French were no more than 'conversations', an exploration of the possibilities; to Wilson and the French High Command they evinced a firm commitment on Britain's part.

This planning activity was to prove useful in 1914, though it was without any official sanction. The British Government had made *no open formal alliance* in support of the French, and had still not done so when war broke out in 1914. The fact that it was tacitly accepted that Britain *would* send a force to France was largely due to Wilson's efforts during the immediate pre-war years. The latter saw himself as the architect of Franco-British understanding and therefore a major player when war broke out, as being the only man in Britain who *really* knew what was going on.

Wilson was already angry with Kitchener for reducing the size of the BEF, and further embarrassed that Britain had not declared war on Germany on 1 August, the day Germany declared war on France. Britain, he believed, should have mobilised on that day and thereafter kept pace with French mobilisation, but now the country was dragging its feet and letting *la belle France* down. Wilson records the War Cabinet meeting of 5 August as 'an historic meeting of great men, mostly entirely ignorant of their subject'. Clearly he had forgotten that these 'great men' were either his political masters or his superior officers, something which was to lead him into error when the French emissary, Colonel Huguet, reached London.

Huguet arrived on the afternoon of 6 August and was immediately snapped up by Wilson. The two men had a long talk in Wilson's office, after which Huguet went straight back to Paris. News of his visit had by now reached Kitchener, who sent for Wilson and demanded to know why he had seen fit to interview the French Government delegate without bringing him directly to meet the British Secretary of State for War. Kitchener was further infuriated when it transpired that Wilson had told Huguet all about the Cabinet discussions of 5 August, and had assured him that the BEF would start crossing the Channel on Sunday, 9 August. Wilson's diary entry for the 5th concludes with the comment that, 'I answered back, as I have no intention of being bullied by him, especially when he talks such nonsense . . . he is sending troops from Aldershot to Grimsby, thus hopelessly messing up our plans.' 'Our plans', we must presume, were the plans Wilson had been at pains to prepare with the French before the war.

Wilson's biographer, Callwell, does not conceal his opinion that his subject was entirely wrong in this episode. Field Marshal Kitchener was the Secretary for War; moreover, he spoke good French. Kitchener naturally wanted to see Huguet, and had every right to do so without either obstruction or unwanted assistance from Henry Wilson. The latter's attitude to Kitchener was unfortunate and caused friction between the two men from then on. It was also a portent that, in matters concerning France's involvement in the war, Wilson was determined to take his own line and press his views – and those of the French – on his British colleagues and superiors, and not least on that ever-susceptible field marshal, Sir John French.

Up to a point, Wilson's intensely francophile leanings were no bad thing. Britain and France were allies, and it was essential that their political and military leaders should communicate, that their forces should co-operate and their plans should coincide. The problem was that Wilson went beyond that point; his actions, though undoubtedly well-meaning, were not always helpful to his superiors in the British Army, who were already in some difficulty with their new allies.

On arriving in France on the evening of 14 August, Field Marshal French and his staff drove to Paris, where the Field Marshal met the President of the Republic, M. Raymond Poincaré, and the Minister of War, M. Messimy, on the afternoon of the 15th. On the following day he drove to the French general headquarters – GQG – at Vitry-le-François, where he had his first meeting with the French Commander-in-Chief, General Joffre.

French recorded that his first impression of Joffre was of

> a man of strong will and determination, courteous and considerate, but firm and steadfast of mind and purpose and not easily turned or persuaded . . . These were all first impressions but eveɪything I then thought of General Joffre were far more confirmed throughout the year and a half of fierce struggle in which I was associated with him. History will record him as one of the supremely great commanders.

The immediate task before him was tremendous and nobly did he arise to it.' (*Life of Field Marshal French*, pp. 204–5.)

History has not, in fact, been so kind to General Joffre. In this, history has been unjust to another Great War general who, from the outbreak of war until his dismissal two years later, was undoubtedly the most influential military leader on the Allied side, the man who saved the French nation – and thus, arguably, Europe – from disaster in the early months of the war. Joseph Jacques Césaire Joffre was born at Rivesaltes, a village at the foot of the French Pyrenees, in 1852. He came of humble stock and from a large family, for his father, a cooper, had eleven children to support. In 1870, when Joffre was still a student, he found himself serving a cannon against the Prussian Army and he continued with the artillery during the Siege of Paris in 1871, but had joined the Engineer Corps before being sent to Indo-China, then under French control, in 1873.

Joffre's military career was largely spent in the French Empire. He was involved in the Timbuktu Expedition of 1894, then served in Madagascar before returning to become Director of the Engineer Corps in 1904. He then sought a field command, and spent the years from 1906–10 commanding first an infantry division, and then an army corps, both in Metropolitan France. In 1910 he became a member of the French War Council and in 1911 Chief of the General Staff. In this role he introduced three-year conscription, increased the work then being done on the fortifications along France's eastern frontiers and, with the assistance of General de Castelnau, finalised the details of Plan XVII. The Chief of the General Staff was also *de facto* Commander-in-Chief of the French Army, and in this role Joffre was less successful.

As to his character, various traits stand out. A modern historian has described Joffre as 'a man with immense patience, enormous strength, great courage and few nerves; he was not an intellectual but he had intellectuals in his entourage and he listened to them.' (John Hussey, letter to the author, 1997.) The single quality that attracted the greatest amount of comment at the time, however, was Joffre's prodigious appetite; he ate gargantuan meals, followed by long siestas, and woe betide any officer or courier who interrupted either of these events, even with a vital dispatch. In his *The Price of Glory*, Alistair Horne has described Joffre as 'a true viscero-tonic, a man who thought with his belly rather than his mind'.

Joffre did not study strategy before the war, nor was he to show any interest in how the war was fought in the years after the Armistice. The basis of his great contribution to victory and the survival of the French nation in the early months of the war might well be described as 'gut-feeling', an instinctive understanding of the battlefield and a stubborn, phlegmatic refusal to panic, a state which he maintained in adversity, however bad the news from the front. Joffre's calm, somewhat dour nature, his refusal to let his decisions be swayed by events, was to save his country from disaster when the German war machine swept over the frontiers of France in the summer of 1914, when the news from the front was very bad indeed.

Joffre's judgement on his colleages and subordinates is more suspect, though he was ruthless in sacking any general who failed to live up to his expectations. Field Marshal French soon found fault with one of Joffre's opinions, namely that General Lanrezac, commanding the French Fifth Army, the force that would lie on the right flank of the BEF, was one of the finest officers in the French Army. French drove directly from Vitry-le-François to Lanrezac's headquarters at Rethel for a meeting that was to affect the BEF considerably in the days ahead. French records that Lanrezac was, 'a big man with a loud voice and his manner did not strike me as very courteous'. This comment might be regarded as an understatement, for at this first meeting between the two commanders General Lanrezac was extremely rude.

It was now 17 August, and General Lanrezac was a worried man. He had good reason to be worried. The French Army was poised to implement Plan XVII, which called for four out of the five French armies, a force totalling around 800,000 men, to surge through Alsace and Lorraine into the heart of Germany with the aim of dislocating the enemy war machine before it could swing into action.

The French First and Second Armies would attack south of Metz, and would be connected by the Third Army with Lanrezac's Fifth Army to the north of that city, while the Fourth Army remained in reserve. Plan XVII was taking shape, but Lanrezac had the distinct impression that something formidable was taking place in the north and threatening his left flank along the Belgian frontier, on the Rivers Sambre and Meuse. That flank was at present 'in the air' since the British Army had *not* mobilised with the French Army on 1 August, and the BEF had therefore *not* arrived as expected and taken up position on Lanrezac's left. Apart from a French cavalry division and some territorial units, the country between Lanrezac's left flank and the French Channel coast was completely devoid of troops . . . and Lanrezac blamed the British for this situation.

Nor could he persuade Joffre or anyone else at GQG to pay any attention to his fears that the Germans now rampaging across Belgium were intent on encircling his left flank, though Joffre had allowed him to realign some of his troops along the Sambre, just in case there was some substance to his fears. Lanrezac had not received any reinforcements for this move and was therefore thinning out his centre in order to strengthen his left, a process known as 'taking ground to the flank'. He was also becoming steadily more peeved with the still-absent British, so that when French and his staff drove into Fifth Army's headquarters on 17 August they met with a frosty reception. As they got out of their cars Lanrezac's Chief of Staff greeted them with, 'Well here you are, and about time too . . . If we are beaten, it will be thanks to you.'

Fortunately, this remark was in French. Only Henry Wilson and Lieutenant Edward Spears, a British liaison officer with the French Fifth Army, understood it, for Field Marshal French's language skills were extremely limited. In spite of this, French and Lanrezac withdrew into a side room for a private discussion, re-emerging swiftly when they realised that they could not understand each other. The generals then consulted the war map, while a French staff officer gave an assessment of the situation, including the view that the Germans had reached the River Meuse. French found the Meuse on the map and, putting his finger on one of the bridges at Huy, asked Lanrezac, in his stumbling French, what he thought the Germans were doing there? Lanrezac replied that he thought the Germans had gone there to fish.

The Field Marshal did not fully understand this reply, but he caught the tone of it and realised that Lanrezac was being sarcastic and insulting. Like many French officers, Lanrezac did not care for the British, regarded the British Army as an amateur force, and felt no need to go out of his way to treat his country's ally with courtesy. The atmosphere in the room became tense and after a few moments French made his brief goodbyes and withdrew. 'I left General Lanrezac's headquarters believing that the Commander-in-Chief [Joffre] had overrated his ability.'

This meeting had the most unfortunate repercussions. It was vital that the two armies, Lanrezac's Fifth and the BEF, should co-operate closely in the hard days ahead, but the commanding generals had already formed an unfavourable impression of each other and French had no particular desire to meet Lanrezac again. He hurried on to Le Cateau, where his own headquarters were then being set up. There he would be surrounded by his own officers, men with manners, men who knew more about war than any arrogant French upstart.

However, when he arrived at Le Cateau on 17 August, French met more bad news. One of his officers, Lieutenant-General Sir James Grierson, the commander of II Corps and a personal friend, had collapsed with a heart attack on a train near Amiens and died. A new commander must be sent out, and sent quickly, for the troops, the front-line battalions of the BEF, were now coming up, long columns of infantry, cavalry and artillery flooding over the cobbled roads of France, and concentrating around Le Cateau before advancing towards the Belgian frontier. The Field Marshal therefore sent a request that Lieutenant-General Sir Herbert Plumer should be sent out from Britain with the utmost dispatch to take command of II Corps.

While waiting for the arrival of his new subordinate, French held a conference at Rethel, during which he outlined the current situation, in so far as it was known, to Major-General Edmund Allenby, commanding the single cavalry division of the BEF, and General Haig of I Corps. Most of the news he had to give them came, via Henry Wilson, from the French. The burden of this intelligence was that some five German corps were about to move across the northern French frontier on a line between Brussels and Givet. This was only a part of the force so deployed, but even so the fact that the Germans were massing in the north did not seem to be causing Joffre any undue alarm. Few things did, but on this occasion 'Papa' Joffre's normal state of calm was leading him rapidly into error.

On 18 August he concluded that: 'The enemy may engage only a fraction of his right wing north of the Meuse. While his centre is engaged frontally by our Third and Fourth Armies, the other part of his northern group, south of the Meuse, may seek to engage the flank of our Fourth Army.' In making this assessment Joffre appears to assume that Moltke was as obsessed with Plan XVII as he was, and that the German general was deploying his forces in the north with the sole purpose of taking the French armies in the flank *as those armies pushed to the east*. The notion that the Germans were, in fact, preparing a great, westward thrust into France from Belgium had not occurred to Joffre. He told Lanrezac that the BEF and the Belgians were 'quite capable of dealing with the German forces north of the Meuse and Sambre' – an optimistic forecast in view of the large number of enemy troops involved. As a result of this intelligence Field Marshal French held to the same opinion and resolved to lead his forces north as soon as they had assembled.

The 20th was a significant day on many sections of the embryonic Western Front. On 20 August, the German First Army entered Brussels. On 20 August, RFC patrols reported long columns of German infantry and artillery heading south and west, straight for the British section of the front. These reports were rejected by Henry Wilson, in charge of operations at French's GHQ, who declared that the RFC information was 'somewhat exaggerated . . . only mounted troops or jägers [i.e. light infantry deployed for scouting] are in your area'. On 20 August, those French armies pushing into Alsace and Lorraine were met and counter-attacked by the advancing German forces of Crown Prince Rupprecht of Bavaria, a counter-attack which was to have a grave effect on the operation of the Schlieffen Plan. On 20 August, French reported to Joffre that his forces had all arrived and he was about to march north towards the Belgian frontier and take up his position on the flank of the French Fifth Army.

This march commenced on the following day, the 21st. On that day the new commander of II Corps arrived, not General Plumer as French had requested, but General Sir Horace Smith-Dorrien, a man Field Marshal French loathed. All seemed friendly when the two men met, however, and the BEF movement forward continued on 22 August. By this time Lanrezac's command had been heavily engaged and pushed back across the Sambre, while the French armies further east were being driven back by the Germans in what came to be called the Battle of the Frontiers. The force of France were already in trouble – and worse, much worse, was to follow.

It is time now to consider the other events of the first three weeks of August. On 4 August, the Germans had advanced into Belgium and moved along the River Meuse until, by the 8th, they were besieging the city of Liège. This much the French knew, but exactly which German army was doing all this was as yet unclear. The main German forces appeared to be mustering around Metz or in Luxemburg, ready to advance to the west or the south, depending on what happened at Liège, which was actually under attack from an advanced force of six German brigades and a quantity of super-heavy artillery.

The Schlieffen Plan depended on *speed*. While the German armies were assembling along the frontiers of Belgium, Luxemburg and France, this advanced force had crossed into Belgium to invest Liège, which elements of the German Second Army entered on 5 August. The city itself was abandoned on the following day, but Liège was surrounded by a network of fortifications and many of these still held out. It took six days to bring up the siege cannon and another four days for these heavy guns to reduce the Belgian outposts to rubble. The Liège fortifications finally fell on 16 August, but this stern resistance to the Germans put the first crimp in the Schlieffen Plan.

This delay in the west was matched by a German defeat on the Eastern Front, where the Russians sent two barely mobilised armies into East Prussia and took the Eighth Army, the only German army guarding that part of the Reich, completely by surprise. The Austrians were also shocked when they invaded Serbia, suffering their first defeat of the war on 12 August at the hands of the hard-fighting Serbian Army. The Austrians sent in massed infantry attacks, and their men went down in swaths under the artillery and rifle fire of the Serbs. On the 17th the Russians entered East Prussia, and four more Russian armies began gathering along the Austrian frontier in Galicia.

But if the Central Powers were not doing well in the east, by 16 August the fog of war in the west was enveloping Joffre and his staff at GQG. It appeared that a large German force was attempting to pass the Meuse between Givet and Brussels and that another German thrust was developing in the Ardennes, although the main German armies south of Metz appeared to be on the defensive. This suited the French as they prepared to launch their attack in accordance with Plan XVII, but this static German frontier defence was in fact a part of the Schlieffen Plan, which was now starting to develop in the north. The Belgian Army was driven steadily back, Kluck's First Army entered Brussels, and on the 21st the German Second Army invested Namur, another fortress city, at the junction of the Meuse and Sambre. The three armies on the right of the German line, the First, Second and Third, were now sweeping ahead and driving all before them. The French armies charged with implementing Plan XVII, the advance into Alsace and Lorraine, were not so fortunate when they began their attack, though the stiff German resistance they met ran contrary to the Schlieffen Plan, which required a slow German retreat by which the bulk of the French armies would be lured away to the east.

Plan XVII – 'to advance with all forces united to the attack of the German Armies' – was implemented on 20 August. It called for a thrust east by four French armies, with General de Castelnau's Second Army in the van. The planned German reaction to this long-anticipated attack was to hold a defensive line along the Franco-German border with two armies, which would suck the main French forces into battle, while three German armies made the wheeling advance south-west through Belgium and France to circle Paris and take them in the rear. Unfortunately, the German commander on the Alsace front, Crown Prince Rupprecht, could not bring himself to fight a defensive battle or a fighting retreat. He elected to counter-attack the advancing French armies and General Count von Moltke, the German Chief of Staff (effectively the Army C-in-C), gave him permission to do so. The Schlieffen Plan, so long and carefully prepared, at once began to fall apart.

On 20 August, the French First and Second Armies ran headlong into Prince Rupprecht's counter-attack; the result was a slaughter of the French infantry by the German machine-guns and field artillery. The first two 'Battles of the Frontier', at Sarrebourg and Morhange, dealt a devastating blow to Plan XVII. By the following day the French First and Second Armies, having suffered terrible losses, were in full retreat towards Nancy, a city that might have fallen but for the stubborn defence put up by XX Corps, commanded by General Foch.

This drama had the additional effect of diverting Joffre's attention from what was happening in Belgium, leaving him deaf to the pleas for aid coming from General Lanrezac. Never more phlegmatic than in adversity, Joffre refused to be upset by the frontier catastrophe, not least because he did not believe that the Germans had the manpower to shatter Plan XVII *and* make any significant advance through Belgium. He therefore ordered another attack, this time by the French Third and Fourth Armies in the Ardennes, anticipating that they would strike at the weak centre of the German line and cut the communications serving the advancing German right (northernmost) wing. Joffre had not yet appreciated that the German use of reserve corps enabled their armies to be strong everywhere, and this attack was repulsed with great loss, particularly among the French officers, who led their men forward with great courage and *élan*, and died in scores under the machine-guns.

These first actions of the war provide early proof that it was not only British generals who made mistakes. Prince Rupprecht's decision to attack rather than fight a holding battle, and Moltke's error in permitting him to do so, completely undermined the Schlieffen Plan. While the outcome had the local advantage of slaughtering thousands of French soldiers and about 10 per cent of the French Army's professional officer corps, this small gain could not offset the later effect caused by tampering with a vital strategic plan that *might*, just *might*, have given victory to Germany in the first weeks of the war.

It is also probable that Plan XVII, the French recipe for swift victory, was fatally flawed from its inception. The weapons of the day, given their chance to display their full power against infantry in the open, did awesome execution everywhere during August 1914. The prime cause of this slaughter lay with the plan itself, a plan based on an all-out advance on the enemy, an *attaque à outrance*, an attack that relied on *élan* and the valour of the French infantry, regardless of the terrain, the power of the enemy, the weaponry deployed or the situation at any given time. Neglecting these factors, or completely ignoring them, changed a plan for success into a recipe for slaughter. Plan XVII required, even demanded, gallantry and *élan*; the greater the gallantry shown, the greater the slaughter would be, and the French soldiers of the Great War were very gallant indeed. So, in these first battles of the war, we see Austrian infantry mown down by the Serbs and French infantry mown down in huge numbers by the Germans, all victims of the firepower made available by the weapons of the day. Other nations, in other battles fought in similar ways, were soon to suffer a comparable fate.

The war was not yet a month old, and disaster was staring France fully in the face. Her First, Second, Third and Fourth Armies had been savaged by the Hun, who was now coming on into France in overwhelming numbers as the French armies fell back in retreat. Now, at last, Joffre turned his attention to the northern frontier, where Lanrezac's Fifth Army and the BEF were about to be attacked by yet more German armies. In round figures, three German armies, mustering thirty-four divisions, were about to fall on the ten divisions of Lanzerac's Fifth Army and the four infantry and one cavalry division of the BEF. General Lanrezac was already in a difficult situation, for his movement towards the left flank of the French line had put his army into the salient formed by the Meuse and the Sambre. These rivers met at the city of Namur, and both Namur and Lanrezac's positions on the Sambre were already under attack.

On 22 August, sensing that all was not well, and worried about the situation on his right flank, Field Marshal French decided to make another call on his ill-tempered French colleague, and accordingly set out for Lanrezac's headquarters at Chimay. On the way, French met Spears, the BEF liaison officer at Lanrezac's HQ, who told him that Lanrezac had no intention of advancing any further and was quite prepared to withdraw if the German pressure increased. Spears also told the Field Marshal that French intelligence reports indicated that a large German force was coming in on the left flank.

This news put French in a quandary; his orders from Joffre obliged him to advance, but this news from Lanrezac hinted at retreat . . . and if Lanrezac retreated, and the BEF advanced or even halted, it would soon be dangerously exposed, in a position forward of the French Army, and with a widening gap on its right flank. In this situation the best solution was for the two army commanders to meet and agree a common course of action, but the memory of that first encounter still rankled and French therefore returned to Le Cateau. Lanrezac's army was already falling back but, lacking orders from Joffre, French decided to stay where he was. The BEF was now on the Belgian frontier and there their commander decided they should stay, digging in along the line of the Mons-Condé Canal to await developments or further orders. It was now the evening of 22 August, the eve of the Battle of Mons.

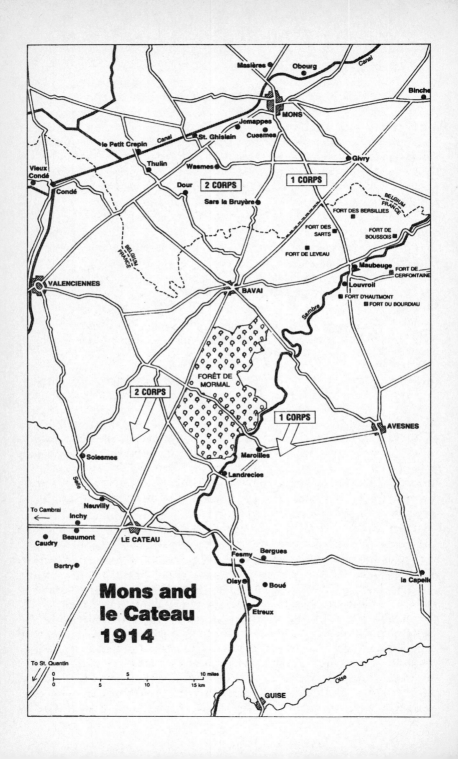

Mons and
le Cateau
1914

CHAPTER 4

ADVANCES AND RETREATS, MONS AND LE CATEAU, 23–26 AUGUST 1914

*'I have seen the Iron Corps of France in the square at Ypres;
I have seen the Canadians marching to St Julien before the
gas attack; I have seen Indian troops going into action for
the first time on European soil; I have seen the Australians
on their way to the attack at Pozières; but I have no
remembrance to equal, in any way, that of the old regiments
of the BEF, marching to the battle of Mons.'*

Captain C.A.L. Brownlow, Royal Field Artillery

While the BEF was marching from the Channel coast to the Belgian frontier, sweltering in heavy kit under the summer sun, many men limping on feet blistered by their newly issued boots, the enemy was assembling his forces for a massive push into France. The main weight of that German advance, a move dictated by the Schlieffen Plan, would come in the north, through Belgium,

It remains a mystery why, in spite of prior intelligence and increasing evidence, the French General Staff remained unconvinced that the Germans were planning to invade in strength through Belgium. The broad outlines of the Schlieffen Plan had been known for years, and even as the war opened, Colonel Repington, Military Correspondent of *The Times*, had produced an article and accompanying map which indicated the disposition of the German forces, clearly showing that the main weight of their arms rested in the north. If further evidence were needed, the fact that the Germans were willing to take the risk – indeed court the certainty – of British involvement if Belgium were invaded should have indicated that such an invasion would be by a large force. The Germans would not have risked a major escalation of the war just to let a few cavalry brigades water their horses in the Meuse.

French moves to counter this developing threat were at best hesitant, in spite of General Lanrezac's pleading, for attention at the Grand Quartier Générale (GQG) was firmly fixed on the implementation of Plan XVII and their major thrusts into Germany east through Alsace, Lorraine and the Ardennes. To trace the events that brought the BEF into action at Mons, it is therefore necessary to go back to a few days before that encounter and consider developments in the north. On 15 August, German cavalry appeared on the Meuse at Dinant, south of Namur. On that day Lanrezac obtained permission to shift the front of his forces from the east, facing the Ardennes, to the north-east, between the Rivers Meuse and Sambre, on a line from Givet to Maubeuge, where Lanrezac's Fifth Army would link up with the BEF. Joffre, now becoming worried that the Germans might indeed be preparing a major thrust through Belgium, also ordered the French Fourth Army, on Lanrezac's right, to prepare defensive positions. Given the French commitment to *l'offensive à outrance*, this represented a major concession from GQG, but it came a little late.

The Germans started crossing the Meuse on 17 August, and French cavalry pickets, observing the crossing, reported that the German divisions were heading north, into Belgium, not south into France. Brussels fell to the German First Army on 20 August and on the 21st the Second Army laid siege to the city of Namur, at the junction of the Sambre and Meuse. By then the Liège forts had already fallen and it became clear that the German First, Second and Third Armies, totalling sixteen corps with six attached divisions and five cavalry divisions, were part of a great movement to the west, one that would swing around the left flank of Lanrezac's Fifth Army and head south into France. On the far, northernmost tip of that left flank stood the four infantry divisions and one cavalry division of the British Expeditionary Force.

The weight of the German First Army was now bearing down upon the BEF as it moved north but on Saturday, 22 August, their advance screened by Allenby's cavalry division, the British divisions took up positions along the line of the wide canal which runs east–west like an arrow for sixteen miles between Condé and Mons, and which provided them with a defensible line. Sixty-four feet wide and averaging seven feet in depth, the canal was spanned by no fewer than eighteen bridges; these, however, could be demolished or covered by fire. When the move had been completed, in the early hours of 23 August, the BEF positions, from the west, were as follows:

On the extreme left lay the newly arrived 19 Infantry Brigade. This had been sent by Field Marshal French to strengthen the flank of Smith-Dorrien's II Corps and fill the gap between that corps and the French 84th Territorial Division to the west. Then, moving east, came the divisions of Smith-Dorrien's corps, starting with the 5th Division, which lined the canal from Le Petit Crépin as far as Mons. Just west of Mons the canal swings north in a wide sweep around the town as far as Oberg, three miles east of Mons, before heading east again into the Sambre. This swing created a forward salient, later called the 'Mons Salient', which, though occupied by troops of the 3rd Division of II Corps, was seen as indefensible if the Germans attacked in strength, as it could be brought under fire from three sides. Smith-Dorrien established his HQ at Sars-la-Bruyère, five miles south of the canal. Communications, other than by courier, were poor. There was no time to lay out lines and establish telephone links along the twenty-mile front held by II Corps, and the existing telephone network was not extensive.

Haig's I Corps was positioned south of Mons, facing east and attempting to stay in contact with the left wing of Lanrezac's army, though the gap was steadily widening. Meanwhile French had established his GHQ at Le Cateau, with his Advanced HQ at Bavai and, thus deployed, the BEF waited for further orders or the arrival of the enemy. If French was unhappy to have Smith-Dorrien commanding one of his two corps, there is little evidence of it from the first days of the campaign, though Kitchener's action in sending out Smith-Dorrien instead of Plumer eventually precipitated one of the great personal tragedies of the war. In a war that cost so many lives, a squabble between two senior officers on one sector of the Western Front must be kept in proportion. It merits inclusion, however, because this quarrel was to cost Britain the services of a good general, and and because it reveals a good deal about the character of Field-Marshal French, who had been nursing a grudge against Smith-Dorrien for years. He was to maintain his enmity even after the war, and far beyond the point of reason.

The roots of French's antipathy to Smith-Dorrien can be traced back to 1907, when French left the Aldershot Command and was followed into that post by Smith-Dorrien. The latter reviewed his new command and at once began to tinker with French's beloved cavalry, ordering fewer exercises with sword and lance and more time spent on rifle practice and infantry tactics. It appeared that Smith-Dorrien intended to turn the cavalry into the much-detested mounted infantry . . . and this within weeks of General French having given up the command.

From such disputes can great resentments grow. Smith-Dorrien maintained his own point of view and insisted that the cavalry units in the Aldershot Command become at least competent in infantry tactics and musketry, a view he stressed in his autobiography many years later:

> It had for a long time been evident to many soldiers that, both in the mounted and dismounted service rapid fire might prove a decisive factor in war, that the days of the cavalry charge in large formations were numbered, and that in a big action their horses would be chiefly valuable to get them into a position quickly where they could dismount and fire. This had been admirably illustrated by the Japanese pressing back the Russian Army at Mukden in 1904.
>
> I was, therefore, not at all pleased to find that the Cavalry Brigade at Aldershot were low down on the annual musketry courses and further, on field days and manoeuvres hardly ever dismounted but delivered perfectly carried out, but impossible, knee-to-knee charges against infantry in action. So, on 21 August 1909 ordering all cavalry

officers to meet me in the 16th Lancers' mess, I gave them my views pretty clearly with the result that dismounted work was taken up seriously. I submit that my action was justified by what happened in the Great War but at the time I am aware that my attitude was resented. (*Memories of Forty-Eight Years' Service*, pp. 358–9.)

Smith-Dorrien had a hot temper, and was not the most tactful of men, while French, by then Inspector-General of the Forces, certainly resented his successor's actions, and nursed this grievance against Smith-Dorrien for years. During his time as Inspector-General, and in spite of the fact that Aldershot was the principal UK command, French never visited Smith-Dorrien unless obliged to do so as part of his duty as ADC to the King, who inspected the Aldershot Command once a year. The last man, therefore, French wanted in August 1914 was Smith-Dorrien, but such is the way of the military world that Smith-Dorrien was the man he got. Although French later went to great lengths to disparage his subordinate general, he was to be well served by his unwanted II Corps commander in the difficult months ahead.

Kitchener was well aware of French's antipathy to Smith-Dorrien. French's successor as CIGS, General Sir Charles Douglas, told the Secretary for War that this appointment would 'put Smith-Dorrien in an impossible position' since French 'had shown great jealousy of and personal animus towards Smith-Dorrien for some years'. Kitchener told Smith-Dorrien that he had doubts about the wisdom of sending him to France but in the end Kitchener stuck to his decision and Smith-Dorrien took up his new command at Bavai, eighteen miles north-east of Le Cateau, on the evening of 20 August. He drove back from there to meet Sir John French and by his own account was greeted 'pleasantly'.

Lieutenant-General Sir Horace Smith-Dorrien was an interesting man. He was born in Hertfordshire in 1858, the eleventh in a family of fifteen children. His father was a soldier, which influenced Horace's decision to join the Army, and he entered the Royal Military College, Sandhurst, in February 1876. Destined for the Rifle Brigade (95th Rifles), he was eventually commissioned into what would become the 2nd Battalion, Sherwood Foresters, in January 1877, and went directly to his regiment in Ireland.

Smith-Dorrien was a tall, hot-tempered man with a lantern jaw and a kindly, although not an outgoing, personality. He was interested in the welfare of his soldiers, and when in command at Aldershot took steps to improve the barrack-room and recreational facilities of the private soldier, and ended the practice of sending pickets of military police about the town in the evening, believing that the soldiers did not need to be harassed in their off-duty time. He studied the elements of his profession, was extremely capable in the field and was widely regarded in the Army as a good soldier. He also saw a lot of soldiering, most of it in India, Egypt and South Africa.

He was sent to South Africa in 1878 and took part in the Zulu War of 1879, where he was one of only five British officers to escape from the massacre of British and African troops by a Zulu *impi* at the Battle of Isandhlwana. When the British line was overwhelmed by the Zulus, Smith-Dorrien fought his way down to the Buffalo River, swam across, rescued a brother officer, and made his way on foot to the town Helpmakaar, twenty miles away, keeping off his Zulu pursuers with shots from his revolver.

After this alarming experience he returned briefly to Ireland and then served in Egypt under Sir Garnet Wolseley during the 1882 Arabi campaign. He then spent some time in India before being seconded to the Egyptian Army for the Suakin campaign against the Dervishes, during which he took part in the Battle of Ginnis, the last occasion on which British soldiers wore their red coats in battle.

From 1887–9 he studied at the Staff College and having passed the course, returned to India, where he saw further action on the North-West Frontier in the Tirah Campaign of 1897–8. He returned to Egypt in May 1898 to take command of a Sudanese battalion in Kitchener's Nile campaign which terminated at the battle of Omdurman. After that victory he accompanied Kitchener upriver to meet the French explorer, Commandant Marchand, at Fashoda.

At the outbreak of the South African War in 1899 Smith-Dorrien was a lieutenant-colonel commanding the 1st Sherwood Foresters, but by February 1900 he had been promoted and had taken command of 19 Infantry Brigade; shortly afterwards he was promoted again, to the rank of major-general. He saw a great deal of active service in the South African War. He had command of a column during the latter stages of that war, and was then dispatched to India as Adjutant-General, serving in this capacity from 1902–3. From 1903–5 he commanded the 4th Division of the Indian Army, and in 1907, by then a lieutenant-general and a KCB, was given the Aldershot Command, a highly prestigious post in what is effectively the home of the British Army. His autobiography records that except for the two years he had spent at the Staff College this was his first posting in the United Kingdom for twenty-seven years.

It was clear that Lieutenant-General Sir Horace Smith-Dorrien was destined for higher things. On leaving Aldershot he was offered command in South Africa, but preferred to take over Southern Command, based in Salisbury, where he became acquainted with Britain's newly formed Territorial troops, part-time soldiers whom he came to admire for their enthusiasm and intelligence. He was still GOC Southern Command in August 1914 when he was sent to France to serve under Sir John French.

If the rest of the Army knew how French felt about Smith-Dorrien, the latter can hardly have been unaware of it himself. No man willingly puts himself under the orders of a personal enemy, but there were exceptional circumstances here, not the least being that for a professional soldier, the only place to be in August 1914 was with the BEF in France. Whatever reservations Smith-Dorrien must have felt about French, he jumped at the offer of a fighting command, and two days after he arrived at Bavai, II Corps went into action at Mons.

On that day, 22 August, as the BEF advanced, Lanrezac began to withdraw, forced back by pressure from the German Second Army which was bearing down on his front and right flank. Allenby's cavalry screen, operating ahead and on the left flank of the BEF, bumped into German cavalry and were soon reporting back that strong enemy forces seemed to be somewhere to their front; these reports, however, like those previously received from the RFC observers, were discounted at French's HQ. The latter's left flank was quite open, with nothing to screen it but French Territorial troops and General Sordet's French Cavalry Corps, but the BEF commander was more concerned with his right flank, where Haig's corps seemed to be losing touch with Lanrezac's Fifth Army. This was a legitimate concern, for by the evening of 22 August the BEF was some ten miles ahead of the Fifth Army, with a growing gap between the flanks of the two armies. The more Lanrezac withdrew or the BEF advanced, the wider that gap would become.

French eventually decided to halt his advance on the line of the Mons-Condé Canal, rejecting a request from Lanrezac on the 22nd that the BEF should wheel right on the following day and attack any German thrust threatening the left flank of Fifth Army. That night Lanrezac informed Joffre that, far from being out in front, the BEF were actually 'echeloned in rear of 5th Army', which was not only quite untrue, but obvious nonsense. Something close to chaos was reigning between the HQs of the BEF and the French Fifth Army as the British infantry drew up to the south bank of the Mons-Condé Canal later that night, and began to dig in.

The situation of the BEF was critical, but that was not the fault of Field Marshal French. He had been ordered by Kitchener to co-operate with the French Army, and that was what he was trying to do by obeying Joffre's orders to advance to the north. The error lay with the actions of the French Fifth Army, which was crumbling before the German pressure, thus allowing the German Third Army to push itself forward at Charleroi and into the growing gap between the Fifth Army and General Langle de Cary's Fourth Army on Lanrezac's right. Lanrezac himself was prepared to abandon the British allies on his left flank in an attempt to stay in touch with the French army on his right. The answer to the problem lay in closer co-operation and in the maintenance of a common BEF-Fifth Army front against the developing attack from the north-east, but neither came about. As for French, he elected to hold his ground along the canal and prepared to give battle at Mons.

The country around Mons is not ideal for a defensive battle. The Official History describes the area as 'one huge unsightly village, traversed by cobbled roads and overlooked by pit heads and slag heaps, often over 100 feet high. It is a close and blind country such as no army had yet been called upon to fight against a civilised enemy in a great campaign.' (Volume I, p. 63). General Smith-Dorrien, coming up to review the position, saw that the area around the 'Mons Salient' was not defensible and proposed withdrawing his troops from the salient and preparing a second, shorter, defence line a mile or so south of the canal. His corps front, currently stretched along the canal and round the town of Mons, extended for over twenty miles, far too long a front for two divisions and one attached brigade. However, the canal was a useful barrier and II Corps stayed in position. The weight of the German onslaught was to fall on Smith-Dorrien's II corps, and not on Haig's I Corps further east.

At 0600 hours on the morning of the 23rd Field Marshal French called a corps commanders' conference at Smith-Dorrien's HQ, reviewed the situation and told his subordinates that, 'at most', two enemy corps and perhaps a cavalry division were facing the BEF. According to Smith-Dorrien, French was 'in excellent form' . . . and clearly blissfully ignorant of the true situation. The C-in-C ordered his commanders to be prepared to move forward, though he also ordered them to strengthen their outposts, while II Corps engineers were to prepare the canal bridges for demolition.

Smith-Dorrien pointed out the inherent weakness of his line along the canal, especially in the Mons Salient which, in the event of attack, would come under fire from three sides, and added that he had already issued orders for the preparation of a second defensive line two miles south of Mons. French approved of this arrangement, but the opening shots of the Battle of Mons were already being fired as he talked to his commanders at Sars-la-Bruyère.

The Battle of Mons features in some detail in many accounts of the Great War, but it was in reality a short, small-scale engagement. The British outposts started bickering with the advance German scouts around 0600 hours, and at 1000, as he was driving through Jemappes, Smith-Dorrien saw a German shell burst on the road in front of his car. The enemy artillery had been pounding Mons for about an hour and fighting now became general around the Mons Salient and along the canal. Vastly outnumbered, the last British units withdrew at 1800 hours that evening, so the entire battle of Mons only lasted about twelve hours, and, on the British side, involved just one reinforced infantry corps.

Mons was an 'encounter battle', fought out between the advancing troops of General von Kluck's German First Army, wheeling south and west from Brussels, and the infantry of the BEF dug in along the Mons-Condé Canal. Kluck's cavalry and infantry scouts cannot have got much information back to their general, for he had no idea that British troops were in the line at all until his troops came under heavy and accurate rifle fire from British positions around the Mons Salient. Slowly, as the First Army came wheeling south, more German troops filtered forward towards the canal, and the fighting spread along it to the west.

Two of Kluck's corps, the III and the IX – four divisions, plus a cavalry division – were soon heavily engaged with Smith-Dorrien's divisions, while Haig's I Corps sector remained quiet. More German divisions soon came up and were sent into the attack at Mons. According to the German General Staff account, the 3rd Division was attacked by three and a half German divisions and the 5th Division by two and a half divisions – a total of six German divisions against the two British divisions of II Corps. This should have been enough men to swamp the British line, if the attacking troops were well handled and supported by artillery, but the German troops were not well handled and the British infantry had command of the killing ground.

In South Africa, the British infantry had learned how to take up good, concealed positions and hit what they aimed at with their rifles, a skill kept up with constant practice. The average infantryman of the BEF could get off twenty *aimed* shots a minute and many soldiers could do even better. The German tactics simply provided these marksmen with excellent targets. At Mons it was the German infantry that came on 'in solid blocks, standing out sharply against the skyline', and the dug-in British troops were soon pouring fire into the massed ranks of the enemy, a fire so heavy and accurate that the latter came to believe they were facing machine-guns.

Nor was it just heavy rifle fire; there was method behind it. The British officers had their men hold fire until the Germans were close and fully exposed before giving the order to open fire. The senior NCOs told off the better shots in their sections to mark the German officers and NCOs in the advancing formations and shoot them down. What happened then was sheer slaughter. Their leaders dead, their ranks blasted by accurate fire from positions they could not see, the German infantry attack faltered. While it did so, however, the German artillery came into play, and began to probe the British line with shellfire. 'All at once,' says one British account, 'the sky began to rain down bullets and shells.'

The Great War on the Western Front was to become an artillery war – some 58 per cent of all British casualties in France and Belgium between 1914 and 1918 were due to shellfire – and if the shelling at Mons was a trifle compared to later bombardments it was still bad enough for troops that were not used to it. This battle, of infantry and artillery, of massed infantry attacks, plunging shellfire and the rattle of rifles, went on all morning, spreading slowly west along the canal as more German battalions came up and were engaged.

As has been said, the German forces engaged by II Corps at Mons consisted of III and IX Corps plus the 9th Cavalry Division from II Cavalry Corps, all from Kluck's First Army. The British troops in the Mons Salient were engaged on three sides by a full German division, the 18th Infantry, and were soon in trouble, but along the canal the enemy were held off without great difficulty. Nevertheless, Smith-Dorrien was well aware that his position was inherently untenable. German strength was increasing as more divisions came up, and he had no reserves to put into the line, which was too long and too thinly held to begin with. The Germans had more and heavier artillery and a greater number of troops, so that sooner or later they would cross the canal and turn Smith-Dorrien's flank.

The British rifle fire had dismayed the Germans; the writer Walter Bloem, then serving in the Brandenburg Regiment, recalls his battalion commander lamenting the loss of 'my proud, beautiful battalion . . . shot to pieces by the English, the English we laughed at'. For the morning and part of the afternoon that was the situation all along the front; the German infantry came on in solid masses and were shot down in quantity. This tactic should be borne in mind when accusations are made that the British generals – and, it seems, only the British generals – expended their men in this fashion. The German tactic at

Mons sought to overwhelm the British line by pouring in the infantry, accepting heavy casualties in the process. Only in the late afternoon did German numbers begin to tell, so that Smith-Dorrien was then faced with the problem of disengaging his troops when they were still in close contact with the enemy.

Fortunately for Field Marshal French, who took no part in this engagement but spent the day touring other units of his force, General Smith-Dorrien knew what he was doing. By mid-afternoon it was clear that the Mons Salient was no longer tenable and he therefore ordered the battalions holding it to pull out. The 4th Royal Fusiliers, defending the bridges in Mons itself, withdrew first, and then the whole of the British line, starting on the right and shifting steadily left, began to pull back. This was not a ripple movement from right to left, but a piecemeal process as and when companies and platoons found themselves able to beat down the enemy fire to their front and pull back to deeper cover. There was plenty of cover among the gardens and houses, so the move, carried out by experienced, disciplined troops, went off without undue difficulty; in no sense was it a forced withdrawal, and far less a rout. The blowing of the canal bridges was the signal for a general withdrawal, and by 1640 hours most of the British line had disengaged and was moving back to the previously prepared positions two miles south of the canal.

Only in the salient, where elements of 8 Infantry Brigade were surrounded by advancing German forces, was there any significant loss. In an attempt to carry this position the Germans put in another attack at about 1730 hours, which was met with artillery fire and more scorching rifle fire from the Royal Scots, the Gordon Highlanders and the Royal Irish Rifles. The Germans held back; then their bugles began to sound the 'Cease Fire', halting any further attacks that day. The German soldiers had discovered what British infantry could do, and had not enjoyed the experience.

That was the famous Battle of Mons. It lasted twelve hours and, where senior officers were concerned, apart from a few tactical decisions during the day and the order to pull back in the early evening, even General Smith-Dorrien did not have a great deal to do. From the moment the first shot was fired, the outcome rested on the steadiness and shooting ability of his soldiers and the tactical skills of his battalion commanders; neither let him down. Total casualties in II Corps were just over 1,600 men killed, wounded and missing, and the corps lost two guns. Haig's I Corps suffered just forty casualties, and Allenby's cavalry division even fewer.

Since this was a II Corps battle, they should have the credit for it. As for the blame, such as it is, for pitting Smith-Dorrien's corps against so many German divisions, the finger must point at General Lanrezac and, to a certain extent, at Field Marshal French, who had failed to keep a grip on the campaign, declined to consult his French allies or insist on an obviously essential conference with Lanrezac and let the BEF march on unsupported towards the advancing Germans.

Night fell while II Corps were pulling back from direct contact with the enemy. The troops were inevitably in some disorder, in need of sorting out, a meal, and, if possible, some rest. As for their commander, Smith-Dorrien, he had to regroup his forces, resupply his men and contact French to report the situation and get fresh orders. In the meantime, he pulled his men back to that defensive position two miles south of the canal and ordered them to dig in for a renewal of the battle on the following day. The weary soldiers of II Corps were carrying out this order when, at 2300 hours that night, instructions arrived from French, ordering Smith-Dorrien to send a staff officer at once to GHQ at Le Cateau, and get fresh orders.

The background to this call, according to Henry Wilson, is as follows. On the afternoon of 23 August, while II Corps were engaged at Mons, Wilson had calculated that the forces opposing the BEF did not exceed two corps. This being so, he had drafted orders on behalf of French which ordered II Corps, the Cavalry Division and 19 Infantry Brigade to put in an attack north-east of Mons on the following day, the 24th. Fortunately, fresh information then arrived from Joffre giving a much higher estimate of German strength, with the result that this BEF attack was shelved. GHQ then received the alarming news that the French Fifth Army, on the right flank of the BEF, were falling back, and fresh orders were hurriedly prepared, instructing the British force to retreat towards a line between Maubeuge and Valenciennes. These orders now had to be relayed to the troops, and it was for the purpose of receiving them that a senior II Corps staff officer, Brigadier-General Forestier-Walker, was sent to GHQ.

It is necessary to understand the state of communications in Northern France in the second decade of the twentieth century. Haig's HQ had telephone contact with Le Cateau, but Smith-Dorrien did not. Hence the order to send the II Corps staff officer to receive GHQ's instructions, though since French had made up his mind to retreat, it is hard to understand why orders to that effect were not sent directly to Smith-Dorrien by courier, as they were passed directly by telephone to Haig.

As it was, several precious hours were wasted while Forestier-Walker drove to GHQ and back again. Nor were the orders he brought of great help, or of great complexity, for they contained no plan for the retirement, only the advice that the arrangements for withdrawal were to be worked out between the two corps commanders, though the idea seemed to be that I Corps should cover the retreat of II Corps. It was now 0300 hours on 24 August, daylight was at 0500, the men had not slept for two nights, and the battle was sure to be renewed as soon as it was light enough for artillery commanders to spot the fall of shot. German artillery actually began firing against the new II Corps position at 0515 hours, so if the corps were to retire safely there was no time to be lost.

I Corps was on the move by 0530 hours, but when the German attack against II Corps developed, at around 0700, their infantry was again greeted with a storm of rifle and machine-gun fire from the well-concealed British infantry. The 3rd Division of II Corps fought its way clear without undue loss but the 5th Division, fighting off three German divisions which were attempting to outflank the left of the British line, was pinned by artillery fire and then hit by a heavy infantry attack. The British Regulars blasted the advancing German line and a spirited charge by the 9th Lancers and the 4th Dragoon Guards extricated some guns in danger of capture. Only then could the infantry withdraw.

Some of Smith-Dorrien's battalions sustained heavy losses and not all of them got away; the 1st Cheshire Regiment was cut off and forced to surrender when the survivors ran out of ammunition. Even so, by the end of the day II Corps had beaten off all the German attacks and had managed to disengage, for the loss of another 2,000 men killed, wounded or captured. Haig's corps again saw very little fighting and lost only 100 men from all causes on 24 August. The BEF was still intact and still full of fight, but the men were very weary and in urgent need of sleep and food.

Field Marshal French had also been busy, although his actions were of no great help to his units or the Allied cause. On the 24th he sent a message to Lanrezac telling him that 'should the left flank of the BEF be threatened, he intended to withdraw on his lines of communication [i.e. south-west towards Amiens] in which case General Lanrezac must look after his own left flank and the British would no longer hold themselves responsible for covering it'. This tit-for-tat message may have given French considerable satisfaction, but it was a remarkably petty and foolish one. His left, or western, flank was already under attack, so that he had no option but to withdraw due south and somehow maintain contact with the French Army.

Lanrezac did not reply, but sent the message on to Joffre, who suggested that if Field Marshal French had to withdraw the BEF, he should do so in the direction of Cambrai. French then sent a telegram to Joffre telling him that he proposed falling back towards Maubeuge and Valenciennes. He had spent most of 24 August at his Advance HQ at Bavai, but he left it to visit Haig and to have a meeting with General Sordet, commanding the French Cavalry Corps. He also went to greet General Snow's 4th Division, elements of which were now coming forward. For some reason, however, he did not try to meet Smith-Dorrien, commanding the only corps heavily engaged with the enemy that day. In the late afternoon French returned to Bavai, where Smith-Dorrien arrived at 1800 hours and asked for instructions as to further retirement. According to Smith-Dorrien French told him that 'he could do as he liked', but that Haig intended to start his corps retreating again at 0500 hours on the following day, 25 August.

Anxious to avoid yet another dawn entanglement with the enemy, Smith-Dorrien stated that he intended to get his men on the move by midnight and be across the Valenciennes-Bavai road by daylight. A similar order was then issued to the whole BEF – which had now learned that the three French armies on their right flank were in full retreat – and, after a delay while Sordet's Cavalry Corps crossed their line of retreat, the BEF began to move southwards early on the 25th, with French shifting GHQ south from Le Cateau to St Quentin.

There was then a problem. Across the path of the BEF lay the Forêt de

Mormal, a thick wood with excellent communications east and west but no roads through it from north to south. This being so, and to prevent congestion, I Corps passed down east of the forest and II Corps passed to the west. The two corps were supposed to swing inward and meet up as soon as they had cleared the forest but this did not happen and a gap of some miles opened up between Smith-Dorrien's troops and Haig's that was not to be closed for another six days. Smith-Dorrien records that on 25 August, as the march began, 'Communication with I Corps was a matter of supreme difficulty . . . I heard nothing from I Corps throughout the day . . . and no information was sent to me by GHQ concerning it. I imagined we would meet up at Le Cateau in the evening, according to orders.'

By 1800 hours that evening, after another hot and exhausting march, I Corps was moving into billets at Landrecies and Maroilles. Haig's command had seen little of the enemy and had lost very few men, though blisters, heat exhaustion and lack of sleep were taking their toll of everyone. II Corps, 19 Brigade and Allenby's Cavalry Division, on the other hand, had been continually engaged by elements of the German First Army, which was attempting to hook round their western flank and either cut them off or drive the entire BEF into the fortress of Maubeuge, where it could be surrounded and eliminated at some future date. In the event, II Corps and their cavalry colleagues were able to beat off these German probes, but the inevitable result was that the corps and its supporting elements became strung out and scattered. The difficulties of keeping units together were compounded by the crowds of French and Belgium refugees cramming the roads, fleeing before the advancing German armies.

'It will be difficult to realise the fog of war which surrounded us that night', writes Smith-Dorrien in his memoirs:

> Communication was most difficult and although the Corps signal-lers performed miracles with their wires and cable it was impossible to find out the position of units until hours after they had reached them. Then it was not only as if I had II Corps to deal with, for mixed up with them was the Cavalry Division, the 19th Infantry Brigade and the 4th Division, none of which were under me but were reporting their movements and getting their orders from GHQ, twenty-six miles to the rear. It is true that GHQ issued an order at 1pm [1300 hours] 25 August, placing the 19th Brigade under II Corps but it was then with the Cavalry Division and heaven knows when it got the order . . . I only succeeded in collecting them next morning when they were starting south from Le Cateau.

The Germans were now pressing hot on the heels of the retreating British and their Uhlan scouts were probing the I Corps positions at Landrecies by the evening of August 25. Just after dark there was a brisk exchange of fire in Landrecies, when 4 (Guards) Brigade fought a brief engagement on the outskirts of the town. Haig, who was with this brigade during the fight, made his way back to GHQ with some difficulty, arriving there around 0100 hours on the 26th, where he told French that the situation at Landrecies was 'very critical' and requested that II Corps, then at Le Cateau, eight miles south-west of Landrecies, should go to the Guards Brigade's assistance.

French went further than this; at 0500 he sent Colonel Huguet, who was now the French liaison officer at GHQ, to Lanrezac's HQ, telling him that 'I Corps has been violently attacked in its billets between Le Cateau and Landrecies and is falling back – if it can – on Guise to the south; if not, south-east in the direction of La Capelle. Tomorrow the BEF will continue its retreat towards Peronne. Can Fifth Army come to FM French's aid by sheltering 1 Corps until it can rejoin the main body of the British forces?'

Once again a lack of communications was causing confusion. The action at Landrecies had been brisk enough for some hours, but it was a skirmish compared with the fighting at Mons and on the first day of the retreat. However, it took place in the dark, no one was quite sure what was going on, and since there was no way of quickly finding out the true situation, fears escalated. French's message galvanised Lanrezac into ordering his left wing to help Haig if possible, but by that time the Germans had drawn off from Landrecies and I Corps was able to continue its retreat at dawn on 26 August. As the men marched south they heard the sound of heavy artillery and rifle fire from the direction of Le Cateau, where II Corps, the 4th Division and the cavalry were now heavily engaged.

To understand the situation leading to the battle at Le Cateau on 26 August, it is necessary to go back to the previous evening. When Smith-Dorrien's staff reached Le Cateau at around 1730 hours on the 25th, they knew that Haig's corps was some eight miles away to the north-east. As Smith-Dorrien's account indicates, II Corps had been scattered in the fighting that day; units of the 3rd Division were still coming in to Le Cateau at midnight. Snow's 4th Division, though not under Smith-Dorrien's command, had been fighting at Solèmes, north of Le Cateau, and did not reach its billets until after 0330 hours on the 26th, while 19 Infantry Brigade was marching with Allenby's Cavalry Division. The men of all these units had been marching or fighting or digging trenches for three days (two days, in 4th Division's case), and were very tired.

Smith-Dorrien had established his HQ in the village of Bertry, three miles south-west of Le Cateau. At around 1800 hours he received a note from Henry Wilson, a 'warning order', telling him that orders would shortly be issued for a continuation of the retreat. These duly arrived at 2215 hrs, when the situation of II Corps was as described in the preceding paragraph; the units were scattered, some battalions were only now coming in, and the whereabouts of many others was still unknown. There was no help for this, nor was it anybody's fault. The heavy fighting that day, and the state of military communications in 1914, created the difficulty, but it put Smith-Dorrien in a quandary; how could he get the order out to his scattered, weary forces when he could not locate many of them . . . and when those units he could locate were in no state to continue marching?

Smith-Dorrien was still talking the situation over at 0200 hrs when General Allenby arrived and announced that since his cavalry brigades were also much scattered and his men and horses 'pretty well played out', he would not be able to occupy the heights overlooking II Corps' line of retreat next day. He therefore urged Smith-Dorrien to move at once and get away in the dark, for otherwise he would be forced to fight at daylight. Smith-Dorrien thought this over, and then consulted his two divisional commanders. Both told him that their men were tired out, and that their battalions were still coming in. The conclusion reached was that II Corps could not move before 0900 hours, at the earliest. Smith-Dorrien then asked Allenby if he would act under his command, should he be forced to make a stand at Le Cateau. 'Allenby replied in the affirmative,' says Smith-Dorrien, 'and I remarked "Very well, gentlemen, we will stand and fight and I will ask General Snow to act under me as well."'

Snow was contacted some time before 0500 hours and agreed to put the 4th Division under Smith-Dorrien's command, and with that much decided the troops began to prepare for battle. Smith-Dorrien sent a note of his decision to GHQ at St Quentin, explaining the circumstances which caused him to stand and fight rather than continue to retreat as ordered. His message arrived at St Quentin at 0500 hrs, and French rapidly sent back a reply:

> If you can hold your ground the situation appears likely to improve. 4th Division must co-operate. French troops are taking the offensive on right of 1st Corps. Although you are given a free hand as to method, this telegram is not intended to convey the impression that I am not anxious for you to carry out the retirement and you must make every effort to do so.

This communication cheered up Smith-Dorrien considerably. He had no intention of getting into a prolonged battle or asking for further help, and he assumed from this message that Field Marshal French understood his reasons for making a stand and approved of his decision. Smith-Dorrien – as he told Henry Wilson later that day – intended only to 'give the enemy a smashing blow and slip away before he could recover', and he felt he had a good chance of doing that. Wilson replied 'Good luck to you . . . yours is the first cheerful voice I have heard in three days.'

Like the Battle of Mons, the action at Le Cateau did not last long, or place any great demands on the skill of the generals. It required the British Army to do what it did best, to occupy a position and defy eviction, take a toll of the attacking enemy, force them to halt and deploy, and then break off the action before it was overwhelmed. This was Smith-Dorrien's sole intention at Le Cateau, and he succeeded brilliantly.

Smith-Dorrien drew up his forces with the 3rd Division facing north along the Le Cateau-Cambrai road, and the 4th Division on their left, echeloned south but facing west. Beyond the 4th Division, Sordet's cavalry covered the open, western, flank, and beyond that a French territorial division held Cambrai. The ground around Le Cateau is hilly, and there are commanding heights north of the Cambrai road and along the Selle valley, which runs south from the town. The 5th Division occupied Le Cateau itself and held the ground to the south, above the valley of the Selle, while Allenby's cavalry brigades were in support, in rear of the infantry divisions or on the flanks. The eastern flank was open, for Haig's corps was too far away to give any assistance. Smith-Dorrien's men therefore held a thin, curving line, some ten miles in length, and cannot have expected to hold it for long.

The British position at Le Cateau has some similarities with the position at Mons and General von Kluck attacked it in much the same fashion, sending in four army corps piecemeal against the British line. The German IV Corps attacked Le Cateau and soon forced the defending soldiers, from the East Surreys and the Duke of Cornwall's Light Infantry, out of the town and on to higher ground to the south. There, aided by dismounted troopers from 3 Cavalry Brigade, they stemmed the German advance on the slopes.

The morning was misty and under cover of a thin fog the Germans managed to infiltrate through the 5th Division positions and down the valley of the River Selle. As more and more German units came up and were engaged by the British artillery and infantry, the fighting spread west as the enemy attempted to find a way round the British line. The German artillery was a sore trial to the defending infantry and took a steady toll of the exposed British batteries, but the great weight of the fighting fell to the British infantry battalions, which broke up attack after attack with their fast and accurate rifle fire. The infantry brigades on the right flank held off the German attack for six hours, while the troops in the centre held up any advance across the Le Cateau–Cambrai road.

It soon became clear that the Germans were determined to lever the left flank loose, and to achieve that end they concentrated a lot of their artillery fire on the 4th Division. In fact, the weak point in the British line was the right flank, since it was not covered by Haig's corps, which was still withdrawing to the south. Eventually, around 1200 hours, the German pressure on the 5th Division began to tell, and men began to fall back, in small parties and then larger groups, moving from one patch of cover to another, turning back at intervals to engage the enemy. It was time to pull out the guns – the BEF was always very anxious about its guns – and great skill and considerable courage were employed in getting the batteries of the divisional artillery off the forward slopes, which were under heavy German fire. With the guns back and in position to cover a further withdrawal, the infantry began to pull out, pushing their way past the advancing patrols of the German III Corps, which was moving up to cut them off from the Selle valley.

Not all the British units got away from Le Cateau – the 2nd Suffolks were cut off and overwhelmed in the middle of the afternoon – but most of the other battalions disengaged without undue difficulty. By early evening the men of his corps were seen by General Smith-Dorrien streaming down the road past his position 'like a crowd coming away from a race meeting', smoking their pipes and completely unconcerned. Thanks to the stout fight put up on the flanks by the 4th and 5th Divisions, the 3rd Division in the centre got away smoothly though another battalion, the 1st Gordon Highlanders, did not receive the order to retire and fought on until they were overrun. The Germans did not pursue their opponents and later that night, as II Corps continued to withdraw, German shells were still falling on their empty positions.

Le Cateau was a neat little battle, and the credit is entirely due to General Smith-Dorrien, the dauntless troops of his corps and of the two divisions, the 4th and the Cavalry, which had given him such unstinting support. Smith-Dorrien also records his debt to Sordet's French cavalry who held up the German advance on the left flank and used their 75-mm guns to great effect against the German infantry during the afternoon. In the words of the Official History, 'With both flanks in the air II Corps had turned on an enemy of twice their strength; struck him a hard blow and withdrawn – except on the right flank of 5th Division – practically without interference.'

Smith-Dorrien's 'stopping blow' at Le Cateau was highly effective. It was twelve hours before Kluck got his divisions together and took up the pursuit, and Smith-Dorrien records that for the next twelve days of their retreat, his corps was not seriously troubled, 'except by mounted troops and detachments which kept a safe distance'. There was, as always, a cost. The British casualty figures for Mons and Le Cateau come to 7,812 men killed, wounded and missing, including 2,600 taken prisoner, and the loss of 38 guns.

With two battles – which, if not outright victories, were certainly not defeats – under their belts, this might be the time to take a look at the three British generals most closely involved to see how they are performing. For Haig, commanding I Corps, there is little to say, for his troops had barely been engaged, and his testing time had yet to come. For Smith-Dorrien praise is certainly due, for he had done all he set out to do, and done it well. He had twice met a stronger enemy in terrain which offered him no particular advantage and fought that enemy to a standstill, skilfully extricating his men to fight another day. In the face of such evidence no charge of incompetence against Smith-Dorrien can stick, though such charges were made by his commander, Field Marshal Sir John French, years after these battles. Significantly, however, French did not make them at the time.

The BEF's Commander-in-Chief was not having a good war, nor is it hard to pick holes in his performance. He had got off on the wrong foot with Lanrezac, though that was not entirely his fault, but by 25 August he seems to be out of touch with the situation of his soldiers. His order that II Corps should continue to retreat at Le Cateau was issued in ignorance of the circumstances governing Smith-Dorrien's ability to carry out that order. The chronic communications problem bears some of the blame, but French had made no effort to find out what was going on with II Corps, the Cavalry Division, 4th Division or 19

Brigade, yet all were under his command and the last three units were reporting directly to GHQ. These three units were in action all day on the 25th and that fact alone should have indicated that II Corps might be in difficulty.

Field Marshal French did little to influence the course of events either during the battles at Mons and Le Cateau, or during the intervening retreat. Telling the corps commanders to make their own arrangements for the withdrawal from Mons is, at best, a strange course of action for any army commander to take, not least because it appears to be an abnegation of responsibility. French seems to have spent a great deal of time away from his Headquarters and this may have left him out of touch with the situation, especially as it affected II Corps. Perhaps he felt happier and more confident out with the troops on the ground, but the impression remains that the scale of this war, so different from anything he had encountered before, had overwhelmed the Field Marshal's powers of judgement. That apart, from the evidence in his own memoirs, too much of his attention was devoted to brooding over the shortcomings, real or imagined, of his hard-fighting subordinate, Horace Smith-Dorrien. For a while though, French kept these doubts to himself.

Even given the C-in-C's failings, however, a fair summary of the two actions at Mons and Le Cateau would not reflect badly on any of the British generals. On the other hand, if General Lanrezac is to be condemned it must also be appreciated that the situation in which he found himself, and to which he was forced to react, was the very one about which he had been warning GQG for some time. That the British Army recalls these successful actions with pride is understandable, but Mons and Le Cateau were small battles which had little effect on the outcome of the titanic struggle then taking place on the Western Front between the armies of France and Germany.

French would not have agreed with that assessment, and his first official Dispatch, written on 7 September 1914 and covering the actions at Mons and Le Cateau, is full of praise for his army, his field commanders, and especially for Smith-Dorrien:

> I cannot close this brief account of the glorious stand of British troops without putting on record my deep appreciation of the services rendered by General Sir Horace Smith-Dorrien. I say without hesitation that the saving of the west wing of the army under my command on the morning of 26 August could never have been accomplished unless a commander of unusual coolness, intrepidity, and determination had been personally present to conduct the operation . . . it is impossible for me to speak too highly of the skill evinced by the two generals commanding Army Corps.

This is fulsome, if well-deserved, praise, but before too long French had chosen to forget Smith-Dorrien's service at Mons and Le Cateau, and he eventually issued a revised opinion of his unfortunate subordinate.

Five years later, the Field Marshal published a book, *1914*, his personal account of the early months of the war. Coming from a former Commander-in-Chief of the BEF, such a book might have been invaluable, an insight into what was happening in those desperate days, both at the front and at GHQ. Instead, the main theme is one long complaint against General Smith-Dorrien, nor does the book shrink from distortion and lies in order to smear a man who was by then in no position to defend himself. Sideswipes are also taken at Field Marshal Kitchener, French's political master (and military superior) in 1914, and dead for three years when the book appeared.

1914 is not only unkind, it is unfortunate, to such an extent that one can only wonder what persuaded French to write it – not least because many of the 'facts' he inserts in orders to denigrate Smith-Dorrien could easily be refuted by reference to his own dispatches, to unit war diaries, or to the recollections of many people then living, many of whom came forward willingly to put the truth of the matter before the British public.

In *1914*, French withdraws his praise of Smith-Dorrien:

> In my despatch of September 1914 I refer eulogistically to the battle at Le Cateau . . . It [the Dispatch] was completed, of necessity, very hurriedly, and before there had been time to study the reports immediately preceding and covering the period of that battle, by which alone the full details could be disclosed . . . accepted without question the estimate made by the commander of II Corps as to the nature of the threat against him and the position of the German forces opposed to him . . . (*1914*, pp. 79–80.)

French does not go so far as to withdraw his Dispatch entirely, but the inference is plain; Smith-Dorrien had not deserved such praise, and French now wished to amend it. His explanation for doing so – that the Dispatch was written too hurriedly and too soon after the battle – does not bear close inspection. Twelve days passed between the fight at Le Cateau and the issuing of the Dispatch . . . and five years more before French saw fit to refute much of what it had contained. The truth of the matter is that French did not know the situation of II Corps when it arrived at Le Cateau, and Smith-Dorrien was perfectly correct in disobeying the order to retreat. Such an action was covered in the then current edition of *Field Service Regulations* (Para. 13, Section 12, Part 1): 'If a subordinate, in the absence of a superior, neglects to depart from the letter of his order, when such departure is demanded by the circumstances and failure ensues, he will be held responsible for such failure.'

Written five years after the events it pretends to describe – and dedicated, curiously enough to David Lloyd George, a man who was no lover of the Great War generals – *1914* might be ignored, were it not for the insights it offers into the mind and character of Sir John French. If his own words are any indication he seems to have been in a state of detestation amounting to paranoia regarding Smith-Dorrien, a fact which can be illustrated by some further examples. French's message to Smith-Dorrien on 26 August, clearly gives tacit support to the latter's decision to stand at Le Cateau, even to the point of saying the 4th Division must support him.

In his book, however, continuing his comments on the September Dispatch, French writes: 'In more than one of the accounts of the retreat from Mons, it is alleged that some tacit consent at least was given at Headquarters at St Quentin to the decision arrived at by the commander of II Corps. I owe it to the able and devoted officers of my staff to say that there is not a semblance of truth in that statement.' (*1914*, p. 80.) Readers are invited to look again at the message French sent to Smith-Dorrien again and judge the truth of French's statement.

Then, still on the subject of this message, there is the matter of timings. French states (*1914*, p. 82) 'It was not until 8 am on the 26th that I knew that the left wing of the Army was actually committed to the fight . . . Staff officers were sent to General Smith-Dorrien carrying peremptory orders to break off the action and continue the retreat forthwith.' This is a lie, and an easily detectable lie. The reply sent by GHQ to Smith Dorrien – the reply later refuted by French in his book – was timed at 0500 hours – three hours *before* French claims to have heard that Smith-Dorrien had decided to commit his corps to action.

French then refers (*1914*, p. 84) to 'the shattered condition of the troops which had fought at Le Cateau', overlooking the fact that these same troops, though undoubtedly weary, marched more than thirty miles on the two days *after* the battle and had re-formed their battalions by the end of the second day. French knew this statement to be untrue, for he had stood beside the road at Ham on 28 August and watched the troops march by 'whistling and singing', and records in his book (*1914*, p. 89) that: 'Their one repeated question was "When shall we turn round and face them again?" and then they would add, "We can drive them to hell".' Men like that are hardly 'shattered', but French is so anxious to belittle Smith-Dorrien that he frequently contradicts himself.

French told another lie in the casualty figures he gave – this time a deliberate falsification of fact rather than a statement arguably open to interpretation. In *1914* he claims that Smith-Dorrien lost 'at least 14,000 officers and men and at least 80 guns', in the fighting at Mons and Le Cateau. This is roughly *twice* the actual losses in these engagements, which were 7,812 men and 38 guns, and though Great War casualty figures are always hard to pin down, a mistake of this order cannot be ascribed to statistical error.

There are also many distortions. French states that on the night before the action at Le Cateau, 'Sir Horace asked General Allenby what, in his opinion were the chances if he remained and held the position, adding that his troops were so exhausted as to preclude the possibility of removing them for some time to come.' This reversal of the actual conversation – a typical ploy of the Field Marshal, as we shall see – was part of an attempt to take the credit for the stand at Le Cateau from Smith-Dorrien and give it to Allenby. The actual situation is as described above, and was confirmed by Allenby himself after French's book appeared in 1919. Then again, at Mons, according to French, the actual German forces opposing Smith-Dorrien – two army corps and a cavalry

division with more corps coming up, six full divisions by the German count –
are dismissed and the battle becomes a skirmish between cavalry patrols.
Sneers are also directed at Smith-Dorrien for evacuating the Mons Salient,
though a glance at any map reveals that this position was untenable . . . And so
it goes on, for page after page. Reading *1914* is not a pleasant experience.

It is also noticeable, and even wryly amusing, that in his book French goes
out of his way to praise the actions of Douglas Haig and his corps even
though, as has been shown, Haig's corps saw little action at Mons or Le
Cateau and by comparison with Smith-Dorrien's command, was hardly
troubled during the early days of the retreat. Swamped with jealousy and
suspicion of Smith-Dorrien, French seems unaware that his real enemy at
that time was Sir Douglas Haig, who was informing anyone who would
listen that the Field Marshal was not up to the job and should never have
been appointed Commander-in-Chief of the BEF. French may not have
known this in 1914, but he must have known it by the time he sat down to
write his book in 1918. Yet to make Smith-Dorrien look incompetent, Haig
must be presented as the highly professional, loyal subordinate.

The publication of *1914* caused an outcry. Sir John Fortescue, the
distinguished historian of the British Army, wrote sadly:

> On the whole we must pronounce this to be one of the most
> unfortunate books that ever was written. It is the spirit of the
> whole work which gives us pain. The author has descended to
> misstatements and misrepresentations of the clumsiest and most
> ludicrous kind in order to injure the reputation of a subordinate
> who is forbidden to defend himself.

This last comment refers to the fact that when Smith-Dorrien asked for a
right of reply and an inquiry into French's allegations, the Prime Minister –
Lloyd George, the man to whom French dedicated *1914* – refused both
requests on the grounds that Smith-Dorrien was still a serving officer. So, by
virtue of his rank, since field marshals do not retire, was Sir John French,
but that point seems to have escaped Lloyd George's notice. A correspondence in *The Times* and the *Daily Telegraph* ensued, and Smith-Dorrien
again requested that a commission be convened to examine the relevant
records. The Secretary of State for War decided, however, to prevent any
public reply by Smith-Dorrien, 'because if we once allow officers on full pay
to get writing to newspapers it seems to me there will be no end to the
amount of damage it will do to the Army'. Sir Horace did not pursue the
matter, but his friends saw to it that the true state of affairs in France in 1914
were brought to the attention of a wider public.

There will be more of this distressing business, but now it is time to return
to the battlefield where, in the last week of August 1914, the British
Expeditionary Force, much battered but still a fighting force, is retreating
south towards the Marne.

CHAPTER 5

THE MARNE
TO FIRST YPRES,
SEPTEMBER–OCTOBER 1914

*'As, day by day, the trench fighting developed I came to
realise more and more the much greater relative power which
modern weapons had given to the defence . . . and so, day by
day, I began dimly to realise what the future might have in
store for us.'*

Field Marshal the Viscount French of Ypres
(later first Earl of Ypres) on the battle of the Aisne, *1914* (1919)

After following the BEF in their retreat from Mons and Le Cateau it is
necessary to take a brief look at the general situation on the Eastern
and Western Fronts, if only to keep the actions of the British Army in
context, as a small force operating on one front, in a major and spreading
war. On the Eastern Front and in the Balkans, the Russians and Serbs had
acted with a vigour that had dismayed their German and Austrian attackers.
The Germans had hoped that these fronts would remain quiet while France
was crushed, but the Serbs were giving the Austrians considerable trouble
and the Russians had swung into action with surprising speed. By 20 August
Russian forces were well inside East Prussia and two full armies were
advancing on Königsberg.

The German commander in the east, General von Prittwitz, was
promptly sacked and replaced by General Paul von Hindenburg who,
called back from retirement for this task, took with him as his Chief of
Staff, Major-General Erich Ludendorff, the man credited with taking
Liège. Should these men not be able to turn the tide in the east quickly,
Moltke was prepared to divert large forces to assist them from the Western
Front, where the Schlieffen Plan was already disintegrating. This failure of
the German master plan was not yet apparent to the French commanders,
who had seen their own Plan XVII dissolve under the German guns, and

whose armies were now in full retreat, instead of pushing hard into Germany.

Depressing as it was for the soldiers on the ground, slogging along under the blazing summer sun, or drenched by sudden and torrential thunderstorms, at least the retreat kept the French armies together. The Belgian Army was also still intact and had now withdrawn west to the forts around the port of Antwerp. There they intended to hold off the advancing Germans while waiting for assistance from their French and British allies. Nor was the picture entirely without bright spots. In Alsace and Lorraine the French were falling back slowing, fighting for every metre of ground, while in the centre Generals Ruffey and Langle de Cary were regrouping their forces in order to launch counter-attacks. General Lanrezac was falling back from the Meuse, with the BEF hanging on his left flank and resisting the temptation to seek the doubtful shelter offered by the fortifications of Maubeuge. The Anglo-French forces, if in full retreat, were still in being and presenting a common front to the foe.

The German armies on the western flank were not so united. That 'stopping blow' at Le Cateau had confused Kluck and, believing that the British would retreat south-west towards Amiens and the sea, he set out in that direction. This caused the First Army to lose contact with Bulow's Second Army on its right and a gap began to grow between them, a gap which attracted the attention of General Haig, who brought it to the attention of Lanrezac. On the 28th, while the retreat continued, Haig sent a liaison officer to Lanrezac's HQ, pointing out that the south-westward direction of Kluck's advance presented his left flank towards them, providing the chance for a counter-attack, Haig also offered to support Fifth Army with I Corps if Lanrezac cared to attempt such an attack. Since Joffre had already ordered Lanrezac to attack Kluck, the French general took up Haig's offer with alacrity.

Then came the snag. Haig had not consulted French about this proposal and now had to tell Lanrezac that the participation of I Corps depended on his chief's approval. French, however, did *not* approve, and Lanrezac had to attack alone. 'For the first time I felt we were in the wrong,' records Lieutenant Spears, the British Liaison Officer with Fifth Army. 'The great British complaint against General Lanrezac had been that he could not be induced to attack. Now that he was about to do so, nothing would induce the British to co-operate . . . they were doing as they had been done by.'

That first interview with Lanrezac still rankled with Field Marshal French, but he had an excuse in his orders from Kitchener, which had told him to consider carefully before 'participating in forward movements where large bodies of French troops were not engaged and where your forces may be unduly exposed to attack.'

It is pleasant to record that Lanrezac handled his army with considerable skill and nerve in the battle that followed. There was a gap between his Fifth Army and Langle de Cary's Fourth Army, and as the former moved against

Kluck at St Quentin, the German Second Army came in on Lanrezac's right flank at Guise. Undaunted, Lanrezac swung his army about and defeated the Second Army decisively at what came to be called the Battle of Guise, driving it back three miles on a twenty-five-mile front. The Second Army commander, Bülow, called for help from Kluck, who was forced to respond. It was this action on 29–30 August that forced General von Kluck to abandon the Schlieffen Plan's principal requirement, to turn east *south* of Paris. Instead, to aid his colleague Bülow, he turned east *north* of the capital, so exposing his right flank to an attack from the French armies now mustering south of the Marne.

This victory at Guise greatly encouraged Joffre, but the time for a counter-attack had not yet arrived. In the west, the French armies and the BEF were still off balance and falling back, and the German advance, though it was slowing down, was still relentless. The BEF managed a rest day on 29 August while the French were engaged at Guise, and on that day Joffre fitted in a visit to Field Marshal French at the latter's new HQ at Compiègne, to urge on him the necessity of keeping the BEF in the field and in line with the French left. He left without any certainty that the British C-in-C appreciated this point.

By 1 September, the Anglo-French situation on the Western Front was critical. To the east, French attacks along the German frontier had been thrown back, while the German right wing had succeeded, though at some cost, in forcing the French left wing and the BEF into full retreat. The German armies were now sweeping south and west, and in spite of the victory at Guise there seemed no way of stopping them in their headlong march towards Paris.

There were still, however, a few hopeful signs. The French and British soldiers falling back towards the Rivers Oise and Somme were exhausted, but so too were their German pursuers. The Germans were also outmarching their supplies, in spite of the frantic efforts of their engineers to repair the Belgian and French railway lines and link them up with those of Germany. Moreover, the German losses and reverses on the Eastern Front obliged Moltke to order two corps from the Western Front to entrain for East Prussia, and this was only one reduction to his western power. Other German forces had been diverted to invest Antwerp or take up the siege of Maubeuge, which held out until 6 September, or to guard and garrison every town and river crossing they had taken west of the Rhine. And so, little by little, the strength of the German thrust into France leaked away.

The French Fifth Army's attack at Guise on 29 August jarred the Germans considerably and enabled the BEF to make good its escape to the next river line, along the Aisne, which it reached on the 30th. On that day the German armies in the east shattered the Russians at Tannenberg, one of the great German victories of the war and the one which established the reputation of Hindenburg. On the other hand, the Austrians, attacking in Galicia and Poland, were flung back by the Russian armies and forced to retreat for some 200 miles, losing over 300,000 men in the process. Then, on 31 August, while the balance of advantage swung to and fro in the east, Field Marshal French flung a bombshell into the Anglo-French alliance in the west.

For the past week, ever since the Battle of the Frontiers and the German thrust from the north, General Joffre had been intent on reinforcing his left wing, which he now recognised as the weak part of his front, the extreme left of which was occupied by the BEF. French's volatile nature and unpredictable conduct did not add to the confidence of Joffre, who naturally wanted all the troops on this critical flank under his direct command. Joffre did not lack nerve, and he had now begun weakening his right flank to find units for a new army, the Sixth, which was now being formed under General Maunoury and moving to a position on the left flank of the line, beyond the BEF. The Sixth Army began to form north of Paris as the BEF continued to retreat under the blazing summer sun. Among those falling back were the men of the newly formed III Corps, which began to muster on 30 August under the command of Lieutenant-General W.P. Pulteney, made up from the weary troops of the 4th Division and 19 Infantry Brigade.

Exhausted though these men were, they were more than ready to fight, but on 30 August, convinced that the situation was desperate, French informed Kitchener and Joffre that he intended to exercise the privilege of independent command and withdraw the BEF to a safe haven south of Paris and keep it there until it was refreshed, re-equipped and reinforced. Only then would he bring his army back to the battle.

'I could not forget', French wrote,

> that the 5th French Army had commenced to retreat from the Sambre at least 24 hours before I had been given any official intimation that Joffre's offensive plan had been abandoned. Only due to the vast superiority of our cavalry and the marching and fighting powers of our troops had we been saved from an overwhelming disaster ... It is impossible to exaggerate the danger of the situation as it existed. Neither on this day or for several subsequent days did one man, horse, gun or machine-gun reach me to make good deficiencies. (*1914*, pp. 94–5.)

If carried into effect, this decision to pull the BEF out of the line would leave a yawning gap between the French Fifth and the new Sixth Army. French's announcement caused consternation in London and Paris and messages poured in to GHQ from the French and British Governments, urging the BEF's commander to drop this proposal. What induced him to take such a decision can only be guessed at, but like most of his soldiers, French was dog-tired. He was a man in his sixties and a week of battles, retreats, lack of sleep and worry had taken their toll. He was also deeply depressed at the state of his army, and refused to believe any evidence which told him that the men were in good heart. Indeed, when Smith-Dorrien told him as much after Le Cateau and during the retreat, French rebuked his subordinate in front of his staff for being 'over-optimistic'.

Inevitably, French later attempted to place the blame for his decision to pull out of the line on Smith-Dorrien (*1914*, p. 93). Recalling the corps commanders' conference at Compiègne on 29 August, which discussed the state of the BEF, the Field Marshal writes, 'Horace Smith-Dorrien expressed it as his opinion that the only course open to us was to retire to our base, thoroughly refit, re-embark and try to land at some favourable point on the coast-line. I refused to listen to what was the equivalent of a counsel of despair.' There is no evidence that Smith-Dorrien said anything of the sort and in his own memoirs he records that it was French who 'was insistent that the BEF must continue withdrawing as it was not in a fit state to fight'. The records show that on 29 August French warned Major-General F. S. Robb, the Inspector-General of Communications, that he had decided to make 'a definite and prolonged retreat, due south, passing Paris to the east or west'.

In June 1919, after *1914* was published, Smith-Dorrien wrote to the other senior officers present at the Compiègne meeting asking if they recalled him proposing a retreat to the sea, and received the following replies (ranks given are as held in 1919):

> Can I remember you saying anything at Compiègne which was of the nature of a counsel of despair or indeed anything which could be twisted round to have such a meaning? I can honestly say that I have no recollection of your having done such a thing. (Field Marshal Sir Douglas Haig.)

> I remember the conference at Compiègne but I have no recollection of your expressing an opinion to the effect that the only course was to return to base, re-embark and land elsewhere. (General Sir Edmund Allenby.)

> I have not the least recollection of your urging at Compiègne on the 29th August a return to base and re-embarkation. You are perfectly at liberty to make that statement, as also that I have never known you in the least pessimistic but on the contrary full of optimism at all times. (Lieutenant-General Sir Archibald Murray, French's Chief of Staff in August 1914.)

The responsibility for this decision, the thinking behind it, and the trouble it caused all clearly rest with Field Marshal French. The first reaction came from Joffre, who hurriedly asked the French Prime Minister, M. Viviani, to intercede with and beg him 'not to retire too rapidly and at least contain the enemy on the British front'. The British Government, equally aghast, sent Field Marshal Kitchener hurrying to Paris. From there the Secretary for War summoned French for an urgent conference at the British Embassy on

1 September, a meeting which began in the presence of the Ambassador, Sir Francis Bertie, and caused yet another row.

The meeting got off to a very bad start when French took exception to the fact that Kitchener was in uniform; since Kitchener was the senior field marshal, French took this as an attempt to 'pull rank'. Kitchener then informed French that he wished to visit the BEF and inspect the condition of the troops, a request which also did not go down well. French pointed out – abruptly – that he was the Commander-in-Chief in France and he declined to permit Kitchener to visit the troops. His manner was so close to insolence that Kitchener suggested they retire to another room and continue their meeting in private.

According to French, when they were alone Kitchener said that he resented the other's manner. French then

> told him what was on my mind . . . that I had the Command in France and I alone was responsible for whatever happened and that on French soil my authority as regards the British Army must be supreme until I was legally superseded . . . I further remarked that Lord Kitchener's presence in France in the character of a soldier could have no other effect than to weaken and prejudice my position . . . and while I valued his advice I would not tolerate any interference with my executive command and authority as long as His Majesty's Government chose to retain me in my present position . . . we finally came to an amicable understanding.

Given French's usual standards of veracity, this version of the meeting, and certainly the final words, may be regarded with some scepticism. Kitchener did not leave an account and we can only judge what probably happened by subsequent events. As soon as the meeting was over, Kitchener cabled London, telling the Cabinet – much to their relief – that 'French's troops will now remain in the line and will remain there, conforming to the movements of the French Army.'

For his part, French wrote to Joffre that day, suggesting that the BEF take up a defensive line along the Marne and hold that 'for as long as the situation requires, provided our flanks are not exposed'. The evidence suggests, therefore, that in spite of French's bluster, Kitchener overruled his decision of 30 August and either ordered or persuaded him to keep his troops in the line. It is a further indication of French's state of mind that six days later, when he might have had other things to worry about, he was writing to Winston Churchill, then the First Lord of the Admiralty, venting his resentment at Kitchener for wearing uniform and for wanting to see the troops. That Kitchener, as a field marshal *and* Secretary for War, was perfectly entitled to do both, seems to have escaped French's notice.

While this spat was taking place in Paris, on 1 September the BEF were in action again at Néry, where the cavalry and horse artillery fought a small

but successful battle against a German cavalry division, and at Villers-
Cotterêts, where 4 (Guards) Brigade were attacked by strong German forces
and lost 300 men in a day of savage fighting. On that day the two corps of
the BEF, separated for almost a week, finally regained contact.

Also on 1 September, Joffre finally reached the decision that was to
reverse French fortunes, a decision spurred by the finding of documents on a
dead German officer which revealed the dispositions and intentions of
General von Kluck's First Army. At last Joffre knew what the German
armies were trying to do, and the moves he had already made, to strengthen
his left wing and shore up his centre, now paid off. The captured documents
revealed that Kluck was about to abandon the Schlieffen Plan and, alarmed
at the widening gap between his own First Army and Bülow's Second Army,
was already starting to swing east, preparing to march his army to the north
of Paris. This offered Joffre the opportunity for a counter-attack against the
right flank of Kluck's forces, and this duly took place between 6 and 9
September, astride the River Marne.

Part of Joffre's preparations for this battle required the dismissal of
General Lanrezac, who was sacked on 3 September and replaced by the
forceful and efficient General Franchet d' Esperey. Lanrezac was not the
first or the last French general to go, for in this desperate hour any officer
who was not up to his job was swiftly replaced, while only those ready and
willing to fight and win were promoted to higher command.

The Battle of the Marne involved the French Third, Fourth, Fifth, Sixth
and Ninth Armies, with the BEF sandwiched between the Fifth and Sixth, a
Franco-British force totalling well over a million men. It proved to be a great
victory for France, and by the end of the battle, with some assistance from
BEF, these French armies had driven the Germans back more than sixty
miles to the River Aisne. Among such numbers the BEF's contribution
could only be small, but it was not without significance and the French were
duly grateful.

On 5 September the BEF was south of the Grand Morin river, just east of
Paris, but although French had kept his promise to remain between the Fifth
and Sixth Armies he was not in line with them but some fifteen miles, or a
day's march, in rear of his allies. Joffre needed every man he could get for his
attack and – perhaps with some reason – he had doubts that French would
commit his men to this battle. He therefore visited GHQ, now at Melun,
and, having explained the details of his plan, made a personal appeal for
British support, on behalf of France, to the Field Marshal. This appeal was
so effective – and so emotional ('Monsieur le maréchal, c'est la France qui
vous supplie') – that it reduced French to tears. But he was speaking for his
soldiers when he said to his interpreter: 'Dammit, I can't explain. Tell him all
that men can do, our fellows will do.'

Since leaving Mons on 24 August, the BEF had marched and fought over
a distance of some 200 miles. Now the days of retreat were over and they
were going to hit back, hard. Spirits soared in the cavalry regiments, in the

gun batteries and among the infantry battalions, as the men tightened their equipment and gave their weapons one last going-over. Then they began to march, not south, away from the enemy as on previous days, but north and east, towards the rumble of the guns . . . and as they continued to advance, on 6 and 7 September, they realised that the Germans were retreating.

The Battle of the Marne ended German hopes of a quick victory. General von Moltke still persisted in trying to return to the Schlieffen Plan, failing to see that all the actions since the Battles of the Frontier had combined to render it useless. Neither did he try to cope with the situation affecting his armies east of Paris, which were now falling back under pressure from the French, for he issued no orders to his troops as their retreat continued. To some of their more thoughtful leaders this reverse on the Marne marked the beginning of their ultimate defeat. Moltke saw this much at least, for on 9 September he wrote to his wife: 'Things are going badly and the battles east of Paris will not be decided in our favour. This war which began with such hopes will go against us and we must be crushed in the fight against East and West . . . and we shall have to pay for all the destruction we have done.'

Moltke was right. The battle on the Marne marked the end of the Schlieffen Plan, which alone had offered Germany the chance to fight and win a war on two fronts. Moltke did not live to see his other predictions come to pass, for he died in 1916, and on 14 September 1914, just six weeks after he had sent his armies into Belgium, he was replaced as Chief of the German General Staff by General Erich von Falkenhayn.

Helmuth von Moltke was not the right man to command the German armies in such a desperate venture as the Schlieffen Plan. He did not have the nerve to put all his assets into that one bold stroke, or the intelligence to realise that the more he attempted to hedge his bets, the more certain he was to lose all. To his credit, he realised his shortcomings, for he was a decent, sensitive man who owed his army career and his elevation to high office to the reputation of his uncle, the Prussian Marshal Count von Moltke, who had shattered the French Army in the war of 1870, and so earned the gratitude of the Hohenzollerns.

The younger Moltke's successor, Erich von Falkenhayn, the Prussian Minister for War, was a stern and decisive soldier who immediately took firm control of the German armies on the Western Front and began to co-ordinate their actions, while Moltke, though relieved of his command, was ordered to stay at OHL, the German military headquarters at Coblenz, in case news of his dismissal should leak out, and be seen as an admission of defeat in the west. Falkenhayn ordered the German armies to go over to the offensive at all points, to bombard Antwerp and press home the siege, while the generals in France were to continue with what was left of the Schlieffen Plan by enveloping the French left wing. He also ordered the rapid formation of a new army, the Ninth, and the mustering of six and a half new reserve corps. He was appointed too late, however, to prevent a major defeat on the Marne and the subsequent retreat to the Aisne.

Falkenhayn was fifty-three when he took over command of the German armies. In his photographs he appears as a typical Prussian Junker, hair cropped, heavy moustache over a grimly set mouth, an unblinking stare at the camera. Opinions vary as to how much this appearance lived up to the reality. Falkenhayn did not lack nerve, but given time to think he tended to become overcautious. He owed much of his advancement to the favour of the Kaiser, who had been impressed with Falkenhayn's dispatches from China during the Boxer Rebellion of 1900. He had become Prussian War Minister* in 1913 and played a major part in formulating the final plans for the attack on Belgium, and he was also to be the architect of the 1916 attack at Verdun. As a field commander, however, his touch was less sure, and from September 1914 his actions around Ypres were to cause severe losses to the cream of the pre-war German Army. After taking command of the armies, he retained his post as War Minister until February 1915, and was therefore doubly responsible for German strategy – and casualties – in the battles in Champagne and at the First Battle of Ypres which occupied the final months of 1914.

During the Battle of the Marne the BEF operated in the Brie country, east of Paris, in an area enclosed by various tributaries of the Marne, the Ourcq, the Grand Morin and the Petit Morin. On the first day of the fighting, the task of the BEF was to march to the north-east and reach or cross the Grand Morin, heading towards Montmirail. This advance went well, in spite of heavy skirmishing, and on the following day the BEF, with Smith-Dorrien's II Corps in the lead, crossed the Grand Morin. By 8 September, Field Marshal French was able to issue fresh orders to his troops covering further advances over the Petit Morin and on to the Marne.

This was a war of movement and French handled his troops well, pushing them on behind a thick cavalry screen, while the men, buoyed up by advancing after weeks of retreat, marched at their best speed, taking plenty of prisoners and a quantity of guns. In the six days from 6–12 September, the German First and Second Armies were driven back more than sixty miles, but this was not a rout. The Germans fought well, gave ground reluctantly when pushed back by superior numbers, and were always seeking a position where they could halt and dig in to stop the Allied advance. Such a position was eventually discovered on 12 September, on the River Aisne.

The First Battle of the Marne ended on the night of 12–13 September. That night also marked the end of the retreat for the German First and Second Armies, which withdrew across the Aisne and dug in for the next phase of the struggle, the First Battle of the Aisne which, according to the British Official History, took place between 12 and 15 September. These fixed dates for particular battles are simply a historical convenience; they

---

* Prussia, the largest and most powerful of the German states which were united into the German Empire in 1871, retained, as did some other states, a degree of self-government; furthermore, as well as being the German Emperor, William II was also King of Prussia.

should not be taken to mean that there was no fighting before or after those dates, or that no preliminary moves were made before the 'battle', or that nothing much happened after it. Battles are simply fixed points in a campaign; they are the result of what happened before and a cause of what followed, but by and large the fighting continued all the time in greater or lesser degrees.

Field Marshal French mentions that the first surprise on the Aisne came when his troops came under heavy fire from German 8-inch howitzers hurried down from Maubeuge (which had fallen some days before) 'to support the German defensive position along the Aisne, our first experience of an artillery much heavier than our own' (*1914*, p. 144). On 12 September French established his headquarters at Fère-en-Tardenois and went forward to a point on the Aisne south-east of Soissons, where the 4th Division of Pulteney's III Corps were assisting an attack by the French Sixth Army. From the ridge on the south bank the Field Marshal could look down on the valley and was astonished by the intensity of the shellfire; 'the river seemed to be ablaze, so intense was the artillery fire on both sides' (*1914* p. 145).

On the River Aisne in the middle weeks of September 1914, six weeks into the war, the nature of the fighting changed. As French now saw, the artillery piece was beginning to dominate the battlefield and would continue to do so until the end of the war. The Aisne also saw the start of 'trench warfare' which began, not as part of any deliberate, strategic plan, but for two simple, tactical reasons. On the Aisne the Germans found a position they could defend and from it defy eviction; to hold it they dug trenches and artillery positions. Secondly, when the Anglo-French armies came up to assault these positions, they came under the fire of that artillery, and dug trenches to shelter from it. The Allies then tried frontal assaults from their trenches, and when these attacks failed attempted to outflank the German position with a hooking attack to the north and west, only to find that the Germans had extended their right flank, dug-in, and could beat them off again.

The process then repeated itself, day after day, and so, hooking and digging, hooking and digging, the trench lines of both sides slowly crept north and west. They might have crept south and east, and indeed they eventually did so, right up to the frontier of Switzerland, but in September 1914 both sides were attempting to get round the 'open' or western flank of their foe, hoping to roll up the enemy's line, force a final battle and end the war. However, as Field Marshal French soon noticed, the defence was beginning to dominate the battlefield and stifle the war of manoeuvre. So the great trench system – the 'Old Front Line' of the Western Front – gradually came into being, not as the concept of some great commander, but simply as a means whereby soldiers of all armies on that front could hold ground and protect themselves from shellfire.

The Germans gained the benefit of this procedure, for they had the choice of ground. Though neither side had visualised a war in fixed positions, the Germans had an adequate supply of trench stores like barbed wire, spades and duckboards, and useful weapons like hand grenades and trench mortars. The French and British had none, or almost none, of these assets. As the Allied advance continued, the Germans therefore fell back until they found some position which offered defensive advantages, and then they would dig in. Such a position was usually on higher ground, where the height gave them good observation and the reverse slope could conceal their artillery and supply lines and screen them from direct fire. Their pursuers – the French and British – were therefore obliged to take up inferior positions on lower slopes, positions which could be observed from the higher ground occupied by the enemy, and from which the mounting of attacks was made just that much more difficult. The trench lines thus created were not always continuous, and not always below ground – the high water table in Flanders often forced both sides to build sandbagged entrenchments partly above ground level – and the Germans did not always enjoy the advantages of terrain, but that is the general picture which developed in the autumn of 1914, one that should be borne in mind from now on.

The BEF's part in the Aisne battle began on the morning of 13 September, when French ordered his three corps, after crossing the river, to make an advance of some five miles from the north bank of the Aisne to the foot of a long, low ridge that ran across their front. Along the top of this ridge ran a carriage road, which, since it had been built in the eighteenth century by King Louis XV so that his Court ladies could take the air, was known as the Chemin des Dames. From this ridge various spurs run down towards the Aisne, while the entire country between the ridge and the river, a tumbled mixture of fields, woods and copses, was overlooked from German positions on the heights of the Chemin des Dames above.

Pulteney's III Corps, reinforced for the later stages of the battle by the newly arrived 6th Division, had already established a bridgehead across the Aisne and although all the bridges had been destroyed, the two wings and then the centre of the BEF managed to get across without undue difficulty and in a wide variety of ways, from rafts and small boats, to clambering over the remains of demolished bridges. So the advance continued, under shellfire which did little damage at the time, for the British troops were advancing on a broad front and in open order or 'artillery formation'. A German officer, Hauptmann (Captain) Walter Bloem, watched the advance of Haig's I Corps near Chivres:

> From the bushes bordering the river sprang up a second line of skirmishers, with at least ten paces from man to man: the second line pushed nearer and now a third line, two hundred metres behind that and then a fourth wave. Our artillery fired like mad, but all the shells could hit were single men, all in vain; a sixth line appeared, a seventh, all with good distance and intervals between the men. We were filled with admiration.

The whole plain was now dotted with khaki figures, coming ever nearer, the attack directed on the corps on our right. Now our infantry fire met our attackers but wave after wave flooded forward and disappeared from our view behind the woods.

These advances, however well handled, were not without cost; the 6th Division had a bloody baptism, losing 1,500 men in its first engagement on the Aisne.

This advance to the Aisne was the last piece of truly open warfare the Western Front was to see for the next three and a half years but although the German First and Second Armies had fallen back steadily from the Marne to the Aisne, the Allied armies, including the BEF, were not moving fast enough in pursuit and their tardy advance gave an advantage to the retreating enemy. Haig saw this as the advance began, recording in his diary for 7 September: 'I thought our movements very slow today, in view of the fact that the enemy was on the run. I motored and saw both [Major-Generals] Lomax and Monro [commanding respectively the 1st and 2nd Divisions in Haig's corps] and impressed on them the need for quick and immediate action.'

The secret of a maintaining a successful advance is *to keep contact with the enemy and prevent him gaining enough ground and time to reorganise, find a good defensive position and dig in.* A retreating enemy has to be kept moving and hustled out of any likely defensive position before he has time to use it. This the Anglo-French forces failed to do as they pushed the German armies back from the Marne, and they paid for it on the Aisne. The Germans had time to dig in, their supply lines were shortening, heavy guns were brought up, the Allied advance was checked and the enemy, pivoting on that position along the Chemin de Dames, were able to fend off further attacks as the trench lines crept north and west. The main reason for this failure was excessive caution on the part of the Allied army commanders.

French had become obsessed with protecting his flanks and keeping the BEF in line with the French Sixth and Fifth Armies. This may have been to show Kitchener that he intended to do what he had been ordered to do at the meeting in Paris, or because of some genuine fears of a German counter-attack against his front or flanks. Equally, it may also have been from sheer petulance, resulting from Kitchener's insistence that he work closely with the French. Whatever the reason, the effect was to slow the Allied advance, for the French were also reluctant to push ahead and the three armies acted like men in a three-legged race, each unwilling to move unless the others kept pace. The pace became that of the slowest, with the result that the Germans were given the chance to disengage, get away . . . and dig in.

The result was a stalemate on the Aisne and great losses as each side strove to break through the other's line. According to the German official account (pp. 108–114), 26 September

was the bloodiest battle . . . of the whole of this period of the war. Nowhere had the Armies won any ground worth mention, far less beaten the enemy. A great part of the German Armies suffered an irreparable loss of officers and men and what was shaken was the hitherto unshaken belief in the irresistible might of the German attack, which the Marne had not destroyed.

The Allies also lost heavily in the Aisne fighting, and after some initial thrusts up the southern spurs of the German-held ridge, Field Marshal French ordered his men to dig in and hold their positions against the German attacks and the ever-increasing shellfire. He issued no further operational orders to his command for two whole weeks, between 16 September and 1 October, the period during which 'trench warfare', with all its attendant horrors, first began. It was by then becoming clear that the Allied armies could not break through with frontal attacks on the Aisne, and Joffre therefore decided on an outflanking movement – the so-called 'Race to the Sea' – which began in early October. By this time the French and Germans were already facing each other in a trench system that ran for over ninety miles, from the Aisne north and west towards Béthune and La Bassée, two towns between Arras and Ypres. This movement was not a 'race' but, as already described, a series of flanking movements, a fact which gives the lie to the popularly held belief that the generals of the Great War only thought in terms of frontal attacks. The trench system on the Western Front was actually created by *weeks* of flanking attacks, each one stifled by the enemy's defence line.

This shifting movement to the north-west caused French to review the position of his army. At the end of September he proposed to Joffre that the BEF, currently sandwiched between two French armies in the centre of the Allied line, should resume its position on the left, beyond La Bassée, and with the aid of Belgian units, fill the gap between that town and the sea, a distance of some forty miles. This offered various logistical advantages, for it would put the BEF close to their cross-Channel supply ports at Calais and Boulogne.

Joffre was less than enthusiastic, but on 1 October the British commander told him that, with or without French agreement, he intended to shift his forces north and west. Having little option, Joffre then agreed to this move and the BEF began to travel north on the night of 2 October. The 2nd Cavalry Division went first, by road, followed by II Corps, which began to move by rail from Compiègne to Flanders on 5 October, followed a short time later by Pulteney's III Corps and later still by Haig's I Corps. GHQ moved to Abbeville on 8 October, and on the 13th French established his HQ at St Omer. As these British units came into line in the north, German units arrived in line to the east, just in time to oppose them.

This move took the British away from the Aisne, but the fighting for the Chemin des Dames went on for the rest of the war, making that barren ridge a byword for slaughter among the French military. The tardy approach of the Allied forces to the Aisne contributed to the deadlock which began to grip the front as winter came on, and the Official History's verdict on the BEF at the Aisne seems both fair and accurate:

> The race was lost mainly owing to a failure to make a resolute effort to reconnoitre the enemy's dispositions on the river . . . and to push forward parties to seize the bridges on September 12/13. When the divisions made a rather cautious and leisurely advance they should have been reminded of the old adage that 'Sweat saves Blood'. In GHQ orders there was no hint whatever of the importance of time.

The account goes on to add that, after the Germans were known to have dug in, 'There was no plan, no objective, no arrangements for co-operation, and the divisions blundered into battle.' (Volume I, p. 465.)

During the British move north, the infantry by rail, the cavalry and artillery by march route, all arms took great care to conceal their movements from the prying eyes of German airmen. Aerial reconnaissance, unknown two months before, was now playing an important role on both sides of the line, and the information the pilots and observers provided was to prove of increasing value in the months and years ahead. The BEF's movement north continued, and by 20 October, I Corps had arrived in Ypres where they linked up with the 7th Division and the 3rd Cavalry Division, which had landed from England at Ostend and Zeebrugge and covered the retreat of the Belgian Army from Antwerp to their new positions north of Dixmude.

Antwerp, that city-port on the Scheldt into which the Belgian Army had retreated in August and where, with some aid from the British in the shape of a Royal Marine Brigade, they had at first resisted a German siege, had soon proved unviable as an Allied outpost behind the German front. The city lies up the estuary of the Scheldt (as the Rhine becomes in this part of Belgium), forty miles from the sea, and the Germans soon had heavy guns in position to sink any ships attempting to run up the river and supply the garrison. Falkenhayn had assembled some of the heavy siege guns released by the fall of Maubeuge and with their support some four and a half divisions of German infantry were ready to overwhelm the defenders of Antwerp. The Belgian forces further south were reinforced by the British 7th Infantry Division and the 3rd Cavalry Division, a force commanded by Lieutenant-General Sir Henry Rawlinson. These, plus the Royal Naval Division, arrived on 7 October, just in time to cover the retreat of the Antwerp garrison.

On 8 October, with German artillery fire and infantry probing the defences, the Belgian field army withdrew down the coast to Ostend, and a week later had taken up positions on the coast from just inside the Belgian frontier at Nieuport to the town of Dixmude on the River Yser. Antwerp fell on 10 October, by which time Rawlinson's forces had been transferred to the

BEF. Renamed IV Corps, they arrived in time take part in the First Battle of Ypres.

The focus now turns to the British front which, by mid-October 1914, lay between the La Bassée Canal and the Flanders cloth town of Ypres, a city of some 20,000 inhabitants situated a few miles south of Dixmude. The German forces were slowly converging on Ypres, where the three armies, German, Anglo-French and Belgian, were set to fight one of the major battles of the war. Before proceeding to give an account of that month-long engagement, however, it is necessary to explain the location of the forces and the nature of the ground.

According to the British Official History, the First Battle of Ypres ('First Ypres') actually consisted of four engagements: the Battles of La Bassée (10 October–2 November), Armentières, (13 October–2 November), Messines (12 October–2 November) and Ypres (19 October–22 November), with the latter further broken down into three distinct engagements, at Langemarck (21–24 October), Gheluvelt (29–31 October), and finally Nonne Bosschen on 11 November. A glance at the map will reveal that the battle-line ran from south of Ypres at Béthune-La Bassee, north to the edge of the soon-to-be-notorious 'Ypres Salient', and then round the low hills that form the eastern rim of the Salient to Langemarck, which lies in a shallow valley.

The broad term 'First Ypres' embraces the entire front line, for in this battle the fighting did not die out in one place only to flare up in another. Once it began, First Ypres continued with growing intensity, generating a slaughter which consumed tens of thousands of lives, British and Belgian, French and German, largely destroying the old regiments of the BEF in the process. Though 'First Ypres' is often regarded as a 'British' battle, it could not have been fought and won without the French and Belgians; moreover, it was here that the first of the Empire contingents, the Lahore Division of the Indian Army, appeared in France for the first time.

When the battle began the disposition of Allied forces from the south was as follows: the French Tenth Army, under General Maud'huy, were holding the front from south of Arras to Vermelles, four miles south of the La Bassée Canal. Then came two French cavalry corps, commanded by Generals Conneau and de Mitry, and Smith-Dorrien's II Corps. Then, east of St Omer, came Pulteney's III Corps, then Allenby's cavalry, now a full corps, then the two divisions of Rawlinson's embryonic IV Corps (7th Infantry and 3rd Cavalry Divisions) holding the line at Ypres, with two French territorial divisions linking them with the Belgian Army along the River Yser. These positions were fluid, for the front had not yet settled down and Haig's I Corps had not arrived when the battle began. In order to control this motley Allied force, on 11 October General Foch was appointed Commandant de la Groupe des Armées du Nord (GAN), which would include the Tenth Army and any French forces north of Arras, and with which the British and Belgian forces were obliged to co-operate.

The fighting at First Ypres is best imagined as a brawl, and that is the image to retain in mind, for the battle was a pell-mell struggle which allowed neither time nor opportunity for major tactics. The Allied generals and their men had to hang on, patch up the defence line, muster troops for yet another attack, and keep fighting. First Ypres was an 'encounter battle' between the Anglo-French and Belgian forces trying to advance east past Lille and turn the enemy's line, and the Germans attempting to push west, take Ypres, drive the British into the sea, and then turn south along the Channel coast. There was little time or space for manoeuvre or fancy plans or any refinement of tactics. The German pressure was so strong and so constant that the Allied defenders were forced to throw in battalions and brigades wherever they were needed to shore up the line – 'puttying up', in the jargon of the time.

Necessity takes no account of corps or regimental boundaries, and at various times during First Ypres every British soldier who could stand and fire a rifle – including cooks, signallers and Sappers – would be flung into the fighting. This included the cavalry, who left their horses and took on the infantry role. In the weeks for which the battle lasted – had the situation permitted – many men, and perhaps a few senior generals, might have taken thought and thanked the man who insisted that the British cavalry should be equipped with an infantry rifle, learn to shoot it accurately, and have a grasp of infantry tactics.

An understanding of the fighting around Ypres is not possible without a mental image of the terrain (see map, p.112). The popular image of Flanders is of a flat country seamed with waterways. This vision is neither inaccurate, nor entirely true. Flanders is criss-crossed with waterways, canals and drainage ditches and has two significant rivers north and south of Ypres, the Lys, which runs south-west from Menin, and the Yser, as well as the Yser Canal, which runs south from Dixmude and passes just west of Ypres. There are a number of small but steep hills, beginning in the west with the hill crowned by the town of Cassel.

Then, heading east, comes the Mont des Cats, the Monts Rouge and Noir and the steep-sided Mont Kemmel, which glowers down on the Ypres plain to the north-east and offers views to the south as far as the slagheaps of Loos. Beyond Kemmel the ground falls away to a much lower ridge at Messines and Wytschaete, and this high ground runs east to Gheluvelt and Passchendaele. Ypres itself is frequently described in the histories as 'lying in the centre of a saucer'; the rim of this saucer runs from Messines in the south to Passchendaele in the north-east, falling away from there to the east bank of the Yser Canal at Bixschoote, and from the main ridge other, lower, ridges run towards Ypres, like the spokes of a wheel. Those who have never visited the area should not imagine that the Ypres–La Bassée area, although low-lying, is either wholly flat or utterly featureless.

When fighting in relatively flat, open country even small elevations take on significance, and this is especially so in a war dominated by artillery. The small mounts and low ridges of the Ypres Salient seem insignificant to the civilian, but to soldiers in 1914 they offered to whoever occupied them the advantage of observation and the opportunity to direct artillery fire on to targets on lower ground, as well as protection on the reverse slopes for trenches and dugouts, and also artillery positions. Look at the ground with the eye of an infantry soldier or an artillery officer and the need to gain and hold some slight rise becomes instantly apparent.

Walk the Ypres Ridge today, up from low-lying Langemarck to Passchendaele and then on round to Messines: the gain in height over the plain towards Ypres seems imperceptible, but the observation obtained is easy to appreciate. The towers of Ypres are always in view, so that a man with a pair of field glasses and a telephone line to a gun battery could bring down fire upon any point in the Salient below. Between 1914 and 1918 this ridge, nowhere more than 200 feet high, was the vital piece of ground in the Ypres sector, for whoever held the ridge could dominate the battlefield. Most of the fighting at First Ypres and in the years that followed would be for the possession of this feature, and the vast British cemetery at Tyne Cot is only one memorial to the severity of that struggle.

As for Ypres itself, a glance at a large scale-map will reveal its military importance. The town was, and is, a road, rail and canal centre, the key to Bruges, Calais and Dunkirk, and the vital Channel coast. The army that held Ypres had the key to the coast in its pocket. Ypres was also politically important, since it was the only significant Belgian town free from German occupation, and retaining it was taken to be a symbol of Allied resolve. These factors, the importance of Ypres and the necessity of holding the ridge around the Salient in order to retain the town, explain the years of bitter fighting for which the place became notorious; it was not fought for simply because the generals were too stubborn to abandon it. From 1914 to 1917 the British Army held Ypres and the Germans held the ridge that overlooked it. How that came about is the story of First Ypres.

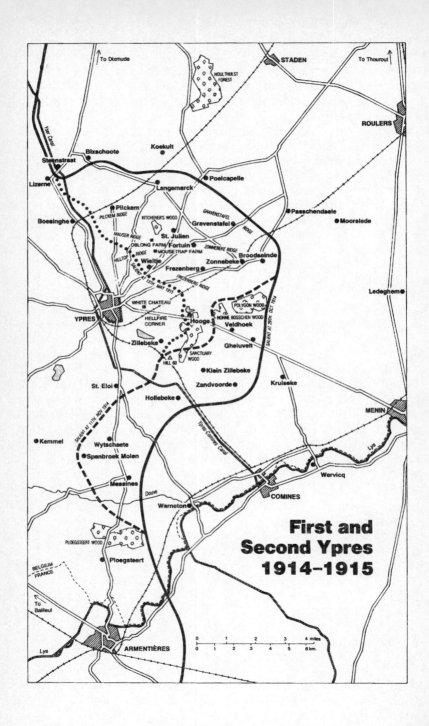

First and
Second Ypres
1914–1915

CHAPTER 6

FIRST YPRES,
October–November 1914

*'The line that stood between the British Empire and ruin was
composed of tired, ragged and unshaven men, unwashed,
plastered with mud, many in uniforms that were little more
than rags. But they had their rifles and bayonets, and plenty
of ammunition.'*

Brigadier-General Sir J. E. Edmonds,
Military Operations France and Belgium, 1914, Volume II

First Ypres was a terrible, scrambling battle, the graveyard of the
original, Regular BEF, and the first real test for Lieutenant-General
Sir Douglas Haig, commander of I Corps. Though Field Marshal French
dates it from 15 October, the battle lasted a full month, from 10 October to
11 November, swaying this way and that, stretching north from the La
Bassée Canal to Dixmude, and the result was not finally decided until the
afternoon of the last day, when the Prussian Guard finally fell back down
the Menin Road, leaving behind the remnants of the British Regular Army
that had fought the German Army, by which it was greatly outnumbered, to
a standstill.

The first engagements of the battle that came to be known as First Ypres
took place some distance south of both the town itself and the Salient, along
the La Bassée Canal and at Armentières, a small town just south of the
Franco-Belgian border. These battles featured Smith-Dorrien's hard-
fighting and long-suffering II Corps. Its battalions had been much reduced
by the fighting of the last few weeks and in particular by the battle on the
Aisne, in which the BEF lost 10,000 men killed, wounded, or missing. A
third of these losses came from II Corps but the soldiers, if tired, were now
fit and still full of fight.

The BEF needed rest and reinforcement, but first, as has been said,
French wanted it at the western end of the line, a position in which it would
be as close to the Channel ports as possible, with all the benefits that would

then accrue from short supply lines. The Anglo-French armies were always 'a day late and a corps short,' relative to the Germans, in this outflanking march to the north, but these movements set the tactical pattern for the greater part of October. Smith-Dorrien was ordered to make just such an outflanking attempt at La Bassée when his corps came north.

He was also charged with keeping touch with Maunoury's Tenth French Army on his right and – when it arrived – Pulteney's III Corps on his left, a diversity of tasks that was to create difficulties in the days ahead. The opposition on the II Corps front at this time came from the German I and II Cavalry Corps, but it has to be remembered that German cavalry divisions included Jäger battalions and plenty of artillery. In order to advance and take La Bassée II Corps had to do a good deal more than simply brush aside a cavalry screen, and more German units were coming up all the time.

So, having detrained at Abbeville, II Corps and III Corps marched north, meeting steady and increasing resistance as they approached the Belgian border, where the Germans had established the new Sixth Army of four corps behind Lille. Having taken Lille this army began to deploy across the path of II and III Corps. Other German divisions, released after the fall of Antwerp, were now marching south and taking up positions opposite the Belgian Army around Nieuport and Dixmude, from where French troops took up the defence of the Allied line down to Bixschoote, five miles north of Ypres. The front was fluid, but this is the general position: Belgians and French in the north, more French in the south, and the BEF slowly coming up in the centre, between the La Bassée Canal and the Ypres–Menin road.

In front of this Franco-Belgian force, north of the Menin Road, General von Falkenhayn was forming yet another new army, the Fourth, consisting of four reserve corps. This Army took up position east of Ypres, circling the town south to north in a line from Menin to the sea, with the Sixth Army on its left flank. Like the Sixth Army, the Fourth was supported with a large amount of artillery and greatly outnumbered the Allied forces on its immediate front. The composition of this new German army is worth noting, for it was full of recently recruited volunteers, the German equivalent of the enthusiasts now flocking to join Kitchener's New Armies across the Channel. The ranks of the Fourth Army contained artisans, students, office workers, and factory hands, but there was also a good stiffening of regular soldiers, as well as officers and NCOs, the latter the backbone of all the German armies, to provide the leadership. This was not an entirely untrained or inexperienced force; indeed, given such enthusiasm and such leadership, the Fourth Army was a formidable military machine.

Myth has it that all the men in this army were half-trained students borne along by patriotic fervour, and there is some truth in that belief, at least where the lower ranks were concerned. The fighting of the past months, which had strained French and British resources to the limit, had done much the same to the Germans, who also had a war to fight in the east. Both sides cherished the fading illusion that one more effort, one more attack, one extra ounce of energy and courage, could turn the opposing front and therefore decide the outcome of the war. The Germans needed every man they could find to bring this war to a rapid conclusion, and so these eager volunteers were sent marching into battle outside Ypres against the finest professional infantry in Europe. What happened when these forces met is another of the great tragedies of the war.

British military historians have written many books on the slaughter inflicted on British troops on the Western Front during infantry assaults. It is worth remembering, however, that not only British generals sent their men into such assaults, and that it was not only British soldiers that fell in great numbers before massed rifle and machine-gun fire. This is not to excuse the practice, but to place it in context. Other generals, German and French, Italian and Turkish, Serbian and Austrian, tried the same tactics, with the same dire results – though without, or so it would appear, the same castigation from posterity.

The German infantry had already sustained heavy losses attacking British troops, and were to sustain more when their forces met II Corps along the La Bassée Canal on 10 October. This engagement followed French's Operation Order No. 33, directing the BEF – or, to be exact, II and III Corps – to 'advance and meet the enemy, prolonging the French left'. Smith-Dorrien's Corps met the Germans astride the La Bassée Canal, and from there the fighting spread steadily north towards Ypres, being taken up by the Cavalry Corps and III Corps in their turn. Sir John French had hoped that II Corps could swing behind the German line, take La Bassée and advance to Lille, if not Brussels, but when the 3rd and 5th Divisions of II Corps and the 6th Division of III Corps were brought to a halt, this eastward advance stopped on a line between La Bassée and Armentières. (This process is easier to understand if it is followed corps by corps and with the aid of the map on page 112.)

II Corps began its advance on 12 October and soon ran into heavy opposition. According to the Official History, II Corps was opposed by four German cavalry divisions, supported by infantry battalions, but pressed on nevertheless and reached Givenchy where there was a considerable battle on 13 October. It was then that a problem began to develop, for this advance, wheeling south towards La Bassée, was gradually exposing II Corp's left flank. On the following day, therefore, advised by reports from the Royal Flying Corps that a large German force was massing around Lille, Smith-Dorrien halted his advance, dug in and waited for III Corps to come into line. That night the Germans introduced a new tactic, making night attacks and infiltrating through the British line.

On 14 October the 3rd Division suffered a setback when its commander, Major-General Hubert Hamilton, was killed by shellfire. His death is another statistic which should give the lie to that popular belief that the British generals spent their time in safe, cosy châteaux well behind the lines. The 3rd Division was to have four more commanders before Major-General Haldane took over command on November 22.

The 14th is a significant date in the history of the Great War. On that day the 'Race to the Sea' ended with the completion of a trench line from Belfort on the Swiss frontier to the Channel coast at Nieuport. This line was not yet very thick, and did not begin to approach the dense defensive state into which it would be developed over the next months and years, but its completion signalled the effective end of open warfare and the start of trench warfare. On that day, the British having taken Bailleul and Messines, the German High Command ordered the Sixth Army to halt its offensive push towards Givenchy, Armentières and Menin and wait until the Fourth Army was in position on its right, north of the River Lys. Only then would the Germans attack again, planning to sweep forward in force and drive the British out of Ypres, back to the Channel coast and into the sea. Meanwhile, the battle along the La Bassée Canal crept north, with French taking Rawlinson's IV Corps under command on 15 October.

Field Marshal French dates the opening of First Ypres from 15 October, and admits in *1914* (p. 216) that on that day

> I thought the danger was past. I believed that the enemy had exhausted his strength in the great bid he had made to smash our armies on the Marne and capture Paris. The fine successes gained by the Cavalry and III Corps, did much to confirm these impressions on my mind . . . In my heart I did not expect I should have to fight a great defensive battle. All my dispositions were made with the idea of carrying out effectively the combined offensive which was concerted between Foch and myself.

Orders to implement that Anglo-French plan were issued on the afternoon of 15 October.

Between 16 and 18 October II Corps took Givenchy and swung south and east to Aubers Ridge. This was the limit of their advance, and La Bassée was to remain in German hands for the next four years. On 20 October II Corps suffered the loss of the crack 2nd Battalion, Royal Irish Regiment, which was overrun by the Germans at the village of Le Pilly on Aubers Ridge. This was a considerable disaster, for nearly 600 officers and men were lost, only 30 soldiers regaining the British lines. French's estimates of German numbers on his front was seriously flawed and he should have known it, for information about the enemy formations and numbers on his front was pouring into GHQ, from the RFC reconnaissance aircraft, from cavalry patrols, from the interrogation of prisoners, and from the examination of the shoulder tabs of the German dead. By mid-October the Germans could count on *sixteen* infantry divisions and *five* cavalry divisions already in the line around Ypres, with another five divisions marching west to join them. In mid-October the BEF mustered a total of seven infantry divisions, three cavalry divisions and the two newly-arrived divisions of the Indian Army, the Lahore and Meerut Divisions – less one brigade left at Suez – and had no reserves at all. Should the British line need shoring up, the reserve forces would have to be provided by the French.

The Belgians had six divisions north of Ypres, and General Foch, commander of the Northern Army Group, had the French Second and Tenth Armies with which to stem the German thrust, but the weight of the developing attack was centred on Ypres, for the excellent reason that whoever held the town held the key to the Channel ports. Ypres was defended by I Corps of the BEF under Haig, and it is with the actions of his corps that this chapter is chiefly concerned, though the actions of the other British corps and their allies should not be overlooked.

Sir John French had now been in command of the BEF for two months, and certain of his command characteristics were becoming evident. The first and most damaging of these was a refusal to face facts or accept the information provided by his own Intelligence officers. The second was too great a willingness to believe that his own men were in danger, or worn out, or for some reason unable to fight. The third was his constant underestimation of the enemy forces opposed to his own.

The first and third of these faults were making an appearance during the fighting for La Bassée, but there may have been – and almost certainly was – another factor, the pervasive influence of Henry Wilson, his Sub-Chief of Staff. Wilson's francophilia – or francomania – was being reinforced by the presence of his much-admired mentor, Foch, who now commanded the French forces in the north and was therefore in daily touch with French's HQ. The push by II and III Corps towards La Bassée and Armentières was one result of this influence, for on 10 October Foch and French had agreed on a combined attack eastwards, with the BEF passing to the north of Lille. If Foch thought an advance was possible, Wilson was the man to urge Field Marshal French to support it. The order was given and the BEF duly advanced, but it did not get far against stiffening German resistance, and every yard of the advance was made at a considerable cost in lives.

The left flank of II Corps had been exposed by the wheel south towards La Bassée and, anticipating a German counter-attack, Smith-Dorrien had begun constructing a new defence line to the rear, between Givenchy and the village of Neuve Chapelle. Materials to build a really formidable line were not available but these trenches offered some protection in the event of a retreat. On the night of 22–23 October, after General Conneau's cavalry division, on the left flank of II Corps, had been driven back, Smith-Dorrien, having consulted French, pulled his troops back to this line – a line that became the 'Old Front Line' of the BEF for much of the next four years. The Germans followed up on 26 October with an attack on Neuve Chapelle, pressing the assault for four days before at last falling back. On the night of 29–30 October, II Corps was relieved by the newly arrived Indian Corps, but most of its battalions were soon sent back into action to shore up the British line at Ypres.

With the situation of II Corps stabilised, it is time to look at the dispositions of the other corps along the northern sector of the Western Front, looking first at III Corps and the Cavalry Corps. Obeying French's order to 'advance east, engage the enemy and pass north of Lille', these formations had made some progress towards Armentières. By the evening of 19 October they stood on a line from Violaines to Ploegsteert Wood, north of Armentières and just inside the Belgian frontier. The Cavalry Corps, on the left flank of III Corps, had linked up with the 7th Division of Rawlinson's IV Corps, in position on the Ypres–Menin Road. On the southern flank of III Corps, Conneau's French cavalry division occupied the space between III and II Corps, and was to give the British on its flanks stout assistance in the days ahead. (Close inspection of the map on page 112, which shows the Salient at different dates, will be helpful at this point.)

On 16 October, III Corps' troops were engaged at Armentières, which they captured on the 17th, though the Germans pounded their positions with heavy artillery and put in strong counter-attacks. As at Neuve Chapelle these attacks lasted four days and then the Germans pulled back, having sustained heavy losses, though not without inflicting grievous blows against the depleted British forces. On that day General Haig arrived at St Omer and had a meeting with Field Marshal French, who told him that he did not intend to commit I Corps until it had fully concentrated at Ypres and had had a few days' rest. The interview could not end without a few jabs at Smith-Dorrien, whose corps, said French, 'has not done well', and Haig added the comment in his diary that the 3rd Division of II Corps 'had never recovered from Le Cateau and done nothing on the Aisne'. How Haig came by this opinion is not clear, but he would soon have more to worry about than the actions of his colleague's corps.

While II Corps, III Corps, the French Cavalry divisions and Allenby's Cavalry Corps were fighting south of the River Lys, Rawlinson's IV Corps was pushing south and east from Ypres, down the Menin Road. On its left, towards the Channel coast, lay a number of French and Belgian divisions, for the First Battle of Ypres, which was now about to open, was by no means only a British 'show'. French and Belgian troops were involved from first to last, and the fact that this book concentrates on the BEF should not obscure the actions of its allies.

On 18 October, the situation was roughly as follows: the British line ran north-east from Givenchy to Herlies, where II Corps handed over to Conneau's French Cavalry Corps of three divisions, based at Fromelles. Then came III Corps, set astride the River Lys, its line running east of Armentières and up to Messines. There the dismounted British Cavalry Corps took over and there the Ypres Salient began, the line running north but edging east to Hollebeke on the Yser Canal, where the 3rd Cavalry Division, currently part of IV Corps, took over a line heading almost due east to Kruiseeke, just south of the Menin Road. That road was also the boundary between the German Sixth and Fourth Armies.

At Kruiseeke, the 7th Division of IV Corps took over and held the line to

Zonnebeke, where Haig's I Corps took on the task, the 2nd Division holding the line to north of Langemarck and the 1st Division holding positions which ran west from there to the Yser Canal, where General de Mitry's French forces, cavalry and territorial divisions, carried the line north along the canal to link up with the Belgians.

Thus were the forces poised when the main part of the First Battle of Ypres began. It should be noted that this was not a carefully prepared defensive line, but the 'start line' for an advance to the east, and that First Ypres began as an encounter battle between the two opposing armies. In line with the Foch–French plan of 10 October, all the Allied forces north of the La Bassée Canal were to advance on their respective fronts. Foch hoped to achieve a breakthrough east of Ypres; after that his left wing would wheel north while the rest of his forces, including the BEF, would turn south, rolling up the German line. French's part in this plan was to hold the line to the south of Ypres with the Cavalry Corps, III and II Corps, and send Haig's I Corps driving eastward to make the breach in the German line.

The scale of the enemy forces that would counter this Anglo-French attack and strike west was still unknown. The Germans, however, also intended to attack, and their plan – a breakthrough, albeit in the opposite direction, followed by rolling up the Allied line – was roughly the same, though their forces were much larger. The Sixth and Fourth Armies were to pierce the Allied flank at Ypres and then wheel south and west, pinning the British against the Channel coast, taking Dunkirk and Calais and pressing on to the south; in short, to attempt a re-run of the Schlieffen Plan. The opening rounds of this battle had been the engagements at La Bassée and Armentières; the major encounter would come at Ypres, where the weight of the fighting would be borne by Lieutenant-General Sir Douglas Haig's I Corps.

On 19 October, General de Mitry's French cavalry, duly advancing east, met the new German Fourth Army outside Roulers. On the same day the German III Reserve Corps in the north mounted an attack against the Belgian Army, opening an engagement that became known as the Battle of the Yser – a battle which the Belgians only won by opening the sluices and letting the sea in to flood Belgium from the coast to Dixmude, a drastic step that made the north flank of the Allied line secure for the rest of the war.

Meanwhile, Rawlinson had sent the 7th Division down the road towards Menin. The division got as far as the village of Gheluvelt, on the ridge east of Ypres and six miles from Menin, and there it halted, under heavy artillery fire from the guns of the German Fourth Army. On the left of the 7th Division British cavalry were also moving east, 3 Brigade reaching Ledeghem and 6 Brigade reaching Passchendaele. These cavalry brigades met with very little opposition, for Falkenhayn was biding his time. As Rawlinson's IV Corps advanced towards Menin it created a sharp forward salient which Falkenhayn intended to bite off in due course.

Fortunately, before that could happen, sanity returned to the Allied higher command. General de Mitry, the officer commanding the French cavalry north of the BEF, realised that a whole German army was on his front. He hurriedly pulled his forces back from Roulers, a sensible move, but one which had the unfortunate effect of exposing the left flank of the British 3rd Cavalry Division. GHQ had also totted up the information about German forces across the British front and realised that the BEF was facing not just one powerful German army – which would have been bad enough – but two.

Though the weather on 18 October was poor, restricting visibility and limiting air patrols, it improved on the following day, when information that large enemy forces were on the northern front came pouring in from the pilots and observers of the RFC. Their reports were proving exceptionally useful as the trench line began to form and cavalry patrolling became impossible. Though variable weather – and an increasing tendency for the Germans to move their divisions at night to avoid such reconnaissance – was curtailing the number of sightings, the German moves could not be entirely concealed, so that the build-up of forces east of Ypres became obvious.

Whatever the assessments GHQ had made, Field Marshal French was still clinging to the idea that the opposition on his front at Ypres was negligible. In spite of all evidence to the contrary, on 19 October, having decided that the German 'reinforcements' were directed at the BEF south of the Lys, he told Haig that I Corps 'would not be opposed by more than one German Reserve Corps' and ordered him to advance east, via Thourout, to capture Bruges and drive the enemy out of Ghent.

The right of I Corps was to pass through Ypres and, having reached the top of the low eastern hills, Haig could decide whether to attack the enemy in the north or the north-east. Haig would be supported by de Mitry's cavalry to the north and by Major-General the Hon. Julian Byng's 3rd Cavalry Division of IV Corps to the south, while the rest of the BEF were to continue their present operations, pushing east if possible, or holding their present positions if not, but always 'leaning' on the enemy line. The eyes of GHQ were now fixed on Haig's corps, and great things were anticipated. The snag was that though French estimated that 'the whole forces of the enemy north of the Lys did not exceed three and a half Army corps', facing the French and Belgians as well as I Corps, they actually consisted of some five and a half corps – eleven full divisions – of the German Fourth Army. On 20 October, this army, and the German Sixth Army to the south, flung all their divisions against the Allied line, and the two advancing forces collided.

On that day French finally decided to abandon the II Corps attack on La Bassée. He did not abandon the idea of an outflanking move to the south-east, but for the moment he ordered II and III Corps and the Cavalry Corps to stand fast and wait until Haig's corps could push ahead at Ypres. Even now, French was *still* convinced that the total German strength in the north did not exceed two – or at the most three – army corps around Lille, and perhaps another two corps behind Armentières.

Whole books have been devoted to First Ypres, and it it is not the purpose of this book to follow every stage of that battle. The points of interest here concern the actions of the generals and how they responded to the changing circumstances of the battle. Though the details are extremely complicated, the broad outline of the battle is fairly clear, so that a judgement can be made on the performance of the senior Allied commanders.

Smith-Dorrien, unaware that French was still nursing his enmity and biding his time, had done well at La Bassée, handling his tired but willing troops with considerable skill. To comply with his orders had been difficult, for he could not advance on La Bassée *and* keep in contact with the French on his right flank; he simply did not have enough men, which in turn meant that whatever he did, he would have a gap on one flank. Forced to choose, he elected to keep in touch with the French forces on his left, and Conneau's cavalry duly came in to fill the gap between II Corps and III Corps on Smith-Dorrien's right. This was the correct decision, and though he was forced to give ground and occupy a line at Neuve Chapelle, this line held, for he had taken the precaution – as at Mons two months before – of seeking out a better defensive position some distance in his rear in case a withdrawal became necessary.

Smith-Dorrien had again demonstrated his ability to make difficult decisions and anticipate problems, but the reduction of his forces in the fighting eventually became the overriding factor affecting his corps. Between 9 and 18 October, II Corps lost another 2,500 men and though it was then withdrawn into rest, his brigades and battalions were soon sent back to 'putty up' the line; for a while Smith-Dorrien found himself a corps commander without a corps.

Allenby, Rawlinson and Pulteney, commanding the Cavalry Corps, IV Corps and III Corps respectively, were also handling their men competently. Their troops were comparatively fresh and, unlike the divisions of II Corps, their units had not been badly 'written down' in the marching and fighting since Mons. The actions of Allenby's corps, now fighting as infantry, must reflect particular credit on their commander. Both he and Rawlinson will come under close examination later, but for the moment it is sufficient to say that they were handling their forces competently in a difficult situation, and no particular criticism can be levelled against them.

Haig was to meet his first great test in the First Battle of Ypres, and how he responded to that challenge will be looked at later. There remains Field Marshal Sir John French, who was about to face the greatest challenge of his career. He was not displaying the qualities of a great commander, and it is idle to pretend otherwise. His volatile character, his mood swings between optimism and pessimism, denied him the ability to reach clear decisions and form a picture of what was actually happening from the huge amount of confused information he received.

It is easy to feel a little sorry for French, an elderly soldier pitched suddenly into such a large-scale campaign, one so different from anything in his experience. It is less easy to find excuses for him. He ignored facts that were staring him in the face, disregarded information that did not match his preconceived notions, and failed to get a grip on his subordinate commanders. Commenting on the opening stages of First Ypres, the Official History remarks carefully (Volume II, p. 157) that 'the Commander-in-Chief apparently either placed no reliance on the details of the strength of the enemy gathered by his Intelligence or else he considered the new German Reserve Corps of small account.'

French also listened for far too long to the siren-like tones of Henry Wilson, urging him to follow Foch's lead and press on with the move east, however much the evidence indicated the rapid adoption of a defensive position. Another, wiser, commander, with his emotions under control, might have taken time to consider the mounting evidence of German strength, calculated their intentions and taken a different course. French ordered his men to face disaster, and when disaster did indeed confront them he relied on their fighting ability to get him out of it. On 20 October, after two days of fighting, his Army Operation Order No. 39 opened with: 'The enemy today made determined attacks on the II, III and IV Corps which have been successfully repulsed. The Commander-in-Chief intends to contain the enemy with the II, III and Cavalry Corps and the 7th Division of IV Corps and to attack vigorously with the I Corps.' This order ignored the fact that the German attacks were not only still continuing, but were mounting in strength, and that it remained to be seen if the enemy could be 'contained'. Fortunately for French and the BEF, his corps commanders were starting to take their own line and adopt defensive measures.

On the 20th, Pulteney realised that his advance at Armentières had been checked and ordered his men to halt and dig in, in anticipation of a counter-attack. This duly came in later that day when the German XIII Corps pounded the 6th Division with artillery and then sent in the infantry, the advancing troops covered by heavy machine-gun fire and moving in 'tactical bounds', forward movements of a few hundred yards at a time, covered by artillery fire. The Germans continued this attack after dark and by dawn on 21 October Pulteney realised that his force was directly opposed by two corps, the XIX as well as the XIII, both from Sixth Army. He managed to hold on, but his position was precarious, for his corps held a front of twelve miles and he did not have the forces to man it properly.

Allenby's corps was driven back by superior numbers. Cavalry divisions are much smaller than their infantry equivalents, and his two divisions only mustered some 9,000 rifles. Against them came no fewer than six German cavalry divisions, plus four supporting Jäger battalions, a total of some 24,000 men. The Cavalry Corps duly fell back before this force and dug in that night around Ploegsteert and Messines, while Allenby sent appeals to III Corps for assistance.

Both German armies were on the move to the west, thrusting into the

Allied front, and on 21 October battle was gradually joined all along the line north from Armentières. III Corps and the Cavalry Corps held their positions in the face of heavy German artillery bombardments followed by infantry assaults which they drove off with loss, flaying the advancing German infantry with rifle and machine-gun fire. Villages were lost and recaptured on the 6th Division front, but the cavalry managed to hold Messines, though the château at Hollebeke was taken by the Germans. IV Corps also held its position astride the Menin Road and attempted to dig in as the Germans pounded their lines with artillery and again sent in infantry in force. Rawlinson's men managed to hang on while I Corps came up on their left flank, with Haig still intent on obeying the instructions for his corps contained in French's Operation Order No. 39: 'to march in the direction of Thourout using the road Ypres-Passchendaele and roads to the north. This Corps will attack the enemy wherever met.' That meeting occurred a mile or so east of Ypres.

On 21 October, I Corps advanced across the Zonnebeke–Langemarck road and met heavy artillery fire and massed infantry attacks from the five German divisions opposing their advance. The 2nd Division ran into a large body of German troops from the 52nd Reserve Division, and the field gunners of I Corps literally had a 'field day', sending a storm of shrapnel into the advancing waves of German infantry. Ammunition was clearly in adequate supply for once, for one Royal Artillery battery fired 1,400 shells on that day alone. Those Germans who survived the shelling were then met with rifle fire, and the young soldiers went down in swaths before the rapid and accurate shooting of the British infantry. Eventually, though, numbers will tell, and that evening the 2nd Division was brought to a halt and forced to entrench around Zonnebeke. The 1st Division had also met stiff resistance from the outset but had managed to advance about 1,000 yards before it too came to a halt, on a line between Poelcapelle and Koekuit. The German Fourth Army had suffered severe losses and its attack had been halted, but the position of Haig's Corps was not secure and was further threatened when the French cavalry of General de Mitry, on its left flank, was seen to withdraw towards the Yser.

Here was another example of the problems caused by a divided command. If the French – or the British – generals wanted to withdraw or were ordered to do so by their superiors, the effect on the Allied formations on their flanks was treated as being of secondary importance. Thus a successful withdrawal without causing problems for flanking units all depended on the good sense and good will of the local commanders; on this occasion, fortunately for General Haig, the commander of the French 7th Cavalry Division, on the left of I Corps, saw the problem his withdrawal would cause and decided to stay where he was. This division held its line until again ordered to withdraw at dusk and that gave Haig time assess the situation and issue fresh orders. At 1500 hours, like the corps commanders to the south, he ordered both his divisions to stop attacking and dig in. His corps had already lost 932 men killed and wounded, about one for every yard of his advance, and the Germans were still coming on.

By evening, seven and a half British infantry divisions and five French and British cavalry divisions, fighting as infantry, were holding a front of some thirty-five miles, against eleven German infantry divisions and eight German cavalry divisions backed with a quantity of heavy artillery and well supplied with machine-guns. It was clear to everyone – at least outside GHQ, where Field Marshal French was convinced, according to a telegram he sent to Kitchener at 1212 hours on the 22nd, that the enemy 'is vigorously playing his last card and I am convinced that he will fail' – that these German forces were intent on a major offensive. That day's fighting had at least persuaded French that his troops should halt until the German reaction had been 'contained'. An order was issued placing the BEF on the defensive, so the troops – those who were not already doing so – now had to dig trenches and prepare to hold on against whatever force the Germans could bring against them. On the evening of 21 October the BEF had just fifty-three heavy guns along that thirty-five-mile front, which meant that the British defence depended largely on field artillery and the rifles of the infantry.

The attacks against the British line were renewed on the 22nd, and were concentrated along the front from Messines to Bixschoote, though the German Sixth Army kept battering away north of La Bassée and the Fourth Army pounded the Belgians and French along the Yser Canal. The fighting in this First Battle of Ypres hardly stopped for the next month, with attack and counter-attack taking place all along the line, which swayed to and fro under the pressure. On 22 October the German infantry were again shot down in quantity as they pressed home their attacks at Langemarck, their dead piling up before the British trenches, while German shells rained down continuously on the British outposts, taking a pitiless toll of the ragged infantrymen in their shallow trenches. These attacks on the 22nd caused a great many casualties on both sides. They did not seriously dent the British line, but they did force the Belgians on the Yser to withdraw to the west of the canal after an attack east of that waterway by French territorial troops had been driven back. More French divisions were now coming into the Ypres Salient – the French 17th Division took over the front of Haig's 2nd Division on 22 October – and a heavy German attack on Langemarck on that day was driven back with great loss. The advancing Germans made a wonderful target and some British infantrymen claim to have got off about 500 rounds that day, firing their rifles until they were too hot to handle. The British Official History (Volume II, p. 178) records what happened to the German infantry: 'Struck by gun and machine-gun fire as soon as they came well into sight, the German masses staggered . . . their dead and wounded were literally piled up in heaps . . . but, led by their officers, some still struggled on, only to meet their fate at the hands of the reserve companies.'

For hour after hour, these young German soldiers pressed home their attacks against the British infantry. The attacks were hopeless, but they continued nevertheless, until the ground before the British line was carpeted with field-grey uniforms, the silent dead, the wounded crying out for aid or, most pitifully, for their mothers, their cries unheard under the thunder of the guns and the relentless crackle of rifle fire. These engagements around Langemarck on 22 October, and the others that were to follow during First Ypres, have entered German history as the '*Kindermorde von Ypern*', the 'Slaughter of the Innocents at Ypres'. Today, the vast German cemetery at Langemarck, where most of these young people lie, has become a place of pilgrimage for their countrymen.

On the 23rd the four British corps again managed to hold their own against renewed attacks, and Sir John French even sent a cable to London stating that the situation was 'in hand and that the French and Belgians might be able to drive the Germans out of Ostend within the week'. The Field Marshal remained optimistic that the battle was going his way, although reports were coming in of fresh German concentrations at Courtrai. On that day he also issued an Order of the Day to his troops, 'congratulating them on their bravery and endurance and reminding the troops that the enemy must before long withdraw troops to the east and relieve the tension on our front'. French records that this was 'my great hope', that the Russian invasion of East Prussia would force the German Army to withdraw troops from the Western Front.

Such relief was urgently required, for the BEF had suffered severe losses in the recent fighting. The 7th Division of IV Corps had already lost 45 per cent of its officers and 37 per cent of its men. A number of battalions had been gravely reduced, with the 2nd Scots Guards, the 1st Royal Welsh Fusiliers and the 1st South Staffordshire Regiment losing over 500 men apiece – and these battalions had not been up to full strength when the battle began. The generals were having to fight with battalions mustering a couple of companies, brigades at half strength, and a declining supply of artillery ammunition. On the other hand, the German infantry, especially those volunteers of the Fourth Army, had been shot down in droves, the Sixth Army units also losing men in quantity. The British were now fighting a largely defensive battle and this gave them a small but useful advantage in what was becoming a battle of attrition.

Further south, the Indian Corps, which had taken over from the battered II Corps on October 28, was in action around Neuve Chapelle, which had been captured by the Germans on 27 October. A counter-attack on the 28th failed to drive the Germans out, however, and the Battle of La Bassée ended – officially – on 2 November. It had lasted for over three weeks, since 10 October, and had cost II Corps nearly 14,000 casualties. Although they had held the German attacks on their line after 18 October, they had not gained a yard in return. Further north, Pulteney's III Corps was outnumbered two to one and under unceasing attack, especially along its right wing. Here as elsewhere, the British line held – just – and the Battle of Armentières ended, again officially, on 2 November. The Cavalry Corps also managed to hang on and inflict heavy casualties on the Germans attacking Messines, so Field Marshal French had some reason to feel hopeful.

The German offensive had been held, if not actually repulsed, and French telegraphed London on the 24th that if all went well the battle was practically won. On the following day he sent word that the situation was 'growing more favourable by the hour', concluding on 27 October that it was 'only necessary to press the enemy hard in order to achieve complete success and victory'. He also ordered the offensive to continue . . . but victory continued to elude him, and there was now another problem, a shortage of artillery ammunition. On the day he ordered the renewed attack French also warned Kitchener that unless fresh supplies of shells were soon available 'the troops will be compelled to fight without the support of artillery.'

On the night of 24–25 October the BEF held the southern half of the salient around Ypres with the French 17th, 18th and 87th Divisions holding the northern half, and the Belgian Army continuing the French line to the North Sea. A new Allied attack, confirmed to the BEF in French's Operation Order No. 40 of 24 October, required I and IV Corps and the Cavalry Corps to advance east in support of the French, while II and III Corps and the Indian Corps contained the enemy to their front from Messines to Neuve Chapelle. The order also contained a significant flaw. Concerned as always about his flanks, French directed that the three corps ordered to advance should 'dress by the left' and stay in line with the units on their flanks. Thus Haig's advance was constrained by the progress made by the French IX Corps on his left, while IV Corps on his right had to wait for Haig's battalions to get forward, and so on right down the line to the Lys.

This continued, and even compounded, the failures of the advance to the Aisne. There, to keep the various corps in line, the advance was made at the speed of the slowest unit and the enemy was able to break contact and get away to dig in. Here the assumption was that only one flank, the left, would set the pace, and that whatever happened elsewhere along the line, everyone must conform to the pace of that flank. French did not grasp that flank protection, though desirable, worked both ways. If any of the advancing British and French corps could effect an advance or force a breach in the German line, that breach could be used to weaken or outflank the German forces on either side. Such a breach, if exploited, could be beneficial to the advancing troops as a whole, wherever it occurred. By insisting on a linear advance, however, Field Marshal French denied his troops the opportunity to take advantage of any local successes they might gain in their attack.

The Allies were therefore compromised before the attack began. French's optimism was also premature, for the Germans were about to renew their offensive. While the battles south of the Lys were petering out, the German

Sixth Army was preparing to mount another major effort further north, pushing down the Menin Road to Gheluvelt. The fighting was particularly heavy but French remained full of hope, believing, as he said in a cable to Kitchener on 27 October, that the enemy had suffered such losses they were now 'quite incapable of making any strong or sustained attack'. Three days later the enemy put in a strong and sustained attack at Gheluvelt, a thrust that was to threaten the entire British line in front of Ypres.

Like the British, the Germans had adopted the tactic of holding the line with part of their forces and attacking with the other part. The Fourth and Sixth Armies took it in turns to mount attacks, using most of the artillery from both forces to support whichever army was attacking. This did not mean that the front of the holding force became quiet; far from it. It was necessary to keep up the pressure everywhere, if only to prevent the enemy from transferring forces from one part of the line to another, but the effect was that of a counter-puncher, blocking a blow with one fist while striking with the other. Unfortunately for the commanders on both sides, these assaults caused great loss to the attackers, yet failed to penetrate the enemy line in any decisive way. The Fourth and Sixth Armies did not achieve a breakthrough, and neither did their Anglo-French opponents. The lines held, with small advances to and fro, while the fighting continued and the losses mounted. A breakthrough would require more men, more guns, and fresh units not yet shattered by weeks of battle.

Falkenhayn therefore decided to form a third army of three corps, totalling six divisions, under General von Fabeck, who was currently commanding XIII Corps. Fabeck was also provided with a cavalry corps and a further six unbrigaded battalions of infantry, plus a quantity of artillery, over 250 heavy guns in all. This force, 'Army Group Fabeck', was deployed between and behind the flanks of the Sixth Army and tasked with pushing a way through to the vital Messines-Wytschaete ridge and on to the Gheluvelt plateau. The attack was set for 30 October and would consist of the right and centre of Sixth Army, the whole of Fourth Army, and Army Group Fabeck. On the 29th, while Fabeck's men were mustering behind Sixth Army, two German army corps and a Bavarian reserve division would put in an assault against Gheluvelt as a prelude to the main attack.

Field Marshal French had no more units available. Rawlinson's IV Corps had now been broken up and Rawlinson had returned to England to take command of the 8th Division, a Regular Army unit. When it was ready he would bring the division to France and join it with the 7th Division to form a new IV Corps. In the meantime, the 7th Division went to I Corps and the 3rd Cavalry Division to the Cavalry Corps. Haig placed the latter division astride the Menin Road, and it was there on 27 October when GHQ telephoned Haig with the news that they had intercepted a German wireless message ordering XXVII Reserve Corps of Fourth Army to attack towards Gheluvelt on the 29th.

Haig decided to forestall this attack – which became the three-day 'Battle of Gheluvelt', – by strengthening his line, registering his artillery on the likely line of attack, the area around Polygon Wood, and digging in astride the Menin Road, though he still intended to continue pressing east with the 2nd Division if possible. This action was still in hand on the misty morning of 29 October, when, at 0530 hours, the German attack came in from the north-east. The Germans promptly overran a position manned by the 1st Black Watch and the 1st Coldstream Guards. The day did not go at all well for the British, for even the Guards battalions were pushed back. By the evening of the 29th, I Corps had lost 500 yards of trench, the vital Gheluvelt crossroads, and the best part of three Regular battalions, cut to pieces by shellfire or in hand-to-hand fighting. The advance of French troops north of Ypres had also been held by German units which 'were numerically strong and well entrenched and whose heavy artillery becomes day by day unceasingly stronger'.

None of this perturbed Field Marshal French. He issued orders for the advance to be continued on the 30th, and told Kitchener that 'if the present success can be followed up it will lead to a decisive result,' adding that 'slow but decided success is being made everywhere.' One can only wonder where the Field Marshal was getting his information. More troops were going to be needed to ensure this 'success', and he therefore intended to take II Corps out of the line and send it north, but the only fresh troops available on the night of 29 October were from a Territorial battalion, the London Scottish (14th Battalion, London Regiment), which had arrived at Ypres that night and were in reserve when the second phase of the German thrust developed. This was the attack by Army Group Fabeck, fresh infantry divisions supported by 260 heavy and super-heavy guns, an attack which came pushing up towards the Menin Road from the south-east on the 30th.

General Haig's estimates of the situation on his front were considerably more cautious than those of his C-in-C. He noted the order to resume the advance on the 30th, but ordered his three divisions to entrench on favourable ground, reorganise and carry out an active reconnaissance at daylight, adding that 'orders as to the resumption of the offensive will be issued in the morning, when the situation is clearer than it is at present.'

Fabeck's force was set to overwhelm the 7th Division, the three cavalry divisions of the Cavalry Corps, equivalent to perhaps two infantry brigades in firepower, and two Indian infantry battalions, which had the 1st Division in close support. The Germans should have overrun the British with comparative ease, for there was no continuous trench line, little wire, and no heavy artillery to support the tired infantry. It was indeed a near-run thing, with Haig throwing everything he had into the line to hold the German advance, 'putting up' the gaps in his seven-and-a-half-mile front with a battalion here and a company there, just to keep the enemy out.

On this section of the front the Germans enjoyed a manpower superiority of three to one, but their attack did not at first enjoy much success and, as usual, the British infantry shot down the advancing enemy in quantity, swiftly repulsing the attack on their left which came in against the 1st and 2nd Divisions at 0630 hours. As the day wore on, though, the pressure increased, and the heavy and constant artillery fire, a major feature of German attacks from now on, began to intensify. Heavy artillery fire helped the German infantry into Zandvoorde, which was held by squadrons of the 1st and 2nd Life Guards from 7 Cavalry Brigade and infantry of the 7th Division. A counter-attack failed, and by 1500 hours Haig feared that the enemy were going to break through south of Ypres, where the Cavalry Corps were in difficulties. He therefore asked the French on his left flank for assistance, pointing out that if the Germans succeeded in breaking through in the southern sector they could cut the Allied line in two. General Pierre Dubois, commanding French IX Corps, reacted at once and sent his corps reserve of two battalions up to Zillebeke.

Fortunately, the German attacks south of Ypres died out at dusk, but by then they had taken Hollebeke and Zandvoorde and forced the British centre back for more than a mile between Messines and Gheluvelt – and the loss of Hollebeke put them within three miles of Ypres. They had also inflicted heavy casualties on the 7th Division, one of whose battalions, the 1st Royal Welsh Fusiliers, had been overwhelmed, only eighty men returning to the British line. That night, Field Marshal French visited I Corps HQ, which Haig had established a couple of units from the front line in the White Château at Hellfire Corner, east of Ypres, and requests were sent to Foch asking for more French assistance as soon as possible. Foch promised to send five infantry battalions and some artillery to I Corps on the following day. Haig was now busy establishing a new line, running from the Ypres-Comines Canal at Hollebeke, north to a point east of the village of Gheluvelt, the last defensive position in this sector in front of Ypres.

At 2200 hours on 30 October heavy German artillery fire began to fall on Messines, and Haig summoned all the available BEF reserves to beat off the major attack that was clearly coming in at dawn against his right flank. The only significant force available was the London Scottish, 750 strong, which was sent up to the Cavalry Corps and attached by General Allenby to the 2nd Cavalry Division, before being sent to bolster the defenders at Messines. On that day, too, so great was the pressure on the extreme left of the Allied line, the Belgians opened the sluices in their dykes and let the sea flood their country north of Dixmude.

The BEF was now in serious trouble. The troops had been fighting continuously for ten days and few reserves were available, other than from the French. The French units on the BEF's left flank were co-operating wonderfully well, but their reserves had also been committed and little more than defensive fighting could be expected on their front. Meanwhile, a major attack was clearly about to come in against the Cavalry Corps positions south of I Corps.

The attack on Messines, a village which, though in British hands, lay just *outside* the main British line, came at 0430 hours on 31 October, while it was still dark, but at 0800 German heavy guns joined the bombardment and soon reduced most of the remaining houses to rubble. Men of twelve British cavalry squadrons from the 1st Cavalry Division held Messines and, with the support of some infantry, they continued to hold it for most of the day against twelve German infantry battalions – odds of at least six to one. The cavalry troopers were slowly forced out of the village and off the ridge, but at noon help finally arrived in the shape of four British infantry battalions. These were of varied strength, with the 2nd King's Own Yorkshire Light Infantry (KOYLI) and the 2nd King's Own Scottish Borderers (KOSB) down to around 300 men each; only the London Scottish – the first Territorial battalion to go into action in France – was up to full strength. With this assistance the cavalry were able to hold most of Messines village and even mount local counter-attacks. Heavy German assaults were also going in against the 2nd Cavalry Division at Wytschaete, but these, made by infantry with artillery support, petered out by 1830 hours, and a further attack at 2230 that night lasted only half an hour before the enemy were driven off. The scale of the fighting can be gauged from the fact that the London Scottish, which arrived at Messines 750 strong, had lost 321 men killed, wounded and missing, by the end of the day. French records that 'for close on 48 hours these troops held the Wytschaete–Messines ridge against the utmost efforts of two and a half German Army Corps to dislodge them. Here was the centre of our line of battle and had it given way, disaster would have resulted to the entire left wing of the Allied line.'

The 1st Division had meanwhile been engaged at Gheluvelt, where the Germans sent in thirteen battalions against five much-reduced British battalions. These were odds of perhaps ten to one, for six of the German infantry battalions were quite fresh and the five well-worn British battalions could only average around 200 men apiece. The initial attack was made against the 1st Division line at 0615 hours, the young German soldiers singing as they advanced, some men walking arm-in-arm towards the British trenches, where a line of weary, muddy soldiers, with clean rifles and neat piles of ammunition clips to hand, lay waiting to receive them.

When the Germans were well within range, the British infantry opened a rapid fire. Once again the bolts flew and once again a hail of rifle fire drove the Germans back. Unable to believe that bolt-action rifles alone could produce such a volume of fire, the Germans later reported that the BEF were equipped with quantities of machine-guns. These attacks were repulsed, but the German artillery then began to pound the British line and this process, alternating infantry attacks with artillery bombardments, went on all morning. In spite of the losses to their infantry, the Germans pressed home their attack, and by just before noon Gheluvelt was in their hands.

This was a major disaster for the Allies. Gheluvelt was the high point on the plateau, and from there the Menin road ran like an arrow down to Ypres, less than five miles away. The front of the 1st Division had been broken and many of the men were now pulling back, in good order, towards

Ypres. British losses had been severe in the struggle for Ypres; the 2nd King's Royal Rifle Corps (KRRC) was reduced to just 150 men and other battalions had suffered in proportion, but the 1st and 2nd Division commanders, Major-Generals S.H. Lomax and Charles Monro, respectively, had an agreement for mutual support and at 1015 hours Monro had placed one of his reserve battalions, the 2nd Battalion, Worcestershire Regiment, at the disposal of Lomax. These officers were conferring at Hooge Château but at 1300 Brigadier-General Charles FitzClarence, VC, Commanding 1 (Guards) Brigade of the 1st Division, ordered Major Hankey acting CO of the Worcesters, to take his battalion and 'counter-attack with the utmost vigour against the enemy in Gheluvelt and re-establish our line there'.

The loss of Gheluvelt was not the only setback. At 1315 hours disaster befell the staffs of the 1st and 2nd Divisions in their joint HQ at Hooge, when four shells struck the château, mortally wounding General Lomax, GOC of the 1st Division, stunning and concussing General Monro of the 2nd Division, and killing several members of the divisional staffs. Other staff officers were severely wounded, in a catastrophe which yet again disproves the popular notion that the Great War generals and their staffs kept well out of danger.

Haig's corps was now in serious trouble. Gheluvelt had been lost, the Germans were within five miles of Ypres and were pushing hard all along his line – and now his principal subordinate Commanders were wounded or out of action. This last news reached Haig at the White Château, just down the road from Hooge, at about 1400 hours. Fortunately, he was a phlegmatic man, not easily ruffled, and in this desperate situation he appears at his best. He kept his head; tugging on his moustache (the only sign he gave of any inner agitation), he scratched up more men to shore up the line, sending Sappers, cooks, clerks, anyone who could hold a rifle, up to the front. Moreover, he elected to go up to Gheluvelt and see the situation for himself, summoning his mounted escort and riding up the road towards Hooge, stopping to encourage the troops he met along the way.

He then returned to the White Château, received confirmation that the 1st Division front had broken, and ordered the urgent preparation of the defence line in front of Ypres, to which his troops could retire if the 1st Division line was driven back still further. This seemed all too possible in the early afternoon, when Field Marshal French arrived at I Corps HQ to find Haig and his staff officers occupying the wrecked conference room – for shells were now falling around the château – and attempting to cope with the situation in the HQs of the 1st and 2nd Divisions.

The Field Marshal had no reserves to offer, and left to see what troops could be obtained from Foch, while Haig prepared to take over direct command of the 1st Division. It was a dark moment but then, just as French was leaving, up the drive galloped Brigadier-General Rice, the Commander, Royal Engineers (CRE) of I Corps, fresh from the front line and bearing good news. The 2nd Worcesters – a reduced battalion of just 7 officers and

350 men – had charged across open fields and retaken Gheluvelt at the point of the bayonet. The battalion had lost 3 officers and over 180 men in the process, but they were in the village and holding their positions and the Germans were falling back in some disorder.

The attack of the 2nd Worcesters deserves a mention in any account of First Ypres, but it was one gallant deed among many. The German attack was being pressed home with great strength all along the line and being beaten off by men who, though having little left to give, still found the means to fight back. In such a battle generals can do little but muster men, organise and reorganise the lines as they ebb and flow under enemy pressure, and keep urging their troops to hang on.

After leaving Hooge, French had a meeting with Foch and obtained the promise of help in the shape of a counter-attack by French troops at dawn on the following day. The Field Marshal's state of mind may be judged by the fact that he allegedly told Foch that unless such support was sent, 'There is nothing left for me to do but go back up and die with I Corps.' French and Foch told Haig of the plan for a French counter-attack next day, while urging him, in separate messages, to hold on at all costs. Such exhortations were hardly necessary, and besides, holding on was all that Haig could do. In the event, it was enough to turn the tide. That night Haig decided that, for various reasons, mainly a shortage of men, Gheluvelt should be abandoned and the British line moved back to the reverse slope of a low ridge slightly closer to Ypres.

The fighting in other parts of the line had been equally severe. The right wing of III Corps had been heavily engaged and was ordered to pull back to a line between Klein Zillebeke and Frezenberg. With German infantry swarming all over his front, General Bulfin, who was commanding a composite unit – 'Bulfin Force' – on the Zillebeke-Frezenberg front, ordered his men to give the Germans one 'mad minute' of rifle fire, loosing off as many rounds as they could manage, and then charge them with the bayonet. The effect of this storm of fire and the charge of the cheering British infantry was dramatic; the Germans fled to the rear and the British found themselves standing on an empty battlefield, surrounded by heaps of enemy dead. From there they advanced for half a mile, driving all before them, and then dug in. Here again, though, losses were very high, with 21 Brigade, nominally 4,000 strong, having just 750 effectives left at the end of the day of which half were in one battalion, the 2nd Bedfordshire Regiment. How much more of this attrition the BEF could stand was the question in everyone's mind when night fell.

Haig spent the night of 31 October–1 November adjusting his line and pulling his men back to better positions. This included abandoning the village of Gheluvelt, captured at such cost on the previous day, but no longer tenable with the scanty forces available. The Worcesters were withdrawn a mile nearer Ypres and took up positions around the village of Veldhoek. During that night German artillery pounded the Allied line, concentrating much of its attention on Fabeck's chosen objective, the ridge line between Wytschaete and Messines, and deploying one battery of 8-inch howitzers for the destruction of Wytschaete alone. This bombardment was followed, at 0100 hours on 1 November, with an assault on the village by nine battalions of the 6th Bavarian Reserve Division – odds of twelve to one against the British. This attack was accompanied by a general assault all along the Messines Ridge, a sector held by cavalry of the Dragoon Guards and part of the London Scottish, and these units were slowly driven back.

The following day, 2 November, was one of mixed fortunes. The French reinforcements promised by Foch arrived, but General Fabeck had captured Messines and thus had a foothold on the Messines Ridge. Fabeck continued to press towards Ypres, battering the defenders around St Éloi. This day marked the crux of the First Battle of Ypres, for both sides were exhausted. The battle had become a contest of wills, the Germans doggedly pushing on towards Ypres, the Allies determined to keep them out. There was little scope now for generalship – provided the generals kept their heads – for it all depended on the men in the line, on their willingness to 'stick it' and go on fighting. The Germans were not quite fought out, but that evening, as Falkenhayn records, OHL, the German High Command, debated the wisdom of diverting their efforts to some other part of the Allied line. In the end the decision was made to try one more major attack at Ypres, and this went in on 11 November, after another week of front-line fighting.

The situation of the BEF on 2 November can be briefly summarised. The French counter-attacks north of Ypres had yielded little but casualties, and it was only with difficulty that they could hang on to Bixschoote. Meanwhile Field Marshal French was rightly concerned about his casualties and especially about his officer casualties, for some battalions had only three or four officers left. He was also troubled by the exhaustion of his men and the acute shortage of artillery ammunition.

Still the fighting continued. Wytschaete, now held by the French, fell to the Germans on 2 November. On that day the British 7th Division, which should have had 12,672 men in its three fighting brigades, could muster exactly 2,434, and the 1st Division had just 3,583. This shortage of men was not to be easily remedied. At a meeting in Dunkirk on 1 November, attended by Field Marshal Kitchener, Generals Joffre and Foch, the President of France and a representative of Field Marshal French, Kitchener told the French leaders, who were pressing for immediate reinforcements from Britain, that 'to send untrained men into the fighting line was little short of murder, and that no very important supply of British effectives could be looked for until the late Spring of 1915 and that the British Army would only reach full strength, its high-water mark, during the Summer of 1917,' a statement which, with hindsight, appears to have been totally correct. When French queried this statement with the War Office he was told that there were practically no Regular troops left in the United Kingdom, and that the total number of reinforcements currently available to him was just 150 officers and 9,500 other ranks -- roughly two brigades.

During 3, 4 and 5 November, little changed in the battle for Ypres. The enemy's artillery fire increased in weight and frequency, but his infantry attacks failed time and again before the fire of the British and French soldiers, cavalry and infantry, who were grimly hanging on. Although the Battles of Gheluvelt and Messines ended officially on 31 October and 2 November respectively, this happy fact was not apparent to the troops on the ground. French counter-attacks soon petered out and in anticipation of further German onslaughts, Haig ordered his men to construct all-round defensive positions covering every flank, and to lay in supplies of ammunition. Large French reinforcements, which would allow the British units to pull back for a much-needed rest, were constantly promised but did not arrive, and here and there the German line crept forward. On 5 November the Spanbroekmolen position near Messines was lost by the French.

The French now occupied the Ypres Salient from Bixschoote to the Ypres–Roulers railway line, where Haig's battered I Corps and the 1st Cavalry Division held the front as far as Zillebeke. Then the French XVI Corps took over and held the line south to the River Douve, where the BEF's Cavalry Corps and III Corps linked up with II Corps, though many of the latter's battalions were now at Ypres where, on 5 November, they relieved the 7th Division in the line. On 6 November these II Corps battalions were formed into a division, 'Wing's Division', under the command of Major-General F. D. V. Wing. The general impression held at GHQ was that the fighting, if not over, was at least petering out, and at a corps commanders' conference on the 5th, General Haig was surprised – and by no means pleased – to note that the chief topic discussed was winter leave. On 9 November, French informed Kitchener that Joffre believed the Germans were now in the process of withdrawing troops from the west and sending fifteen army corps to Poland, where Hindenburg was in full retreat before the Russian Army. Meanwhile, the Germans were mustering for their final attack at Ypres, which came in just forty-eight hours later.

General von Falkenhayn had elected to persevere with the Ypres offensive, and Crown Prince Rupprecht had concluded that the attack could not succeed unless Fabeck had more men and more guns. Artillery and vast quantities of ammunition were therefore transferred to Army Group Fabeck, while a comb-out of units from the other armies produced six more divisions and the formidable Prussian Guards Corps for this final attack. While these forces were being mustered, the Fourth and Sixth Armies continued to strike the French and BEF lines at every opportunity.

For this fresh attack the German High Command created another new formation, II Corps, consisting of the 4th Division and a composite Guards Division, under General Linsingen, supporting it with no fewer than 230 guns. This corps would form the centre of the attack on the BEF, with XV Corps on the left and XVII Reserve Corps on the right, a total force of twelve and a half divisions attacking on a front of nine miles between Messines and Polygon Wood. The main weight of their attack fell on Wing's division, though the battle began with a *coup de main* assault which gained the Germans a bridgehead across the Yser at Dixmude. This success convinced the French that the weight of the German attack would come against their line north of Ypres.

The battle of First Ypres ended *officially* on 22 November, but the bulk of the final fighting took place between the 10th and the 12th, culminating in the defeat of the Prussian Guard at Nonne Bosschen, east of Ypres. German artillery opened the battle at 0630 hours on the 10th with heavy concentrations of fire all along the front, but a particular weight fell on Wing's division, which could muster only about 4,000 men. This bombardment went on for three hours, and other parts of the British line on the 1st and 2nd Division fronts were also pounded, but though infantry attacks were threatened, none were actually delivered.

The fighting on 11 November was of a different order, one of the hardest days of battle in the entire war, for besides the main attack on the front from Messines to Polygon Wood, diversionary attacks were made at the La Bassée Canal and north of Ypres. As on the previous day, the German artillery started pounding the British line at 0630 hours. This bombardment grew in intensity, the heaviest shelling falling on MacCracken's and Shaw's brigades in Wing's division and on Brigadier-General FitzClarence's 1 (Guards) Brigade in the 1st Division.

At 0900 hours the Germans came in to the attack, twenty-five battalions of fighting infantry totalling 17,500 men, pressing home their attacks against some 7,500 British infantry at Nonne Bosschen, taking terrible casualties from British field artillery and, as always, from the rapid rifle fire of the British Regulars. During the morning the German battalions attacked again and again but were driven back with loss. They tried again at 1600 hours and were again cut down, until the shell-pocked fields before the British line were carpeted with field-grey dead.

North of the Menin Road, the Prussian Guard, the elite troops of the German Army, were attempting to break the centre of the British line. The German 4 Guards Brigade was driven off with loss by the 1st Lincolnshire and 2nd Duke of Wellington's Regiments, but the German 2nd Guards Grenadier Regiment broke through the line further east and two counterattacks by the 2nd Royal Sussex Regiment and the 1st Royal Scots Fusiliers could not drive them out.

The outcome hung on the third encounter, in which – curiously – the German 1 Guard Brigade, consisting of two full regiments, met the British 1 (Guards) Brigade by Polygon Wood – though this latter formation only contained one Guards battalion, the 1st Scots Guards, the other two battalions in this small brigade being the 1st Black Watch and the 1st Cameron Highlanders, totalling about 800 men. The Germans advanced at the trot, crossed the first line of trenches and attacked the British positions with the bayonet, taking severe losses from close-range rifle fire. Their attack was broken up but not turned back and the Camerons and Black Watch were swiftly overwhelmed, though the Scots Guards hung on to their strongpoint in a farm and defied eviction. By midday companies of the Prussian Guard had fought their way into Nonne Bosschen, but in front of Polygon Wood the 1st King's (Liverpool Regiment) had beaten off all attacks and raised a wall of German dead in front of their position. In other parts of the line the Prussians were kept out by the fire of cooks, gunners and clerks, who snatched up rifles and ran to take part in the fighting. The battle hung in the balance until Haig sent in his only reserve, 500 men of the 2nd Oxfordshire and Buckinghamshire Light Infantry, who attacked the Prussian Guard with rifle fire and the bayonet. By dusk the Nonne Bosschen position had been retaken and the Germans were in full retreat.

First Ypres was effectively over when the Prussian Guard fell back from Nonne Bosschen, but the outcome had been a near-run thing. This fact is underlined by the comment of a wounded German officer captured at Nonne Bosschen, who asked a British artillery officer, 'Where are your reserves?' The latter pointed wordlessly to the guns. The German then asked, 'And what is there behind?' When he was told 'Divisional Headquarters', he shook his head in amazement and said, 'God Almighty!'

That night, Brigadier-General FitzClarence was killed leading a column of troops up to the line. Over the next few days more men died as the First Battle of Ypres slowly petered out. British losses for the period 14 October to 30 November total 58,155 men, killed, wounded and missing, the killed and missing totalling 25,833, with 614 officers, 6,794 British and 522 Indian other ranks being definitely recorded as killed. The figure for the missing includes men taken prisoner, but the bulk of the missing are men whose bodies were never found and whose names are so recorded on monuments all over the Western Front.

German losses are given as 134, 315, killed, wounded and missing for the period from 15 October to 24 November. This figure is suspect, for the German method of calculating wounded differs from that used by the British. Only those wounded actually kept in the dressing stations or sent back to base are included in the German figures while the British figures include all those treated, even if they immediately went back to duty. The German killed in this period total 19,230 men, and given the losses sustained in their massed infantry attacks against British rifle fire, this may be an accurate figure. The other armies involved, the Belgian and the French, suffered in proportion.

The result of First Ypres was a stalemate which enabled both sides to claim the victory. Neither side achieved its first ambition, a breakthrough, but since the Anglo-French and Belgian forces did succeed in hanging on to Ypres, they can, perhaps, be awarded a victory on points, though operations in and around the Salient were to prove a great drain on British resources in the years ahead.

As for the generals, few accusations of incompetence in this encounter can be sustained against the British generals, while the French, if tardy in committing it, were constant in support. First Ypres was not an exclusively 'British' battle, though this book, and many others, concentrate on the British actions. On 31 October the British held twelve miles of the front and the French fifteen; by 5 November the French share had risen to eighteen miles and the British share shrunk to nine. Since the French had more men this is hardly surprising, but it should not be overlooked. First Ypres was not a battle that left much room for fine plans or the display of tactical skills, but there are plenty of instances where the generals acted with foresight and displayed both competence and courage. It was a question of hanging on, doing your best, putting in what men there were to 'putty up' the front, and trusting to the skill and courage of the men in the line. If those men lacked reinforcements and artillery support – and they certainly did – the fault lies with the politicians and the electorate who had failed to build up an army and a munitions industry in peacetime that could cope with the shock of modern war.

The actions of the German generals are less easy to excuse. They had quantities of artillery and an abundance of shells and yet, time and again, at Langemarck at the start of the battle and at Nonne Bosschen and Polygon Wood at the end of it, they sent their men in mass attacks against entrenched infantry, only to have them mown down like summer corn by that fast and accurate rifle fire. Their attacks had great weight and cohesion but it is hard to see where much use was made either of ground or of sensible tactics; the Germans, too, had a lot to learn about this new form of war. Their current tactic consisted of battering the Allied line with shellfire and flooding it with manpower, and this was not sufficient to cause a breach, as well as being expensive in men. Since the Germans were fighting in a country where they had no right to be, they at least had the option of withdrawal, a choice not open to the Allied armies.

Now winter was coming on. The men in the line had more hanging-on to do, waiting in water-filled trenches for whatever fortune would bring them in the spring. On both sides of the line, those men who had rushed to war, expecting to be home 'by the time the leaves fall', or that the whole business would be 'over by Christmas', began to realise that they were in for a long, hard war.

CHAPTER 7

SECOND YPRES,
APRIL 1915

*'The cardinal principle of the defensive scheme of this
Division is a determination to hold our front-line trenches at
all costs.'*

Lieutenant-General Edwin Alderson, GOC 1st Canadian Division, 4 March 1915

The fighting on the Western Front in the months immediately following the outbreak of war was only part of a growing conflict. The war was spreading, like some untreatable cancer, eating away at the flesh and fabric of European society, moving out from the initial contestants to invade other territories. On 11 August two German warships, the *Goeben* and the *Breslau*, evaded the British Fleet and took shelter in the then neutral port of Constantinople, where their presence played a major part in persuading Turkey to join the war on the side of Germany and Austria-Hungary. Turkey had entered into an alliance with Germany two days before the war began, but it was not until 31 October 1915 that the Ottoman Empire officially joined the war.

Italy, undecided which side to join when war broke out, had elected to ignore her treaty with the Central Powers and declared herself neutral, waiting until May 1915 before declaring war on Austria, until August 1915 before declaring war on Turkey and until August 1916 before declaring war on Germany, her decisions swayed by Allied promises of territory from Austria once the war had been won. The Central Powers would acquire another ally in September 1915, when Bulgaria, the most powerful of the Balkan states, entered the war, with the promise of Serbian Macedonia when the war had been won. There was fighting in East and South-West Africa, German commerce raiders, operating against Allied merchant shipping, were being chased in the Pacific and the Indian Ocean, and German submarines were active in the North Atlantic and the Western Approaches. The Allied High Command had a lot to think about as winter came on in 1914.

Following the petering out of the offensives that comprised First Ypres on 22 November, a certain amount of adjustment to the Anglo-French line took place. By 1 December the BEF occupied a continuous line from Givenchy in the south, by the La Bassée Canal, north to St Éloi on the southern edge of the Ypres Salient, which was largely held by the French. From the south this BEF front of twenty-one miles was held by the Indian Corps, IV Corps, III Corps and II Corps respectively, with Haig's I Corps and the bulk of the Cavalry Corps in reserve. The entire force was urgently re-equipping and attempting to build up stocks of artillery ammunition. The BEF was ill-equipped for trench warfare or the winter weather, and the men suffered considerably in their shallow trenches as winter rains began to flood the fields.

On Christmas Day 1914, his command having increased considerably in recent weeks, Field Marshal Sir John French told his senior corps commanders to form two full armies on the following day, the First Army under General Sir Douglas Haig consisting of the I, IV and Indian Corps, and the Second Army, comprising II and III Corps and the 27th Division – and, later, V Corps – under General Sir Horace Smith-Dorrien. Allenby's Cavalry Corps and the Indian Cavalry Corps remained under French's direct command at GHQ.

Although not chronologically correct, for the battle of Neuve Chapelle on the First Army front took place in March 1915, this chapter will deal with the affairs of Smith-Dorrien's Second Army and especially with the Canadian Division, which arrived at the front early in that month, and with the Canadian Brigadier-General Arthur Currie, one of the outstanding soldiers of the Great War, a man who first came to prominence during the Second Battle of Ypres in April 1915. The battles fought in 1915 by General Sir Douglas Haig and the First Army at Neuve Chapelle, Aubers Ridge and Festubert, south of the Ypres Salient, will be covered in the next chapter.

The BEF entered the New Year with a considerable number of problems. Firstly, though the force now contained eleven infantry divisions and five cavalry divisions (by the end of January it would number some 350,000 men), the fighting since August, and especially the First Battle of Ypres, had effectively exhausted the available manpower of the Regular Army. By the end of 1914 the BEF's losses totalled just under 90,000 men; only an average of 1 officer and 30 men remained of the original 64 battalions, each 1,000 strong, which had landed in France in August. During 1915 the BEF would increasingly come to rely on the Territorial Force, which had two full divisions in France by March 1915, with a third, the 48th (South Midland) arriving in early April. In addition, a large number of Territorial battalions had been sent out piecemeal to shore up the thinning ranks of the Regular divisions. There were also contingents from the Empire, in particular from Canada which provided the first non-Regular Army division to join the BEF. The Indian Army had two divisions in the line by the end of October

1914, but the bitter winter weather and a shortage of suitable rations were to prove sore and additional burdens to troops used to warmer climes.

If manpower was one problem, it was also apparent that the BEF was seriously short of all the impedimenta necessary for the successful conduct of an entirely new kind of war, and a war much larger in scale than anything previously envisaged. Pre-war planning had assumed a war of manoeuvre; now they were facing siege warfare and lacked the means to prosecute it.

The BEF lacked sappers in sufficient numbers, and those it did have were short of entrenching equipment, barbed wire, timber for revetting trenches, and sandbags – these last were essential for building breastworks in the Ypres Salient, where men digging trenches struck water at two feet. Picks and shovels were in short supply everywhere, and the fighting divisions lacked grenades, mortars and, most particularly, heavy guns and an adequate supply of shells, especially the high-explosive shells needed to destroy trenches and strongpoints.

These deficiencies in guns and shells meant that the British generals had to rely on infantry armed only with rifles, far too few machine-guns, a small amount of artillery and a rapidly falling supply of shells to stave off German attacks which were always supported with a great quantity of artillery delivering tremendous and crushing bombardments. Most of the difficulties faced by the British commanders in 1915, and most of the casualties suffered by the troops, can be traced back to this lack of artillery. Nor can the blame for this be laid entirely on the generals. True, the senior British generals should have pressed for a higher scale of high-explosive ammunition, which was in fact available (except for the 18-pounder field guns), but the real reason for this shortage of guns and shells lies, as has been said, with the politicians and the British people, who would not provide the necessary funds to create the powerful, well-equipped army a Continental conflict would require.

In the years before 1914, British politicians, though they knew that a European war was probably coming, did little to prepare for it. Everyone supposed that, if and when war came, the British contribution would be small and the war would not last long. This being so, the country's munitions and armaments industry was also small, barely sufficient to supply the needs of the existing army. When war came, and was quickly recognised as a large and enduring struggle, there was no immediate way in which the Army's crying need for guns and shells could be swiftly met. Munitions factories cannot be built overnight, and those in existence could not cope with the demand. New plant had to be built, machine-tools designed, ordered and installed, staff trained and – a very British dilemma – trade unions persuaded to adopt a more flexible approach to manning levels and the use of non-union labour. Then specifications had to be prepared for the new weapons needed for this new kind of war – trench war – such as heavy howitzers, mortars and hand grenades.

The existing armaments factories did increase their production considerably but much more needed to be done, not least in abolishing the restrictive trade union practices which inhibited an immediate expansion in production. In March 1915, a survey revealed that only one-fifth of all the machinery in the armaments factories was used on night shifts and most of the remainder was only in use for eight hours out of twenty-four. Trade union rules prohibited semi-skilled or unskilled men doing work reserved for skilled men, and women from doing men's work. The unions also insisted on 'one man to one machine', placed a limit on the amount of work that a factory hand might produce, and enforced trade-demarcations rules about union men working with non-union labour . . . all this while other working men were fighting and dying on the Western Front for lack of artillery support. This state of affairs was eventually sorted out, but it took time.

Arms production cannot easily be farmed out to small component manufacturers, for some parts – like shell fuses – require skilled hands and special machinery. Quite apart from the overall shortage of shells, large stocks of artillery ammunition could not be used through a lack of fuses, and the constant cries for artillery support sent back from the front-line infantry meant that existing stocks of fused shells, already inadequate, were rapidly depleted and could not be rebuilt. In August 1915, a year after the outbreak of war, Britain had a stockpile of 25 *million* shells which could not be used because they had no fuses. The country needed a new and vastly expanded armaments industry, and though steps were swiftly taken to create one, this too all took *time*.

The Official History rightly devotes considerable space to the shell, gun and grenade situation, and a few statistics will reveal the extent of the problem that the front-line soldiers and the generals had to cope with. Various kinds of hand grenade were improvised by the troops from the first weeks of the war, many involving gun-cotton or dynamite pressed into jam tins. In November 1914 *the entire BEF* had a total ration of 70 hand grenades and 630 rifle grenades per week. The first 'Mills bomb' – known to a later generation of soldiers as the '36' grenade – was introduced in March 1915; a year later the armaments factories were turning out 800,000 a week. The first experimental trench mortars, high-angle-fire weapons capable of lobbing a projectile into an enemy trench, did not arrive at the front until December 1914; even then, only twelve were available and they proved inaccurate. The Stokes 3-inch mortar, a highly effective weapon, was not brought into service until November 1915.

As discussed earlier, the water-cooled, belt-fed, Vickers machine-gun, so effective against enemy infantry and cavalry, had been issued pre-War on a scale of just two per battalion, the same scale as in most of the other European armies. This was soon seen to be inadequate, but the production of the Vickers MMG was limited to 200 a week because the factories did not have the machine-tools or skilled men capable of producing more. Nor could all the weapons available be sent to the BEF. The Territorial and New Army battalions now being raised and trained in Britain also needed such weapons, so that demand always ran ahead of supply. Machine-gun belts were also in short supply, and Vickers ammunition was not yet supplied in belted form; filling the 250-round ammunition belts was a constant and most unpopular infantry task. Another useful weapon, the drum-fed, air-cooled, light and portable Lewis machine-gun, which would give a great boost to the firepower of infantry sections, was still in the development stage and would not reach the armies in any quantity until the end of 1915. One advantage of both the Vickers and the Lewis, however, was that, at .303-inch calibre, they fired the same round as the SMLE service rifle.

The greatest need was for artillery ammunition, but here too the picture was bleak. In November 1914, the 3rd Division of II Corps had just 363 rounds of field artillery ammunition for each gun, and the average across the BEF amounted to just one day's supply at the normal rate of fire. To conserve ammunition and build up stocks for attacks, the BEF field guns were at one point restricted to firing four shells *per day*. The consumption of ammunition on the Western Front exceeded any previous calculation, but it was soon all too apparent that without an abundance of heavy guns – and a superabundance of ammunition – the BEF would be hard pressed to defend its line, let alone carry out attacks.

There was also a shortage of trained men, especially NCOs and junior officers, for the fighting of 1914 had taken a particularly heavy toll of corporals, sergeants and young lieutenants. Officers were being sought at the universities and among the professional classes but they had to be trained in their duties before they would be of any use in the field, or fit to command the flood of volunteers now entering the Army at home . . . and above all there was a shortage of trained staff officers. All this would be put right in time, but not in 1915, which was to prove a hard year for the soldiers of the BEF in the front-line trenches.

At the end of December 1914 the British front line ran north from the junction of the First Army with the Tenth French Army at Cuinchy up to St Éloi in the Ypres Salient, where the Second Army met the French troops under General Putz, commanding the Détachement de l'Armée de Belgique, a five-division force largely composed of French colonial or territorial troops. Overall command of French troops in the northern sector of the line was held by General Foch, and the British were under continual pressure from the French GQG both to take over more of the line and to mount attacks against the enemy.

Field Marshal French did not have the troops to do both but, ever-mindful of his orders to co-operate closely with the French, he carried out various attacks throughout December, with a special effort to recapture the vital Messines-Wytschaete Ridge. This seemed feasible, not least because the Germans had been withdrawing troops from the Western Front to buttress their armies in the east. In Flanders they now had only six and a half divisions opposing the ten British divisions, and nine divisions to oppose ten French divisions. On the other hand, they were working hard to improve their defensive line, pressing Belgian civilians and Russian prisoners into service to complete and develop their fortifications.

The BEF's II and III Corps were duly tasked with retaking the Messines ridge and this attack, with French support on the left wing, went in on 14 December. No progress was made, the German artillery pounded the Franco-British line heavily, and further attacks on the two following days also got nowhere. Yet more attacks followed but were equally unsuccessful. One effect of this failure was to leave the French with the impression that the British Army was reluctant to fight and was only good for holding trenches. The fact that the French had done no better, and had lost even more men, was overlooked. The truth of the matter was that until the troops in the line could be reinforced, trained in the correct tactics and supplied with heavy guns, the German line was impregnable. Until that time the BEF went on the defensive and endured the mud, misery and steady losses of men from shelling, sniping and 'trench foot', during their first winter in the line.

Behind that line plans were being prepared for the coming year. There were already genuine fears that Russia might collapse, which would free vast numbers of German troops for a major campaign in the west. Whether that were to happen or not, the Allied commanders, and especially General Joffre, were convinced that the war would be won or lost on the Western Front. Field Marshal Kitchener was less certain and, urged on by Winston Churchill, was contemplating some diversions. On 2 January 1915 the Secretary for War wrote to French:

> We must now recognise that the French Army cannot make a sufficient break in the German line to bring about a retreat of the German forces from Belgium. If that is so, then the German lines in France may be looked on as a fortress, that cannot be carried by assault and cannot be completely invested, with the result that the lines may be held by an investing force while operations proceed elsewhere.

Once again Kitchener was displaying foresight and good sense. He recognised that the strong German defences – which were growing stronger every day – were impervious to assault without unacceptable losses. 'Trench warfare', the popular name given to the fighting on the Western Front, is not in fact an accurate description; as Kitchener now recognised, this was really siege warfare. It would remain as such until 1918, when the German 'fortress' eventually fell, as fortresses had done throughout history, from a combination of starvation and a failed sortie, in this case the suffering of the German population from the Allied naval blockade and the failure of the German 'Michael' offensive of March 1918 and their subsequent attacks from then until July. If, therefore, as Kitchener pointed out, the German front could not be breached, it must be outflanked. This conclusion, while perfectly sound in itself, led to the disastrous Dardanelles expedition and the fruitless campaign in Salonika.

Both of these ventures lie outside the scope of this book, but since they had their military and political supporters in London – the so-called 'Easterners' – the possibility of success in these theatres might be briefly covered now. The attempts to break out from Salonika in order to aid the Serbs and knock Bulgaria out of the war went on for years, and their failure speaks for itself. The Dardanelles expedition might have achieved great things but the British and French – and, for that matter, the Australians and New Zealanders who now lay strong claims to that campaign – had so little knowledge of amphibious warfare that the expedition was doomed from the start.

Hindsight is not always useless; indeed, historians would be lost without it. Hindsight can enable a later generation to see where a previous generation went wrong, so that with the greater experience drawn from numerous amphibious operations in the Second World War it is easy to see where the Dardanelles expedition of 1915 went awry. The idea was to force a passage through the Dardanelles, capture Constantinople and seize the sea passage to the Black Sea. These were high and worthy aims, for had the operation succeeded it might well have driven Turkey out of the war; furthermore, by ensuring a steady supply of war material brought by ship through the Black Sea, it might have enabled Russia to fight on against Germany and even, perhaps, to avoid revolution.

The snag is that the operation was bungled from the start. There was no *surprise*, the first requirement for any attack. By preliminary bombardment of the Turkish shore batteries dominating the Narrows – the north-eastern end of the Dardanelles, the latter being the passage from the Aegean into the Sea of Marmara, and thus to Constantinople itself – the Royal Navy and French ships alerted the Turks to the possibility that an attack was being mounted. When ships were lost, mainly to mines, in an attempt to sail through, the naval attack was abandoned, so that when the troops went ashore on the Gallipoli Peninsula some time later, all surprise had been lost and the Turks had brought up enough men and guns to contain the Allied beachheads. Once the troops were ashore they failed to 'peg-out claims' well inland to give the landing beaches security from Turkish shellfire. In round figures the British lost 20,000 men, the French 10,000 and the Anzacs 7,000 in the Dardanelles, and all for nothing, for the operation had to be abandoned and the troops withdrawn by early January 1916. (The evacuation, however, was a masterpiece of military planning, with not a single man lost.)

It remains doubtful, in the light of more extensive Second World War experience, whether the Dardanelles landings of April 1915 could ever have succeeded. Matters improved over the months as the operation proceeded, but the training, experience, logistical capacity and technology needed to force a way ashore, found so vital in 1943–44, and deployed with differing success in Sicily, at Salerno, Anzio and on D-Day, were simply not available in 1915. The Great War troops and their commanders did not have the kit or the competence in 1915 to mount an amphibious attack against a determined, courageous and well-commanded enemy.

However accurate Kitchener's appreciation, and however enthusiastic the 'Easterners' for the opening of a second front in the Balkans or the Mediterranean, these found no favour with Field Marshal French, and even less with Joffre and the French politicians. At a meeting of the War Council in London in January 1915 French stated that: 'Breaking through on the Western Front is simply a matter of larger supplies of ammunition and especially of high-explosive ammunition, and until the impossibility of breaking through on the Western Front had been proved there was no question of making the attempt somewhere else.' (Official History, 1914, Volume I, p. 65.)

The French reasons were at once more emotional and more pragmatic. The Germans stood on the sacred soil of France and must be swiftly evicted, whatever the cost in lives. In addition, since that is where the bulk of the Germans were, that was the place where they could be killed in large numbers, until their leaders lost their enthusiasm for European domination, and to that end all efforts must be addressed. The first step to be taken in 1915, therefore, would be an Anglo-French offensive at Neuve Chapelle, as soon as the ground had dried out. For this and subsequent offensives more men, guns and shells would be urgently needed. Meanwhile, the BEF dug in and endured the rain and mud as best it could, Haig's First Army taking over the sector from astride the La Bassée Canal at Cuinchy to Bois Grenier in the Lys valley, while the Second Army continued the line north, through Armentières and round to the eastern side of the Salient, where their positions were overlooked by the German positions on the Wytschaete-Messines Ridge.

On 15 February 1915, the BEF received a small but significant reinforcement when the 1st Canadian Division disembarked at St Nazaire. This division spent some time with the First Army and took a small part in the Battle of Neuve Chapelle in March, before being sent to Smith-Dorrien's Second Army in the Ypres Salient, a move which introduced to the Western Front one of the Great War's most famous and effective fighting corps.

The Canadians were – and are – justly proud of the exploits of the 1st Canadian Division, and the British can share this pride, for, according to the Canadian historian Daniel Dancocks, of the 30,617 men who sailed from Canada in October 1914, nearly 20,000 were British-born; this first contingent also included 762 Americans. In one newly formed regiment Princess Patricia's Canadian Light Infantry, which became a crack unit of the BEF, no less than 87 per cent of the soldiers – 950 of the first volunteers – were British-born, and most of the PPCLI recruits – 1,049 out of 1,089 – had formerly served in the British Army and could display a total of 771 decorations for gallantry or compaign medals.

The Canadians were to become one of the great fighting contingents of the war, earning the respect of soldiers on both sides of the line, but they retained their own particular style and way of doing things as well as a somewhat *laissez-faire* attitude to the niceties of military life, an attitude summed up by the following popular joke:

> *British sentry*: 'Alt, oo goes there?
> *Voice*: The Scots Guards.
> *BS*: Pass, Scots Guards.
> *BS*: 'Alt, oo goes there?
> *Voice*: The Buffs.
> *BS*: Pass, The Buffs.
> *BS*: 'Alt, oo goes there?
> *Voice*: Mind your own goddam business.
> *BS*: Pass, Canadians.

Such troops took careful handling, but both of their British commanders, Alderson and Byng, came to adore their tough outspoken soldiers and left their command with great regret, in Byng's case in tears. Lieutenant-General Edwin (later Sir Edwin) Alderson, the Canadians' first commander in France and Flanders, was an experienced and humorous British officer, then aged fifty-five. Though no great success as a field commander, Alderson was an efficient trainer of troops, had served with Canadian units in the South African War, and the men liked him. The brigadiers were all Canadian, and included one man who was to prove a considerable soldier, Arthur Currie.

Arthur Currie was not a professional soldier. Before the war he had been a Territorial officer in Victoria, British Columbia, where he worked as a realtor – an estate agent. He was eventually to become the commander of the Canadian Corps and one of the most successful generals of the Great War, but when war broke out in 1914, Currie was a lieutenant-colonel commanding a militia battalion, the 50th Gordon Highlanders of Canada, and nursing a shameful secret.

Currie had been speculating in real estate, but when his schemes went awry and he was facing bankruptcy he made up the gap in his finances by taking money, the then considerable sum of C$11,000, from his regimental funds, money that had been earmarked for new uniforms. Currie could not repay the money, and when war broke out he hoped for a command that would leave him in Canada until he could put the money back. His soldierly qualities, however – and his theft of the funds – were known to one of his officers, Major Garnet Hughes, the son of Canada's Minister of Militia, Sam Hughes.

Major Hughes wrote to his father, praising Colonel Currie, with the result that Sam Hughes offered the errant realtor command of 2 Infantry Brigade in the 1st Canadian Division. This offer was impossible to turn down, but Currie sailed for Europe with the debt unpaid and fear of discovery preying on his mind. 'It was,' he said, 'the first thought that struck me when I woke in the morning, and the last thought in my mind when I turned in at night.'

In fact, Currie's peculation had already been discovered. Before sailing for Britain, he had written to a friend, Arthur Matson, telling him what he had done and asking Matson to arrange for him to have the time to pay the money back. Instead, Matson wrote to the Canadian Prime Minister, Sir Robert Borden, enclosing Currie's letter with one of his own in which he begged the Premier to delay the impending investigation and allow Currie the necessary time in which to repay the debt. Fortunately, Borden had met Currie and formed a high opinion of his abilities. He therefore did as asked, although other letters were sent from Victoria to the Prime Minister's office demanding that Currie be arrested and tried for theft.

The matter was not settled until after the war, though the missing sums were repaid in September 1917 with money borrowed from two of Currie's subordinates. The theft was to dog Currie for the rest of his life, but as the Canadian Division prepared for war he was earning golden opinions for his good sense and soldierly qualities. Those accusations of callousness and incompetence levelled at other Great War generals were never made against Arthur Currie.

In truth, Currie did not look much like a soldier. He was a big, pear-shaped man who stood 6 feet 4 inches tall and weighed 250 pounds, thirty-eight years old in 1914, with a large belly, a sagging behind, a heavy jowl and a uniform that bulged in a less than martial fashion. What marked him out, however, were his common sense, his quick brain and his ability to analyse swiftly any military problem. His theft of the money also indicated that if he saw a quick way out of a problem he would take it and worry about the consequences later. Yet people liked and respected him, and with good reason. 'His sincerity and forcefulness was marked, he was good-natured, natural, cheerful, imperturbable,' wrote Colonel Birchall Wood, a British officer attached to Canadian Headquarters. Such personal qualities are useful in a soldier, and since his two fellow brigade commanders were not stamped by brilliance, Arthur Currie quickly stood out as the coming man in the Canadian Division.

'From the first, he was the outstanding commander among the Canadians' said Canadian Prime Minister Borden. 'I felt convinced he was the ideal man to command a Brigade and was delighted when he was given one,' said HRH the Duke of Connaught, Governor-General of Canada and a field marshal in the British Army. These golden opinions continued when Currie reached England. 'Currie is out and out the best of the Brigadiers,' said his new commanding officer, General Alderson, and great things were expected from him when the division reached France.

The Canadians were introduced to the front line gently, on attachment to British formations, and were greatly impressed with their phlegmatic British cousins. The British were equally impressed, and on 1 March 1915 the Canadian Division took over a section of the line as part of Rawlinson's IV Corps in Haig's First Army. There they played a small part in the battle at Neuve Chapelle, bringing fire to bear on their section of the German line, discovering in the process that their .303-calibre Canadian Ross rifles jammed when used for rapid fire. Although the Ross rifle was greatly inferior to the British Lee-Enfield, this defect had not been made good when the Canadians went north to join Plumer's V Corps in Second Army, and they were still equipped with the Ross when the Germans launched the gas attack to start the Second Battle of Ypres, tearing a huge hole in the Allied line.

In April 1915 the Ypres Salient was a bulge eight miles deep protruding to the east of Ypres from the Canal d'Yser, the front line – that is, the perimeter of the bulge – a seventeen-mile curve from Steenstraat in the north to St Éloi in the south. The terrain of the Salient was so open that even the slightest elevation was worth fighting for. This need to hold the high ground was to be a feature of operations well into 1915, and involved General Plumer's V Corps in a fierce battle to capture Hill 60, an artificially created mound not quite 200 feet (60 metres – hence the name) high south of Hooge, formed by the spoil from the excavation of a cutting on the Ypres–Comines railway line. After a few weeks of mining and tunnelling the hill was captured by the British 13 Infantry Brigade on 17 April. The Germans counter-attacked and pounded Hill 60 with heavy artillery, and in three days of fighting to retain the hill the British suffered over 3,000 casualties, most of them in 13 Brigade.

The British V Corps, commanded by Lieutenant-General Sir Herbert Plumer, now held most of the Ypres Salient, with the Canadian Division joining up with General Putz's forces south-west of Poelcapelle, where two French divisions, the 45th Algerian and the 87th Territorial, continued the line to the north. The Canadian division took over this north-eastern section of the Salient between Gravenstafel and Poelcapelle on the night of 14–15 April, and were still there when, on the warm afternoon of Thursday, 22 April, the Germans sent a cloud of poisonous chlorine gas over the French troops on the Canadians' left and drove them, coughing and gasping as their lungs collapsed, into full and panic-stricken retreat.

Poison gas was a forbidden weapon, barred from use in warfare by the Hague Declaration of 1899 and the Hague Convention of 1907. Germany was a signatory to both these agreements, but had been carrying out experiments with poison gas since 1902. By the outbreak of war they were fully prepared for its use and, although the British and French did not think that any civilised nation would break an international agreement and use such a devilish weapon, they had had received plenty of warnings that a gas attack at Ypres was not only probable, but imminent.

At the end of March, German prisoners had revealed that gas cylinders were being brought up to the line near Zillebeke. On 13 April, a German deserter, August Jaeger, told his French captors that 'an asphyxiating gas would be discharged on French troops, the attack signalled by three red rockets, and carried by a favourable wind into the French lines'. Jaeger, a private, was so full of useful information that the French decided that he had been sent into their lines as a deception, and therefore ignored his information, while General Edmond Ferry, commanding the French 11th Division at Ypres, who passed Jaeger's news to the British, was reprimanded by General Putz 'for communicating directly with our allies, and not through these headquarters'. On 17 April the German press announced, wholly untruthfully, that the British had used asphyxiating gas shells near Ypres, and since the Germans were fond of accusing their enemies of their own transgressions, this should have been another warning sign. Then two more men, another German deserter and a French spy, brought news of an impending gas attack.

All this accumulating evidence was ignored by the French and the British. Though the information was passed on to his divisional commanders by General Plumer, he added that he sent it to them 'for what it was worth', and like him, they paid no heed to it. No thought was given to preventative measures like gas masks, so that the troops were completely without protection when the gas cloud rolled over their trenches in the third week of April.

General Alderson was visiting his artillery batteries on the afternoon of the 22nd when he heard heavy firing from the French divisions on his left. Then he saw 'two clouds of yellow-green smoke, which spread out rapidly from the German line and appeared to merge into each other'. This cloud was chlorine gas, and when it reached the French line the effect was devastating. The French and Algerian troops, unable to breathe and coughing up blood, abandoned their positions and fled. The French field artillery went into action, pounding their own front-line trenches and the advancing Germans with fire, until the gas reached the guns, when they too fell silent, leaving a four-mile-wide gap in the Allied line and completely exposing the left flank of the 1st Canadian Division . . . towards which the gas cloud was now rolling.

Two Canadian medical officers, Colonel Nasmith and Captain Scrimger, out riding behind the 1st Canadian Division lines, were the first to analyse the problem. Nasmith was a chemist, and having watched the gas cloud and got a sniff of it, the officers agreed that it was probably chlorine. They kept their heads, worked out an emergency solution and hastened to send word to the trenches, directing the troops to urinate on their handkerchiefs or any cloth they possessed and hold the wet pad over the nose and mouth. Necessity is mother of invention and knows no laws, and urine was in plentiful supply, so the troops hastened to comply. The uric acid caused the chlorine to crystallise on the cloth and, thus protected, the Canadian infantry began to flay the German infantry with rapid fire, cursing their Ross rifles which soon began to jam.

Three things saved the Allied position that afternoon; the quick thinking of Nasmith and Scrimger, the discipline and courage of the Canadian soldiers, and the fact that the German infantry were also afraid of the gas cloud. Unwilling to get close to it they declined to advance. Moreover, the leading German division, the 52nd, received orders not to advance beyond the southern slope of Pilckem Ridge, so they halted there while other German troops moved south, occupied Kitchener's Wood (a happy translation of the Bois des Cuisiniers) and Mauser Ridge, and dug in to fight off the inevitable British counter-attack. The Germans hesitated just long enough for news of the disaster to spread, and gradually more troops and guns began to bolster the Canadian resistance on the left of the British line.

Mauser Ridge features in many accounts of the fighting at Second Ypres and its importance can be judged by its position. The ridge runs east to west, between Pilckem Ridge and Hilltop Ridge, with Kitchener's Wood and Oblong Farm at its eastern end. It overlooks the ground to the south and west, towards Ypres, offers reverse-slope protection to troops between the ridge and Pilckem, and an easy route towards the Yser Canal. Unless the Germans could be levered off Mauser Ridge the Anglo-French positions in Ypres and St Julian, and in all the defensive positions between those places, were in jeopardy.

There was now understandable confusion at Corps and Army HQs. Moreover, the reports that got back to V Corps and Second Army HQ that evening seemed to say that there were no French troops in the Salient east of the Yser Canal, and that the Canadian Division had also given way. In fact, the Canadians were holding their original positions and organising some form of defence along their open left flank. The German advance had halted and although the entire Salient was now being swept with artillery fire, the threat of an immediate defeat had been averted. Even so, unless the French could counter-attack and restore the original front line, the Salient might have to be evacuated. With the loss of the north-eastern ridges, and the Germans now holding a line from the western edge of Mauser Ridge to Kitchener's Wood and the outskirts of St Julian, thus chopping off the northern third of the Salient, the whole area was open to observed artillery fire.

The Ypres Salient was inherently indefensible. Every inch of ground was under observation from the ridges to the east, and with fire directed from there, German guns could probe into every corner of the Allied position. It would have been much easier, and far more sensible, to withdraw to a line behind the west bank of the Yser Canal. Everyone knew that, yet the Salient was not being held because the generals were blind to the difficulties of holding it, or to the losses that its defence would inevitably entail.

The reasons for clinging on to Ypres were political and emotional. It was one part of Belgium that the Germans had not overrun, and it was also a place that the Allied armies had bought and paid for with quantities of blood the previous November. However great the problems caused by holding the Salient, the idea of giving it up was unthinkable. Besides, the reasons for the First Battle of Ypres, which had created the Salient, still held good. The town was the main bastion before the Channel coast – if it fell, who knew where the Germans could be stopped? So, for one reason and another it was considered vital to hang on to Ypres. The only question was, could the Allies do so if the ridge line was lost?

There was a second defence line, a network of trenches and strongpoints built by the French at the end of 1914, but now in the British sector, running up into the Salient from the south-west and curving round east of Ypres to finish by the Ypres–Langemarck road. This line, known as the 'GHQ Line', could, if extended to the Yser Canal, offer some sort of protection to the troops attempting to defend the northern flank of the Salient.

By early evening on the 22nd, General Plumer had got a grip of the situation. He ordered the Canadian Division to make its left flank secure and at all costs to hold the GHQ Line. As an aid to this end, Plumer sent the 2nd East Yorkshire Regiment up to join the Canadians, the first of thirty-three British battalions that would be sent to fight under General Alderson's command at Second Ypres. A further British reinforcement of two battalions arrived from the 28th Division on the Canadians' right flank and these took up position in the north, with their left flank on the east bank of the Yser Canal. So, slowly, the Allied line was stabilised, with a new position that seemed at least viable, though German infantry had by now dug in on Mauser Ridge and were able to enfilade the GHQ Line.

In the light of this a counter-attack seemed called for, and at 2000 hours an officer from General Putz's HQ came to Alderson's headquarters requesting Canadian support for an attack by the French 45th Division. This division would advance to the Pilckem Ridge, just east of the canal, if the Canadians would mount an assault on Kitchener's Wood at the eastern end of Mauser ridge. If the Pilckem and Kitchener's Wood positions could be taken, the Germans would be forced to withdraw from Mauser Ridge or face attacks from both flanks. Since this seemed a sound plan, the Canadians agreed to co-operate. There was only one thing wrong with it: the French were in no position to mount an attack. The 45th Division had withdrawn to the west bank of the Yser Canal and, having been gassed and shelled a few hours before, was demoralised and in urgent need of reorganisation. Nevertheless, a counter-attack must go in soon or the Germans would secure their positions for another assault.

The Canadians elected to proceed with their advance without the French, making an attack which illustrates how officers and men, acting sensibly and doing their best, can still be defeated by the pressure of events. Two battalions, the 16th (Canadian Scottish) from Brigadier-General Turner's 3 Brigade and the 10th Battalion (Calgary Winnipeg) from Brigadier-General Currie's 2 Brigade, were committed to this attack. Turner took overall command and the attack went in at 2330 hours that night, barely six hours after the first gas attack. The few hours available in which to organise this operation left little time for preparation or artillery support – only thirteen field guns could be committed in support, in any case – and none at all for reconnaissance. The attackers, 1,500 strong, crossed their start line near Mousetrap Farm and had got to within 200 yards of Kitchener's Wood when a storm of fire broke upon them from an undetected German position in the wood. The Canadians reeled, rallied, and then charged into their first battle of the war.

Losing men with every yard, they ran across open fields and into the wood, where they fought the Germans hand-to-hand in pitch dark, the light of flares obscured by the trees. They drove the defenders out of the wood and dug in on the northern edge, well aware that unless help came quickly they could not stay there in daylight. The attack had already cost the two battalions over a thousand men killed and wounded, about one for every yard of their advance, and as they worked feverishly to deepen their trenches and send back the wounded, they came under fire from three sides.

Reinforcements were on the way. Two fresh battalions, the 2nd (East Ontario) and the 3rd (Toronto) from Alderson's Divisional Reserve had been sent up to Brigadier-General Turner, who ordered the 2nd Battalion to get up to Kitchener's Wood as quickly as possible. Once again, however, the chronic problem of battlefield communications reared its head. The 2nd Battalion did not know what awaited them up in Kitchener's Wood and had no means of finding out, but they knew from the wounded men streaming back that a fierce fight had taken place and was probably still going on. The battalion commander, fearing that if he marched on the wood his men might soon be fighting other Canadians in the dark, sensibly decided to carry out a reconnaissance and make contact with the two forward battalions before advancing.

Lack of reconnaissance had led the first two battalions into attacking a heavily defended German position. Time taken for reconnaissance succeeded in delaying the advance of the 2nd Battalion until dawn and the result was another slaughter. An advance that should have been made in the dark took place in broad daylight, so that in twelve hours of fighting on the night of 22 April and the morning of the 23rd, the 10th Battalion lost 623 men killed and wounded out of 816 and the 16th almost 600 of the 800 who advanced, while of the 2nd Battalion fewer than 20 men reached the wood. When daylight came the Canadian positions on the north edge of the wood could not be held and the survivors of the 10th and 16th Battalions pulled back to trenches on the south side, where they were joined by the remnants of the 2nd Battalion.

At dawn on the 23rd, artillery fire began to fall all over the Salient. There were 50,000 British and Canadian troops here, with all their guns and supply wagons, a great quantity of stores, and much 'impedimenta'. All of this, and every yard of ground east of Ypres, was now a target for the enemy's artillery. Over the next few days the German tactics became clear. They would make limited advances, each preceded and supported by artillery bombardments and accompanied by gas released from canisters or delivered by shell, the plan being that this fatal combination would squeeze the British, Canadians and French out of the Salient. It was a race between German artillery and gas-supported infantry attacks and an Allied resistance based on the hunt for some form of defence against gas, and on the guts of the British and Canadian infantry. The role of the French, though not lacking in courage, was of no great help to their Allies, while their actions, or rather their unwillingness to act at all, sealed the fate of one senior British officer, Lieutenant-General Sir Horace Smith-Dorrien.

Just after midnight on 23 April the French again declared that their 45th Division was ready to counter-attack, shortly after dawn, and again asked General Plumer for support. Plumer passed the task to the Canadian Division, and General Alderson passed the task to Brigadier-General Mercer's 1 Brigade. Mercer selected the Canadian 1st and 4th Battalions for this new attack, ordering them to advance up the left-hand edge of the Ypres–Pilckem road in support of two French battalions of the 45th Division, which would be making a simultaneous attack on the Pilckem Ridge up the right-hand side. These orders were issued by Alderson's HQ at 0345 hours on the 24th, and the attack was due to start at 0500, less than two hours later, led by the 4th Battalion.

Other units were also moving forward. After midnight – at 0030 hours – on the morning of the 23rd, General Alderson had created a 'provisional brigade' from four of his available British battalions, the 2nd East Kent Regiment (the Buffs), the 3rd Middlesex Regiment, 5th Kings Own (Royal Lancaster Regiment) and 1st York and Lancaster Regiment. This ad-hoc brigade, commanded by Lieutenant-Colonel A. D. Geddes of the 2nd Buffs and therefore known as 'Geddes Force', was sent up to fill the gaps in the northern front of the Salient, with orders to take position close to Oblong Farm, a post now held by the remnants of the 2nd Canadian Battalion. Meanwhile, the two battalions of Mercer's brigade were waiting for the French to advance. In the event, 0500 came and the French troops failed to appear. Then Lieutenant-Colonel Birchall, commanding the 4th Canadian Battalion, saw movement on his flank. Thinking the French were finally moving, he ordered his battalion to advance.

It was now broad daylight and the two Canadian battalions and the Germans on Mauser Ridge had been observing each other for a full half-hour. The French did not appear – and were not to appear – and the Germans let the advancing Canadians get fully into the open before they opened fire. What followed was slaughter. Brigadier-General Mercer, watching his two battalions being cut to pieces, sought out the officer who should have led the French attack, Lieutenant-Colonel Mordacq, who assured him that some five or six French battalions were on the point of attacking. These battalions still did not appear, and to save what men he could, Mercer ordered his battalions to dig in and hang on while he sought help elsewhere.

Colonel Geddes and his battalions were also moving up. At 0430 hours on the 23rd Geddes sent the Buffs, the Middlesex and the King's Own into the attack, deploying at Wieltje and advancing north over the almost level ground below Mauser Ridge to fill in the gap between the French on the Yser Canal and the Canadians in Kitchener's Wood. The advancing troops came under furious machine-gun fire but managed, as required, to form a thin line spanning the gap. There they hung on, unable to advance or pull back

One of the problems of untangling the threads of a battle is that a great many events happen at much the same time, and often overlap. These can only be understood if they are put into some sort of order, but it has to be remembered that this option was not available to the commanders on the spot at the time. They had to plan or order one attack while another was going on, and do so without having much information as to how matters were progressing. It is clear, *now*, that the Canadians should have been ordered on to the defensive, and not sent out to make a series of attacks which were essentially fruitless without adequate artillery preparation and French support. Nevertheless, after a full day's fighting and three separate disasters, some idea of what was going on should have reached higher authority. The problem, essentially a lack of understanding, seems to have been caused by the fact that the direction of the battle for the Salient was reaching ever higher levels, and now lay in the hands of Field Marshal French and General Foch.

With his northern flank driven in, French at first wanted to evacuate the Salient and pull his line back to the Yser Canal. He therefore went to Foch's HQ at Cassel on the morning of the 23rd to tell him as much. Foch, however, talked the Field Marshal out of it, assuring him that a large number of French troops were already on the way and would be thrown into a counter-attack as soon as they arrived – if the British would support them. This was a wild exaggeration. There was just one French division en route for the Salient, and no sign of French support east of the Yser Canal. Nevertheless, this promise sent Field Marshal French into one of his mood swings. Now full of optimism, he hurried to Smith-Dorrien's HQ and urged the Second Army commander to press on with preparations for another attack, promising him support from other corps and divisions of the BEF.

Smith-Dorrien had already released 13 Infantry Brigade from the Second Army reserve to assist the Canadian Division, and ordered its commander, Brigadier-General Wanless O'Gowan, to report to Alderson's HQ. Smith-Dorrien now went there himself and ordered Alderson and O'Gowan to commit 13 Brigade, and any other troops in the area, to an advance towards Pilckem, on the axis of the Ypres–Pilckem road. The order urged 13 Brigade, having taken the Pilckem Ridge, to press on and reoccupy the front line lost on the previous day. This last objective was, to say the least, over-optimistic, not least because the attack was again to be made in conjunction with the French 90 Brigade under Colonel Mordacq.

There was also the problem of time. The order was issued about noon and the attack had to go in at 1530 hours, half an hour after the French had moved. This allowed no time for O'Gowan to study the ground or properly brief his men, though it was noticed that 13 Brigade and Mordacq's 90 Brigade had been assigned the same objectives, and would therefore probably become entangled. There was also confusion in the fire plan, for the British artillery was ordered to open fire at 1445 to support the French attack. In the event the artillery followed this plan, with the result that the guns ran out of ammunition before 13 Brigade advanced.

Yet again, the hour of attack arrived with no sign of the French. 'Zero' – 1530 hours – arrived and passed, the artillery bombardment ceased, and at 1545, with chaos mounting, General O'Gowan sent a message to Alderson, saying he needed another half-hour before his troops could advance. In fact, it was 1630 before 13 Brigade attacked, and even then there was no sign of the French. O'Gowan took three of his four battalions into this attack, the 1st Royal West Kent Regiment and the 2nd KOSB in the lead, with the 2nd KOYLI in immediate reserve. As they advanced, some French troops finally appeared, a single battalion of Zouaves (French Algerian infantry), who marched in front of the British battalions until, coming under machine-gun fire from the German line, they went to ground and dug in. O'Gowan's men marched on towards Mauser Ridge and deployed for the attack.

The Canadians, pinned down below Mauser Ridge, watched the British infantry coming on. They also saw the German fire from artillery, machine-guns and rifles, start to take its usual, terrible effect. Then they saw the British infantry of Geddes Force rise from their shell-scrapes and trenches, fall in on the left flank of 13 Brigade and join in their advance. Finally, survivors of the Canadian 1st and 4th Battalions also rose up as the British swept past and surged forward with them into the attack. It was gallant beyond belief . . . and quite hopeless.

These men – the two battalions of 13 Brigade, and what was left of Geddes Force and their Canadian comrades – pressed home their attack on the German position. They went on pressing it home for a full ninety minutes, until the fields below Mauser Ridge were carpeted with khaki-clad dead and wounded. The firing died away at dusk and only then did the survivors pull back a few hundred yards and dig in. Midnight on 23 April 1915 brought an end to a terrible day, and one in which, as the British Official History bitterly remarks, 'No ground was gained that could not have been taken, probably without casualties, by a simple advance after dark.' On that day Geddes Force and 13th Brigade alone lost some 1,500 officers and men. The commanding officers of both the 1st York and Lancasters and the 3rd Middlesex were killed at the head of their troops, as was Colonel Birchall of the 4th Canadian Battalion, and 18 other officers and over 800 men of the 1st and 4th Canadian Battalions were listed as killed, wounded or missing.

These fruitless infantry attacks need to be analysed and understood before the blame is shared out. The riposte to a successful attack is a counter-attack, delivered if possible before the enemy has had time to reorganise, consolidate his gains and dig in; if he is given time to do that the counter-attack will be even more costly. The counter-attack to retake the ground lost by the gas attack should have been made by the French, who lost that ground in the first place, but since they were incapable of delivering it, the task fell to the Canadians and their British supports.

There was no point in being chauvinistic about this; the line had to be restored by someone or else the Salient, or at the least a large part of the Salient, would have to be evacuated. That in turn would create a large gap in the Allied line – how large no one could say – and introduce the strong possibility that the Germans could roll up the British line, push west to the Channel coast and threaten the very existence of the BEF. So the Salient had to be held, and that could be done more easily if the Allies held the ridge line, which therefore had to be retaken. The problem was how to do it.

In an ideal world, these counter-attacks would have been supported by heavy artillery fire and delivered by an adequate number of fresh troops, but for reasons already explained, this fire and those troops were not available. Going over to the defensive and digging in until sufficient men and shells were available was not an option, for in the Salient the water table lies close to the surface and it takes time – more of that precious, unavailable time – to build sandbag parapets . . . and there were no sandbags anyway. Besides, with German guns dominating the Salient, any defences prepared overnight would not be substantial enough, and would be blasted out of existence on the following day.

When the options are considered they come down to just two: evacuate the Salient, with all the risks involved; or try to hang on to it by retaking the ridge with the resulting cost in lives. This attack required plenty of artillery with abundant ammunition, but these were simply not available. The Canadians and British only had infantry and so the infantry had to do the job. Meanwhile the German attacks and the relentless shelling continued, ground was steadily lost, and casualties mounted. On the following day, Saturday, 24 April, the Germans renewed their attack against the eight Canadian battalions crammed into the apex of the divisional salient. Again they used chlorine, preceding the gas attack with a heavy bombardment and following it with an assault by thirty-four battalions of infantry. Since the Canadians had only eight exhausted and depleted battalions in the line along the Gravenstafel Ridge, the Germans anticipated a walk-over.

By just after dawn on a beautiful spring day the Canadians had begun to relax. Then came a ten-minute bombardment of their positions from guns of every calibre, and a great, green cloud of gas came across their trenches and rolled on towards Brigadier-General Currie's 2 Canadian Brigade HQ near Fortuin. By now the search for preventive measures against gas was well under way, but the main defence still consisted of holding a wet cloth over the mouth and nose. Buckets of water had been placed here and there in the trenches, although the troops generally relied on urine. With the last traces of gas came the German infantry, and as the chlorine thinned out the Canadian soldiers, many standing on the parapets of their wrecked trenches, opened fire on the advancing enemy.

Currie had not slept for three days, but he was still in command and leading his much reduced brigade with considerable skill. The main German attack fell on the 8th Battalion from Winnipeg, but its soldiers held their trenches and, with help from the 5th Battalion, drove the Germans off. Other battalions were not so fortunate, and the combination of gas, shellfire, infantry assault, and the fact that their Ross rifles jammed so easily, forced a breach in the Canadian line. The 15th Battalion (48th Highlanders of Canada) were overrun and through the gap thus created the Germans were in a position to outflank the entire Canadian line and get in rear of the Canadians defending the village of St Julien.

Other parts of the Canadian line held. Help was on the way from the other Canadian brigades and from the British, with General Alderson sending the 150th (York and Durham) Brigade, which had just arrived from Britain and had been placed under his command, to form a defensive position along the GHQ Line. Meanwhile, the Germans were throwing assaults against the Canadian line, at St Julien and along the Gravenstafel Ridge until the entire Canadian front was in action, the area behind the trenches draped in wisps of gas, the entire area pounded incessantly by shellfire. The Canadians were putting up a magnificent fight, but their position was untenable. Slowly, the troops on the Gravenstafel Ridge were pushed back, the 13th Battalion was blown out of its trenches, and 1 and 3 Canadian Brigades began to pull back to the GHQ Line. However, the units of Currie's 2 Brigade, notably the 8th Battalion, still held their trenches, beating off attack after attack.

At 1200 hours the Germans took St Julien, sending in twelve battalions which advanced into the village in the face of intense rifle fire and Canadian field artillery engaging them over open sights. By 1500 the village had fallen, which put the Germans in a position to enfilade the Canadians in Kitchener's Wood. These soldiers hung on, however, under heavy fire, holding the left of the Canadian line, but elsewhere the Canadians were being forced to withdraw. Brigadier-General Turner's 3 Brigade completed its withdrawal to the GHQ Line by 1530 . . . leaving a gap in the line between the GHQ position and Currie's brigade, whose men were still – just – hanging on to their trenches on top of the Gravenstafel Ridge. To hold this position Currie needed fresh troops, but his appeals for reinforcements either never got back to Division, or went unheard. Finally, at around 1530 hours, he decided to go back himself, find the British battalions that were supposed to be in the GHQ Line to his rear, and bring them forward.

For a general to leave his headquarters in the middle of a battle was not only most unusual, but much frowned upon in 1915. Even if a brigadier could not communicate with his battalions, the divisional commander always wanted to be in touch with his brigade commanders, which in practice meant that they had to remain in or near their headquarters. By taking this drastic step Currie was putting his entire career in jeopardy. He did not shirk a risky decision if no other course was open to him; his brigade needed support, and if the appeals he sent for help went unanswered, he would seek that support in person. Currie set off over open, shell-swept ground to find help for his beleaguered brigade, but such help was not readily forthcoming, for when he finally contacted Brigadier-General Bush of 150 Brigade, the latter refused to move. Currie then went on to Potijze, to the headquarters of Major-General Snow, now commanding the 27th Division. Snow also refused to send help, and is alleged to have said afterwards that if Currie had been a British officer he would have had him shot (Dancocks, *Welcome to Flanders Fields*, p. 193). This tale may have grown in the telling but there is no doubt that the two men had a row, although Snow had already sent some of his battalions to shore up the Canadian line.

Two problems were affecting the situation of the Canadian Division. Firstly, the command structure had broken down. Plumer, Alderson, Snow, and the three Canadian brigadiers were all fighting separate battles and none of them – with the possible exception of Currie – knew what was going on: the now familiar problem of battlefield communications having its usual dire effect. As a result, battalions were mixed up, orders were going astray, and misunderstandings were common and considerable. Alderson, for example, thought that Turner's 3 Brigade was still defending its original line, while Turner thought the divisional general was well aware he had pulled back to the GHQ Line. By nightfall Turner had assembled around 3,500 men on that line, drawn from his own four Canadian battalions and some five assorted British battalions.

For his part, Field Marshal French had spent most of the day urging Smith-Dorrien to restore the line about St Julien, showing his usual inability to grasp what was actually going on. 'Every effort must be made to restore and hold the line about St Julien, or the situation of the 28th Division will be jeopardised. The Germans are numerically inferior to us, as far as we can judge. In fact there can be little doubt about it.'

There was a considerable doubt about it. The Salient now contained some fifty-two British, Canadian, and French battalions, most of them battered and all of them weary, while their opponents mustered sixty-two battalions and had the inestimable advantages of gas and heavy artillery. French, however, had been to see General Foch again, and returned full of enthusiasm for another assault on Mauser Ridge, this time by Brigadier-General Hull's 10 Brigade and whatever extra battalions could be mustered.

There is no need for a detailed account of Hull's attack. It was a repeat of all the other attacks made over the previous days. The plan was for the assault to be launched just before dawn on 25 April, and Hull's force was to consist of no fewer than fifteen battalions drawn from his own brigade and other brigades and divisions already in the Salient. Hull and his staff did not know the ground, and none of the battalion commanders came to his briefing, being too busy moving their men up to the start line: a better recipe for chaos can hardly be imagined. Then the attack was postponed from 0330 to 0530 hours, but this news did not reach their supporting artillery from the

27th and 28th Divisions, who had fired off all their ammunition before the infantry advance began – in broad daylight.

The Official History provides the epitaph for Hull's force:

> They were called on to attempt the impossible. Without adequate artillery preparation and support, over ground unknown and un-reconnoitred, they were sent to turn an enemy well provided with machine-guns out of a position which had ready-made cover in houses and a wood, and splendid artillery observation from high ground behind it. (*1915*, Volume II, p. 240.)

The attack duly went in, St Julien was not retaken, and Hull's force lost 73 officers and 2,346 men killed or wounded. The Official History calls it an 'annihilation'.

The failure of Hull's attack was followed by further German assaults, a reorganisation of the V Corps line, and a confrontation between General Smith-Dorrien and Field Marshal French. The French were now proposing yet another attack on the vital Mauser Ridge and the Field Marshal had therefore ordered the Lahore Division of the Indian Corps up from the southern sector to support it. Smith-Dorrien entertained doubts as to whether this French attack would take place, and had no wish to expose the Indian troops to a dose of chlorine gas.

He confided these views to French, but was told that the latter did not wish to give up any ground; on the other hand, the Field Marshal added, unless the French could retake the ground lost on the 22nd, the Salient might indeed have to be evacuated. French suspected that the Germans were attacking in the Salient to weaken the Allied attack planned for Aubers Ridge, and he was determined that they should not succeed in this ambition. He wanted the situation in the Salient quietened down, and told Smith-Dorrien that 'since the French had got the Second Army into this difficulty the French would have to get them out of it,' a remark that might have been made with greater force, and better effect, to General Foch.

Smith-Dorrien reluctantly agreed to commit the Lahore Division in support of the forthcoming French attack but returned to his HQ to discover that General Putz was up to his old tricks. The time of the attack had been changed to 1400 hours on the 26th and the size of the attacking French force had been reduced. Smith-Dorrien therefore contacted GHQ again but was told to carry out his orders. The result was a catastrophe as the Lahore Division put in yet another attack over the corpse-littered ground before Mauser Ridge. Two British battalions, the 1st Manchester Regiment and the Connaught Rangers, plus battalions of, Sikhs, Baluchis and the 57th (Wilde's) Rifles, six battalions in all, were greeted with shell and machine-gun fire as they advanced and never reached the German line, losing 95 officers and 1,734 men killed and wounded in the attempt. A supporting attack by 149 Northumbrian Brigade fared even worse, the brigade losing 42 officers, including the commander, Brigadier-General J.F. Riddell, and 1,912 men, over two-thirds of its strength. Part of the French attack was launched at 1400 hours and part at 1500, but after the Germans released gas the French fell back. Apart from some colonial troops that came up abreast of the Lahore Division around 1900 hours but went no further, the French made no other contribution to the day.

On the following morning, 27 April, with the attack due to be renewed, Smith-Dorrien received a copy of Putz's orders for the day, from which he discovered that the French general intended to use even fewer troops than he had on the previous day, and seemed to be proposing nothing more than another round of fruitless attacks. Smith-Dorrien had clearly had enough of this situation and wrote a long letter to Lieutenant-General Sir William Robertson, now Chief of Staff at GHQ, setting out the situation in the Salient and asking 'Wully' Robertson to place his views before the Commander-in-Chief, Field Marshal French.

Having explained the situation, Smith-Dorrien expressed his well-founded doubts about the French doing much or achieving anything. He therefore proposed pulling his troops back to some defensible position close to Ypres, and evacuating every gun and piece of equipment he could out of the Salient where, he said, they were simply a target for the German guns. Smith-Dorrien added that he was 'by no means pessimistic' and believed that the coming offensive – by Haig's Army on Aubers Ridge – would force the Germans to halt their attacks on Ypres. The Lahore Division had again been ordered to support the French attack on the canal at Lizerne on the 27th, but after their losses on the previous day were in no state to do so. The French put in an attack but it was soon halted, and although Lizerne did fall, the Germans were not forced out of their bridgehead on the west bank of the Yser Canal. Meanwhile, Field Marshal French was digesting the contents of Smith-Dorrien's letter.

This letter marked the end of the Second Army Commander's career. At 1415 hours Smith-Dorrien received a terse telephone reply from GHQ:

> Chief does not regard the situation as nearly so unfavourable as your letter represents. He thinks you have abundance of troops and notes especially the large reserves you have. He wishes you to act vigorously with the full means available in co-operation with and assisting the French attack, having due regard to his previous instructions that the combined attack should be simultaneous . . . letter follows by Staff Officer.

This message was sent 'in clear', so that everyone at GHQ, from staff officers to signal clerks, knew of it.

One might judge from this reply that the last four days, so packed with death and disappointment, had never happened or one might conclude that Field Marshal French had failed to absorb what had gone on – the fruitless and costly attacks, the gas, the remorseless shellfire, the daily French promises of attacks or support that never materialised. In fact, Sir John French knew of all these things, but the only thing that mattered to him was to get rid of Smith-Dorrien.

The staff officer, Major-General Perceval, duly arrived with the written draft of the telephone message, a public rebuke which Smith-Dorrien received and acknowledged. Then, at 1635 hours, a further message arrived, also 'in clear', directing Smith-Dorrien to hand over command of all his troops to General Plumer, the commander of V Corps, together with such staff officers as Plumer might require.

Plumer took up his new command at 1730 hrs on 27 April and since Smith-Dorrien had not resigned or yet been formally sacked, this command was designated 'Plumer's Force'. Plumer then received an order from GHQ ordering him to prepare a defensive line east of Ypres in case it became necessary to withdraw from the existing positions and evacuate any unneeded equipment from the Salient. In other words, he was being ordered by French to carry out the action proposed by Smith-Dorrien . . . and which had been derided by the Field Marshal. This Plumer was preparing to do on the 28th when French was again dissuaded from carrying out his plans by General Foch, who protested against any idea of withdrawal and begged the British commander not to move until he had seen the result of fresh French attacks. The Field Marshal, willing as ever, agreed to wait.

The French bombarded the German positions around Steenstraat for six hours, and at 1530 hours on the 28th three regiments left their trenches and advanced, only to be brought to a halt with heavy casualties without getting within 400 yards of the German line. Other French units did not advance at all, and the attacks soon petered out. Even so, Sir John French waited on results and the French put in another attack on the 30th. None of these attacks did anything towards restoring the Salient to the line occupied by the Allies before 22 April. Having suffered so much and waited over-long, the BEF finally pulled back to its new defence line . . . just as had been proposed a few days previously by General Smith-Dorrien.

The British withdrawal was carried out over two nights, between 1 and 3 May, without any direct interference from the Germans, though the shelling, infantry probes and gas attacks continued, notably against Hill 60. Here the German attack was repulsed, though the hill fell to a further gas, artillery and infantry assault on 5 May.

On 6 May, General Smith-Dorrien, who had still not resigned, in spite of the loss of most of his command to 'Plumer's Force', wrote a letter to Field Marshal French, recalling the growing lack of trust he had noticed since February, and suggesting, 'for the good of the cause', that someone else should take command of Second Army. There was no reply to this letter; instead an order arrived from GHQ ordering him to hand over his army to General Plumer.

Smith-Dorrien wrote a few letters to his corps and divisional commanders, thanking them for their support in the previous months and then left for England, his career effectively at an end. Plumer took over command of Second Army, Lieutenant-General Sir Edmund Allenby succeeded him as commander of the V Corps, and Major-General the Hon. Sir Julian Byng took command of the Cavalry Corps.

The new Salient Plumer had to defend was much smaller than the one that had existed until ten days before. It now formed a semi-circle about three miles deep and the front line ran from the shaky French positions on the Yser Canal at Steenstraat southwards, passing just east of Boesinghe, edging east to the southern slope of Mauser Ridge, where the British took over. Then it ran south and east across the GHQ Line to the Ypres-Zonnebeke railway line and Hill 60, running on from there due south to Hooge and Sanctuary Wood and so out towards Armentières, a line which the British Army was to hold, with certain small adjustments, for the next two and a half years.

The crux of the Second Battle of Ypres had passed with the British withdrawal, but the fighting continued: Plumer's units dug in and did all they could to improve their defences, anticipating further German attacks and further engagements. These are listed in the Official History as the Battle of Frezenberg Ridge (8–13 May) and the Battle of Bellewaarde Ridge (8–10 May), two long ridges running west from the Messines-Passchendaele Ridge. The results of these actions were further losses, the Frezenberg battle alone costing over 9,000 casualties. By the time the fighting ended, the total cost of 'Second Ypres' to the British, Canadian and Indian forces involved was 59,275 men killed, wounded and missing. Total German casualties of all types, though calculated on a slightly different basis which tended to reduce the final figure, are estimated in the Official History as 34,933. Most of the missing on both sides were in fact killed, blown to pieces or buried by shellfire, their names, in the case of the British and Imperial soldiers, now recorded on the walls of Tyne Cot Cemetery or on the Menin Gate at Ypres. Their bodies, with a handful of exceptions, have never been found.

What is the verdict on the competence of the generals after this battle? The first point to make is that after the gas attack of 22 April forced the French divisions to withdraw, the entire Salient became inherently untenable. The Germans had the gas and the guns, and the latter especially made any attempt to hold the Salient or prepare a new defence line extremely costly. This would have been the case even if the British had been well supplied with heavy guns and adequate supplies of ammunition, or if the French had given them regular and reliable support. Lacking any of these assets, the British generals attempted, with some limited success, to hold the Salient with infantry. The result is as has been described: severe losses and a curtailed Salient.

When all the factors are taken into account the situation does not offer any obvious alternative to the actions the British generals took, *once the decision had been made to hold on to the Salient.* Everything that happened at Second Ypres stems from that fatal decision, a decision arrived at more through sentiment and political will than through any military requirement or failure in generalship. And yet, if Ypres had fallen, and the Germans, using that successful combination of gas and artillery had been able to exploit their bridgehead over the Yser Canal at Lizerne, the entire Allied front might have crumbled, the road to the Channel ports would have lain open, and the Schlieffen Plan might once more have been viable. Second Ypres prevented that, though at great cost.

There is still plenty of room for criticism. The hurried counter-attacks against Mauser Ridge and St Julien, when whole brigades were thrown in without adequate support, reconnaissance, preparation or rest, or sent to attack ever-stronger positions in broad daylight, are hard enough to describe, let alone justify. And yet, if the Germans were *not* immediately counter-attacked, their defences would grow even stronger, and their heavy guns and gas cylinders would be brought up for yet another lunge forward . . . and infantry alone was all that the British and Canadian generals had to counter-attack with. The actions of the French, who consistently failed to deliver on their promises, are hard to explain, nor should Field Marshal French have listened so often and so long to the blandishments of General Foch. And yet he had been told to co-operate with the French; moreover, if the British and Canadians did not hold the Salient until the French were ready to retake the ground they had lost, then who would?

Even with hindsight, there is no easy answer to the question of whether Ypres was worth defending. There is room for criticism and even guilt, but these must be shared, and the guilty include a government and nation which failed to provide the field army with the equipment and supplies necessary to fight a modern war. But then, who in Europe, nine months before Second Ypres, could have imagined such a battle and such slaughter?

CHAPTER 8

HAIG'S YEAR, 1915, NEUVE CHAPELLE TO FESTUBERT

'As soon as we were supplied with ample artillery ammunition I thought we could walk through the German lines at several places.'

Lieutenant-General Sir Douglas Haig, conversation with
Colonel Charles Repington of *The Times*, 22 January 1915

To carry this story forward it is now necessary to return to March 1915 and cover four battles that took place south of the Ypres Salient, between Armentières and Vimy Ridge. This is not chronologically correct, for one of these – Neuve Chapelle – took place before the Second Battle of Ypres, and the Battle of Aubers Ridge took place while Second Ypres was still in progress. Nevertheless, it has the advantage of gathering together the battles conducted by General Sir Douglas Haig in 1915, before he came to replace Field Marshal French as Commander-in-Chief of the British Armies in France.

Many of the accusations about the Great War generals focus on Douglas Haig, and his handling of the armies tends to be the yardstick by which all the other British generals are judged. Just how well or ill he handled his awesome responsibilities will be seen in subsequent chapters, but the background to the man and his career should be known now, when he first moves to centre stage as the officer directly responsible for the planning and conduct of battles. At First Ypres, Haig was a lieutenant-general and corps commander, acting under the direct control of Field Marshal French. Now he was a full general in change of an army and responsible for its actions, though French was always hovering at his elbow, in a position to influence his decisions.

Douglas Haig, the youngest of eleven children, was born in Edinburgh on 19 June 1861. He was, therefore, just fifty-three and one of the youngest

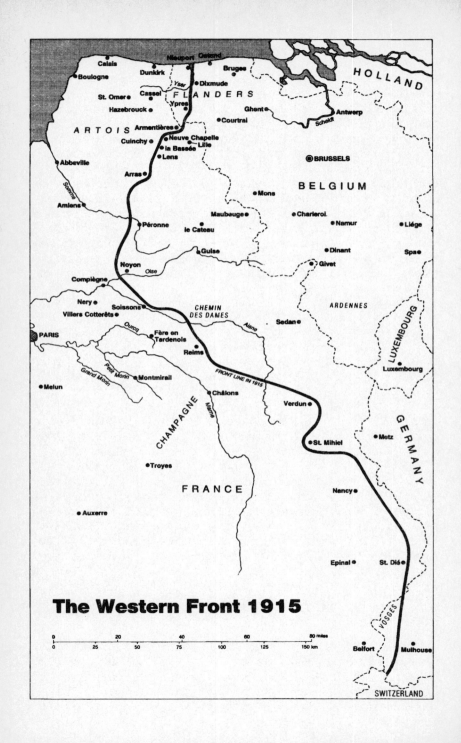

The Western Front 1915

lieutenant-generals in the Army when he went to France in August 1914. The family came from ancient Border stock with a seat at Bemersyde on the Tweed near Kelso, though Haig's father came from Fife and was a distiller of whisky. As a result the family were comfortably off but, being 'in trade', were not regarded as members of the landed gentry. Like John French, Haig was a cavalry officer, having been commissioned into the 7th Hussars in 1885 at the somewhat advanced age of twenty-four because he had been to university. He spent three years at Oxford, where he did well academically but, having missed a qualifying term, left without taking a degree. He then went to the Royal Military College, Sandhurst, in 1884 as a university candidate, and passed out first of his class after the one-year course.

Haig was the exception to many officers of his time in that he devoted a great deal of energy to the study of his profession. This still left plenty of time for leisure pursuits, however. Haig excelled at polo, and had the money to buy good ponies; the 7th Hussars won the Inter-Regimental Polo Cup in 1886, and Haig was in the British team which beat the USA in an international match later that year.

In December 1886 the 7th Hussars went to India, and by July 1888 Haig was a captain and adjutant of the regiment. He spent four years as adjutant and then took command of a squadron in 1892, before returning to England to sit the Staff College entrance exam, which he failed. He returned to India and the 7th Hussars, and devoted himself to his regimental duties until recalled to England as ADC to the Inspector-General of Cavalry. This appointment lasted a year and when it ended Haig joined the staff of Colonel John French, who had recently been charged with writing a new Cavalry Drill Book. When French went to another appointment, Haig took on the task and the new – or much revised – Cavalry Drill Book, by Colonel French and Captain Haig, duly appeared, in two volumes, in 1896.

This work brought Haig to the notice of the High Command and in February 1896 he was nominated for a place on the next staff course, entering the Junior Division at Camberley without having to sit the entrance examination again. This two-year staff course was attended by a number of men who would feature in Haig's future career: Edmund Allenby of the cavalry; James Edmonds, a Sapper who would later become the Official Historian of the Great War on the Western Front; as well as various competent officers, like Captains T.E. Capper and William Robertson, who were also at Camberley at this time. Haig clearly did well, for the Chief Instructor, Lieutenant-Colonel G.F.R. Henderson, is alleged to have remarked that he would one day be the Commander-in-Chief of the British Army.

Douglas Haig next saw some active service, joining Major-General Kitchener's 1898 campaign in the Sudan against the Dervishes, a war which culminated in the Battle of Omdurman, and during which Haig served in the Egyptian cavalry. Though still a captain in the British Army, Haig was appointed Major – bimbashi – in the Egyptian Army, and served as Chief of

Staff to the commander of the cavalry, Colonel Broadwood, at the Battles of the Atbara and Omdurman.

After this campaign Haig became a brevet major, a man marked for promotion, and returned to the UK in November 1898 to become Brigade Major of 1 Cavalry Brigade at Aldershot, under the now Major-General John French. The two men already knew each other and this acquaintance-ship must have deepened, for later that year Haig loaned French the then considerable sum of £2,000 to cover losses French had suffered from speculating in South African gold shares. This action enabled French to pay his debts and remain in the service, which soon took both men to the South African War of 1899–1902, French as commander of the cavalry, Haig as his Deputy Acting Adjutant-General (DAAG). They arrived in South Africa on 10 October 1899, the day before the Boers declared war.

Like French, Haig had a 'good war' in South Africa, and he emerged from the conflict with an enhanced reputation and some useful promotion, rising from brevet major to lieutenant-colonel. He also took area responsibility for part of the Orange Free State, and was appointed to command of the 17th Lancers. (Later, on the Western Front, his personal escort would always be found from this regiment.) He had gained some useful experience in that three-year débâcle, but – like French – he remained firmly convinced that the shock of the *arme blanche* cavalry charge was still a battle-winning tactic, and was also a stout opponent of the growing use of mounted infantry as a replacement for the cavalry in its traditional role.

Haig returned to England in 1902 in command of the 17th Lancers, relinquishing that post in 1903 to go to India as a colonel, rising on arrival to the rank of local major-general and taking up the post of Inspector-General of Cavalry under the Commander-in-Chief India, Lord Kitchener. In 1906, after three years in India, Haig returned to Britain, but the period had been marked by two significant events. In 1905, after a whirlwind one-month courtship, he married Dorothy Vivian, sister of a brother officer, Lord Vivian, who had served in the 17th Lancers during the South African War. The Honourable Dorothy was one of the Queen's ladies-in-waiting, and this match therefore marked a further advance in Haig's already extensive social connections.

Haig also wrote a book, a worthy if misguided work entitled *Cavalry Studies, Strategical and Tactical*. This book draws on his experience as Inspector-General of Cavalry in India and contains much good advice on the handling of cavalry regiments, but it also offers some intriguing insights into what Haig saw as the cavalry's part in a major war.

'The role of cavalry on the battlefield will always go on increasing,' he avers, and 'the greater range and killing power of modern weapons will cause panic and render troops ripe for attack by cavalry'. What such weapons would do to cavalry formations is not discussed. Haig also considered that cavalry action will be favoured by 'the introduction of the small-bore rifle, the bullet from which has little stopping power against the horse'.* It is true that a horse will run a good way after being hit by a bullet, but the outcome of rifle or machine-gun fire against cavalry formations cannot be in doubt, so this is a very curious assertion indeed. General Sir James Marshall Cornwall, otherwise a great supporter of Haig, sums up these and other comments as indications that the latter 'could certainly not be considered among the prophets', and that his faith in the future role of cavalry was 'a pipe dream'. (*Haig as Military Commander*, 1973.)

Haig's views on cavalry, if disparaged today, were received with respect in 1906, and he came to be considered as both a thinking soldier and a coming man. On returning to England in 1906 he was snapped up as Military Secretary by another Lowland Scot, Richard Haldane, later Lord Haldane, Secretary of State for War, the man charged by the Liberal Government with reorganising the British Army and completing the reforms started in the previous century by Cardwell.

Haig stayed at the War Office from 1906 to 1909 and played a significant part in developing the General Staff concept, the development of the Territorial Force and the all-important reorganisation of the British Army into an Expeditionary Force of six infantry divisions and a cavalry division. His next appointment was as Director of Military Training (DMT), responsible for training areas, methods, schools of instruction and the writing and publication of training manuals. In 1907 he was appointed Director, Staff Duties at the General Staff Directorate, remaining there until 1909 when he went to India as Chief of the General Staff to the new Commander-in-Chief India, General Sir O'Moore Creagh. On taking up this appointment Haig was knighted by King Edward VII at Balmoral, and spent a few days with the royal family before sailing with Lady Haig for India. During this latest period of service there his Assistant Military Secretary was the then Captain John Charteris of the Royal Engineers, the man who would become Haig's Intelligence Chief during the Great War.

Haldane did not forget his useful subordinate and in 1911 he wrote offering Lieutenant-General Haig the Aldershot Command, which he only took over from Smith-Dorrien in March 1912. The assumption was that the officer commanding at Aldershot would automatically take command of I Corps of the BEF should Britain go to war during his appointment, and so it proved: when war broke out in August 1914 that post duly fell into General Haig's lap. From this circumstance a great deal followed, so that it is useful to see what conclusions can be drawn from Haig's life and career up to that date.

From the military point of view, Douglas Haig must be regarded as an officer of much experience and considerable efficiency and therefore an ideal man for this challenging task. He was clearly very ambitious and socially

---

* Apart from greatly increasing the power, and thus the range, of weapons, the coming of 'smokeless' propellants also allowed a reduction in rifle calibres; the British service rifle dropping by nearly 33 per cent from .455-inch (black powder) to .303-inch. Other nations also reduced the calibre of their service rifles.

well connected, no bar to promotion at any time, and was particularly useful in the British Army in the years before the Great War when the monarchs – both Edward VII and his successor George V – took a great interest in military affairs and exerted considerable influence on staff and command appointments.

The later doubts that arose, and which continue to arise, over Haig's professional competence often seem to stem from his personal manner and private actions. The Border Scots tend to be dour, but even so Douglas Haig was noticeably taciturn, if not actually inarticulate, much given to long and heavy silences, often interpreted as rudeness or indifference. He was certainly not above intrigue and back-stabbing. During his service in the Sudan he wrote private letters to Field Marshal Sir Evelyn Wood, then Commander-in-Chief of the British Army, criticising the actions of his superior officer, Major-General Kitchener, and he was to repeat this clandestine correspondence in 1914 and 1915, writing to Kitchener and the King about the performance of his current superior officer, Field Marshal French.

Haig was apt to denigrate anyone who he felt might bar his path to the top, but there is little doubt that he was a very efficient soldier. He was also a far more decent human being than he is usually given credit for. His private Great War diaries, while they contain some unkind comments about his colleagues, also record him shopping with his wife before attending meetings of the Cabinet, and taking his children to a pantomime before rushing off for an audience with King George V. During the Great War he felt the losses among his men deeply, took great care of his wounded and, according to his son, would have visited field hospitals more frequently had the sights there not made him physically ill. Haig knew that his inability to express emotion told against him, and there is a sad note to that effect in a letter he wrote to his wife in April 1917:

> I am very glad to hear from you that those serving under me have an affection for me. As you know, I don't go out of my way to make myself popular, either by doing showy things or by being slack in the matter of discipline – I never hesitate to find fault but I have myself a tremendous affection for those fine fellows who are ready to give their lives for the Old Country at any moment and I feel quite sad at times, when I see them march past me knowing as I do how many must pay the full penalty before we can have peace.

Haig was the man in command, the man who had to order the attacks, and take the blame if and when they failed. He carried a great weight of responsibility for what happened, and the burden not only clearly told on him, but grew heavier with the years. To portray Douglas Haig as a bloodless, unfeeling autocrat is to pervert the truth.

Even so, Haig was not without faults, some of them decidedly distasteful. He certainly had a good opinion of his own abilities, and his backstairs manoeuvrings to obtain the BEF command can stick in the throat of anyone who reads about them. From the moment of his appointment as Commander of I Corps in 1914, he carped to the King and anyone else who would listen, about the character and competence of Sir John French – his friend – whom he declared to be both temperamentally and professionally unsuited to the post of Commander-in-Chief. While motoring around the lines at Aldershot in August 1914 with George V, Haig told the King that while he was 'sure Field Marshal French would do his utmost to carry out any orders the Government might give', he felt grave doubts whether French's temper was 'sufficiently even or his military knowledge sufficiently thorough to enable him to discharge properly the very difficult duties which will devolve upon him during the coming operations, though he thought it sufficient to tell the King that he had doubts about French's selection.' (Robert Blake [ed.], *The Private Papers of Douglas Haig*, 1952.) The fact that Haig was right in this assessment does not make his actions at the time – and later – any less distasteful. Haig also took care to bask in French's public approval, as expressed in the latter's letters and dispatches from France, and also gently to fan the flames of French's antagonism against Haig's colleague and rival, General Sir Horace Smith-Dorrien.

In the context of a great war, these petty squabbles among the generals, this evidence that they were not above spite and envy, might not seem to matter. The only point at issue is, or should be, were they efficient? Did they act wisely and do their best to win battles at a minimum cost in lives? Whether they did or not was largely determined by the circumstances of the time, but neither can the *character* of the individual general be ruled out of the equation. A reckless general will take chances, a cautious general will hesitate, a man subject to outside influences – like Field Marshal French – will be constantly changing his mind.

Haig's character too requires consideration. Clearly, he was a steady, careful, resolute man, one of the kind who plan carefully, which is all to the good, but are then reluctant to change their mind or admit defeat, however obvious the signs. The one accusation that can certainly be levelled against Haig is that he did not always know when to give up. Behind that dour façade he was, perhaps surprisingly, an optimist, always convinced that one more effort, one more attack, one last heave would win the day and justify the losses so far. Haig had not heard of, or did not grasp, the law of diminishing returns, though it is a law that applies on the field of battle as well as in the field of economics. His failure to understand this would cost Haig's armies dear in the years ahead.

This chapter will look at three short battles in 1915, all of them in the First Army area: Neuve Chapelle, Aubers Ridge and Festubert (the Battle of Loos will be described in the following chapter). Unlike the fighting at First and Second Ypres, these were all 'setpiece' battles, at least initially, in which a plan was drawn up for every stage of the engagement before the first round was fired. The fact that these plans went wrong is hardly surprising, for such plans – for any battle, in any war – rarely survive the first encounter with the enemy. What these three battles will illustrate, however, is what Haig was trying to do throughout 1915, and why it went wrong.

During 1915 the BEF was still the junior partner in the Anglo-French alliance, fighting battles which were either thrust upon it, as at Second Ypres, or which formed part of a French offensive campaign. The main strategic aim of General Joffre was to cut off the 'Noyon Salient', that great bend in the French line which came to an apex near Noyon, just fifty-five miles east of Paris, and which marked the limits of the German advance in 1914. Joffre's plan for 1915 was to attack this bulge in the enemy's line from the north and south – that is, from Artois and Champagne – and force the German troops in the Noyon Salient either to retreat or to allow themselves to be cut off. For this he required as much assistance as he could get from the gradually expanding BEF.

Haig's First Army occupied the line on the right of the Second Army, holding the ground roughly between the southern end of the Ypres Salient and the flatlands below the steep slopes of Vimy Ridge, where the British line ran into that of the French Tenth Army. Field Marshal French intended to 'box' with his two armies, putting Smith-Dorrien's Second Army on the defensive at Ypres while using Haig's First Army to strike some telling blows south of Armentières, because, Haig records in his diary, 'he [French] could never be certain of getting satisfactory results from Smith-Dorrien and because my troops were better.' The Germans, however, were not party to this decision and struck some telling blows of their own at Second Ypres. Before that, though, Haig took his army into action at Neuve Chapelle.

The Battle of Neuve Chapelle was planned as part of a combined Anglo-French attack, in which the British would break through the German line and take Aubers Ridge, while the French on their right captured Vimy Ridge. Aubers Ridge, twenty miles long and about forty feet in height, spanned the British front north from La Bassée, at a distance of between one and four miles east of the British trenches. Taking the ridge was an appealing plan, for behind it lay higher, drier ground and easy access to the town of Lille. The first step towards its capture was to eliminate the German salient at the village of Neuve Chapelle, a mile west of the ridge.

With these commanding features in their possession the Anglo-French armies would then seize the coalpits and factories of the Douai plain. In mid-February 1915, however, Joffre commenced a series of attacks in Champagne, and the effort there gradually drained his commitment to an attack in March on Vimy Ridge, though he did not tell Field Marshal French that this attack had been cancelled until 7 March. In such circumstances – and bearing in mind the chronic British shortage of heavy guns and artillery ammunition – it would have been wise to cancel the Neuve Chapelle operation, but French was anxious to disabuse his ally of the notion that the British Army was only useful for holding a defensive line, but no help at all in driving the enemy out of France and Belgium. It can be said, therefore, that the battle of Neuve Chapelle in March 1915 was fought as much to prove a point as to achieve an objective.

However, the attack did have a physical objective. The country around Neuve Chapelle is dreary, a flat plain devoted to arable farming, seamed with narrow streams and wet ditches, overlooked by the slag heaps of the local coalmines, by the loom of Vimy Ridge to the south and, a mile or so behind the German line, by the long shoulder of Aubers Ridge. Today, cloaked with trees and dotted with houses, Aubers Ridge is easy to overlook but in 1915 any piece of higher ground was vital, as had been proved in the Salient. Aubers Ridge provided the German artillery with the height that allowed good observation, and also barred the road to Lille and the Douai plain; its capture would be extremely useful. The road on to Aubers Ridge lay through the village of Neuve Chapelle, which the Germans had seized in 1914. Their front-line positions now lay just west of the village, which was in ruins, while behind the village lay a trench, now, of course, in German hands, dug by II Corps soldiers in 1914 and therefore known as the 'Smith-Dorrien Line'. These three positions, the German front line, the village and the Smith-Dorrien Line, were the immediate objectives of the Battle of Neuve Chapelle. (See map on p. 194.)

Haig's Operation Order No. 9, dated 8 March 1915, laid out the plan for the attack that would take place two days later. The aim was to force the enemy's lines at Neuve Chapelle and drive his forces back from the line Aubers–Ligny-le-Grand, with the object of cutting off his troops holding the front between La Bassée and Neuve Chapelle. This attack enjoyed the advantage of superior numbers, for the German Sixth Army line at Neuve Chapelle was thinly held. The German VII Corps had only two divisions facing the six divisions of First Army between the La Bassée Canal and the Bois Grenier, and Haig was able to tell his men on the eve of the battle that he was 'sending 48 battalions to attack a locality held by three German battalions'. This assessment was quite accurate, but did not allow for the German heavy guns, or a flat terrain ideal for the deployment and use of machine-guns, or the enemy's ability to move up reinforcements rapidly.

The assault would be made against the salient jutting into the British line at Neuve Chapelle, between two points known as the Moated Grange and Port Arthur. The initial attack would be made by Lieutenant-General Rawlinson's IV Corps and Lieutenant-General Sir James Willcocks's Indian Corps, the 8th Division of the former corps attacking from the west, and the Meerut Division of the Indian Corps attacking from the south. Their attacks would be supported by a short but fierce thirty-five-minute bombardment by the corps and divisional artillery. The available artillery totalled 530 guns of various calibres, over half of them being 18-pounder field guns which were detailed for wire-cutting. The German line was thin as well as thinly manned, but it was supported by various strongpoints equipped with machine-guns and platoons of men, in Neuve Chapelle itself, at the flanks, and along a shallow stream called the Layes Brook that ran behind the village. The problem for the British on this narrow front was not so much a shortage of guns, but a lack of ammunition, especially high-explosive ammunition capable of destroying entrenchments, defensive positions and barbed-wire entanglements.

In fact, Field Marshal French had now taken steps to minimise the effects of the artillery shortage. Firstly, divisional artillery was taken from divisional control and placed in 'zones' along the front. This was a sensible move, as divisions were always being moved about and shifted between corps, and their artillery would otherwise have had constantly to re-lay and register their guns on fresh targets. Now they provided gunfire support for a section of the front, whatever division was holding or attacking in that section. The second move was an attempt to make the best use of the heavy guns – 8-inch calibre and above – which were now organised in Heavy Artillery Reserve (HAR) groups, each commanded by a brigadier-general, from which they were allocated by GHQ to any army which had particular need of them, though before long each army had its own HAR group. But even these moves, however useful, could not make up for the fact that the BEF was very short of artillery, especially heavy artillery, and chronically short of shells.

For the coming attack, the bombardment would start at 0730 hours and lift at 0805, when the British and Indian infantry assaulted the German front-line trenches before Neuve Chapelle and the Bois de Biez, which lies just to the south-east of the village. While they were doing so, the barrage would lift to pound the village for a further half-hour and the infantry, having taken the German front line, would advance on the village at 0835. Other units in First Army, including I Corps and the Canadian Division (which was then part of First Army), would act or 'demonstrate' on their front with rifle or artillery fire to indicate a pending attack, and so prevent the Germans moving reinforcements to Neuve Chapelle.

Neuve Chapelle was not envisaged as a major engagement. This was a 'bite and hold' operation on a frontage of just 2,000 yards, as part of an overall plan to seize a useful objective – Aubers Ridge – and would initially involve just two divisions plus whatever artillery and ammunition the BEF could spare. When and if the Neuve Chapelle position had been breached Haig would then press on to Aubers Ridge. The shortage of artillery ammunition was to bedevil Haig in March as much as it was Smith-Dorrien in April, and the former's plan for Neuve Chapelle allowed for the fact that he only had enough ammunition for three days, though the short opening bombardment – just thirty-five minutes – also offered the useful advantage of surprise.

Haig made careful preparations for his attack, and these cannot be faulted. The three brigades listed for the assault – the Garhwal Brigade from the Meerut Division of the Indian Corps, and 23 and 25 Brigades from the 8th Division of IV Corps – were withdrawn from the line on 2 March for rest and training. This last included a careful briefing of every officer, who then, equally carefully, briefed the men on what was to happen and what they were to do. Supplies of ammunition, food and water were moved up to the front, the German front line was carefully but unobtrusively registered by the guns, and at 0730 hours on 10 March 1915 the artillery blared out before Neuve Chapelle. Half an hour later the infantry went over the top.

At first all went well, for the initial bombardment had done its work. The German wire had been cut or levelled, their trenches had been destroyed by shellfire and those of the enemy who were not dead or wounded had either fled to the rear, or were too shocked to offer much resistance. The assaulting infantry from the 8th Division took the first-line trench and moved on to occupy the support trench about 200 yards in the rear, waiting there while the artillery did its work on the defenders of Neuve Chapelle. The bombardment lifted again at 0835 and the infantry advanced swiftly into the village and out to the country beyond, to the Layes Brook and the Smith-Dorrien Line. This latter position was reached by the Indians at 0900 hours and since the trench was found to be full of water, the troops took up position fifty yards in rear and began to dig in.

The enemy front had been broken as planned, though only on a front of 1,600 yards, for the Germans still held strong positions on either flank. The British and Indian troops were now advancing to and even beyond the Smith-Dorrien Line, where they were held up by the fire of their own artillery pounding the country ahead.

Contact was established between the leading troops of the 8th Division, attacking from the north, and the Garhwal Brigade of the Indian Corps coming from the south, reserve brigades of both divisions were coming forward, and by mid-morning all seemed to be going well. The only snag was the heavy machine-gun fire coming from enemy strongpoints on the flanks, and a steadily increasing weight of artillery fire from German guns behind Aubers Ridge. By 1330 hours all the first-phase objectives had been taken, including the village of Neuve Chapelle and the Smith-Dorrien Line. The only German position still untaken from the first objectives was a 200-yard length of trench at Port Arthur on the Indian Corps' front. The advancing brigades had done well, and were now ordered to consolidate, hold the ground gained and wait for the arrival of reserves.

Delays plagued the attack at Neuve Chapelle, and these delays had begun early in the operation. At 0900 hours, hearing that the German line had been breached, Haig asked Field Marshal French to move up at least one cavalry brigade so that if the enemy front collapsed he would be able to keep contact with the retreating Germans and prevent them digging in again. Two hours later French ordered 5th Cavalry Brigade to Estaires, three miles north-west of Neuve Chapelle, where Haig anticipated a further advance by the rest of IV Corps and the Indian Corps. Nothing happened.

The crux of the problem was the difficulty of communication with the front-line units. Rawlinson did not intend to move his reserves forward until the situation on his front was clear, and at that time he believed that some of the German positions were still untaken. Lacking precise information, he did not move the 7th Division forward to support the 8th until 1315 hours, and it was not until 1400, *five hours* after the German positions and strongpoints around Neuve Chapelle had been taken, that the former division was ordered to advance towards Aubers Ridge. A similar delay had occurred on the Indian Corps front, where General Willcocks was still encountering resistance from the German salient at Port Arthur, and was waiting for news of IV Corps before advancing. The two corps commanders were determined to move together and Willcocks was not yet ready to advance on his next objective, the Bois du Biez. This led to further delays in the two corps

At 1445 hours, both corps commanders received a message from Haig, saying he was 'most anxious' that they should advance. The damage had been done, however, for this five-hour delay after the initial breakthrough permitted the ever-resilient Germans to muster their reserves and dig in on their second line, a good position near the crest of Aubers Ridge from where a heavy crossfire from rifles and machine-guns could rake any troops advancing from Neuve Chapelle. The British advance began again, though it was not until 1730 hours that the two leading battalions of the 7th Division moved out towards Aubers Ridge. Other battalions did not move until 1800, when it was starting to get dark, and none got very far among the ditches and fences. Those troops advancing over open country between Neuve Chapelle and Aubers were subjected to heavy fire and brought to a halt, and it was no better to the south-east, where the Indian Corps had advanced into the trees of the Bois du Biez and encountered stiff and increasing resistance. By nightfall, the attack at Neuve Chapelle had clearly stalled.

Even so, if all had not gone exactly as planned, General Haig was not entirely dissatisfied. His men had advanced about 1,200 yards on a 4,000-yard front, and had taken Neuve Chapelle and the trenches beyond it. They had not taken the German second line or any part of Aubers Ridge, but much might be done on the following day. During the night both sides were busy, bringing up reinforcements and preparing to renew the battle at first light. The Germans brought up more machine-guns, dug deeper trenches on their second line and reinforced their strongpoints, they also sent up a fresh brigade, 14 Bavarian Reserve Brigade, specifically tasked to counter-attack and retake Neuve Chapelle at dawn, without artillery preparation. Fortunately for the British this brigade was delayed and its attack was therefore postponed, but other German units were now speeding in from either flank to seal the breach in their line at Neuve Chapelle.

Haig's orders for 11 March were to continue the attack and press on, IV Corps towards Aubers Ridge, the Indian Corps in support with an advance through the Bois du Biez. This advance was to commence at 0700 hours and 'to be pressed vigorously as from information received it appears the enemy before us is in no great strength'.

Haig's 'information' is best described as sketchy. Air reconnaissance the previous day had seen German units marching on Neuve Chapelle but had not sighted any troop trains, so Haig assumed that the only German reinforcements likely to have arrived overnight were from local divisions. In fact, by dawn on the 11th, the German Sixth Army had mustered twenty battalions in front of Neuve Chapelle ready to stem the British advance and it should have been obvious that on the second day, with surprise lost and the enemy strength and defences improving, the task before Haig's troops would be harder than on the first day.

So it proved. The day was misty, making artillery registration on the new German trenches or battery positions ineffective, though the advancing British infantry soon came under fire from German artillery and machine-guns firing blindly into no man's land. In the 7th Division 20 Brigade lost heavily, while the men of 21 Brigade were forced to halt and dig shell-scrapes. In the 8th Division 24 Brigade was unable to get forward in the face of machine-gun fire. The German bombardment on the area in rear of Neuve Chapelle was so heavy that all the telephone lines were cut, and runners from the advancing battalions of the 7th and 8th Divisions were unable to move across the open ground to let commanders know what was going on. Telephone lines had been run forward overnight but these were soon cut by the heavy German artillery fire that began just after dawn.

The same tale applies to the Indian Corps, which encountered heavy resistance from the start. There was also a confusion over orders, with the commander of the Dehra Dun Brigade convinced that he should not advance until 25 Brigade of the 8th Division arrived in his rear at Neuve Chapelle. The latter brigade was in fact in divisional reserve so, as the Official History observes, the Dehra Dun Brigade 'waited in vain for its arrival'. The Jullundur Brigade took cover in and around Neuve Chapelle but otherwise the Indian Corps did not move at all, and as communications broke down all along the front under the rain of shells and the sweep of machine-gun fire, so the second day's attacks petered out. The Germans had by now managed to dig in and establish a second defence line in front of Aubers, but Haig and his corps commanders were not yet aware of this. Even had they been informed, the sheer impossibility of contacting the front-line units would have prevented the proper organisation of another attack. The only order that went forward was that the attack 'must be pressed home vigorously' and this the leading brigades and battalions were already trying to do, supported by artillery that had not yet registered its guns on the new enemy line and therefore failed to hit it.

As a result, casualties were mounting, and some battalion commanders were already ordering their men to stop advancing and dig in where they were. Lieutenant-Colonel Pritchard of the 1st Worcesters (24 Brigade, 8th Division), called off his battalion attack, telling his brigade commander that 'It is a mere waste of life, impossible to go to 20 yards, much less 200 yards. The [enemy] trenches have not been touched by artillery.' By this time

24 Brigade had already suffered severe casualties, another battalion, the 2nd Northamptonshire, Regiment having been reduced to 12 officers and 320 other ranks. Other battalions in both corps suffered in similar proportion.

There is no need to go on describing this part of the battle. Communications had broken down, the British artillery had not been able to register on the new German positions, and chaos was reigning. The Germans had recovered from their initial surprise; already strong, they were growing stronger as more men and guns were brought up to contain the breakthrough around Neuve Chapelle. Haig's ability to co-ordinate a viable plan for the second day of his battle had been fatally compromised by the fact that he was unable to communicate with the front-line battalions, or to co-ordinate the fire of the artillery on to the defence lines the Germans had flung up overnight.

The first day of 'setpiece' battle, which had gone broadly according to plan, had disintegrated into another series of 'advance to contact' engagements along the front. These actions saw the British and Indian infantry rise from their trenches to be met at once with a storm of machine-gun and artillery fire from positions which would need to be reduced by artillery before they could be overcome. To his credit, Haig realised this. He went forward to view the battle on the evening of the 11th and ordered the guns to be brought up closer to the front and ranged on the enemy trenches, intending to renew the attack towards Aubers Ridge at 1030 hours on the following morning.

When a commander is not otherwise engaged he cannot be more usefully employed than in calculating what the enemy might be doing. General Haig had a great deal to do on the night of 11–12 March, but had he considered the enemy's reaction, it would have been clear that the Germans would be reinforcing their line and probably preparing to counter-attack, the latter being the usual military response to any seizure of ground. This is exactly what the Germans were doing, bringing six fresh battalions into the line and preparing for a push west on a front between Mauquissart and the Bois du Biez; other units also arrived until by dawn on the 12th the Germans had ten battalions in the front line, four in support and six in reserve – ten battalions which, at an average of 800 men per battalion, gave them 8,000 men for the counter-attack. This was delivered at 0500 hours after a violent half-hour artillery bombardment. Mist shrouded the ground and the German infantry were within sixty yards of the British line before they were detected.

In the event, the counter-attack failed with great loss, as the German infantry withered away before the rifle and machine-gun fire of the British and Indian soldiers – once again proving that the practice of sending in waves of infantry to take well-defended positions was not confined to the British generals. The French and – as demonstrated here – the Germans, also used this tactic with the same dire results. The Germans left over 400 dead before the trench of the 1st Sherwood Foresters (Nottinghamshire and

Derbyshire Regiment). Two hundred Germans, dead and wounded, lay before the trench lines of the Garhwal Rifles and another hundred dead before the trenches occupied by the (2nd Yorkshire Regiment better known as the Green Howards). The survivors of the attack on the 2nd North-amptonshire retired to their trenches, as the Official History puts it, 'pursued by bullets and losing heavily'.

The enemy's counter-attack might have been repulsed, but in Haig's command poor communications between divisional and brigade HQs and the front-line battalions meant that that the repulse was not followed up, and no attempts were made to turn the Germans out of their defences. General Haig was determined to stick to his original plan for a setpiece attack, and did not intend to be diverted from this aim by any local success along his front.

The problem now rested with the artillery. Communications were difficult and visibility restricted, for that mist which had concealed the German infantry at dawn still concealed their trenches a few hours later. The British guns were reduced to 'firing off the map', with no idea where their shells were actually landing, and no information from which to correct the fall of shot. The attack was to go in at 1030 hours after a half-hour bombardment, but at 0920 General Rawlinson reported that certain German strongpoints on his front had not yet been hit, let alone subdued. Haig therefore put back the attack until 1120 hours, to allow time for the mist to clear and the artillery to engage the German line. The assault finally went in at 1230 and met with mixed fortunes.

In 8th Division's sector, 25 Brigade lost heavily in the first half-hour, after which Brigadier-General Lowry Cole halted the attack and told the div-isional commander, Major-General Davies, that it was pointless to attack again until his advance was concealed by darkness. The other brigade earmarked for the assault, 24 Brigade, had not fully reorganised after repulsing the German counter-attack and did not attack at all, while the last brigade in the division, 23 Brigade, remained in divisional reserve. On the 7th Division front, the message postponing the attack did not reach the leading battalions, for the runners bringing it had been killed. The two leading battalions, Scots Guards and the 2nd Border Regiment, therefore advanced at 1030 hours and were brought to a halt by machine-gun fire after a hundred yards. They stayed in the open while artillery fire pounded the German defences and then advanced with the bayonet, taking some 400 prisoners. Once again, though, communications between the front line and Divisional HQ broke down, and this led to further confusion as to the extent and location of the division's advance towards Aubers Ridge

The advance of the Indian Corps went in at 1300, half an hour after the attack by IV Corps. The two leading formations, the Sirhind and Jullundur Brigades of the Lahore Division, pushed towards the Bois du Biez but encountered heavy machine-gun and artillery fire and came to a halt by 1345 hours.

Confusion caused by poor communications was now seeping into Haig's HQ, where messages recounting the repulse of the German counter-attack that morning were only now being absorbed. The notion that the 7th Division had actually succeeded in breaking through the German defences along the Mauquissart road north of Neuve Chapelle and before Aubers Ridge, had also taken hold, and at 1506 hours Haig sent an order to his troops for a further attack: 'Information indicates that enemy on our front are much demoralised. Indian Corps and IV Corps will push through barrage of fire regardless of loss, using reserves if required.'

It is hard to see how Haig came by the idea that the Germans, though repulsed that morning, were also 'demoralised'. The order to attack 're-gardless of loss' was foolish, for if casualties are too high an attack cannot be sustained. It seems likely that, frustrated by the delays in communication that had plagued his battle so far, Haig now wished to seize the moment, this 'promising situation' as he called it, when – according to reports from 7th Division HQ – there was a gap in the German line which he must exploit before it was closed.

Haig can hardly be blamed for any of the delays in information reaching his HQ, or for that information's inaccuracy. He can, however, be blamed for failing to calculate the probable enemy reaction, and for failing to allow for the limitations imposed by the state of the communication of the time. Battlefield communications in 1915 were primitive, aerial observation during the operation was inhibited by mist and shell smoke, and for two days he had been trying to push his men forward quickly before the enemy could regroup, only to be thwarted by a succession of delays. After the successful repulse of the German counter-attack a rapid advance was the right thing to do, at least in theory. Haig therefore ordered up reserves, asked Field Marshal French to send the cavalry forward, and prepared for a general advance. Unfortunately, thanks to the mist and the chronic lack of accurate information, this intention was based on a false premise, for the new German line before Aubers Ridge had not been breached at all.

Due to the inevitable delays in passing orders forward, the attacks went in late. On the Indian Corps front it was not until 1700 hours that the Ferozepore Brigade of the Lahore Division advanced on the Bois du Biez, while further delays in organising artillery support held up the advance of the Sirhind and Jullundur Brigades of the same Division. This last brigade had suffered nearly 900 casualties during the attacks that day, about a quarter of its rifle strength, and was in no state for further action. Moreover, any advance on the left of the Indian Corps by the Ferozepore Brigade, brought up from reserve, was inhibited by fire from a still-untaken strong-point on the Layes Bridge, east of Neuve Chapelle. So the time for the new attack slipped back, to 2030 hours and then to 2230, at which time Brigadier-General Egerton, commanding the Ferozepore Brigade and in temporary command of the other two brigades, telephoned his divisional commander and stated that, in his opinion, the attack ordered was unlikely to succeed. The corps commander, General Willcocks, concurred and cancelled the attack entirely.

Similar events, all the result of poor communications, were taking place on the IV Corps front. The corps artillery was growing short of ammunition and did not fire on the Mauquissart road line, believing that it was in British hands. The 8th Division's 25 Brigade attacked as ordered at 1745 hours, only to report back within minutes that the attack had failed, every man who rose from cover being shot down, though the brigade commander, Lowry Cole, declared that he was willing to try again under cover of darkness.

The two other 8th Division formations, 23 and 24 Brigades, put in a confused attack at 0130 hours on the 13th, after more delay caused by difficulties in rounding up the battalion commanders for briefing. Those companies that did attack ran into barbed wire and machine-gun fire and the assault was called off. The rest of the night was spent by the brigade and battalion commanders trying to find out what was going on, a task made more difficult by the fact that after three days and nights without rest, the men went to sleep whenever they stopped, and were hard to find on the corpse-littered battleground. The IV Corps commander, Rawlinson, realised that his troops were fought out and needed rest and reorganisation before they could be used again.

General Haig was coming to the same conclusion. It was now clear that the German positions before Aubers Ridge had not been breached, and that the enemy had managed to construct a new line and were reinforcing it by the hour. At 2240 hours on 12 March, therefore, after talking to the corps commanders, Haig ordered that all attacks should be cancelled and that the troops should dig in and hold the positions they now occupied. This order also took some time to relay to the forward troops, with the result that local attacks were put in some hours after the Battle of Neuve Chapelle had been officially called off.

On the following morning Field Marshal French sent a cable to Lord Kitchener telling him that 'a cessation of the forward movement has been ordered owing to the fatigue of the troops and a shortage of ammunition.' Both these statements were true, but they did not tell the whole story. The weight of the battle had fallen most heavily on the divisions engaged on the first day, and these units had not been relieved or rested until after the battle had ended. It was clear from what happened that the pressure of battle quickly exhausted the attacking troops, and that adequate reserves were necessary to take over and continue the advance. The expenditure of ammunition necessary to support the initial attack, cut the wire, defend the ground taken and support any further advances far exceeded the wildest estimate made by any of the commanders. To give two explanatory statistics, the three days of Neuve Chapelle used up one-sixth of all the 18-pounder ammunition in France, and it would take seventeen days' production from Britain's entire munitions industry to replace it. Above all there was the matter of communications, the problem of finding out what was going on at the front and of passing the necessary orders forward to the infantry and back to the artillery.

Neuve Chapelle showed the new face of warfare, and underscored the difficulties any commander would face in attempting to force a passage through a defended locality. To a certain extent, Haig's opinion, as expressed to Colonel Repington in January 1915 and quoted at the head of this chapter was quite correct. Given surprise and a heavy weight of artillery it *was* possible to break through the German front – at least if that front was lightly held and not well prepared for defence.

The battle at Neuve Chapelle also enhanced the reputation of the British Army. The attack shook the commanders of the German Army, who had so far not yet taken the offensive capability of the BEF very seriously, and opened the eyes of the French to the capabilities of British troops, for this was the first occasion on which the German front line had been broken. The problems came later, when the breach had to be held and widened, further advances had to be made and the bastions of the defence, strongpoints equipped with resolute defenders, came into play and began to strafe the advancing troops. The lessons of Neuve Chapelle seemed to be that the initial attack, if successful, required an instant follow-up by fresh troops, and a great deal of pre-registered artillery support if it was to have any chance of subsequent exploitation. The cost of learning these lessons, for the British and Indians, was 12,982 men killed, wounded and missing, for a gain of about 1,000 yards and one much-battered village. How these lessons were to be applied with the existing methods of communication had still not been settled two months later, when Haig was obliged to attack again in what became the Battle of Aubers Ridge.

On 24 March, ten days after Neuve Chapelle, Joffre wrote to Field Marshal French, proposing another joint attack at some time after the end of April, partly to further his own plan for operations on the Western Front in 1915, partly in the hope that an attack in the west might blunt the large German offensive pending in Russia. Joffre also requested that the British take over more of the front line by relieving two French corps at Ypres, so that these could be employed in the coming French offensive. The BEF's commander might have pointed out that he could not take over more of the line *and* build up reserves for a major attack, but he agreed to an extension of the British line northwards into the Salient, and directed First Army to build up supplies of men and munitions for a further attack.

These plans were disrupted by the German gas attack at Second Ypres on 22 April, but before this battle began Joffre sent Field Marshal French a plan for a joint offensive in Artois, the French Tenth Army attacking between Arras and Lens towards Vimy Ridge and the Douai plain, and Haig's First Army moving on their left for yet another attack on Aubers Ridge. The details of this plan were to be worked out by Field Marshal French and General Foch, now commanding the French Northern Group of Armies (GAN).

Foch pressed his views first, proposing that the French Tenth Army, fourteen divisions and a thousand guns, should attack first on a four-mile front with Vimy Ridge as its main objective, while the British First Army was to attack a day later, the main assault between Festubert and Neuve Chapelle to be made by I Corps and the Indian Corps, supported by an attack by IV Corps thrusting in the direction of Aubers Ridge. Though Field Marshal French was usually mesmerised by Foch, on this occasion he demurred, insisting that the British attack should go in at the same time as the French assault and demanding a precise date for the launching of the combined offensive, for which he was prepared to commit ten infantry divisions, supported by six hundred guns – a hundred of them heavy – and five cavalry divisions.

By 2 May Foch was able to inform the Field Marshal that the Tenth Army would attack five days later, on the 7th. He also requested that the British attack be made on the following day – so it appears that he had again persuaded French to follow his wishes. The French Tenth Army's attack was eventually postponed, finally taking place at 1000 hours on 9 May, five hours after the British began their assault on Aubers Ridge. Since this book is principally concerned with the British generals, the Tenth Army's attack can be dealt with quickly, though the battle lasted five weeks, from 9 May to 14 June, while the battle for Aubers Ridge lasted for just one day.

Foch's offensive was preceded by a six-day-long artillery bombardment, during which the French field artillery fired 1,813,490 shells and their heavy guns 342,372. As a result of this, Tenth Army's gallant and spirited attack breached the German lines on a four-mile front and penetrated for up to two and a half miles, some small parties reaching the crest of Vimy Ridge in less than two hours. Then came a problem already all too familiar to the British generals; the French reserves were not ready for such a sudden success. Before they could be brought up to enlarge the breach and press on towards Lens and the Douai plain, the Germans had brought in reinforcements and counter-attacked, using a multitude of heavy guns. The French were pressed back from the crest of Vimy Ridge, and bitter hand-to-hand fighting went on for weeks without avail. Tens of thousand of lives were lost; indeed, the French cemetery at Neuville-la-Targette, just west of Vimy Ridge, where many of the dead now lie, is one of the largest military cemeteries in France.

The British attack on 9 May was a much briefer affair. It lasted just one day before it was called off, making the Battle of Aubers Ridge one of the shortest of the Great War engagements on the Western Front. This had not been the original plan, however; French, Haig and the corps commanders approached the battle with great optimism, believing that they had learned some useful lessons at Neuve Chapelle, and that they knew both how to breach the enemy line, and how to exploit forward thereafter. Unfortunately, the Germans had also learned a few lessons from Neuve Chapelle, and had taken steps that were to nullify all the hopes of French, Haig, and their subordinates.

French's orders were that 'The First Army will . . . break through the enemy line on its front and gain the La Bassée-Lille road, between La Bassée and Fournes [i.e. east of Aubers Ridge]. Its further advance will be directed on the line Bauvin-Don.' This called for an advance of some two miles across open country under the loom of the ridge, a place were no British soldier had yet advanced more than a thousand yards. The idea was to breach the enemy line at two points, three and a half miles apart. The two forces would then converge, I Corps and the Indian Corps advancing east, IV Corps south-east, trapping the German defenders between them and forcing a withdrawal, a small-scale version of Joffre's plan for the Noyon Salient.

It was a good plan, but one which depended on the artillery and the assaulting troops breaching the enemy line – and on the rapid movement of reserves to exploit forward thereafter. If the line could be breached, as at Neuve Chapelle, then Field Marshal French had a large reserve, consisting of the Cavalry Corps, the Indian Cavalry Corps, the 1st Canadian Division, the 51st (Highland) Division and the 50th (Northumbrian) Division (the two last being Territorial formations) standing by at two hours' notice ready to move to Haig's assistance. One lesson of Neuve Chapelle, the need for rapid support by reserve formations, appears to have been learned.

Haig explained his plan to his divisional commanders at two conferences on 27 April and 6 May. Of his two assaults, he had elected to make one north and one south of Neuve Chapelle. Once through the German line, the three corps would converge for a solid advance towards Aubers Ridge, 3,000 yards away, mopping up such strongpoints as the German position at La Cliqueterie Farm as they went, aiming to get up on to the ridge before the Germans had time to establish a new defence line. That advance should succeed in trapping a number of German battalions between the advancing British and Indian forces. That done, and with the ridge taken, the British troops would move on to their final objectives, crossing the La Bassée–Lille road to the Bauvin–Don position along the Haute-Deule Canal. This last position was *four miles* east of Aubers Ridge.

The attack would be supported by another short, violent, artillery bombardment, of only 40 minutes' duration, and for this First Army had 516 field guns and 121 heavy pieces, with the 18-pounders again detailed for the vital task of wire cutting. Haig had also laid plans for the rapid movement forward of artillery pieces, and batteries of mortars were attached to the assault battalions for use against enemy strongpoints. These mortars and some light artillery – 3-pounder Hotchkiss and 'mountain guns' – were to be sent forward on lorries or armoured cars. Clearly another lesson of Neuve Chapelle, the need for the rapid shift forward of artillery support, had also been noted by General Haig.

Haig also laid plans to disperse the 'fog of war' – lack of information on the position of his troops – by having three RFC machines tasked with flying 'contact patrols' over the front, and reporting back constantly on the movement of troops. To aid this task the infantry were equipped with white observation panels which they were to lay before any static position. Much of this may sound primitive today, but these air-to-ground contact practices became common, worked fairly well, and remained in use even in the Second World War. Their introduction here shows a degree of foresight and initiative on Haig's part, as well as a readiness to face problems and seek workable solutions. In addition to these new ideas a great deal of work was done preparing the troops for the task of crossing wide ditches, providing them with light bridges and with accurate maps prepared from aerial photographs.

In sum, General Haig had decided to repeat the methods of Neuve Chapelle, having taken steps to remedy what he saw as the faults in that engagement. He opted for a short bombardment because that had given him the advantage of surprise at Neuve Chapelle, and he had taken steps to remedy or reduce the problems encountered in that battle of sending up reinforcements, supplying artillery support, and finding out what was actually going on. When, therefore, he gave the order for the Aubers Ridge attack, he felt confident of success. Many of his troops felt much the same way.

The prospect of success was enhanced by the fact that although the Germans had good views over the British front line from Aubers Ridge, they did not seem to notice preparations for the pending attack until the day before the battle began. However, their defences were already much stronger than they had been in March. There were now three strong enemy divisions on the First Army front between the La Bassée Canal and the Bois Grenier – the 14th, 13th and 6th Bavarian Reserve – and every night for the last two months the German commanders had sent out working parties to improve their defences and build more strongpoints. Parapets were heightened to six or seven feet, deep bunkers, equipped with pumps to keep out the water, were dug into the ridge to shelter the troops; sandbagged breastworks, too strong for the shells of field artillery to pierce, were erected. They had also sited more machine-guns to enfilade the front, and laid thickets and hedges of barbed wire. As a result of all this the Battle of Aubers Ridge would prove to be a good deal harder than that of Neuve Chapelle.

What happened on 9 May can be quickly told. The bombardment began at 0500 hours, and at 0540 the guns lifted from the German front line and the infantry went over the top. On the I Corps front the assault was delivered by Major-General Richard Haking's Ist Division, with Major-General Henry Horne's 2nd Division in reserve . . . three miles behind the front line. Haking's leading battalions, which had moved out into no man's land before Zero hour, rose up when the bombardment lifted – and were greeted with a curtain of fire from the German line. The supporting waves were shot down as they left their trenches, and within minutes the Ist Division's attack had stalled before German positions untouched or unsubdued by the artillery.

The Indian Corps attack was led by the three brigades of the Meerut Division (the Dehra Dun, Garhwal and Bareilly Brigades), with the Lahore Division in reserve. It was the same story; the troops were unable to advance more than a few yards from their trenches before being shot down. The initial bombardment had completely failed to quell the enemy machine-gunners or do much harm to the German defences; that shortage of heavy, trench-smashing artillery was having the usual effect. Moreover, the fire plan had been too optimistic and the bombardment had moved on too quickly. The shell cover was now falling well behind the German trenches, so that their defenders were able to move about in safety, serve their weapons, and take a heavy toll of the British and Indian infantry now stuck in the open.

There was no means of calling the guns back, for the telephone lines from the front line to the artillery battery positions had already been cut – unlike the barbed wire before the German trenches, which had hardly been cut at all. By 0720 hours General Haking was reporting the situation to Corps HQ, asking for permission to commit 1 (Guards) Brigade, but adding that even if the entire 2nd Division came forward from reserve, it could not achieve much against uncut wire and undamaged defences. In the last hour his division alone had more than 2,000 men killed and wounded, and the British attack had stalled all along the line.

By 0800 news of the check to the initial attack had got back to Haig's headquarters, but the full extent of the problem had not been realised. He therefore decided to try again at noon, ordering I Corps and the Indian Corps to reorganise their units for another push. He then went to visit the headquarters of the Indian Corps, and there realised for the first time the seriousness of the position. Responding to this, Haig ordered the artillery to repeat their original fire plan for the second attack and pound the German trench line thoroughly, switching the 18-pounders from wire-cutting shrapnel ammunition to high-explosive shells directed against the enemy trenches. This was a sensible tactic, for barbed wire is only an effective defence if it is covered by fire; if the artillery could knock out the machine-guns and riflemen, the wire could be penetrated. Even so, it was clear that the Indian battalions had been severely mauled, and Haig therefore postponed his second attack, first to 1440 and then to 1600 hours.

The British artillery had not been idle meanwhile, firing steadily on the German support trenches in an attempt to inhibit the forward movement of reserves. In this they were successful, but they could not muster the weight of shot to dent the existing defences or subdue the defenders; moreover, their ability to do so was declining steadily, for they did not have an adequate supply of high-explosive ammunition. Further losses therefore followed. At 1600 hours 1 (Guards) Brigade attacked and reached the German parapet, but were then driven back into no man's land with heavy loss. A further assault preceded by a ten-minute bombardment and put in by the troops pinned down in no man's land simply led to more casualties.

The infantry of I Corps and the Indian Corps continued to press their attacks home with great gallantry, while their generals attempted to supply what support they could find, calling back the artillery again and again to pound the German defences. These, however, were simply too well built and too stoutly defended to be overwhelmed by any volume of fire the British guns could then produce. In attempting to put in another assault, the Bareilly Brigade got just twenty yards before being held up by a ditchful of wire, and lost more than 1,000 men in a few minutes. At 1700 hours General Haig called a halt, telling the troops to dig in and hang on to the ground they already held; at the same time he sent the 2nd Division up to relieve the much-reduced 1st Division, having ordered the former to prepare for another attack.

The attack by Rawlinson's IV Corps, on the northern side of Neuve Chapelle, got off to a more encouraging start but also petered out before the German defences. Part of the reason for the initial success was that Rawlinson had used mines, tunnelled under the German lines, to reduce a number of strongpoints on his front. The IV Corps attack was led by the 8th Division with the 7th in close support. Once through the German front line the idea was that the 8th Division should hold the breach while the 7th exploited forward towards Aubers Ridge. The bombardment started at 0500 hours, some of the assault battalions moved out into no man's land to reduce the distance they would have to advance under fire – the distance varied from 100 yards to more than 300 – and at 0540 the mines were detonated, the barrage lifted and the infantry advanced.

The assault by 25 Brigade of the 8th Division was initially successful, with the troops of the 1/13th London Regiment actually getting into the German third-line trench. This success was not widespread, however, for the German line generally held and the attacking troops were soon pinned down in the open, taking heavy casualties. Forty minutes after the infantry had gone over the top 25 Brigade's commander, Brigadier-General Lowry Cole, arrived in the front-line trench to find it crammed with wounded men and the rest of his brigade scattered across no man's land, all forward movement having ceased. He ordered more troops forward, only to see his leading waves falling back from the German trenches. While he was standing on the parapet trying to stem their retreat he was hit by machine-gun fire and mortally wounded.

By 0830 hours the situation on the IV Corps front was grave. The infantry had managed to enter the German line at three points but could make no further progress, nor could they be supported, reinforced or withdrawn, for German artillery and machine-guns were raking the flat ground between the lines. This situation was reported to General Haig, who already had enough to cope with; according to reports reaching his HQ, the French were storming on to Vimy Ridge, but his ability to support this success was hampered by the defeat already inflicted on I Corps and the Indian Corps. Haig ordered Rawlinson to press his attack vigorously, but there was little the latter could do. The First Army's assault had foundered and at 1800 hours Haig cancelled the order to attack again at 2000, calling all three corps commanders to meet him at the Indian Corps HQ.

There they discussed the merits of a further attack in the dark, or a renewal of the offensive at dawn. The first decision taken was to delay any further attack until daylight, but long before dawn casualty returns revealed just how grievously the Haig's command had suffered in the previous day's battle. In twelve hours of fighting, First Army had lost 458 officers and 11,161 men killed, wounded and missing, nearly as many as in the three-day battle of Neuve Chapelle. Furthermore, the artillery, which had been firing constantly all day and were still delivering harassing fire on the German trenches, reported that their stocks of ammunition were not adequate to sustain a further assault and that many of the guns were virtually useless, their barrels and recoil mechanisms worn out by incessant firing.

It was clear that the German defences could not be beaten down without artillery, and artillery heavier and better supplied with high-explosive ammunition than any currently in the British line. These views, with a recommendation that the attack should be called off, were sent to Field Marshal French, and the attack was cancelled, pending further orders, at 1320 hours on 10 May.

The blame for the failure at Aubers Ridge was placed squarely on a shortage of heavy guns and high-explosive shells . . . or, to put it another way, on the fact that the German defences were simply too strong for the methods available for reducing them. The casualties caused in one fruitless day called for an explanation and the blame was swiftly fixed on the Government and the munitions industry. There was an outcry in the press over what came to be called the 'Shell Scandal', because of which, to quote *The Times* of 14 May, 'British soldiers died in vain on Aubers Ridge because more shells were needed.' Further articles attacking the Government followed, and it became clear that the figures relating to ammunition supply, if not the interpretation put on them by the press, stemmed from a source close to or in Field Marshal French's HQ.

The attempt on Aubers Ridge had petered out but, with the French apparently storming ahead at Vimy, Joffre insisted that the British renew their attacks quickly, if only to prevent the Germans shifting their forces to stem the French advance. In fact, the French attack was already running out of steam for, having penetrated the German line at Notre-Dame-de-Lorette and crossed the intervening valley, their advance ground to a halt on the lower slopes of Vimy Ridge. Nevertheless, ever eager to help his ally, Field Marshal French ordered Haig to resume his attack, with the result that a fresh battle, an extension of the Aubers Ridge engagement, began on 15 May. The first moves of what became the Battle of Festubert took place on 10 May, when the 7th Division was transferred from IV Corps to I Corps and went into the line north of Festubert.

Unlike Neuve Chapelle and Aubers Ridge, the battle at Festubert lasted a long time, twelve full days, before it was called off on 27 May. Following the hang-up before the German defences at Aubers Ridge, Haig abandoned surprise and the sudden, short bombardment, for two days of steady shellfire which would, he hoped, shatter the German defences and demoralise the defenders. The German line was to be breached in two places, by the 7th Division north of Festubert and by the 2nd Division 600 yards to the south. The depth of the attack was to be no more than 1,000 yards, and when that much had been achieved the advance was to stop. The prime purpose of this offensive was to help the French by holding German troops on the British front, and in this task, at least, the British succeeded. Any other success at Festubert was strictly limited, and was obtained at considerable cost.

Nevertheless, the evidence is that General Haig was adapting his methods to a constantly changing situation, and learning from the snags that each battle threw up. He was also showing initiative, especially in his use of the air arm. Following the use of aircraft for observation, reconnaissance and contact patrols, the RFC was tasked to undertake bombing operations during the Festubert engagement, attacking German troop trains and military headquarters, as well as flying contact patrols. If the ability to follow a steep 'learning-curve' is one of the marks of a flexible-minded general, Haig was showing promise in 1915.

The artillery bombardment at Festubert began on 13 May and continued steadily, though not continuously, until the infantry assault went in at 2330 hours on 15 May, when Horne's 2nd Division, with the Meerut Division in support, went over the top. General Horne had opted for a night attack by his division, whose men knew the ground around Festubert well, while the 7th Division, being new to this sector of the front, was to follow up at dawn. This first attack was made by some 10,000 British and Indian infantry and proved partially successful, for 6 Brigade of the 2nd Division got into the German front line and support trenches and was able to consolidate. However, 5 Brigade and the Garhwal Brigade were not so lucky. Diversionary fire alerted the Germans and the advancing infantry ran into machine-gun and rifle fire, swiftly supported by artillery. The Germans had an adequate supply of excellent flares and rockets with which to illuminate no man's land, and were able to shoot the British and Indians down in quantity. When Haig heard of this, at around 0540 hours, he ordered 6 and 5 Brigades to hold on while a fresh Indian brigade moved up behind the 2nd Division.

While the 2nd and Meerut Divisions were thus engaged, the 7th Division attack went in at 0315 hours on the 16th, closely supported by the fire of six guns which had been brought forward into the front-line trench. These fired high-explosive shells at the German trenches with some success but the attack of the leading brigades was met with such heavy machine-gun fire that the advance was suspended for fifteen minutes until the enemy trenches could again be dosed with shellfire. In the event this did little to quell the defenders and the attack stalled, not least because some of the advancing battalions ran into the British bombardment and suffered heavily from their own gunfire.

At 0900 hours, Lieutenant-General Sir Charles Monro, now commanding I Corps, visited the headquarters of the 2nd and 7th Divisions, and assessed the situation. This was not promising, for the two divisions had not managed to link up and only one brigade had actually entered the German trenches. Monro ordered the two divisions to effect that link, but this proved difficult in broad daylight across ground flayed by shells, machine-gun and rifle fire. In the afternoon Haig came up to visit the HQs of the Indian Corps, I Corps, 2nd and 7th Divisions, and concluded that an advance by his right wing offered the greatest chance of success. The objective of the battle also changed at that time, from a 'bite-and-hold' operation designed to grab a portion of the enemy front, to one of simple attrition: 'the main object to aim at for the present is to continue to wear down the enemy by exhaustion and prevent him detaching troops to oppose the French.' (Letter from Haig, recorded in the Official History, Volume IV, p. 65.)

To do this required further attacks, so the battle, having sputtered on all night, was renewed at dawn on the 17th. The rest of First Army – IV Corps and 'Barter's Force' comprising the 1st and 47th (London) Divisions – was to remain on the defensive, with the Canadian Division moving into First Army reserve. The attacks for that day and the 18th were hampered by communications difficulties, which increased with every day of battle, and by the constant and heavy German artillery fire. The Germans had also started preparing a second defence line, 1,000 yards behind their existing front line, and were beginning to pull back towards it. This line was observed by RFC patrols but its significance was not appreciated, while poor weather, including heavy rain, inhibited air observation patrols.

An attack by the 2nd and 7th Divisions ran into British as well as German artillery fire, but the German front line was taken and the advance continued to the new defence line, where the attack was held, not least because British artillery fire was again falling on the British infantry. The artillery fire plan had got out of phase with the infantry advance, and with no air observation and no way to contact the guns other than by runner, the attack faltered. The advance was further checked when the infantry encountered wide dikes previously undetected and deep enough to drown those laden men who attempted to swim across. In the afternoon a further advance was stopped by enfilading machine-gun fire which decimated the ranks of 4 (Guards) Brigade of the 2nd Division, while an attempt by the Sirhind Brigade to support them also led to heavy losses. The Guards halted their advance and dug in, and all along the line other British units did the same.

That night, 18 May, the Canadian Division took over from the 7th

Division and the 51st (Highland) and 47th (London) Divisions (the latter, like the 51st, also a Territorial formation) began to take over from the 2nd and Meerut Divisions. These changeovers were completed by the 20th and for the next week, until the Battle of Festubert officially ended on the 27th, the three divisions – grouped as 'Alderson's Force' – consolidated on their new front.

In terms of ground gained, the twelve-day battle at Festubert had managed to push back the German line – or force a tactical withdrawal – for about 1,000 yards, so that the new line now ran from just south of Port Arthur, the right flank for the engagements at Neuve Chapelle and Aubers Ridge, to just west of Givenchy, two miles to the south. No apparent tactical advantage had been gained, and Aubers Ridge was still in German hands. As for the 'benefits' of attrition, the British had lost 16,648 men killed, wounded and missing during the Battle of Festubert, and the Germans about 5,000. Attrition cuts both ways, and at this rate Britain would run out of men long before Germany did. As for the main objective, the French did not take Vimy Ridge and their attacks, which continued until 18 June, proved equally costly, with losses rising to over 100,000 men before Joffre called off his offensive.

Three battles in three months; British casualties totalling some 41,000 men, and nothing to show in return but a strip of muddy, bloodstained ground, two miles long and a thousand yards wide, littered with shell holes and corpses. Is it possible to add this up and still find some merit in the actions of General Haig? Could the war be won by these present methods? And if it could be won, was the cost of winning it simply too high?

The first answer must surely be 'yes' – Haig was learning, and learning fast. The answer to the second question must be 'no'. The defensive combination of barbed wire, heavy artillery and machine-guns could not be overcome by any force or method presently available to the Anglo-French armies . . . and to that defensive combination one must add the skill, tenacity, fighting ability and sheer guts of the German professional soldier. As to the final question, that could only be answered by the politicians and the public; the job of the generals was to fight the war, and to win it if they could.

If the war could not be won, it must be ended, but on what terms? The Germans held virtually all Belgium and much of Northern France. Their armies were intact and their initial defeats on the Eastern Front had been contained and turned into victories, while of their allies, Austria-Hungary was holding her own, and Turkey was in the process of inflicting a further defeat on the Allies at Gallipoli. There was no reason for the Germans to seek a peace, and the Entente Powers had no means of forcing them do so. The last solution to this bloodbath was surrender to German aggression, a course which would give much of Western Europe into the hands of a ruthless militaristic society. Since that was no solution at all, no one even considered it.

For these reasons, therefore, the war would go on, until one side or the other could fight no longer. At the moment it appeared that a stalemate was developing, in which whatever side attacked lost the greater quantity of men. Some new methods had to be found or some great commander take over, a man who could devise a solution to the problem of cracking the German defences on the Western Front. The question, of course, was who?

Field Marshal French, that volatile general, had almost shot his bolt, but what of General Sir Douglas Haig, who had planned and commanded in these last three battles? He had failed to win any decisive victory or gain any useful territory, and had lost a large number of very good men in the process, but had he behaved *incompetently*? So far, surely, the evidence suggests that Haig, the thinking, educated soldier, was using his brains and doing his not inconsiderable best. He was fighting a new kind of war and he did not yet have the resources, in guns and shells and manpower, let alone in new equipment and methods, to fight it properly.

Haig had not shown much in the way of innovation so far, but he was learning lessons and attempting to put them into practice. The allegation that he always attacked in the same way is not substantiated by these three engagements, for if something went wrong in one battle, Haig took steps to correct that error in the next engagement. His efforts did not always work, for the Germans too were adjusting their methods, making them a difficult enemy to outguess, but Haig was trying – and trying hard – to make some sense of this constantly shifting, technological war. He was varying his plans and making some use of air power, an arm not even considered by the generals nine months before, thus starting a process that would only reach its full potential on the battlefields of the Second World War, long after Douglas Haig was dead.

This book is not designed to whitewash Haig or any other general, but if this war could not be ended – and therefore had to be fought – it is hard to see anyone doing better. Moreover, it is even harder to see what could have been done instead. Haig had to work out his solutions as he went along and find some way to breach the German line, for another Anglo-French attack was already being planned by Joffre, one which would commit Haig's army to an all-out attack at Loos.

CHAPTER 9

LOOS,
JUNE–DECEMBER 1915

*'An attack on an entrenched position is not merely a matter
of a commander making a good plan and getting it rehearsed
and understood. Once released, an attack does not roll on to
its appointed end, like a play. Innumerable unforeseen
situations, apart from the loss of actors by casualties, begin
at once to occur. Troops must be led, there must be leaders
of every rank and in the later part of 1915 these leaders were
in the making.'*

Brigadier-General Sir J. E. Edmonds,
Military Operations France and Belgium, 1915, Volume IV

Reflecting on his experiences during the Second World War, for most of
which he had been Prime Minister, Winston Churchill remarked that
'the greatest cross I had to bear was the Cross of Lorraine,' a reference to
that prickly commander of the Free French forces, General Charles de
Gaulle. British commanders in France during the Great War would have
relished such a comment and broadly agreed with the sentiment, for Anglo-
French relations were dogged, if not dominated, for much of the war by the
wishes of the French commanders.

Throughout the early battles of 1915, the BEF had acted in support of, or
in concert with, the actions of the French forces on their flanks. This had
been the case during Second Ypres and at Neuve Chapelle, Aubers Ridge
and Festubert. The latter engagement ended on 27 May, but even before it
ended Joffre was planning another assault on an even grander scale, and was
once more demanding the full support of his British allies.

This Field Marshal French was willing to supply, for as has been said, on
taking up the BEF command in 1914 he had been ordered to 'act in full co-
operation with the French', an order he had consistently tried to fulfil. He
had also been told that his was an independent command and that he was
not under the command of any other general, although this part of his

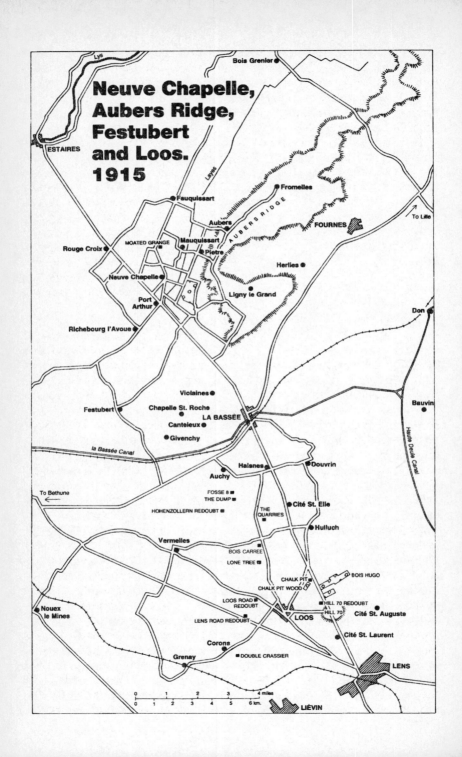

instructions was tacitly contradicted by the point about co-operation. Given the fact that in 1914–15 the BEF was small in comparison with the French forces, was using French ports, roads, airfields, railways and communication facilities, and was fighting on French soil, such co-operation was necessary, but it had the effect of putting the British commanders in a subordinate position vis-à-vis their French opposite numbers.

The French, with the assistance of that relentlessly-scheming francophile, Henry Wilson, and of Field Marshal French's almost pathological inability to resist the wiles of General Foch, were prepared to push this instruction to co-operate as far as it would go. While Joffre and Foch did not actually issue orders to the BEF, it was made very clear that they expected the British commanders to fall in line with their wishes. This left the French free to complain that if the British did not do so in every respect, they were not pulling their weight in the common struggle. The answer to the problem of inter-Allied co-operation was to appoint a Supreme Commander acceptable to both allies, but neither country was yet ready to accept such a step. The matter of co-operation became a struggle of wills, a point well illustrated by the preliminary steps taken before the Battle of Loos.

Festubert had ended and another offensive was pending. This time Joffre was planning his two-pronged attack from Champagne and Artois, to eliminate the Noyon Salient, that great curve in the French line which had its apex at Noyon, just fifty-five miles north-east of Paris, and not much more than ten from Compiègne. Four French armies were to thrust north from Champagne, while the French Tenth and the British First Armies drove east in Artois, these forces aiming to join up somewhere in the Ardennes, trapping the German First and Second Armies behind their advancing lines. If all went well, said Joffre, this would be a great victory, and one that might well end the war.

There were, inevitably, a number of snags, especially on the Artois front. Firstly, the French had not taken Vimy Ridge, a bastion in the German line. Secondly, the French needed to shorten their line in order to build up reserves for the forthcoming offensive. This meant that the BEF must occupy more of the front – a continual demand of General Joffre's – and this Field Marshal French was unwilling to do. The British C-in-C was well aware that the French armies held a disproportionate share of the front, but he had his own problems and for once these took priority.

Like Joffre, French had to build up reserves if the BEF was to play any part in the forthcoming offensive. He could not do this and take over more of the line. Granted, more British divisions were coming out to France, but the British professional army of pre-war days was gone, destroyed in the battles that culminated with First Ypres, and the troops coming out now were Territorials, or the first of the New Army divisions. Six first-line Territorial divisions – the 46th (North Midland), 47th (1/2nd London), 48th (South Midland), 49th (West Riding), 50th (Northumbrian) and 51st (Highland) – had all arrived by April 1915, and the first of Kitchener's

New Army divisions – the 9th (Scottish), 12th (Eastern) and 14th (Light) were in France by May. Other divisions, New Army or Territorial, were on the way. All these units needed more training, more equipment – especially artillery – and some experience of Western Front conditions before they could be of use.

There was also the chronic problem of finding trained, efficient staff officers for these new units in the rapidly expanding British armies. To train a private soldier took about six months, provided good instructors were available, but staff officers, men able to plan, organise and conduct the movements of corps and divisions in the field, and to perform a hundred other tasks such as the gathering and assessment of intelligence or the co-ordination of transport and supplies, were harder to find and inevitably took much longer to learn their complicated duties. This shortage of staff officers was to blight the performance of the British Army in the coming year, though again, nothing could be done about it quickly. Suitable candidates for staff duties were simply not available.

Nor was the front line quiescent. In the weeks after Festubert BEF casualties were running at around three hundred a day – or some nine to ten thousand men a month – even though there was no major battle in progress. Between June and September the BEF fought significant 'actions' in the Salient at Givenchy, Bellewaarde and Hooge, which pushed this total higher and drained away more trained soldiers. There was also, as always, the chronic problems of artillery ammunition and heavy guns.

Joffre sent a draft of his plan for the Artois offensive to Field Marshal French on 4 June, when the possibility of taking Vimy Ridge was still on the cards, expressing the hope that the new offensive could take place in July and calling on the British to support the French attack in two ways: firstly, by taking over twenty-two miles of the French front between the Somme and Hébuterne, south of Arras, thereby relieving the French Second Army for the offensive; secondly, by making an attack on the immediate left of the French Tenth Army, on a line between the La Bassée Canal and Lens, as their part in the northern thrust. This latter action would become known as the Battle of Loos.

On 19 June, the day after the French called off what came to be called the Second Battle of Artois, Field Marshal French met Foch to discuss these proposals and came away having agreed in principle to both of them, his acquiescence being the usual outcome of any meeting of the two men. Foch, as commander of the French Northern Group of Armies, hoped the British would be ready to launch their attack on or about 10 July, and on returning to GHQ, French sent an order to General Haig, whose First Army would conduct this operation, asking him to look at the ground and submit plans for the attack. Haig duly looked at the ground . . . and did not like it at all.

Having consulted his corps commanders, Haig reported his conclusions to Field Marshal French:

It would be possible to capture the enemy's first line of trenches, say on a length of 1,200 yards opposite Maroc, west of Loos, but it would not be possible to advance beyond because our own artillery could not support us, as ground immediately in front cannot be seen from any part of our front. On the other hand the enemy has excellent observation stations for his artillery. The enemy's defences are now so strong that, lacking ammunition to destroy them, they can only be taken by siege methods – the ground above is so swept by machine gun and rifle fire that an advance in the open, except by night, is impossible.

The battlefield at Loos has not changed a great deal since 1915. Lying under the bulk of Vimy Ridge, which overhangs it to the south, the country between the La Bassée Canal and the town of Lens is one of the most charmless areas of France. The word 'dreary' would be flattering to this part of Artois, for this is mining country, dotted with grimy villages and the great black humps of slag heaps – *crassiers* – and dominated by the winding-gear of the pits. The fields around the villages are small, devoted to market gardening and arable farming; there are numerous isolated farm buildings; the land is criss-crossed by ditches, hedges and fences; and apart from Vimy Ridge the only rising ground lies to the east, beyond the large village of Loos, offering perfect observation points to the Germans. From the La Bassée Canal to Lens the countryside is flat and open, totally devoid of cover.

German observation posts, and thus German guns, covered every foot of ground in front of the British line, and their defences – deep trenches and wide thickets of barbed wire – were growing stronger every night. Moreover, the low water table of the Salient gives way here to chalk, so that the Germans were able to excavate deep shell-proof dugouts in this absorbent, easily worked material. Anywhere in Northern France in 1915 less suitable for an infantry assault it would have been hard to imagine, and Haig said so in his memorandum, clearly and forcibly. Field Marshal French went to see for himself, and came back in full agreement with the First Army commander.

Haig now proposed that, if an attack on the left flank of the French Tenth Army was deemed essential, then subsidiary attacks could be made south of the La Bassée Canal, while his army launched yet another major assault on Aubers Ridge to the north of it. French endorsed this proposal, and passed it on to Joffre. Before Joffre could react to this new scheme, however, the French and British Ministers of Munitions – the latter being David Lloyd George, newly appointed to the post – met with the Commanders-in-Chief of the French and British Armies at Boulogne, to discuss the problems of artillery support.

Following the failures at Neuve Chapelle and Aubers Ridge, it was clear that the German defences could only be overcome with an abundance of heavy guns and a constant supply of high-explosive ammunition. It was also necessary to find a shell that could cut wire, to which end a fuse of sufficient sensitivity to detonate a shell on contact with wire – the Direct-Acting Fuze No. 106 – was even then at the testing stage. The big problem was that the Germans, who had a long start in preparing for this war, had as a result a preponderance of heavy guns, and they were likely to maintain their lead for some time. In 1914 the Germans had over 10,000 artillery pieces, of which more than a third were heavy or super-heavy guns. In mid-1915 the BEF had just 71 heavy guns (of over 6-inch calibre) and 1,400 field guns. The French and British had to rely on field artillery, mainly the famous 75-mm Soixante-Quinze and the 18-pounder respectively, which had high rates of fire but no great weight of shot. The two Munitions Ministers agreed that their countries must maintain their production of field artillery but press on with heavy guns, until there was one large-calibre weapon for every two field pieces. The French Minister declared that the ultimate aim would be a ratio of 1:1, but the fulfilment of both ambitions lay well in the future.

There was also the problem of the supply of artillery ammunition for the BEF, which was still inadequate and likely to remain so until the British munitions industry expanded or the large supply of shells ordered from the USA arrived. Logistical and supply factors were to dog BEF operations for the first three years of the war, and it is to their credit that ministers and generals realised that fact and appreciated the consequences, though this appreciation did nothing to ease the armies' problems in the field. Time was needed to rectify the situation, but time was not on the BEF's side.

There was another, tactical, problem related to the question of ammunition and guns. In the wake of Neuve Chapelle and Aubers Ridge, it was obvious that these limited, short-front offensives would never work. A narrow breakthrough simply created a small salient and the men in it could be brought to a standstill by heavy guns pouring in shells from all three sides. The conference at Boulogne decided that to have a realistic chance of success an offensive must have a continuous front of at least *25 miles*, and that the assault must be made by at least 36 divisions, supported by a minimum of 1,150 heavy guns and howitzers and at least the same number of field guns. Asked to give a date for the provision of this power, the Ministers suggested the spring of 1916. What was to be done in the interim was left to the judgement of the generals.

The necessity for adequate heavy artillery support has been aired so often in this book that the snag with the basic premise of this proposal for massive assaults on very broad frontages will be obvious. Clearly, a wide-front assault gave a better chance of avoiding the problems of a narrow salient. However, to have any chance of achieving a breakthrough, wide or narrow, the assault must be supported by a *concentration* of heavy guns and a continuous bombardment . . . but if the front was widened, the artillery support would be correspondingly thinned out, at least until such time as there were more heavy guns available than were actually needed for normal operations. This was the nub of the problem, and no easy solution to it appeared on the table at Boulogne.

General Joffre tackled this conundrum by ignoring it. It could be argued that unless he, his political masters, and the French people were prepared to do nothing for a year, there was little else he could do other than follow the pattern of attacks so far established. Joffre called another conference at the BEF's HQ at St Omer on 11 July, during which he blandly informed French and Haig that he disagreed with any notion of postponing offensive operations until 1916, and also disagreed with Haig's proposals for an attack *north* of the La Bassée Canal. He followed this with a letter to French in which he said that if the British looked carefully and avoided the built-up area of Lens and Liévin, their attack would 'find particularly favourable ground between Loos and La Bassée'.

Joffre did not offer any evidence to support this contention, probably because there was none. There then followed a considerable amount of to-ing and fro-ing between the two headquarters, but it was a dialogue of the deaf, at least on the French side. The French wanted an all-out infantry attack between Loos and La Bassée, and they maintained the pressure on their ally until they got it.

Field Marshal French's resistance was also crumbling when it came to other issues. He offered to help France's front-line manpower problems by relieving two French divisions north of Ypres, but that did not satisfy General Joffre. Finally, French agreed under pressure to establish his newest army, the Third, commanded by Lieutenant-General Sir Charles Monro, astride the River Somme, between the French Tenth and Sixth Armies, thus taking over a wide section of the French line. Field Marshal French did not like doing this for it split his command, placing a French army between the British First and Third Armies, but he never resisted Joffre's demands for long. This relief could not take place before 8 August, thus putting back the Artois offensive to the end of that month at the earliest.

Meanwhile General Haig, a man of sterner stuff than his C-in-C, was still fighting for an attack north of the La Bassée Canal. At a BEF conference at Frévent on 22 July, he reiterated his objections and again the Field Marshal concurred. There was then another meeting with Foch, at which French, while stressing his eagerness to aid the Tenth Army attack, pleaded that he could do this equally well, and far more usefully, by sending in his men at, say, the Messines-Wytschaete position, as well as against Aubers Ridge. These areas had been fought for time and again since December – surely those attacks had not been without purpose? Why not repeat them, therefore, with more men and artillery, and thus a greater chance of success?

Foch would not hear of it. He admitted that an attack against the Lens-Liévin position would probably be a disaster, but maintained that if the British attacked north of this position and the Tenth Army attacked south of it – and this time took Vimy Ridge – success was guaranteed. He did not believe that an attack anywhere north of the La Bassée Canal would have the useful effect of keeping German reserves away from the French attack at Vimy.

For once, French returned to his Headquarters unconvinced, not only about a British attack at Loos, but about the whole Artois offensive. He did not think the French could break the German line with the resources currently at their disposal. Having thought it over, he wrote to Joffre expressing his doubts, and offering, yet again, to attack at Aubers Ridge. The latter discussed this letter with Foch – and how one would like to have had a report of this conversation – and wrote back saying that he still insisted on an attack around Loos. 'I agree entirely with General Foch,' he wrote, 'and I cannot suggest a better direction of attack than the line Loos–Hulluch and the ground extending to the La Bassée Canal, with the final objective Hill 70 and the Pont à Vendin.' These places, as yet unknown to the Army or the public, were to feature in British dispatches over the next few weeks as fields of slaughter, and graveyards for the British dead.

Haig demurred yet again, whereupon Field Marshal French sent Joffre another proposal. He began by stating that since the French were set on a British attack at Loos, he would say no more . . . but that the British attack would take the form of reinforcing the artillery of First Army and directing it to hold the Germans on that front by neutralising the enemy's guns. On 7 August he sent instructions to Haig confirming this decision: 'The attack of the First Army is to be made chiefly with artillery, and a large force of infantry is not to be launched to the attack of objectives which are so strongly held as to be liable to result in the sacrifice of many lives.'

General Joffre erupted. This was not what he wanted, not what he had been promised; an artillery attack would not do *at all*. He then went further. If the British would not support his schemes willingly, perhaps they could be coerced? His proposal, which went first to M. Millerand, the French Minister for War, and then to Lord Kitchener, was worded as follows:

During the period in which the operations of the British Army take place on French territory . . . the initiative in combined action of the French and British Armies devolves on the French Commander-in-Chief notably as concerning the effectives to be engaged, the objectives to be attained and the dates fixed for the commencement of each operation.

The proposal – or formula – concludes: 'The Commander-in-Chief of the British Forces will, of course, fully retain the choice of means of execution.' In short, the French will decide *who* the British will attack, *where* they will attack, and *when* they will attack. All the British generals have to do is work out how to do it.

This breathtaking piece of arrogance was duly presented to Lord Kitchener who, after a prolonged conversation with Joffre and M. Millerand, agreed to it – for the forthcoming operation only. Kitchener then had to break the news of his decision to French and Haig. It was not an easy task.

'Lord K came to my writing room,' writes Haig in his diary for 19 August,

> saying he was anxious to have a few minutes' talk with me. The Russians had been severely handled and it was doubtful how much longer they could withstand the German blows. He favoured a defensive policy in France but . . . the situation had arisen in which the Allies must act vigorously to take some of the pressure off Russia. He had heard from the French that Field Marshal French did not mean to co-operate to the utmost of his power when the French attacked in September and were anxiously watching the British on their left . . . and he had decided that *we must act with all our energies and do our utmost to help the French even though by so doing, we suffered very heavy losses indeed* [Haig's italics].

Even if the reasons for this decision are valid, which is a very big 'if' indeed, this is an appalling situation. The Russians had indeed been driven out of Warsaw on 5 August and lost a great many men, but how was a fruitless (as Haig saw it) attack in Artois to remedy that far-off situation? Here was the British Secretary of State for War ordering his generals to launch an attack, an attack which they had decided – correctly, and for very good reasons – would be a disaster, costing thousands of British lives for no tactical gain, simply to please the French. Quite apart from the fact that Kitchener was an officer in the British Army, and an officer's first responsibility is the welfare of his men, what purpose would be served in launching an attack which those who would have charge of it believed would prove little short of catastrophic?

Kitchener fully agreed with the field commanders' summation of the attack's chances, and knew the French were being intransigent, but he still wanted Haig to attack anyway. Perhaps he felt the Russian situation to be really serious; perhaps he felt that Joffre must be supported to the limit. The French had been offered full British support anywhere else but at Loos, but refused to accept anything other than compliance with their demands . . . and Kitchener ordered Haig and French to meet these demands in full. Perhaps French and Haig should have resigned rather than accept this order, but their soldiers could not resign, and what generals knew the situation better than these two? They had to stay, and do their best.

These meetings, conferences and exchanges of letters and proposals reveal the deep divisions that underpinned the working of the Anglo-French command. The French commanders clearly saw the BEF as an ancillary force of the French Army. The BEF was most useful for holding part of the French line and pinning down German reserves during French attacks. Therefore, if British attacks did not succeed or resulted in heavy losses, *tant pis.* Provided they occupied the attention of the German commanders and held down German reserves while the French broke through elsewhere, they would be useful. The French did not really care if the attack they insisted on, north of Loos, succeeded or not. Their only concern was that it should be a major, all-arms attack on a sufficient scale to occupy large elements of the German Army and keep them away from Vimy Ridge.

From the French point of view this attitude, if harsh, was reasonable. After all, there was a war on, French losses had far exceeded British losses, and sacrifices should be shared. Field Marshal French and General Haig did not – could not – agree with this. They were willing to commit their forces, but only on the understanding that the attack should stand some chance of success. To make an attack in the full knowledge that it will fail is little short of murder, an action that falls well within the limits set by Liddell Hart's dictum that 'to throw away men's lives where there is no reasonable chance of advantage is criminal.' This, however, is the course that the BEF were now set upon.

The French were not so inflexible when it came to the actions of their own forces. On 31 August, Joffre informed Field Marshal French that the offensive could not begin before 15 September, and a few days later the attack was put back yet again, to 25 September. It transpired that Joffre had finally decided to look at the ground in front of his Tenth Army, on the British right, and decided that it would need a good deal more softening up by artillery before the French infantry went in. He had also decided to move the attack in Champagne to another, more open, habitation-free area of the front, for he considered that the ground originally chosen was not suitable for an attack, since it contained too many villages and farmhouses offering strong defensive positions to the Germans. The existence of villages, farmhouses, miner's cottages and strongpoints on the front at Loos had not however, struck Joffre as a reason why the *British* attack should be moved to more suitable ground.

The best answer would have been for Kitchener, French and Haig to refuse to launch an attack at Loos at all and go ahead with an attack at Messines and Aubers Ridge, telling the French they could take it or leave it. The probability is that, *faute de mieux*, the French would have agreed. Now, however, Haig's army was committed to the attack at Loos, an attack which he knew would cost his army dear. He could not know that it was to cost the British Army 59, 247 men killed, wounded and missing, most of them in just two days of pointless assaults. From the moment the order to attack was given, the fate of the First Army at Loos was sealed, but Kitchener did have one sweetener to sugar this bitter pill – poison gas.

British anger at the German use of gas at Ypres in April did not prevent them developing their own chemical weapon. By the end of the war the British had launched more gas attacks than any other combatant, and gas attacks, either by shell or by the release of gas from the front-line trenches, continued after Loos for the rest of the war. Gas masks were standard issue on both sides of the line by mid-1915, but despite its horrors, gas was still seen as a useful assault weapon. The thought of using it to aid the initial assault at Loos eased Haig's mind somewhat as he prepared his orders for the attack, now scheduled for dawn on the 25 September, with the French Tenth Army, which wanted daylight for its final bombardment, attacking five and a half hours later. Over the days before the battle, gas containers were moved into the British front-line trenches, and the gas was ready for release just before the infantry assault, which was to be preceded by a long artillery bombardment.

Haig intended to start his attack with a forty-minute discharge of gas, since the German gas masks were known to be effective for only half an hour. There would be a preliminary four-day bombardment by 110 heavy guns and 841 field guns, and Haig's artillery commanders had calculated that they had enough shells for this, and for up to six days of subsequent fighting. To ensure continued artillery support after the breakthrough, some guns would be shifted forward as soon as possible after the initial assault, and spotting would be aided by RFC observers whose aircraft were now equipped with wireless sets which put them in direct contact with the gun batteries. The infantry assault would be made by the six divisions of I and IV Corps, ranging from the 2nd Division astride the La Bassée Canal, south through the 9th (Scottish) Division, the 7th, 1st, 15th (Scottish) and finally the 47th (London) Division, which had the French Tenth Army on its right. To widen the breakthrough, the 2nd and 47th Divisions were directed to pivot outwards on breaching the enemy line and make a front, guarding the flanks of the attack and protecting the guns which would be brought forward in support. The total weight of the assault by these British divisions amounted to 75,000 men. They were opposed by only four German regiments, thirteen infantry battalions of the Sixth Army, mustering perhaps 11,000 men. These regiments kept one battalion in the line, one in the support trench anything up to 1,000 yards behind the front line, and the third at rest in billets miles to the rear. The only immediately available reserve was the 2nd Guards Reserve Division, which was seven miles behind the front, and the 8th Division, which was at Douai, twelve miles back. The Sixth Army general reserve, three Landwehr divisions, was in Lille and Valenciennes, and was not expected (by the British, at least) to reach the battle area until twelve hours after the attack began. The Germans therefore had far fewer men and far fewer guns, but they had good, well-wired defensive positions, established strongpoints, excellent observation and plenty of machine-guns.

The matter of deploying reserves so that they could rapidly follow up the assaulting divisions had also been carefully considered by French and Haig after previous problems at Neuve Chapelle and elsewhere. Since every man would be needed to effect the breakthrough, the corps reserves had been committed to the attack, so for the battle itself all that was left was the GHQ reserve. This was XI Corps, consisting of two New Army divisions, the 21st and 24th, plus the newly formed Guards Divisions, under Lieutenant-General Haking.

Field Marshal French intended to retain control of these divisions, releasing them to Haig when the need arose. In conjunction with the Cavalry Corps, which was also standing by to exploit the breakthrough, XI Corps was dispatched to an assembly area around Lillers, the infantry divisions marching up over two nights from around St Omer, a distance of some forty miles. The corp's two New Army divisions had only just arrived in France, had not been in the line for training, had inexperienced staffs and were already very tired, even before the battle began, but the XI Corps commander had been assured that his men would only be committed after the breakthrough, and used to pursue a retreating enemy.

To prepare his men for the battle Haig also took each brigade out of the line in turn and had the officers and men go over a rehearsal area where the ground they had to attack and the obstacles they would face had been marked out with tape. He also decided to mix smoke shells in with the gas, in an attempt to screen the advancing troops from direct aimed fire, while newly arrived infantry weapons, like the Stokes 3-inch mortar and the Lewis light machine-gun, then coming into service, were incorporated into his battle plan. It is therefore fair to say that – given the difficulties of the ground and the strong German defences – Haig did everything he could do to produce a workable plan, and to give all the assistance in his power to the men making the attack.

It was clear to Haig that the success of the Loos assault depended almost entirely on gas. To get the gas cloud flowing over the German trenches depended on a good, steady westerly wind, but winds are notoriously fickle and there was a risk that the gas would either hang about in no man's land and impede the attack, or drift back into the British trenches. At 0500 hours on 25 September, Haig was waiting anxiously in the garden of his Advanced Headquarters. The wind rose and fell away again, but finally there came a slight but definite south-westerly breeze. He therefore ordered the release of the gas at 0550 hours, and the start of the attack at 0630.

What happened at Loos was determined long before the infantry left their trenches, and it is not the intention to describe events after that in any great detail. A broad outline of the actions of the various divisions gives a good picture of what happened on each section of the front, and of the problems faced by Haig and his corps commanders.

On the far right flank of General Rawlinson's IV Corps, the 47th Division had the unenviable task of attacking with one flank in the air, since the French to their south were not planning to attack for another five hours, though the latter's artillery was pounding the German line and keeping heads down. The division, a Territorial formation composed largely of Londoners, was to advance through the village of Loos to the Lens–La Bassée road, and their attack faced two significant obstacles, a high slag heap on their right flank called the Double Crassier, about a thousand yards in length and some thirty-five yards high, and another slag heap close by called the Loos Crassier. Behind that stood a pair of linked pit wheel houses known to the British troops as 'Tower Bridge'. The two right-hand brigades of 47th Division were to form a right flank between these two *crassiers* while the rest of the division surged on through Loos.

The 47th Division infantry found that the gas had reached the German trenches; moreover, their advance was concealed by the thick smokescreen laid by the Stokes mortars. The enemy was therefore reduced to unaimed fire, and most of the defenders in the German front line fled as the British infantry came charging out of the murk. A number of flanking machine-guns still caused considerable loss in the attacking battalions, but by 0730 hours the Londoners had got into the German support line and were frantically preparing it for defence. The division lost 1,200 men killed, wounded, and missing in the first hours, but by 1000 hours had taken most of its objectives, held the right flank of the attack firmly, and was ready to defend it. The guns were coming forward to support them, so in this sector of the assault all was going well.

The same cannot be said of the 15th (Scottish) Division, on the 47th's left. This division had to assault due east between two roads, the Béthune–Lens and Vermelles–Loos roads, a distance of some 1,500 yards. Its main objective was the village of Loos itself, after which it too was to press on to the ridge crossed by the Lens–La Bassée road. The main obstacles here were various strongpoints, particularly the Lens Road redoubt and the Loos Road redoubt, as well as Loos itself, Hill 70 and the Hill 70 redoubt. Behind all that lay the German second line, which was also a divisional objective.

The 15th Division had to tackle one of the strongest defensive systems on the entire First Army front, and there was a strong possibility that its advance beyond Loos would be enfiladed by machine-guns from either flank, from German positions in the Bois Hugo and Chalet Woods, north of their line, and from the suburbs of Lens to the south.

The Scots advanced in extended-line formation, with fifty yards between each line, and at once ran into machine-gun fire. The gas had not flowed well here; pockets of it hung about in no man's land, choking the troops as they ran, urged on by the bagpipes. Apart from the limited effect of the gas the smoke screen screen was also too thin, and the German machine-guns did grisly work amongst the advancing troops, while snipers took a particularly heavy toll of officers.

Nevertheless, nothing could stop this indomitable infantry. On they went, over the German line and into Loos, bombing their way across the trenches and supports. After ninety minutes Loos was in their hands and by 0915 hours the leading companies had reached the Lens–La Bassée road. However, poor visibility due to smoke and pockets of gas, plus the constant raking by machine-gun fire, had begun to cause confusion. By now the troops of 44 and 46 Brigades had combined into one jumbled mass of men, perhaps 1,500 in all, surging out of Loos to attack Hill 70, 500 yards to the east; one regimental diary records the sight as 'resembling a Bank Holiday crowd'. More to the point, however, the 15th Division was getting out of line; its axis of attack, which should have been directly east, was swinging away to the south.

This swing was caused by the poor visibility, compounded by the fact that a great many officers, especially battalion COs and company commanders, had been lost in the first hour of fighting. The troops were increasingly leaderless, and simply attacked whatever obstacle stood in their path or appeared most obvious, their original orders being either unknown to the junior officers and senior NCOs struggling to take charge, or ignored in the general excitement as the Scots chased the Germans fleeing from Loos towards the Hill 70 redoubt. To give just one example, 44 Brigade, which should have had its right wing aligned on Hill 70, had its *left* wing so aligned. This caused 46 Brigade to its right to push over to the south, where the troops came under heavy fire from German positions in the Cité St Auguste, behind Hill 70.

The advance continued, in the face of increasing opposition. As the Scots crossed Hill 70, their leading platoons were heading almost due south, towards the Cité St Laurent, a suburb of Lens, an area their commanders had been most anxious to avoid. The Germans were manning the Cité St Laurent defences in strength and met the Scots with a hail of fire, bringing their advance to a halt, with terrible losses, only eighty yards from the St Laurent line. By 1130 hours the 15th Division attack had been stopped and the Germans were pounding and raking the survivors with fire while preparing a counter-attack. Fortunately, at noon the French attack began south of Lens, with the result that no German troops could be spared to assault the Scots hanging on south and east of Lens. The division spent the rest of the day consolidating the ground already gained, attempting to evacuate the wounded – a task not completed for another full day – and bringing up reserves.

The 15th Division had taken Loos village and gained positions between the German first and second lines, on a front between the Double Crassier and the Chalk Pit Wood beyond the Bois Hugo, but the cost had been high; 124 officers and 4,151 men killed and wounded were lost from 44 and 46 Brigades alone. Whether the positions gained at such cost could be held was yet to be seen.

The division to the north of the 15th was the veteran 1st Division, one of the original BEF units, though very few veterans remained in its ranks after over a year in the field. The 1st Division had originally been tasked as corps reserve but was eventually committed to the initial assault, attacking on a line between the Vermelles–Hulluch road and a point just north of the Vermelles–Loos road. The German trenches here were only some 300 yards from 'jumping-off' trenches which had been dug in no man's land before the British front line. These trenches had, however, been sited on a small reverse slope, which effectively meant that troops coming over the crest would be immediate and obvious targets. The 1st Division objectives were the Lens–La Bassée road, which lay just in rear of the German line, and beyond that the German second-line position south of the village of Hulluch. After that, all being well, the division would press on to the Haute-Deule Canal. Taking these objectives would involve an advance of some 2,500 yards though two defence lines and various strongpoints, an ambitious aim.

Two features of this attack were the gap of some 600 yards between the right of the 1st Division and the left of the 15th, and the remains of a cherry tree that stood on a low ridge projecting from the German line. This, known as 'Lone Tree', marked the dividing line between the two assault brigades, 1 and 2 Brigades, where yet another gap was to occur. The former brigade would attack due east from the north of Lone Tree, while the 2 Brigade attack would bear south-east, to regain touch with the 15th (Scottish) Division on the right flank. The two brigades would therefore diverge as they advanced, and to fill the growing gap in the centre a two-battalion formation, 'Green's Force', consisting of one battalion from each brigade, was formed under the command of Lieutenant-Colonel E.W. Green. Green's Force contained the 1/9th King's (Liverpool Regiment) and the 1/14th London Regiment (London Scottish).

The gas was duly discharged and at 0630 hours the 1st Division assault began. The wind then veered and drove the gas back into the British trenches, forcing men to leap out and take cover behind the parados in the rear, and many men were feeling the effects of the gas as they recrossed the trench and advanced into no man's land. Untroubled by gas or smoke, the Germans at once opened fire with machine-guns and trench mortars, and 2 Brigade soon discovered that the wire on its front, set like a hedge on the reverse slope to a depth of some ten yards, was quite undamaged. The men had wire clippers, but as they tried to open up a path they were ruthlessly cut down by machine-gun fire and snipers. This delay gave the Germans time to man their trenches in strength and call up reserves, while the British supports soon fell back, leaving the first wave of attackers isolated. The attack by 2 Brigade had stalled within an hour of starting.

On the left, 1 Brigade did rather better, for though the gas attack failed here too, the assault wave advanced in three extended lines, each line fifty yards apart, and in spite of intense machine-gun and rifle fire pressed home its attacks and took the Bois Carrée, the Germans abandoning their front-line positions and fleeing back toward Hulluch. According to the Official History, however, 'The 10th Gloucesters had been destroyed as a battalion and only sixty survivors continued the advance.' The rest of the brigade pressed on east, towards the outskirts of Hulluch, and dug in to await the arrival of Green's Force.

News of this expensive success encouraged 2 Brigade to try again, and the 2nd Royal Sussex Regiment, with two companies of the 1st Northamptons attached, was ordered to push ahead, picking up the remnants of the first assault battalions as they advanced. At 0805 hours this attack was reported as successful, but at 0901 another report came back, denying the first and saying that the Royal Sussex and Northamptons were hung up on uncut wire south of Lone Tree and taking a terrible beating.

The fate of 2 Brigade, 1st Division, at Loos is an archetype of a Great War attack, the stuff of nightmares. The brigade had now put in two attacks. Its soldiers had been poisoned by their own gas, and lacked any cover provided elsewhere by smoke. They had twice run into uncut wire and taken casualties from machine-guns untouched by the previous days' bombardments or by the gas. Now they were pinned in the open and ripe for slaughter, with enemy artillery and machine-guns raking no man's land, denying them either retreat or support. The Germans were now working their way north to outflank the brigade and being taken on by elements of 1 Brigade, but 2 Brigade was in deep trouble and needed prompt support.

Major-General A.E. Holland, commanding the 1st Division, had a fair grasp of the situation by 0900 hours. He knew that the 2 Brigade attack was stuck in front of the German wire, but that 1 Brigade had managed a limited breakthrough. He also knew that the divisions to his south, the 15th (Scottish) and 47th (London), had broken though and taken Loos. The snag at the moment was the failure of 2 Brigade to maintain its advance, and this had to be put right. Two obvious courses were open to General Holland: either to send his reserve 3 Brigade in behind 1 Brigade, ordering it to work south, or to send it into the gap between his division and the Scots and order it to advance north; either decision stood a fair chance of easing the situation of 2 Brigade. However, General Holland believed that there was only a weak German battalion on the 2 Brigade front. He also believed that these enemy soldiers must soon surrender, as they were outflanked on either side and about to be overwhelmed, either by his own troops or by the Scots of 15th Division, now bombing their way along the German trenches.

He therefore decided to reinforce 2 Brigade directly, putting in Green's Force to the left of it, while 3 Brigade went up on the right of 1 Brigade. He then ordered Green's Force to make yet another assault on the uncut German wire. Orders for this attack went out at 0910 hours, but three runners were killed trying to get them forward, and the orders did not reach Colonel Green until 1055. It was therefore after midday before his attack went in, with one battalion deployed on either side of Lone Tree.

It was a slaughter. The men were shot down as they rose from cover and ran forward to join the survivors of 2 Brigade, still pinned in the open before the German wire. In half an hour the London Scottish lost 260 men, and the King's Liverpool 235; all this in addition to the 1,728 men, killed, wounded and missing, already lost by 2 Brigade – a total of 2,223 men killed or wounded that morning, without gaining a yard. By reinforcing failure – itself a basic military mistake, as any second lieutenant could have told him – General Holland had simply added to the casualties. There was, and is, no excuse for it. He knew what was going on, had a grasp of the facts, yet he made a stupid decision based either on excessive optimism, or a complete misjudgement of his enemy. To assume that German soldiers, soldiers who were shooting his attack to pieces and who were snugly hidden behind wire, would elect to surrender before their position became untenable, was simply fatuous, but it cost a lot of lives to drive that fact home.

To mount another such assault was obviously stupid, and at 1315 hours Holland abandoned frontal attacks and sent what was left of his infantry round to the south, ordering 2 Brigade and Green's Force to leave some men to hold the line while the rest came back and went south, crossing the German line through the gap created by the 15th Division and wheeling north 'to get behind the Germans holding up your [2] brigade'. This move succeeded, for the Germans, 400 men of the 157th Infantry Regiment – commanded by a captain – were taken in the rear and duly surrendered two hours later, having held up the British advance for nine hours. As they did so, a strong German counter-attack came in from Hulluch but was repulsed by 1 Brigade. The survivors of 2 Brigade and Green's Force then moved up to the Lens–La Bassée road, which they reached at 1720 hours. The 1st Division had lost about half of its infantry; of the 6,000 men of the first two brigades who had attacked that morning only 1,500 were still fit to fight at dusk. Moreover, the gap which Green's Force had been created to fill was not closed overnight, and was to cause further losses and fresh disasters on the following day.

On the left of the 1st Division, I Corps, commanded by Lieutenant-General Hubert Gough (as he had now become) took over the attack from IV Corps. Gough had three divisions, the 2nd, 7th and 9th (Scottish), and was responsible for breaking through the German line on a two-mile front up to the La Bassée Canal, and then pressing east to the German second line and the Haute-Deule Canal. All this was to be achieved without any pause in the advance which might give the Germans time to gather reserves. This sounded a formidable task, as indeed it was, but Gough's divisions were opposed by only three German regiments and he felt confident of success, though the ground over which his troops were to advance was very open. It was also well supplied with slag heaps, quarries and groups of miner's cottages, most of which had been turned into mortar- and machine-gun-equipped bastions. There were five lines of trenches and the entire advance would be overlooked by the 'Hohenzollern Redoubt', a German strongpoint that lay just inside the 9th Division area. These defences had been virtually untouched by the British bombardment and were ready for action when the assault went in.

Major-General Capper's 7th Division attacked between the Vermelles–Hulluch road and the Hohenzollern Redoubt. Gas release was inhibited by the fact that the south-westerly wind would tend to blow it over the British front, so not all the cylinders were turned on; even so, where gas and smoke were employed they worked fairly well. The leading battalions of the 7th Division managed to enter the German front line in less than fifteen minutes, though they took heavy losses, for the wire had not been well cut. Casualties were especially high among the officers, a fact indicated by losses in the 8th

Devonshire Regiment, where only three officers out of the nineteen who went over the top made it to the German line. By the end of 24 hours this battalion had lost, killed or wounded, all its officers and 600 men out of the 750 who had attacked at 0630 on 25 September. All the officers of the 2nd Royal Warwickshire Regiment were killed or wounded, and only 140 of the battalion's NCOs and other ranks were unwounded at the end of the day.

Other battalions suffered in proportion, so that the 7th Division advance, though made with great resolution, was also made at great cost. Even so, the division advanced and took its first objective on the Vermelles–Hulluch road. Though originally detailed to press on to the German second line and the Haute-Deule Canal, by evening the division had already lost around 5,000 men and at 1930 hours Gough ordered it to consolidate and hold the ground gained, north-west of Hulluch and roughly between the German first and second lines. The divisional staff work was good, the guns came forward, Sappers came up to improve defences and lay telephone wires, and the new front was supported at dusk by three brigades of artillery and some howitzers.

The 9th (Scottish) Division, to the left of the 7th, had to take certain German front-line positions, including a 20-foot-high slag heap called 'The Dump' and the Hohenzollern Redoubt, as well as 1,500 yards of the enemy's front-line and support trenches. It had then to press on to the Lens–La Bassée road, moving on from there to reach the Haute-Deule Canal. At first all went well. The gas was successfully launched, the infantry had cover from a thick smokescreen, and the wire had been well cut. The assaulting troops of 26 Brigade bombed their way into the Hohenzollern Redoubt within the hour. The advance here should have continued towards the village of Haisnes but was hampered by a lack of success on the left flank, where 28 Brigade had been held up before their objective, Madagascar Trench, partly because the gas failed to take effect, and partly because the wire had not been adequately cut. The infantry duly suffered; one battalion, the 6th KOSB, was reduced from 750 to just 70 men; moreover, the whole 9th Division front was now being flayed by a machine-gun crossfire.

At 1115 hours General Gough ordered a renewed attack by 28 Brigade, assisted by the artillery of the 9th and 2nd Divisions. The losses of the first attack had not been reported, and Corps HQ did not know that three German strongpoints on the 28 Brigade front were still in action. This second attack failed with great loss. At 1330 hours the 28 Brigade commander reported that his force was incapable of further offensive action and it was ordered on to the defensive.

This reverse affected the entire division, which now had to devote all its strength to defending its north-eastern flank in front of a German position called Fosse 8, since the attack of the 2nd Division to their left had failed. There was still a divisional reserve, 27 Brigade, which came up to support 26 Brigade, but there was then a breakdown in communications between the 27 Brigade commander, Brigadier-General Bruce, and Divisional HQ.

General Bruce had been given two conflicting sets of orders. Half 26 Brigade was tasked to assault Fosse 8, and if the attack failed he was to reinforce it. On the other hand, if its attack went well he was to support the *other half* of 26 Brigade in its advance towards Haisnes. In the event the attack did go well; and Fosse 8 fell at 0800 hours and so Bruce was cleared to move on Haisnes, but the timing of the move was unclear. The divisional commander, Major-General G. H. Thesiger, wanted Bruce to wait for an order to proceed, whereas the latter understood that he should move his men as previously ordered, as soon as he had definite news that Fosse 8 had fallen. He therefore ordered his three leading battalions to advance on Haisnes.

The 9th Division commander, unaware that Bruce had already acted, now sent an order that only two of 27 Brigade's four battalions should assist the attack on Haisnes. Ten minutes later, Gough, who seems to have taken a close interest in the brigades of the 9th Division, told Thesiger that the 7th Division had taken Hulluch and he was to send the whole of his reserve – that is, Bruce's brigade – to take Haisnes. There were too many people giving orders at this time, but Bruce and his battalions were already en route for Haisnes, so this should not have been a problem. Then it transpired that a gap in the line had opened up between 26 Brigade and the shattered 28 Brigade, so that Bruce received *yet another order*, to send only three battalions against Haines and send the fourth to plug the gap. Order and counter-order usually add up to disorder, and so it proved here.

In view of all these conflicting orders, Bruce elected to proceed with his current plan, supporting the 8th Gordon Highlanders in their move on Haisnes. There the attacking battalions were soon caught up in a maze of trenches, German artillery began to range on the advancing troops, and the balance of the battle here, which had been in the British favour, began to tilt back. General Bruce was unable either to restore the position or to advance, and by nightfall his brigade had halted, that position then becoming the British front line. Brigadier-General Bruce's nightmare was not over, however, for that night he was captured in a counter-attack, the first British general to go into captivity.

Apart from a certain amount of meddling by Gough, the 9th Division had been well handled, but the results were meagre and had cost over 5,000 men. Among those to die in the battle was General Thesiger, the GOC, who was killed by shellfire near the Hohenzollern Redoubt. Gough was of the opinion that more could have been done that day if a greater degree of support had been available, and this opinion was spreading as night fell on the first day of the Battle of Loos.

Finally, there is the fate of the 2nd Division of I Corps. The Official History sums up this division on 25 September: 'The 2nd Division awoke to a day of tragedy, unmitigated by any gleam of success,' and the fate of its brigades and battalions can be briefly recorded, for this was simply an extension of what had already happened elsewhere along the front.

The prime task of the 2nd Division, which was commanded by Major-

General H.S Horne, was to form a defensive flank in the north-east to protect the four assault divisions in the centre and provide cover for the forward movement of the guns. To do this three brigades were drawn up astride the La Bassée Canal: 5 Brigade on the north bank was to advance east through Canteleux and Chapelle St Roch, while 6 and 19 Brigades on the south bank were to attack towards Auchy and occupy a German communication trench, Canal Trench, which ran parallel with the canal, and turn it into a defensive flank.

As well as gas and artillery fire, this attack was to be assisted by the explosion of three mines under the German front-line trench. This trench was just 100 yards from the British line, but the Germans had recently evacuated it and moved to their support position a short distance to the rear, which was held by six battalions. The Germans here had turned their support line into a fire trench, equipped with a firestep and loopholed parapet, so thickening their defensive position, which was further covered by enfilade machine-gun fire from the brickworks of La Bassée.

The gas and smoke were launched at 0550 hours, but came drifting back into the British trenches. Two of the mines went off at 0620 hours and the attack went in at 0630, but many of the men had either been gassed or were wearing fogged-up gas masks, there was no smoke to conceal their advance, and the Germans were fully on the alert after the explosion of the mines. On the right, 19 Brigade advanced in extended line, but the attackers were forced to bunch at the mine craters and to pass through gaps in the British wire, thus presenting splendid targets to the German riflemen and machine-gunners. The latter had set up their weapons on the parapets of their trench and cut the British down with sustained bursts of fire. As a final blow, when the British infantry approached the German wire they found it uncut. In the first hour 19 Brigade lost 857 men, with a high number of officers in the leading battalions becoming casualties; the 1st Middlesex Regiment lost sixteen out of seventeen officers, the 2nd Argyll and Sutherland Highlanders fifteen, the 2nd Royal Welsh Fusiliers seven.

Elsewhere 6 Brigade, advancing on the bank of the La Bassée Canal north of 19 Brigade, met a similar fate. The ruin of the 2nd Division's attack was complete. The men had been gassed, the enemy wire was uncut, and since the Germans had fallen back from their front-line trench before Zero Hour the mines exploded under it did them no harm. The advancing infantry were raked with fire from the occupied support line, and though some progress was made by the South Staffordshires along the canal towpath they were soon driven back by showers of grenades and intense machine-gun fire.

Meanwhile, on the north bank of the canal, 5 Brigade was also taking a beating. This brigade had elected to attack in two places half a mile apart, near the canal and near Givenchy. Once again the gas failed to reach the German trenches, and the machine-guns flayed the advancing infantry. On the right the attack of the 1/9th Highland Light Infantry petered out within yards with the loss of 8 officers and 350 men killed and wounded.

The left-hand attack, put in at 0600 hours, half an hour before the main assault, was made by 5 Brigade's other three battalions, heading for a line between the villages of Canteleux and Chapelle St Roch, a distance of some 800 yards. These battalions reached the German wire without undue loss and found it well cut, but again the front-line trench was empty, negating any effect of the third mine, which was exploded before the attack. The Germans were in their support line, from which they greeted the advancing British infantry with mortar bombs, machine-gun fire and showers of grenades. They then mounted a counter-attack down the communication trench and forced the British back into no man's land.

By 0830 the division's attack had stalled in front of the German wire and casualties were mounting. General Horne ordered the artillery to bombard the German line for another half-hour before the infantry tried again, but as the guns opened up Brigadier-General Daly, commanding 6 Brigade, reported that 'The gas was a complete failure, our men have suffered heavy casualties and are not in a position to attack again.' Further reports from the battalions stated that after another twenty minutes of shellfire the German strongpoints and machine-gun posts were untouched. Horne was a man who listened to his subordinates, and at 0945 hours the attacks of 6 and 19 Brigades were halted until further orders; for its part, 5 Brigade was now back in its trenches. The 2nd Division attack had failed.

Attacks continued all along the Anglo-French line for most of the day, but no further advantage was gained. Subsidiary attacks by the Indian Corps to the north got nowhere, and the losses in the French Tenth Army to the south were as horrendous at those of the British First Army opposite Loos. The French assaulted at 1255 hours, more than six hours after the British, and the results may be summed up in their own words: 'Insignificant on the right of Tenth Army, slight in the centre but very satisfactory on the left where the 70th Division and the XXI Corps reached all their objectives. On the other hand the British offensive had been very successful.'

It is hard to see where this final morsel of information came from, and the descriptions of the French performance seem optimistic in the extreme. Any ground taken by XXI Corps was retaken by the end of the day, while elsewhere the German line held firm. By that evening General Joffre was asking Foch if it was worth while renewing the attack on the following day, or whether reserve divisions on the Artois front should not be switched to Champagne, though the attack there had not been significantly more successful. Foch then went to see Field Marshal French, who told him that he intended to resume the attack at first light with a push by three reserve divisions. Foch therefore decided to renew his attack as well, with another push on Vimy Ridge. There seems to be some disagreement as to who actually took the initiative in deciding to resume the attack, but since both Allied generals were in agreement, it duly went ahead.

The situation on Haig's First Army front at midnight on 25 September was that some advances had been made in the south and centre of the line, though at great cost. In the south, the British had taken Loos and pushed some companies up to the Bois Hugo and actually crossed the Lens–La Bassée road at one point. In the centre some forward elements had pushed forward 1,000 yards. Elsewhere the British troops were back in their own trenches, and everywhere their losses had been terrible. With the exceptions noted above, the troops had been well handled and although there had been the usual and inevitable amount of battlefield confusion, Haig's plan had achieved some success. The snag was that success or failure had depended on the gas and on a certain amount of luck, for the ground was unsuitable for an infantry attack, a fact indicated by the losses suffered in the assaulting battalions. Now the decision had been made to keep up the attack, and this meant reinforcing the battalions now embedded in the German defences.

The weight was now to fall on the reserve formations, Lieutenant-General Haking's XI Corps, consisting of the newly formed Guards Division and the 21st and 24th (New Army) Infantry Divisions which, with the two Cavalry Corps, formed the GHQ Reserve for Loos. All these units were under the direct orders of Field Marshal French. The deployment of the GHQ reserve divisions, and the timing of their release to First Army, was to be the cause of much argument between French and Haig in the weeks after the battle, but much of this argument is irrelevant to what happened when these formations were committed to the battle. Given the circumstances of their employment not even Alexander the Great could have averted a catastrophe, for the New Army divisions should not have been employed at Loos at all.

These new, half-trained and inexperienced divisions began their march to the front from St Omer on the night of 20 September, the Guards Division following a day later. Night marches were now commonly employed to screen the movement of reserves from enemy aircraft, and the men should have rested in billets during the day. The divisions arrived at Lillers, sixteen miles from the front, on the eve of the battle, by which time the men were already tired and in some disarray, for the staff work had not been good, with the result that some units had not been fed, and arrangements for rest had either not been made or not been enforced.

Before the battle, discussions had taken place between Haig and French on the vexed question of deploying reserves. The battles of 1915 had underlined the fact that the *prior deployment* of reserve formations *close to the front* is crucial to the continuation of a battle after the assault divisions have shot their bolt. Crucial, but not easy, for if the support divisions were placed well forward to permit their swift deployment, they might equally well be within range of enemy artillery. In any event, their logistical requirements would add to the difficulties of the assault divisions, which must have prior call on the available roads. In 1915 a division on the march took up some seventeen miles of road, and getting the assault battalions through to the forward area required skilled staff work.

Better then, perhaps, to keep the reserves out of the ruck and away from shellfire until they could be sent in at some suitable point. The problem, however, lay with getting them to the front by route march, up roads crammed with wounded men coming the other way, and jammed with ambulances, staff vehicles, artillery, and ammunition and supply wagons. This problem was compounded, as always, by the difficulties of communication, of getting orders back to the reserve's corps and divisional commanders, telling them where to go and how to get there. Haig had brooded on these twin difficulties and concluded that, whatever the risks, he wanted his reserves as close to the front as they could safely get and under his command from the outset. Field Marshal French had disagreed with this conclusion and continued to disagree, even when Foch pointed out that, in his opinion, reserve formations should be placed no more than a mile and a half behind the assault divisions before the battle started.

Haig was right in wishing to have his reserve divisions close up and under command, not least because the First Army had no army reserve or corps reserves; every division of his two corps was in the line, and unless the GHQ reserve was committed swiftly, and at the right point, the assault divisions would have no support at all. Matters were not helped by the fact that just before the battle, French moved his headquarters to the Château Philomel, three miles south of Lillers, which not only had no telephone communications with Haig's headquarters, but was also hard to find. Moreover, there was no wireless link with First Army, and messages went to and fro by staff car or dispatch riders.

Haig pressed for the prior commitment of reserves, but French remained adamant. The GHQ reserve, consisting of XI Corps, had only begun to form under Haking on 29 August, and on 18 September French told Haig that the troops of First Army were already more than sufficient for the attack, and that he intended to keep the reserve divisions at Lillers, miles from the front line, and under his direct command. Haig, never one to give up easily, kept up the pressure, writing to ask French to put the leading troops of XI Corps at least as far forward as Noeux-les-Mines, three miles from the front. On the evening of 19 September Haig was told that the 21st and 24th Divisions would be assembled 'in the area mentioned in your letter by dawn on the 25th'. Haig therefore began the battle believing that his view had prevailed, and that these two divisions would be at his disposal for instant deployment as he saw fit.

In fact, this was not so. Field Marshal French still retained control of these divisions, and proved hard to contact when Haig looked around for support on the afternoon of 25 September. Meanwhile, the staffs of the two New Army divisions were not doing well, and the men, so recently arrived in France and lacking any experience of battle, were tired, hungry and thirsty. The battalions had lost their transport and cookers, and rations were not reaching them. They were committed to another night march and their officers, equally inexperienced, had not insisted that their men spend the waiting daylight hours asleep, or at least resting. The march up to Noeux-les-Mines was by roads crowded with traffic, and although it was only six or seven miles it took most of the night, so that the men arrived at their billets on the morning of 25 September exhausted, hungry and in some disorder.

So the attack was launched and the confusion of battle added to the difficulties of the day. At around 0700 hours, hearing that elements of I and IV Corps had breached the German line, Haig sent a staff officer to Château Philomel to report this success. As time wore on doubts entered his mind, and at 0845 he requested that the divisions of XI Corps should be placed under his command and moved up to the British front-line trenches, which should by now be clear of the attacking battalions.

According to Haig's ideas, the British front-line and reserve divisions should make their respective moves forward as one, the reserves entering the front line as the assault troops left it. As far as that plan went, two hours had already been lost, while the true situation of the attacking battalions was as previously described, in many cases verging on the perilous . . . and the reserves were not available. The latter did not actually get on the move from Noeux-les-Mines until 1115 hours, nearly five hours after the assault commenced. These delays continued, and it was not until 1320 that Haig was finally informed that the two New Army divisions of XI Corps were under his command. Field Marshal French retained control of the two Cavalry Corps and the Guards Division.

The move-up of these two divisions to the front line was a horrific experience for the young, inexperienced soldiers. They marched past ambulances crammed with muddy, bloodstained wounded, saw corpses for the first time, and – again for the first time – came under shellfire as they marched towards the thunder of the guns. By the time they reached the front the true facts of the situation among the assault divisions had reached General Haig, much reorganisation was needed, and there were doubts whether the attack would be renewed at all after the first day's battering. The two divisions marched on towards the Loos sector and halted just forward of Vermelles, with the 24th Division deployed to the north and the 21st to the south, both formations waiting for the dawn and further orders.

Fighting continued during the night along the front line, with German counter-attacks probing the British advanced positions. One such counter-attack, at 0100 hours on the 26th, forced its way into the lines of I Corps, and another succeeded in recapturing the Quarries strongpoint. In the fighting here on that day Major-General Capper of the 7th Division was mortally wounded, when up with his attacking battalions. The Germans were rushing troops to the front and, when dawn broke on the 26th, their position was as secure as on the day before, while the ability of the British to breach it was considerably reduced.

On this day there would be no gas discharge, no smoke cover, no culmination of a four-day bombardment, no trained, experienced, well-rested troops, no surprise: any development depended on two tired divisions of inexperienced infantry. At 1100 hours Haig ordered a general assault along the front, from Hill 70 north to Hulluch. The weight of the attack would be provided by the 21st and 24th Divisions, which were to break through on a narrow front between Bois Hugo and Hulluch and then advance some five miles to the apparently unreachable banks of the Haute-Deûle Canal – over ground where no British troops had yet advanced more than 1,000 yards. The assault was launched, the men moving forward in broad daylight across shell-pitted ground carpeted with the dead and wounded from the day before, marching toward German wire draped with British corpses, a sight to quell the most dauntless spirit.

All the attacks failed. The 15th (Scottish) Division failed to retake Hill 70. The 1st Division failed to capture Hulluch. As for the 21st and 24th Divisions on this, their first day of battle, their men were slaughtered by machine-guns and artillery as they advanced past Lone Tree towards the Lens road.

The attack began about 1200 hours when, according to German accounts, 'Masses of infantry, estimated at about a division, began to advance in about twenty waves on a front between Loos and Chalk Pit Wood, towards Hill 70.' This was the 21st Division, and as its tired volunteers advanced machine-guns from Bois Hugo and Chalk Pit Wood caught them in enfilade. They pressed on but, as the Official History recounts, 'Before the men reached the Lens-La Bassée road they reached the limit of endurance and though some held on most fell back in an orderly manner across the Loos-Hulluch road.' The 'limit of endurance' can for once be quantified; in the case of 21st Division that morning it was the loss of 4,051 officers and men killed, wounded or missing.

While the 1st Division was attacking and failing before Hulluch and the 21st was enduring that Calvary before Bois Hugo, the 24th Division was also going in to the attack. The troops advanced steadily, though they came under shell, mortar and machine-gun fire from the moment they rose from cover. Their attack, like that of the 21st Division and all the other divisions on that front, was pressed home with great resolution, but again without success. The 24th Division lost 4,178 men before the German wire that morning. The slaughter was so terrible, and the situation of the troops so hopeless, that the Germans ceased firing along part of the front to let the survivors fall back and stretcher-bearers come up to clear away some of the thousands of wounded. Perhaps the most pitiful remark was made by one of the survivors: 'We did not know what it would be like . . . but we will do better next time.'

The Battle of Loos lasted, officially, until 8 October. British losses, counting subsidiary attacks, exceeded 59,000 men killed, wounded and missing, the killed and missing totalling over 15,000, most of whom died in the first two days. As has been said, among the casualties at Loos were eight British generals; Major-General Wing was killed on 2 October, and Brigadier-General Wormald of 5 Cavalry Brigade was killed by shrapnel on the following day. Brigadier-General Pereira was wounded and Brigadier-

Generals Pollard and Nickells were killed during the battle. The deaths of Major-General Capper and Thesiger, and the captured Brigadier-General Bruce, have already been recorded.

Nothing of significance was achieved at Loos, or in the Anglo-French offensive as a whole. The French did not take Vimy Ridge, the Noyon Salient remained intact, and German casualties did not exceed 20,000, of whom fewer than 5,000 were killed. The British had taken parts of the German line and demonstrated their commitment to the common struggle. But the cost had been terrible, and when the extent of the loss was realised in Britain there was an outcry.

The generals were in dispute about the reasons for this failure even before the battle ended, and the British public, stunned by such losses for no apparent gain, were asking hard questions and insisting on answers. Lord Haldane and other politicians came out from England and questioned the commanders closely, and there was a considerable row between Haig and French over the matter of reserves after the publication of French's Dispatch on the Battle of Loos, which appeared on 2 November.

In this dispatch, French stated that he had placed the 21st and 24th Divisions under Haig's command at 0930 hours on 25 September, and the Guards Division under his command on the morning of the 26th. Haig at once wrote to the Field Marshal, including copies of the relevant signals, which showed that Haig had not taken command of the two New Army divisions until 1430 hours on the 25th, too late for use that day, and had not taken command of the Guards Division until 1615 on the afternoon of the 26th, when the 21st and 24th Division had already been decimated. Haig's request that Field Marshal French amend his dispatch to correct these statements was rejected, with the remark that French's statements were 'substantially correct'. Relations between the First Army commander and his superior, while they did not achieve the status of an open breach, were no longer warm, and Haig missed no chance of telling Kitchener, the King, and anyone else who would listen, that the time to replace French had long passed, and that this was amply proved by the failure at Loos. Haig himself attributed that failure to the lack of reserves, which arrived too late to support his initial attack, writing to Kitchener that 'My first attack was a complete success.' This letter, dated 29 September, does not reflect a view that posterity accepts, or that the men of the divisions who had carried out the attack on 25 September had reason to share.

This account has covered the main causes for the failure at Loos. The first mistake was to attack there at all. The blame for that can be laid on Lord Kitchener, who gave in to French pressure and ordered French and Haig to do as Joffre wanted. As for the attack itself, given the inherent problems of the ground selected for the attack, Haig did his best with the resources available, at least on the first day, but the committal of the two New Army divisions on 26 September was a clear mistake. If an attack did not succeed with the advantages of a four-day bombardment, a degree of surprise, gas and fresh troops, it would not succeed on the second day when none of these advantages were on offer.

Haig knew that the enemy line was thinly held, and knew also that if any breach was to be made it must be made quickly, before the Germans had time to bring up reserves. He also knew that the GHQ reserve must be brought up quickly; otherwise its deployment would simply add men to the casualty list. In the event the first attack stalled on the German wire along much of the front and the British reserves, held up by Field Marshal French, arrived too late to do any good. It remains doubtful, however, whether these untrained and inexperienced divisions could have achieved much against an alert and aggressive German defence, manning strong positions with considerable courage and fortitude.

The other problems of the first day were the familiar ones, with the battalions of the 15th (Scottish) Division veering off track having lost most of their officers, and other divisions being cut to pieces in front of uncut wire before they could even reach the enemy line. There were, of course, many other errors, but errors in battle are inevitable and too much can be made of them, though the sum of small errors contributes to the overall cost. The Official History comments that 'the staff work was very far from perfect,' but this was due, as has been said, to the rapid expansion of the Army, and was not the fault of the generals in the field. There were not enough fully trained officers of any kind, let alone experienced staff officers, and suitable candidates had first to be found, and then trained in their duties. As to field commanders, certainly one division, the 1st, was badly handled, making frontal assaults again and again when the enemy flanks lay open to exploitation, but this seemed small beer compared to the magnitude of the whole disastrous operation. Someone, clearly, had to answer for the entire débâcle and the most obvious candidate, was the man in charge, Field Marshal Sir John French.

French had not helped his troops by consenting to attack at Loos in the first place, and even less so by holding back the reserves on the first day. In the light of this, the British Government saw that he had to go. His period as Commander-in-Chief of the BEF was brought to an end on 8 December, when he tendered his resignation to the Prime Minister . . . and General Sir Douglas Haig – once French's friend, now one of his most implacable detractors – became the new Commander-in-Chief of the British Armies in France.

CHAPTER 10

THE ROAD TO THE SOMME, DECEMBER 1915–1 JULY 1916

'Information often comes late; it is nearly always inadequate and often contradictory. Hence it is only by keeping firmly to the main lines of his plan that a commander can carry out his task and impose his will on the enemy.'

French Field Army Regulations 1913

The Battle of Loos ended officially on 8 October 1915, although fighting continued around the Hohenzollern Redoubt. The British Army did not launch another major offensive on the Western Front until July 1916, when the Fourth Army and two divisions of the Third Army attacked on the Somme. This is not to say that the British sector of the front remained quiet, the armies inactive or the generals idle. Between December 1915 and July 1916, the BEF suffered more than 125,000 casualties either in 'actions' falling short of all-out battle, or through the usual day-to-day attrition of trench warfare.

Throughout this period the BEF was steadily expanding. New Army divisions were arriving, more of the line was being taken over from the French, new weapons, like the Stokes mortar and the Lewis light machine-gun, were being brought into general service, artillery and artillery ammunition were at last arriving in large quantities, and fresh plans were being laid for future operations. To cope with this expansion, and in an attempt to redeem the strategic, tactical and command failings of Field Marshal French, a number of changes were made in the higher command.

General Sir Douglas Haig took over command of the BEF on 19 December 1915, and set about reorganising his forces. Third Army was taken over briefly by General Sir Charles Monro, but this officer was then sent on a mission to assess the viability of the Dardanelles operation and his place was taken for a while by Lieutenant-General Sir Henry Rawlinson. Henry Wilson, formerly the Sub-Chief of Staff at GHQ, took over Rawlinson's IV Corps on 22 December 1915, and Lieutenant-General Sir

William Robertson, Field Marshal French's Chief of Staff, was promoted general and sent to London as Chief of the Imperial General Staff, where he was to serve as Haig's staunchest ally in the years ahead.

Lieutenant-General Sir Launcelot Kiggell came out from the War Office, where he had been Director of Home Defence and Assistant to the CIGS, to serve as Haig's Chief of Staff, and Brigadier-General John Charteris, who had served as an Intelligence Officer to Haig since 1914, arrived from I Corps as Chief of Intelligence. Robertson, Kiggell and Charteris were to work closely with Haig for the next two years; all of them, but particularly Kiggell and Charteris, would share some of the blame that has in later years been heaped on Haig for the conduct of his various battles.

William 'Wully' Robertson was one of the success stories of the British Army, a man who rose from the ranks to the post of CIGS and ended up a field marshal. Like Haig, he was a cavalryman, joining the 16th Lancers as a trooper in 1877, aged seventeen. He did not come from a military family and his mother lamented that she would 'rather see him dead than in a red coat', but 'Wully' enjoyed the Army and, as is the way when a man enjoys his work, he became good at it and rapidly earned promotion. Within a year he was a lance-corporal, recording in his memoirs that he 'felt greater satisfaction in becoming a lance-corporal in 1878 than in becoming a baronet forty years later'.

For social as much as for military reasons, it was not easy for an ordinary soldier to rise far in the Victorian Army, and Robertson must have had some exceptional qualities. By 1885 he was a troop sergeant-major, and three years later he was commissioned into the 3rd Dragoon Guards and went with that regiment to India. There he served on the staff as an Intelligence Officer, and saw action on the North-West Frontier, where he took part in the Chitral Expedition of 1895 and in the operations of the Malakand Field Force, for which he was mentioned in dispatches and awarded the DSO. He rose steadily in rank, attended the Staff College from 1895–7, and during the South African War served as an Intelligence Officer on the staff of Lord Roberts. Intelligence work underpinned most of Robertson's duties, but he took every opportunity to widen his experience, travelling in the Empire and the United States. From 1910–12 he was Commandant of the Staff College in the rank of major-general, then Director of Military Training at the War Office in 1913, and he was sent out to France in 1914 as Quartermaster-General (QMG) on the staff of Sir John French. He did well in this role, or as well as anyone could in those difficult early days, cutting through the red tape to see that the troops were at least fed and clothed and supplied with ammunition. Early in 1915, by then a lieutenant-general, he replaced Murray as French's Chief of Staff. Now Kitchener and Haig had him in London as CIGS, a post which required him to act as the Government's chief military adviser and the link between the Secretary of State for War and the commanders in the field.

Wully Robertson was a dour, hard-working, intelligent officer. His lowly origins were not often held against him and he was generally held in high esteem, but there was one factor in his makeup that made him a less than ideal partner for General Sir Douglas Haig. Like the latter, Robertson could be a model of clarity and concision in his written communications, but when it came to talking he was, also like Haig, extremely taciturn. He was not greatly interested in conversation, and even less interested in argument. His normal response to any criticism was a series of ferocious grunts, or the blunt comment, 'I've 'eard different'. This unwillingness or inability to carry an argument or maintain his point of view verbally when confronted by politicians was to prove a severe handicap in the difficult years ahead, especially when dealing with David Lloyd George, currently Minister of Munitions but clearly the coming man in British politics.

Again like Haig, Robertson was a convinced 'Westerner', and this too rapidly brought him into conflict with Lloyd George. If Haig had to fight the Germans, and to a lesser extent the French, Robertson had to protect his back in England, where the politicians were becoming restive at the lack of success and the heavy casualties on the Western Front. He did this to the best of his considerable ability, and it can be said that but for Robertson's staunch support and sound advice, Haig's position would have often been untenable in the years ahead.

Lieutenant-General Launcelot Kiggell was a staff officer of considerable experience, but a soldier who had spent little time in the field, though like most of these Great War generals he had served on the veld during the South African War. When he came out to France in 1916 as Haig's Chief of Staff he had just spent two years as Commandant of the Staff College after four years as Director of Staff Duties at the War Office, in which post he had succeeded Douglas Haig. The BEF's new C-in-C had therefore acquired one of the best-trained and most experienced staff officers in the Army, and a man with a wide range of connections. For all that, however, Kiggell remained unpopular. He had no command experience, was generally in poor health, and was not well known among the field commanders, most of whom had already soldiered together in some part of the Empire. Nor is he popular with historians bent on proving that all the British generals, and especially Haig, were incompetent butchers.

The persistent criticism that has followed Kiggell in the years since the Great War does not relate to his professional abilities, however, but to the allegation that, two months into the Battle of Passchendaele in 1917, he visited the front, saw the conditions and, or so it is said, burst into tears, exclaiming, 'Good God, did we really send men to fight in that?' Careful research, as well as enquires among a large number of Great War experts, have failed to find any truth in this allegation, and it is most unlikely that Kiggell ever said it. He must have been well aware of the conditions at the front, for he shared the same mess as General Charteris, Haig's Intelligence chief, and the latter was certainly aware of the conditions. Kiggell had probably been up to the reserve trenches, at least, at some time; then there were aerial photos, after-action reports, gun-laying reports and maps etc., casualty returns, requisitions for duckboards, waders etc., medical reports of trench foot – and so on, but that the two men could sit at the same table twice a day for two months of a major offensive, and not mention the situation of the troops or the state of the terrain over which they were fighting is simply not credible.

Brigadier-General John Charteris has also come in for considerable criticism. The main charge levelled against him is that he provided Haig with intelligence information that was either totally inaccurate, or skewed in such a way as to tell the C-in-C whatever Charteris thought he wanted to hear. This last allegation has even been used by the pro-Haig faction as evidence that Charteris, and not Haig, was to blame for the decisions to press on with attacks long after they had run out of steam. Though Sir Douglas Haig's dour exterior concealed the soul of an optimist, Charteris's detractors maintain that he concealed the true conditions or the more uncomfortable facts about what was actually happening at the front, and so led his master to continue attacks which, had the truth been known, might have been broken off earlier.

It is even alleged that in order to prove the declining state of the German Army, Charteris would remove healthy, strong German prisoners from the camps close to the line, so that Haig would see only the weedy, shell-shocked and demoralised ones. It is hard to find any evidence to support this particular allegation, and Charteris's own war memoirs, *At GHQ*, which is largely composed of his diary notes and extracts from letters to his wife, gives no indications that he ever felt obliged to 'over-egg the pudding' in his daily reports to his chief. Charteris believed in balanced reporting, and in his diary for 28 October 1916 referring to the state of the German Army he notes:

> Of course everyone agrees that undue optimism either in Press or Council is unwise. I think there a distinct risk however lest we go to the other extreme. All our captured documents, all our prisoners' examinations, more important still all our own commanding officers in the front line do actually point to the same story, viz. that the German, though he is very far from being a demoralised enemy, is most undoubtedly not of the same calibre as he was this time last year.

This is a fair, balanced and accurate summation of the state of the German Army after three and a half months of fighting on the Somme, written ten months after Charteris took over his post at GHQ. There is no reason to believe that his other reports to Haig were less honest or less balanced, although it is fair to add that his estimates of German strengths and morale did not always meet with general acceptance, even within his own department, while a number of other officers at GHQ and in the War Office felt his information or assessments frequently needed correction. His judgement may have been faulty, and he may have put a gloss on the intelligence he and his staff collected, but there is no evidence that he ever attempted to deceive his Commander-in-Chief.

The BEF's plans for the offensives in 1916 were drawn up in close consultation with the French, and Haig's instructions from Kitchener on taking over command reinforced those given to Field Marshal French in August 1914: he was to '*co-operate closely*' with the French, but his was 'not a subordinate command' and '*you will in no case come under the orders of any Allied general . . . further than the necessary co-operation referred to above.*' (Author's italics.) This last, of course, was a qualification which left considerable scope for debate and disagreement between the Allies. In practice, Haig always tried to act in conformity with the wishes of Joffre and his successors, unless – or until – he felt that, by so doing, he was placing his troops in unacceptable situations.

As it happened, one of Haig's first moves on taking up command was to pay a visit to General Joffre. The commanders met on 23 December 1915, and during the meeting Haig agreed to take over more of the French line as soon as possible by filling the twenty miles of front between the Third Army on the Somme and the First Army north of Vimy, a sector currently held by the French Tenth Army. This he was soon able to do, for on 1 January 1916 the strength of the BEF had increased to around 987,000 men, mustered in thirty-eight infantry divisions, two of them Canadian, and five cavalry divisions, two of them Indian. The Indian cavalry were to stay in France until the war's end, but the bitter winters in Northern Europe had proved a sore trial to the Indian infantry, and it was decided to send them to other theatres. The Indian Corps ceased to exist on 8 December 1915, and by the end of that month its troops had left France for Mesopotamia (now part of Iraq), where a hard campaign was being fought against the Turks.

In spite of losing the doughty Gurkhas and the splendid Indian infantry, the overall rise in the BEF fighting strength was a great leap forward, but the infantry units were still short of establishment by some 75,000 men, and many of the divisions were not fully trained or accustomed to the routine and rigours of trench warfare, or equipped with the necessary artillery. The GHQ Staff directing this force consisted of just 101 officers, while the 'Third Echelon Staff', responsible for such vital functions as signals, supplies, ordnance, medical and veterinary services, transport, and the all-important postal service, so essential to morale, had risen from 45 in 1914 to 129 in January 1916, though trained, competent staff officers were in short supply at corps and divisional level.

A large number of the battalions in these new divisions were composed of men from 'Kitchener's Army', units raised from the million or so volunteers who had rushed to the Colours in 1914. Among these were locally raised battalions – the 'Pals' battalions, as they came to be called – which were to bring a special flavour to this war and, in the tragedy of their destruction, add immensely to the nation's grief and subsequent bitterness. The Pals did not make up the majority of the battalions formed for the New Armies, and only certain regiments had such battalions at all, but their unique composition was to make a particular mark on the Great War.

It will be recalled that in 1914 Lord Kitchener had let it be known that he had little time for the already established Territorial Force. 'I prefer to have men who know nothing to those who have been taught a smattering of the wrong thing,' he told Margot Asquith, the wife of the Prime Minister. This was an unwise and unjust conclusion, for the Territorial battalions swiftly rendered sterling service at the front and continued to do so throughout the war, during which time the Territorial Force raised no fewer than 692 battalions either for General Service or Reserve, as against the 557 'Service' and Reserve battalions of the New Armies.

In August 1914, however, Kitchener wanted to raise a 'New Army' of men enlisted for the long struggle he – almost alone of senior officers – had foreseen, and his famous call, 'Your Country Needs You', produced such a flood of volunteers that the recruitment resources of the Army were swamped. On 19 August, therefore, Lord Derby, Chairman of the West Lancashire Territorial Association, suggested that Liverpool people and the local authority could take over the task of recruiting on Merseyside. This initiative proved extremely successful and just five days later, on 24 August, the 11th (Service) Battalion, the King's (Liverpool Regiment) was ready to begin training. This was not a Pals battalion, for though all such units were raised locally, not all local battalions were made up of Pals. In the event, Liverpool raised four Pals battalions, the 17th, 18th, 19th and 20th King's, in the months that followed. The 11th King's (Liverpool) were followed to the training camps a day later by the 10th (Service) Battalion, the Royal Fusiliers, another entirely volunteer force raised from among office clerks in the City of London.

This local enthusiasm was then increased by the promise that 'those who join together will serve and fight together.' Thus peer-group pressure was added to the national outburst of patriotism – and a national tragedy was in the making. In every city of the land, but especially in the industrial towns and cities of the north, in Burnley, Sheffield, Bradford, Accrington, as well as in Bristol, Belfast, Glasgow and London, in a hundred towns and cities, large and small, local men flocked to the Colours . . . and they often went in groups composed of friends and colleagues.

Football and rugby teams cancelled their winter fixtures and went in a body to the local recruiting office to enlist as a section or a platoon. Factory workers joined with their shift mates, and office workers left their desks to sign up and fight together. Four hundred men from the staff of Harrods went into the service, and workers from the Burnham estate in Buckinghamshire received a £10 bounty from His Lordship when they volunteered en masse for the Army. They formed platoons and companies and whole battalions, and whatever their official Army title, they knew why they had joined, and took care to remember it. They were soldiers now, but they had always been 'Pals'.

They were the 'Bradford Pals', the Glasgow Tramways battalion, or the 'Grimsby Chums' or 'Bristol's Own', men who had grown up together, played together, been to school together, gone to dances with each other's sisters. Many were brothers, or brothers-in-law. Others worked for the same companies or played in the same teams, but the great bond was that they knew each other or came from the same communities. The 10th Royal Fusiliers, referred to above, became known as the 'Stockbrokers Battalion' for it was raised in the City of London from the office workers, 1,600 of them. Having mustered in the street outside the Guildhall they marched in a body to the Tower of London where they were sworn in for service by the Lord Mayor. Similar recruitment was taking place in other cities establishing units like the Hull Tradesmen's Battalion (11th East Yorkshire Regiment) or the North-Eastern Railway Battalion (17th Northumberland Fusiliers), and scores more, local units full of local men, fuelled by patriotism and local pride.

It was a magnificent response, and it had advantages, for the men were keen to do well and quick to learn. Some men – particularly those who had rushed in from factories needed for war work, and especially the manufacture of arms and munitions – had to be culled out and sent home again, but the bulk stayed on and became good soldiers, though there was initially a woeful shortage of arms, equipment and clothing, as well as of trained officers and experienced NCOs to guide the recruits into the basics of military life and the use of arms. Theirs was a glorious response, by any standards, yet, as has been said, in that flood of patriotic enthusiasm lay the makings of a great tragedy.

The tragedy, however, came later, when these locally recruited battalions were sent into battle. In units raised from all parts of the country losses in action, however heavy, are diffused across the nation as a whole. When a Pals battalion went into battle and the casualty lists came home, the impact on a close-knit local community was considerable. After news of what had befallen the Accrington Pals (11th East Lancashire Regiment) and the Sheffield City Battalion (12th York and Lancasters) when they went into the machine-gun fire at Serre on 1 July 1916 the opening day of the Battle of the Somme, reached home, the blinds came down in streets across Accrington and Sheffield, where many households had lost husbands, fathers, brothers or friends. Families and local communities were close in those now-distant days, and the effect of a death spread far beyond the immediate family.

Nor were such disastrous local losses confined to Britain. Newfoundland raised a regiment of two battalions to fight in the Great War, many of its men coming from the island's capital, St John's. The 1st Battalion served at Gallipoli and went into action in France for the first time at 0905 hours on 1 July 1916, attacking a German position at Y Ravine, at Auchonvillers, near Beaumont Hamel on the Somme front. Some 800 officers and men went over the top, down the slope towards the German line and into machine-gun fire. Within a few minutes and a few yards the battalion had lost 710 men killed and wounded – and Newfoundland has still not recovered from the losses of that dreadful day. Thus, from these few examples – of many – it can be seen that the creation of the Pals battalions, however well-intentioned, served in the end to compound and increase the agony of the war. 'It is worth pointing out,' says Peter Simkins, Senior Historian at the Imperial War Museum and an acknowledged expert on the Pals battalions, 'that the authorities realised this and as a result the whole training, drafting and casualty replacement system was changed in August-September 1916 to prevent this happening again.' (Letter to the author, 1998.)

By the end of 1915 the war was flourishing on other fronts, and spreading. On 14 October Bulgaria had declared war on Serbia and entered the struggle on the side of the Central Powers. In December the newly-formed British War Cabinet decided, after consultation with the French, to pull out of Gallipoli, where the attempt to relieve the pressure on the Western Front had proved a disaster. The French wanted the Gallipoli troops sent on to Salonika, where the Anglo-French Expedition had arrived on 5 October but most of them, including the men of the Australian and New Zealand Army Corps, the Anzacs went to the Western Front. Except on the Russian front, where fighting ceased before the end of 1917, action continued in other theatres until the end of the war – notably Italy, Palestine and Mesopotamia, and the Balkans, while the Allied naval blockade and the German U-boat campaign were also maintained to the finish – and British politicians made many attempts to woo their generals from a total commitment to France. From the end of 1915, however, the Western Front was regarded as the principal theatre of operations by the British Army. All efforts were now directed towards finding a solution to the problems of trench warfare and of achieving a breach in the German line.

Joffre wanted yet another combined offensive in the west, timed to coincide with attacks on the armies of the Central Powers in Italy, Greece and Russia. At a conference at GQG at Chantilly on 29 December, Haig listened carefully while the French C-in-C proposed that the Western Front part of this scheme should take the form of a grand offensive by both French and British armies on a sixty-mile front astride the Somme in the mid-summer of 1916. This idea was pressed on Haig in a follow-up letter next day, after which he agreed to take over the lines held by the French Tenth Army, south of Lens, as more British divisions became available.

Joffre also proposed a series of attacks along various parts of the front, starting in the early spring, with the aim of 'wearing down' the German Army and using up its reserves. The snag with this part of the scheme will be obvious – namely, that such attacks would also 'wear down' the Allied armies – emphasised by the fact that in the 17 months of fighting since August 1914, the French Army had already suffered casualties of *1,932,051* men. Although this book concentrates on the British side of the war, the far greater losses suffered by France should never be overlooked. Haig declined to join in with these attacks, or to make any preliminary ones of his own, saying that he intended to conserve his men and resources for the combined attack in mid-summer.

Regarding that combined assault, Joffre wanted Haig to join in the main offensive on a front of at least 20,000 yards – roughly 12 miles – north of the River Somme, and in mid-February 1916 the two commanders agreed to make a combined offensive on or about 1 July. Seven days later, on 21 February 1916, the German Army launched a powerful offensive at Verdun.*

The Germans attacked Verdun for two reasons. Firstly, Verdun was a place that the French were bound to defend. A dreary fortress-city on the eastern frontier of France, it had held out against the Germans in 1870 and, surrounded by its network of forts and fortifications, it held out again in 1914. Like Ypres to the British and the Belgians, Verdun was a symbol of French defiance and resistance. Secondly, the Germans knew that to defend Verdun the French would throw in every man and gun they had. The German hope was that, in holding Verdun, the French Army, in Falkenhayn's gruesome phrase, 'would bleed itself to death' under the German guns. The Battle of Verdun was a battle of attrition, fought not to gain ground, but to kill soldiers, with the added advantage to the Germans that, if they won, the city's loss would seriously affect French national morale.

The siege and defence of Verdun, which cost both the French and German Armies an appalling number of casualties, falls outside the main scope of this book, but the battle was to have an immediate and drastic effect on the Somme offensive. Because Verdun sucked in more and more French reserves, including units designated for the combined offensive, there was a fall-off in the French commitment to the Somme, coupled with growing demands from Joffre that the British should take over more of the French line, launch preliminary attacks, and bring forward the date of the Somme attack. By the time the battle opened, the French share of the assault front had shrunk from twenty-five miles to just eight.

The Battle of Verdun provides a background to the British preparations for the attack on the Somme, but while those preparations went ahead the British had their own battles. A series of actions, some of considerable size, took place in the north, around the Ypres Salient and along the front before Loos, though again with no significant result. The Canadian forces had expanded to a corps of three divisions and the 1st Division was now under the command of Major-General (as he had become) Arthur Currie. The Anzacs had arrived in France early in 1916 after their exploits at Gallipoli and were resting before taking their place in the line, so that, with more troops at his disposal, Haig was able to expand his armies.

---

* For a full and vivid account of the Battle of Verdun, readers should turn to Alastair Horne's masterly *The Price of Glory: Verdun 1916*.

On 4 February Haig ordered Lieutenant-General Sir Henry Rawlinson to take command of the newly created Fourth Army and join General Sir Edmund Allenby of the Third Army in studying the ground north of the Somme, where the British were to launch their main offensive as part of what was still regarded as an Anglo-French affair. Haig now had a force of one and a half million men under command, organised in forty-three divisions making up twelve corps in four armies, the First under Monro, the Second under Plumer, the Third under Allenby, the Fourth under Rawlinson. The Reserve (later the Fifth) Army, under Lieutenant-General Sir Hubert Gough, was created in May 1916.

With all his other responsibilities Haig could not himself draw up detailed plans for the deployment of his individual armies, even for a major offensive. The practice in the British Army (as also in the French and German Armies) was to delegate that task to the individual army commanders, the men who would command the forces making the attack. They would be told the strategic objective and the factors affecting the attack such as the number of reserve units and guns available, and left to reconnoitre the ground and come up with a viable plan, which they would then submit for the C-in-C's comment, amendment and eventual approval.

This would not be achieved without a great deal of discussion and even argument, but in the end it was usual, *though by no means inevitable*, that in case of doubt, the views of the army commander rather than the C-in-C would prevail, on the sensible ground that the former was the man who would actually have to fight the battle, knew the ground and the men involved, and had a better idea of what was actually possible. Once the overall plan had been agreed this process repeated itself, in a declining scale, to corps, division, brigade, battalion, company and even platoon commanders.

Allenby and Rawlinson began their task with a survey of the ground and Rawlinson liked what he saw: 'It is capital country in which to make an offensive *when we get a sufficiency of artillery*, for the observation is excellent and *with plenty of guns and ammunition* [author's italics] we ought to be able to avoid the heavy losses which the infantry have suffered on previous occasions.' (Rawlinson Papers, National Army Museum, London.)

This comment on the ground is interesting. The Somme country is open downland and rolling grainfields, with plenty of 'dead ground',* woods and copses, and the deep groove of the River Ancre cutting across it from the north-east. It therefore offered the infantry far better cover than they had enjoyed at any of their battles in 1915. Rawlinson's approval of the ground as a place for the offensive was, however, subject to not one but two qualifications, both concerning guns and ammunition. Even after one look

---

* 'Dead ground' – ground into which an enemy cannot fire directly because of land features (usually hills, ridges etc.) between weapon and target.

at the ground, the Fourth Army commander believed that the success or failure of his attack would depend on the weight of shellfire supporting the troops. In other words, victory on the Somme would depend on the artillery.

The offensive known to British military history as the Battle of the Somme officially consisted of twelve separate battles, none of which actually took place astride the River Somme. They were fought in the *département* of the Somme, but north of the river, several in rising country astride the River Ancre, a tributary of the Somme, which flows through the town of Albert and enters the main river at Amiens. From Albert, which lay just behind the British front line in 1916, a road follows the route of a Roman highway to the north-east, running almost dead straight across the open downs towards Bapaume, climbing two miles outside Albert to cross a stretch of higher ground known as the Pozières Ridge. This road was to provide the direction of the British attack – the 'axis of advance', in military jargon – and most of the fighting on and after 1 July was for the possession of villages or German positions in or on either side of the Ancre valley or on the Pozières Ridge. Before the Somme offensive this had been a 'quiet' sector of the front, for when no battle was actually in progress the French and Germans adopted a 'live and let live' policy.

Not so the British. When the Third Army took over the Somme front in the autumn of 1915, the British infantry and artillery started stirring things up, dominating no man's land with fighting patrols, raiding the German trenches, bombarding the enemy positions. As a result, the Germans had been working hard all winter to strengthen their line, thickening up the wire and digging deep, exceptionally well-constructed dugouts in the chalk to shelter their troops.

The German front line ran from the just north of the River Somme at Maricourt then west to the village of Fricourt, west of the Pozières Ridge, and then north towards Gommecourt, crossing the Ancre valley just below the village of Thiepval. This line clung to the high ground, though many of the German positions were on the reverse slope, hidden from view and direct shellfire. They had also constructed a second defence line, spanning the Pozières Ridge, and marked out a third position, four miles behind the second line, which cut the Albert–Bapaume Road at the village of Le Sars.

The Battle of the Somme would consist of a series of attempts to penetrate these defence lines, and both Allenby and Rawlinson saw at once that this would not be easy. The Germans possessed the basic advantage of higher ground, giving them good observation over the British lines, and by the early summer of 1916 they had converted their Somme front into one of the finest defensive positions on the Western Front. From the Schwaben Redoubt at Thiepval they were able to look across to the lower ground on the west bank of the Ancre and directly into the British trenches. When the Third Army shifted north to take over the ground previously held by the French Tenth Army its positions were taken over by Rawlinson's Fourth Army, and since the main brunt of this offensive would fall on that army, this officer now moves forward into the ranks of the Great War generals.

Henry Rawlinson was an old Etonian and, unlike Haig and French, an infantry officer, having been commissioned into the King's Royal Rifle Corps (60th Rifles), though after eight years in that regiment he transferred to the Coldstream Guards in 1892. Born in 1864, he was just fifty when the war broke out, and had by then already amassed a great deal of military experience in India, Burma, Egypt, the Sudan, and South Africa. He married in 1889 and, having decided to stay in the Army, he had passed the course at the Staff College, where his talent had caught the eye of the great G.F.R. Henderson, and where he formed a firm and lasting friendship with Henry Wilson. Rawlinson served on the staff of the Aldershot Command as a brigade major in 1895–6, and then arranged a posting to Cairo where he hoped that the climate would improve the health of his wife. He was therefore on hand when Kitchener launched his Omdurman campaign, in which Rawlinson served on the former's staff, with particular responsibility for the mustering and supply of reinforcements.

During the South African War he was with the British force that was trapped in Ladysmith, where he used his initiative to get some artillery into the town before the Boer ring closed; he stayed there, helping with the guns, until the town was relieved in March 1900. He then went to join the staff of the new C-in-C, Lord Roberts, whom he greatly admired. Roberts and Rawlinson got on well, and the latter was invited to join the Field Marshal's mess and lodge in the Field Marshal's house, where he was presently joined by his old friend, Henry Wilson.

In 1900, assuming the war to be as good as over, Roberts went home, taking Rawlinson with him. When the guerrilla war flared up in the Cape Colony and Natal, however, Rawlinson came back, joining Kitchener (who had succeeded Roberts as C-in-C) as a column commander and taking an active part in the fighting, even having a horse shot under him in one brisk engagement. He established a sound reputation as a fighting commander in South Africa and returned with some firm views on the Army and the way it should be trained for the field. He was convinced that the day of the *arme-blanche*, lance-and-sabre cavalry soldier was over. 'Infantry remains the only arm that can decide a battle,' he wrote, 'and the cavalry must be trained to fight on foot as weapons increase their range and power.' Inevitably, these views did not endear Rawlinson to Sir John French, who became one of his most bitter enemies.

He then went to the War Office as Acting Adjutant-General (AAG), a senior staff officer with the rank of brigadier-general in the new Department of Military Education, and followed that with three years as Commandant of the Staff College at Camberley, like his slightly older contemporary, William Robertson. He was next appointed to command of 2 Infantry Brigade and then, in the rank of major-general, to command the 3rd Infantry Division in Southern Command. Despite his rise, however, Rawlinson was not entirely devoted to his Army career. On several occasions he toyed with the idea of leaving the service for a more lucrative position in the City, but the Army sent him about the world and, like Haig, he had established a reputation for himself as a thinking soldier. Rawlinson – or 'Rawly' to his intimates – had proved himself able to absorb the lessons of the US Civil War and of the even more relevant Russo-Japanese War, during which the Japanese machine-guns, heavy artillery and entrenchments had been deployed with great effect against the Russian infantry.

In August 1914, Major-General Rawlinson was on half-pay, having just relinquished command of the 3rd Infantry Division. He was offered the important post of Director of Recruiting, a job which brought him back into contact with Kitchener, but this appointment did not last long, for he was sent to France to take command of the 4th Division, arriving just too late to take part in the Battle of the Aisne. He was then recalled to England, given command of the 7th Division and the 3rd Cavalry Division, and sent to aid the Belgian Army trapped in Antwerp, escaping from that all but impossible mission to join French's army in time for First Ypres, his force having now been renamed IV Corps. He fought at First Ypres, where he did well, though according to his diaries he fell out continually with French. This was certainly not difficult for any officer to do, but the Field Marshal already detested Rawlinson and was quick to find fault with his actions.

It is fair to say that Henry Rawlinson was a man of definite views, with a strong streak of independence, the ability to stand up for himself, and that Old Etonian gift of mixing easily with all levels of society. By 1916 he was an experienced battlefield general who had served and fought as both a divisional and a corps commander and done well at each level, though his time in France had not been without criticism. Rawlinson and Haig (his immediate superior, since IV Corps formed part of Haig's First Army) did not always see eye to eye, for Haig set a high value on personal loyalty and did not fully trust Rawlinson, a man who had a habit of arguing with his superiors and going his own way.

He was also very thick with the arch-intriguer Henry Wilson, but though this made Haig suspicious, it is not likely that Wilson's mischief-making ever had much influence on Rawlinson. The latter had a sense of humour and Wilson was very amusing; but while Rawlinson may have enjoyed Wilson's jokes, he was far too intelligent to accept the Irishman's ideas at face value, or to become a party to his schemes. Rawlinson could also be wily himself, however, and was not above blaming his subordinates for his own mistakes.

In March 1915, Lieutenant-General Sir Henry Rawlinson nearly lost his command, IV Corps in Haig's First Army, over the matter of Major-General Davis, GOC of the 8th Division, a man unjustly accused by Rawlinson of being responsible for the delayed advance at the Battle of Neuve Chapelle. Davis protested to Haig, the whole case was reviewed, Davis was vindicated, and Rawlinson had to admit that the fault had been his. Field Marshal French then wanted to sack the IV Corps commander, but the matter was kept inside First Army, and as Rawlinson's diary records 'I know I shall get justice from DH' [Douglas Haig] – which he did, though he also received a clear warning, relayed from Field Marshal French, not to let this sort of thing happen again, 'or next time he will lose his Corps.' The truth was that Haig, while he certainly viewed Rawlinson's friendship with Henry Wilson with a wary eye, recognised his subordinate general's abilities and valued his experience. Thus Rawlinson was entrusted with the Fourth Army and the main effort in the 'Big Push' of 1916, the coming Anglo-French offensive on the Somme.

The objective of this offensive was to force a breach in the German line and break through into open country around Bapaume, before 'rolling-up' the German line. The breach would be effected by Rawlinson's Fourth Army, after which the cavalry of Gough's Reserve Army, which was forming close behind Fourth Army, would come thundering through the gap, and mobile warfare would return again to the Western Front.

That entire front was a fortress, but the walls were not equally strong at every point. The German position on the Somme, however – where deep dugouts had been cut in the chalk, where there were three prepared defence lines, where the commanding heights of the Pozières Ridge offered the enemy good observation, and where the thick belts of wire before his trenches and the good supply of machine-guns and artillery guaranteed a stout defence – was a very strong position indeed, especially when backed by the strongpoints established in the villages of La Boisselle, Ovillers, Fricourt, Mametz, Thiepval and the rest, each one a bastion in the German line.

The divisions and regiments defending the Somme position were from the German Second Army, commanded by General Fritz von Below, part of the army group commanded by Crown Prince Rupprecht of Bavaria. The Second Army had no reserves, for these had been sucked away to Verdun and the Eastern Front, but as preparations for the Anglo-French assault became more obvious it was reinforced with artillery units, some of which remained silent and undetected until they opened fire on 1 July.

All this being so, it is a matter of some wonder that the Somme was ever chosen as a suitable place at which to attack, but there were two main reasons for this decision. Left to his own devices, Haig would have attacked at Aubers or in the Ypres Salient, but the Somme attack had been planned as a *combined* offensive and the French wanted it to be made there for the simple reason that, since this was where their two lines met, the British were bound to take part and act in concert with French wishes. A natural boundary between the two armies would have been the River Somme itself, but Joffre insisted that at least one corps of the French Sixth Army should be kept on the north bank, ostensibly to protect the French left flank, actually to act as a check, if not a brake, on any British attempts to vary the pace or direction of their advance. A second reason was that a breakthrough on the Somme offered strategic advantages, in that, if successful, it would split the German armies and thereby force a withdrawal.

The first point that had to be settled between Haig and Rawlinson, following the latter's survey, with Allenby, of the ground, was the proposed extent, in width and penetration, of the British advance. Here the first dispute arose, for Haig favoured a rapid breakthrough into open country smashing directly through the three main German defence lines in the first battle while Rawlinson felt that taking the German first line was all that could be achieved in the initial assault.

This was the great tactical argument of the Great War. What was the best aim for a general to pursue – a 'breakthrough' into open country, to deploy the cavalry, roll up the enemy line, and restore open warfare? Or a more cautious – but more certain – 'bite-and-hold' operation, seizing a part of the enemy line, beating off the subsequent counter-attacks, consolidating that position and bringing up the guns to cover the advance before pushing on again? Haig aimed for a breakthrough on the Somme, Rawlinson advocated a bite-and-hold attack or series of attacks, beginning with the German front line. What they both agreed on, given the chronic problems of communication and the need to be able to move reserve rapidly, was that the attack must be a 'setpiece' battle, planned to the last detail, with the artillery, the detonating of the mines, and the advance of the infantry all co-ordinated in one carefully timed plan.

These generals held different points of view as to the nature of the offensive, and it cannot be said that either was entirely wrong. Haig, as Commander-in-Chief, necessarily had to take a wider view of the conflict than Rawlinson, the Fourth Army commander. If the latter was concerned with winning the battle, Haig was equally concerned with winning the war . . . and how many bite-and-hold attacks would it have taken to advance the BEF from the Somme to the Rhine?

There was also the matter of their experiences in 1915. Haig had already seen attack after attack fall apart, and thousands of lives be lost for nothing, because attacks were not pressed on or fell apart after an initial success. This time, with a large force and an adequate supply of guns and ammunition at his disposal, he intended to make a real thrust for open country, without giving the Germans any chance to bring up reserves and seal the breach. Rawlinson, though almost equally experienced, took a different view. He simply did not believe that it was possible to make an advance of several miles through three German defences lines; it had not been done in the war so far, and he did not believe it could be done now. He therefore wanted to bite and hold, and chew his way through the German lines. Since Haig never got his breakthrough and four and a half months of effort did not see Rawlinson through the German lines, both proved to be wrong in practice, but either might have been right in principle. After the battle, everyone can 'play general'; real generals, however, have to make their decisions in advance.

Rawlinson felt that with the forces at his disposal in Fourth Army and with the aid of part of Third Army, he could attack on a front of 20,000 yards (a little over 11 miles). This would enable him to attack on a line from the junction with the French at Maricourt north as far as Gommecourt. As for pushing through the German lines, while his artillery could provide fire for an advance of up to 5,000 yards, he did not believe that the New Army and Territorial formations which made up the Fourth Army could advance that far without falling into confusion. He therefore elected for an average advance of 2,000 yards, which would take his army through the German first line and on to the top of the wide Pozières Ridge. The extent of the penetration varied in different sectors of the assault front because no man's land ranged in depth from 200 yards to the best part of a mile, but if his army had established itself on top of the Pozières Ridge by the end of the first day, Rawlinson would be well content.

There were other disagreements. Haig still believed in the benefits of surprise, and wanted a brief but overwhelming artillery bombardment before the assault. By contrast, Rawlinson wanted to ensure the German wire was thoroughly cut and insisted on a pre-assault bombardment of at least seven days, the method advocated by Foch. As he had reported after seeing the ground, Rawlinson felt that *if* the artillery did its work well and cut the German wire to pieces, the rest would be easy. So those fatal 'ifs' began to accumulate, even as the battle was being planned. Haig wanted a dawn attack, Rawlinson and the French wanted daylight for the final bombardment. Haig wanted the attack made in strength against different parts of the German line, Rawlinson wanted an attack delivered with equal force right along the front.

The Fourth Army commander was adamant in his belief that he should not send his infantry further out than the effective range of his artillery. When the guns had been brought forward, registered on new targets, and had cut the next line of German wire, then he would send the infantry forward again. Haig, on the other hand, wanted to take advantage of any confusion among the enemy, and to use any opportunity provided by the initial assault, to push ahead and gain better ground. These arguments were not egotistical differences of opinion; both generals were simply trying to work out the best means of carrying out an attack which both knew would be extremely difficult, however good their plan might be.

On 12 April, having argued the matter out with Rawlinson, Haig encapsulated his decision in a formal letter of instruction. The Fourth Army assault would form part of a general offensive in close co-operation with the French, and would run from Maricourt north-west to about Hébuterne, with the aim of first establishing a strong defensive flank on the spur running south-east from Serre to Miraumont and the high ground – the Pozières Ridge – running south to Fricourt through Beaumont Hamel, Thiepval, Ovillers, La Boisselle . . . in other words an advance *east* to take the German front line. This line swerved east at Fricourt and therefore 'a simultaneous attack should be made on the enemy trenches east of Fricourt to the point of junction with the French' at Maricourt. The direction of this latter push would be *north*. Haig stressed that during this attack at the southern extremity of Rawlinson's front the village of Montauban and the ridge from there to Mametz were vital features to be seized as soon as possible, since 'their possession will be of considerable tactical value in the second stage of the operations.' The directive continued:

> After gaining the ground described above, your next effort must be directed to capturing by attacks from the west and south, the Ginchy–Bazentin le Grand ridge, then pushing eastwards along the high ground towards Combles in order to co-operate with the French Army on your right, in effecting the passage of the River Somme.

This last move must involve breaching the German second line, which ran in front of Bazentin-le-Grand, while Combles was almost on the German third line. There is no mention of whether these two advances were to be made in one attack or two, but the implication is that Haig, while insisting on a rapid breach of the enemy's second line, was prepared for this to be effected in a follow-up attack, provided that attack was not unduly delayed. The directive went on:

> Operations subsequent to those outlined above must depend on the degree of success obtained and on developments which cannot be foreseen . . . but the objective will be to continue to prevent the enemy from re-establishing his line of defence and exploit to the full all opportunities opened up for defeating his forces within reach, always however with due regard to the need to assist the French Army.

Ten minutes spent studying the map on p. 250 will be most useful at this point. Put simply, Haig was making an ambitious proposal, an advance on a front of some fourteen miles to an *average* depth of about a mile and a half. Since, as has been said, the distances between the British and German front lines varied to take account of the ground, and since a similar variation existed between the German first and second – and, indeed second and third – lines, the actual distance of the proposed penetration varied from just over a mile at Thiepval to well over two miles on the British right, and rather more on the extreme left. That was what had to be done; the problem was how to do it.

The main attack would be delivered by the Fourth Army, as set out in Haig's directive, but on their northern flank two divisions of Allenby's Third Army would attack and pinch out the Gommecourt salient that projected into the British line north of Serre. Rawlinson had five corps for his attack, VIII in the north, on the boundary with Third Army, followed, moving south and east, by X, III and XV Corps, all of which would attack *east*, and finally XIII Corps, which would push *north* from Maricourt where the British right flank met the French XX Corps.

The infantry assault would be preceeded by seven days of bombardment, as Rawlinson had required, with the aims of, first, cutting the enemy wire; second, destroying the German front-line trenches; third, cutting off the supply of food and reinforcements to those trenches; and fourth, demoralising the troops occupying those trenches. Since the success of the preliminary bombardment was crucial to the success of the infantry assault, it would be as well to examine this phase now and see what happened to each of these aims.

The bombardment to cut of the wire entanglements was still entrusted to the 18-pounder field guns, firing shrapnel. In the event, as at other battles in this war, the wire was either not completely cut, or not cut at all. There were, as always, exceptions to this rule, but that is the general picture. The main bombardment, in which the heavier guns joined, did destroy or break down much of the German front-line trench system and made a mess of the support trenches, but it had little impact on the second-line position – as Rawlinson had always feared – while those Germans sheltering in the deep dugouts on the front line and in the support trenches endured a nerve-racking time but suffered few casualties. They did suffer from shortages of food and water, and, prevented by the shelling, reinforcements did not get forward in any numbers, but their weapons – especially their machine-guns – and adequate supplies of ammunition remained safely below ground. Finally, although there is plenty of evidence that many German soldiers were driven to distraction by the constant shelling, the fact remains that enough of them were still able and willing to fight when the bombardment lifted, and these rushed up from below to their shattered trenches in time to open fire on the advancing British infantry.

It is also a fact that the effect of the bombardment was much reduced by ammunition failure and by the great *width* of the attack front, as well as by the need to shell *two* German defensive positions. To put the first point simply, a large number of the shells fired before 1 July did not explode. The fact that the Somme battlefield today, eighty years after the war's end, can still produce an annual harvest of some thirty tons of unexploded ordnance is proof of this point, as is the evidence provided by the heaps of rusty shells any visitor can still find beside the roads, awaiting collection by bomb-disposal squads. By mid-1916 the British Army was receiving an adequate and increasing supply of artillery ammunition, but its quality was poor. When he became Minister of Munitions in mid-1917, Winston Churchill was to forecast that 'In the first year you get nothing, in the second year a bit more, in the third year as much as you want.' In terms of quantity of shells, this had also been quite true a year earlier. Unfortunately, however, in 1916 the rush to grant munitions contracts and get the shells flowing to the front had led to a severe drop in quality control, not least in the manufacture of fuses. The result, a growing crop of unexploded shells, many of American manufacture, could be seen littering the slopes above the Ancre in the days before the assault.

The second problem was inherent in the plan and was created by the need to attack on a wide front and thereby avoid the creation of a narrow salient. In *Command on the Western Front*, their excellent analysis of Rawlinson's Somme offensive, Robin Prior and Trevor Wilson point out that although Rawlinson had a large number of guns – more than 1,000 field guns and 400 heavy guns and howitzers, twice the number available at Loos – these had to tackle a larger number of targets and a much longer trench line – or, rather, lines. The German positions were pounded by 1,010 field guns, 808 of them the wire-cutting 18-pounders, by 182 heavy guns, 4.7-inch calibre and 60-pounders, and by 345 heavy howitzers, of 6-inch calibre and above; 100 of these heavy howitzers were French guns deployed on the right of the British line at Maricourt, but engaging targets in the British sector.

According to the Official History, this total gave one British field gun to every twenty-one yards of German trench, and one heavy gun to every fifty-seven yards. Expressed like that, the artillery concentration does not sound overwhelming, and though these guns fired a total of 1,508,752 shells in the week before the assault, and another 250,000 shells on the first day itself, and although this bombardment was supported by trench mortars and medium machine-guns, it was not sufficient to subdue the enemy on 1 July, and was a much less heavy weight of shells than would be expended in later battles.

The result was that, yet again, the bombardment was not sufficient for the task, was spread too thinly, and did not achieve anything like the success in dominating the enemy and destroying his capacity to resist on which Rawlinson's entire strategy depended. To this can be added the fact that the gunners' accuracy, especially in counter-battery fire, was still not good. A great many targets were not hit at all, or not hit hard enough or often enough. Military historians have criticised Haig and Rawlinson for what they see as a failure to provide sufficient artillery, but this is hindsight, untroubled by any understanding of the realities of the time. The truth is that the generals provided all the guns they could find and more than had been mustered for any other offensive, to produce a shattering bombardment which lasted for more than a week. By any normal calculations it should have succeeded in crushing the life out of the German lines. That it did not was certainly not because the generals failed to try to their utmost to provide sufficiently overwhelming gunfire support.

That said, however, it is true that even if there had been signs of significant German resistance, the attack would still have gone in on 1 July. War has its own dynamic, and a major, and intensely complex, attack like the one on the Somme started to unroll when the first troops were committed to battle, and could not be stopped at the last minute because part of the preparations had not gone to plan.

This situation – that an offensive, once begun, could not be stopped – was not unique to the Somme, or one faced only by the Great War generals. On 6 June 1944, during the invasion of Normandy, Lieutenant-Colonel (later Major-General) J. L. Moulton, commanding 48 (Royal Marine) Commando found himself on the beach at St Aubin-sur-Mer, with less than half his unit ashore and his objective not yet taken.

> It was a shambles but we had to press on. I looked back down the beach, which was covered with dead and dying infantry, ours and the Canadians, wrecked tanks and burning landing craft and realised that something close to disaster had struck 48 Commando. But behind the surf there was a great armada approaching the beach, hundreds of craft coming in to land. It was too late to turn back and the invasion could not be stopped. That is the crux of it . . . the show had started and we had to press on and do the best we could with what we had. (General Moulton, in conversation with the author. It is worth noting that Colonel Moulton's much-reduced commando captured its objective, the strongpoint at Lagrune-sur-Mer, on the following day.)

So much for D-Day 1944, and so it was on the Somme on 1 July 1916, just twenty-eight years earlier.

At a meeting between Rawlinson and Haig on 16 May, Haig agreed that the infantry should not attack until the corps commanders were convinced that the German defences on their fronts were sufficiently reduced; this agreement however, stood no chance of being adhered to. The French continued to insist on an early attack, the build-up of men and stores, reserves and supports, guns and shells, the preliminary work and the start of the bombardment, all these were steps leading up to that moment when the infantry would go over the top. There would be enormous weight behind this attack, and that weight would push the British infantry into no man's land on 1 July whether the German defences had been subdued or not.

Apart from the bombardment, the initial assault on 1 July would also be aided by the detonation of mines beneath the German positions. Mining operations were now a regular feature of trench warfare, and three huge charges and a number of smaller ones were laid to support the assault, two of the former in the shallow valleys on either side of La Boiselle – known to the British as 'Sausage Valley' and 'Mash Valley' (the first of these creating a crater known as 'Lochnagar', which still exists) – and the third under the Hawthorn Redoubt at Beaumont Hamel, in the VIII Corps area. The Hawthorn Redoubt mine was set to be detonated ten minutes before the troops went over the top, the other two eight minutes later – that is, two minutes before Zero.

The arrangements for artillery support, reinforcements, communications and supply were immensely complicated, and once the plan started to develop, its momentum mounting day by day and peaking at the moment of assault, it became virtually impossible to call a halt to its inexorable progress. As the weeks went by, Haig wanted the attack put back to September, but he came under increasing pressure from the French not only to launch the attack on the agreed date, 1 July, but actually to bring it forward if at all possible. The French Army was being ground to pieces at Verdun and unless the British offensive opened soon and forced the Germans to slacken or even call off their attack there, France's army might well be destroyed.

In the days and weeks before the attack, reports came in from the RFC, and from infantry night patrols up to the German line, all providing plenty of evidence that the enemy's wire was largely uncut. These reports were, however generally ignored. Nothing could be done about the situation anyway, except to continue what was already being done, to pound the German wire and trenches with artillery fire. When that pounding had achieved all it could, the infantry must take their chances. How good those chances might be would largely depend on the tactics adopted for their advance.

The standard tactic for advancing under fire, one used by the British infantry in 1914–18 and still used by infantry today, is the process known as 'fire and movement', described earlier in his book. The basics of this tactic can be employed by any number of men, within reason, but it is usually a minor tactic used up to platoon or company level, and consists of one part of the force providing covering fire, thus keeping the enemy's heads down, while the other moves forward. The process is repeated until an assault line is established close to the enemy position, after which a final blast of fire is delivered and the assault goes in to finish the job with small-arms fire, grenades and the bayonet. This tactic was not generally employed by the British infantry on the first day of the Battle of the Somme, but the popular notion that all the troops advanced in extended line and at walking pace is not correct either. There was a large variation in both the method of advance and the speed of the attack.

On 17 May 1916, Rawlinson issued a pamphlet, *Fourth Army Tactical Notes*, directing that this be read by all ranks down to captain – that is, to company commander level. These notes called for an attack in extended line: 'the leading lines should not be more than 100 yards apart and the men in each line should be extended at two or three paces' interval, the number of lines depending on the distance and the nature of the objective.'

In practice, therefore, the men were to get out of their trenches, file through the gaps cut the night before in the British wire, and form into long lines abreast, facing the German trenches. That done, they were to proceed in line, at a steady pace, right across no man's land and into the German trenches. 'The idea,' says the pamphlet, 'is for the artillery to keep their fire immediately in front of the infantry as the latter advances, battering down all opposition with a flurry of projectiles.' In this, Rawlinson was actually proposing the first steps of what would become a standard Western Front tactic, the 'creeping barrage', in which the infantry advances as close as possible to the supporting barrage, which 'lifts' a specified distance of specific intervals – thus troops and barrage advance together. The problem was that this type of barrage could only be controlled visibly or by setting timed phases which the infantry had to follow. Therefore if the infantry were to keep close behind the creeping barrage of shells as they exploded, they *must advance in line*. Small groups dashing about all over the place would have simply run into their own shellfire. Battlefield visibility was rapidly reduced by smoke and shellfire and the infantry could not usually keep up with the movement of the barrage; moreover, voice-radio, to control the guns or adjust the barrage if need be, had not yet been perfected, and the primitive wireless sets were in any case far too heavy and unwieldy to carry into action.

It also has to be appreciated that in the days before the Somme offensive was launched, and particularly in the final week of the bombardment, it was widely believed – not least by General Rawlinson – that the German defences and the soldiers manning them would have been blown to pieces. If so, the British advance would be, literally, a 'walkover'. If, on the other hand, if – that fatal '*if*' again – the bombardment had not done its work, the advance would be a slaughter.

Since the possibility of failure should at least have been considered, the reasons for adopting this 'extended-line' tactic need examination. At a meeting of his army commanders on 15 July Haig, a cavalryman, queried the tactic and suggested that an advance in small groups might be better than an extended line. His army commanders, however, all disagreed, stating that 'the advance of isolated detachments except for reconnoitring purposes should be avoided. They lead to the loss of the boldest and best without result. The enemy can concentrate on these detachments and the advance should be uniform.'

Writers should resist the temptation to 'play general', but these statements cannot be allowed to pass unchallenged, not simply because they are wrong, but because they were known to be wrong at the time; furthermore, they also flew in the face of accepted pre-war Army practice. These is also a strong element of contentiousness in the phrasing. For example, the enemy soldiers cannot 'concentrate on these detachments' – that is, the 'movement' group – if the 'fire' group is keeping their opponents' heads down. The army commanders' statement implies that a few unsupported bands of heroes would duck and weave their way across no man's land, achieving little until, inevitably, they would be left hanging on the German wire. This is a travesty of what a proper attack can be if the ground is suitable and fire-and-movement tactics are correctly employed. No man's land on the battlefield of the Somme, especially after a week's bombardment, would be pitted with shell holes, and the ground is in any case rolling and provided with a good supply of dead ground, terrain masked by higher features from direct enemy fire and observation. This fact did not escape the notice of either the divisional commanders or the men who were about to advance into no man's land, and there are plenty of instances where Rawlinson's *Tactical Notes* were ignored by the front-line commanders.

The essence of fire and movement, as used by the British Army before the Great War, is that the attackers should make use of the ground and of covering fire to work their way forward without undue loss, until a spot can be found from which an assault against the enemy position can be launched at close range with some chance of success. This process is greatly aided by the use of one or more light machine-guns by the 'fire' section, but the British riflemen of 1914–18 could produce a high volume of rapid fire, as they had demonstrated at Mons and elsewhere. The men advance to their assault position in a variety of formations, in columns, small knots of one or two or three men, or by individual rushes. Only when forming for the actual assault do they adopt extended-line formation, which is done so that every man can bring fire to his front without the risk of hitting one of his own side, and to ensure that the final attack achieves the maximum impact. Had 100,000 men, the number committed to the first assault on the Somme on 1 July 1916, worked their way forward in short rushes, covered in the open by fire from their own trenches and from the 'fire' groups of their own platoons and companies – not least from the Lewis gunners who were now a fixture of any battalions fire plan, for the Vickers MMGs had been withdrawn from the battalions and formed into special brigade companies which operated as supporting-fire groups – the outcome of that fateful day might have been very different.

General Rawlinson estimated later that success or failure on the Somme came down to a matter of some *three minutes*, the time it took to cross no man's land before the German infantry could man their trenches. This seems a tight schedule but if it is correct then three minutes of close fire from the attacking infantry on the emerging German defenders could have made a difference. The Official History mentions that Rawlinson's pamphlet omits all reference to rifle and machine-gun covering fire, the essential feature of pre-war training, adding that 'it was perhaps taken for granted'. This, however, was not so; if the extended-line tactics ordered in the pamphlet were implemented then the pre-war, commonsense tactic of fire and movement became impossible. There was simply no provision for fire and movement and the two tactics are incompatible.

Among the reasons advanced for proposing this extended-line formation was the belief that the men in the New Army divisions had not been trained in fire and movement and so could not have managed it effectively. This seems, at best, dubious, on two grounds. The most obvious question is, if not, why not? The majority of these infantry had had over *one and a half years* in which to learn such tactics – and fire and movement is not hard to learn. It could have been taught in a matter of weeks, and months of practice should have made it second nature to even the most stupid soldier. It was also maintained that the extended-line formation delivered such a weight of attack that even if there were heavy losses, some – enough – men would still get through to carry the enemy position. Most battalions attacked in four lines, each line comprising one rifle company, the theory being that the first and second lines might fall, the third might suffer heavy casualties, but the fourth line would do the business and thereby justify the losses of the rest.

This is a 'human-wave' tactic, and a dangerous practice on two grounds. Firstly, it will not work against an unreduced position manned by a resolute enemy equipped with an abundance of automatic weapons. Secondly, it was based on the assumption that the entire position – fixed defences, defenders and weaponry – would have been destroyed by days of artillery bombardment. This, however, was only an *assumption*, not a proven fact. There was plenty of evidence, and even more experience since 1914, to suggest that this assumption was dangerous, or even fatal. Given sufficient ammunition, one machine-gun, correctly deployed and courageously manned, could mow down an extended line without difficulty, and go on doing so for hours, cutting down wave after wave of attackers.

A machine-gun is not used, as it is often portrayed in films, to spray fire forward into no man's land. Ideally, it is fired in short, four-second, bursts from an echelon position, that is, across the front of the advancing enemy line, and not directly ahead into that line. This makes the best use of the weapon's elongated, cucumber-shaped 'beaten zone', the area where the bulk of the bullets fall. If a number of weapons are employed in this fashion so that their fire criss-crosses – and the Germans had over 1,000 machine-guns on the Somme – no man's land becomes impassable. A machine-gun is a *machine*; it does not get tired, or sick of slaughter, and the water-cooled medium machine-guns of the Western Front, each with a cyclic rate of fire of 600 rounds a minute, could go on firing for hours.

There was also the matter of smoke. Smoke had been used at Loos and even in that bloody débâcle, it had helped many battalions to get across open ground with a reduction in losses. It is hard to hit a man you cannot see and blind firing into smoke is, obviously, far less effective than aimed fire, even with tripod weapons like machine-guns. Though Rawlinson was worried that his men might wander of their axis of advance in the thick haze of a smokescreen and knew that smoke would inhibit the artillery observers (Forward Observation Officers, or FOOs), he did not ban its use. Neither did he insist on it. Instead, he left the decision to his divisional and corps commanders. Some used smoke and some did not, but those who did, notably the two Third Army divisions attacking Gommecourt, the 46th (North Midland) and 56th (1/1st London), seem to have advanced with relatively small losses, though they were mauled later by German counter-attacks and artillery fire.

However, it should not be thought that the officers and men in the assault battalions went into this attack like sheep. In many cases they took precautions to minimise their losses and reduce the time spent in the open.

In places trenches were dug in no man's land to provide advance jumping-off positions for the assault. Some battalions sent out skirmishers and fire groups, and many battalion commanders urged their men to be on the look-out for gaps in the enemy wire, to seek ways round any strongpoints, and to avoid frontal attacks on well-defended positions. Others ignored entirely the instruction to advance at a steady pace in extended line, and flung themselves forward at the enemy positions, which was anyway the natural thing to do. Other units advanced in small groups or section 'blobs'. The idea that all the British infantrymen on the Somme advanced in extended line at a sedate walk is another Great War myth.

All these moves, however small, may have prevented the attack on 1 July 1916 from being a greater disaster than it was, but nothing can alter the fact that it was the failure of the bombardment to beat down the German wire, destroy the German trenches and demoralise the defenders which lay at the heart of the catastrophe. When the British infantry fell into line and advanced across no man's land, a very great number of them were marching to their doom.

It is possible to go on picking holes in the plan for the Somme offensive. The Official History does so for pages, but the volume covering the preparations for the battle and the action on the first day was published in 1932, and so enjoyed the inestimable benefits of hindsight. Nevertheless, an examination of the Official History reveals that while many options were considered the final plan left too much to chance and too much to the infantry, and that some obvious options – like a night attack or a pre-dawn advance, or even a heavy blanket of smoke – were either rejected or not even considered, or, as in the case of smokescreens, were optional. This is curious, for Rawlinson had no real faith in Haig's overall plan, which aimed to take two German defence lines in one day, if not in one bound, yet he rejected, and was allowed to reject, some of Haig's sensible proposals over tactics.

To these details one can add the old problems of 1915, most of which had still not been eliminated. There were many more guns, but still not enough heavy howitzers, and Rawlinson's insistence on an equal weight of attack along the entire line denied the possibility of an overwhelming rate of fire at any one spot. Communications were still a nightmare; forward of the front-line trench the assault battalions had to depend on runners or carrier pigeons. This is not to say, however, that the communications difficulties went untackled, simply that the means to solve the basic problem – reliable contact with the forward units – did not yet exist.

Behind the front line, the Sappers, Pioneers,* and the 'resting' infantry slaved to dig miles of narrow, six-feet-deep trenches to protect the telephone

---

* Pioneers are infantry whose additional role is to dig entrenchments, lay tracks, strengthen defences, set up wire entanglements, and so on. Each infantry division of three brigades, each of four battalions, also had a Pioneer battalion attached, making thirteen battalions in all. First and foremost, however, Pioneers are fighting infantry.

wires, but these still got broken by shellfire. Attempts were made to eliminate this problem, or to back up the telephone with alternative methods, but forward of the front-line trenches the infantry were out on their own. The Royal Flying Corps flew contact patrols, each of two aircraft, one machine using wireless to communicate with the ground, the other dropping messages directly on GHQ or the corps command posts, but these operations were of little effective use. The RFC also provided observation aircraft for artillery spotting, again with wireless contact to the batteries, but this too was not always effective. It is worth nothing here that, throughout the war, command of the air went to and fro over the Western Front as the opposing sides brought in new and better aircraft; in July 1916, however, air superiority belonged to the British.

While these preparations were in progress the British Army – indeed, the British nation – received an unexpected blow. On 5 June Field Marshal Lord Kitchener, the Secretary of State for War, was drowned when HMS *Hampshire*, the ship taking him on a mission to Russia, struck a mine and sank off the Orkneys. Kitchener was a British icon and his loss was felt deeply not only among the ranks of the Regular Army, but especially among the young soldiers of the New Armies – or Kitchener's Army, as they preferred to be called – who had responded to his call in 1914.

Among the higher echelons of the military and in government his loss, if publicly lamented, was less strongly felt, for by 1916 Kitchener had become a declining force in public affairs. His reluctance to work in committee and his open contempt for politicians told against him, and some of the blame attached to the failure of the Dardanelles expedition and the reverses of 1915 was also charged to his account. The public and the Army mourned the passing of Britain's greatest soldier, but his place in the Cabinet was quickly filled by David Lloyd George, and the shock of his death was soon forgotten in the greater losses on the Somme.

The first shot of the four-and-a-half-month-long Battle of the Somme was fired on 24 June, six days before the date originally fixed for the infantry assault, 30 June. This was the beginning of the bombardment, and the first two days were devoted entirely to wire-cutting and the registration of guns on to specific targets. Wire-cutting was to continue for the next three days, though some batteries were also turned on the trenches and support lines as well. This bombardment included fire from 3-inch trench mortars, as well as heavy howitzers, and covered every kind of artillery tactic, from counter-battery fire to the pounding of strongpoints, wire and trenches. The batteries paused from time to time, to bring up more ammunition, to clean and service the guns or to let them cool, or to permit the crews to have a rest and a meal, but then the firing began again. So it continued, day after day, for seven days, the bombardment being extended to the morning of 1 July after rain on 30 June forced a twenty-four-hour delay in the infantry assault.

Visibility was not good during that week, for the weather was overcast, and low cloud, mist and rain seriously disrupted the registration of targets and the accuracy of fire. Much of the registration work and observation of targets was carried out by the RFC, and its reports tended to indicate that, despite the poor visibility, the artillery fire was doing its work against the German wire. Night patrols from the British trenches returned with far less optimistic findings, however, but when the patrol commanders' reports reached the heights of division or corps they were all too often ignored. On one occasion such a report produced the comment that the people filing these gloomy accounts of uncut wire were 'scared' – a jibe which, apart from being grossly unfair overlooks the fact that if the German wire was uncut on the day of the attack, the men had every reason to be scared. In fact, some of this news did penetrate to the higher command, for the 18-pounder guns were ordered to concentrate all their power against the wire.

On 27 June, Haig moved to his Advanced HQ at Beauquesne, twelve miles north-west of Albert. Final arrangements were now made for the attack, with the movement of the assault infantry into the line, the testing of communications, and the last briefings of the troops who would go into action. The men had been well trained for the attack, and every soldier knew what his task was when his company went over the top. Then came heavy rain, and on the 28th the attack was postponed by one day, until 0730 hours on the morning of 1 July.

On the night of 28–29 June, fighting patrols sent into no man's land found the German trenches strongly manned and their defenders aggressive, though a large patrol from the 12th Middlesex was able to enter the German trenches on the right of the line near Maricourt, and stayed there for an hour before withdrawing. The German High Command knew of the impending attack, partly from monitoring British Army telephone messages, which could sometimes be intercepted, partly because a British Cabinet minister, in a widely reported speech, had asked factory workers to delay their holidays until after the beginning of July – 'a fact that should speak volumes', but mainly because the long bombardment obviated the possibility of surprise; moreover, the Germans had a good view over the British lines from the heights above Thiepval. However, according to German deserters and prisoners, the High Command's information about an impending British attack had not reached the front line, while there was always the possibility that the British bombardment here was simply a feint, designed to draw attention from a strong attack in some other area. So the seconds, minutes and hours ticked away, until the last hour before the attack arrived and the British guns opened a final, furious bombardment of the German line. At 0720 and 0728 hours on 1 July the three great mines were detonated, one on either side of La Boisselle, one at the Hawthorn Redoubt, the latter serving to alert the defenders, who had ample time to man the parapets for the attack they now knew was coming. On many parts of the front, the British infantry had already moved out of their trenches and lines of troops were lying in no man's land, as close as they dared go to the German wire, waiting for the bombardment to lift and the whistles to blow for the assault.

At last Zero hour – 0730 – came. Officers' whistles shrilled, and the shellfire paused briefly while the guns were lifted and re-laid. During that pause 120,000 British soldiers got to their feet or climbed out of their trenches along fourteen miles of front, filed through their own wire, and began to advance towards the tumbled mass of rusty wire and white streaks of chalk that marked the German trenches. A minute or so later, the enemy's machine-guns, rifles and artillery began to play upon them.

CHAPTER 11

THE FIRST DAY ON
THE SOMME, 1 JULY 1916

*'Great attacks were carried out in thick irregular lines with
small columns following close behind . . . to this must be
attributed the heavy British losses in their attacks, though
they were certainly made with conspicuous courage.'*

German official monograph, *Somme-Nord Offensives, 1916*

Whole books have been devoted to what happened in the next hours,
days, weeks and months along the Ancre and astride the Pozières
Ridge. It is not the intention to re-fight the Battle of the Somme in this book,
or to give a blow-by-blow account of events in every sector of the line during
that offensive. What does need to be done, however, is to examine the plans
of Rawlinson and Haig, and then to see how the assault worked out for each
of the attacking corps.

The essence of Rawlinson's plan, and the idea accepted by Haig, was an
even-handed approach to the problem of making a breach, with roughly
equal amounts of artillery and men spread evenly along the front. This may
have seemed an equitable approach, but the distance the men had to cover
and the obstacles they had to face, man-made or natural, varied considerably. Much adverse comment has also been attracted by Haig's diary entry
for 30 June 1916, in which he wrote that 'The wire has never been so well cut
nor the artillery preparation so thorough,' though both statements were
perfectly true. The tragedy is that the wire was not cut *well enough*, and the
artillery bombardment, the longest and heaviest – the most 'thorough' – of
the war so far, had not destroyed the German defences or shattered the will
to resist of the troops manning them. Broadly speaking, the attack on the
first day of the Somme battle succeeded on the right flank, failed with great
loss on the left flank, and met with mixed fortunes in the centre. Total
casualties at the end of that day totalled 57,470 men killed, wounded or
missing, of whom 19,240 were killed. Unlike the assault, these terrible losses
were not spread evenly along the front.

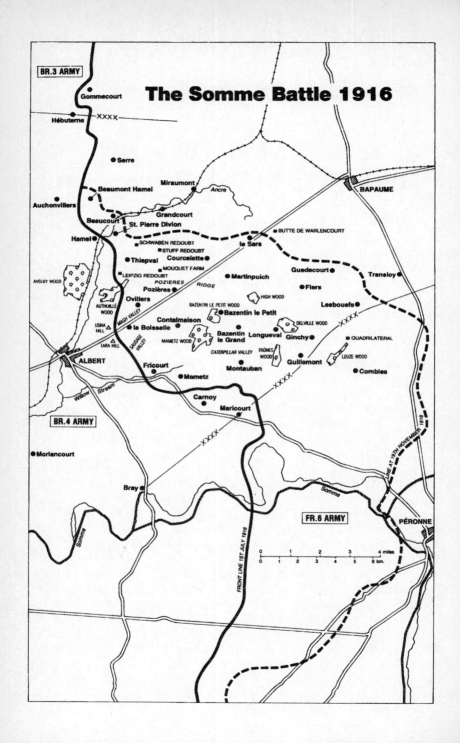

The Somme Battle 1916

BR.3 ARMY

Gommecourt

Hébuterne XXXX

Serre

Beaumont Hamel

Miraumont

Ancre

BAPAUME

Auchonvillers

Grandcourt

Beaucourt

St. Pierre Divion

BUTTE DE WARLENCOURT

Hamel

SCHWABEN REDOUBT

le Sars

STUFF REDOUBT

Thiepval

Courcelette

MOUQUET FARM

Guedecourt

Transloy

AVELUY WOOD

LEIPZIG REDOUBT

POZIÈRES

RIDGE

Martinpuich

Fliers

Pozières

HIGH WOOD

Ovillers

BAZENTIN LE PETIT WOOD

Lesboeufs

AUTHUILLÉ WOOD

Bazentin le Petit

DELVILLE WOOD

XXXX

USNA HILL

Contalmaison

MASH VALLEY

la Boisselle

Bazentin le Grand

Longueval

Ginchy

QUADRILATERAL

TARA HILL

SAUSAGE VALLEY

MAMETZ WOOD

CATERPILLAR VALLEY

TRÔNES WOOD

LEUZE WOOD

ALBERT

Fricourt

Montauban

Guillemont

Mametz

Combles

Willow Stream

Carnoy

Maricourt

XXXX

BR.4 ARMY

Morlancourt

XXXX

Bray

Somme

FR.6 ARMY

PÉRONNE

FRONT LINE 1ST JULY 1916

LINE AT 19TH NOVEMBER 1916

Somme

Somme

| 0 | 1 | 2 | 3 | 4 miles |
| 0 | 1 | 2 | 3 | 4 | 5 | 6 km. |

Above: Haig and his army commanders, Cambrai, 31 October 1918. From left to right: General Sir Henry Rawlinson (Fourth Army), General the Hon. Sir Julian Byng (Third Army, behind Rawlinson), Field Marshal Sir Douglas Haig, Lieutenant-General Sir Henry Horne (First Army), Lieutenant-General Sir Herbert Lawrence (Haig's Chief of General Staff, with cigarette), General Sir William Birdwood (Fifth Army).
(Photo: The Trustees of the Imperial War Museum, London)

Left: General Count Alfred von Schlieffen, Chief of the German General Staff from 1891 to 1906, and author of the Schlieffen Plan.

Above: Field Marshal Sir John French
Commander-in-Chief of the British
Expeditionary Force from August 1914
to December 1915, with a group of
staff officers, 1915.
*(Photo: The Trustees of the Imperial
War Museum, London)*

Left: Field Marshal Lord Kitchener of
Khartoum, Secretary of State for War
from 1914 until his death at sea in
1916, leaves a conference in Paris,
1915.
*(Photo: The Trustees of the Imperial
War Museum, London)*

Above: From left: General Joseph Joffre, C-in-C of the French Armies of the North and North-East, President Raymond Poincaré of France, HM King George V, General Ferdinand Foch, commanding the French Army Group of the North, General Sir Douglas Haig. This photograph was taken in August 1916, more than a month into the Battle of the Somme. *(Photo: The Trustees of the Imperial War Museum, London)*

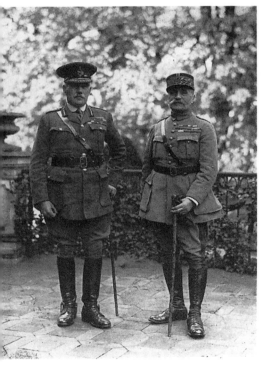

Left: General Sir William ('Wully') Robertson with Foch, by now a Marshal of France. *(Photo: The Trustees of the Imperial War Museum, London)*

Above: Major-General John J ('Black Jack') Pershing, commander of the American Expeditionary Force, lands in France, June 1917. *Below*: The Generals, Vimy Ridge, 1917. From left to right: Major-General Arthur Currie, commanding 1st Canadian Division, Major-General M. S. Mercer, commanding 3rd Canadian Division, and Lieutenant-General Byng, commanding the Canadian Corps. *(Photos: The Trustees of the Imperial War Museum, London)*

Above: Kaiser Wilhelm II, Emperor of Germany and King of Prussia (centre), with Field Marshal Paul von Hindenburg, Chief of the German General Staff (left), and General Erich Ludendorff, First Quartermaster-General. *Below*: Hindenburg inspects a German regiment on the Western Front, June 1918. Although the tide was by now beginning to turn against the German Army, the quality of its troops is evident from this photograph. *(Photos: The Trustees of the Imperial War Museum, London)*

Above: King George V prepares to knight Lieutenant-General John Monash, commander of the Australian Corps, August 1918. Just as his corps was among the finest formations on the Western Front, so Monash proved to be one of the best Allied field commanders. *(Photo: The Trustees of the Imperial War Museum, London) Below*: Lieutenant-General Sir Arthur Currie, who succeeded Byng in command of the Canadian Corps, with Field Marshal Sir Douglas Haig, 1918. Like Monash – and despite his rather unsoldierly appearance – Currie proved to be a superb field commander. *(Photo: National Archives of Canada)*

To break this down and see what happened the story begins on the right flank, with XIII Corps, commanded by Lieutenant-General Walter Congreve, VC, which held the line from contact with the French XX Corps at Maricourt westwards to beyond Carnoy, with three divisions, the 9th (Scottish), 18th and 30th, the former including the South African Brigade. Congreve's corps was supported by its own divisional and corps artillery and by French heavy guns firing on its front, and was opposed by nine German battalions, drawn from three divisions, occupying a front-line position spanning two spurs. The Germans also had a second-line position some 3,000 yards behind the first, in front of High Wood and Delville Wood, and a marked-out but as yet unbuilt third line beyond that.

Congreve divided his attack into three phases, with the 30th and 18th Divisions spearheading the attack and the 9th in reserve. Their first objective was the village of Montauban, reached by pushing north and taking the German front line and reserve trenches, which would require them to cover a distance of about three-quarters of a mile. From there the attack would proceed to take Montauban and then the ridge running from that village to Mametz, high ground which would provide good observation over the ground to the east. Then XIII Corps was to pivot and advance east to the German second line, keeping in phase with the French XX Corps on its right flank. The XIII Corps artillery was to provide a constant barrage, the heavy guns switching to the second line at Zero hour 'while the field artillery was to creep back [i.e. lengthen its range] by short lifts' in support of the infantry – the first time the word 'creep' was used for a barrage on the Western Front.

This meant that the field guns should alter their aim very gradually, and to stress this point the artillery orders added 'it is preferable that the infantry should wait for the barrage to lift than that the latter should lift prematurely and allow the enemy to man his parapets.' This order was to make a considerable difference to the casualties, not least because the commanders in XIII Corps had elected to advance without a smokescreen, maintaining that it had caused confusion at Loos. Laying down smoke would also have hindered an accurate view of the advancing infantry by the artillery observation officers, on whom close gunfire support largely depended.

There was more good fortune for XIII Corps. In front of the 30th Division the wire was well cut, with the result that the division was able to gain most of its objectives in just over an hour, and the rest by the end of the morning. The 18th Division, commanded by that very efficient officer, Major-General Ivor Maxse, was assisted by the explosion of two small mines on its front, where no man's land was only about 200 yards wide. It stormed ahead through the German front line, though not without loss before some of the German strongpoints and redoubts. The French XX Corps on the right also attacked at 0730 hours and attained all its objectives without undue difficulty, and the French Sixth Army divisions south of the Somme also got ahead, capturing all of its objectives by the end of the day, and taking more than 4,000 prisoners.

The afternoon was quiet on the XIII Corps front, but by nightfall its assault divisions had taken the Montauban ridge and were digging in. This success was due to their rapid advance through well-cut wire, to the narrowness of no man's land, to their efficient use of artillery, to their prior training, and to their post-assault concentration upon mopping up the German position, thus ensuring that no enemy soldiers would emerge from shelter and fire on the backs of the advancing British troops. It still cost XIII Corps some 6,000 men killed and wounded; their German opponents lost around 3,500.

The next corps on the left, Lieutenant-General Sir Henry Horne's XV Corps, consisting of the 7th, 21st and 17th Divisions, had to attack the hinge of the German line at the Fricourt salient. The German positions here, between the villages of Fricourt and Mametz, were particularly strong, a 1,200-yard-deep maze of trenches, wire and fortified houses, with strong bastions at Fricourt and Mametz. On the other hand, the enemy did not have enough troops to man this position properly, just six battalions of the 28th Reserve Division in the front-line and support trenches, while the German artillery covering this section of the front had been largely destroyed by the bombardment. The defence therefore depended chiefly on machine-gun and mortar fire and the tenacious, hard-fighting qualities of the German infantry soldier

The British attack here was supported by the explosion of three mines, detonated more to disturb the enemy and throw up protective earth barriers against enfilade fire than in any hope of destroying enemy soldiers. Rather more faith was placed in the artillery programme supporting the assault. General Horne was a Gunner and he took a considerable and personal interest in the proposals for support offered by his artillery commander. The word Horne's orders employed in reference to the forward movement of the shellfire was 'drift', and the gun-layers were directed to lift their sights by no more than fifty yards a minute, 'drifting the fire forward', while the infantry were told that if they reached an objective before the artillery could strafe it they were to wait until the shells had done their work before attacking. The guns were to pave the way for the infantry, and to aid this process artillery officers (FOOs) were attached to the assaulting battalions, to spot the fall of shot on the enemy defences.

Since, however, they had no means of communicating with their batteries it is hard to see what these officers hoped to achieve, other than by asking battalion commanders to adhere to the fire plan. In the event the barrage was of considerable benefit to the advancing infantry, but it had insufficient weight to shatter the German defences, and once the British infantry got into the German lines even the guns' lift of aim of fifty yards a minute proved too fast. The barrage soon moved away from the infantry and the German machine-guns began to take a heavy toll of the two assault formations, the veteran 7th Division, a relic of the 1914 BEF, and that New Army 21st Division which had suffered so grievously on the second day at Loos. Only the divisional titles remained the same, though; most of the men of these divisions who had fought on the Aisne or at First Ypres or Loos had long since disappeared.

The 21st Division was to push east, take Fricourt and Mametz, and press on up the axis of the Willow Stream towards Mametz Wood. By nightfall it had taken ground to the north of Fricourt, while the 7th Division had succeeded in taking Mametz and had then lined up along the south side of the Willow Stream and linked up with the 18th Division on its right. Then, however, their attacks were held. The assault on Fricourt was halted after terrible losses, one company of the 7th Yorkshire Regiment (Green Howards) being utterly destroyed by the raking fire of just a single German machine-gun. When the Green Howards put in an attack against the strongest part of the Fricourt position they found only four small gaps in the German wire. Mustering to pass through these they were subjected to a murderous fire from machine-guns and rifles, and within three minutes the battalion had lost 15 officers and 366 men. The 7th East Yorkshires, coming up in support, suffered a similar fate, losing 5 officers and 150 men in the first few yards before their advance was called off.

By the end of the day XV Corps could claim that it had made good progress on the flanks of its attack, and had taken over 1,500 prisoners. On the other hand, the Fricourt bastion was still unsubdued and the corps had lost 8,791 men killed and wounded, nearly half of them from the 21st Division. Firing from the German line ceased at dusk, and the British stretcher-bearers were left undisturbed as they collected thousands of wounded men from in front of the German wire.

The next corps to the north, Lieutenant-General Sir W.P. Pulteney's III Corps, comprising the 8th, 19th and 34th Divisions, straddled the Albert–Bapaume Road, the axis of the British advance in the Battle of the Somme. The road led over the crest from Albert, dropped into the valley at La Boisselle, on the road itself, and then rose again to the top of the eastern ridge at Pozières. The German battalions had a strong entrenched position astride the road, with strongpoints in the villages of Ovillers, at the head of Mash Valley and left of the road, and in La Boisselle itself. Moreover, the British lines were overlooked by the higher German defences and could be reached by machine-gun fire from the Thiepval spur, beyond Ovillers.

This advantage of observation was, however, shared by the British artillery observers who, from their posts on the western ridge, had a clear view over the German positions. This sector of the ridge, 'Tara Hill' to the British, was occupied by a support trench known as the 'Tara-Usna Line' from which communication trenches snaked down to the British front line just in front of La Boisselle. The snag was that British reinforcements and attacking infantry moving east of Tara Hill were in full view from the German positions, whose defenders, drawn from four regiments, did not need to expose themselves at all in order to fire upon their attackers.

The Ovillers–La Boisselle position was among the strongest on the entire front, occupying a naturally strong site astride three ridges from which the ground in between could be covered by interlocking fields of enfilade machine-gun fire. The right of III Corps faced the western slope of the Fricourt spur, the centre that of La Boisselle, the left that of Ovillers. No man's land varied in width from 800 yards at Ovillers, to less than 50 yards at a much-mined point just south of La Boisselle known as the 'Glory Hole'. Of the two shallow valleys on either side of La Boisselle, Sausage and Mash, neither was more than 1,000 yards long. Finally, as has been said, the whole III Corps front could be overlooked from Thiepval.

The Germans had fortified their position with thick belts of wire, strongpoints and redoubts in the villages of La Boisselle and Ovillers, as well as a series of trenches leading back to the second line running across the Pozières Ridge from Bazentin-le-Petit to Mouquet Farm, with a third line three miles behind that. The 34th Division was to attack La Boisselle, Sausage Valley and the Fricourt spur, the 8th Division was to capture Mash Valley and Ovillers and all the German positions north of the Bapaume road. The 19th Division was in corps reserve, but its guns were deployed in support of the assault divisions. The task of III Corps was to advance two miles to the east, up to the German second line, on a front of 4,000 yards – a task which meant taking two fortified villages and six lines of trenches.

The La Boisselle-Ovillers position was recognised as difficult and the artillery concentration here was stronger than elsewhere, with ninety-eight heavy guns and howitzers plus some French artillery made available to reduce the defences; the deployment averaged one field gun per twenty-three yards of front and one heavy gun every forty yards. After some days of bombardment, night patrols up to the German wire found much of it still uncut; as a result, in front of La Boisselle and Ovillers a battery of Stokes mortars was added to the barrage at Zero hour. The attacking infantry were supported by a carefully timed fire programme calling for eight slow 'lifts' of the heavy artillery – an advance up to the German second line calculated at about two miles – which were to be made in precisely one hour and forty-seven minutes. The divisional field artillery was to lengthen its range very gradually and 'rake' the ground between the trench lines while the infantry advanced behind it.

It can be seen, therefore, that with their 'creeping', 'drifting' and 'raking' fire programmes, the corps commanders were trying to give close artillery support to their infantry battalions. This effort was largely wasted, however – since the only means of controlling this fire was by adhering to strict timings – because the infantry, fighting their way through strong enemy defences, could not keep up with the barrage, and because the lack of battlefield communications meant that the artillery fire could not be adjusted if the timings went awry. None of this was the generals' fault; the communications of the time were simply not good enough.

The assault was also to be aided by the explosion of the two large mines at the heads of Sausage and Mash Valleys. The Y Sap crater in Mash was filled in a few years ago, but the Lochnagar crater, blown under the redoubt in Sausage Valley, still remains; it was created at 0728 hours on 1 July by the detonation of 60,000 pounds of ammonal. Two minutes later the infantry assault went in.

The 34th Division sent twelve battalions over the top, deployed not in extended line but in 'columns of battalion', each column four battalions (i.e. one brigade) deep and about 400 yards wide. These columns were not to hurl themselves directly on the La Boisselle strongpoints but to pass on either side of it, dropping off platoon bombing parties and men with Stokes mortars and Lewis guns, to attack the position from the flanks. This method was used because Rawlinson had assured General Pulteney, the corps commander, that La Boisselle would be shattered by artillery fire and the supporting redoubt positions completely destroyed by the two mine explosions. None of these things actually came about, and the advancing troops took a terrible beating from a mass of sustained and accurate fire.

As the leading brigades rose from their trenches, they were met with a hail of machine-gun and artillery fire. Within ten minutes some 80 per cent of their men had become casualties, and as the bombardment moved on, more and more enemy machine-guns and mortars began to rake the British infantry. The Germans swarmed up from their dugouts directly the gunfire lifted, manned their defence line and cut the four advancing columns of the 34th Division to pieces.

The brigades attacking Sausage Valley and La Boisselle – 102 (Tyneside Scottish) and 103 (Tyneside Irish), consisting of battalions of the Northumberland Fusiliers – pressed home their attacks with great resolution. The casualties of the 34th Division were the highest recorded of any division that day, but in the noise and dust and confusion of battle it was not until 0900 hours that Divisional HQ realised the attack had failed. Some artillery had already been ordered to move up in support but apart from a small advance on the Fricourt spur and possession of a section of the redoubt in Sausage Valley, the infantry were pinned down under heavy fire in no man's land. By the end of the day the 34th Division had lost 6,380 men killed, wounded and missing, and had advanced barely a hundred yards.

Meanwhile the 8th Division was attacking up Mash Valley towards Ovillers. Since the ground over which the division would advance was overlooked by flanking positions and covered by interlocking machine-gun, mortar and artillery fire, the divisional commander, Major-General Hudson, had proposed to hold back his attack until the 34th and 32nd Division (the latter from X Corps) on his flanks had taken their objectives. This suggestion was rejected. In another attempt to reduce his inevitable losses, Hudson ordered his front-line troops to move out into no man's land, which varied here from 300 to 800 yards in width, and so reduce the distance they must cover. This action saved lives, but did not help the division take the enemy position.

At least two German machine-guns were playing on the front-line parapet even before the infantry went over the top, and as they pressed on up Mash Valley and on to the Ovillers ridge the soldiers were seen to be leaning forward into the fire, as into driving rain. Within minutes, whole battalions were being shot down. Only about seventy men of 23 Brigade reached the German trenches, where, sheltered from the machine-gun fire, they held out for two hours before withdrawing. Artillery pounded the troops advancing up Mash Valley, which was totally devoid of cover, and with machine-guns from either flank and from Thiepval calmly raking their ranks from side to side, the men fell dead in orderly rows before their attack disintegrated. It was soon clear that General Hudson had been quite correct; unless and until the flanking defences had been reduced, an attack up Mash Valley into Ovillers was not possible. The cost of underlining that conclusion was 5,121 officers and men killed, wounded and missing.

Immediately to the north, X Corps had the task of capturing the Thiepval spur, south of the Ancre, and the left bank of that river up as far as Beaucourt. This corps, commanded by Lieutenent-General Sir T.L.N. Morland, consisted of the 32nd and 36th (Ulster) Divisions, which would mount the assault, and the 49th Division, which was in reserve. The German positions, held by eight battalions, completely overlooked the British line, but the Ancre valley winds about and the trees in Aveluy Wood on the valley floor, since they were largely undamaged by shellfire, still had their leaves, so most of the British preparations went unseen.

This proved of little advantage on the day, however, for the Thiepval position was extremely strong. Thiepval village contained sixty houses, all of which had been fortified and though shellfire had destroyed the buildings, the cellars remained intact and provided ideal shelter for a quantity of machine-guns. These cellars were linked by tunnels and the machine-guns could enfilade any attack coming up directly from the Ancre valley or from either flank. The Thiepval spur itself was covered by the Leipzig Redoubt, another fortified position, and the interlinked trench lines included a triangle of trenches known as the Schwaben Redoubt, which overlooked the ground before the British line, and another German strongpoint further down the slope, in the hamlet of St Pierre-Division. Finally, this position enjoyed the advantage of linked, supporting enfilade fire from Ovillers. It was said later that only bullet-proof soldiers could have taken Thiepval on 1 July 1916, and so it proved.

The task of X Corps was to take the enemy position in the first rush and get well forward on the Thiepval spur. If they could do so, not only Ovillers but all the German defences up to Serre, on the extreme left wing, would be outflanked and might, possibly, be rolled up. What actually happened after 0730 hours may be quickly told, though the fighting went on for most of the day.

There was no arrangement here for any form of creeping barrage, but the 18-pounders were directed to move up in ten lifts, from trench to trench. There would also be a gas discharge at 0700 hours, but in the event this had little effect, while the artillery bombardment soon ran away from in front of the advancing soldiers. As elsewhere on 1 July, everything would depend on the infantry.

Some battalions of the 32nd Division, the 17th Highland Light Infantry (HLI)* for example, sent their troops out into no man's land early, and the men were lying within forty yards of the German trenches when the bombardment lifted. As a result, they were over the wire and at the entrances to the dugouts before the Germans scrambled out, but though they captured their share of the German front line they were stopped from advancing further by machine-gun fire and showers of mortar bombs and grenades when they attempted to move forward. Other battalions suffered severely as they advanced, for the artillery support had moved on, and since Divisional HQ came to believe that the Thiepval spur had actually fallen to the attack, no further artillery fire was directed on to the village. By 1030 hours the 32nd Division had halted, and its men were ordered to hang on grimly to whatever ground they held.

The 36th (Ulster) Division went into the attack with considerable élan and in great spirits, for 1 July is the revised date for the Battle of the Boyne in 1690, when the Protestant William of Orange (William III) defeated the forces of the Catholic James II – a great anniversary for the Protestant community in Northern Ireland. The division's attack on the German front line was completely successful except down on the bank of the Ancre. At Zero hour, the men advanced in the approved GHQ formation, each battalion in four extended lines, each line fifty yards apart, every man a few paces from his neighbour. Bayonets fixed, rifles at the high port, the infantry swept into no man's land at a steady pace and, by some miracle, crossed the 300–500 yards of open ground before the Germans could get into action, aided by the fact that here at least the wire had been well cut.

Resistance then began to stiffen. More and more German machine-guns stuttered into life, but by 0830 elements of the division had advanced up to one mile through the German defences beyond Thiepval Wood and had taken some 400 prisoners. Matters were not going so well on the right bank of the Ancre, however, where two battalions of the Royal Irish Fusiliers and one of the Royal Irish Rifles were tasked to advance on Beaucourt station. These battalions had elected to move out of their trenches before Zero hour, but were caught by the enemy machine-guns as they passed through their own wire and were raked again as they advanced steadily across the 600 yards that separated them from the German front line. The outcome was seen by a British artillery officer, who stared into no man's land through his field glasses and then asked his companion why the men out there were not moving. 'Because they are all dead,' was the brief reply.

This litany of slaughter need not continue. The 36th Division flung all its

---

* A New Army unit, styled the 17th (Service) Battalion, HLI (Glasgow Chamber of Commerce).

weight into the attack at Thiepval but could not overcome the strong defences and the massive volume of fire produced by the German machine-guns. By-mid morning the two divisions of X Corps were embedded in the German positions at various points, most deeply at the Schwaben Redoubt, which the 36th Division had penetrated, and the corps commander was faced with the choice of deploying his reserve division to extricate the 32nd Division, or of reinforcing the 36th in the hopes of a breakthrough.

The golden rule in such situations, as has been said, is to reinforce success, and since the 36th Division had forced its way through the German positions between Thiepval and St-Pierre-Divion and had got on to the Thiepval plateau, that was where the reserves could best be used – if they could get up there. However, the defences of Thiepval and St-Pierre-Divion were now producing a prodigious amount of interlocking fire and an advance up the slope to Thiepval was impossible – nor was it possible to take one of these mutually supporting positions without overcoming the other. In addition, the 36th Division troops had not had time to 'mop up' the trenches and dugouts in their rear, with the result that German snipers and machine-guns were now active behind them, preventing any movement across no man's land. It was also necessary to get a grip on the artillery fire and direct it back on to the main German defences. None of this could be managed; a setpiece attack suffers from the great disadvantage of inflexibility and it was not possible to refocus the corps' attack and put the main weight behind the Ulster Division

The advance units of the 36th Division could not be supported and as the afternoon wore on their grip on the Thiepval plateau began to slip; casualties mounted, ammunition and grenades began to run out, the ever-resilient German defenders began to work their way forward down the trenches. By 1400 hours the Germans were ready to deliver a heavy artillery bombardment on the division's position and mount a counter-attack. The Ulstermen were forced to pull back, taking heavy casualties as they withdrew from the German trenches. The division had lost a great many men by this time – the highest ranking officer left alive in the companies holding the Schwaben Redoubt was a major – and at dusk the order was given to retire, the men pulling back in good order at about 2200 hours. At 2330 orders came that two brigades were to recapture the Schwaben Redoubt. In the event, however, the two commanding brigadier-generals agreed that this was impossible and the attack was cancelled. So the attack of the 36th (Ulster) Division, so gallant and initially so successful, finally petered out, with the loss of 5,104 men killed, wounded and missing – more than half the total casualties suffered by the entire X Corps. It took two full days, until 3 July, to move all the wounded men off the slopes above the Ancre.

If the other corps astride or north of the Albert–Bapaume Road suffered – as they did – various degrees of terrible loss and made little or no progress, no units suffered so badly for so little gain as the brigades and battalions of Lieutenant-General Sir Aylmer Hunter-Weston's VIII Corps, on the extreme left of the Fourth Army line. This strong corps, consisting of the 4th, 29th, 31st and 48th Divisions, was charged with breaking the German line north of the Ancre and taking the villages of Beaumont Hamel and Serre.

As elsewhere on the Somme front, the enemy defences here enjoyed the advantage of higher ground, and the Germans had enhanced this advantage with deep dugouts, barbed wire, interlocking machine-gun fire and an abundance of trench mortars and artillery. No man's land averaged 500 yards in width and was open and bare of cover except for a sunken lane running north from the Auchonvillers–Beaumont Hamel road. The Official History describes the German defences here as 'a form of amphitheatre, confronting the VIII Corps with tiers of fire . . . and offering the enemy complete observation.'

The corps plan of attack required the 4th and 29th Divisions to advance eastwards, through the German front line and across the valley containing Beaumont Hamel, thence on to the Beaucourt spur and the German second line, a distance of 4,000 yards. For this they were allowed three and a half hours. Meanwhile, the 31st Division, on their left, was to form a defensive flank and take the village of Serre, and the 48th Division was to stay close up, but in corps reserve.

The assault infantry were to move out of their trenches before Zero hour and take up positions in no man's land not more than 100 yards from the enemy line. Ten minutes before Zero a large mine was detonated under the Hawthorn Redoubt, the German strongpoint in front of Beaumont Hamel, in the hope that the explosion would throw up debris and screen some of the advancing infantry from direct fire. In fact, this explosion only served to alert the Germans to the imminent assault. Risking the shellfire, they were out of cover and manning their defences when the British infantry attack came in.

The advance here was supported by a creeping barrage, the lifts calculated from the map and timed for an infantry advance of fifty yards a minute. The corps artillery orders, as detailed in the Official History, added the accurate but ominous reminder that 'The times, once settled, cannot be altered. The infantry must therefore make their pace conform to the rate of artillery lifts. If the infantry find themselves checked by their own barrage they must halt and wait until the barrage moves forward.' This instruction does not allow for the alternative situation, however: namely, that the infantry, far from advancing too rapidly, might advance very slowly, or not at all, and so lose the vital assistance of close artillery support. The orders conclude: 'The success or otherwise of the assault largely depends on the infantry thoroughly understanding the "creeping" method of the artillery.' The infantry understood the principle well enough; their problem lay in keeping closed up to the barrage in the face of barbed wire, manned trenches and all the defensive fire the enemy could put down.

The task proved impossible. The German machine-guns were supported by field artillery from behind the Beaucourt spur, which blanketed the enemy front with fire, while heavy artillery came in to pound the British front line and support trenches down which the follow-up waves were moving. The fate of the 1st Royal Newfoundland Regiment, cut to pieces before Y Ravine at Beaumont Hamel, and of the two Pals battalions from Sheffield and Accrington falling in their ranks before Serre, has already been told. What happened to these battalions is only an extreme example of what was happening elsewhere.

When the advance stalled, attempts were made to bring the artillery barrage back, but since no one at either Divisional or Corps HQ knew exactly where the leading battalions were, this was of little practical assistance. The German artillery commanders, with the aid of good observation, were able to pound the British line at will and moved their guns about to pulverise the British line and the battalions trapped in no man's land, which rapidly became pockmarked with shell holes – as a part of it still is, eighty-two years later. At the end of the day, and for the loss of over 14,000 men killed, wounded and missing, VIII Corps had only managed to establish a small foothold on part of the German line at the Quadrilateral position between Serre and Beaumont Hamel. Serre had not been taken, and Beaumont Hamel, 500 yards from the British front line and an objective for the first day on the Somme, did not actually fall until the last days of the battle, four and a half months later.

The final assault on this terrible day was delivered north of Beaumont Hamel by two divisions from Lieutenant-General Sir Edmund Allenby's Third Army. These two divisions, the 56th and 46th of Lieutenant-General Snow's VII Corps, were to attack the Gommecourt salient, which projected into the British line and could therefore enfilade the advancing battalions of VIII Corps.

The Gommecourt salient was to be pinched out by an attack from two sides, the 46th Division attacking from the north, the 56th from the south. This attack seems to have been doomed from the start, after a German observation aircraft flew over a Third Army practice area where the unmistakable outline of the Gommecourt defences was marked out in white tape on the ground. The attack was not designed to achieve a breakthrough or even to draw enemy reserves away from other areas under assault; its sole purpose, according to General Haig's instructions, was 'to assist the operations of Fourth Army by attracting on to itself the fire of artillery and infantry which might otherwise be directed against the left flank of the attack on Serre'. The Gommecourt salient was another heavily defended position and to attack it frontally was to invite disaster, a fate which was duly delivered. The attack itself was a complete failure, and VII Corps suffered nearly 7,000 casualties. It is hard to see what benefit this sacrifice brought to the men of VIII Corps as they pressed home their attacks against Serre.

The Somme is the Great War battle that every Briton remembers. Not even Passchendaele is so firmly etched in the popular imagination, and most of the folk memories that surround the Great War consist of images, real or imagined, from the first day on the Somme. That day, 1 July 1916, was the worst a British army had suffered since Hastings in 1066; at a cost of some 57,000 casualties, the maximum advance into the enemy line was no more than a mile deep and perhaps three and a half miles wide . . . and on many parts of the front there had been no gains at all. The first day was a defeat, and a terrible one – but how much of what happened can be blamed on the generals?

In so far as they planned and conducted the battle, Haig and Rawlinson (and, to a much lesser extent, Allenby) may quite fairly be blamed for all of it. Had the offensive succeeded they would certainly be entitled to all the credit, and it is not possible to have it both ways. This does not mean that Rawlinson and Haig were either callous or incompetent. The accusation of callousness can be refuted in the case of the former by the great attention he paid to the care of his men even before the battle began, ensuring that there were enough dressing and casualty stations to get his wounded treated, and enough trains standing by to get them to hospital.

As for his competence, his plan was sound. Although it is possible to pick holes in it, much of the criticism is made with the benefit of hindsight, rather than in the light of circumstances as they prevailed at the time. Considering the situation as it appeared in 1916, it is hard to do more than suggest minor alterations to the plan. Yes, it might have been a good idea to strengthen the attack at some points, rather than attack with equal weight all along the line. More guns would definitely have helped, but Rawlinson used all the guns he could get and he had plenty of ammunition, even if not all of it was reliable – and he cannot be held responsible for that. The order to attack in extended line, which has come in for a great deal of criticism, was frequently ignored by the attacking troops, so that formation may not have caused as many casualties as is commonly supposed. As Dr John Bourne writes:

> The fate of the infantry battalions on 1 July had very little to do with the attack formation they adopted. On the southern front, units took all their objectives whether they advanced in extended line or in skirmisher formation; on the northern front they failed disastrously no matter whether they went over the top shoulder to shoulder, or using the state-of-the-art, pre-war, fire-and-movement tactics. The key to success was artillery. (Letter to the author, 1997.)

Greater use should have been made of smoke; some divisions used it, but the reasons for not doing so – that it would hinder artillery observation and cause the attackers to lose direction – are also valid, especially when it is recalled that a number of divisions used some form of 'creeping barrage' and needed to be able to observe its effects. It is possible to criticise many minor points in the planning and conduct of the battle but while eradicating all the errors would have helped, any one error contributed just a small part to the whole tragedy. The crux of the problem, the dominance of the defence in this war, lay deeper, and was currently insoluble.

The first day on the Somme was a tragedy of epic proportions, an example of the simple, awful truth that the German defensive positions on the Western Front could not be taken by any means available to the Allied generals in 1916. Until some way could be found of providing the troops with close support, these losses would continue. The only other alternative was to stop the war.

CHAPTER 12

THE ADVENT OF TANKS, JULY–SEPTEMBER 1916

'It is not too much to claim that the foundations of final victory on the Western Front were laid by the Somme offensive of 1916.'

Brigadier-General Sir J. E. Edmonds,
Military Operations France and Belgium, Preface to *1916*, Volume II

Although the Battle of the Somme lasted for four and a half months, this chapter pays particular attention to just one major action which took place during that time; Rawlinson's night attack of 14 July. It also looks at the fighting on General Gough's Reserve Army front, north of the Albert–Bapaume Road and aims to reveal how the three commanding generals, Haig, Rawlinson and Gough, handled some specific parts of these encounters. Finally, it will also trace the development of that trench-breaching weapon, the tank, before it made its battlefield debut at Flers in September.

Given the casualties of the first day, one option open to Haig and Rawlinson on 2 July was to call the battle off, hang on to the slender – *very* slender – gains made on that day and prepare another setpiece offensive for the forthcoming weeks. This option was not taken for a number of reasons, not least because the exact extent of the casualties suffered on 1 July was not finally known until the 6th. At midnight on 1 July, the Director of Medical Services in Fourth Army reported to Rawlinson that the number of wounded admitted to field ambulances and dressing stations was 526 officers and 14,146 men, a total of 14,672.

To this had to be added the dead, who had not yet been counted, but at the usual rough ratio of around 1 man killed for every 3 wounded, the total casualties for 1 July might be estimated at around 20,000; bad enough, in all conscience. On the evening of 3 July, the total reported wounded for Fourth Army had risen to around 41,000 men and it was not until several days later that the casualty figure reported reached the actual total for 1 July of nearly

60,000 men killed, wounded, missing and made prisoner. It takes time to clear a battlefield and the doctors had more urgent work to do in the first days of July than count the number of patients in their wards.

Rawlinson's oft-quoted comment of 3 July that 'I do not think that the percentage of losses is excessive', and the remark in Haig's diary for 2 July that 'This [the casualties] cannot be considered severe in view of the numbers engaged and the length of front attacked' – both often cited as evidence of callousness in the High Command – are not, therefore, unreasonable in the circumstances. Quite apart from the fact that these two comments are taken out of context, the generals simply did not *know* the full extent of the losses when they were penned.

As so often, though, there are discrepancies in the figures. In the same diary entry for Sunday, 2 July, Haig refers to casualties of over 40,000, although these figures were not yet available on that date. He might, of course, have been writing up his diary a day or two later; indeed, since these figures were not even known to the Director of Medical Services on 2 July, this is the only reasonable conclusion.

Rawlinson's full statement, which was contained in a letter, reads: 'The casualties have, of course, been heavy, but when we consider that 29 brigades – over 100,000 infantry – were taking part in the first assault, I do not think that the percentage of losses is excessive,' while Haig's diary entry was based on a report just received from the Adjutant-General which had also underestimated the true figure. Haig and Rawlinson had already experienced the severe losses at Loos, and the casualties on 1 July, though extremely high, were from an army numbering over half a million men. By the time the true figures reached the two generals, the decision to continue to press ahead with the Somme offensive had been taken.

How it was pursued thereafter was greatly influenced by the French, but that the British commanders would press on with their attack was made certain by other factors. As has been said, it is an accepted military truth that a general does not 'reinforce failure', but seeks to take advantage of whatever opportunity success has brought, even on the most disastrous of fields. The subsequent and justified outcry over the casualty figures should not conceal the fact that the fighting on 1 July did provide some successes.

On the right flank, the assaulting divisions had succeeded in taking most of their objectives, and the fortress of Fricourt fell on 2 July. The French XX Corps, on the right of XIII Corps, had done well, as had the rest of the French Sixth Army south of the Somme. The success of these attacks offered a number of possibilities, not least because the British troops attacking between Fricourt and Maricourt on the right flank, were attacking *northwards*.

The possibilities are clearly seen from a study of the map on page 250. If the British attack on the right wing could be continued, and was supported on the flank by the French, there was a strong possibility that the breach here could be ballooned out across the German second line at High Wood, once Delville Wood and Longueval had been taken. If this could be done, then the top of the Pozières Ridge would have been gained. From there the British might push north and east to outflank and undermine the strong German defences around La Boisselle and Thiepval, and so north, wheeling on firm ground above the Ancre valley. Rawlinson's first decision was to push on north of the Albert–Bapaume Road and take the objectives the X and VIII Corps had failed to take on 1 July. Haig overruled him, however, directing his reserves to the right flank in order to develop his attack from there towards Delville Wood and Longueval . . . and was immediately checked by General Joffre.

Joffre did not really care if the British made a breakthrough on the Somme. If they did that would be a bonus, but he had two other aims, one immediate, one long-term, both of which he considered more important than any local success. Firstly, he needed to ease the German pressure at Verdun, where the French Army was in dire straits, by forcing the Germans to transfer troops to the Somme front. Secondly, he wanted to write down the strength of the German field army by a battle of attrition, to do to the Germans on the Somme what they were currently doing to the French at Verdun. The instrument he would use to achieve this end was the British Army; a concentration of effort on the right flank of the British front would not – at least in Joffre's view – assist in achieving either of these two aims. Moreover, Haig's plan would also involve the French Sixth Army and suck in more reserves, while Joffre wanted any available French reserves for use at Verdun. The Somme was therefore to be a British battle, and Joffre wanted it to be a big one.

On Monday, 3 July, Joffre and Foch descended on Haig's headquarters to discuss, 'future arrangements'. The French C-in-C began by stressing the importance of taking Thiepval, in the centre of the 1 July assault area. Haig demurred: 'having pointed out the progress made on my right near Montauban and the demoralised nature of the enemy troops in that area, I was considering the desirability of pressing my attack on Longueval. I was therefore anxious to know whether the French would attack Guillemont?'

Joffre's reaction to this enquiry was volcanic. According to Haig's diary, he 'exploded in a fit of rage. *He* could not approve of it. He *ordered* me to attack Thiepval and Pozières and said if I attacked Longueval I would be defeated, etc . . .'

Joffre and Foch were now to discover that they were dealing with a very different kind of British general from Field Marshal French. Haig, though taken aback, waited until Joffre had finished and then calmly reminded the French generals that 'I am solely responsible to the British Government for the actions of the British Army,' going on to say that he had approved the plan to push on at Longueval with his right wing and saw no reason to change that decision. Joffre realised he had gone too far, at least for the moment, and became conciliatory, assuring Haig 'that he knew this was the

"English battle", adding that France expected great things from me'. He received in turn an assurance that Haig had only one object, to beat the Germans, and that France and England marched together. French medals were then distributed, with hearty smacks on the cheek, to various members of Haig's staff.

The outcome of this somewhat fraught meeting was still a compromise, for the French agreed to discuss ways of assisting the British attack at Longueval, while Haig agreed to press the attack on other sections of the Somme front. As a result, against the background of the specific actions described in this chapter, the 'battle of attrition' desired by Joffre continued on other parts of the Somme front, bleeding the German strength, certainly, but having a similar effect on the British forces. The problem was to a certain extent tactical, for while Joffre could not *order* Haig to make another all-out attack along his entire front, he could certainly inhibit the British intentions of pushing ahead on the right.

The British right flank did not rest firmly on the River Somme, but on the left of the French XX Corps, which as Joffre had insisted was placed north of the river. If the British pushed ahead and the French held back, a gap would open on the right of the British line; yet the only way in which Rawlinson could advance on to the Pozières Ridge and push along it to the north was if the French covered his flank, which Joffre and Foch were not willing to do. There was, also, that further, chronic complication – that part of Haig's orders requiring him to 'co-operate closely' with the French.

Turning to their maps, the British commanders prepared to attack at different points all along the front, though their offensive on the Somme had already done its work at Verdun. The German attacks there began to peter out on 12 July, and by the 14th their bid to take the city was at an end. Though the fighting at Verdun continued for several more months, the crisis had passed and the French, under Generals Pétain and Nivelle, now proceeded to drive the Germans back from their gains astride the Meuse.

On the Somme front, however, the battle was only beginning. On 3 July, the Fourth Army was split in two. General Rawlinson retained command of the three southern corps (III, XV and XIII Corps), for operations astride and south of the Albert–Bapaume Road, while Lieutenant-General Sir Hubert Gough, currently commander of the Reserve Army, took command of the two northern corps (X and VIII Corps) and, with his existing infantry and cavalry divisions, assumed responsibility for the front from north of the Albert–Bapaume Road up to the junction with the Allenby's Third Army at Gommecourt. Gough's Reserve Army was renamed as the Fifth Army, during the course of the battle.

Hubert Gough is one of the tragic figures of the Great War. His final ruin came after the collapse of his Fifth Army in the 'Ludendorff Offensive' of 1918, a collapse for which he was hardly to blame; even so, his period in command between 1916 and 1918 was marked with constant controversy. He had been a competent officer at lower levels of command, but it remains doubtful whether he had the broad grasp necessary to exercise the effective command of a full army. In the military parlance of the time Gough was a 'thruster', a man who plunged ahead and got the job done; he was, however, a 'thruster' who attacked regardless of the situation, and his troops suffered in consequence.

At Loos he had thrown his troops forward without adequate artillery support and Major-General E.S. Bulfin, commanding one of Gough's divisions, was only the first of several officers who declared that he never wanted to serve under him again. It was this reputation as a thruster that earned Gough the command of the Reserve Army for the Somme, for if a breach *was* achieved, rapid exploitation by the cavalry was clearly essential. General Haig attributed the futile and tragic events of 1915, at Neuve Chapelle and Loos, to a failure to commit the reserves quickly. This time he wanted a man in charge of the reserves who would not hang back at the crucial moment, but since 1 July had not provided that essential break-through he now decided to give Gough a large force and responsibility for part of the front. The latter's first day in command was not marked by any particular good fortune, for his attacks on Ovillers and Thiepval on 3 July both failed with loss, and the village of La Boisselle, attacked on 1 July, did not finally fall until 6 July.

Rawlinson's main task, south of the Albert–Bapaume Road, was to breach the German second line at Longueval. Before he could do that he had to clear his front by capturing Mametz Wood and Contalmaison, but it was evident that any advance up the road beyond La Boisselle, on the axis of that advance, would be impossible unless the villages of Ovillers and Thiepval were in British hands. La Boisselle was finally captured on 4 July by troops of the 19th (Western) Division.

On 7 July, therefore, Fourth Army concentrated its efforts on Mametz Wood and the village of Contalmaison, but these attacks were driven off. Haig severely criticised the handling of the 38th (Welsh) Division during this attack and on 9 July, while the fighting continued, the GOC 38th Division, Major-General Ivor Philipps, was sacked. General Philipps was a protégé of Lloyd George, the Secretary of State for War. On 12 July another divisional commander, Major-General T.D. Pilcher of the 17th (Northern) Division was relieved of his command and sent home. The idea that incompetent commanders were left in place is yet another Great War myth.

Meanwhile, just across the Albert–Bapaume Road, the Reserve Army's attack on Ovillers succeeded in penetrating to the outskirts of the village but cost the attacking brigade 50 per cent casualties. On the Fourth Army front, Contalmaison fell on 10 July and Mametz Wood was finally in British hands on the 12th. Rawlinson then proceeded with the next phase, a dawn attack on the German second line, though Gough's divisions were still held up north of the Albert–Bapaume Road. The main problem affecting the Fourth Army's attack was the 1,500 yards of open ground between the British forward positions and the German second line. Covering such a distance and then assaulting an entrenched enemy position was a daunting task. Rawlinson, however, thought he had the answer.

Having consulted his artillery and infantry commanders, he decided on a dawn assault, following a stealthy night advance of his infantry up to a point close to the German line, and a final but very short 'hurricane' bombardment. The enemy wire would be cut by a continuous bombardment over the previous days, but one put down in such a way as not to seem an obvious precursor to an assault, while an attack in the grey light of dawn should not provide the German machine-gunners with too many good targets. Haig expressed doubts that the infantry and staff of the four divisions chosen for this night attack, the 3rd and 9th (Scottish) from XIII Corps, and the 7th and 21st from XV Corps, were well enough trained to handle a night advance and a dawn attack, but Rawlinson felt certain that it could be done. His corps commanders agreed with him and, after a considerable amount of argument and discussion, Haig decided to let him go ahead.

The allegation that the British troops fighting on the Somme were not well trained surfaces continually in many accounts of the fighting. While the allegation has some truth in it, it applies in particular to *staff officers*. There had been plenty of time since 1914 to train the men, NCOs and junior officers in their duties, though the process had not been aided by a shortage of equipment and of suitable instructors, or by the fact that many of those instructors who were available had learned their expertise in wars very different from the one now being waged on the Western Front, and was further inhibited by the fact that in the rapidly expanding British armies instructors of any kind and of any level of ability were inevitably in short supply.

Staff officers – the administrative element in any sizeable military formation – were also in short supply, and that shortage would take even longer to make up. The peacetime Staff College course took two full years, but in the current emergency any form of staff training was of much shorter duration – it had to be, since otherwise the divisions necessary to man the line and do the fighting could not have been formed at all. It was inevitable, therefore, that many staff officers did not know their duties or were not fully competent, and the abuse heaped on them – 'incompetent swine', in Sassoon's words – fails to take account of this fact. Most of the staff officers with the BEF had to learn 'on the job'; while they were doing so, the administration of the armies and the organisation of attacks was bound to suffer.

The planning for Rawlinson's attack was somewhat disrupted when, on 8 July, he learned that the French XX Corps on his right would not, as had been promised, support his operations with an attack on Guillemont. The French elected to remain on the defensive, and expressed their belief that the Rawlinson's attack would be a disaster. This refusal did, however, provide Rawlinson with a small advantage once he realised that, since the French declined to be involved in his attack, he had no need to consult them. He could therefore make a plan in the best interests of his army, without the usual inhibitions caused to British planners by the views of the French. For his part Haig, keeping his part of the bargain with Joffre and Foch, was meanwhile maintaining pressure all along the German line on the Ancre.

On 11 July Haig and Rawlinson held another conference to discuss the preparations, and on the following day the latter issued his final orders. The attack would go in before dawn at 0325 hours on 14 July, after a hurricane bombardment of just five minutes' duration. This was at the request of the two generals commanding the 3rd and 9th (Scottish) Divisions of XIII Corps, who said that any longer barrage simply put the Germans on the alert. Rawlinson had about 1,000 guns of various calibres to support the infantry, but since the front on 14 July was much narrower than that attacked on 1 July, the weight of shot falling on the German line would consequently be much heavier. The guns were only to use high-explosive shells with delayed-action fuses, so that the shells would explode in the wire and among the trench defences and not be detonated by prior contact with trees and buildings. This tactic proved so successful that purely shrapnel barrages were rarely employed again.

The 22,000 men of the four attacking divisions had to make a night advance uphill to their assault line, the 3rd and 9th about 1,200 yards, the 7th and 21st of between 350 and 600 yards, to a position some 500 yards from the enemy trenches. From there they were to assault the enemy positions on a line from Delville Wood through the centre of Longueval village, then on through the southern edge of Bazentin-le-Grand village and wood, and so to the southern edge of Bazentin-le-Petit wood. With this much achieved, the next stage would be the capture of Delville Wood, the rest of Longueval village, and Bazentin-le-Petit village and wood. The Indian cavalry would then pour through this breach to capture High Wood, a dominating position on the Pozières Ridge a mile west of Longueval.

General Rawlinson's night attack – actually a night advance and dawn attack – of 14 July 1916, just two weeks after the 1 July catastrophe, was a great, significant, and now largely forgotten success. The staff work on this occasion was excellent, secrecy had been maintained, the guns had been registered and the wire cut without revealing the point of attack, and the men carefully briefed on what they had to do. The operation was aided by an attack made on the same night, 13/14 July, at Trônes Wood, on the right-hand edge of the main assault, by General Maxse's 18th (Eastern) Division, and by various diversions staged by VIII Corps north of the Albert–Bapaume Road. Nevertheless, the credit for the idea and its execution rests with Henry Rawlinson.

After a five-minute storm from artillery and machine-guns, the infantry went forward in the gloom at 0320 hours and reached the German line without undue difficulty, while the enemy's counter-barrage fell behind them, in Caterpillar Valley. The wire was found to be well cut, the German trenches wrecked and most of the defenders either dead or in full retreat. By mid-morning the attackers were up to the edge of Delville Wood, fighting in the ruins of Longueval, and had established contact with the 18th Division on their right. They had obtained a grip on the main Ginchy-Pozières ridge in one bound, on a front of some 6,000 yards, captured some 1,400 Germans and were now consolidating their gains and mopping-up the trenches they had so recently overrun. That the Germans would react swiftly to contain this advance, and would fight tenaciously for Delville Wood and High Wood in the ensuing weeks, was only to be expected. This cannot detract from the fact that their second line had been breached, and that the ground taken in Rawlinson's attack was held.

However, in the Great War there were few absolute victories and the second stage of Rawlinson's plan, the attack on High Wood by elements of the 2nd Indian Cavalry Division was a costly failure. There was also the problem of deploying the reserves before the Germans could seal off the breach. Taking High Wood was crucial and this might have been done before 1000 hours on the 14th, for the Germans were falling back from their second line and several senior British officers, who were well forward in this attack, reported that the way up to the wood was wide open. Major-General H. E. Watts, commanding the 7th Division, therefore proposed rushing his reserve brigade, 91 Brigade, up to High Wood at once but was ordered not to do so, firstly because this task had been delegated to the Indian cavalry, and secondly because Rawlinson anticipated a German counter-attack and needed to keep the assault divisions' reserves available to beat it off. This was a sensible, professional precaution, for consolidating captured positions and beating off counter-attacks are what reserves are for, and Rawlinson cannot be faulted for taking it. Moreover, the decision to use units from the Cavalry Corps was also reasonable, provided the enemy fire could be suppressed, since cavalry was the only force capable of moving forward rapidly on a battlefield in 1916.

The problem was that a delay arose in bringing the 2nd Indian Cavalry Division up. It had been kept back at Morlancourt, four miles south of Albert, and when it was called forward, at 0820 hours, it had to make its way up roads crowded with supply and ammunition wagons and over ground pitted with shell holes, trenches and belts of wire. As a result it was 1415 hours before it reached the front and was ordered on to attack High Wood, which had meanwhile been assaulted by troops of the 7th Division. By now, German counter-attacks were starting to develop and a certain amount of confusion was arising at the HQs of XIII and XV Corps and at Fourth Army HQ, concerning the state of affairs in Longueval, where the fighting was still going on. It was not until 1900, nearly twelve hours after they had been ordered up, that the cavalry, one squadron each from the 20th Deccan Horse and the 7th Dragoon Guards, began to advance towards High Wood. They rode into machine-gun and shellfire that rapidly brought their attack to a halt with heavy casualties, a sad conclusion to an otherwise satisfactory day. Losses on 14 July amounted to some 9,000 men, killed, wounded and missing from the four divisions involved. In return, the British had driven a salient into the German second line, but Delville Wood, parts of Longueval, and the all-important High Wood were still untaken.

Some severe fighting still lay ahead to complete the task begun on 14 July. In the coming weeks, the South African Brigade, part of the 9th (Scottish) Division, would suffer terrible casualties in the long-drawn-out struggle for Delville Wood, and the Australians would be thrown into the attack against the Pozières position, a mile north-east of La Boisselle.

With La Boisselle taken on 4 July the next obstacle on the British axis of advance up the Albert–Bapaume Road was the village of Pozières. This straddled a high point on the battlefield, on the top of a slope leading to the main ridge. It took many weeks of stubborn fighting to edge up the road towards Pozières and the task of finally taking it was delegated to the 1st Australian Division, which was now serving in Gough's Reserve Army.

After arriving from Gallipoli the Australian and New Zealand Army Corps had been rested and then attached to Plumer's Second Army. On 7 July, Haig ordered the 1st Australian further into GHQ Reserve in the Fourth Army area and then attached it to Reserve Army on 19 July, relieving the 34th Division in III Corps. The 5th Australian Division joined Horne's First Army for the ill-conceived attack on Fromelles, near Aubers, between 19–20 July, in which it lost over 5,000 men, killed, wounded and missing, but the first major battle fought by the Australians in France began on 25 July 1916. On that day the 1st Australian Division attacked Pozières the first of a series of attacks between then and 3 September which are officially referred to as the Battle of Pozières Ridge.

At this battle, and in every other battle from their arrival in Egypt in 1914 until Lieutenant-General John Monash took command of what had become the Australian Army Corps in May 1918, the Anzacs were commanded by a British general, an officer of the Indian Army, Lieutenant-General William Riddell Birdwood – 'Birdy' to his much-loved 'Diggers'. Birdwood was born in 1865 in Poona, India where his father was Under-Secretary to the Governor of Bombay. The Birdwoods were a military family; two of his brothers entered the Army and died in service, one in 1894, the other while serving with the 4th Gurkha Rifles in Mesopotamia in 1914.

After attending Clifton College, Haig's old school, Birdwood went to Sandhurst, was commissioned in 1894 and joined his regiment the XII Lancers in India. This family were not wealthy, however, and after a year in India young Birdwood had to transfer to a less expensive Indian Army regiment, the 11th Bengal Lancers. Birdwood clearly loved India. He saw service on the Frontier, taking part in the Tirah Expedition of 1897, during which he was present at the Battle of the Heights of Dargai, when the Gordon Highlanders, supported by Gurkhas and Sikhs, took the ridge from the Afghans at the point of the bayonet. It was an exciting life, full of sport and adventure. Birdwood enjoyed it thoroughly and rose steadily in his profession, especially after his service in South Africa during the Boer War, where he met and was taken up by General Kitchener. The two men remained close friends for the rest of Kitchener's life; the Field Marshal was godfather to Birdwood's daughter, and his loss at sea less than a month before the Somme battle started came as a great blow to General Birdwood, a tragedy which, he said, 'overwhelmed me . . . I mourned him no less as a personal friend than as a great soldier and administrator.'

While serving in India Birdwood married the niece of Lieutenant Gonville Bromhead, one of the officers who had won the VC defending Rorke's Drift against the Zulus in 1879. Birdwood went on to make his name during the South African War, when he renewed his acquaintance with many of his former Sandhurst colleagues in the British Army, established his reputation as a good commander of fighting troops and, in 1900, joined Kitchener's staff as Deputy Assistant Adjutant-General (DAAG). After the South African War he returned to India as Military Secretary on Kitchener's staff and remained on it through the years of difficulty between Kitchener and the Viceroy, Lord Curzon. When the Great War broke out Birdwood was a major-general and Secretary to the Indian Army Department in Delhi. On 18 November 1914, however, he received a telegram from Kitchener offering him command of the Australian and New Zealand divisions, then en route for Egypt. A month later Birdwood, now promoted lieutenant-general and a corps commander, joined the Anzacs in Cairo, and began one of the happiest and most fruitful periods of his long and distinguished military career.

According to popular myth, the Australian troops, in particular, did not take kindly to British officers, considering them effete, chinless and class-ridden, short of soldiering ability and far too keen on saluting – a view nowadays reinforced by films like *Gallipoli* (1981), as well as books and television programmes. There is, however, very little contemporary evidence to support that belief. Had it been true, the appointment of a British professional soldier – and from the caste-ridden Indian Army, no less – would not have been the wisest choice. As it was, Birdwood and his Anzac soldiers got on wonderfully well from the start, an affection that endured until his death. His memoirs are studded with references to 'my beloved Australians', and during his post-war visit to Australia in 1919–20 he was greeted everywhere by thousands of his former soldiers, cheering him and demanding his autograph. At one dinner during his visit, *700* former Diggers asked him to sign their menus. Birdwood's unfulfilled wish was to become Governor-General of Australia, but although he was disappointed in this hope, his daughter married an Australian, and he himself visited Australia several times and came to regard it as his second home.

Birdwood commanded the AIF or Australian Imperial Force at Gallipoli, where he was responsible for the final evacuation, during which not a single man was lost – and took them to France in 1916, where the AIF split into two corps, with Birdwood in command of I Anzac, the 1st and 2nd

Australian Divisions, and Lieutenant-General Sir Alexander Godley commanding the 4th and 5th Australian Divisions in II Anzac. Now Birdwood's men, those 'beloved Australians', were committed to the fighting on the Somme.

The attack at Pozières, which began on 23 July, was preceded by a three-day bombardment, and the infantry from the 1st Australian Division were supported by the British 48th (South Midland) Division attacking on their left. The assault brigades worked their way to within 200 yards of the German trenches before the attack and took Pozières Trench, south of the Albert–Bapaume Road, in the first rush. The 2nd Australian Division took up the battle some days later, and I Anzac then began to batter its way up the road, taking heavy casualties as it did so.

Nor were matters any better south of the road. Rawlinson had always preferred 'bite-and-hold' tactics to all-out attempts at a breakthrough, but as July turned to August these nibbling attacks, made in battalion or brigade strength, cost heavy casualties and gained very little ground. On 24 August Haig, growing increasingly dissatisfied with Rawlinson's progress, urged him to adopt a more co-ordinated approach: 'the attack must be made a general one, engaging the enemy simultaneously, along the whole front.' So the fighting continued as the summer wore on, the British slowly gaining a little ground by a number of attacks, in return for a high toll of casualties. It was not until two full months after Rawlinson's successful attack on 14 July that the British made another significant gain at the Battle of Flers-Courcelette, in which a new instrument of war made its debut on the battlefield – the tank.

The prime reason for the horrific death toll on the Somme, and on many other battlefields of the Western Front during the Great War, was that the tactics of the time were dominated by defensive weapons, most specifically by a combination of barbed wire, artillery and machine-guns. This was the problem faced by any attacking force, for against this lethal combination the infantry of every army, French and German as well as British, hurled themselves in vain. This is not to say, however, that the problems of breaking through on the Western Front were not appreciated either by inventive minds or by higher authority.

A possible solution to the problems confronting the British Army on the Western Front had first been put down on paper not quite five months after the outbreak of war, on Christmas Day 1914, by Lieutenant-Colonel Maurice (later Lord) Hankey, then Secretary to the War Council and the Imperial Defence Committee. In a memorandum to the Prime Minister, Asquith, and the Cabinet, Hankey summarised the situation which had developed on the Western Front since the armies had dug in for the winter, and pointed out that since the situation there was now deadlocked and likely to remain so, there were only two ways out: 1) to attack the enemy at some other point and so outflank the Western Front; or 2) to devise some method or means of overcoming the defensive combination of artillery, machine-guns and barbed wire. Both Hankey's solutions were eventually adopted. The first led to a holocaust among the British, French, Gurkha, Australian and New Zealand troops landing at Gallipoli in 1915. The second led to the invention and development of the tank.

Armoured fighting vehicles were not new, even in 1914–15. Armoured trains had been used during the South African War of 1899–1902, and in September 1914 the Royal Naval Air Service (RNAS) had started to use armoured cars – actually civilian Rolls-Royces covered with boiler plate – to patrol the flat country east of their base at Dunkirk, and for the recovery of shot-down pilots. This activity led to more aggressive patrols, suggested by the Director of the Admiralty Air Division, Commodore (later Rear-Admiral Sir) Murray Sueter, who added machine-guns to the boiler plate and sent the cars out to harass the enemy's cavalry patrols; Sueter had also been influential in the formation of the RNAS shortly before war broke out.

Handled aggressively and imaginatively, these vehicles did good work during the 'Race to the Sea', but when the trench line settled after First Ypres in 1914, the opportunity for mobile action disappeared. Apart from any other considerations, the armoured car was road-bound, and in June 1915 the remnants of this little naval force were handed over to the Army, sent to the Middle East and used later by Colonel T.E. Lawrence and his Arab army in the fight against the Turks.

Although Winston Churchill was the prime mover, no one man can claim to have invented the tank, and in the true meaning of the term, the machine was assembled rather than invented, for the basic elements of engine, armour plate and caterpillar track already existed. One of the earliest advocates for something like the tank was Lieutenant-Colonel E.D. (later Major-General Sir Ernest) Swinton, an officer of the Royal Engineers. Sent to France as an official war correspondent in 1914, he had seen the war of movement stop with the formation of the Western Front, and had conceived the idea of breaking the deadlock using armoured vehicles running on tracks, based on an existing agricultural machine, the Holt Caterpillar Tractor.

Swinton first put these ideas to his chief, Colonel Hankey, thereby sparking the thoughts which led to Hankey's memorandum of Christmas 1914. However, if anyone can claim to have initiated the early development of what became the tank, that man is Winston Churchill, First Lord of the Admiralty in early 1915. Churchill picked up Hankey's memorandum, and thereafter pushed for the development of a tracked armoured vehicle which could cross trenches, flatten barbed-wire entanglements and provide close support for the infantry.

In the early days, therefore, the tank was a naval project, and was referred to as a 'landship', while the naval group set up to develop it was known as the 'Landships Committee'. The original landships ordered by Winston Churchill in 1915 were armoured vehicles, 40 feet long and 13 feet wide, with

0.24 inch (6 mm) of roof armour and 0.31 inch (8 mm) of side armour, designed to carry storming parties of fifty men armed with Lewis machine-guns. This project foundered when Churchill was driven to resign his office as First Lord following the failure of the Dardanelles expedition, of which he had been one of the chief advocates, but the idea was followed up by the Minister of Munitions, David Lloyd George.

Swinton had continued developing his idea and in June 1915 he produced a memorandum of his own, entitled 'The Necessity of Machine-Gun Destroyers'. These, he suggested, might be 'petrol tractors of the caterpillar type which can travel at up to 4mph, cross a ditch up to 4 ft wide and scramble over heathland'; 'They should be armoured against German steel-cored bullets and armed with two Maxims and a 2-pounder gun.' This was a considerable step forward from the troop-carrier of the previous year, for what Swinton was now proposing was an armoured *fighting* vehicle (AFV).

A specification was drawn up by the War Office and sent to the Landships Committee, who ordered a prototype called the *Tritton* after its designer and later christened *Little Willie*. Construction began in August 1915, and the work proceeded rapidly as the main elements, the tracks and the engine – a 105-hp Daimler – were readily available, though the design was changed constantly as the work progressed. The name 'tank' was first used to preserve secrecy about the weapon during transit – the tarpaulin-covered vehicles on railway wagons being labelled 'water tanks' – and gradually drifted into accepted usage. The first completed, if much modified, model, christened '*Big Willie*', crawled into the daylight on 8 September 1915.

Work continued on the prototype throughout the autumn and winter of 1915–16, and on 2 February 1916, it was formally introduced to the Government and senior Army officers. By now, *Big Willie* had grown. The complete vehicle was 31 feet 3 inches long, 8 feet high and 13 feet 8 inches wide, and weighed over 28 tons when loaded with men, fuel and ammunition. It carried a crew of eight, and either machine-guns or a 6-pounder naval gun in the side sponsons – semi-circular turrets which permitted a degree of lateral, as well as vertical, movement of the gun. The demonstration took place in Hatfield Park, Hertfordshire, where *Big Willie* successfully negotiated a series of trench obstacles, though the best speed it could manage was no more than 2 miles per hour.

This success in the trials met with a varying response. Commodore Sueter thought the Army should order 3,000 of these monsters at once, but Lord Kitchener was rather non-committal, so that the first order was for just 40 machines, later increased to 100. This order was placed on 11 February 1916, less than five months before the start of the Battle of the Somme. In that time there was a lot to do: the machines had to be built and tested; men had to be recruited and trained; and the problems of the new weapon's tactical deployment had to be thrashed out by those responsible for the project. Above all, the whole business had to be kept secret.

Colonel Swinton was appointed to raise and train the infant tank force, although it was at once made clear that he should not – indeed, must not – expect to command it or lead it in battle. Once convinced of the potential usefulness of the tank, the army commanders in France began to agitate for their swift deployment in the field, a move Swinton attempted to resist. He also produced a series of 'Tactical Instructions', both as a guide to battle training and, he hoped, a blueprint for the way tanks would later be employed in action.

The successful development of a new weapon is far from being the end of the story. The weapon, in this case an armoured fighting vehicle, will have a designed range of technical features and benefits, but at least half the effectiveness of any weapon *in battle* will depend on how it is manned and deployed. The manner in which a weapon *is used* is therefore as critical to its success as its designed technical performance. Early advocates of the tank, having appreciated this point, had very definite views on how, when and where this new weapon should be employed in battle.

Swinton's main proposal was that the tanks should not be tied to the infantry. Since, however, it had been developed as an infantry support weapon this is surprising. His Tactical Instructions also insisted that the new weapon should not be used in 'driblets' but deployed in large numbers, as part of one great combined operation with the infantry, artillery and air force, employing the considerable advantages of surprise in the assault, and speed in the subsequent exploitation. Secrecy was essential to ensure surprise, but when the tank was first deployed, speed was not possible. The heavily armed and armoured machines were painfully slow over heavy ground and not as nimble over shell holes and trenches as the enthusiasts had hoped. This was simply a reflection of technology of the time; the engines and transmission systems of 1916 were not powerful enough, in the case of the former, or reliable enough, in the case of both, to heave such a heavy load over difficult terrain.

In the months which followed Swinton's appointment, the tanks were built and the embryo Tank Corps took shape. The latter began life as 'The Armoured Car Section of the Machine-Gun Corps', which later became the no-less-unwieldy 'Heavy Branch, Machine-Gun Corps'. Men who were felt to have an aptitude for machines were recruited or transferred to this new formation, many coming from the RNAS or the Machine-Gun Corps. They and their tanks first went into action at the Battle of Flers-Courcelette on 15 September 1916.

Before this battle is examined in detail, we must return to the matter of deployment, a factor that affects all weapons. Even if the original specification is excellent and the resulting weapon capable of its designated task, no such device will achieve its full potential unless those who use it are properly trained and those who command it have some idea of its employment in conjunction with other arms, and of its battlefield capabilities – this combination being covered by the term 'tactical deployment'.

With a new, even a revolutionary, weapon, its *tactical* use is a matter of heated debate. In the case of the tank this argument began with an attempt to define exactly what sort of weapon this machine *was*. Was it a mobile fort, fitted with machine-guns, which supported the infantry in the assault, or was it, if used in force, actually armoured cavalry, capable of thundering through the enemy lines into the open country beyond and so restoring mobility to the battlefield? In the event, the British tank experts, not surprisingly a small band in 1916, decided that the tank was an infantry support weapon, a decision that was to have far-reaching consequences

This argument was not academic. Depending on the view taken, so the tactics would vary, as would the specifications for new tank models or further marks of the existing AFV, specifications affecting their speed, armour, armament, range, manning, and tactical organisation. Tank tacticians also had to consider where tanks, in whatever role, could be successfully deployed, and what type of terrain best suited their employment. The last two points may seem blinding glimpses of the obvious, but this basic question of tank deployment, either in twos and threes to support the infantry, or en masse as an armoured spearhead to break the enemy front and restore mobility to the battle, went to the heart of the argument about this new and revolutionary weapon.

The conclusion that the tank was an 'infantry support' weapon affected British tank design until the middle years of the Second World War. When that war started Britain's main battle tank was the heavily armoured but lightly gunned Matilda; it had a top speed of around 8 miles an hour which, though very slow, was more than enough to stay with the infantry. The Germans, who did very little with tanks during the Great War, had adopted the other viewpoint and decided that tanks were actually 'armoured cavalry'; their panzers, fast, heavy-gun machines, were to spearhead the rapid German blitzkriegs in France and Russia in the first years of that struggle. The tanks employed at Flers-Courcelette in 1916 were undergunned, underpowered, inadequately armoured and unreliable, a chronic list of faults that Second World War tank crews in the Western Desert in 1941–2 would have found all too familiar.

While the tanks were being brought in secrecy to France and the crews trained in their use, fighting on all parts of the Somme front had continued. Slowly and painfully, the British line was pushed east. By 14 September the British line ran from its junction with the French at Leuze Wood, just west of Combles, then past the north edge of Delville Wood to the Albert–Bapaume Road. Just behind the German line, on the right-hand side of the road, lay the village of Martinpuich; another village, Courcelette, lay on the left-hand side of the road, 800 yards away The village of Flers, 1,500 yards behind the German line, lay north of Delville Wood and here, between the two latter villages, on the open ground east of Pozières, tanks were first employed in battle.

Sheer necessity – the mother of most inventions – accelerated the requirement for the tank. This urgency meant that its reliability could not be fully tested in trials before it went into service. The tank was one of those weapons that its operators learned to use and fight on the battle-field, not on exercises; it is hardly surprising, therefore, that the early machines were unreliable or that mistakes were made in their use. The most frequent criticism levelled at General Haig over his use of tanks is that he flew in the face of expert opinion and threw away their first advantage – surprise – by employing them too soon, in small numbers scattered among the assaulting infantry battalions, and on unsuitable ground. These last statements are perfectly true, but beg a further question: if these were such obvious mistakes, why did Haig make them?

The answer lies in the situation confronting Haig and his army comman-ders in mid-September 1916. The Battle of the Somme had been going on for two and a half months. There had been some gains, though at great cost, but in many parts of the front – for instance, along the Ancre – the line had not advanced by so much as 50 yards. Autumn had arrived, winter was coming on, casualties had been massive; something had to be done to justify the cost of this offensive. Somehow the German line had to be breached.

Now there was this new invention, the tank, a weapon that could make a breach, crush the wire, defy the machine-guns, and spearhead an advance by the infantry. The tank 'experts' were telling Haig to wait, but they were also telling him that the state of the ground was crucial to their machines' success . . . yet if he waited, the state of the ground, under yet more shelling and the autumn rains, would certainly deteriorate still further. That secrecy they were so keen on could not be maintained much longer, so that if the tank was to be used at all it 1916, it must be used *soon*. Making critical decisions is never easy, but apart from all these points Haig had to consider another factor.

Every day he waited, every day the infantry went without tank support, more men were being killed. Many historians have alleged that Haig was foolish to deploy the tank at Flers-Courcelette in September 1916 because he deployed it too soon. It is not hard to guess, however, what they would have said – or would say today – had Haig kept back this wire-crushing, trench-breaching weapon at Flers-Courcelette, and let his infantry go into the assault without it.

Academics and historians of armoured warfare can choose the ground on which to deploy their arguments, and can stress the particular features that make their points, while concealing or ignoring others that weaken their cases. General Haig did not enjoy such luxuries. He had the interests of his army as a whole to consider, he was the man in charge, the commander with the ultimate responsibility. If he felt that the new weapon could help his assault at Flers, he would have been neglecting his duty not to use it. Besides, the tank was still an *experimental* weapon. Sooner or later it must go into battle – and then the soldiers would see how all the theories about what it could do stood up to battlefield realities.

The truth is that there were no tank 'experts' in July 1916, The weapon had not yet been used in battle and all the suggestions made for its tactical deployment by Swinton and others, and later by Lieutenant-Colonel J.F.C. Fuller and his apostles (who will crop up later in this narrative), were theories, nothing more. It therefore made good sense to test in action and see what happened, before placing orders for hundreds of machines, deciding on improvements, diverting thousands of men to form tank crews and scarce industrial resources to tank manufacture. The so-called 'experts' knew no more about tanks in battle than Haig did, for this was an entirely new weapon, as yet unproven in the field.

The aim of the Battle of Flers-Courcelette was to push through the German lines with a phased attack between those two villages, through a series of objectives drawn on the map and known, beginning with the nearest, as the Green, Brown, Blue and Red Lines. The farthest, the Red Line included Morval and Gueudecourt, and taking it would leave Martinpuich and Flers well inside the British lines, representing an advance of some 2½ miles on a front of 3½; given the previous advances on the Somme front, this target must be regarded as ambitious.

This attack would be made by the, from left to right, III, XV and XIV Corps of Fourth Army, supported on their left by the Canadian Corps of the Reserve Army, who were to take the village of Courcelette, and on the right by the French XX Corps, whose objective was the village of Combles. In reserve, to exploit any breach, were five cavalry divisions. Rawlinson selected 0620 hours on 15 September as Zero hour, and drew up a careful plan for all the varied elements of his army.

As has been said, the Battle of the Somme was actually a series of separate engagements, so that by the time of Flers-Courcelette a large number of lessons had been driven home. Rawlinson was full of admiration for the courage and resource of his New Army battalions, but was well aware that on 1 July they had shown their lack of training and experience. Now, in the harsh school of battle, they were learning fast. So too, were the generals.

By September 1916, innovative practices such as creeping barrages, the rapid deployment forward of guns and reserves, the use of smoke, counter-battery fire, the attachment of artillery FOOs to infantry brigades and battalions, the careful mopping-up of trenches and dugouts after successful attack, tactics regarded as radical, if not dangerously so, on 1 July, were now becoming widespread. Rawlinson gave orders for the implementation of such tactics in a special Fourth Army instruction, which accorded particular priorities for the use of roads during the advance.

The mud of the Somme had already become notorious, and as shellfire further churned the ground the roads leading across the battlefield, though targeted by enemy guns, became increasingly vital for the rapid movement of troops and supplies. These made roads were few and narrow, so orders had to be issued for their use. After an assault, first up would be the guns, to support the advancing troops. Then the cavalry had priority, to widen the flanks and take advantage of any breakthrough. When the cavalry had gone ahead, light wagons with food and ammunition for the infantry could pass, taking the wounded to the rear on the way back. While all this was going on, Sappers and Pioneers would be at work, repairing the roads and tracks, smoothing out paths over the cratered ground, doing all they could to speed up the rate of advance.

A realistic command timescale for the coming attack was also established, one which assumed that it would take *six hours* for an order to pass from corps to the front-line companies, and which stressed that this meant an early issue of orders so that the battalion and company commanders would have adequate time to survey the ground, make a plan, issue their orders, and rest and feed the men. In this attack, no one would be hurled into battle at short notice and over unreconnoitred ground, if prior thought and careful planning could prevent it.

Signal arrangements were also overhauled. An integrated system was worked out involving RFC observers – Flers-Courcelette provides the first instance of a British commander referring to air superiority – and FOOs advancing with the infantry brigades, while every available kind of communication, from carrier pigeon to wireless, from telephone line to runners, cyclists and horsemen, was employed to get messages, and the true picture of what was happening at the front, back to the divisional and corps headquarters.

The artillery had been reinforced. By the time the troops advanced Rawlinson could deploy one heavy gun or howitzer for every 29 yards of enemy trench and a field gun for every 10 yards, roughly twice as many as were employed, on a much wider front, on 1 July. Moreover, the British artillery was also becoming a far better-trained and more integrated force, capable of coping with the various kinds of fire required, from counter-battery bombardment to creeping barrage, able to register its guns quickly, change ranges and targets rapidly and bring down a weight of shot which the Germans were beginning to fear. Each corps now had a senior artillery officer, a Brigadier-General, Royal Artillery (BGRA), in charge of the guns, and the role of the artillery, always vital on the Western Front, was at last receiving the attention it needed at corps and army level.

Special consideration was also paid to the requirements of the tanks. To prevent them being held up by shellfire or churned-up ground, wide 'corridors' were left in the creeping barrage, down which the machines could move. This sensible decision produced mixed results, however. Since many tanks did not make it to the start line, got lost later, 'ditched' (bogged down), broke down or were damaged by enemy fire, these corridors created unattacked, undamaged portions of the German line, from which machine-gunners could cut up the troops advancing on either side. German machine-gunners had also started moving out from their trenches, which were now being accurately shelled, to take up posts in no man's land. Though the creeping barrage dealt with many of these machine-gun nests, the tanks would have been ideal for rooting out these scattered positions – if only they could have got forward.

These rapid improvements in artillery and tactics did not always get the welcome they deserved. David Lloyd George, now Secretary of State for War in succession to Lord Kitchener, made a visit to the Somme front in September 1916, heard the complaints about the ammunition used in the early stages of the battle and the shortage of heavy guns, and returned home to state that 'The garrison artillery* in France is entirely untrained, it cannot shoot and is quite unfitted to work the perfect weapons which I [when Minister of Munitions] have provided.' This outburst was the first indication that Lloyd George was not going to be an easy man to work with, nor was he going to take the blame for the fact that while 'his' guns might be good, the quality of the shells coming from the munitions factories still left much to be desired. General Rawlinson, when asked to comment on Lloyd George's statement by Major-General Noel Birch, the Major-General, Royal Artillery, at GHQ and Haig's chief artillery adviser, had no hesitation in declaring himself 'perfectly happy' with the work of the counter-battery and heavy howitzer batteries in the battle so far.

The infantry had been prepared, the guns were ready, the communication and logistical arrangements had been overhauled. There remained the tanks. For the assault at Flers, between Albert and Bapaume, where the tanks were employed in battle for the first time, it was decided that, as 'infantry support' weapons, they should advance with the infantry companies and operate in pairs. Sixty tanks had arrived in France by 6 September, but only forty-eight were available for the battle. These were distributed among the assault divisions, with sixteen going to the XIV Corps, eighteen to the XV Corps, eight to the III Corps and six to the Canadians. In the event, only thirty-six tanks made it to the start line to take part in the Battle of Flers-Courcelette.

* The Royal Garrison Artillery, one of the three arms of the Royal Regiment of Artillery at that time, operated the heavy guns and howitzers; the Royal Field Artillery supported the infantry with field guns; and the Royal Horse Artillery the cavalry with lighter fieldpieces.

CHAPTER 13

FLERS AND THE ANCRE, 15 SEPTEMBER– 19 NOVEMBER 1916

'The British Army learned its lesson the hard way during the middle part of the Somme battle, and for the rest of the war was the best army in the field.'

Charles Carrington, *Soldier from the Wars Returning* (1965)

Flers is an interesting battle. It introduced a new weapon to the battlefield and provided the generals with the means to break that German defensive system which had stymied their efforts for two years – and yet it still took the Allies another two full years to win the war. This latter fact indicates that even a war-winning weapon takes time to reach its full potential, a potential that the tank never actually achieved in all the battles of the Great War. Armour would dominate most of the battlefields of the Second World War, and carry all before it in Poland, France, the Western Desert and Russia until tactical air power limited its use. The tanks employed in the Great War had no such chance of glory. Even so, when the first machines lumbered forward on 15 September 1916, they changed the face of war.

The British bombardment for the Battle of Flers-Courcelette opened at 0600 hours on 12 September, and was kept up without ceasing until Zero hour on 15 September, stopping briefly from time to time to let the RFC overfly the German defences to see what points needed further attention. Around 100,000 shells were fired on the first two days and 120,000 on the third, while 288,787 shells struck on or close to the German line in the 24 hours before the infantry assault. Not only did the guns engage the Germans in the front and support lines, but they bombarded the German rear areas as far as Bapaume, using gas as well as high-explosive. Thus supported, and with the new-fangled tanks trundling along as well, the British infantry went over the top.

On the right flank, Lieutenant-General the Earl of Cavan's XIV Corps found the tanks useful, not least because although many of the tanks ditched or broke down before even reaching the start line, the single machine that made it to Combles Trench in the 56th (1/1st London) Division's area 'thoroughly frightened the enemy'. This may have been the first reaction, but the German soldier is always resilient, and enemy troops were soon hitting back at this new and fearsome weapon. One tank was knocked out by a shell soon after Zero hour, another shed a track and a third, according to the Official History, 'cruising about for some time by the enemy front line became ditched and was boldly attacked by German bombers [i.e. soldiers with grenades]'.

The 6th Division had three tanks tasked to tackle the Quadrilateral, a German strongpoint east of Ginchy. Unfortunately, only one made it to the start line, and that got off to a bad start by opening fire on British troops, before blundering off towards the German front line. The infantry were held up by machine-guns and barbed wire and the tank eventually returned with an abundance of bullet holes in its armour. It soon transpired that the German infantry were using armour-piercing bullets, of the kind they normally used to penetrate the steel loopholes put up along the British line by snipers, against this new weapon.

The Guards Division attacked from Ginchy in line of platoons, nine waves in all, four platoons in line on a frontage of about four hundred yards, with ten tanks in support. Almost all these machines met with misfortune; one failed to arrive at all, two started late and veered off towards the German trenches on their own, one broke its driving wheel and could not leave the start line, and others lost direction and went off across the front of the 6th Division. The Guards therefore attacked without tank support but behind a creeping barrage that moved just thirty yards ahead of the advancing troops. A terrific volume of enfilade fire from the Quadrilateral, on the 6th Division front, drove 2 Guards Brigade off course, but their advance continued through well-cut wire and by 0715 hours, though much reduced in numbers, they had taken their first objective. Meanwhile 1 Guards Brigade also took its first objective, though it arrived there in considerable disorder and, having reached the decision that they had in fact captured their third or 'Blue Line' objective, sent a carrier pigeon back with that message.

In fact, their Blue Line objective was still more than a thousand yards ahead. This error was eventually picked up by an RFC patrol, but not before it had caused a certain amount of confusion. After more heavy fighting, a party from 2 Guards Brigade made its way up to the Blue Line position but could not take it. Thinking the entire Guards Division had got to their third objective, however, the 6th Division on their right asked for the Guards to 'cut in behind the Boche at the Quadrilateral'. When it became clear that the Guards were on their first objective rather than their third, the two divisions were told to hang on to the gains they had made until the following day, pending a further bombardment by the artillery. Tanks and the new communications arrangements had clearly not done much to help XIV Corps.

In the meantime, the XV Corps had taken Flers. Fourteen tanks had been tasked to assist this corps and most of them were deployed to deal with strongpoints in the village before moving on to tackle the wire and trenches of Gueudecourt. Before the main attack, three tanks were attached to two companies of the 6th KOYLI to clear a pocket of resistance east of Delville Wood, but only one turned up. This machine started at 0515 hours, drove off a few Germans with its machine-gun but was then hit by a shell which destroyed its steering gear. The KOYLI companies were then raked by machine-gun fire and, after losing all their officers, were rallied by their NCOs and joined in with the main advance.

Three tanks should have assisted the advance of the 14th (Light) Division but suffered varied fortunes. One ditched before Zero, another went off on its own towards Gueudecourt, but the third moved ahead of the infantry making towards Flers, a spirited advance that overran several German trenches before the tank was hit by shellfire and brought to a halt. The 14th Division then got ahead of the divisions on its flanks and came under fire from three sides as it pushed past the east side of Flers towards Gueudecourt.

The 41st Division, attacking from just north of Delville Wood, had the task of capturing Flers and here at least the tanks had a great and public success. Ten tanks were tasked to support this attack, four moving up the main Longueval–Flers road, and six moving across country against the centre and western end of the village. Again, however, not all the tanks made it to the start line. Only seven turned up, but as they did not arrive in time to move ahead of the infantry assault, they advanced with it. The leading infantry waves had deployed in no man's land before Zero and their first and second objectives were taken without difficulty. On the division's left, 122 Brigade had the support of several tanks and reported that the barrage had been 'excellent and just what the men had been trained to expect', and the tanks provided useful support until one was ditched, one was hit by a shell which killed or wounded the entire crew, and one, having got as far as Flers Trench, the second objective, was hit and forced to withdraw.

Now there were just four operational tanks left with 41st Division. With their aid 122 Brigade stormed Flers, one tank leading the infantry down the main street in what the Official History describes as 'a scene without precedent in war'. Flers was in British hands by 1000 hours and an RFC observer reported back to GHQ that he had sighted 'A tank in the main street of Flers, with large numbers of troops following it.' This message was translated by the British press into: 'A tank is walking up the High Street of Flers, with the British Army cheering behind it.'

This was a considerable, if pardonable, exaggeration. The first effect of the tanks was immediate and dramatic, for some German soldiers took one look at them and fled. The machines crunched over machine-gun nests and crushed barbed-wire emplacements with ease, often sending the enemy scurrying in panic to the rear. In general, however, the advent of the tank on the Flers-Courcelette battlefield was rather less successful than the capture of Flers suggested. As we have seen, most of those deployed did not make it to the start line, several were knocked out by artillery fire, others broke down or shed their tracks, many became ditched in the trenches and shell holes. Then there was the enemy, who did not take long to hit back.

Although startled by these monsters rumbling upon him out of the mist, the German soldier of the Great War was a resourceful and tenacious fighter. Field guns were swiftly manhandled into position to engage these apparitions, the use of armour-piercing bullets soon spread, and lone tanks without infantry support were soon under attack by small groups of German soldiers armed with grenades; the fact that their machines needed infantry support was one lesson that had not been apparent to the tank 'experts' on the training grounds.

While one tank led the infantry up the main street of Flers, the other three roamed about the outskirts of the village, smashing down strongpoints and firing at point-blank range into houses containing machine-gun nests. With Flers taken, 122 Brigade now had to pass through the village and take the Blue Line position, but most of the officers had become casualties and a certain amount of confusion was reigning, aided by the euphoria of the tank attack. Eventually, the brigade drifted back to the captured German trenches south of Flers, though some companies did press on to their third line objective, just as heavy German artillery fire began to fall on the village.

The left-hand formation of XV Corps was the New Zealand Division, which had to advance east of High Wood and reach a position north-west of Flers. Four tanks were available to this division, but though all made it to the start line none arrived in time to lead the advance. The New Zealanders attacked with great élan, captured their second objective inside an hour, and fought their way forward to take their third objective at Flers and Fat Trench by 1030 hours, assisted in the attack by two tanks which overran the German wire and dealt with a number of machine-guns. By 1030 XV Corps had seized all their second line objectives and were preparing to advance on the Blue Line, around Gueudecourt. This advance began at around 1100 hours, aided by a heavy bombardment and the actions of a lone tank, which had wandered away from its appointed task of assisting the 14th Division attack from Delville Wood, and advanced alone towards Gueudecourt, where it knocked out a battery of field artillery and shot up the German defences before being hit by a shell and set on fire.

Although the fighting was now intense along XV Corps' front of XV Corps, little ground was gained between 1100 and 1400 hours. The corps commander, General Horne, therefore ordered a further bombardment and told Fourth Army that he would push on again at 1700 hours, but at 1500 Rawlinson, who now had a grasp on the situation, cancelled all further attacks for that day. The assault divisions were instructed to hold on to the positions they had taken and prepare for a renewal of the attack on the morrow. Meanwhile, the artillery took up their bombardment tasks again.

Lieutenant-General Sir William Pulteney's III Corps was not directly involved in the battle for the villages of Flers-Courcelette. His corps had the highly important task of protecting the flank of Fourth Army, and they achieved two definite successes, capturing High Wood – that small, blood-stained copse on the skyline that had cost the lives of over 6,000 men in the fighting since 1 July – and the village of Martinpuich. The capture of High Wood by the 47th (1/2nd London) Division was crucial to the advance of the New Zealand Division of XV Corps, but the former division soon became involved in some of the worst of the fighting of the battle and lost over 4,500 men in four days. 'The divisional commander, Major-General St L. Barter, was removed from his command and sent home a few days later, "at an hour's notice", because of these heavy losses but the man who should have gone was the corps commander, Pulteney, who refused to listen to advice concerning the use of tanks.' (Colonel Terry Cave, letter to the author, October 1977.) Barter later appealed against his dismissal, but his formal request for an inquiry was ignored.

Eight tanks had been allotted to Pulteney's corps, of which four were tasked to pass through High Wood, where the opposing lines were too close for normal artillery support, and four sent to help the attack on Martinpuich. The first task was a fundamental and obvious mistake, for tanks are not much use in woods. Although High Wood had long since been levelled by shellfire, the stumps and mud-filled shell holes and the jumble of wire, trenches and fallen trees created an impenetrable obstacle, with the result that the infantry were left unsupported and chaos reigned. One tank fired on the British troops by mistake, another managed to get into the wood but was then hit by shellfire, another slid into a shell hole and got stuck, its crew baling out to fight with the infantry, though returning later to dig their machine out, while the fourth tank was set on fire and burnt out. The infantry of the 47th Division finally took High Wood in mid-morning, after a fifteen-minute hurricane bombardment of the German positions by a trench mortar battery. Martinpuich had already fallen to troops of the 15th (Scottish) Division, assisted by a solitary tank which shot up machine-gun posts and rolled over dugouts on the outskirts of the village as the infantry worked their way in.

Across the Albert–Bapaume Road, the Canadian Corps of Gough's Reserve Army were playing their part in the battle by attacking Courcelette. The attack was to be made by Major-General Turner's 2nd Canadian Division, on the right of the Canadian Corps line, supported by six tanks and a creeping barrage. These tanks were deployed on the flanks, three down the axis of the Albert–Bapaume Road on the right, three on the left flank, all moving with the infantry and fifty yards behind the creeping barrage. The attack went very well, with the troops keeping close behind the barrage and reaching Courcelette by 0730 hours. The tanks had been unable to keep up with the barrage but the troops apparently enjoyed having them along, and although two fell out with mechanical trouble, the remaining four joined up with the infantry around Courcelette and did good work among the German defences. The 2nd Canadian Division pushed on in the afternoon and had consolidated around Courcelette by dusk.

By mid-afternoon the British attack had been halted, either by German resistance or on Rawlinson's orders, and most of the tanks had been knocked out, or in some way disabled. The attack at Flers-Courcelette had achieved some positive gains, for large sections of two German defence lines, 6,000 yards of the first line and 4,000 yards of the second, together with High Wood and the Bazentin ridge, had been taken and held. How much more might have been achieved had more tanks been available, or had those which were there been used as a concentrated armoured spearhead rather than in 'penny packets', remains a matter of speculation. The chances are that if more tanks had been available, more would have made it across the start line, but the percentage loss among them would have been the same. This, the first tank engagement, demonstrated that a lot had still to be learned about fighting and maintaining tanks in battle, quite apart from the fact that the machines were not reliable and their crews lacked experience.

Yet the tanks had certainly proved their worth, even if very few managed to get far forward. The Official History reports that of the thirty-six machines that crossed the start line only about a dozen played an active part in helping the infantry cross the German wire and beat down the machine-guns, the task for which they had been designed – but at least a start had been made. Haig was satisfied with their debut, telling Swinton that, although the tanks had not achieved all that had been hoped for at Flers, they had saved many lives and amply justified their employment, adding that 'wherever the tanks advanced we took our objectives, and where they did not advance, we failed.' He followed this up with a request for 1,000 machines, to be delivered as soon as possible.

At Flers-Courcelette the tanks achieved a great deal, not least in convincing both sides that a new and significant force had appeared upon the battle-field. After 15 September the development of new models and the provision of more tanks became a major priority with the tank enthusiasts. With Colonel Swinton kept from field command, Lieutenant-Colonel Hugh (later General Sir Hugh) Elles was appointed to command the 'Heavy Section' in France, but in October 1916 Swinton was relieved of his duties and transferred back to the War Cabinet Secretariat, the first of many tank enthusiasts who were to be removed just when their experience could have been most useful. It was not until 1934 that Swinton's great contribution to the development of the tank was finally recognised with his appointment as Colonel-Commandant of the Royal Tank Regiment.

After Flers the next major action for the tanks took place in April 1917, east of Arras, in the rolling country of Artois. By the time of this attack the Tank Corps, as the Heavy Section, Machine-Gun Corps became, had expanded, first to four battalions and then to three full brigades. One of the staff officers appointed to this growing force in 1916 was the then Major J.F.C. Fuller of the Oxfordshire and Buckinghamshire Light Infantry, an intelligent, far-sighted officer, a leader in the development of tank tactics but a bitter enemy of Haig and the Great War generals, especially those who did not value his precious tanks as he did. During the winter of 1916–17 Fuller revised the training schedules, and helped to prepare the Tank Corps for further armoured attacks when good weather and firm ground returned to the battlefields of France.

Meanwhile, fighting continued on the Somme. At the end of the first day at Flers, Rawlinson had advanced on his selected front for an average of around 4,500 yards, reaching the Blue Line (third objective) and taking High Wood, Flers, Courcelette and Martinpuich. Parts of the Blue Line position around Morval and Gueudecourt had still not been taken, and there was still no breach for the waiting cavalry to exploit. On the right flank of Fourth Army, the French Sixth Army had made no progress at all, and called off their attack on the afternoon of the first day, 15 September. Rawlinson therefore told Haig that he would not renew the attack until another heavy artillery bombardment had softened up the third German line. Over the next week the attacks continued, but when the offensive was finally called off on 23 September, the British line, though secure, was not far in advance of where it had been on the evening of 15 September. Morval, Lesboeufs and Gueudecourt were still in German hands, and the village of Le Sars remained a distant objective on the Albert–Bapaume Road.

Rawlinson and Haig realised that the Flers-Courcelette offensive would be their last major attack in 1916, but the latter did not suspend the fighting or order his troops on to the defensive when the operation petered out. The attack at Flers was followed by the Battle of Morval, which began on 25 September and lasted until the 28th, and then by the Battle of the Transloy Ridges, which ran from 1 October until the 18th, a series of seven all-out attacks, made in steadily deteriorating weather, which ran from 1 October until the 18th. On 29 September, Haig even began to plan for a general attack using the Third, Fourth and Reserve Armies, with the ultimate objective of taking Cambrai, more than twenty miles away. The purpose of the Somme offensive had changed. It had begun with hopes of a break-through. It was fought now with the aim of 'attrition' – of killing German soldiers.

Haig would gladly have stopped all attacks when the autumn rains turned the Somme countryside into a quagmire, but the French, having achieved their first ambition, a halt to the German attacks at Verdun, were now pressing hard to fulfil their second aim, a 'battle of attrition' to wear down the fighting divisions of the German Army. This is what the Battle of the

Somme now became, a steady descent into murderous fighting, in which the various actions were simply excuses to engage the enemy and kill his soldiers . . . losing a lot of British and French soldiers in the process.

Joffre pressed Haig to keep on attacking, slipping steadily back into his old, peremptory style, spiced with strong hints that the British were not pulling their weight. On 19 October, Haig was again obliged to remind the French C-in-C that the commander of the British Armies in France was the sole judge of what that army and its Australian, Canadian, New Zealand and South African contingents could undertake . . . and when they could or would undertake it.

By the end of September, constant battering by the British on the Somme had driven a large salient into the German line of 1 July, most of it south of the Albert–Bapaume Road. By 30 September, the British front line lay before the village of Le Sars, overlooked by the white, shell-scraped mound of the Butte de Warlencourt, a prehistoric burial mound set just beside the road. Gueudecourt had finally fallen, as had Lesboeufs and Morval, Thiepval and Mouquet Farm, but across the Ancre the villages of Beaumont Hamel and Beaucourt, objectives for the attack on 1 July, still remained in German hands.

It was to the Ancre that the focus of the battle now shifted. Here, on 1 October, the Canadian Corps under Lieutenant-General the Hon. Sir Julian Byng, attempted to gain possession of Regina Trench, the key position on the Thiepval ridge, their attack forming part of General Gough's push with his Reserve Army north along the Ancre. This attack, pressed home with great resolution, became the cause of considerable antipathy among the Canadians for Gough. After the fight for Regina Trench, they were reluctant to serve under him again, and at Passchendaele in 1917 General Currie, by then a lieutenant-general and commanding the Canadian Corps, flatly refused to have his corps transferred to Gough's command.

The problems at Regina Trench began at 0730 hours on 1 October when Major-General R.E.W. Turner commanding the 2nd Canadian Division, told Byng that he did not consider that the bombardment of the German positions at Regina Trench had been sufficient, for the wire was still uncut. The wire-cutting barrage therefore continued up to the moment of the assault, but when the Canadians advanced at 1515 hours they were first severely machine-gunned, and then caught in the open by artillery fire, and had great difficulty forcing a way into the German trenches. Those Canadians who got into Regina Trench were then attacked with grenades by strong enemy forces coming down the communication trenches. This bombing fight went on for much of the day, and eventually the Canadians were forced to retire. Vicious fighting continued in this part of the front over the next several days, until 8 October, when a fresh attempt to take the rest of Regina Trench was launched by Major-General Currie's 1st Canadian Division. This attack went in during a rainstorm at 0450 hours on the 8th.

At first the advance went well, but in the early afternoon the Germans counter-attacked. After heavy fighting the Canadians, greatly outnumbered and out of grenades, were forced back to their jumping-off trenches. The 16th Battalion (Canadian Scottish) had got a foothold in Regina Trench but was driven out when the battalion on its right fell back and that on its left suffered heavy losses to machine-gun fire. The 3rd Canadian Division then attacked, but did no better. Fighting for Regina Trench went on until 21 October, when, after the 4th Canadian Division had replaced the 3rd Division, the entire Canadian Corps, less the 4th Division, was withdrawn from the line, having suffered losses and endured conditions, according to the Official History, 'as difficult and as harassing as any which prevailed upon the Somme'. The 4th Canadian Division remained in the line as part of II Corps, completed the capture of Regina Trench and remained with that corps until the end of November. Canadian casualties on the Somme, according to their own Official History, totalled 24,029 men, killed, wounded and missing.

The Canadians believed, with some reason, that they had been ill used in the fighting for Regina Trench. Gough had a reputation for pushing his men hard, and they felt that he had pushed them too hard. In part, however, this was because the fighting on the Somme was now becoming a contest of endurance as the weather deteriorated and the mud deepened – and as the French policy of attrition began to assume dominance.

By 1 October, the Allied offensive on the Somme front had formed a deep salient in the German line. On the Albert–Bapaume Road the British stood just short of Le Sars, their line falling away to the west north of the road, but bulging slightly forward to include Gueudecourt and Lesboeufs south of it. The French IX Corps, which had replaced XX Corps north of the Somme, now had a pronounced dent in their line, thrusting to Combles, but otherwise the French line was roughly level with that of the British, and by now included Morval, near the junction with Rawlinson's army. The obvious task was now to push on up the Ancre in the north and straighten out the British front, roughly on a line running north–west from Le Sars to Miraumont, Serre and Gommecourt.

After the Battle of the Transloy Ridges petered out on 20 October, Gough's Reserve Army – which was renamed the Fifth Army on 30 October – took up the main weight of the advance in what had become the Battle of the Ancre Heights. This began on 1 October with a preliminary attack on Stuff Trench, east of the river, and another thrust against Regina Trench, as part of a drive north by II Corps of Gough's army towards the Ancre between St-Pierre-Divion and Grandcourt. The attack on Stuff Trench by the 39th Division was completely successful, and most of Regina Trench was taken by the 4th Canadian Division on the night of 21 October. This Fifth Army attack petered out on 11 November only to be renewed north of the Ancre on 13 November, when it became the Battle of the Ancre, an engagement which lasted until 19 November and finally brought the Somme battles to an end.

Bad weather continued to harass the troops, with gales, constant rain and falling temperatures. The men were now in a pitiful condition, a fact brought to the notice of Haig and Rawlinson by a letter from the XIV Corps commander, Lord Cavan, on 3 November:

> An advance from my present position [at the eastern extremity of Rawlinson's front] with the troops at my disposal has practically no chance of success on account of the heavy enfilade fire of machine-guns and artillery from the north and the enormous distance we have to advance against strongly prepared positions . . . I perfectly acknowledge the necessity of not leaving the French left in the air . . . and I assert my readiness to sacrifice the British right rather than jeopardise the French, for a sacrifice it must be. No one who has not visited the front-line trenches can really know the state of exhaustion to which the men are reduced.

Haig did know. His diary for Tuesday, 31 October, records:

> In the afternoon I rode to HQ, Fifth Army, at Toutencourt. I wanted definite information as to the state of the front-line trenches, and whether the winter leather waistcoats had yet been issued, also whether an extra blanket per man had been sent up. Malcolm [Gough's Chief of Staff] assured me that everything possible was being done for the men but the mud in front is quite terrible.

Mud, rain, the growing cold and the exhaustion of the troops was bringing the Somme offensive to a long-overdue halt, but even so the attacks continued. Slowly and painfully, the objectives on the Fourth Army front were taken. On the Fifth Army front Regina Trench and the whole of the Thiepval ridge were finally in British hands by mid-November, the right, Fourth Army, flank was pushed out to a point some three miles due south of Bapaume, but in the centre Le Sars and the Butte de Warlencourt – the former in British hands, the latter in German – marked the limit of the British advance. On the following day Rawlinson told his commanders that Fourth Army would restrict itself to 'modified operations' designed only to prevent the Germans switching troops to other parts of the front, but Gough still had one more battle to fight, in the Ancre valley.

The second phase of the Battle of the Ancre lasted from 13 to 19 November, most of it taking place in terrible weather. Gough used two corps in the battle, II Corps south of the river and V Corps north of it. The objectives were those of 1 July, Serre, Beaumont Hamel, St-Pierre-Division, Grandcourt, and the rationale for the offensive was provided by the fact that Haig was about to attend yet another high-level conference in Paris and needed a victory to put on the table. 'The British position will be much stronger, as memories are short, if I could appear there on the top of the

capture of Beaumont Hamel, for instance, and 3,000 German prisoners.'
Gough was assisted in this action with all the artillery and ammunition that
could be spared from Third and Fourth Armies, as well as fifty-two tanks.
The General, his officers and men, all seemed confident of success.

Since it was obvious that this was to be the final attack of the year, no one
expected much from it. Haig visited Gough on the afternoon of 12 November and told him that the assault need not proceed if the risk of failure
seemed too high, but added that a victory would raise spirits at home and
hearten Britain's allies. The ground was now deep in mud and the Ancre in
flood, but Gough, ever the thruster, elected to go ahead with his 'limited
offensive' between the Albert–Bapaume Road and Serre. The main weight
of the attack fell on Lieutenant-General Fanshawe's V Corps – from south
to north the 63rd (Royal Naval), 51st (Highland), 2nd and 3rd Divisions,
with the 37th Division in reserve – which held the front north of the Ancre
between Auchonvillers and Hamel.

The German defences were still intact, but it was hoped that the four
months and more of constant battering since 1 July had taken the heart out
of the defenders. The assault divisions could take some encouragement from
the fact that earlier attacks, though constantly repulsed, had at least pushed
their front line up to within 250 yards of the German trenches. Even so, the
Ancre engagement would be over the same ground as that attacked on 1 July.
It remained to be seen what the British would do with their second chance at
the enemy line here.

Gough split his attack into three phases. The first called for an advance of
just 800 yards, to capture the Beaumont Hamel valley and the ridge up to
Serre, requiring a thrust through three trench lines, and in some places a
fourth. The next bound was longer, between 600 and 1,200 yards, a thrust
across the valley south of Serre and round to the eastern edge of the village
itself. With the high ground thus taken, the final attack would be up the
Ancre valley to Beaucourt. Gough had an abundance of artillery; on the V
Corps front he could deploy roughly 1 heavy gun to every 31 yards of trench
and a field gun or howitzer for every 13 yards. South of the Ancre II Corps,
which was to attack up the valley on the steep, south slope between St-
Pierre-Divion (still in German hands) and the Schwaben Redoubt (captured
by 39th Division a month earlier), had an even heavier concentration.

Both corps would attack together on 13 November – on V Corps' left, the
31st Division of XIII Corp was to advance to form a defensive flank – after a
daily hurricane barrage lasting anything from half an hour to an hour on
previous days had, it was hoped, lulled the enemy into indifference. The
attack at 0545 hours, would be supported with heavy fire on the enemy
trenches, but 25 per cent of the artillery were to shorten their range and lay a
curtain of fire 50 yards in front of the enemy front-line trench, to screen the
advance of the infantry. This barrage would then creep forward at the slow
rate of 100 yards in 5 minutes and thus supported, the infantry were
supposed to be on their first objective in exactly 56 minutes, and on the

second an hour after that. The attack on Beaucourt by the 63rd Division was timed for 3 hours 20 minutes after Zero, and every gun available would pound the village before the division – which had one brigade of sailors, another of sailors and Royal Marines, and a third of Army battalions – went in. Compared with the attack hereabouts on 1 July – which failed totally – the differences could hardly be more striking. Gough's men would have surprise, a dawn attack, heavy artillery support, some tanks and a creeping barrage. The question was, would all this be sufficient?

The attack began just before dawn and was both screened and hampered by a damp and heavy fog, which restricted visibility to around 30 yards, and heavy ground which prevented the advance of the tanks. The first waves of 56 Brigade, 19th (Western) Division, on the right of II Corps, got into the German trenches without difficulty and by 0800 hours had taken their first objective for the loss of just 200 men killed and wounded, having captured a large number of Germans and killed about 150. To their left the 39th Division, tasked with clearing the slopes on the south bank of the Ancre, made steady progress behind the creeping barrage, though some battalions lost their way in the fog. The attack went well and by 0830 most of the II Corps units had captured their objectives with – in Great War terms – comparatively small losses of around 1,300 men, mostly wounded. The corps reported that the enemy losses in dead and wounded were very heavy.

North of the Ancre, the attacks of the V and XIII Corps enjoyed a more varied mixture of success and failure. In the former corps the 63rd Division, which had not taken part in any Western Front offensive and had been carefully trained for this attack, at first made good progress, following a carefully timed plan. The troops were anxious to do well, pushing their attack forward with great élan and keeping close behind their barrage. The star performer in this division was Lieutenant-Colonel Bernard Freyberg, commanding the Hood Battalion of sailors, the man who was to command New Zealand's forces in the Second World War.* Wounded twice, Colonel Freyberg won the VC for his actions this day, pushing his battalion ahead, spearheading the advance of the Royal Naval Division through to their second-line objective, though at the cost of heavy casualties. The division did not manage a great deal of progress, but by dusk they were embedded in the enemy line and waiting for support, including six tanks, to help their attack on the following day.*

The 51st (Highland) Division on the left of the Royal Naval Division, made their attack after yet another mine had been detonated beneath the Hawthorn Redoubt. The division attacked with two brigades up, and the struggle in the fog soon became a battle of small units, with companies and platoons tackling whatever opposition they encountered while pressing on

---

* As Lieutenant-General Sir Bernard Freyberg, VC, DSO and three Bars, and later to become Lord Freyberg. In all he was wounded six times in the Great War; among other distinctions, he was one of the pallbearers for the poet Rubert Brooke in 1915.

steadily over the ground. Beaumont Hamel was entered at around 1030 hours, the German reserve line was penetrated, and by mid-afternoon the village was in British hands, though a lot of mopping-up was needed before the enemy defenders were rooted out. The advance units were then ordered to push on towards Serre, and this action was still continuing at nightfall.

The other two divisions of V Corps, the 2nd and 3rd, pressed home their attacks behind the barrage and made good progress initially before being held up by machine-gun fire, uncut wire and deep mud; indeed, the mud slowed the advance so much that even the lavish time-scale allowed proved insufficient. The barrage moved steadily away, the fog hampering the work of the artillery observers, who might otherwise have seen the problem and brought it back. As a final snag, some of the assault battalions lost their way in the fog, and the attack, which had begun so well, gradually got out of control.

The troops of the 3rd Division, on the left of V Corps, ran into waist-deep mud and uncut wire covered by machine-guns, with the result that the attack by their two leading brigades failed completely. Attempts were made to call off the action after a few hours but some detachments, isolated in the fog, had penetrated the German line and hung on waiting for reinforcements. At 1245 hours 3rd Division HQ informed General Fanshawe that their attack had failed, and that a renewed assault on that part of the front held out no prospect of success.

The final attack, by the 31st Division of XIII Corps, an attack designed to cover the flank of V Corps, also went awry, through no fault of the divisional commander, Major-General Wanless O'Gowan, the officer who had seen much hard fighting as commander of 13 Infantry Brigade at Second Ypres. His division attacked at Zero on a 500-yard front and had soon taken the German first line and part of their support line. Then the enemy artillery came into play, laying a carpet across no man's land which effectively cut the assault battalions off from support – and since the 3rd Division attack on their right had failed, these troops were isolated. A German counter-attack was beaten off with loss but the telephone lines linking 31st Division with the 3rd on its right had been severed. Now, with the Germans bombing their way in from the untaken trenches in front of the latter division, its leading troops were in an untenable position and taking heavy casualties. At around 1500 hours they were forced to withdraw, and by 2130 were back in their own trenches.

In many respects, the Fifth Army attack on the Ancre was a small-scale re-run of 1 July. Gough's attack prospered on the right, but failed totally on the left. Nor was it broken off after the first day, for on the evening of 14 November he issued orders for a further advance. When a copy of this order reached Haig, however, who was now attending that inter-Allied conference in Paris, he ordered that no more large-scale operations were to be undertaken until he returned. Gough ignored this instruction and Beaucourt fell on the same day, the advance into the village being led by the indefatigable Colonel Freyberg.

Haig now wanted to halt all the attacks but Gough and his corps commanders persuaded him that one last thrust would succeed in clearing the Ancre valley. With some reluctance, Haig therefore permitted them to go ahead. His opposition, however, led Gough to re-examine his plan, and he finally settled on a more limited assault on 18 November tasking II Corps with a 500-yard advance towards Grandcourt, and V Corps with a push along the Ancre valley on the left. Snow was now falling, which had the advantage that the mud froze, but conditions were terrible as the men prepared for the final assault. The attack went in at 0610 hours on the 18th and succeeded in pushing forward the British line a little beyond Beaumont Hamel, and somewhat further to form a small salient beyond Beaucourt. There the Germans held firm, and the Battle of the Ancre petered out, having added another 23,274 casualties to the total roll-call on the Somme. The successes of the first day had been blighted, as all too often before, by the losses caused in follow-up attacks which lacked the surprise, artillery support and careful planning which had been given to the original assault.

The final result of the Somme battle provides very little comfort for any supporter of the Great War generals. When matched against the anticipated gains for 1 July alone, this four-and-a-half-month battle provided a small return for a vast expenditure in lives. No breakthrough was achieved, and the balance sheet of the Somme is heavily weighted by this terrible loss of life.

The profit side can be looked at first, for it is shorter. The British Army advanced about six miles on a front of about twenty, and after four and a half months finally took most, though not all, of the objectives listed for the first day. The British, Dominion and Imperial soldiers learned a great deal about this new kind of war, introduced a number of tactical refinements, and improved the battlefield performance of almost every arm and level of command, besides introducing and testing a potentially war-winning invention, the tank.

They had also destroyed the backbone of the great German field army, by killing a large number of those superb officers and senior NCOs on whose abilities the German war machine largely depended. The failure of the Verdun offensive also led to the dismissal of General von Falkenhayn, who was sacked as Chief of the German General Staff at the end of August. He was replaced by the formidable Field Marshal Paul von Hindenburg, who, with his even more formidable Chief of Staff, General Erich Ludendorff, had hurried over from operations against the Russians in the east and made a first inspection of the Western Front in early September. As First Quartermaster-General, Ludendorff was effectively to run the German war effort from now on.

Peter Simkins, Senior Historian at the Imperial War Museum in London, also points out that the German generals did not cover themselves with professional glory during the Somme battles:

> British generalship was not at its best on the Somme and those differences in concept between Haig and Rawlinson, whether to go for a breakthrough or settle for a series of bite-and-hold attacks, should have been sorted out early on. The losses have proved the heaviest charge made against the British generals but consider the German losses – and the reasons for them. Erich von Falkenhayn ordered that any ground lost should be retaken by an immediate counter-attack, pressed home 'regardless of loss even to the last man'. Von Below, who commanded the Second Army, also demanded sacrifices, saying that the British should have to 'make their way into the German line only over a pile of [German] corpses'. Those orders, and the zeal with which they were carried out bled the German Army white on the Somme. Captain von Hentig, a staff officer with the Guard Reserve Division, described the Somme as . . . 'the muddy grave of the German field army'.

As for the British generals, Haig, Rawlinson and Gough, their performance on the Somme is best regarded as adequate. The attempts at breakthrough failed, and the battle of attrition that replaced it was at best a draw. Rawlinson has to be given a large share of what little credit there may be, for his night attack of 14 July and for recognising that since a breakthrough was clearly impossible, bite-and-hold operations offered the only realistic tactic. For his part, Gough seemed to be developing an unfortunate habit of squandering his troops and upsetting his senior subordinates. The common failing among senior commanders on the British side, however, was an apparent inability to break off an action when the main benefits had been obtained, or when the price of continuing had become too high. Battering away at strongpoints only caused further losses among the attacking troops. Since this had also been the case in the engagements of 1915, some lessons should have been drawn from the experiences of that unhappy year, not least by the Commander-in-Chief, General Haig.

Haig's performance in the Somme battle is a reflection of his character; the dour and determined part urged him to press on, while the optimistic side of his nature led him to believe that one more push would do it, that the German Army was on the wane as a fighting force, that victory was always within his grasp – if always just a fraction out of reach. Haig pushed his men hard on the Somme, and was to push them even harder at Passchendaele. Though both battles contributed considerably to the eventual collapse of the German military machine, this was not one of the prime objectives of either offensive; rather, it was a reason thought up later to justify the costs. And yet, with all that said, Haig remained popular with his troops, and was regarded by most of his peers as the only man who could deliver victory to the Allied arms.

The great lesson of 1915, and the common factor in all the battles on the Somme, was that a carefully planned and well-supported attack – especially if that support included lavish amounts of artillery and, latterly, some tanks – could achieve useful results for (in Great War terms, anyway) relatively small losses, *at least in the early stages*. Battles rarely go exactly as planned, and the British generals cannot have been surprised that their attacks did not enjoy equal success at every point along the front of the assault. There is also a natural tendency to press on with an attack, especially one which is hanging in the balance, in the hope that one more try will tilt the balance, thereby justifying the losses suffered so far.

That tactic of continuing an action rarely paid off on the Western Front, however. If the initial attack failed or faltered, any attempt to renew it resulted at best in another battering-ram advance, most costly in lives. Haig's attacks always had a strategic element; he dreamed of a break-through, a return to mobile warfare, the possibility of absolute victory – but then Haig was the Commander-in-Chief. Rawlinson, in a less demanding position, had smaller ambitions and would settle for bite-and-hold opera-tions, for attacks that nibbled away at the enemy's line and sapped his strength. Gough, a 'Haig man' through and through, tried to achieve breakthroughs when to bite and hold was the best option available, and wore out his men in the process.

When Haig failed to achieve that breakthrough to Bapaume and beyond on 1 July, or indeed on 15 September, the nature of the Somme battle shifted Rawlinson's way. His bite-and-hold tactics suited both the terrain and the constant demands of General Joffre for a battle of attrition. The Somme offensive's descent into a battle of attrition was aided by the orders of Falkenhayn to the German Army, that every foot of ground was to be held, and any ground lost was to be retaken immediately by counter-attack. So it came about that all the armies on the Somme battered themselves to pieces.

It is fair to say that the British Army learned its trade on the Somme. For the rest of the war it was the finest army on the Western Front, but the cost of that instruction had been extremely high. The casualty figures for the battle are still disputed, but the most commonly accepted 'round figures' will serve to draw up the profit-and-loss account – the totals are so massive that any arguing about a few thousand here or there becomes simply petty.

Total casualties among the combatants, for the entire Somme battle, are estimated at 1,300,000 men, British, French, and German, killed, wounded, missing, or taken prisoner. The British share in this catastrophe included the losses of Australia, Canada, South Africa and New Zealand, and amounted to something over 400,000 men. Most of the 'missing' were in fact killed and their names are recorded among those having 'no known grave' on the great memorial at Thiepval and elsewhere about the Great War battlefields, the Canadians at Vimy, the Australians at Villers-Brettoneux, the New

Zealanders at Polygon Wood, the South Africans at Delville Wood. Taking the Great War as a whole, the number of 'missing' on the Western Front almost equals the number of 'known dead', the latter being those who have graves and gravestones.

The numbers actually killed were, as usual, much less than the total casualty figure. Major-General Sir Frederick Maurice, in his life of General Rawlinson (1923), calculates that the total of German killed and missing on the Somme amounted to 164,055, a figure supplied by the Reichsarchiv. As always, though, there are differences. The relevant volume of the British Official History, published in 1938, lists the German total casualties as of the order of 660,000 to 680,000 (some estimates put German casualties as 'low' as 437,000), and the Anglo-French total, for killed, wounded and missing, as 630,000. The French killed and missing amounted to 50,756, and the British to 95,675. Far more men were wounded, but some 83 per cent of the British wounded recovered and eventually returned to their units. Even allowing for error, these figures are appalling.

The French lost some 200,000 men on the Somme, to add to the casualties they had already suffered at the Battle of Verdun, for which the *official* French casualty figure is 377,231, of which 162,308 were killed – figures roughly equal to the German losses in that battle. This means that if the Germans lost something over 600,000 on the Somme, killed, wounded and missing, about the same as the combined Franco-British casualties, the accounts for both battles had been evenly balanced.

To put it another way, the brutal fighting of 1916 had achieved precisely nothing. Territorial gains had been slight, and the battles of attrition that Falkenhayn had desired at Verdun and Joffre had wanted on the Somme had killed just as many of their own men as of the enemy. If the fighting continued like this, the Great War would be won by the last soldier to be left alive.

Europe
in 1917

CHAPTER 14

THE GENERALS
AND THE FROCKS,
NOVEMBER 1916–APRIL 1917

*'Henceforward the increasing divergence of views between Mr
Lloyd George and Generals Haig and Robertson should be
borne in mind.'*

Brigadier-General Sir J. E. Edmonds,
Military Operations France and Belgium, 1916, Volume II

The winter of 1916–17 in Northern France and Flanders was an
exceptionally harsh one, arriving early and staying late. The last battle
of the Somme offensive in November 1916 was fought partly in a snow-
storm, and when the Canadians advanced on Vimy Ridge in April 1917,
sleet and snow fell heavily on their backs. In the intervening months, while
the soldiers suffered and endured in their wet, freezing trenches, the fighting
continued along the Western Front and the toll of casualties mounted daily.

This war, which had begun in the summer of 1914 with the idea that it
would be 'over by Christmas', and that the men would be 'home before the
leaves fall', had now lasted more than two years and the losses, in killed,
wounded and missing (who had usually been killed) now ran into millions.
Thoughts at home and abroad, on both sides of the line, turned increasingly
to how this terrible war might be brought to a close, for it was more and
more obvious that the cost of continuing the fighting was going to be a
further holocaust of lives.

The failures in command and staff work, the terrible effects of modern
technology and modern weapons, the lack of training and the inadequacy of
support and supplies, these were but the instruments of catastrophe, and as
the armies learned how to fight this new and terrible kind of war, these initial
problems were gradually resolved. As a result the killing simply became
more efficient. The root cause of all this endless suffering was not the guns,
or the shells, or the gas, or the grenades and mortar bombs, but the *war*

itself. Since this vast conflict could not apparently be won, it should – indeed, it must – be ended. The question was how, and on what terms?

Such thoughts were not new. Steps to prevent or to end the war had begun before the first shots were fired and had continued intermittently ever since, with initiatives from among others, the Pope and the United States, but no basis for a peace existed, not least because the combatants could not agree on who started the war, who was to blame for it, or indeed what they were actually fighting about.

Most of Europe blamed Germany, and in particular the Kaiser, but the Germans did not believe that they had started the war, and were willing to argue about that accusation even at the Versailles Peace Conference in 1919, when German leaders refused to accept Article 231 of the Treaty which obliged their country to accept full responsibility for 'causing all the loss and damage to which the Allied and Associate Governments have been subjected as a consequence of the war imposed upon them by the aggression of Germany and her allies'.

Yet although Germany rejected this accusation, subsequent investigations by Professor Franz Fischer into the records of the Wilhelmine era have revealed that Europe at large was right. The militaristic Germany of the pre-1914 era, dominated by the Junkers and the Army, *had* been planning an aggressive war, aimed at France and Russia, in which Belgium and probably Holland, as well as vast tracts of Russia, would be overrun and seized. All the European nations had mobilisation plans, and many French generals and politicians lusted for the reconquest of Alsace and Lorraine and revenge for the Prussian defeat of 1870; but only Germany had mobilisation plans which would inevitably lead to the outbreak of a war of conquest. The time factor inherent in the Schlieffen Plan made German mobilisation not a defensive move, but a decisive step on the road to all-out war.

More than a million casualties in a single year concentrated minds, however, even in Berlin. The capture of Bucharest by the Central Powers in December 1916 (Romania having entered the war on the Allied side) enabled the German Chancellor, Theobald von Bethmann Hollweg, to suggest that the Kaiser and the High Command could offer as a result peace terms to the Allies without the prospect of humiliation or of displaying signs of weakness. The generals and admirals did not object, the former because they knew they had hurt the French and British more than they had been hurt, the latter because, if these peace proposals were rejected the Chancellor could no longer maintain his opposition to unrestricted submarine warfare, which the German Navy regarded as the only certain way to win the war. Some German commanders, notably Hindenburg, wanted the war ended because they knew that the losses of Verdun and the Somme had dealt a grave blow to the German armies, and that further battles on that scale could only have one outcome. At a conference at Pless in January 1917, Hindenburg is recorded as having said that 'Things cannot be worse than they are now. This war must be brought to an end by the use of all means, and as soon as possible.' This was quite true, but if Germany wanted peace, her stated terms were not the way to achieve it.

The Allies had no difficulty rejecting the German proposals, for the conditions were outrageous. In return for a ceasefire Germany required possession of the Belgian Congo and of the French industrial area around Briey-Longy. She would permit the re-establishment of Belgium, but it would be under German influence; moreover, the Belgians would be required to hand over Liège. Germany would also, of course, retain Alsace and Lorraine. The Austrian frontier would be adjusted to take in some rich areas of Italy, and the Austro-Hungarian Empire would absorb Serbia. So the conditions went on, for pages. The object was to obtain for Germany at the conference table all that she had as yet been unable to obtain, or was able to retain only at great cost, on the battlefield.

Germany's view was that the war had been forced upon her because of the 'encirclement' of her territory by an aggressive alliance comprising France, Russia and Great Britain, and there are good reasons for accepting, or at least considering, that argument. At the end of 1916 Germany saw no real reason to seek peace at any price. If peace was offered to end the slaughter then the bargaining would begin with a good deal in Germany's favour – hence this stunning list of demands.

The Entente Powers were no less intransigent. France would settle for nothing less than the return of Alsace-Lorraine and reparations for her losses in the war so far. Britain had gone to war to ensure the neutrality of Belgium – and to strike down a potential maritime aggressor before it grew too powerful. The restoration of Belgian sovereignty was the very least that Britain would settle for, but the German fleet must also be destroyed, since its continued existence was a threat to British maritime supremacy.

That threat still existed, for not only were German submarines taking a heavy toll of Britain's merchant fleet, they were also causing significant losses to the Royal Navy. Even Britain's surface fleet was not proving too successful. At the Battle of Jutland, in May 1916, the Royal Navy, though claiming a strategic victory over the Imperial High Seas Fleet, actually suffered a tactical defeat. Britain lost 6,000 men, three battle cruisers, three heavy cruisers, and eight destroyers, to German losses of one battleship, one heavy cruiser, three light cruisers, eight destroyers and around 2,500 men.

Nevertheless, apart from short forays, after Jutland the German High Seas Fleet spent the rest of the war in port, but the Royal Navy's century-old mastery of the seas had received a severe setback, and it had yet to find an effective way of countering the growing menace of the U-boats. The Allied – mainly British – blockade of German ports was slowly strangling that country's economy and already starving her people, but the German submarines appeared to be capable of reversing that process, not least because the Lords of the Admiralty flatly refused to introduce the convoy system for British and Allied shipping.

When every factor has been considered, deadlock was the likely result of any peace negotiation, for while all the major Powers professed a willingness to seek peace, none was willing to contemplate the concessions necessary to bring that peace about. As we saw, an interlocking system of treaties and alliances had brought about the rapid spread of the war in 1914–15. Now it seemed that without a general agreement peace was impossible, for all sides had agreed that the making of separate peace treaties between any of the warring parties was not to be contemplated.

Besides, there were spoils to be had if total victory could be achieved. Italy, which, in spite of her membership of the Triple Alliance with Germany and Austria, had opted for neutrality at the end of August 1914, had finally entered the war on the side of the Entente – but only against Austria-Hungary – in May 1915. The Italians hoped for territorial gains in the Tyrol and around the Adriatic if the Austro-Hungarian Empire could be shattered by this war, or if the new Emperor Carl, who had succeeded to the Habsburg throne on the death of Franz Joseph in November 1916, proved less committed to the German-Austrian axis.

Other nations, Greece, Serbia, Bulgaria, Romania, Britain, France and Russia, had their eyes fixed on parts of the Turkish Empire which had been on the point of disintegration even before the war began. For her part, Germany intended to secure her eastern frontier against the Russians and the Poles, besides her other ambitions in France and the Low countries, as well as in Africa and the Pacific. Austria-Hungary hoped to settle once and for all with Serbia, and to crush nationalist aspirations throughout the Balkans. The war had turned out to be longer and more costly than any of these nations had contemplated. After such a sacrifice, surely victory could not be just a dream, and all these losses for nothing?

One nation pressing unreservedly for peace was the United States of America. Under its President, Woodrow Wilson, the USA had kept strictly neutral in this struggle so far, and even the sinking of the passenger liner *Lusitania* by a U-boat in May 1915, with a heavy loss of American lives, and other losses caused by Germany's submarine fleet had not driven Wilson away from that policy. In January 1916 he sent his close friend and political adviser, Colonel Edward M. House, as his personal emissary to Europe, to assess the chances for peace. House duly travelled to all the warring capitals, talked to the leaders of all the main political factions, and reported back to Washington that he could see no grounds on which the United States could usefully intervene with peace proposals.

At the end of 1916, having been re-elected for a futile four-year term, Wilson tried again, hoping that the terrible losses of Verdun and the Somme would have produced a change of heart among the belligerents. He also ordered that no further financial credits were to be granted to any of the belligerents, an action which nearly brought on an economic crisis in Great Britain, the banker of the Entente's war effort. Colonel House did get the two sides to declare their war aims, but the Central Powers remained convinced that the Entente Powers were bent on their destruction and declined to talk, while the French refused to discuss anything unless and until the provinces of Alsace and Lorraine were returned to France.

Allied war aims included the restoration of Belgium with full sovereignty, reparations for damage to France and Belgium, return of territories seized in the past by the Central Powers, the liberation of Czechs, Serbs, Slavs and Romanians from Austria-Hungary, and the expulsion of the Ottoman Empire from European soil. The German aims were based on the idea that they should retain at least some of their gains in this war. Faced with these unreconcilable intentions from both sides Colonel House once more returned to the USA with nothing to offer his President.

The Germans were still afraid that America would eventually join the Allies and in the winter of 1916–17, seeking to keep the United States occupied with domestic problems should she join the war on the Allied side, they were trying to foment trouble between the USA and Mexico. German diplomats and politicians were secretly urging the Mexicans in the event of an American declaration of war on Germany to invade the United States and retake 'lost' Mexican territory in New Mexico, Texas and Arizona, promising them aid in this struggle, a fact eventually revealed to the US President and Congress by the Zimmerman Telegram, a missive intercepted by the British, decoded and sent on to the State Department. Meanwhile, the war in Europe and the Middle East continued.

Since 1914, a number of theatres of action had been tried as the Entente armies had probed about the periphery of the Central Powers, and in late 1916 some of these campaigns were still in progress. The Dardanelles Expedition had ended in January of that year, but the campaign against the Turks continued in Mesopotamia where, in May 1916, the British and Indian Army garrison in Kut-al-Amara, on the River Tigris some 100 miles from Baghdad, had been forced to surrender after a six-month siege. The British commander at Kut, Major-General Charles Townshend is one Great War general who does seem to conform closely to the popular stereotype, being both incompetent and indifferent to the fate of his men – who were abysmally treated by their captors – after the capitulation, but his failings lie outside the scope of this book. The war against the Turks, in Mesopotamia and in what were then Palestine and Arabia, would continue, sucking in British, Dominion and Imperial troops that might have been used on the Western Front where Hindenburg and Ludendorff were now in command of the German armies.

The Chief of the German General Staff and the First Quartermaster-General were a partnership, rather like that of Foch and his Chief of Staff, Colonel (later General) Maxime Weygand. They worked as mutually supportive teams, each supplying a range of talents that, together, formed a perfect whole, but while Weygand was never regarded as anything other than a prop to General Foch, Hindenburg and Ludendorff were equal partners. While the Field Marshal was the senior officer – indeed, effectively the Commander-in-Chief of the entire German Army, of which the Kaiser was the nominal head – Ludendorff was the *de facto* commander of the field army and the man most directly responsible for planning and operations.

Hindenburg was born in 1848, and had been retired for three years when the Great War began. He was another of those archetypal Prussian officers and a Junker, a member of the aristocratic, landowning, though often impoverished, military class which dominated Germany in the time of the Kaisers, and whose aims were the preservation of their identity and of their extensive social and political privileges. He had served in the Austro-Prussian (1866) and Franco-Prussian (1870–1) Wars, with no more than competence, and had retired in 1911 with the rank of general. He had been recalled to service in 1914 and sent to take command of the Eighth Army and check the sudden and alarming successes of the Russians on the Eastern Front; Ludendorff, then a major-general, went with him as Chief of Staff. Their successes led to Hindenburg's promotion to field marshal and command of all Eastern Front operations, which they had conducted with such success that when Falkenhayn came to be replaced as Chief of the General Staff in August 1916, only one man could be considered for the post. It went to Paul von Hindenburg, and he came west with Erich Ludendorff.

Ludendorff was, at least in appearance, another Junker, a typical Prussian officer with the cropped hair, stern manner and unflinching gaze of the senior German commander. This impression was deceptive, however, for he was by no means typical of the Prussian officer class. His background was humble; born into a family of merchants, his rise through the ranks of the Prussian Army came not through any aristocratic influence or patronage, but by the ability he showed in a series of staff appointments. Born in 1865, he was only a child when the Prussian Army crushed the French and Bismarck created the German Empire for the first Kaiser. Hard-working, intelligent and energetic, he had attracted the attention and praise of both Schlieffen and the younger Moltke, who had appointed him Chief of the Operations Section of the General Staff in 1904. After the outbreak of war Ludendorff proved his ability in the field with the siege and capture of Liège in 1914.

It was during their time in Russia that the two men came to form a team. Though Ludendorff's rank was Quartermaster-General, he was in reality Hindenburg's Chief of Staff, and in practice the power behind their joint success. Hindenburg admired Ludendorff deeply, and pays tribute in his memoirs to the 'intellectual powers, the superhuman capacity for hard work and the untiring resolution of my Chief of Staff'. When they came west in 1916 and Hindenburg became Chief of the General Staff, Ludendorff was offered the title of *Second* Chief of the General Staff, which he abruptly declined, taking the title of *First* Quartermaster-General, to demonstrate that he was second to no one.

Both generals were competent, professional, ruthless and accustomed to command, but that could be said of many generals, on either side of the wire. What made them so formidable was their combined and *complementary* characters. Hindenburg was phlegmatic, composed, and possessed a great depth of personal control. In times of trouble or great difficulty he was the one to steady his more volatile colleague, for Ludendorff was restless, temperamental, nervous and prone to depression. Nevertheless, he was a military genius, if of a somewhat limited kind, but first and foremost he was a man of action, one who had to be on the attack, an officer for whom defensive fighting was little short of torment. Above all, he did not believe that the war could be won by staying on the defensive. Expressing this belief in his memoirs, he writes: '. . . We could – indeed we must – attack. The offensive is the most effective means of making war; it alone is decisive. Military history proves it on every page. It is the symbol of authority.'

Ludendorff's tactical ideas were sound and his grasp of command absolute, but Hindenburg was not just a figurehead in this alliance, or certainly not at first. Ludendorff had flaws; for all his hardness and resolution he had a tendency to panic in times of crisis, and was not always able to handle the pressures inherent in his responsibilities. Hindenburg supplied the ballast; always on hand to steady his colleague in times of trial, he was the rock that stood firm and solid when Ludendorff's more fragile façade seemed in danger of cracking. The combination was both proven and effective. These two formidable soldiers had done great things together in Russia, and were to strive with some success for a fuller reward on the Western Front in 1918, after the collapse of Russia had supplied them with a vast new supply of trained fighting men.

As the war dragged on into 1917, however, Russia was still in arms – if only just. The main Revolution was still ten months away, but in spite of the great if temporary gains of the 1916 Brusilov offensive, Russia was a failing power, not least because her armies did not have those quantities of heavy guns and ammunition necessary to sustain themselves against the German and Austro-Hungarian offensives. This fact was underlined by the failure of the Dardanelles campaign which, had it succeeded, would have given Allied munitions ships access to the Russian Black Sea ports. Even so, while Russia continued to fight, her influence on the Western Front was considerable.

The Germans had discovered in 1914 that they could defeat large Russian formations. For their part, the Russians were able to drive off any Austrian army, but fell back swiftly before German offensives, a situation that still obtained even after Hindenburg and Ludendorff had left for France. This obliged the Germans to maintain in the east large numbers of troops which they might otherwise have employed on the Western Front, in order to support their Austrian ally. As the war entered 1917, though, Russia was clearly failing; the plight of her armies and the need to keep German reserves away from the Eastern Front was another in the long list of factors which obliged the Franco-British forces to continue their offensives in the west.

In the Balkans, where the war had begun, war continued. Serbia had fought a long, hard struggle against the Austrians, but a major Austro-German offensive in October 1915, followed by a winter campaign had finally defeated the Serbian Army, the remnants of which had, by the spring of 1916, joined the Anglo-French expedition in Salonika, in neutral Greece. This expedition, under the French General Maurice Sarrail, had been dispatched in October 1915 to aid the Serbians against the Bulgarians, but arrived too late to have any effect on Serbia's defeat. Nevertheless, the Anglo-French force remained in Salonika for the next three years, absorbing troops that might have been better employed elsewhere, but otherwise achieving very little except extremely high casualties, mainly from disease; Allied casualties in Salonika were 18,000 from battle and 481,000 from malaria

Of the other Balkan nations, Bulgaria had signed an accord with the Central Powers in September 1915 and entered the war with an attack on Serbia a month later. Now, at the end of 1916, she too was in decline. A junior partner in the Central Powers, Bulgaria's views were ignored by her allies, and a great deal of her produce, at best barely sufficient to feed her own population, was being taken to feed the hungry people of Germany; voices suggesting that their country withdraw from the war could already be heard in the Bulgarian Government. Albania, which had only gained her independence from Turkey in 1913, was split among several competing political factions. At the end of 1915 the Austro-Hungarian Army had invaded the country and occupied much of it, absorbing some or all of Albania as part of the spoils of war.

The various actions in the Middle East and the Balkans absorbed a certain amount of attention and a considerable number of troops from the French and British Armies; on the credit side, they did at least tie up large numbers of Turkish, Bulgarian, Austro-Hungarian and German troops, as well as a great deal in the way of enemy resources. By the end of 1916, however, it was becoming clear that the focus of the war was now on the Western Front, and that the prerequisite for peace was the total defeat of the German Army in that theatre. This fact was now bearing down on the politicians and senior military commanders in France and Great Britain, and here too there were changes.

In Britain, the Liberal Government of Herbert Asquith had been replaced in May 1915 by a coalition 'National Government'; still under Asquith, its Cabinet included the fiery and politically astute David Lloyd George, another Liberal. After a spell as Minister of Munitions and Secretary of State for War, Lloyd George replaced Asquith as Prime Minister in December 1916. The latter's grip on the Government, and thus on the war effort, had been slipping for some time, and the loss of his son in the fighting on the Somme may have played a part in his decision to stand down. Even so, Conservative members of his government had agitated for him to go, an end to which Lloyd George had also worked assiduously. The resulting long and bitter fend between the two men effectively destroyed the Liberal Party as a political force by 1925.

By the end of 1916, the future course of the war had become abundantly clear. Neither side would, or could, settle the argument, and thus the fighting on the Western Front would go on until one side or the other was simply unable to fight any longer. To say that the general acceptance of this state of affairs represents a complete failure of political will, or of human ingenuity, is to understate the case; none the less, it threw the problem of ending the war back into the laps of the military and naval commanders.

The generals' task now was to wear down the enemy's armies and kill his soldiers by the thousands and tens of thousands until the will to fight on – or even the means to do so – was gone. Meanwhile, the admirals would attack the civilian population, by sinking ships and blockading ports until starvation did for civilians what shells, bullets and poison gas were doing to their husbands, sons and brothers on the battlefield. When that policy did eventually succeed, the winning British generals were vilified while the politicians, whose failures had set the generals upon this course of action in the first place, walked away unspotted, later to join in the general chorus of condemnation.

Apart from the fact that the policy of attacking the German Army on the Western Front had the wholehearted support of the French, it also followed that well-established article of strategic doctrine which states that a nation or coalition faced with an array of enemies should attempt to defeat the strongest one first. This done, the weaker elements may collapse, and will certainly be easier to subdue. Though sound, this doctrine is sure to cause controversy, for the various allies will have separate priorities. Besides, the strongest enemy is usually causing most of the casualties and there is an understandable tendency to seek a less expensive way of bringing him down, by knocking away his subordinate, supporting props.

Plans for the Western Front offensives in 1917 had been discussed at the Chantilly Conference on 15 November 1916. While the army commanders were meeting at Chantilly, their political masters were in conference in Paris and on the following day, the 16th, the two groups met for a joint session. According to the Official History, the atmosphere at this conference was 'soberly optimistic'. Although French casualties had been horrific, the German attack at Verdun had been defeated; the British were still pushing on in the final days of Battle of the Ancre; and General Alexei Brusilov's offensive in Russia in June 1916 had reaped a harvest of 400,000 prisoners, mostly Austrian, and 400 guns. After an advance in May 1915 across their extreme north-eastern border into Austria (an area now part of Slovenia), the Italians had fought various battles along the River Isonzo and, although they were no nearer taking Trieste, the object of their advance, they had at least kept the Austro-Hungarian forces occupied.

As for the British, there was the fact, often overlooked, that although the fighting on the Somme had been both terrible and costly, the army that emerged from it was vastly more effective and efficient than the force that had opened the battle on 1 July. Moreover the morale of the British Army was still intact despite the losses of the Somme. The artillery was growing in power and expertise, and the ammunition failures were declining. The tactical handling of the infantry was also improving, with commanders like General Maxse setting an example in tactical training that others were to follow. The Royal Flying Corps, which had maintained air superiority over the Somme front for much of the battle, had become both more powerful and more effective, strafing and bombing the enemy trenches and supply lines, observing the effect of artillery fire and reporting the registration of the guns, carrying out reconnaissance and contact patrols with the infantry, identifying targets, providing photographs of enemy defences and dispositions. Moreover, under the inspired leadership of Trenchard the RFC was becoming a strategic force, which would soon be able to reach Germany and bomb targets there.

The Royal Engineers, those gallant and hard-working Sappers without whom the army could not move at all, were now expert in mining operations, in road building and trench construction, and in providing an ever more sophisticated range of signalling and communication equipment. Then there were the tanks, whose advent on the battlefield, if not decisive at the time, gave hopes of better things to come once this new weapon had been technically improved, and its parent corps expanded.

As for the infantry, though they had suffered grievously, here too matters were changing. Their tactics had been studied and were being modified and improved; their firepower had increased with the widespread issue of the Lewis gun; and their advances were benefiting from creeping barrages and the increasing use of smoke. The problems caused by the enemy emerging from deep dugouts after the assault, and harassing the next wave of advancing troops, or firing into the backs of those who had moved forward, had been tackled by the 'mopping-up' wave, a small group of soldiers, equipped with grenades and Lewis guns and charged with clearing all the enemy trenches and dugouts after the assault wave had passed through.

Infantry assaults, if still costly, were also achieving greater success because of a gradual improvement in that essential co-ordination between the infantry advances and the shifting artillery fire – the creeping barrage. Moreover, the British artillery now had more heavy guns, 1,517 in December 1916 as against 761 on 1 July; more artillery pieces were arriving all the time and the worn-out, obsolete 4.7-inch weapons were being phased out and replaced by the 60-pounders. A wire-cutting fuse was now generally available, and if the artillery could cut the German wire on a regular and reliable basis, one great obstacle to successful infantry attacks would be removed.

The most persistent problem remained that of communications, despite many and constant improvements. Hundreds of miles of trenches, six to eight feet deep, in which to bury telephone cables had to be dug behind the front line in a bid to prevent them being cut by shellfire. This measure met with with only limited success, and forward of the front line communications were far more a matter of luck than technology or expertise, though runners, carrier pigeons, flag and lamp signals, and primitive radios were all regularly employed by commanders. Wireless sets were still unreliable, as well as bulky and very heavy, and generally had to be carried in trucks or aircraft, though it would not be long before the tanks found another useful role as radio vehicles. On the whole, though, communications were to bedevil the generals' plans until the end of the war.

The popular belief that those generals continued to use the same methods in all their battles, and thereby caused great losses through their inability to learn and modify their tactics, is simply not true. The most important development by 1916 was that the British commanders, especially at corps and divisional level, had learned how to handle large forces in this new and constantly evolving form of warfare. They had begun to master the essential elements of attack and defence in trench fighting, and had learned the vital importance of co-ordination between the infantry and the artillery and, latterly, of co-ordinating their tactics with the RFC and the tanks. They were learning how to overcome the problems caused by the lack of reliable communications, and were beginning to calculate accurately just what was and was not possible in the attack. New techniques in infantry tactics and artillery fire, like the use and refinement of the creeping barrage introduced on the Somme, were coming into play and were already proving invaluable.

So, in spite of the losses of the last twelve months, it is not too surprising that the mood at Chantilly on 15 November was 'soberly optimistic'. Joffre and Haig were in accord in their belief that the war would be won on the Western Front where, with any luck and a good deal of judgement, the tank would provide the means to prise open the German fortifications and grant the Anglo-French armies their long-sought-after breakthrough in 1917.

The British forces in France had now risen to over 1,500,000 men, mustered in 5 cavalry and 56 infantry divisions. These units were divided between five armies, numbered from the First to the Fifth. Plans for the deployment and action of this force in 1917 were prepared, as usual, in co-ordination with the French, and began, again as usual, with the British taking over more of the French line. Haig's army took over the entire line north of the Somme on 12 December, adding about ten miles to the front of Rawlinson's Fourth Army. The Chantilly Conference had also concluded that the British Army was to continue operations throughout the winter whenever and wherever possible. This was sound thinking, for it was essential not to allow the German Army any time to recover from the later reverses on the Somme and at Verdun.

Joffre's proposals for the spring included an attack on two parts of the line, the British on a twenty-five-mile front from Bapaume to Vimy, with a major attack in the north against Vimy Ridge, and the French attacking between the Oise and the Somme. This would leave an eight-mile gap between the two assaults, roughly between Bapaume and Péronne, and this part of the front would be held defensively by the British. This plan was agreed between the Allies without undue difficulty and provisionally set for a date in the early spring. However, the British had an additional scheme in mind, an amphibious landing on the Belgian coast to neutralise the German submarine base at the inland part of Bruges by seizing the exits to the canals at Ostend and Zeebrugge, through which the U-boats reached the North Sea. This project – or others very similar – came up at regular intervals throughout the war. Of all the operations of war, however, an amphibious landing is the most difficult to carry out successfully, and it is probably fortunate that this scheme, though often raised, was never adopted* – though its existence was not to be without relevance to the operations of Haig's armies in 1917.

In Paris on 17 November, Joffre and Foch met Asquith, at that time still Prime Minister, and Lloyd George, Secretary for War, together with Prime Minister Aristide Briand of France and various other members of the French Government. Joffre briefed the politicians on the discussions at Chantilly and Lloyd George raised the question of supplying further Anglo-French forces for Salonika, but the broad conclusion of this meeting was support for the proposals outlined at Chantilly. After a further meeting of Britain's naval and military commanders in London on 22 November, however, a letter was sent to Joffre by the CIGS General Sir William Robertson, urging that an amphibious landing, timed to support a land offensive in Flanders, should be included in the Allied plans for 1917. Then, within a few weeks of these successful meetings, everything fell back into the melting pot.

On 7 December, David Lloyd George replaced Asquith as Prime Minister and head of the Coalition Government. Five days later General Joffre was sacked from his post of Commander-in-Chief of the French Armies, even though Haig made a personal appeal to Prime Minister Briand, claiming that Joffre's continued presence was vital to Allied co-operation.

The dismissal of Joffre came as a result of the terrible losses suffered by the French Army at Verdun. As an exercise in preserving *amour-propre*, his and France's, he was raised to the rank of Marshal of France, and then removed from operational duties and given the largely ceremonial post of President of the Supreme War Council (he was first offered a post as military adviser to the French Government, which he refused). Haig was shocked at this dismissal, which was to bring about, albeit indirectly, one of the great Allied disasters of the war. Joffre had earned the gratitude of the French people by his stubbornness on the Marne in 1914, and the British generals who had served with him since that time seem to have regarded him with affection, and viewed his departure with regret. His replacement was General Robert Nivelle, the hero of Verdun, a man who promised his political masters an attractive mixture of great victories and smaller casualty rolls.

---

* In April 1918, however, a daring combined operation – Royal Navy and Royal Marines – was launched against Zeebrugge and Ostend with a view to blocking the canals. Blockships were sunk successfully at Zeebrugge, but the raid failed at Ostend, and a second attempt was made there in May, which partially succeeded. As a result, the larger U-boats and a number of destroyers were bottled up in the canals.

General Nivelle was an artillery officer. Aged fifty-eight in 1914, he had soared in a year from command of an artillery regiment to command of an army corps. The strategy he promised was based on the use of powerful artillery support, deployed suddenly to overwhelm the enemy artillery and defences, followed by a creeping barrage of great depth in order to assist the infantry in the capture of the enemy's entire defence system '*in one day, up to and including the enemy batteries* [in other words, right through to the German rear areas]'. If that could be done, the Germans would have to pull back and a breakthrough would indeed be achieved. Nivelle claimed that he had done exactly this at Verdun when recapturing Fort Douaumont, where his assault, carefully planned and well supported by artillery, had seen its objectives captured within a few hours.

In early December 1916, he repeated the feat, rapidly recapturing three former French positions at Verdun and taking over 10,000 prisoners. The trick, according to Nivelle, was to avoid frontal attacks on strongly held positions, but to seize the greatest amount of ground possible while still enjoying the benefits of surprise, and then to call the attack off, consolidating any gains. There was enough sense in all this to make the strategy sound plausible, and Nivelle convinced the French politicians that his methods could succeed in larger battles on any part of the Western Front. He came to the command of the French armies convinced that if he were given absolute control over all the forces on the Western Front, British and Belgian as well as French, he could deliver victory on the battlefield in forty-eight hours and without great loss, for in the unlikely event that victory was not won in that time, he would simply call off the attack.

Nivelle's reign as Commander-in-Chief was not to last long, but he had a charming, forceful personality and spoke excellent English, learned from his British mother. Above all, he promised rapid victory without great loss. This promise alone was enough to endear him to Lloyd George, who had seen attack after attack start well, only to peter out with small gains and big casualties. 'We have the formula,' Nivelle told his political masters, and Lloyd George believed him.

David Lloyd George, one of the stars of the Liberal Party, first came to wide public notice in 1908. As Chancellor of the Exchequer, a post he held for seven years, he was responsible for the 'People's Budget' of 1909, still recognised as a major step on the road to widespread social welfare, and introduced such popular measures as the old-age pension. Born in England, he was raised in Wales and, after studying for the Bar, entered Parliament in 1890 as Member for Carnarvon, a seat he held for more than fifty years.

Lloyd George was a small, excitable, dazzling man, a brilliant speaker and a shrewd politician. A lawyer by training and a politician from conviction, he inherited the worst traits of both professions, being at once wily, devious, persuasive, and economical with the truth. He could also be hypocritical and vindictive, as his campaign against the generals, and especially Haig, would demonstrate. He came to Downing Street, aged fifty-four, determined to get a grip on the war and to harass those generals who, though promising victory, seemed unable to deliver it. Lloyd George was as determined to win the war as Haig or Clemenceau (who would become Prime Minister of France in November 1917) – the snag was that he wanted to win it without casualties. As a means to that end he intended to find some way of bringing the Central Powers to the conference table, probably by attacking and defeating their smaller allies in the Balkans.

This division on strategic policy, between the 'Westerners' – the French, King George V, Haig and the CIGS, Robertson – men who saw Germany as the main enemy and the Western Front as the principle theatre of war, and the 'Easterners' – Lloyd George, the Italians and the Greeks – who saw almost anywhere except the Western Front as likely to be more productive of victory, was to sour relations between the politicians and the generals (or the 'Generals and the Frocks', as Henry Wilson called the ministers, frock coats still being the chosen garb of senior politicians) for the rest of the war. It would also cause that deep rift between Haig and Lloyd George which would inspire the Prime Minister to attack the reputations of Haig and the other Western Front generals in the years after the war, though such deep and long-lasting enmity must have had other, more personal, roots.

The two men first collided when, as Minister of Munitions, Lloyd George was touring France in the summer of 1916, and disliked the complaints he received about the lack of heavy guns or the quality of the ammunition. He and Haig did not get on, which is hardly surprising; temperamentally, they were poles apart – a dour, inarticulate, Border Scots general, a soldier who made a plan and drove it through in spite of all the difficulties, and a loquacious, mercurial, Welsh politician who believed that there was a solution to every problem, if only a man had the wit to find it. The losses on the Somme had appalled Lloyd George and he placed the blame squarely on the British generals, especially Douglas Haig, believing that the offensive had gone on too long and that the results were a costly and bitter disappointment. Other people, at the time and in the decades since, have come to the same conclusions.

Lloyd George was not the kind of man to listen to advice or explanations from a professional soldier, and especially not one apparently unable either to muster his arguments coherently in council, or to win victories on the Western Front. One of Lloyd George's first moves as Prime Minister was to create a small 'War Cabinet', with himself as its chairman, a committee that would take over the strategy for fighting the war and issue orders to the various commanders-in-chief via the CIGS, General Robertson. Thus another burden, the mistrust of his political masters, was added to those on the shoulders of Sir Douglas Haig – who became a field marshal on New Year's Day, 1917. Haig did not trust Lloyd George. He did not think him 'straight', and regarded him as a man wholly ignorant of war. Haig had good reasons for these beliefs, but Lloyd George was now his political master. It was a most unhappy situation, and it soon became a great deal worse.

For the rest of the war Haig was to be confronted by a political chief who doubted his abilities, did not trust him with the command of armies, and laboured continually for his replacement. Lloyd George's attitude is, however, something of a paradox, for if he did not trust Haig to fight the war properly then he should have dismissed him. He was the Prime Minister, and if he wanted to get rid of the commander of the British forces in France – which he clearly did – he had only to issue such an instruction or request Haig's resignation. Haig said later that if the Government had ever asked for his resignation they could have had it, but that he would not resign of his own accord.

Lloyd George did not act to remove Haig for two reasons. Firstly, though not short of courage, he lacked the nerve to sack Haig, for the bulk of British opinion was firmly behind the Field Marshal. Whatever Lloyd George thought, the Army, many ministers and politicians, the King, and most of the public believed that Haig was doing a good job in difficult circumstances. If he was sacked, and his replacement did no better, a great deal of fury would descend on Lloyd George's head, and if he was driven from office for having made what would be perceived as such a poor decision, he might never get back. He might also lose the war.

The second reason was that Lloyd George could not find a replacement for his unwanted Commander-in-Chief. This was not for want of trying. The Prime Minister even asked Foch and Joffre for their views on the British generals, and sent his cronies about the Western Front to check up on Haig and to find out whether any one else might do better. The spectacle of the Prime Minister conspiring to force out his Commander-in-Chief is unedifying, to say the least; moreover, it is fair to say that Lloyd George would have appointed Fred Karno* to command the British Army if anyone had supported the basic idea of replacing Haig. Haig knew of all this, but although it upset him, and drove him to the brink of resignation, he concealed his feelings and hung on to his post, believing that no one could do better.

The Prime Minister hoped that by constant harassment he might provoke Haig's resignation, for which he, Lloyd George, could not be directly blamed, but that dour quality which marked the Haig's method of waging war stood him in equally good stead against the pressure and provocations exerted by the politician. Haig was popular with the soldiers and with the bulk of the British population, a popularity that was to endure until his death. He and Robertson never found favour with Lloyd George, but while Wully Robertson was eventually disposed of, Haig managed to keep the command of the British Armies in France until victory was finally achieved. In early 1917, however, Lloyd George found an ally in his undeclared war on Field Marshal Haig – General Robert Nivelle. Early in 1917 the Prime

* The stage name of Fred John Westcott, a comedian and producer of burlesques who enjoyed enormous popularity in Britain at the time. The New Armies were nicknamed 'Fred Karno's Army', and a parodic song of that title was popular with British soldiers.

Minister had a meeting in London with Bertier de Sauvigny, a French liaison officer at the War Office, during which he confided that he wanted to sack Haig but, being unable to do so, intended to ask Nivelle to help him ease the Field Marshal out of office. This attempt took a little time to arrange, but there is no doubt that the French were involved in the plot right from the start.

Nivelle first met Haig at Cassel, the headquarters of Plumer's Second Army, on 20 December 1916. The two men apparently took to each other – in his diary, Haig described Nivelle as, 'a most straightforward and soldierly man' – and, in a two-hour meeting Haig learned that Foch, General Édouard de Castelnau and General Louis Franchet d' Espery, three of the best generals in France, were to be removed from their commands, and Nivelle's own men were to be appointed army commanders. In addition, some major revisions were to be made in the Anglo-French plans for 1917. While the plan was still to destroy the German Army on the Western Front, this was now to be done by a large-scale – indeed, a massive – attack on the Chemin des Dames in the Aisne sector, designed to be a repeat of Nivelle's success at Verdun. This was to be an entirely French affair, but the British were asked to support the offensive with a major thrust east along the River Scarpe, south of Vimy Ridge.

The enemy's forces were to be pinned in position then his front was to be broken and all his available reserves destroyed, after which the French Army would storm through a massive breach created by artillery in the German line to begin the final stage of the battle . . . a breakthrough. To achieve this, said Nivelle, it would be necessary to create a huge French reserve – a *masse de manoeuvre* – of three full armies or at least twenty-seven divisions. To do this, however, the British must take over still more of the French line, some twenty miles from the current French left, at least as far as the Amiens–Roye road. This relief was to be completed by 20 January.

A part of the original Joffre plan would serve to pin the enemy in position, namely, the British attack between Bapaume and Vimy. Nivelle added that the proposed landing on the Belgian coast would be postponed for the moment since, if his offensive was completely successful, the Germans would be forced to evacuate the coast anyway. The British need not carry out further attacks on the Somme, although the atrocious winter weather then prevailing there made any decisive attack impossible anyway.

On the whole, Haig welcomed Nivelle's plan. He had no objection to the French taking over the major role in the forthcoming campaign, and his own preference was for a major British offensive in the Ypres Salient, to retake Messines and then, aided by a seaborne landing, push north and take Ostend and Zeebrugge. Nivelle's battle, as Haig understood it, was to be in three phases. In the first, the French and British would attack on their respective fronts, to suck in and then pin down the German reserves. The French *masse de manoeuvre*, that vast reserve of three armies, would then burst through the German centre. Finally, the French and British armies would deploy all available resources to exploit the breach and follow up the defeated enemy. Haig's one caveat was that if the Nivelle offensive failed he should be free to carry out his own offensive around the Salient, and the French must then take back some of their line to free British divisions for this task. All seemed to be in accord, but then Nivelle sent a letter to Haig in which he mentioned that the forthcoming battle might result in a prolonged struggle – 'une durée prolongée' – which was not the 'success-in-forty-eight-hours-or-we-call-it-all-off' attack he had thus far been promising to deliver.

Haig did not want another battle of attrition, even to draw in the enemy reserves. His understanding was that the first phase should last between one and two weeks, at which point the three French reserve armies would be flung in. Then, and only if the second phase was so successful that complete victory was deemed possible, the exploitation phase would be launched. In other words, everything hung on a rapid French breakthrough by the *masse de manoeuvre*. If that failed or bogged down, then the whole offensive would be called off and Haig would be free to deploy his troops in an attack elsewhere – specifically out of the Ypres Salient to clear the Belgian coast.

Relations between the two generals now began to grow strained. Haig was more than willing to support Nivelle's offensive, but the new War Cabinet in London were also pressing him to clear the Germans from the Belgian coast that summer and take the ports of Ostend and Zeebrugge, which the Admiralty believed – wrongly – to be the main bases for the German submarines harassing British shipping. He therefore wanted an assurance that the Nivelle offensive would be of limited duration. Since the latter had promised that it would either succeed in a few days or be called off, Haig failed to see that there was a problem . . . unless, of course, Nivelle was not being quite straight with him. This point, apparently so simple, could not be cleared up, and meeting after meeting between the two Allied Commanders-in-Chief failed to resolve it.

Then came a further snag. At an inter-Allied conference held in Rome between 4–7 January 1917, Lloyd George offered the Italian Army several hundred heavy guns for their spring offensive, and suggested that the French do the same. The thought of giving way almost 700 heavy artillery pieces *before* their own assault did not go down well with either Haig or Nivelle and after yet more discussions the idea was dropped. On the way back from Rome, however, Lloyd George and Nivelle had a long discussion about the coming offensive in France.

The French general's command of English, his articulate speech and ability to handle complex arguments in that language – so different from the gruff manner and halting speech of Field Marshal Haig and General Robertson – completely won Lloyd George over. Here was a general he could work with, here was a general who *understood* the problem, here was a general who promised a victory and had already demonstrated that he could deliver on that promise. So far as the British Prime Minister was concerned, whatever Nivelle wanted he could have, and when Lloyd George grasped that what Nivelle really wanted was complete control over Field Marshal Haig and the British Armies in France, that seemed a solution to both their problems. Steps to this end began at once, for the CIGS, Robertson, was instructed to write to Haig ordering him to conform to Nivelle's wishes, 'in letter and in spirit'.

Matters came to a head a few weeks later, at a conference in Calais on Monday, 26 February 1917. This conference, called ostensibly to resolve certain problems concerning the allocation of railway track and wagons, was in fact an ambush, laid by Lloyd George and Nivelle for Haig and Robertson. The matter of transportation was set aside after an hour. Lloyd George then told the gathering that he was aware that differences had arisen between Haig and Nivelle, and that he wanted them to speak 'with the utmost frankness' and clear the air.

Nivelle explained his plan yet again: an attack by the British between Arras and Bapaume, an attack by the French between the Oise and Avre rivers, a major French thrust between Reims and the Aisne, and a rapid follow-up through the breach thus created by both armies . . . 'et voilà'. Nivelle then stated that his only disagreement with Haig was over the flank deployment; the latter wanted to extend the attack to the north and take Vimy Ridge – which Nivelle regarded as impregnable – while the former wanted the British attack extended south, well below the River Scarpe, which runs through Arras.

Haig then explained his reasons for including Vimy Ridge, not least that if he attacked south of the Scarpe he would immediately be confronted with a new defence line which the RFC reported the Germans were constructing east of Arras. Secondly, the capture of Vimy Ridge would secure the left flank of the attack east from Arras, and lastly, the ridge was a vital position, dominating the surrounding countryside, which ought to be in Allied hands. General Louis Lyautey, the French Minister of War, chimed in to support Haig's proposals.

Lloyd George then sprang his trap. He deliberated for a while and then asked Nivelle to retire and put on paper his ideas for a 'System of Command', the rules he considered should guide the conduct of relations between himself and Haig. If Nivelle could do this before dinner, said Lloyd George, then he, Haig and Robertson would discuss it over their wine. This was a ruse for, as Lloyd George was well aware, the French had already prepared their proposals, and had brought the relevant paper with them. The game had to be played out, however, so the French withdrew and returned later with their draft proposals. These were, to put it mildly, audacious.

From 1 March, said Nivelle, the French Commander-in-Chief – that is, himself – should exercise authority over the British Armies in France for all matters connected with the conduct of operations, the plans and their execution, the strength and boundaries of the various British armies, and the allocation of supplies and reinforcements. To execute his orders, the

French Commander-in-Chief would have at his headquarters a British Chief of the General Staff and the Quartermaster-General, who would be Nivelle's conduit for communication with the British War Cabinet – headed by Lloyd George – and with the British armies in the field, to whom the British CGS would communicate the French commander's orders. The five British armies would now come directly under the orders of General Nivelle, though the British C-in-C would retain control over his forces in matters affecting discipline and personnel. This left Field Marshal Haig without his armies, and Wully Robertson, the Chief of the Imperial General Staff, with nothing to do but shuffle paper in Whitehall.

These proposals were met with a stunned silence. Then General Sir William Robertson, never a man to mince words, told Lloyd George that rather than submit to these proposals he would resign. Lloyd George then examined Nivelle's proposals and said that they went too far. This may have been true, for Nivelle was not the first or last French general to push a British proposal – in this case Lloyd George's own – as far, or even further, than it would fairly go, and to assume that the British would go along with their amendments, if only from politeness or sheer embarrassment. On the other hand, it seems unlikely that Lloyd George, who was behind this plan from the start, was completely unaware of what the French were up to. Either way, the long-term result of the Calais Conference was to destroy altogether the essential trust that must exist between a British commander-in-chief and his political masters.

In fact, the Nivelle proposals might have been justified, at least in part. Setting national feelings aside, some form of unified command was clearly necessary on the Western Front. Although the two armies had co-operated quite well since 1914, there was no compulsion for them to do so, with the result that Allied efforts were often fragmented. On the other hand, it was the French who had frequently declined to commit their forces to an Anglo-French assault, or had tinkered with the timings, or had broken off the attack when it suited them, or had promised to help and had then failed to do so. Instances of such failures went back via the Somme and Loos to both the battles at Ypres.

As in all matters concerning the Western Front, however, there are few absolutes, and there were many more instances, especially at a local level, where the French had loyally supported their British allies, often at considerable cost, while every British soldier acknowledged the relentless courage of the ordinary French *poilu*. That said, the fact remains that French interests dominated French thoughts and actions; the Anglo-French alliance came second, and the interests of Britain and the British Army last by a long way.

Nor can it be said that the French had produced an outstanding battlefield commander, one whose abilities so outshone those of all the other generals that he was both entitled to the High Command and cheered to that post by public acclamation. No nation produced a Great War general to rank with the great commanders of history, men like Napoleon, Wellington or Marlborough, though many senior French officers were quite convinced that a French general – any French general – was automatically better than any foreign general, and much, much better than any British general.

In the first years of the war Joffre had moved smoothly into the role of strategic commander, deferred to by Field Marshal French and Haig as 'Generalissimo', because the British were fighting on French soil, because the French Army was much larger than that of Great Britain, and because the British commanders had been directed to co-operate with him. Now Joffre had gone, the British Army was much larger, better equipped and more experienced, and the performance of the other French generals in the last two years had failed to impress anyone, having produced a catalogue of defeats and a terrible list of casualties. The thought of handing over command of their five armies to French control in 1917 was anathema to the British commanders, partly on a point of principle, partly for fear of where such an action might lead.

Nivelle's proposals were not for the establishment of a Supreme Allied Command on the lines of the one proposed by Haig and filled by Foch in 1918, let alone like the position occupied by General Eisenhower at the head of the Allied Expeditionary Force in 1944. Instead, he was seeking to remove an entire top layer from the British command structure and put the British army commanders *directly* under French control – thereby increasing the French forces by five armies and 1,500,000 men, enough to replenish the ranks thinned in France's battles of 1915–16. The effect of this proposal on the British troops in the field – and especially on the Dominion contingents, whose own governments had not been consulted – had not even been considered by Lloyd George. The Australian, Canadian, New Zealand and South African Governments might not take too kindly to the idea of their men being placed under French command.

After more discussions, the result of the opposition of Robertson and Haig was a scaling-down of the Nivelle proposal to one which bound Haig to obey the French C-in-C's orders for the forthcoming offensive only. The day after this agreement was reached, however, Nivelle pushed for more, including – inevitably – that General Sir Henry Wilson, that relentless francophile, should become Head of the British Mission at GQG, effectively taking on that post of 'British Chief of the General Staff' for which Nivelle had pushed on the day before, an idea which the British generals had emphatically rejected.

News of Lloyd George's machinations had by now reached the War Cabinet, which had had no prior knowledge of his plot. The Prime Minister had not consulted his Cabinet colleagues about this plan – or plot – and nor had the King been informed. When the Cabinet found out what was afoot they agreed with Haig and Robertson that the terms of the 'Calais Agreement', as it came to be called, at least needed to be carefully defined, and should not be subject to being tampered with or modified by the French.

The French, however, were already pulling on the reins of power. On 27 February Nivelle wrote Haig a letter which, as the latter recorded in his diary, was couched in 'very commanding tones', and which, he continued, was 'not the type of letter which any gentleman could have drafted'. Knowing he had the support of Lloyd George, Nivelle clearly intended to keep Haig in a subordinate position, and had meanwhile persuaded the French Prime Minister, Briand, to send a note to the British Government complaining that Haig was acting 'with the same reticences as formerly', and had not yet submitted his plans for Nivelle's approval. 'It is too sad,' Haig added in his diary, 'at this critical time to have to fight with one's Allies and the Home Government in addition to the enemy in the field.'

Eventually, after another conference in London, more precise terms for this Calais Agreement were drawn up. The French C-in-C would communicate with the British Army only through its Commander-in-Chief. In turn, the latter would send copies of his orders to the French C-in-C and report on their execution. The British armies in France would remain under the orders of their own commanders and of their own C-in-C. The Liaison Mission at GQG was to maintain touch between the two commanders, but it – or General Wilson – might be employed in drawing up instructions for Field Marshal Haig that would go out over Nivelle's signature; furthermore, the Mission would keep Nivelle informed of the situation of the British armies in France, both the orders given by Haig and the army commanders and the developing situation on the British front. So, at last, the problem of Allied command was resolved. A great deal of time and energy had been devoted to this issue, time that might have been spent studying the actions of the Germans, who were currently engaged in a course of action that would pull the rug from under Nivelle's much-vaunted spring offensive.

At the end of October 1916, an RFC patrol reported that the Germans appeared to be constructing a new defence line east of their current front line, roughly between Arras and Quéant, twelve miles to the south-east of Arras, and another line fourteen miles east of the village of Monchy-le-Preux, just south of the River Scarpe. RFC reconnaissance of this interesting earthwork was inhibited by bad weather and by the fact that British air superiority over the front had been ended by the appearance of two new German fighters, the twin-gun Albatros and Halberstadt machines. Powerful squadrons of these aircraft, one of them the 'Flying Circus' commanded by Rittmeister Freiherr Manfred von Richthofen – the 'Red Baron' – quickly swept the British machines from the sky.

Nevertheless, during the winter of 1916–17, more news filtered in, from German deserters and prisoners, or escaped Allied POWs, that the enemy were constructing a new defence line to the east, a line that was being supplied with all the wire, dugouts, strongpoints and machine-gun posts that German arms and ingenuity could provide. This position was known as the Siegfried Stellung, and although the British came to call it the 'Hindenburg

Line', the German title should have provided an indication of what the Germans were doing.

A *stellung* is a position, line or earthworks, and especially one heavily fortified – and the defences the Germans were building east of Arras and the Somme battlefield, on a line that would eventually run from Neuville-St-Vaast by Vimy, all the way south to Missy, west of the Chemin des Dames, was like nothing the Western Front had seen before. The Germans had reached the same conclusion as the Entente generals, that a front line could be penetrated given sufficient artillery and enough troops; moreover, they had come to see that a co-ordinated attack, pressed home with tanks, artillery and sufficient infantry reserves, might one day achieve that break-through the French and British had been seeking for over two years. Lastly, the German commanders had also realised that putting troops forward to repel such attacks simply led to tremendous losses from the ever-increasing artillery fire.

Their solution was 'defence in depth', based on a system of strongpoints and wide – sometimes hundreds of yards wide – belts of wire, covered by an interlocking field of machine-gun and artillery fire, trenches and strong-points equipped with deep dugouts; to all this were added well-concealed observation posts on higher ground, deeply dug communication and tele-phone lines, and adequate supplies of food, water and ammunition. These positions would then be manned by well-trained, resolute troops. Depth is the essence of defence, and the German defences here, the 'Forward Battle Zone', the 'Rear Zone', the lines of dugouts and trenches, the interlocking fields of fire, gave the Siegfried Stellung a depth in many places of between 6,000–8,000 thousand yards, say between 4 and 6 *miles*. Comparison with the trench systems already met at Ypres on the Somme, in Champagne and at Verdun is impossible, for the Siegfried Stellung represented defence of a different order of magnitude.

The Germans hoped that in attempting to penetrate the deep defences of the Siegfried Stellung, the Allies would suffer such insupportable casualties that no attack could succeed. In the north, around Ypres, where the construction of deep trenches was rendered impossible by the high water table, the German line was already studded with reinforced concrete pillboxes, equipped with more machine-guns covering more belts of wire. The Siegfried Stellung, however, and its fall-back extension line, known to the British as the Drocourt-Quéant Switch and to the Germans as the Wotan Stellung provided the bastion of the German front-line defences from the spring of 1917 until the end of the war.

To construct this line in the winter of 1916–17 the Germans employed large numbers of Russian prisoners of war – thereby breaching the Hague Convention – as well as Belgian civilians and thousands of their own soldiers. From the late winter of 1917, beginning around 23 February on the Ancre, up until the middle of March, the French and British forces began to discover that the enemy positions opposite their lines were suddenly empty. Slowly, hesitantly, the Allied troops moved forward, bumping into strong enemy rearguards, taking casualties from booby traps, finding that the country they were cautiously advancing across had been totally wrecked, trees gone, bridges down, riverbanks breached and country flooded, roads destroyed. Anything and everything that could make the ground east of the old front line usable by an advancing army had been pulled down or destroyed or taken away – and all this within three weeks of the time set for Nivelle's offensive. General Nivelle refused at first to believe that any of this was actually happening, and then that such a move would affect his plans.

The German decision to fall back to what can now be called the Hindenburg Line was due to various causes. Firstly, it shortened their front by around twenty-five miles and thus enabled them to move fourteen full divisions into reserve. It also eliminated the two salients, the one between Arras and Bapaume, created by the British advance on the Somme the previous summer, and the long-established Noyon Salient, which pushed into the Allied line between Péronne and the Aisne. Further, although the Germans did not know this, it removed the objectives from Nivelle's imminent offensive, which had now to be recast, except in the north at Vimy Ridge and in the south along the Aisne, where the old German lines were still occupied. It was impossible to mount an attack across the territory vacated by the Germans until the roads, water points, support and communication trenches necessary for an attack had been extended across this newly devastated wilderness.

This work was immediately put in hand along the British front which, after the relief of the French Third Army on the left on 13 February, ran south from Boesinghe at the northern end of the Ypres Salient all the way to Genermont, a village south of the Amiens–Roye road, below the Somme. The spring offensive was recast, with Nivelle's army attacking east of Soissons to start the Second Battle of the Aisne on 16 April, and the British, Canadian and Australian forces attacking at Vimy, Arras and astride the Scarpe on 9 April. Preparations for these attacks were well advanced when the Allies received some good news.

Following the rejection of their peace proposals in January, the Germans had reintroduced their policy of unrestricted submarine warfare. The move carried the risk of provoking America, but offered the possibility of forcing Britain out of the war before the US Army could make any decisive intervention. German U-boats began sinking ships in all parts of the North Atlantic, including waters close to the United States coast, and the vessels sunk included neutrals and those flying the US flag. As a result, on 6 April 1917, three days before the British infantry assaults at Arras and Vimy, the United States of America declared war on Imperial Germany.

CHAPTER 15

ARRAS,
APRIL–MAY 1917

'On the day before the assault, Sir Douglas Haig told Sir
William Robertson that never before had he seen his
subordinate Commanders so hopeful or so well satisfied with
the preparations for an attack.'

Brigadier-General Sir J. E. Edmonds,
Military Operations France and Belgium, 1917, Volume I

Field Marshal Sir Douglas Haig did not want to fight at Arras in 1917. He was convinced that the Somme battle had done grievous harm to the German field army, and he wanted to hurt it still more. Left to his own devices, he would have followed the plan advocated by General Joffre, namely, to continue wearing down the German Army by fighting along the Somme throughout the winter, thereafter mounting a major attack in Flanders in the spring, bursting out of the Salient to clear the enemy from the Belgian coast, this latter move being pressed upon him by the War Cabinet as a matter of some urgency. Both these actions should further reduce the German Army as a fighting force. Then came Nivelle, and this plan had to be changed. In late March 1917, after the Germans completed their withdrawal to the Hindenburg Line, the plan had to be changed yet again.

The German withdrawal did not totally disrupt Nivelle's plan for a major offensive on the Western Front. The withdrawal really affected the area in front of the British Fourth and Fifth Armies, which had been engaged on the Somme, and the French holding back the Germans at the Noyon Salient. In the area of the bulge between Arras and Soissons the Germans laid waste to the ground as they fell back. Crown Prince Rupprecht objected strongly to such barbarism and wanted to resign his command, but while he refused to sign the order for this devastation, most of the troops carried out the work with relish. The Allied forces followed the German Army across the shattered country, entering Bapaume on 17 March and Péronne and Noyon

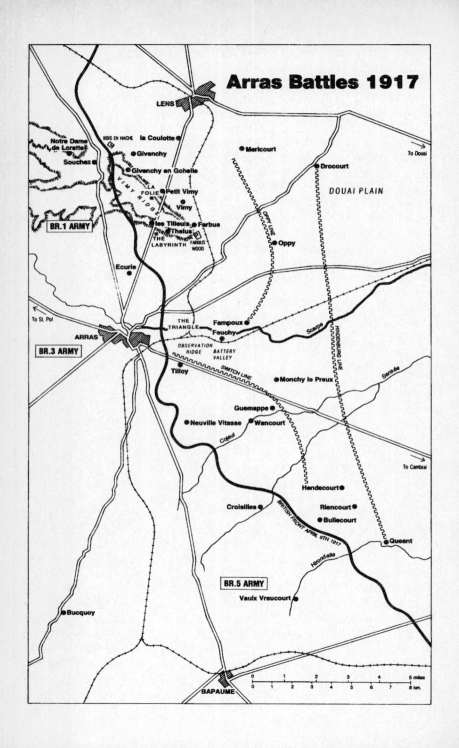

on the 18th, while preparations were pushed ahead for further attacks in Artois and along the Oise and Aisne.

Nivelle's plan required the British Third Army to attack south of Vimy Ridge and push through the German lines towards Cambrai, down the axis of the Arras–Cambrai road, both attacks to precede a massive French assault on the Aisne and in Champagne. Haig had extended his Arras attack by Third Army, along and astride the River Scarpe, to include an assault on the German bastion of Vimy Ridge by the Canadian Corps of First Army, claiming, correctly, that he could not go forward from Arras and leave this fortress in his rear. The British had taken over the Vimy section of the front in the spring of 1916, and in the past year had got to know it well. Vimy Ridge is solid chalk, ideal for mine warfare, and both sides had spent the intervening months in a form of siege warfare, digging under its muddy, shell-pocked slopes, driving tunnels and saps under the front lines, in which they set charges to blow up each others' trenches.

From just north of Arras to around Béthune the front was held by Lieutenant-General Sir Henry Horne's First Army, with the strong Canadian Corps facing Vimy Ridge. Horne is the 'unknown' general of the Great War. He kept no diary, wrote no autobiography, had no biographer, and is referred to only in passing in the numerous accounts of the time. His wife destroyed his letters, and his entry in the *Dictionary of National Biography* is extremely brief. This is a great pity, for Horne was a competent officer. Born in 1861, he was commissioned into the Royal Artillery in 1880, rose steadily to become Inspector-General of Horse and Field Artillery between 1912 and 1914, and was BGRA in Haig's I Corps from August to December of 1914. In 1915 he took over command of the 2nd Division, and in 1916 he was promoted lieutenant-general and given XV Corps, which he commanded during the Battle of the Somme. Now he had an army command. He handled his army with skill and was respected, if not greatly loved, by all who served with him.

The Canadian Corps now had a new commander – Lieutenant-General Sir Edwin Alderson having left to take up the post of Inspector-General of Canadian Forces – a forceful and determined cavalry officer, Lieutenant-General the Hon. Sir Julian Byng. A good soldier, he swiftly became popular with the Canadian troops, who sometimes referred to themselves as 'The Byng Boys' after a popular music-hall act of the day. Byng came from a military family, listing among his ancestors a brigadier-general of the Guards who had held the Château of Hougoumont during the Battle of Waterloo, and that unhappy Admiral John Byng who was shot by a firing squad on his own quarterdeck in 1757, either for failing to show sufficient zeal in preventing the French from taking Minorca, or, according to Voltaire, 'pour encourager les autres'. Julian Byng looked like a soldier; a compact, wiry man, with a firm chin and piercing gaze, he did not suffer fools gladly, but was always willing to listen to advice from any sensible source.

He made his mark with the Canadians even before taking up his appointment when he told Sam Hughes, Canada's bombastic Minister for War, that while, as a matter of courtesy, he would inform Hughes whom he wished to promote or appoint to commands within the corps, if the latter attempted to interfere or override his suggestions he would resign. Byng was not over concerned with such things as dress – before the war he had been criticised by King George V for wearing old clothes and well-worn uniforms – but he knew a great deal about soldiering, and possessed a wealth of common sense. He quickly came to love and admire his Canadian soldiers; when he left the corps to take command of Third Army he was almost in tears. By the time the Canadians came to attack Vimy Ridge Byng had been their commander for eleven months, since the start of the Battle of the Somme, during which he had led them at Flers-Courcelette and at the débâcle of Regina Trench. In this time he had formed some very decided views on their employment and was determined that when they attacked they should have both a sound plan and every possible support.

Like Haig, French and Allenby, Julian Byng was a cavalry officer. The youngest son of the Earl of Strafford, he was born in 1862, was commissioned into the 10th Hussars in 1883, and was not quite fifty-two when the war broke out. He had distinguished himself in command of the South African Light Horse, which he had raised, during the South African War. In 1809 he was promoted major-general and given command of a Territorial division, with which he served in England and Egypt, his first experience of commanding infantry. On the outbreak of the Great War he had commanded the 3rd Cavalry Division at Ypres, and when Allenby was given command of Third Army, Byng was promoted to command the Cavalry Corps. In 1915 he was sent to Gallipoli to command IX Corps, and played an important part in the evacuation of the peninsula, after which he returned to the Western Front. Now he was commanding the Canadian Corps, which was generally regarded, not least by those in it, as one of the crack formations on the Western Front. He was a successful commander and after the war was a popular Governor-General of Canada, greeted enthusiastically by his old soldiers wherever he went in the Dominion.

During the winter of 1916–17 Byng spent a great deal of time working out the necessary tactics for storming Vimy Ridge. To this end he sent Arthur Currie, now a major-general commanding the 1st Canadian Division, and the man regarded as the pick of his subordinates, to study the tactics employed by the French and Germans at Verdun, in an attempt to learn the secret of their successful offensives. Byng rapidly came to agree with the views of General Joffre, who had said in 1915 that Vimy could only be stormed with the aid of an abundance of artillery: 'It is essential to concentrate on the front to be attacked with sufficient artillery, heavy and field, enough to crush all resistance.'

Byng agreed with this, but knew that artillery concentrations alone were not enough. The attacking troops needed to be shielded from enemy fire and assisted by a creeping barrage right on to and through their objective. Counter-battery fire must also be perfected or the enemy artillery would disrupt the forward movement of reserves. The assault infantry must be carefully trained to clear the ground as they went so as not to leave pockets of resistance behind to fire into their backs, hold up support waves or impede the forward movement of the guns. That apart, the old problem of the Somme battles, the dire combination of wire and machine-guns, must also be overcome. Byng and his men continued to ponder this problem while awaiting the order to attack, though they began a series of trench raids and mining operations against the enemy's Vimy Ridge positions which gave them a good knowledge of the ground, although at the cost of considerable casualties.

South of the Canadian Corps lay the 51st (Highland) Division of XVII Corps in General Allenby's Third Army. Third Army was charged with carrying out much of the assault along and astride the River Scarpe in the forthcoming Battle of Arras, and the Highlanders had been ordered to keep their advance tied in with the Canadians on their left. General Allenby was to make a great name for himself in Palestine fighting the Turks, but that still lay in the future. His task in the spring of 1917 was to breach the Hindenburg Line and push on to Cambrai, and to that end he laid careful plans.

Edmund Allenby was born in Nottinghamshire 1861 and was already in his fortieth year before he first saw action in South Africa. He had no great wish to be a soldier, and had in fact tried for the Indian Civil Service, failing the entrance exam twice before electing to enter the Army. He sat the exam for the Royal Military College, Sandhurst, in 1880, and on passing out was commissioned into the 6th Inniskilling Dragoons a year later. He then joined his regiment in South Africa, where he was to remain, with occasional visits to England, from 1882 until 1890. South Africa was a troubled land, and much of Allenby's time was spent on patrol in Zululand and Bechuana-land. He was regarded as an efficient officer rather than a clever one, with a good sense of humour, but as he rose in rank this humour either faded or came to be concealed, to be replaced with a dour determination to do his duty and carry out his orders, backed by an explosive and seemingly uncontrollable temper.

In March 1889, now a captain, he became adjutant of his regiment, and changed within days into a thoroughgoing martinet. The Adjutant and the Regimental Sergeant-Major (RSM) are responsible for the turnout, discipline and routine of a cavalry regiment or infantry battalion. Neither job is suitable for a man who courts popularity, but Allenby clearly went too far, not simply in demanding high standards, which was his duty, but in shouting and raging at anyone who failed to achieve them. Such behaviour usually indicates some insecurity, a sense of inferiority, or a man who is simply not up to the job, but by all accounts Allenby, while sacrificing his previous popularity, was soon marked for further promotion, although it was a while in coming. In the meantime, he married, and in 1896 took the Staff College course, passing in twenty-first out of thirty-two candidates, the only cavalry officer to enter that year through the exam competition. Another cavalry officer, Douglas Haig, entered by selection, and the two men met for the first time at Camberley.

The relationship between Allenby and Haig is complex. Clearly, an unadmitted rivalry existed between them and although each made great efforts to be pleasant to the other, there was a lack of any sincere regard between them. Allenby was a steady, solid, regimental officer who allegedly had brains. He could be jolly, especially when away from his job, and had a range of interests outside the Army, including sketching, botany and travel. For his part, Haig was studious, devoted to his profession, and lacking in humour; he had also already developed powerful connections.

Their unspoken competition extended to their sporting life at Camberley, notably when Allenby was elected Master of the Drag Hounds in place of Haig. The latter, though a keen sportsman, had always devoted a great deal of time to his studies, and was not over-popular with the other students. This may have been because, as a selected entrant, Haig felt the need to demonstrate his ability to the students who had entered by examination, but the then Captain J.E. Edmonds, later the Official Historian of the Western Front, was also a student at Camberley and did not care for either of these cavalry officers, writing later, 'We elected him [Allenby] Master of the Drag because none of us wanted Haig.'

In spite of his notorious temper, to which were added taciturnity and habitual unpunctuality, Allenby was promoted to major while at the Staff College. Haig was still a captain, though he was soon to overtake his fellow student both in battlefield experience and in rapidity of promotion. After Staff College, Allenby went to Ireland as Brigade-Major to 3 Cavalry Brigade, Haig to Egypt and the Omdurman Expedition under Kitchener. When the two men met again in South Africa, Haig was a major on the staff of Major-General French's cavalry division.

Allenby did well in South Africa, where he at first commanded his own regiment, with which he fought in numerous engagements until given command of a column in the war's later stages. He worked hard enough to make himself ill, and finished the war in 1902 as a lieutenant-colonel, as did Douglas Haig. Both soon became full colonels, their promotion published in the same gazette. Allenby was also made a Companion of the Bath and on his return to Britain was appointed to command the 5th Lancers.

Allenby made a name for himself in the long and hard South African campaign. He detested war but liked soldiering, especially if he had a detached command and could make his own decisions. In the field he was cheery, hard-working, decisive and popular, although he had no time at all for sycophants or fools. Privately, he was an agreeable man who adored his wife, was very fond of children, walking, and natural history, and doted on his only son, Michael, who was to be killed on the Western Front in 1917 while serving as an officer in the Royal Artillery. Allenby was never happier than when with his wife and son, or out with his sketchbook, or playing with children. Only when on duty, in barracks, or under the stress of command did his evil temper surface, but it was always there, ready to burst out at the slightest provocation.

In 1906 he was promoted brigadier-general and placed in command of 4 Cavalry Brigade, where he soon made himself most unpopular with both officers and men. His biographer, Field Marshal Earl Wavell, who served with Allenby in France and Palestine and admired him greatly, wrote of him at this time that: '. . . increasing authority brought increasing asperity. He had been a noticeably easygoing young officer . . . he then became a strict colonel, an irascible brigadier and an explosive general.' Allenby's many admirers have made the point that his explosions of wrath did not last long and were soon forgotten – at least by Allenby – but the people he raged at were his subordinates, men in no position to argue back, and there is no doubt that this tendency to rant at his officers in public is the unattractive side of his complex personality. Inevitably, he made enemies, even among those who admired him as a soldier.

On a personal level, however, those who knew him, although they realised that he could be difficult to get on with, they forgave him because behind that brusque exterior, they found a brave, sensitive and intelligent man, with a broad range of interests inside and outside the military world, and one who was more often than not a kind and amusing companion. He did not bear grudges, took any blame on himself, and let any praise go to his subordinates. Serving under Allenby cannot have been easy, but those who came to know him seem to have liked and respected him.

In 1909 he was promoted major-general – six years after Haig had reached that rank – and was appointed Inspector-General of Cavalry, with Brigadier-General Hubert Gough, as his Chief Staff Officer. The two men did not get on, and Allenby's time as Inspector-General, which lasted for two years, was plagued by continual strife with the rest of the cavalry, mainly over the trivial matter of chinstraps. Cavalry soldiers liked to wear their chinstraps on the peak of their caps. Allenby, seeing how their caps flew off when the troopers broke into a gallop, ordered that chinstraps be worn under the chin. By insisting on this point, with his now habitual lack of tact, to which he added intolerance and occasional ranting at those who offended him, he made an enemy of the entire Cavalry Corps. By the time he took the Cavalry Division to France in 1914, Allenby was known throughout the Army as 'the Bull'; this nickname, which had followed him since 1909, although sometimes used admiringly, was not usually intended as a compliment.

Whatever the flaws in his character, however, Allenby was a thinking soldier. Though a supporter of the cavalry role, he could see that modern weapons were going to have a fundamental effect on battlefield tactics. Lecturing at the Royal United Services Institute in London in 1910, he said: 'We do not make sufficient use of machine-guns for the weapon is not properly understood. Personally, I believe that it is going to have an enormous future before it as a cavalry weapon.'

Allenby led the cavalry in support of Smith-Dorrien's II Corps at Le Cateau, and fought again at First Ypres, where his troopers served as infantry. When the number of cavalry divisions reached corps strength he became their corps commander, but mounted troops had no real role in the battles of 1915, other than as infantry. By May 1915 Allenby had become a lieutenant-general and commander of V Corps which he led at the Battle of Frezenberg Ridge, from 8–13 May, during which the corps suffered 8,000 casualties, but held on to its ground. His insistence on immediately counter-attacking to retake any enemy gains during Second Ypres made him even more unpopular; however, the reasons for such a policy have already been explained.

Allenby's admirers – and there are plenty of them – maintain that while he disliked the policy, he was determined to obey any order he was given, whatever the cost. This remained his approach; Field Marshal Wavell wrote that 'Duty, and not ambition was the key to Allenby's character'. This tendency to push on regardless of loss did no good to his reputation as a battlefield commander, and it plunged to an even lower level at the time of Loos when, his corps having been ordered to make a diversionary attack at Ypres, he elected to attack Hooge, a point which had resisted all previous attacks. The assault at Hooge was repulsed with great loss after the Germans counter-attacked using flamethrowers, though this reverse seems to have done Allenby no great harm with Field Marshal French, who promoted him full general in October 1915 on a temporary basis, and gave him command of Third Army. With that formation he held his share of the line, twenty miles from the Somme to Arras, and VII Corps from his army conducted the costly and abortive diversionary attack at Gommecourt on the first day of the Battle of the Somme.

Relations with Haig had not improved over the years, and were generally on a basis of formal, even frigid politeness, though it was noticed how at the weekly army commanders' conference, the C-in-C would frequently break in while Allenby was speaking to solicit another opinion; he was especially given to doing this if the other general from whom he wanted to hear was his old friend Hubert Gough. Whatever his relations with Haig, however, Allenby was generally considered a competent commander, if one without any great flair or special gifts. In reality he must have been rather more than that to reach and retain high command under the eyes of Haig, who was neither an admirer nor a friend. More damaging, though, was the fact that it was also widely believed that, as long as the end result was achieved, the position held or taken, Allenby cared little about the loss of life incurred in the process. This was probably an exaggeration, or even the result of rumours spread by his numerous enemies, for Lloyd George who kept a careful eye on the casualty figures, respected and even admired him; again, however, this may have been because of the antipathy between Allenby and

Haig. As will be seen from the discussion of the Battle of Arras, Allenby would not commit his men to action unless he felt there was a reasonable chance of success. He was also capable of seeing the larger picture, and invariably willing to tackle his superiors directly and forcefully – another reason for his nickname – in order to get the assistance his men needed and which the task required. He was scrupulous in his care of the sick and wounded, ordering that nothing likely to become an artillery target, such as an ammunition dump or a depot, should be sited anywhere near a hospital. He visited hospitals and casualty clearing stations constantly, and the usual explosion of wrath followed any shortfall in the arrangements. If he was not over-popular with his men, despite his concern for their welfare, he was certainly well known to them, for he made frequent visits to the front-line trenches. These occasions did less for morale than they might have done, however, as the General's inspections usually ended up with him shouting at some hapless subordinate in a company dugout, or berating the men for some minor infraction of his rules.

Allenby took easily to modern war, and his use of artillery and air power in France and his deployment of cavalry in Palestine later show that he was not devoid of imagination. He could also be very charming, as he again showed in the Middle East, where he gained the co-operation of eccentrics like Colonel T.E. Lawrence and the respect of the proud and fiercely individualistic Arab leaders. He was, too, capable of making independent judgements, the type of man who worked better when free from the bounds of direct authority. When forced to rely on his own judgement, as in Palestine, he blossomed. In France, he had to endure the limitations in decision-making forced on all the British generals, directly or indirectly, by the need to fall in with French demands, and to meet time-scales that did not always fit with his own army's needs. In the context of the Great War generals as a group, his success in Palestine, when compared with his mediocre performance on the Western Front, might be an indication that the conditions on that front limited any general's power of manoeuvre, so that in a more conventional campaign he flourished. That, however, was in the future; in the spring of 1917 Allenby had a major battle to fight in France, as the greater part of Britain's contribution to Nivelle's offensive.

Allenby's Third Army was tasked with breaking through the German front south of Arras and pushing on towards Cambrai with the Canadian Corps covering his left flank and Gough's Fifth Army – especially I Anzac Corps – covering his right at Bullecourt. This attack was to be made on 9 April, and its purpose was to attract German reserves to the British front before Nivelle launched his offensive on the Aisne and in Champagne on 16 April. How the various generals prepared to carry out these tasks is the next point to consider.

General Haig's first task was to take over more of the French front south of the Somme, to the line of the road linking Amiens with St Quentin. The Third Army was then allotted eighteen divisions, instead of its original ten,

received more field artillery and shifted its front north slightly, so that it now
lay astride the Scarpe. Thus strengthened, it was then ordered 'to capture the
German defensive line which runs from Arras to St Quentin by turning it
and attacking it from flank and rear, continuing to operate in the direction
of Cambrai.' Horne's First Army had the task of taking Vimy Ridge and
received another corps of three divisions either to help exploit this gain by
advancing on to the Douai Plain, or to reinforce the Third Army to the
south or Plumer's Second Army in the north. Rawlinson's Fourth Army was
to continue to keep up what pressure it could on the Hindenburg Line east of
Péronne, and Gough's Fifth Army was to pinch out the German stronghold
at Bullecourt, a task Gough delegated to I Anzac Corps.

It can be seen, therefore, that while the purpose of the entire British
offensive in April 1917 was to help the French by pulling in German
reserves, the main task fell to Allenby's Third Army, with the First, Fourth
and Fifth Armies playing important but subsidiary roles. The main secondary assault was against Vimy Ridge, but the overall success of Haig's
spring offensive depended on General Allenby. His task was formidable, for
the German defences before Third Army were strong, deep and well
defended.

One accusation frequently levelled against the Great War generals is that
they tended to assault the strongest parts of the enemy line, when it would
have been better to attack at some point where the defences were weaker,
penetrate the line there and roll up the enemy from the flank and rear. There
is some truth in this allegation, and there have already been several
examples, notably during the fighting at Loos and Pozières, where commanders continued to attack frontally when a flank was wide open. These
attacks, however, while costly, were local attacks, involving divisions or
even brigades rather than corps or entire armies.

The critics are less vocal in suggesting where these weaker points might
have been found. Indeed, taking the Western Front as a whole, there is little
or no merit in this charge, for the German defences were strong everywhere.
Certainly, their line was stronger in some parts – like the Somme, Vimy and
on the Chemin des Dames – than in others, usually because the ground there
added to the strength of the defence provided by the enemy in terms of guns
and wired-in positions, or because these positions protected some asset or
some region – the Lens-Douai coal mines behind Vimy, for example – which
the Germans were anxious not to lose. Given the vast preparation needed
for an attack, and the existence of air reconnaissance, surprise was not
usually available, so that assaults needed weight if they were to penetrate the
carapace of the German defences and achieve any strategic gain. This was
true everywhere along the line, and there was little the generals could do
about it, except to give their assaulting troops all the artillery, tank and
other assistance available.

The German defences east of Arras consisted of three or four lines of
trenches, set 75 to 100 yards apart and linked by communication trenches.

Some way behind lay a support line, linked into the Hindenburg Line defences, and behind that a strongly held reserve line, with what the Official History describes as 'a veritable fortress' barring the main Arras–Cambrai road, the axis of the Third Army's advance, at Feuchy Chapel.

The Hindenburg Line eliminated the former German salient at Gommecourt and ran on south, past Quéant. Finally, four miles in rear of this line lay the new Drocourt-Quéant Switch Line – or Wotan Stellung – which ran from Drocourt, south-east of Lens, to Quéant, north-east of Bapaume. The Hindenburg Line and the Drocourt-Quéant Switch Line came together just south of Bullecourt, a ruined village on the Hindenburg Line which the Germans had converted into a bastion. The entire defensive position facing Allenby was extremely strong, and it would take both force and judgement to achieve anything against it.

Allenby proposed to restore the element of surprise to the battlefield with a short but intense bombardment lasting only forty-eight hours – a proposal that shocked Field Marshal Haig – and intended to rely on trench mortars to destroy the enemy wire while his heavy guns concentrated on counter-battery work. His intention was then to punch his way through the enemy defences in just eight hours and forty minutes, capturing the vital hilltop village of Monchy-le-Preux, behind the Hindenburg Line east of Arras, by nightfall on the first day. His plan depended on surprise and speed, specifically on a hurricane bombardment and a rapid advance supported by a creeping barrage. This plan was duly submitted to Haig, who demanded changes.

Haig did not like this plan. He considered that a forty-eight-hour hurricane bombardment, during which the firing stopped only to cool the barrels or let the gun crews eat, would cause excessive wear on the guns and exhaust the men, and that trench mortars alone would not cut the wire adequately. Neither did he believe that Allenby could achieve surprise. 'It may be said,' he wrote to the latter, 'that in view of the great and prolonged preparations required, the enemy cannot be surprised as to the general front of an attack, but only to some extent as to its exact limits and the moment of assault.'

These criticisms effectively demolished the key elements of the plan, but Allenby was not the kind of officer to be easily dissuaded. He replied, rebutting all Haig's points, but was then tackled by the GHQ artillery adviser, Major-General James Birch, on the elements of his fire plan, which Birch maintained was flawed by the fact that such a volume of fire concentrated over two days would make it difficult to observe the effect it was having and that Allenby's gunners were not well enough trained to maintain such a barrage – and they also lacked adequate supplies of the vital graze fuse with which to destroy the wire. Allenby's own artillery adviser, Major-General Holland, thought that the artillery could easily handle this task, and indeed had recommended the two-day bombardment, but Birch disposed of Holland by having him promoted to a corps command; his replacement favoured a longer bombardment of the enemy trenches and wire. Birch also had the support of Haig, so the fire plan was eventually rejigged, extending the barrage to five days.

These plans were drawn up at the end of winter, but, as we have seen, after the German retirement to the Hindenburg Line Haig's entire plan had to be recast. The attack would now be made on a 10-mile front by three full corps of Third Army supported by some 1,700 guns, of which more than 700 were medium or heavy weapons. Some forty tanks were also found for this attack, spread out along the front to assist the assault brigades. Allenby would attack on a front between Croissilles, the junction with Fifth Army, to a point known as the Commandant's House, south of Farbus Wood and the junction with First Army. Third Army was to break through the Hindenburg Line and then roll it up by attacking it in flank and rear, and then advance on Cambrai. As this was going on the First Army, attacking at the same time, was to take Vimy Ridge, while the Fifth Army would attack at Bullecourt at some later date. (A short study of the map on page 326 will be helpful at this time.)

Allenby's three attacking corps – VI, VII and XVII Corps – were each to work to a precise time-scale. The initial objective, the German first line, was to be taken in thirty-six minutes by the VI and XVII Corps and the assault troops would stay there until Zero plus two hours while the guns were brought up. Then all three corps were to advance on the enemy's second line, which was to be reached in about 2 hours 45 minutes. They would stay there, consolidating, until Zero plus 6 hrs 40 minutes, and then advance to the Feuchy strongpoint which was to be reached by Zero plus 8 hours. Reaching this objective represented an advance of around four and a half miles; once there, all being well, the Cavalry Corps would be brought up to exploit success, two of its divisions being attached to Third Army and one to Gough's Fifth Army for this purpose. A Third Army reserve would also be formed, under Lieutenant-General Sir Ivor Maxse of XVIII Corps, so that Allenby would eventually have under command no fewer than five full corps, a total of sixteen divisions. Two other divisions previously allotted to Third Army were kept back and held in GHQ reserve.

The large amount of artillery – 1,720 pieces of heavy or field artillery – Allenby could deploy represented 1 gun to every 12 yards of front. When the artillery of the Canadian Corps and the rest of First Army are added to this, the total deployed along the assault front comes to a massive 2,817 pieces – 1,800 *more* than the defending Germans could deploy in opposition. Nevertheless, the German defences still represented a formidable obstacle to any attack, let alone one designed to succeed in eight hours. The infantry advance would be supported by a creeping barrage lifting at the rate of 100 yards every 4 minutes, most of this barrage being provided by the 858 18-pounders, while the heavy guns concentrated on counter-battery work and shelling the strongpoints ahead of the advancing infantry. There would also be a bombardment of gas shell before the assault, as well as a discharge of gas by cylinder a quarter of an hour before Zero, on the VI and XVII Corps fronts only.

The German forces facing the British at Arras and Vimy, though numerically inferior, were good, steady troops, and four of the five divisions manning the defences opposite Third Army were fresh. Three divisions under General Ritter von Fassbender formed the 'Vimy Group' and occupied the trenches from Givenchy-en-Gohelle, just north of Vimy Ridge, as far south as the north bank of the Scarpe. The 'Arras Group', on Fassbender's right, had four divisions, including the 220th Reserve Division of Sixth Army, and all these had been ordered to hold their ground and to counter-attack immediately to retake any position lost. Haig and Allenby had given code names to the various objectives in German position, beginning with the 'Black Line' – the old, pre-Hindenburg Line, front line – passing east through the 'Blue', 'Brown' and 'Green Lines'. Breaking through the defences on to these lines was the entire object of the battle, though the French officers who visited GHQ or Allenby's headquarters thought these objectives far too easy. 'À Berlin, à Berlin,' they cried, and departed to join the forward lunge of General Nivelle, whose main attack was about to take place on the Chemin des Dames.

Haig was quite right in stating that a major offensive like the one planned could not be fully concealed, but the actual hour, and perhaps even the day, of attack could be kept secret if the movement of troops up to the front line could be shielded from view. Troops and supplies coming forward to the Scarpe front and Vimy had to pass through Arras, and the ground beneath this town was already honeycombed with tunnels where the men could shelter from shellfire. In the weeks and months before the attack these tunnels were extended towards the front line and provided with deep shelters and dugouts in which large bodies of men and quantities of supplies could be concealed.

There were two main tunnels, the Ronville tunnel and the St Sauveur tunnel, running out towards the front line astride the Cambrai and Bapaume roads, linked to Arras via the sewer network and supplied along their length with large dugouts capable of holding thousands of men; one of these even contained a fully equipped hospital. The initial success of the 'First Battle of the Scarpe' (as this phase was officially called), which opened the Arras offensive, owes much to the men of the Royal Engineers and the Pioneers who cut these vast shelters in the chalk. 'Now it is possible,' wrote the author of one regimental war diary, 'to get from the crypt of the cathedral to the German wire without braving one shell in the open.' The working parties of Sappers, Pioneers and infantry had also dug hundreds of miles of narrow trenches in an attempt to protect the vital telephone cables from artillery fire. In short, all that could be done to ensure the success of the Third Army attack, was done, and Allenby must be given due credit for these skilful preparations.

Third Army would also have the benefit of air power and the support of tanks. The battlefield deployment of the latter was a skill the British Army had still to master, however. The forty tanks tasked to help the infantry were to start from up to a mile behind the front line and only join the infantry on the Black Line, the first enemy position on the original German front line. They would then be deployed, Somme fashion, in 'penny packets', two attacking one position, four another, although eighteen machines were tasked to attack the strongpoint at Feuchy Chapel, and having broken through there, were to roll up the Wancourt–Feuchy line and take part in the attack on Monchy-le-Preux. It was important to take this village, since it stood on high ground and thus offered its German occupiers an extensive view over the assault front. But despite the care that had gone into the plans for tank deployment, they were not to be relied on. Experience had already shown that tanks – and these were Mark Is, the type used at Flers-Courcelette – had a tendency to break down or get lost or bogged before they could reach the start line. Any assistance they could offer was therefore regarded by the infantry as a bonus, rather than something upon which they could depend.

Air power was at a more advanced stage, for the RFC had made great strides since 1914, in the quality, reliability and number of machines, and in their tactical deployment. Third Army would have the services of two wings, the Twelfth and Thirteenth, which could muster a total of nine squadrons, each of between sixteen and twenty-four machines, for such tasks as offensive and contact patrols, bombing, artillery registration, attacks on observation balloons, and photography. In addition there was the Ninth Headquarters Wing, of eight squadrons, which was tasked to support both the First and Third Armies. German air superiority, so strong in the latter stages of the Somme battles, was now again in decline, for new aircraft, the Sopwith Pup, the two-seater Bristol F2B Fighter and, latterly, the SE5, were coming into service, enabling the RFC to regain control over the Western Front.

Haig had supplied Allenby with a considerable force, and it remained to be seen what he would do with it. But the Battle of Arras, or more precisely the Battles of Vimy, the Scarpe and Bullecourt, would in fact test the mettle of three generals, Byng, Allenby and Gough, as well as their commander, Field Marshal Haig. Third Army had ten divisions in the forward zone, packed into an area ten miles long by two deep, and a large proportion of the infantry, more than one out of three of the one hundred and twenty battalions committed, came from Scottish regiments. The bombardment duly began at 0630 hours on 4 April, and the attack went in at dawn on Easter Monday, 9 April 1917.

The first day of the Battle of Arras, the 'First Battle of the Scarpe', was typical of most assault days on the Western Front – one of mixed fortunes. The assembly in the assault trenches went well, thanks to British command of the air, the counter-battery fire of the previous days, and the tunnels and dugouts. In addition, a strong westerly wind was driving sleet and snow into the enemy lines, so that all the Germans who could were keeping under cover; equally, though, the sleet turned roads into muddy swamps which held up the movement of supplies and the advance of the British tanks and guns.

While there was heavy fighting all along the front where the ten assault divisions and two of the reserve divisions were in action, the attention here must focus on the objectives chosen by Allenby and Haig, to see how their plan held up to the stress of battle. Not all these objectives were attained, but on the first day Allenby's army took over 6,000 prisoners and many guns, as well as making advances of up to three and a half miles. The axis of advance was down the Arras–Cambrai road, and VII Corps, commanded by the veteran General Snow, on the right flank of Third Army, already had possession of the old German front line and therefore had the Hindenburg Line as their first objective, after the other corps had come up into line by taking their initial objectives.

As a result, the attack of the 21st Division of VII Corps, on the right, did not take place until late afternoon, the men advancing in section columns rather than extended line. The attack was well controlled, with Stokes mortars being deployed to beat down any uncut wire, and all went fairly well until the advancing troops ran against the trenches of the Hindenburg Line. On this northern part of the front these trenches lay behind the former German front line, and the ground between the two sets of defences was still occupied by German troops. The attacking infantry therefore had a lot to do before they even arrived at their main objective, and were held up and reduced in numbers before the outer defences of the main Hindenburg Line position were attained.

The 30th Division ran into machine-gun fire from emplacements on that line, one battalion of the Wiltshire Regiment alone losing 342 men in fruitless assaults on the German trenches. The 56th (1/1st London) Division, on the left of the 30th, had a formidable task, having first to advance through Neuville-la-Vitesse and through the first German defences just to get to the Hindenburg Line, then penetrate the line and advance a further 2,000 yards to the Wancourt–Feuchy position, a German defence line running between the villages of Wancourt, south of the Cambrai road, and Feuchy, just to the north of the road and due east of Arras. The advance was handled well, the division pushing forward for over a mile for the loss of 881 men, a small cost in the Great War, but they still could not penetrate the Hindenburg Line. The last division of the VII Corps, the 14th (Light), had the assistance of fourteen tanks, but eight of these were rapidly knocked out or became bogged in the mud, and the German machine-gunners emerged from deep emplacements and raked the advancing infantry with fire.

The attack ground to a halt at dusk, and at 2240 hours General Snow ordered his artillery to bombard the Wancourt–Feuchy line – the Brown Line – at daylight, after which the 14th and 56th Divisions, aided by the 3rd Division of VI Corps, would attack again. Snow now appreciated, rightly, that until the Wancourt–Feuchy position was reduced there was no prospect of breaking through the Hindenburg Line on his front. Even so, by past standards, his corps had done well, advancing for between a mile and a half and two miles, overrunning powerful German defences and taking many prisoners, for the loss of around 4,000 men killed, wounded and missing.

On Snow's left, VI Corps had to attack between the village of Tilloy and the Scarpe and also take the Wancourt–Feuchy line, which was set astride their axis of attack on the Arras–Cambrai road. The corps attacked with three divisions in line, each tasked with taking a section of this objective, which lay two miles in front of their trenches. The fourth division, initially in reserve, was then to pass through and take the Green Line at Guémappe, a further mile and a half away.

The tunnels from Arras proved their worth on this section of the front, for the troops of the 12th (Eastern) Division, advancing along the left of the Arras–Cambrai road with their right flank on the road itself, went into battle fresh and ungalled by artillery fire. The division also used smoke, which concealed their advance from enemy fire, and put down a machine-gun barrage on the enemy trenches from twenty-four Vickers guns which overawed the German infantry waiting to repel their assault. The Vickers machine-guns had been taken away from the battalions and replaced with a much larger number of Lewis guns early in 1916, and were now being used as long-range weapons, formed into machine-gun companies for use in the 'artillery' role, for strafing and harassing fire. The 12th Division went racing ahead, took Observation Ridge and swept into Battery Valley, a ravine crammed with German artillery, which the advancing British infantry rapidly overran, shooting down the gunners and capturing thirty-one guns. The 3rd Division, on their right, was not doing so well, however, and could not get within 650 yards of the Wancourt–Feuchy line before their leading battalions were driven to ground. Moreover, much of the wire before this position was still uncut.

The 37th Division were charged with capturing the villages of Guémappe and Monchy, but since the Wancourt–Feuchy line was still unbreached, the task was beyond them. This Wancourt–Feuchy position – in fact a double line of well-wired trenches set astride the Arras–Cambrai road – which appears in all the divisional reports, was clearly the crux of the problem, but the time for storming it had passed. As the day wore on, German opposition stiffened and it was clear that another full-scale attack would have to be mounted before this line could be cleared.

The last division of VI Corps was the 15th (Scottish), which made their assault with the aid of two tanks, both tasked to attack first the strongpoint in the maze of railway embankments and cuttings known as the Railway Triangle, and then, inevitably, the Wancourt–Feuchy line. The Railway Triangle held up their advance for a while, until the artillery was called back to give it another pounding and it was finally taken by 1230 hours. The Scots also entered another part of Battery Valley and like the 12th Division on their right, got among the enemy guns, capturing another thirty. The division then pressed on and by 1730 had captured all the Brown Line – the now notorious Wancourt–Feuchy line – along their front, aided by a single tank that had somehow made it up to the front of the advance. Monchy-le Preux remained in German hands but, thanks to that tank and the skill and aggression of the 15th Division, a major obstacle had been overcome.

XVII Corps had to attack with its right flank on the Scarpe and its left butting against the Canadians on Vimy Ridge. The most crucial part of this attack lay on the left, where the 51st (Highland) Division had to keep pace with the Canadians, who could not advance unless their flank was covered. The object of the attack was the village of Fampoux and the southern limits of Vimy Ridge and eight tanks were attached to the corps for this offensive. The 9th (Scottish) Division stormed ahead behind a creeping barrage and, screened by smoke, took all their objectives, capturing 2,100 prisoners, for very little loss. The three battalions in the forefront of the battle suffered sixty-nine, eighty-four and eighty-eight casualties, almost negligible losses in a Great War battle, and the division, having advanced for over a mile and a half, were eager to go on and do more.

The 4th Division then passed through and took Fampoux behind a howitzer barrage moving at the rate of 100 yards every 4 minutes. Their advance was then checked by heavy machine-gun fire from the right flank but again casualties were light, 12 Brigade, which took Fampoux, losing only 147 men killed, wounded and missing, having captured 230 Germans and 24 guns. On their right 11 Brigade also swept ahead and advanced three and a half miles, crossing the Oppy-Méricourt line, and even capturing a German general. This brigade also set a Western Front record, the furthest advance made in a single day by any belligerent since trench warfare began in 1914 . . . and at the cost of just 302 men, from all four battalions.

In most areas the Black and Blue Lines were taken without much opposition or great loss. In the centre, the troops of the Tyneside Scottish (102 Brigade, four battalions of the Northumberland Fusiliers) took a large number of German prisoners who seemed anxious to surrender having apparently been demoralised by both the long preliminary bombardment and the storm of machine-gun fire sweeping their parapets. The attack on the Brown Line north of Fampoux did not go so well, however, and parts of it were still untaken that evening.

The last division of the XVII Corps, the left-hand division of Allenby's Third Army, was the 51st (Highland), commanded by Major-General George Harper. His attack was complicated partly by the fact that the German defences, the old 'Labyrinth' position which had caused the French great problems in 1915, were still intact and particularly intricate, and partly because the Canadian line on his left was slightly ahead of that held by the Highlanders.

Harper did not believe in tanks and none were attached to his division, which attacked with two brigades in line, each supported by a battalion from the reserve brigade. Their advance ran into problems from the start, with even the Black Line, which fell easily elsewhere, giving trouble. There was a terrible firefight around the Labyrinth, where a platoon of German infantry fought to the last man before the position fell. This delay lost the High-landers the support of the creeping barrage, which had moved on. Heavy machine-gun fire then cut up the advancing battalions between the Black and Blue Lines, and the advance to the Brown Line is described in the Official History as 'a chapter of accidents'. A more appropriate term would be 'a shambles'.

The leading battalions, the 7th Argyll and Sutherland Highlanders and the 4th Gordon Highlanders, having lost almost all their officers, also lost direction and veered across the front of another brigade; one platoon of the Gordons, having gone off with the Canadians, entered one of the the latter's objectives before coming back again. The division managed to make and maintain contact with Currie's 1st Canadian Division but did not reach its final objective, something which was to cause troubles to the Canadian troops fighting to establish themselves on Vimy Ridge.

On the whole, though, the first day of the First Battle of the Scarpe had gone well, the plan made by Allenby and his corps commanders giving the Third Army a good advance for small losses. Even the 51st Division, which had not captured its final objective, had taken 700 prisoners and a quantity of guns.

The British had learned and applied the lessons of the Somme, but so too had the Germans. The continual increase in the volume and weight of British artillery fire in recent months had been noted and remedies had been sought, most noticeably the abandonment of linear defence as being un-tenable in the face of such fire. Ludendorff had therefore worked out a new defence-in-depth arrangement based on an outpost zone, complete with strongpoints and belts of wire, all covered by machine-guns and artillery and acting as a front for strong counter-attack divisions.

Clearly, if they had enough guns and enough guts, the British could get into the German line. Whether they could stay there would be another matter. The enemy had lost men and guns so far because the local commander, General von Falkenhausen, GOC Sixth Army, did not under-stand the new principles of defence. That would soon change, however. The Battle of the Scarpe had only just begun, and the German riposte was already taking shape.

Vimy Ridge is regarded, rightly, as largely a Canadian Corps battle, almost separate from the Arras offensive taking place on its right flank. Although this is not factually correct, it is reasonable to look at what Allenby's Third Army had achieved before returning to dawn on 9 April and seeing how the Canadians fared at Vimy. Third Army had achieved worthwhile gains for what, in Great War terms, were regarded as acceptable losses. The same number of divisions had been employed here as on the first day of the Somme eight months before, and a comparison of casualties is interesting. Rawlinson lost 57,000 men killed, wounded, and missing on 1 July 1916. Allenby lost 8,328 men in the first three days of Arras, and if the casualties of the First Army engaged at Vimy are included, the total for the *first three days* of the Arras-Vimy battle (since daily figures are not available) comes to around 13,000 killed, wounded and missing.

Although this fortunate balance was not to be maintained, the achievement of Third Army on 9 April should not be dismissed. Some divisions had fought with great skill, and had used tried and tested methods – and the quantity of guns and tanks now available – with considerable effect. The British artillery had become a formidable, accurate and efficient arm, the tanks had been at least useful, and the barrages from the machine-gun companies had proved their worth in keeping the Germans' heads down during the infantry advance. Allenby may have had a rough edge to his tongue, but the men under his command at Arras had little to complain about on the evening of 9 April 1917.

It is also a fact that the German Army at Arras was not the force it had been on the Somme. There had been frequent surrenders – more than 5,000 prisoners had been taken, and a considerable number of guns had fallen into British hands. Only on the Wancourt–Feuchy line had there been stiff resistance, and though they had not taken all their objectives, the men of Third Army, and their general, could regard their day's work as well done. Yet this good news was overshadowed in the communiqués by events taking place just to the north, where the Canadian Corps had taken the bastion of Vimy Ridge in one day of hard, intelligent fighting.

CHAPTER 16

VIMY AND BULLECOURT, APRIL 1917

*'I am among my old friends now, those old friends of
1916–17. I do not know that I have a greater affection for
anything on earth than I have for that old Corps.'*

General the Lord Byng of Vimy, Governor-General of Canada,
speech to Canadian Corps veterans, 1922

The Canadian Corps won a great reputation on the Western Front, as
did the two Anzac corps. Since this chapter covers two of their most
notable engagements, it might be useful to examine the reasons why these
formations did so well and came to be so highly regarded both by their
British comrades and by the enemy. Clearly the first reason is that they were
good troops, well trained, well led and highly motivated. Without these
qualities no unit can do well in war, but this has been overshadowed in the
last twenty years by a swelling chorus of self-regarding praise, orchestrated
in Canberra and Ottawa, and, though to a lesser extent, in Wellington,
growing in volume as the veterans of the Great War have died, and
dedicated to the notion that the soldiers of Canada, Australia and New
Zealand were stronger, braver, more intelligent, and better led, than the
troops provided by the Old Country. In fact, few of the Great War veterans
from those countries would have supported that allegation, and a little
thought makes it apparent that such a simple explanation is not necessarily
correct.

Much of this comment can be accounted for by patriotism and a natural
pride in the exploits of the national army in the Great War – or by attempts
to bolster growing republican sentiment in those countries. It is, however,
regrettable that some historians in Canada and Australia have attempted to
elevate the considerable exploits of their Great War forebears by denigrating
the actions and courage of their British comrades-in-arms. Most of the
soldiers in the Canadian Corps were born in Britain (as is detailed in
Chapter 7), as were a significant percentage of men in the Anzac Corps,

so such chauvinism appears to be largely unfounded. In 1914 the over-whelming majority of people of Australia and New Zealand were of British descent; family links were strong and constantly maintained: the amount of mail between Britain and Australia at this time was said to be 'prodigious'. The citizens of the Dominions in 1914–18 were also citizens – and soldiers, many of them – of the British Empire . . . and proud to be so.

For a later generation to imply that their ancestors were duped into offering their service and their lives by the cunning British is both to insult their intelligence and to denigrate their sacrifice, while the notion that the Anzac or Canadian contingents won the war or did the bulk of the fighting is yet another Great War myth. It is, however, perfectly fair to say that they did more than their share. This hogging of the credit is widespread, although not universal. The gallant South African Brigade fought throughout the war but is chiefly remembered for what it did at Delville Wood in 1916. The New Zealand Division was arguably the finest of all the Dominion formations – and yet very little is heard about it at all, other than as part of the 'Australian' (Anzac) forces.

This is not to say that many Dominion generals and commanders did not complain about the British troops at the time, especially in the battles of 1918. Their complaints were often justified, for the troops being sent out from Britain at that time were often new, half-trained conscripts, put into the line after less than three months' training. Britain sustained terrible losses in the war and her manpower reserves were fully stretched and becoming exhausted, a fact that Commonwealth historians often tend to overlook.

It is frequently pointed out that the British generals were always anxious to have Dominion troops under command, and this is also true. However, apart from being good soldiers, it has to be remembered that the Dominion divisions were kept up to strength and the Canadian divisions were not only up to full strength but in 1918, during the 'Hundred Days', their battalions were, in many cases, well over establishment.

Furthermore, while the British manpower shortage had forced a reduc-tion in brigade strength from four to three battalions in 1918, the Dominion brigades all had four battalions, and these, unlike most British battalions, were up to full strength. So, given the choice of a full-strength, four-battalions-to-a-brigade, Dominion division, or a British division in which the three battalions to each brigade were under strength and composed of hastily trained conscripts, any sensible commander would have leapt at a Dominion corps or division – the fact that so many did so is an indication that the British generals were more sensible than they are usually given credit for.

Great War issues are always complex and open to argument, but a little thought – and a little modesty among Commonwealth historians – will indicate that the success of the Dominion units has more complex roots than the public are usually invited to believe. The Dominions provided just twelve divisions (and a South African brigade) to the British Armies in France, and very fine divisions they were – all the rest were British divisions, and most of those were pretty good, too.

The basic myth still needs refuting, for it does great harm. It cannot be a good thing that generations of Canadian, New Zealand and Australian children are being brought up to believe that their grandparents and great-grandparents were sent to their deaths by incompetent British generals, while great numbers of British soldiers stayed in safety, drinking tea. This myth does harm to the mutual understanding and respect that should exist between friendly nations, to historical truth and, not least, to the reputation of brave men. The soldiers of the Anzac and Canadian Corps who fought on the Western Front in the Great War would deplore the words of some of those who decry the actions of their British comrades, and yet neglect to mention some of the more practical causes of the success in battle of these splendid Dominion soldiers.

Some of these elements were analysed by the senior Australian commander of the war, General Sir John Monash, in his account of the Australian soldiers:

> Many stories of the work they did have been published in the daily press and in book form. Seldom has any stress been laid upon the fact that the Australians in France became moulded into a single, complete and fully organised Corps, fighting under a single command and provided with all the accessory arms and services and so able to undertake fighting operations on the grandest scale. It is impossible to overrate the advantages which accrued to the Canadian Corps from the close and constant association of all four divisions with the others – this was the prime factor in achieving the brilliant conquest of Vimy Ridge.

These are the words of a universally respected Australian general, one of the finest of all the Western Front commanders, and they repay study. British corps did not enjoy such homogeneity, suffered because of the lack of it, and should have adopted it. Failure to keep the same divisions in the same corps was a flaw in British command. British divisions were moved from corps to corps constantly, the chain of command suffered, staff work varied, and that essential 'close and constant association' praised by Monash could rarely be achieved in the British Army. The Dominion divisions were also larger than their British counterparts and were kept at full strength when the British units had to be reduced in 1918. In addition, the Australian, Canadian, New Zealand and South African soldiers felt, rightly or wrongly, that they had something to prove. They represented the cream of their country's manhood, and the stirring of their patriotism, as Australians, Canadians, New Zealanders, South Africans, was a spur to achievement and a justifiable source of pride.

Most of the Dominion soldiers – all of them in the Anzac divisions – were volunteers. That fact is worth remembering, for in order to maintain a large number of divisions in the field Britain had been forced to introduce conscription but by the spring of 1917, she still provided, and would continue to provide, the bulk of the front-line troops under British command. Australia never introduced conscription, and there were major riots in Canada when it was imposed in Quebec. By the time of the Battle of Arras Australia had five divisions in the line, Canada four, India two cavalry divisions, New Zealand one infantry division, South Africa an infantry brigade. The Dominions and Empire thus fielded a total of twelve divisions and a brigade on the Western Front in 1917. Britain fielded all the rest, a total of forty-eight divisions.

The Australians and Canadians, South Africans and New Zealanders were all good soldiers. Nothing can detract from that fact, now or at any time. It is simply regrettable that their deeds have been exploited by some national historians in recent years to make unnecessary and unjust sneers against their comrades-in-arms in the British divisions, who fought as hard, endured as much, and suffered as greatly as did the Australians at Bullecourt or the Canadians on Vimy Ridge.

Vimy Ridge runs for some seven miles, roughly north to south, from Notre-Dame-de-Lorette to Écurie. From the west the land rises gradually to the crest, and the 'ridge' itself is not a sharp edge but a wide-topped plateau, half a mile in extent, dropping down steeply on the eastern side for some two hundred feet to the Douai Plain and the outskirts of Lens. That Vimy Ridge was a stoutly defended bastion in the German line has been pointed out in previous chapters; the French had suffered over 150,000 casualties in their various attempts to capture this piece of ground. Now it was the turn of the Canadian Corps and their commander, General Byng, made careful preparations for what could only be a hazardous assault.

General Horne had issued a preliminary warning to his First Army for the attack on Vimy Ridge in January 1917, stressing that the vital areas were the ridge itself, the village of Thélus on the western slope, and Hill 135 immediately to the rear of the village. If these places at the southern end of the ridge could be taken on the first day, then two points on the northern end, Hill 120 ('the Pimple') and the Bois de la Hache, north of Givenchy, could be captured in a separate attack. The southern attack was the task of the four divisions of the Canadian Corps, with 13 Brigade of the British 5th Division, under command, and would be made at the same time as Third Army assaulted astride the Scarpe. The northern attack around Givenchy would be made by the right-hand divisions of I Corps, assisted by the 4th Canadian Division on its flank.

The distance from the British front line, which ran down from the old Loos battlefield and skirted the western slope of the ridge, to the crest itself varied along the front. The troops of Currie's 1st Canadian Division would have to advance 4,000 yards to carry the crest, those of the 4th Division to the north only about 700 yards. Byng elected to attack with all four divisions in line, each with two brigades up and one in reserve. He also had the British 5th Division in reserve, though as has been said 13 Infantry Brigade of that division had already been committed to assist the 2nd Canadian Division. There would be a massive bombardment, with one heavy gun to every 20 yards of front, and one field gun to every 10. A creeping barrage would be employed to support the infantry, although there was a snag here, for the 1st and 2nd Canadian Divisions on the right had to advance a distance of between one and a half and two and a half miles, beyond the range of their artillery established on the gun line, which was well behind the front line. Byng's plan took account of this by digging in eleven batteries by night, close to the front line and in a position to support these divisions through to their objective. These batteries remained silent, other than when firing for registration, and were still undetected by the Germans when the battle opened. The 2nd Canadian Division, which had the task of taking the village of Thélus, would also be supported by eight tanks. Byng and his divisional commanders believed in careful preparation and for weeks before the battle the ground on and behind the ridge was overflown and photographed daily by RFC patrols. German aircraft attacked the British aircraft and carried out reconnaissance missions over the Canadian lines, so that the enemy commanders must have been well aware that a major attack was coming.

The essence of Byng's plan was speed. The infantry assault would go in at 0530 hours and by 0705 the two left-hand Canadian divisions, the 4th and 3rd, were expected to have taken their objectives and be established on Vimy Ridge. The two right-hand divisions, the 1st and 2nd, had further to advance and more obstacles on the way in the shape of defended woods, and villages like Thélus and Farbus. Like the Third Army division on their right, they had four defence lines to penetrate, codenamed 'Black', 'Red', 'Blue' and 'Brown'; the Brown Line, the furthest point of their advance, ran along the eastern edge of the ridge, and the two divisions were expected to be there by 1318 hours precisely on the first afternoon. Byng had therefore allowed his Canadians slightly less than eight hours in which to take a position that had defied every Allied assault for more than two years.

The Canadian divisions were not to advance in line. The 1st and 2nd would still be fighting forward well after the two divisions to their north had – it was hoped – taken their objectives. That was due to the nature of the ground and the position of the German line, but Byng and his divisional commanders had in any case rejected the extended-line formation used on the first day of the Somme. Vimy was to be taken by platoons and sections, using fire-and-movement tactics, advancing in small units with plenty of grenades and Lewis guns, clearing trenches and strongpoints as they advanced, but leaving behind small parties to clean out any pockets of resistance or to clear deep dugouts while the rest pressed on. Byng's plan had assumed that there would probably be a check somewhere, but he did not intend to let that either delay his programme, or lead him into wasting men by reinforcing failure. His orders directed the Canadians that 'if any unit is held up, those on the flanks will on no account check their advance but will press forward themselves and envelop the strongpoint.' Reserves were standing by close to the assault divisions, specifically the 13 Infantry Brigade, which had seen much hard service at Second Ypres and Loos, and was tasked with supporting the 2nd Canadian Division. But if all went well, this flowing tide of artillery and infantry should swamp the defences of Vimy Ridge.

To support the guns and supply the troops, miles of light railway track were laid from Arras to the front, and twelve subways were constructed to move the assault battalions in safety right up to the front line. Six miles of tunnel and many dugouts were created, some of the former, each twenty-five feet below ground, extending for over a mile. The same care was shown in attempts to protect the ever-vital communications. More miles of buried cable were added to the *fifteen hundred miles* of circuit wire already in use, and the latest means of communication, wireless, buzzers and amplifiers, were added to the old ones, field telephones, carrier pigeons and runners.

New mines were also laid up to and under the German front line, carried along saps dug beneath a no man's land already cratered by mine explosions. Finally, the attack would be supported by a release of gas and smoke and preceded by a bombardment which started on 20 March, when half the available artillery began to scourge the enemy defences. On 2 April the rest of the guns joined in, and in the course of the next few days flung over 1 million shells – more than 50,000 tons of metal – on to the battered surface of Vimy Ridge. At night the Canadian Machine Gun Corps, mustering 280 Vickers MMGs, commenced long-range harassing fire on the enemy trenches and for two or three thousand yards behind his lines, taking care to cover the movement of Canadian raiding parties which went out nightly to check the state of the enemy's wire and to probe his defences.

These patrols established that five German regiments faced the Canadian Corps at Vimy, and learned from their prisoners that four of these had been in the line without relief for up to a month. The Germans normally kept two-thirds of their strength in the trenches and the rest in reserve, so the Canadians estimated that they outnumbered the enemy defenders by three to one. There were also two German divisions of the Sixth Army in reserve at Douai, but Byng estimated that it would take them four hours to reach the battlefield . . . and by that time he intended to have the ridge. Patrols on the night of 8–9 April reported that the wire had been extensively destroyed, and at 0530 hours on 9 April the bombardment rose to a crescendo and two mines exploded on the left of the German line. Then the barrage began to creep forward, lifting by 100 yards every 3 minutes, and behind it came the Canadian infantry.

Vimy Ridge was that rare thing, a Great War battle that went according to plan. On the right flank, Currie's 1st Division attacked on a front of 2,000 yards, heading for Farbus and Farbus Wood, and were into the first enemy trenches, just 75 yards from their own line, before the Germans emerged from their dugouts. Parties already detailed off to do so stayed behind to mop up while the rest forged on behind the barrage, but the other German trenches proved tougher and machine-guns were soon playing on the advancing Canadian infantry. Even so, the Black Line, the first German defensive position, fell in half an hour and the western slope of Vimy Ridge was now covered with a mass of Canadian infantry – riflemen, bombers, support sections, carrying parties – all surging forward, scrambling to get on to and across the ridge.

The 2nd Division on the left did equally well, attacking on a front of 1,400 yards with 2 miles to go to their final objective, over the eastern edge of Vimy Ridge where 13 Brigade would join them in their sweep down the eastern slope. Although a German machine-gun section got into action and badly cut up an Ontario battalion before the crews were attacked and bayoneted by Sergeant E.W. Sifton, who was awarded the VC for this action, the division pressed on and took its first objective by 0605 hours. The support battalions of each brigade then came through to follow the creeping barrage to the next objective, passing through the hamlet of Les Tilleuls on the Lens–Arras road, and capturing a large number of Germans in an underground bunker.

The wrecked village of Thélus now lay ahead. By 1000 hours the leading sections were in the outskirts, and by 1045 the entire village was in Canadian hands and the mopping-up parties were rooting the remaining defenders out of the cellars. At 1300 hours both divisions were moving again. On time to the minute, the 1st and 2nd Canadian Divisions reached the far side of Vimy Ridge and saw before them the wide Douai Plain.

The 3rd Division on their left had just two objectives to take and a shorter distance to cover just 1,200 yards. Tunnels had allowed the attacking troops to get up to their front-line trenches unobserved and in safety, and they were in the German lines before the defenders had a chance to man their positions as the creeping barrage passed over. The German first and second line of trenches fell almost without loss, and the division was on the far crest of the ridge and digging in by just after 0800 hours. There was still one problem, however. The left-hand battalions of the 3rd Division were enfiladed by the Germans on the knoll called Hill 145, the highest point on Vimy Ridge and now marked by the Canadian Memorial, which lay in the sector of the 4th Canadian Division. The 4th had not yet taken this position and until they did so the 3rd Division's left-hand battalions were hung up. The rest of the 3rd Division pressed on, down the eastern slope of the ridge towards the village of Vimy, then Petit Vimy beyond Folie Wood, and then a strongpoint at La Folie Farm. The farm fell and an hour later the woods beyond it were in Canadian hands. Only on the far left of the assault, in the sector of the 4th Canadian Division, was there a major hold-up.

The 4th Division had a short distance to cover to the far crest of the ridge, only around 600 yards, but some formidable obstacles lay in their path. To the north, in Givenchy Wood, lay the Pimple, a German strongpoint. Then came Givenchy-en-Gohelle, a large ruined village in which every cellar contained a machine-gun nest. Then, just before the Black Line, came Hill 145. This was to be assaulted by 11 Brigade, and it provided them with a daunting task, for the entire steep-sided knoll had been turned into a strongpoint equipped with dugouts, trenches, machine-guns, trench mortars and wire. These defences had been well-battered by artillery and in an attempt to shorten the assault, tunnels had been constructed from the Canadian lines at Zouave Valley, well behind the British front line, and four deep communication trenches had been dug and extended to the east, all to get the assault troops as far forward under cover as possible.

Attacking to the left of 11 Brigade, 12 Brigade fell victims to a tactical mistake made by the commanding officer of the 87th Battalion (Canadian Grenadier Guards) in 11 Brigade. Hoping to rush the first German trenches, this officer had asked the artillery to leave the German second-line trench alone, intending to use it as a base for a further advance after it had been captured. When the assault went in, the Germans in the second-line trench managed to man their positions and hang on, enfilading the front of 12 Brigade, so that an hour after the initial attack the advance of the 4th Division was faced with *three* untaken strongpoints – this trench, Hill 145 and, on the far left, the Pimple, from which the defenders were pouring enfilade fire across the divisional front.

Under fire from two sides, 12 Brigade could not get forward. To their left 10 Brigade, tasked with taking the Pimple, put off their attack until the following day, when the artillery could have a further chance to soften it up. Hill 145 had to be taken, however, for it was holding up all progress on either flank. Two of 11 Brigade's battalions in turn tried to take the hill by assault but were driven off with loss, and confused messages were soon flooding back to Division and Corps Headquarters. The division had lost many experienced soldiers in trench raids over the previous weeks, and the new recruits who had replaced them were shocked and dazed by the intensity of the fire now being directed at them. Inevitably, 11 Brigade's attack faltered, and by early afternoon had completely stalled.

The brigade commander, Brigadier-General Victor Odlum, needed fresh troops for another assault and had only his reserve battalion available. This was the 102nd Battalion (Nova Scotia Highlanders), a much-depleted battalion – many of the men were sick with mumps – which had never been in action before. There is sometimes an advantage in using unblooded troops; not knowing what to expect, the men are willing to go forward and find out, where a more experienced battalion might assess the difficulties at a glance and shy away. The Nova Scotias' Adjutant, Major J.L Rawlston, summed up the battalion attitude when he told another officer he met on the way up to the start line that his men would 'Take Hill 145, or never come back'.

The Nova Scotia Highlanders took Hill 145 the only way it could be taken that day, with the bayonet, the grenade, the Lewis gun . . . and guts. The sheer vigour of the Highlanders' assault dismayed the defenders and they quickly began to abandon their trenches or surrender to a wave of yelling Canadians, who sprayed the trenches with Lewis-gun fire, flung in grenades and leapt down from the parapets to root out the defenders with the bayonet. Nothing could stop them, and when Hill 145 had fallen the Highlanders pressed on down the far slope of the ridge until their commander called them back. Vimy Ridge, which had held out for more than two years, fell within hours to a carefully prepared and stoutly delivered attack by a first-class infantry corps.

The taking of Vimy Ridge was, and remains, a proud day in Canadian history, and the battlefield is still the scene of regular commemoration services. The British commander of the Canadian Corps, Lieutenant-General Sir Julian Byng, was rightly proud of his splendid troops, and when he was raised to the peerage after the war, he took the title 'Byng of Vimy' in remembrance of what his men did that day.

By nightfall on 9 April, the Battle of Arras was going well. Although it would take two more days of fighting finally to clear the eastern slope, Vimy Ridge was effectively in British – or rather Canadian – hands. Taking it had cost the Canadian Corps 10,602 men, of whom 3,598 had been killed. On the Scarpe, enough had been achieved to give hope of continued advances on the morrow, and the casualties had been – again in Great War terms – acceptable in view of the gains made.

The German Sixth Army commander, General von Falkenhausen, had also made an error. The best answer to an attack is an immediate counter-attack but Falkenhausen had fallen into the trap that had engulfed Field Marshal French at Loos, and kept his reserve divisions too far back. By the time he could assess the effect of the British attack and get them forward the British and Canadians had had time to dig in, bring up their guns and move fresh troops into the line. The counter-attack on Vimy on the night of the 9–10 April never even reached the Canadian lines, and counter-attacks against the Third Army were headed off by further British attacks on the following day towards Monchy-le-Preux. Falkenhausen was relieved of his command and sent to Brussels as Governor-General of Belgium.

Further south, the Battle of the Scarpe did not go well after 9 April. Allenby issued orders that his corps must press on, taking the rest of the Brown Line on the morning of the 10th and then advance to the Green Line, with the cavalry ordered to stand by to exploit the breakthrough. Third Army managed to advance a further mile in front of VI Corps but the old problems were starting to surface: tiredness and losses affecting the advance of the assault divisions; stiffening resistance by the Germans, especially at Monchy-le-Preux where VI Corps were in trouble; and an inability to get the guns forward over wet ground, torn and pitted by shellfire. There was very little that could be done about this falling-off of the assault, given the state of the armies in 1917. An attack needs *momentum* as well as weight, and without some means rapidly to exploit forward – a role played by cavalry before the advent of the machine-gun and barbed wire – the advance was bound to slow down.

On 10 April, Haig met Allenby and Horne at St Pol. He urged Allenby to press on where he could, especially with cavalry south of the Scarpe, not least because Gough's Fifth Army was putting in I Anzac at Bullecourt on the following day. By the 11th, the attack of Third Army, already slowing on the 10th, had degenerated into a series of local attacks and small counter-attacks against stiffening German resistance. Allenby – the 'Bull' side of his nature now in full control – either did not appreciate this, or could not. His orders for that day instructed his men that:

> The Army commander wishes all troops to understand that Third Army is now pursuing a defeated enemy and that risks must be freely taken. Isolated enemy detachments in farms and villages must not be allowed to delay the general progress. Such points must be masked and passed by. They can be dealt with by troops in rear.

If the first sentence was correct and the enemy were indeed retreating, the other sentences are sensible. Otherwise, they are not. Unfortunately for the Third Army, the Germans were not in retreat, nor were they any longer defeated. They *had* been defeated, on 9 April, but were now fighting stubbornly and using the defences of the Hindenburg Line to great effect. The British troops on the front line knew this, and knew, too, that the hoped-for breakthrough, with the cavalry thrusting past into open country, was again a dream. The battle had become one of bite and hold, seizing a bit of line here and there and hanging on to it, often at great cost, as was demonstrated at Monchy, where 111 Brigade of the 37th Division was met with a terrific volume of fire as they attempted to attack.

Allenby, however, did not seem able to accept this. The fighting on 11 April rewarded him with small gains at a greater cost in lives, not least among the cavalry brigades and regiments sent forward to exploit a *success* that did not exist. Monchy-le-Preux fell to a combined assault from tanks, infantry and cavalry, but the losses were considerable, all the tanks being knocked out. The infantry casualties were so heavy that the troopers of the 3rd Cavalry Division, instead of galloping forward to exploit this gain, were forced to dig in to defend the village from fierce German counter-attacks. Only scattered remnants of the battalions which had attacked Monchy were on their feet when it fell, and according to the Official History 'The defence therefore fell entirely on the cavalry.' Counter-attacks duly came in but were driven off. The three divisions of Lieutenant-General Kavanagh's Cavalry Corps had been placed at Allenby's disposal before the battle, but their opportunity, if it ever existed, had now passed, and Allenby ordered the cavalry out of the battle. Apart from taking Monchy and a portion of the German lines, nothing else was achieved on the 11th – and another 8,238 casualties had been added to the Third Army list.

The First Battle of the Scarpe went on for another three days, until 14 April, but little more was accomplished. The first day had gone well but after that, as all too often before, the amount of ground gained was in inverse proportion to the cost of gaining it. Haig called off the attacks for a few days, to rest his troops and study the situation, intending to renew the assault later with a combined attack by the First and Third Armies supported by the Fifth Army, which had just put in an attack at Bullecourt.

Bullecourt was a two-part Australian affair – officially the First and Second Battles of Bullecourt – fought by I Anzac under their British commander, Lieutenant-General Sir William Birdwood, and with the assistance of British divisions. First Bullecourt was fought by the 4th Australian Division and the British 62nd Division, Second Bullecourt by the 2nd Australian Division and the same British division, so although both are now held to be 'Australian' battles, neither was an exclusively Australian affair. Birdwood thus had five divisions under his orders of which three were to take part – one of them on both occasions – in the first two abortive attempts to take Bullecourt.

The place was only a small hamlet, but it stood at a strategic point in the line, being both on the left flank of Fifth Army, and a jutting buttress in the Hindenburg Line at the point – or the hinge – where that line was joined from the north by the Drocourt-Quéant Switch Line. At the actual junction of these two defence lines stood another village, Riencourt, and a mile behind Bullecourt lay Hendecourt. All three villages had been turned into fortresses. Birdwood's I Anzac was on the left wing of Gough's Fifth Army and the planned purpose of the Bullecourt attack, launched in support of the Third Army onslaught to the north, was to punch a hole in the German line and thereby initiate a pincer movement, passing the 4th Cavalry Division through at Bullecourt to link up with the rest of the Cavalry Corps flooding through the breach made by Third Army astride the Scarpe, a few miles to the north.

This attack was originally due to go in with that of the Third Army on 9 April, but Gough then discovered that his artillery had not yet breached the Hindenburg Line wire in I Anzac's sector adequately, and that it would take another week of shelling to prepare it for the assault. Australian patrols confirmed that the German wire at Bullecourt was largely uncut – and up to 35 yards thick in places – so when the Third Army attacked on the Scarpe, Bullecourt was still being pounded by the Fifth Army artillery. When reports of the success of the 9 April fighting at Vimy and the Scarpe arrived, Gough was anxious to join the battle. On the afternoon of the 9th, a Lieutenant-Colonel J. Hardress Lloyd, commanding D Tank Battalion came to him with a proposal. The attack by I Anzac could be reduced to a surprise attack by just one division, the 4th Australian, on a front of

1,500 yards, *if it was supported by all the tanks available*. This amounted to just twelve machines, all of the Mark I pattern used at Flers, which had been assembled in a tank 'company' under the command of Major W.H.L. Watson. These tanks, said Lloyd, would advance ahead of the Australian infantry and cut the German wire by rolling over it, and would then provide close support within the enemy's trench system. Gough seized on this chance to get into the battle – and from that moment matters went seriously awry.

The attack was planned for dawn, 0430 hours, on the following day, which left only a few hours in which to work out a fire plan and issue orders. Birdwood was now having second thoughts about the whole scheme, but the enthusiasm of the tank crews and pressure from Gough made him hesitate to call it off. The latter claimed that the wire, which had inhibited the launching of attacks in this sector so far, was no longer a problem since the tanks would crush it; he added that since the Third Army attack was succeeding, now was the time to throw Fifth Army into the struggle. Somehow the planning and issuing of orders for the attack were managed in the time available, the commander of the 4th Australian Division, Major-General W. Holmes, deciding to attack with two brigades up and one in reserve, the advance led by the twelve tanks and supported by artillery and infantry of the British 62nd Division of V Corps, which would push through on the Australians' left. By 0100 hrs on the morning of 10 April, the Australian infantry were lying out in no man's land, on flat, snow-covered ground, just 600 yards from the enemy trenches, waiting for the tanks.

No tanks arrived. Frantic telephoning from Divisional HQ produced a barrage of reasons and excuses, but no tanks. The tanks were coming. The tanks were held up. The tanks had been caught by the blizzard. The tanks were lost. The tanks would take another hour and a half to arrive. Meanwhile dawn was coming, and daylight would reveal 6,000 Australian soldiers lying in the open, under the muzzles of the German machine-guns.

Finally, and only just in time, the attack was called off. The infantry pulled back, mercifully without loss, but tempers were somewhat frayed; worse, the 62nd Division, tasked with the supporting attack, were not informed of the situation and sent their men forward. Elements of this division actually got into the Hindenburg Line position before realising they were on their own, and were savagely mauled by the machine-guns of Bullecourt before they could withdraw.

The commanders met again that morning and decided to repeat the attack next day, in the same manner, but with a *guarantee* of tank support. The fact that the Third Army attack was no longer going so well had by now trickled through, but an attack on 11 April would be useful to support Third Army's bid for Monchy-le-Preux, Gough told Birdwood that the Anzac attack, which had been essential the day before to support the *success* of Third Army, was essential today to prevent a Third Army *failure*. Thus the reason for the attack had entirely changed, but Gough insisted that it should still go ahead, despite Birdwood pointing out that the Germans had now been alerted all along the Hindenburg Line. That night the Australian infantry went out yet again, to lie in the snow waiting for the tanks.

No tanks arrived. There is some dispute on this point, but the Australian and German accounts agree that while tanks were heard and fired upon and were certainly blundering about somewhere, they played little or no part in the actual fighting. However, reports somehow got back to I Anzac and Fifth Army HQs that tanks had in fact entered Riencourt and Hendecourt, the two villages behind Bullecourt *and inside the Hindenburg Line*. Unlikely as these accounts (which can be found in the Tank Corps records, which include the war diary of that corps' D Battalion, those of Fifth Army of the Commander-in-Chief) seem now – and should have seemed then – they were believed.

As near as can be discovered, the actual situation was as follows: of the twelve tanks committed, eleven actually set out. The four committed on the right had only managed to reach their start line in front of the Australian infantry by 0430 hours. One of these, instead of heading for the German wire, trundled off into the night, was fired on, developed clutch trouble and went back. The next tank went off to the right, crossed the German trench but at a point 500 yards away from the sector being attacked by the Australians and was put out of action by armour-piercing bullets. The third tank followed the first, was fired upon and went to the rear with engine trouble. Three tanks attacking in the centre of the line were also stopped by enemy fire, one hit in the tracks, one in the petrol tank and one in the driver's compartment. The four on the left were all late and two were hit by shells on the way up. A third did fire effectively on a German machine-gun at Bullecourt and even entered the village; it too then broke down. Only two of the twelve tanks survived the action.

The plan for this assault on Bullecourt depended *entirely* on the tanks. It was a Tank Corps idea, proposed by a Tank Corps officer who twice failed to deliver on his promises, his plan seized on by Gough as a way to play a part in the Arras battle. But while the tanks made no gaps for the infantry on this second night, this time the Australians did not pull back. The 4th Australian Division's 4 Brigade went forward and, with 12 Brigade, fought its way through the wire, which turned out to have been better cut than expected, and got into the German trenches. By 0650 hours both brigades had taken a portion of the Hindenburg Line and sent back messages that they could hang on there, if supported.

It was now daylight, and getting troops forward over open ground was impossible. Artillery support was needed as an alternative, in the form of a screening barrage 200 yards beyond the Hindenburg Line to stop German reinforcements coming up and counter-attacking the Australians in the enemy trenches. The artillery commander refused to supply this, however, for the report that tanks were behind the Hindenburg Line now took its dire effect, with the result that he was convinced that if he put down fire as requested he would be firing on his own troops. Brigadier-General Briand of

4 Australian Brigade had a heated telephone conversation with the artillery commander, and the argument went as far as Birdwood, but no bombardment went down. Gough, meanwhile, convinced that the attack had pierced the Hindenburg Line, was ordering up British and Indian cavalry to pour through the breach. At 0935 hours, still persuaded that the attack was going well, Gough ordered the 4th Cavalry Division to move forward, an advance which was soon brought to a halt by a storm of machine-gun fire. The Australian infantry of 4 and 12 Brigades, hanging on grimly in the German line, were on their own.

At 1030 hours Birdwood appealed to the 62nd Division to attack on the left of the 4th Australian Division, to take some of the pressure off his men. This request, however, was based on the assumption, then current at Anzac HQ, that Bullecourt was in Australian hands, something which the commanders in 62nd Division knew was not true. 'They declined,' in the words of the Australian Official History, 'to send their unprotected troops, without tanks, in broad daylight, against half-cut wire, defended by a well-warned enemy, in order to attempt a task which the 4th Australian Division had barely achieved by surprise in the breaking dawn. It would have been madness . . . and the plight of the Australian Division would not have been aided by the useless sacrifice of British soldiers.'

There the Australians stayed, embedded in the German defences, beating off German counter-attacks, until midday, when they withdrew, the troops walking slowly back across no man's land, bringing their wounded and their weapons. Some four thousand men of the 4th Australian Division went in at Bullecourt on 11 April 1917; 2,258 became casualties – killed, wounded, missing and made prisoner – in twelve hours, 12 Brigade alone lost 909. The Germans claim to have captured 27 officers and 1,137 men, for the loss of just 750 of their own soldiers.

First Bullecourt was a terrible battle, a total shambles, a classic of all that a Great War battle is commonly supposed to be – and mercifully rarely was. The men did all and more than could be expected of them, while staff and commanders stumbled about blindly, refusing to accept the true situation, preferring to believe good news, however unlikely, unwilling to listen to a front-line commander begging for help in a desperate situation. The tank commanders, that stubborn artillery commander and General Gough should all have been sacked, if only, like General Byng's lamented ancestor, 'pour encourager les autres', and even Birdwood deserves censure.

There was a twelve-day pause before the Second Battle of the Scarpe, which lasted just two days, 23–24 April. This battle began after a curious incident, when three of Allenby's divisional commanders sent in a 're-solution' protesting, discreetly but firmly, against any further attacks which left the troops exposed to concentrated enfilade fire from the flanks. Instead, they proposed the fortification of Monchy-le-Preux, followed later by a renewed offensive astride the Scarpe. Given Allenby's notorious temper it is surprising that these generals kept their jobs, but he accepted their 'proposals', as he chose to view them, and no more was said.

Besides, any further moves east of Arras would now be decided by Field Marshal Haig who, on 15 April, told Allenby to halt his offensive and wait while preparations were made for a combined attack on a bigger scale, all along the front. On the following day – 16 April, the day General Nivelle opened his offensive on the Aisne – Haig called the commanders of First, Third and Fifth Armies to a conference at St Pol to discuss plans for the renewal of the offensive. The result was a three-part plan, with each army making a push on its section of the front: First Army were to push east, south of Vimy, and capture Oppy; Third Army were to push on astride the Scarpe and down the Arras–Cambrai road; Fifth Army were to renew their attack at Bullecourt and capture Riencourt and Hendecourt, the two fortress villages behind the Hindenburg Line. All these attacks were to be launched to on 23 April.

For various reasons, the Second Battle of the Scarpe was, like the First, mainly a Third Army operation. It was another setpiece attack, albeit on a more limited scale, though parts of it offered very hard fighting indeed. The German artillery was now stronger and their infantry defenders fresher than the attacking British. Some successes were achieved, however. On the right VII Corps advanced another mile and took 1,600 prisoners, but met with stiff resistance at Guémappe and were counter-attacked east of Monchy. The fighting degenerated into a 'soldiers' battle', a series of small engagements fought at platoon and company level by men using Lewis guns, rifles and grenades.

North of the Scarpe XVII and XIII Corps battered their way east, fighting in the streets of shattered villages and taking heavy casualties. The battle was taking on a form, a distinctive shape, becoming a grim business of attack and counter-attack, constantly repeated, the sort of dogged fighting that seemed to suit 'Bull' Allenby's nature. Progress was being made, although slowly and at great cost, but Allenby and Haig seemed convinced that the enemy was getting weaker and that if only the pressure could be kept up, the fighting would become easier. Here again one sees that great flaw in Haig's command, an unwillingness to accept that an attack had achieved all that it was going to achieve and should be called off.

Allenby would obey any order to attack and, like his chief, saw no reason to halt the offensive until some definite advantage had been achieved. Not unnaturally, the front-line troops, growing ever more tired, did not share this view. They were, moreover, finding the German defences a constant problem, for the old Western Front system of a thick front line and an open rear had gone. The German defence was now in depth, and the British infantry's attacks into it simply left them surrounded by unquelled opposition.

The Germans still had thick front-line defences, thicker than ever in parts, but they had built strongpoints and bunkers well behind the front line, fortified the ruined villages and registered their rear-line positions for artillery concentrations. As the British advanced into these positions, the resistance did not decrease – indeed, it may actually have increased – while their ability to bring up the artillery and adequate supplies of ammunition over heavily cratered ground gradually declined. The Germans were also growing stronger in manpower and soon had nine divisions in the line, against nine British divisions taking part in the attacks at Oppy and La Coulotte. By the end of April, the happy results of 9 April had been forgotten. The Battle of Arras was becoming a pounding match; casualties, killed, wounded and missing, for the First and Third Armies had now topped 100,000 men and although the British armies had gained ground, captured a number of guns and a quantity of German soldiers, there was no sign of a breakthrough. So April ended, with the fighting still going on and the generals preparing for the next phase, the Third Battle of the Scarpe, which would begin on 3 May.

Meanwhile, General Nivelle's offensive on the Chemin des Dames had proved a total disaster. The French attack had been thrown back and terrible losses had been sustained. In the first week of the offensive French losses reached 96,000 men, of whom 15,539 had been killed. In spite of his promise that if the attack did not succeed in forty-eight hours he would call it off, Nivelle continued to batter away at the German defences, but even under constant artillery pounding and repeated infantry attacks, the enemy's resistance did not collapse.

What collapsed, after years of fruitless assaults and nearly 2 million casualties, was the morale of the French Army. By May 1917, many regiments of the French Army were refusing duty, the troops sitting down and bleating like sheep when ordered up to the line. Those who did go up said they would hold their positions, but adamantly refused to take part in any more of these pointless attacks. By some miracle, news of these French Army mutinies, which began on 29 April, did not reach the Germans, but it reached the British and caused considerable disquiet among the commanders.

The tragedy on the Chemin des Dames brought one relief to Field Marshal Haig. It led to the sacking of General Nivelle and for a while at least no more was heard of putting the British Armies under French control General (Henri) Philippe Pétain, who had inspired the defence of Verdun before being promoted and replaced by Nivelle, and who now became Commander-in-Chief of the French Armies, was a different kind of soldier. He saw it as his first task to restore the morale and fighting spirit of his men, which he did this by calling off all attacks, improving the rations, and granting more leave.

It also proved necessary, however, to shoot some soldiers, for besides the passive refusals to attack there had been numerous instances of desertion and other military crimes; 412 sentences of death for mutiny and desertion were pronounced in the French Army in the summer months of 1917, and 59 men were actually shot by firing squads, plus who knows how many more who were summarily executed by their officers or NCOs. Yet Pétain saw that bringing the French Army back to where it had been would take time and rest, rather than the executions of brave men who had been tried too far. During that time, he wanted Haig to keep on punishing the Germans. The Field Marshal elected to do that by winding up the Arras battles as soon as his armies could reach a good defensive line, and then turning his attention to his favourite ground in Flanders.

This Battle of Arras was therefore brought to a close, ending officially on 24 May. The Australians had attacked again at Bullecourt on 3 May, in a carefully planned attack quite unlike the first hurriedly prepared and ill-considered affair. This time the attackers breached the Hindenburg Line with artillery support and, having refused any help from tanks, beat off German counter-attacks and held their position. Second Bullecourt lasted for two weeks, until 17 May, and was a much larger affair than the first battle. Nor, again, was it an exclusively Australian affair, for it also once more involved the 62nd Division of V Corps, their combined attack on the Hindenburg Line aiming for a breach of some 4,000 yards. The battle was fought in a small area, and when it ended one observer stated that he had never seen ground so thickly packed with dead. The Australians took Riencourt and the British Hendecourt, I Anzac losing 7,482 men killed, wounded and missing, and V Corps 6,821.

When the Battle of Arras ended the British Army stood a few miles further east than it had done on Easter Sunday, but very little else had been gained. The battle had been fought to aid Nivelle's offensive and that offensive had failed with great losses among the men and severe damage to their morale. Vimy Ridge had been taken and the German Army had been battered, but it is hard to see what overall benefit had accrued from the expenditure of so many lives and so much effort.

Haig had done his best to support Nivelle, for whatever his private reservations, he had acted as a loyal subordinate. Not so General Nivelle, however, who on 7 March 1917 sent a message to Lloyd George asking for Haig's dismissal. This request might have succeeded were it not for the fact that doubts were beginning to creep in about Nivelle himself. even before he launched his attack. This should have gone in on 1 April, but was then postponed to 13 April, and finally to the 16th. Meanwhile the British were fighting on their own. Haig's actions, however, throughout the period of Nivelle's command go a long way to disproving the allegations that he was an unco-operative, mulish commander.

Byng had done well, and his reward was command of the Third Army. Gough, on whom doubts must begin to gather, probably retained his command through his friendship with Haig, for his performance at Bullecourt was far from impressive, and this had come on top of his actions on the Somme. Gough's hour had not yet come, but he was still in command of an army and a further test was in the offing.

As for General Allenby, on 3 June, five days after the end of the Arras battles, he was summoned to London and told that he was to take over the command in Palestine, and would from now on fight against the Turks. His successor at Third Army was to be Sir Julian Byng, who would have to leave his beloved Canadian Corps. Allenby was depressed by this news, fearing that his removal from France was a reflection on his handling of Third Army – as perhaps it was. Certainly few people in that army shed any tears at the news of his departure, and Haig made no effort to retain his services. In Allenby's case, however, it all turned out for the best. He did well in Palestine, capturing Jerusalem and Damascus, and comprehensively defeating the Turks, and thereby made his name as a great soldier – a reputation he would not have gained if the Arras battles of 1917 were all there was to judge him by.

No 'Great Captain' had yet appeared on the Western Front, but of the generals involved at Arras, only Gough could be regarded as a failure. Now Arras had ended and half the year had gone. This battle had cost the three armies involved 158,660 men, of whom 29,505 had been killed. The closing down of the Nivelle offensive on the Aisne on 20 May enabled the French to take over the southern part of the front, freeing British divisions for the next major operation. Field Marshal Haig could now turn his attention to what had been his first choice for the 1917 campaign, the muddy fields of Flanders in the Ypres Salient. His initial orders for the reserves to concentrate in the Salient were issued on the day the Nivelle offensive ended. Moving the troops and supplies north would, however, take weeks of precious time.

CHAPTER 17

MESSINES, JUNE 1917

*'The enemy will not lightly give up the advantage he has held
so long, and his strategic line of advance via Ypres on
Calais.'*

Preliminary to the plans submitted for the attack on Messines by
General Sir Herbert Plumer, GOC Second Army, 12 December 1916

With the end of Nivelle's offensive and the closing down of the Arras
battle, Field Marshal Sir Douglas Haig was free to turn his mind to
the proposed attack along the Belgian coast from the Ypres Salient. This
plan had the support of the Admiralty, who wanted the German Navy
evicted from their submarine bases on the Belgian coast; furthermore it
might also achieve that long-expected breakthrough on the Western Front
and permit the cavalry to range again over the battlefields of North-West
Europe. To make that decisive thrust Haig must first take the Messines-
Wytschaete Ridge, which overlooked the Salient. To achieve that he had at
his disposal the Second Army and its doughty commander, General Sir
Herbert Plumer, an officer with long experience of the Ypres Salient.

General Plumer is one of the few commanders who came out of the Great
war with an enhanced reputation. Even before the war he was known as a
highly competent, popular general, a likable man and a 'soldier's soldier'.
He had come out to France in 1915 to command V Corps in Smith-Dorrien's
Second Army, and once he was established, Field Marshal Sir John French
wasted little time in getting rid of Smith-Dorrien. The way he went about it
met with quiet disapproval from Plumer, who liked Smith-Dorrien and
worked well with him. Plumer voiced his disquiet in a letter to his wife in
April 1915:

> Things have not been made any better by Sir John slighting Sir
> Horace and taking practically all my force [i.e. his corps] away from
> him and leaving me independent of him. It is the last thing I wanted.
> It is not fair because Smith-Dorrien and I were in absolute agree-
> ment as to what should be done and I am only doing now exactly

what I should have been doing if I had remained under Smith-Dorrien.

What Plumer, who succeeded Smith-Dorrien in command of the Second Army, was doing in April 1915 was moving everything possible – men, guns and stores – out of the Ypres Salient and taking up a new defensive position well west of the line of low hills that half-ringed the town of Ypres to the east. Two years and many thousands of casualties later, Plumer and his men were still holding that curtailed position in the Ypres Salient, but anxious for any orders that could take them out of it.

Herbert Charles Onslow Plumer was sixty years old when he led his army at Messines. He came from Yorkshire stock, though he had been born in London, and after attending Eton and Sandhurst, was commissioned into the 65th Foot (later, the 1st Battalion The York and Lancaster Regiment) in 1876. Three years later, aged twenty-two, he was the Adjutant of his battalion. He fought against the dervishes at El Teb in the Eastern Sudan in 1884, and on his return to England took the Staff Course from 1885–87. Plumer was a good soldier, but not a dedicated one. He had wide outside interests and on several occasions thought of leaving the service for some more lucrative appointment in the City, not least because he had a wife and four children to support. He was widely seen as a coming man, however, and whenever he thought of resigning some senior officer always talked him out of it.

In 1896 he served in the Matabele War in Southern Africa, and stayed on in local commands in what became Rhodesia (now Zimbabwe) for some years. During that time he became extremely popular with the Rhodesian settlers, who presented him with a gold-mounted sword in recognition of his services to the colony. During the South African War he commanded Rhodesian, New Zealand, Canadian and South African troops, earning their liking as well as their respect. This may seem surprising, for on first sight Plumer appeared the archetype of the pompous British officer of the Victorian and Edwardian eras, for he looked uncannily like David Low's cartoon character 'Colonel Blimp'. (Another myth is that Low had Plumer in mind when he drew that caricature, but the cartoonist himself has said that he got the idea from hearing a group of former military men discussing the issues of the day in a Turkish bath at some time in the 1930s.) Plumer was a shy, slightly built, if somewhat stout, man, with a rather bemused expression and delicate features concealed behind a magnificent walrus moustache. That amiable air hid a steel core, however, for while not unsympathetic, he was a strict disciplinarian, only his sense of humour preventing him from becoming a martinet.

Plumer also believed in trusting his men and in leading from the front. During the South African War, when some Australian troops refused to join a relief column on the grounds that they were soon due to go home, he had them paraded and told them bluntly: 'There will be no discussion on this matter. I am leading the relief column and you are going with me. Parade dismissed.' Straight talking always went down well with Empire troops, and the Australians duly followed him out of camp.

Plumer was a lieutenant-colonel at the start of the South African War and became a local brigadier-general during it. When it ended in 1902 he was made a Companion of the Order of the Bath (CB) and promoted major-general. In 1904 he was appointed Quartermaster-General and one of the Military Members on the Army Council, appointments that met with general approval. 'Plumer is one of the half-dozen generals the whole Army unites in praising,' said the *Spectator,* but in the following year he fell out with Haldane, the new Secretary of State for War. As a result, Plumer was dismissed from the Army Council and placed on half-pay, though he did receive a knighthood in 1906.

The cause of this dispute remains obscure, but may have been a mis-understanding on Haldane's part, the latter coming to believe that Plumer, as QMG, did not agree with a recent change in government policy. The Conservative Government had intended to introduce a very brief 'short-service' enlistment of just fifteen months in an attempt to create more reserves for the Army. Plumer was in favour of this move, but when Haldane came into office with the new Liberal administration in 1905 the scheme was dropped. As a serving officer, Plumer would have implemented any sensible policy but Haldane wanted all-out approval for amending the short-service scheme. When Plumer declined to supply this, he had to go. He was not on half-pay for long, however. Four months later, in April 1906, he was appointed GOC, 5th Infantry Division, one of the new divisions being formed for the projected BEF. He was promoted lieutenant-general in 1908, but then spent two years more on half-pay until, in July 1911, he was offered the post of GOC, Northern Command, based in York. As it happened, he had just been offered a civilian job, and this time it was his wife who talked him out of resignation. Plumer was still in charge of the Northern Command when war broke out in August 1914.

Plumer did not write his memoirs or keep a diary, and the first biography of him, published in 1935, three years after his death, is largely based on letters to his wife. It was written by his former Chief of Staff at Second Army, the highly effective General Sir Charles ('Tim') Harington, and is so adulatory as to be almost sycophantic, though the task of writing it must have been difficult, for Plumer destroyed all his private papers before his death. Nevertheless, it is clear that Plumer was both efficient and popular, a good soldier who knew his job and took care of his men, who referred to him as 'Daddy' or, sometimes, 'Old Plum-and-Apple' (plum-and-apple jam, packed in 7-pound tins, was a staple of the troops' rations; they longed for strawberry, or any other flavour than the one they got). His watchwords were 'Trust, Training, and Thoroughness', and from the moment of his appointment to V Corps in 1915 he spared no efforts in preparing his men for the fight. It is also said that, at the moment of Zero, when he could do no more for his men, Plumer would sink to his knees in the privacy of his bedroom and pray for the lives of his soldiers.

Most of Plumer's Western Front experience had been in the Salient, and by the time he was ordered to attack at Messines the Second Army had already made most of the necessary preparations. The order finally came on 7 May 1917, when Haig asked Plumer how soon he would be in a position to attack the Messines-Wytschaete Ridge?

'Today in a month, sir,' answered Plumer, and he was as good as his word.

The attack on Messines was the essential preliminary to that series of terrible battles around the Salient that carries the general name of 'Third Ypres', or to the public, 'Passchendaele'. Since Third Ypres has remained etched in the public memory as the most ghastly of all the Great War battles, it would be as well to consider the steps that led up to it and why it was fought. The Allied armies, French and British, had been driven back from the ridges around the city in the battles of Second Ypres in 1915 and forced into a tighter salient which lay below the higher, drier ground, to the east and south. The British had taken over all the much-reduced Salient in the summer of that year, and had hung on there, though at great cost, ever since.

Since German possession of those eastern ridges and the observation they afforded over Ypres made the Salient all but untenable, Haig had a long-cherished plan to take the high ground back. This plan was thwarted in 1915 and 1916 by the need to co-operate with the French at Loos and on the Somme. In 1917, due to the Arras commitment – again to conform with the French – it was the middle of the year before preparations for what came to be known as the Battle of Passchendaele – or, more correctly, the Third Battle of Ypres – could really begin.

The plans for this battle had been maturing for over a year, but they had crystallised in November 1916 when Plumer was asked to submit proposals for an offensive in Flanders, and then to push the preparations forward so that the plans could be implemented in the following spring. These proposals were based on Plumer's previous submissions, and are in line with the plan eventually adopted by Haig: there would be a preliminary attack on the Messines-Wytschaete Ridge, in order to deprive the enemy of his chief observation point over the Salient, and then a phased attack, pushing steadily eastwards or north-eastwards, moving by stages over the encircling ridges, would drive through to reach the open country beyond. This was a sound enough plan, although it depended on the speed with which the guns could be brought up and registered, but the 'phases' it proposed smacked too much of the Somme to Haig, and he therefore asked Plumer to produce another, one that proposed greater speed, and fewer phases.

Haig had now grasped the fundamental problem of any Great War attack – a lack of *momentum*. He had the guns, ammunition and men to force a breach, but the means were just not available to exploit that breach rapidly, before the enemy brought up reserves and sealed it off. This belief – that the means were lacking – though substantially correct in 1917, was not entirely so. Though in embryonic, often unreliable, form, the capacity to 'exploit' a breach was there, in the tank and the aeroplane, but it would take another war before the 'blitzkrieg' – 'lightning war' – tactic could be successfully employed by better, faster and more reliable machines. Haig and his generals, however, had to rely on cavalry and exhortation: 'Rapid action, with a breakthrough of the enemy's defences on a wide front, and the infliction of a decisive defeat on the enemy was to replace the tactics of attrition' – or so said the CIGS, General Robertson, in a letter to Plumer of 6 January.

On 30 January 1917 Plumer duly submitted a revised plan for an attack by two armies, the 'Southern' (presumably his own Second) army, which would attack at Messines, seize the ridge and secure the southern flank, and another force, not yet designated other than as the 'Northern' army, which would make the main thrust north out of the Salient, then across the Pilckem Ridge and over the main ridges to open country. The British front line in the Salient is best imagined as a reversed letter S with the centre just east of Ypres astride the Gheluvelt plateau. Plumer's plan aimed to straighten out these S-bends as the first step out of the Salient, and this called for a simultaneous advance by both armies of not more than 2,000 yards, though on a 6-mile front. If all went well, this was to be followed by an attack north along the coast from Nieuport by French and Belgian forces and supported by an amphibious landing on the Belgian coast by British troops under General Sir Henry Rawlinson. It was, by any standards a sophisticated proposal, but there was a snag.

Between the 'Southern' and 'Northern' armies was a gap of over a mile, from Mount Sorrel and Bellewaarde Lake, and spanning the high ground of the Gheluvelt Plateau. Plumer suggested that this gap should be closed by the inner flank divisions of the 'Southern' and 'Northern' armies converging on each other as they advanced. Once they had met, the ground thus taken in the centre would become the responsibility of the 'Southern' army, which would take over the southern half of the Salient as far north as Broodseinde, east of Ypres, while the 'Northern' army pushed out north-eastwards to Roulers and Thourout and then turned up the coast to take Ostend and Zeebrugge. (See the map on page 380.)

Haig originally had Rawlinson in mind as commander for this 'Northern' battle, and intended to pull the Fourth Army out of the Somme and send it to the far left wing of the BEF. The latter was therefore asked to examine Plumer's plan and make comments. After a visit to Ypres, Rawlinson expressed approval of the plan and only made some small tactical suggestions, including his opinion that, given the massive mining programme Plumer had organised beneath the Messines-Wytschaete Ridge, he thought that the position could be carried in one day, not the three proposed. This view met with Haig's warm approval, for it would speed things up considerably.

Rawlinson agreed with Plumer, however, that the 'Northern' thrust up the coast was entirely dependent on the success of the central thrust across the Gheluvelt Plateau, and suggested that the three attacks – on Messines, Gheluvelt and then Pilckem, should be staggered, the 'Southern', Messines operation being followed after a gap of *two days or more* by the central and 'Northern' attacks. It was further suggested by a study group from GHQ that this central thrust at Gheluvelt could be made by a force of tanks. What was proposed still seemed too slow to Field Marshal Haig, who had by now also become concerned by what he felt were negative attitudes of both Plumer and Rawlinson towards his proposed offensive.

All three generals, Haig, Plumer and Rawlinson, knew the Salient well. All three had commanded corps in the battles of First or Second Ypres, or both. All three had spent at least one winter in the Salient, and had seen what the ground could turn to after prolonged rain and heavy bombardment. They knew that the water table was high, they knew that the drainage systems were vulnerable; but they also knew that the troops in the Salient had survived two winters already, including the terrible winter of 1916–17, and that the ground had endured at least two full-scale battles, as well as daily shelling, without the terrain becoming impossible for an attack. In other words, they thought, from their own extensive experience, that an attack in the Salient, even late in the year, was perfectly feasible.

It has frequently been suggested that the condition of the terrain in the Salient during the various battles of Passchendaele stunned the senior generals involved, even came as a total surprise to them, but, with the exception of Gough, they were all used to the Salient conditions. After two winters and two terrible battles, it seems highly unlikely that the physical or climatic conditions in the Salient during the Passchendaele offensive came as a great surprise to anyone; it was, after all, the *Third* Battle of Ypres. The rains that fell in October were indeed unusually heavy and constant, and were to have a disastrous effect on the offensive, but they did not come as a surprise. It follows, therefore, that those who seek reasons for what happened at Passchendaele must look elsewhere. In the late spring of 1917, the basic argument between Plumer and Rawlinson on the one hand, and Field Marshal Haig on the other, was the old, now familiar one: would this forthcoming offensive aim for a 'breakthrough', or would it be a series of 'bite-and-hold' attacks?

Plumer and Rawlinson envisaged a series of co-ordinated infantry and artillery attacks of the bite-and-hold variety, which, though limited in scope, should at least provide some positive gains. As always, the Commander-in-Chief, Haig, had a *strategic* aim for his offensive. He was seeking a breakthrough, and this larger plan seemed to require an officer with a thrusting disposition. Haig cast about for a commander who shared this vision, and quickly decided to appoint General Sir Hubert Gough and his Fifth Army as the 'Northern' element of this offensive.

This was not a wise appointment. Gough had no experience of the Salient, no concept of what the fighting there would be like. The first error of what would come to be called the Battle of Passchendaele came with the appointment of General Gough.

Hubert Gough had been out in France since August 1914, when he had commanded 3 Cavalry Brigade in the retreat from Mons. As we have seen, before the war he had been closely involved in the 'Curragh Incident' in the spring of 1914, as a result of which he had made a number of enemies in the higher ranks of the Army and among the politicians. On the other hand, he had been well liked by French and was a good friend of Haig, who had promoted him over the heads of more senior corps commanders to command the Fifth Army on the Somme. Haig remained his supporter and friend, even as it gradually became apparent to everyone else that Gough was not up to the job.

Haig was also to stand up for Gough in April 1918, when Lloyd George and the Cabinet were after the Fifth Army commander's head. This friendship is an interesting one for the two men were not very alike; Gough was the typical cavalryman of popular imagination, who would hurl himself, his horse – or his men – at any obstacle, where Haig was much more dour, a pounder rather than a thruster. Perhaps Haig saw in Gough some facet that was missing in his own personality and which he therefore admired. Apart from the fact that he clearly liked Gough personally – and for Douglas Haig, a friend once made was not lightly discarded – he respected him as a soldier. This was an opinion not widely shared by the rest of the army on the Western Front, or by those generals who had served under Gough. Haig was well aware that some of his corps commanders were less than impressed with Gough's abilities; nevertheless, Gough was the man he wanted for the Ypres offensive.

Motives are rarely obvious, but the probable reason for Gough's appointment to command of the 'Northern' battle' at Third Ypres was that Haig believed that his friend and fellow cavalryman saw the need to force a rapid breakthrough and let the cavalry loose in the country beyond. This view, so often disparaged today, did not seem so foolish in 1917; during the Great War and for two decades after it, cavalry was still *the* mobile military arm, the only force that could travel at will and at speed across open country. In 1917 the tanks were too slow and unreliable, the motor transport still road-bound. If, a very big 'if', certainly, but *if* a breakthrough could be achieved, then only cavalry could exploit the breach. It was imperative that such rapid exploitation should follow if mobile warfare was to be restored to the battlefield and final victory achieved.

The reasons why this vision never really materialised – trenches, barbed wire, artillery, machine-guns – have been explained often enough, but to Haig and Gough that was not cause enough for not trying again. In other battles on this Western Front, the *failure* to push on had resulted in heavy casualties for insignificant gains. What Haig wanted for Third Ypres was a general who *would* push on, whatever the odds or the difficulties, and keep on pushing until something gave. This Gough would certainly do, even if what eventually gave was his army. He had pushed his troops on the Somme to such effect that his losses had been considerable, morale in divisions posted to his command had plummeted, and the Canadian Corps had privately resolved not to serve under him again; the Australians, post-Bullecourt, were also less than keen to do so. Haig, however, though not unaware of all this, still saw Gough as the right man for the job. Hubert Gough was his friend, an attacking general who would fight this battle as Haig wanted it fought, and for the moment that was good enough.

As at Arras, Haig was anticipating a cavalry advance after the breakthrough. In the context of the time, this was sensible, strategic thinking, the sort of thinking a commander-in-chief is paid to do, for a battle is not undertaken in isolation, but is the culmination of what has gone before and the stepping stone to what comes after. When planning an attack, therefore, the first thing a general has to decide is the ultimate objective of his battle; once that has been settled he can work back to establish his plans for everything that will precede the achievement of that objective, as well as contingency plans for all sorts of eventualities. To take a more recent example, when the Allies landed in Normandy on D-Day, 6 June 1944, they selected those beaches not only because they were suitable for getting their armies ashore, but because from Normandy they could break out of the bridgehead, take Paris and Brussels, and hustle the enemy back to the Rhine. When preparing the 'Overlord' plan for submission to the Supreme Allied Commander, General Eisenhower, General Montgomery therefore decided on the *final* objective of the plan – to invade and conquer Nazi Germany – and worked back from there, a process which led him and his planning staff to the beaches in the bay of the Seine; getting ashore on 6 June was only the first phase. It is hard for the fighting soldier to think further ahead than the day of battle, but a commanding general has to ask himself constantly, 'What next?' and 'Where do we go from here?'

So it was in the Ypres Salient in the early summer of 1917. The object was a breakout, to clear the Belgian coast of the enemy, neutralise his U-boat bases there, and begin the process of hustling him back to the Rhine. Haig saw no problem in breaking the enemy line. That had often been done before, though with great loss, but the casualties would have been bearable – or at least less painful – if there had been some success to justify them. The problem, as Haig saw it, lay not in breaking the enemy line, but in what happened if his troops yet again became stuck in the enemy defences, unable to push ahead and taking heavy casualties in return for a few metres of ground. Perhaps the answer *was* to use cavalry generals, officers who understood the exploitation business and who would not be so preoccupied with seizing sections of the enemy line, as infantry generals like Rawlinson and Plumer currently seemed to be. So Allenby commanded at Arras, though with no particular success, and so Gough was appointed to take the Fifth Army to the Salient, breach the enemy line, and break out into the open country beyond.

Gough took up this new challenge on 13 May, some days after another Franco-British military conference in Paris. This meeting, on 4 May, was attended by General Nivelle, in his last public appearance as Commander-in-Chief of the French Armies, by General Philippe Pétain, newly appointed Chief of the French Armies and, for the British, by Field Marshal Sir Douglas Haig and the CIGS, General Sir William Robertson. All agreed that the Western Front offensive must be kept up, that only the British had the men to do it, but that the French would support them by taking back a part of the front line and making 'vigorous [local] attacks'. The conference reported to an inter-Allied meeting on the following day, a gathering attended by the national political leaders. In the course of their deliberations, Lloyd George agreed that the attacks must continue, stating that 'We must go on hitting and hitting with all our strength,' but adding: 'It would be no good us doing so unless the French did the same, as otherwise the Germans will simply bring all their guns, ammunition and their best men against us, and then later against the French.' The Prime Minister's enthusiasm for this sort of pounding would not last, but it should be remembered in view of what followed.

Lloyd George confirmed the agreement struck by the generals at the military conference on the previous day, and the French Prime Minister, Briand, promised that French forces would continue attacking, provided their reserves were not squandered. As a result, Lloyd George agreed to Haig's Flanders offensive, 'provided the French played their part along their section of the line'. Nearly two weeks later, however, on 16 May, Robertson received the printed version of the conference minutes, and discovered that the French agreement to support the British attack had been either deleted or omitted. The War Cabinet then telegraphed Haig and told him that they would only agree to support the British offensive plan if the French kept their promise of 4 May, and that he was to be 'very firm' with Pétain and Foch on this point.

In mid-May Haig met Pétain again and sought clarification on the situation regarding French support. By way of reply, Pétain provided full details of the unrest within the French Army, in which mutinies had now been going on for some weeks (in the end, a total of more than 23,000 French soldiers were sentenced for various crimes, though punishments were mostly light), but offered six divisions to support the coastal advance from Nieuport. These, with the Belgian divisions, would provide a total of twelve divisions for the coastal operation, a force that was to be commanded by King Albert I of the Belgians. More than this the French were unable to do, nor could they keep their promise either to attack with their Third Army at St Quentin, or to take over more than a three-division sector of the British line. The twelve-division force under King Albert also failed to materialise, though Pétain sent the French First Army to the line north of Ypres, where it was placed at Haig's disposal. Thus it was that during late May and early June 1917, Haig, with Cabinet approval, continued with his preparations for the main attack out of the Salient, while Plumer organised his army for the attack on the Messines Ridge.

Among the reasons which impelled the Messines-Passchendaele attack were the need to distract the German armies from the weakness and disarray of the French Army caused by the mutinies – which went on from April to September – and to placate the British Admiralty and the War Cabinet, who wanted the Belgian coast cleared and the ports of Zeebrugge and Ostend captured that summer, in order to reduce the attacks by German U-boats on British and Allied shipping.

Subsequent information has revealed that the U-boats based in these ports were only a small proportion of the total number operating around the British Isles, and therefore that a more effective way of neutralising their activities was to introduce the convoy system, a proposal which those admirals pressing for an attack in Flanders were stoutly resisting. It has been alleged that Haig used the admirals' demand as an excuse for launching his Passchendaele offensive, but this seems unlikely. Other people besides the Field Marshal pressed for the coast to be cleared; indeed, a Cabinet minute of 26 October 1916, quoted in the Official History, notes that 'There is no measure to which the War Cabinet attaches greater importance than the expulsion of the enemy from the Belgian coast.'

There were good reasons for clearing the Belgian coast and they played their part in the making of Haig's plan, but they should not obscure the main reason for the Messines-Passchendaele offensive. Haig had maintained an intention to attack in Flanders since the end of Second Ypres, for he saw that a successful breakout there, at the northern end of the front, offered strategic possibilities not to be found elsewhere. The German forces in the south always had the option of withdrawing to the east and had room to do so, but here at the north end of the Western Front their options were fewer. Haig wanted a breakthrough to the Roulers-Thourout line, well east of the Salient, to get the cavalry moving, cut the German supply lines and force their forces along the coast either, to withdraw eastwards or to be cut off . . . and once they were moving, where might they stop?

The question now is whether his plan – to gain back the territory lost at Second Ypres and force a breakthrough from the Salient – ever stood any realistic chance of success. The delay resulting from Nivelle's offensive, the rainy weather which caused the notorious mud, these played their part in turning Passchendaele into a byword for horror in military history, but these factors would have played only supporting roles if Haig's main plan had been flawed. The basis of that plan was for a two-part attack by two armies. The first attack, by Plumer's Second Army, proved to be one of the great successes of the war.

*   *   *

General Plumer had been preparing for the Messines attack for more than a year. On taking over the Second Army in April 1915, he had decided that when the effort to retake Messines was finally made, it should be supported by the explosion of mines beneath the German lines. These were dug deep under the Messines–Wytschaete Ridge, in the blue clay that underpinned the mud-and-shale topsoil, and most of the charges – some twenty-four in all, totalling hundreds of tons of high-explosive – were in position by June 1916. All they needed were the detonators, but by then the focus of the 1916 Western Front campaign had already switched to the Somme. The mines therefore remained unused, maintained in working order by the miners, and their existence kept secret – they were referred to in orders, if at all, as 'deep wells' – and so they remained until the spring of the following year.

By June 1917, Plumer's Second Army had three corps ready for the Messines–Wytschaete attack. These were II Anzac, commanded by Lieutenant-General Sir Alexander Godley, consisting of the 25th British Division, the 3rd and 4th Australian Divisions and the New Zealand Division; IX Corps, with four British divisions; X Corps, with two New Army and two Territorial divisions; and XIV Corps in GHQ Reserve, with the Guards Division and three others. This force, with nine divisions in the front line, had to breach the Messines Ridge position on a front of nine miles, between St Yves and Mount Sorrel, take the fortified villages of Messines and Wytschaete, capture the enemy artillery positions behind the ridge, and consolidate on the far side on a position known as the 'Oosttaverne Line'. This was some 3,000 yards from the British line and represented an advance of roughly twice that originally proposed by Plumer. The assault would be in phases, beginning with an attack on the German front line, then moving up to the crest of the ridge, then on to the German artillery line, and finally to the Oosttaverne Line.

The attacking force was opposed by four German divisions with two more in reserve. Here, as elsewhere in the Salient, the Germans had started to thin out their front-line defences, adopting a system whereby the troops were deployed in depth behind the front-line wire and trenches, spread about in company-sized groups in strongpoints and dug-in defensive positions, or protected by small reinforced-concrete shelters. The latter, once blasted by gunfire, stood out clearly against the dark soil, and thus came to be known from their appearance as 'pillboxes'.

The German front-line defences were not thin and could not be easily penetrated by attacking troops. Those at Messines had been built up over two years and were up to 2,500 yards deep in places, with thick belts of wire and trenches, all studded with strongpoints and pillboxes offering wide, interlocking fields of enfilade fire across the surrounding ground. This system enabled the number of men deployed in the front-line trenches to be kept quite small, but since these pillbox defenders were equipped with plenty of machine-guns and trench mortars they could still produce a high volume of defensive fire. This, and the always formidable German artillery, would delay and reduce an attack, while strong forces – 'Eingriff' divisions (*Eingriff* in this case meaning intervention, disruption, counter-attack) – were kept in close support, to counter-attack and retake any lost ground. In the event, as at Arras and Vimy Ridge, these Eingriff divisions were kept too far back to intervene successfully after the first attack, but even so this defensive system was extremely formidable.

Plumer went to great lengths to ensure the success of this attack, sparing no detail if it saved lives. (One of his characteristics was the policy of 'waste metal, not flesh', a lesson learned well by an officer who served on his staff for a time, a certain B. L. Montgomery.) Since the explosion of mines would be the key to his attack, he even made tests to see how long it took debris to fall after a mine explosion, and, to counter defensive fire, to discover the various distances at which a man could be seen as daylight strengthened with the coming of dawn. He also arranged for massive artillery support. The attack would be preceded by nearly two weeks of bombardment from 2,266 guns, of which 756 were heavy and medium pieces, and the advance would be supported by 72 of the new Mark IV tanks. The bombardment began on 21 May, and concentrated on wire-cutting and counter-battery work. On the 31st the barrage intensified and swept steadily over the ground behind the ridge as far as the Oosttaverne Line, with a great deal of howitzer fire being directed at the villages and at the pillboxes.

Special infantry tactics had also been worked out to deal with the pillboxes, which were to be tackled by sections of men armed with Lewis guns and grenades, the former to provide covering fire while the 'bombers' worked their way forward and lobbed grenades through the loopholes or rear door – another version of fire-and-movement tactics. Zero hour for was set at 0310 hours on 7 June, and the attack would open with the explosion of the mines. Accounts vary as to the actual number of mines, but the commonly accepted version is that twenty-four were dug. Two were lost to German counter-mining and three, in the 'Birdcage' area near Ploegsteert Wood, were not blown – and two others, though detonated, failed to go off, and in time their positions became lost. The unfired mines near Ploegsteert were later dismantled, while one of those lost finally went off in 1955, fortunately without killing anybody . . . and the last one is still there, its exact location still unknown. These nineteen mines, spread along the ridge, contained a total of 957,000 pounds of high-explosive and created the largest man-made detonation using conventional explosives in history. For General Plumer not only intended to storm the Messines Ridge; his aim was to blow it to pieces, and promptly at Zero on 7 June 1917 these mines – or most of them – went up.

The sound and concussion of the explosion were heard and felt in London and, far more violent, for miles around Messines. The citizens of Lille, twelve miles from the blast, thought it was an earthquake, for buildings swayed and shattered glass filled the city streets. The top of the Messines-Wytschaete Ridge simply disappeared, blown to dust by this shattering blast, while the German defences and the men in them – some 10,000 in all – simply vanished, atomised by the blast. The explosions were followed by drenching fire from six brigades of field artillery and batteries of 6-inch and 60-pounder guns, all of which had been brought up and registered before the appointed day, but which did not open fire until Zero. These now laid a creeping barrage, creating a zone of fire over the enemy lines. Aided by this, and by the previous days of barrage, which had cut the enemy wire to pieces – 280 miles of it, according to Second Army reports – the infantry assault went well. The British, Australian and New Zealand troops were in the German front-line positions within minutes.

Plumer had stressed the need to press on, and the troops did as bidden, forging up the western slope behind the creeping barrage, over the shattered ground riven by deep mine craters, and on to the top of the ridge. By 0900 hours the whole ridge had been taken on the designated 9-mile front, and some 80,000 British and Dominion troops were firmly established inside the German lines. There was some resistance from the German garrisons of Wytschaete and at the White Château, south of the Ypres-Comines Canal, but these defenders were soon rooted out and the advance continued down the eastern slope of the ridge. Hill 60, of ominous memory, fell to the advancing troops and by the end of the morning only one portion of the German positions, Battle Wood on the Messines Ridge, north of the canal, was still offering resistance. A German counter-attack at 1430 hours was beaten off with loss by rifle and Lewis-gun fire and Plumer's men prepared to advance down the slope to the Oosttaverne Line. The advance had gone so quickly that the mines under the German position known as 'the Birdcage', near Ploegsteert Wood at the southern edge of the ridge, which were to have been detonated to support the New Zealand Division's attack, were not fired.

Once the troops had gained ground east of Wytschaete, a halt of five hours was ordered to let the guns move up and to give the troops fighting through the villages time to come into line for the final push down the far slope; during this interval, however, strong infantry and cavalry patrols, supported by tanks, were sent ahead to probe the enemy's positions. This time the Germans were given no chance to regroup; the pressure was kept up and the final advance began at 1510 hours, supported as before by a creeping barrage. The advance went well, though resistance was stiffening and casualties mounted in consequence, but forty-eight German guns were taken and the Oosttaverne Line below the eastern slope was captured by nightfall. By now, however, the German artillery was at work, pounding the troops on the ridge, and their guns, plus some short-firing by the British artillery, caused a large number of casualties among the British and Dominion soldiers.

A strong counter-attack on 8 June by three German divisions, the 7th, 24th and 1st Guard Reserve Divisions, was beaten off by the machine-guns and infantry, the latter now dug in on Messines Ridge, supported by artillery, and Second Army continued to push forward throughout the next week. On the 14th they established a new line on the Lys, running from Warneton in the south to Battle Wood, north of the Ypres-Comines Canal. Plumer had seized all his objectives; his army was now in position, ready to support the advance of Fifth Army out of the Salient.

General Plumer had pulled off one of the great victories of the war, an engagement that ranks with the attack at Vimy and some of the actions of 1918. It is right that most of the credit should go to Plumer, for he planned the attack, prepared every element in the assault, and saw to it that his men had all the support possible, deployed in a sensible fashion. Yet it is one of the sadder aspects of the Great War that the British successes are less well known, and arouse less interest, than their defeats and disasters, perhaps because there is less to say about them, and because much of the element of tragedy is missing.

Messines was a textbook operation, one of the few instances of a setpiece Great War battle which went exactly according to plan. In seven days, Plumer's army had taken all its objectives, together with over 7,000 prisoners and 48 guns. British casualties totalled 24,562, of which 3,538 were killed and 3,215 were missing. German casualties, which are calculated on a different basis and exclude the slightly wounded, came to around 25,000, but were probably somewhat higher.

Unfortunately, this startling success at Messines was not exploited. That failure was due, however, to the 'thrusting' General Gough, not to the 'plodding' General Plumer. One task of the 'Southern' army (Plumer's) was to edge its inward flank forward and seize ground on the Gheluvelt Plateau in the centre, while the 'Northern' army (Gough's) did likewise, thereby taking up a part of that ground in the centre previously seen as essential to the success of the overall plan. Plumer was ready to do this, and on the day before Messines, Haig urged Gough to exploit Plumer's anticipated success '*as it will materially help your operations*'. Gough preferred either to include the attack in the centre as part of his own, later, 'Northern' operation, or to take over the two reserve corps, II and VIII Corps of Second Army, and conduct a separate attack in the centre himself.

On 8 June, while Second Army was still fighting forward, these two corps, still under Plumer's command, sent patrols on to the Gheluvelt Plateau and reported strong resistance. Plumer therefore asked Haig for three days in which to bring up his artillery and mount a formal attack against Gheluvelt, using his two reserve corps. He saw this as the next logical stage in the offensive, but the C-in-C did not agree. Instead, wary that an infantry general was slowing the attack down by introducing 'phases', on 9 June he transferred these two corps to Gough's Fifth Army and ordered the latter to commence a minor offensive designed to secure Fifth Army's right flank 'on the ridge east of Ypres'.

Gough did not do so. Days passed, and on 14 June, the day the Messines battle ended, he told Haig's weekly army commanders' conference at Lillers that, having studied the ground, he had come to the conclusion that to thrust forward in the centre – that is, towards Gheluvelt – was to place the troops involved in an exposed salient that it would be difficult to defend. His counter-proposal, to attack simultaneously in both north and the centre at a later date, was approved . . . and thus the benefits of the Messines victory were dissipated.

This was a tragic mistake. The Messines Ridge was a stepping stone into the heart of the German positions around Ypres, but taking the ridge in the south had only been the first step. The second step was to seize the Gheluvelt Plateau in the centre. This was what the Germans expected the British to do, and this was what they most feared. If Plumer had been allowed to bring up his artillery and put in another attack from his firm base at Messines quickly, the Gheluvelt Plateau would almost certainly have fallen. In turn this would have given the British armies a firm foothold on the high ridges leading north, ridges well above those mud-clogged slopes that were to drown all Haig's hopes of success in the coming Battle of Passchendaele.

CHAPTER 18

PASSCHENDAELE – THIRD YPRES, JULY–NOVEMBER 1917

*'One of the most gigantic, tenacious, grim, futile and bloody
fights ever waged in the history of war.'*

David Lloyd George, *War Memoirs* (1933–6)

P asschendaele – the very name is fearful, enough to send a shiver down
the spine. Today, it identifies a small village (now Passendale) on a low
ridge east of Ypres, but in 1917 this unremarkable village and the slopes
around it were places of slaughter. The name seems to have a deeper, almost
Biblical resonance – the Passion Dale – a place where men died for a cause
greater than themselves – or died for nothing.

There are few excuses for the battles fought around Passchendaele from
July to November 1917, and any needed are hard to find. Some reasons can
be offered, however, just as others can be discarded. In the earlier battles on
the Western Front, the prime movers had usually been the French, and the
hands of the British generals had been tied by that firm instruction to 'co-
operate closely with the plans of our ally', many of the subsequent problems
in 1915 and 1916 stemmed from the British Commander-in-Chief's attempts
to obey that instruction.

That reason does apply at Passchendaele. The British Army was now the
strongest on the Western Front, General Nivelle had fallen into a pit of his own
making, and, with the exception of any caveat issued by Lloyd George, Field
Marshal Haig had a free hand with the where and when of his next offensive. He
chose to attempt to fight his way out of the Ypres Salient, pursuing the elusive
grail of a breakthrough to open country. The chief questions to be asked,
therefore, are firstly, was this a wise decision? and secondly, were the plans
made to achieve that end adequate? It is also necessary to consider the
arguments of Lloyd George, the Prime Minister, whose views on the Passchendaele offensive have coloured all subsequent accounts of the battle.

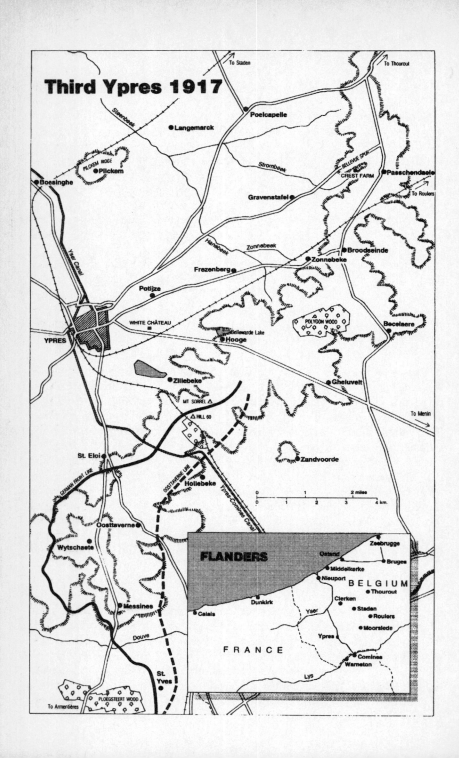

If the war was cutting into the heart of the nation, the battle of Passchendaele came near to breaking it, for every element in British society was now feeling the effects of the struggle. Although it has often been depicted with overtones of class – the aristocratic officer corps and the poor bloody Tommy – the Great War was not a 'class' conflict in which the upper classes gave the orders and the lower classes did the fighting and dying. Everyone felt the effects of the war, and the generals were no less immune or indifferent to the suffering it caused than anyone else, whatever later generations or historians might allege. It was a war that affected and struck at every class and the killing was indiscriminate. It killed the children of the poor but it also killed 1,153 Old Etonians and this grim total came from just one of Britain's many public schools. All the rest sent their former pupils to the trenches and recorded their fate later on panels in the chapel and the dining hall.

The eldest son of Prime Minister Asquith died on the Western Front. So did the only son of the Imperial poet, Rudyard Kipling, and of the Scots music-hall star, Harry (later Sir Harry) Lauder. The war killed working men from the back streets of the industrial towns and labourers on then vast estates, but it also killed the brother of Lady Elizabeth Bowes-Lyon, later wife to King George VI, and the much loved Queen Mother to other generations.

The war killed common folk as well as gentlemen, professional soldiers as well as conscripted civilians. General Allenby had just arrived in Egypt to take up his new command when the word reached him that his only son, Michael, had been killed on the Western Front. Brigadier-General Johnny Gough, VC, brother of the Fifth Army Commander, had been killed at the front in February 1915. General Foch lost his son and his son-in-law on the Western Front. The memoirs of the generals are littered with sad little notes, each recording the loss of an old friend, a relative, a godson. The implacable General Ludendorff lost two stepsons in the war and records how he felt in his memoirs: 'I was deeply attached to my son, as to all my step-children, having no children of my own. He was shot down over the Channel. Not until weeks afterwards did we find his body, washed up on the Dutch coast.' Ludendorff's youngest stepson, also a pilot, was killed a year later, in April 1918; 'The war has spared me nothing', said the general sadly. The Great War laid waste a whole generation, and paved the way for another war two decades later. Clearly, it should have been stopped, but the only people who could stop it were the politicians.

David Lloyd George was a politician, an entirely political animal, a man who saw everything in political terms. The point is worth noting, for the generals who fought on the Western Front came from a different milieu and brought with them a different scale of values. When they were born and while they grew to manhood, politics, like the Army, was an occupation for gentlemen, most often the landed gentry, men with a stake in the stability of the country, who could, and often did, put country before party, even if they put the interests of their class above everything. Lloyd George despised the Great War generals and most of what they stood for, and they in turn had little time for him. They came from a different time, almost a different country, and they saw the fight with Germany in a different way. They wanted to win the war – Lloyd George simply wanted to end it. It is easy to sympathise with his position, but the fact remains that he was wrong. The German terms for peace were not acceptable and peace would not come before victory – and the only place to win a decisive victory was on the Western Front.

The dispute between the British generals – specifically Haig and Robertson – and Lloyd George had been running since before Lloyd George came to Downing Street; it had started when he became Minister of Munitions and thus came into direct contact with the Army's senior commanders. Now Prime Minister and head of the War Cabinet, he was quite determined that things had got to change. Lloyd George believed that there *must* be another way to end the war other than by these ghastly offensives on the Western Front.

Yet the Prime Minister's character was nothing if not mercurial, his opinions liable to sudden and extreme changes. He had believed implicitly in Nivelle, and Nivelle had let him down. He had believed that Nivelle could break through the German line in days rather than months, or else would call off the offensive, yet Nivelle had battered away for weeks and got nowhere. He had believed that Nivelle could fight and win without great loss, and yet Nivelle's offensive had cost France over 100,000 casualties. He had believed that the French Army was better than the British, yet that army was now riven by mutiny. Now, with one of the sudden shifts in view typical of his politics, Lloyd George was willing to believe that Haig was a great commander and that the British Army should hurl itself upon its German counterpart with all its force and skill. Wise men in London and at the front realised, however, that the Prime Minister's new enthusiasm would not last.

Haig's earlier dealings with Lloyd George have already been outlined, but the story can be picked up again on 21 April 1917, two weeks after the taking of Vimy Ridge and one week after the start of the Nivelle offensive, when Lord Esher, a member of the Committee of Imperial Defence, wrote some encouraging words to the Field Marshal: 'He [Lloyd George] has entirely changed his point of view as to the merits of the respective chiefs of the Allied Armies, their staffs and their powers of offence. It is almost comic, to see how the balance has turned. For the moment I do not think you could do wrong.'

Lloyd George's attitude did not signal a change of heart so much as a state of confusion. He had sent the South African Defence Minister, Lieutenant-General Jan Christian Smuts, a former leader of the Boers in their war against the British, now a member of the Imperial War Cabinet, on a tour of the Western Front, asking him to report back on the merits of continuing the struggle there. Smuts returned to endorse Haig's proposal for an attack in

Flanders to clear the Belgian coast. Lloyd George did, however, take some comfort from the South African's addendum that he did not believe a breakthrough was possible, but thought that a decision could be reached on the Western Front by a process of relentlessly wearing down the enemy – 'if we cannot break the enemy's front, we can at least break his heart.'

There were, however, at least two other schools of thought devoted to this subject. One – of which Lloyd George was a student – believed that the war could be won elsewhere, in Italy, or in the Balkans, or in Mesopotamia. If the Austro-Hungarians or the Turks could be defeated, ran this line of argument, the props supporting Germany would be knocked away. This was a reversal of the basic strategic doctrine, as well as wishful thinking. Germany supported – or propped up – Austria-Hungary, Turkey and Bulgaria, the elements of the Central Powers, not the other way round; first knock Germany out of the war and these countries would collapse. Allied support for Italy was necessary, for the Italian Army was not doing well. It was currently fighting the *eleventh* Battle of the Isonzo and still showed no signs of inflicting a decisive defeat on the enemy, nor was there any obvious strategic gain to be had on the Italian front.* As for the Balkan sideshow in Salonika, that had now absorbed half a million Allied soldiers who were achieving nothing in return for very high casualties from sickness, and who should have been employed elsewhere.

The second school of thought held that the best course was to do nothing, or as little as possible, until the United States, with her almost unlimited supplies of men, could make an impact on the Western Front. That would be at some time in 1918 – perhaps a year ahead. This school was strongly supported by the French after their losses at Verdun and on the Chemin des Dames, *provided* that someone, probably the British, continued attacking on the Western Front in the meantime. The snag with this argument was that the Germans still had an unbroken field army and were about to receive a great increase in strength if – as seemed increasingly likely – Russia was knocked out of the war by internal revolution. Tsar Nicholas II had been overthrown and forced to abdicate in March 1917,† Lenin and the Bolsheviks were increasingly challenging the new Russian 'Provisional Government', and while that government had promised to continue the war in the Allied cause, no one knew how long this promise would hold, or what the Bolsheviks would do if they were to gain power.

* Italy's performance – and sacrifice – in the Great War seem largely to be remembered slightingly in this country because of one defeat – Caporetto – and judged by her performance in a later war in which she – or the bulk of her people – manifestly had no heart. Few remember, or give credit for, the crushing Italian victory of Vittorio Veneto in October-November 1918; if Austria had not capitulated, it is likely that the Italians would have occupied Vienna, the capital of the Austro-Hungarian Empire.
† This was the 'February' Revolution of 8–15 March 1917; the anomaly in the months arises from Imperial Russia's use of the Julian calendar after the rest of Europe had adopted the Gregorian calendar. Thus the 'second', 'October', Revolution actually took place on 6–7 November 1917 by the Western calendar.

Freed from fighting a war on two fronts and given a quiet year to re-establish her power on the Western Front, the German position would become invulnerable. Many people, but especially Field Marshal Haig, thought that the only solution was to keep up the pressure and wear the German Army down until its ability to fight had been extinguished. It is clear now that Haig and Robertson were right, and all other arguments irrelevant – the war would be won when Germany was defeated, and the only place where she could be defeated was on the Western Front. Fighting anywhere else was a waste of time and manpower.

The scene now shifts to the conference in Paris on 4–5 May 1917. As we have seen, this meeting and the military conference which preceded it concluded with a general agreement to let Haig attack in Flanders – provided the French gave support elsewhere. Haig therefore assumed that he had been given carte blanche to plan and carry out his Flanders campaign. In this, however, he was mistaken. The French Army mutinies removed any possibility of their forces making any major attacks during the summer, and this falling away of French support took an immediate toll of Lloyd George's resolution.

Nor was he the only one to doubt if the conclusions of the Anglo-French conference were entirely wise. A week after that meeting, the House of Commons held a secret session to discuss the war, during which various Members spoke out vehemently against further offensives. Churchill, who had served as an infantry battalion commander on the Western Front after resigning from the Admiralty, said there should be no further offensives until the power of the United States was in the field. There was the old suggestion that the Italians, if supplied with that universal panacea, heavy artillery, could make a more decisive impact, and there was talk of knocking away the Austro-Hungarian prop by entering into separate peace negotiations with the Austrian Emperor Carl, who was anxious to take Austria-Hungary out of the war through just such a peace. This last idea had, however, already been discussed and rejected by the Entente Powers.

The outcome of this secret Parliamentary session was yet another change of heart. Lloyd George now wanted no more fruitless offensives on the Western Front. At the end of May he told Robertson that Haig must conserve his men because the recruiting situation was not good, and that a continued supply of trained reinforcements could not therefore be guaranteed.

Haig, not unnaturally, would not accept this decision. He had been proceeding with his plans for the Flanders offensive, and on 7 June he was able to provide a stunning victory when Plumer's army took the Messines Ridge, thus securing a jumping-off position for a further offensive. Haig's joy at this victory was short-lived. On the following day, a new committee sat for the first time. This was the War Policy Committee, composed of Lloyd George, Lord Milner, Smuts, Andrew Bonar Law, and Lord Curzon,* with Sir Maurice Hankey (as he had become) as Secretary. Hankey was a friend of Haig and Robertson, with the result that the deliberations of this committee were soon brought to their attention.

The purpose of the War Policy Committee was to 'get at the facts and review the entire policy and strategy of the war'. Since the war had now been going on for the best part of three years the formation of a committee to consider these facts would seem to have been long overdue, but the new body was not simply an instrument for review. Within days it had concluded that the place from which to strike at the Central Powers was in Italy, and that the way to get the Italians moving was not only to provide them with heavy artillery but also to send them *twelve British divisions*. This last move would also curb Haig's ability to undertake a further offensive in Flanders.

Robertson, learning of these plans from Hankey, was appalled. He sent an urgent, secret, warning to Haig, telling him that the War Policy Committee would be sending for him and intended to quiz him closely about his plans for the coming summer. 'Don't argue that you can finish the war this year,' wrote the CIGS, 'or say that Germany is already beaten. Argue that your plan is the best – which it is – and then leave it to them to reject your advice and mine. They dare not do that.'

Robertson was right, but when he and Haig were called before the War Policy Committee on 19 June, they found it a most unpleasant experience. The interviews lasted six full days and began with Haig being asked to explain his plan in detail to the committee. Lloyd George's affability at the Paris conference six weeks previously had now quite disappeared, and the two generals were subjected to a severe grilling. Since Haig and Robertson were two of the most inarticulate men ever to hold public office, the committee's requirement that they should state their case in plain words was a considerable trial to both of them. Haig eventually demonstrated the strategic possibilities of his 1917 plan by making wide arcs with his hands over the map of Flanders and eastern Belgium, each vague sweep moving north and east and finishing up with the little finger of his left hand resting on the German frontier. It was said later that Lloyd George 'never forgave that finger'.

Quite apart from resenting his manner, the generals found that Lloyd George was being economical with the facts, and was not above descending to downright lies when speaking to the rest of the committee. When Haig had finished explaining his plan, the Prime Minister declared that this was

* Lord Milner, one of the architects of the South African War, and of the subsequent reconstruction of the former Boer republics, was a member of the War Cabinet; Law, leader of the Conservative Party, was Chancellor of the Exchequer and Leader of the House of Commons in Lloyd George's Coalition Government (in 1922 he was, briefly, Prime Minister); Curzon, formerly Viceroy of India and another Conservative, was also a member of the War Cabinet.

the first time he had heard of it. He then suggested that Haig and Robertson were seeking to mislead the committee on several crucial points, and that he had never heard of the French Army mutinies until that day. He also declared that had the French generals known of Haig's plan, they would have opposed it, going on to state that the French actually *had* opposed it, and that Haig and Robertson were concealing this fact from the committee.

None of this was true. The conclusions and report of the Paris conference and the minutes of Haig's meetings with Pétain make clear that Lloyd George and the French were fully aware of the former's plan and concurred with it. Conference minutes apart, Smuts, Lloyd George's personal envoy, had reported on all these matters to the Prime Minister in person after his visit to France, and informed him that Pétain, the French Commander-in-Chief, approved of Haig's offensive, not least because *someone* had to fight the Germans on the Western Front and the French Army was currently unable to do so. No one, however, wished to call the Prime Minister of Great Britain a liar to his face, and so his comments were absorbed by the members of the committee and, unopposed, were recorded in the minutes.

In truth, Lloyd George's outbursts were motivated by fear – not for himself, or even for his position as Prime Minister, but fear of further terrible losses if he sanctioned a renewal of the Messines offensive. The losses of 1916 had been appalling, and he no longer believed Haig's optimistic forecasts for the coming campaign. 'During nearly three years of war I have never heard of any offensive to be undertaken without previous predictions of success,' he said, 'yet brilliant preliminary successes are followed by weeks of desperate and sanguinary struggle . . . leading to nothing except the gain of a few miles and a ghastly casualty list.' All this was very true and everyone knew it, but what was the acceptable alternative? If there was none and Lloyd George did not wish to lose this war, what were his proposals for ending it?

Lloyd George knew that he was losing the argument. He knew also that his administration might not survive if he sacked Field Marshal Haig, and there was also the lurking thought that if Haig was forced to resign, and his replacement as C-in-C only produced another disaster, the public outcry would finish him. Haig and Robertson had no intention of resigning, but before the meeting could reach any conclusion, the First Sea Lord, Admiral Sir John Jellicoe, who had commanded the Fleet at Jutland, rose and declared that Haig's Flanders offensive must go ahead, because 'Unless the Army can clear the Germans out of Zeebrugge this year the war is lost; we cannot continue the war through a lack of shipping.'

It is hard to say what prompted Jellicoe's outburst. It may have been faulty intelligence since only ten German submarines were based in Zeebrugge and their effect on the submarine campaign was not significant. It may have been a desire to prevent Lloyd George forcing the introduction of the convoy system, something to which the Navy was wholeheartedly opposed. It may have been the desire of a professional serviceman to aid his Army colleagues in an argument with the 'frocks' – the politicians. Whatever the reason, Jellicoe's statement hit a raw nerve with Lloyd George and his committee, for the losses caused by German submarines – tens of thousands of tons of shipping each month – were the main concern of the Government in 1917. In his backing of the Flanders campaign as essential, Jellicoe was pushing at an open door.

The members of the War Policy Committee found themselves in a quandary, torn between fears of yet another Somme, of the collapse of the war effort from submarine interdiction, or of letting the soldiers have their way, with who knew what outcome. Like all committees, they decided to defer their decision, but told Haig he could continue with his preparations pending their formal report. This took time, more of that precious time, while in Flanders the ground was dry and firm and the good weather was passing. The most important point about this meeting, however, is that it did not *authorise* Haig's offensive, only agreed that he could continue to *prepare* for it.

It was not until a month later, on 20 July, *five* weeks after the end of the Messines battle, that the committee got off the fence, a terrible delay for an offensive that had been planned on the basis of a rapid follow-up to any initial success, as at Messines. The decision was to allow Haig to begin his offensive, but if it showed signs of developing into another long-drawn-out battle, another Somme, it would be stopped. This was to be a re-run of Nivelle's original proposal, a battle that was to show swift returns or be broken off, after which the heavy guns and those twelve divisions could be sent to Italy.

Five days later, on 25 July, Lloyd George changed his mind again. He now proposed that military aid should be sent to Italy at once. As he was to record in his War Memoirs, however, the CIGS, General Robertson, who had enough of this shilly-shallying, 'dug in his heels and refused to budge . . . and held the Cabinet to its assent. We therefore had the choice of dismissing Haig and Robertson and appointing generals who were not so committed, or proceeding with the Ostend operation.' With that settled, Robertson sent a telegram to Haig, telling him that 'The War Cabinet authorised me to inform you that, having approved your plans being executed you may depend on their wholehearted support and if and when they decide again to reconsider the situation they will obtain your views before arriving at any decision as to the cessation of operations.'

Six days later the Third Battle of Ypres – Passchendaele – finally began.

Third Ypres ran from 31 July to 10 November and actually consisted of eight officially listed 'battles': those of Pilckem, 31 July–2 August; Langemarck, 16–18 August; the Menin Road Ridge, 20–25 September; Polygon Wood, 26 September–3 October; Broodseinde, 4 October; Poelcapelle, 9 October; First Passchendaele, 12 October; and Second Passchendaele, 26 October–10 November. These 'battles' are best regarded as phases in a continuing struggle, and it is immediately noticeable that the lengths of the phases vary and that there are gaps between the battles. Some battles last only a day, others several days, the final one two whole weeks, but though the fighting never stopped the phases are not continuous. It is not the intention of this book to examine each battle in detail, but to study how Haig's overall plan, and the plans of the generals for the various phases, were implemented, and what went right or wrong thereafter.

Given a careful study of the map, the names of the individual battles give a good guide to the progress of the offensive. The Battle of Messines, 7–14 June, had given the Second Army a foothold looking north, along the crest of the ridge leading towards the Gheluvelt Plateau. The seizure of the Messines-Wytschaete Ridge gained the high ground overlooking the Salient and enabled Second Army to protect the flank of the 'Northern' army – Gough's fifth Army – as it tried for a breakthrough. The ridge surrounding Ypres to the east ran north and east from Wytschaete towards the village of Passchendaele, and provided the Second Army with firm going, as well as good observation over the positions occupied by the Germans between the ridge and the British lines in front of Ypres.

If the advance of Fifth Army could proceed beyond Passchendaele it would cut the railway lines coming into Staden and Roulers, via Thourout, from Bruges and the north, lines that supplied the German Army along the Belgian coast and at Ypres with their essential supplies. It has to be repeated that motorised transport was in its infancy in 1917.* Rail was the only way to supply large armies, which needed hundreds of tons of supplies each day – and after cutting the railway lines Haig could move on to take Bruges, Ostend and Zeebrugge.

Haig's plan therefore offered various objectives, and even if only one was taken it would be a valuable gain. If the Wytschaete-Passchendaele Ridge could be taken, the German position around the Salient would be untenable. If the railway line at Roulers and Thourout could be cut, the German position in the northern flank would be fatally compromised. If Bruges, Ostend and Zeebrugge could be taken, enemy forces in northern Belgium would be forced to surrender or withdraw and, as a bonus, the Admiralty would be delighted. And if all else failed, the offensive would certainly cause further heavy losses to the German Army, as well as placating the French.

All this made good sense, but there was another factor: for all his dourness Haig, as we have seen, was a great optimist. He believed that with a little luck and some hard fighting his armies could achieve a breakthrough here and let the cavalry through to the open country of eastern Flanders and Belgium. That was why Gough and his Fifth Army seemed the better combination for the northern thrust than Plumer's Second Army, and that is the thinking that underpinned the plans Gough received from Haig for the conduct of his Flanders offensive.

* It is worth noting that the technologically very advanced German Army of the Second World War still relied largely on horses for its transport; in 1945 it had some 2 million of the animals in service.

The Fifth Army were to capture the ridge and form a bridgehead on a line north-east of Ypres, roughly between Passchendaele, Staden and Clerken. These positions, once taken, were to be held by Second Army moving up from the south, while Fifth Army would push on to Roulers and Thourout to cut the railway lines and take the German coastal defences in rear. This decisive thrust, which would surely be strongly resisted, would be aided by a seaborne landing at Middelkerke, commanded by General Rawlinson, made in conjunction with an attack northwards by the Belgian Army and the French First Army, sallying out of Nieuport. This was a viable, if highly optimistic plan, and it might well have worked. The snags were the terrain, the weather, the resilience of the enemy, the depth of his defences, and the character of General Gough.

The key element in Hubert Gough's character was impetuosity. He was born, in August 1870, into a military family, in which there was never any doubt that he was destined for the Army. From Eton he went to Sandhurst, from where he was gazetted into the 16th Lancers in 1889. Gough had his fair share of conceit: in his memoirs, published in 1954 and dedicated to 'The British People', he records that he was the youngest cadet at Sandhurst and, having passed out 'with Honours', was subsequently the youngest captain, commanding officer, brigade commander, general, and army commander, though he has the sense to note that 'perhaps a slower and more steady promotion would have been to my advantage'.

Such rapid promotion indicates that Gough was no fool, but his impetuous nature soon got him into trouble. Posted to India, he took up pigsticking and on his first outing, chasing a wild boar through the bush, he rode his pony at great speed into a nullah (dry watercourse); the pony broke its neck and Gough was lucky to escape with his life. Later, back in England, he fell so heavily while riding over a steeplechase course that he was unconscious for several days. Moreover, he was inclined to be as reckless of danger – to others, as well as himself – in war as he was in the hunting or sporting fields, for on active service this aspect of his character again revealed itself. On one occasion during the South African War, while commanding a regiment of mounted infantry, he led his men, without having made any prior reconnaissance, in a spirited attack on what turned out to be a large Boer commando. A good number of his command were killed and Gough was captured. He managed to escape after a few hours and made his way back to the British lines, but he was under a cloud of official disfavour for a while, although Kitchener eventually forgave him.

Even when not on active service, Gough continued to court trouble, and as we have seen was one of the principal participants in the Curragh Incident in 1914, which brought him into conflict with French and Sir John Seely, then the Secretary of State for War. The British Army had large numbers of Irish officers, a great many of them senior to Hubert Gough, and there had been no real need for him to push himself forward as a martyr for the cause of Ulster. Given his a well-earned reputation as a thruster, however, and the fact that he felt strongly about the Ulster situation, there is a certain inevitability to his actions.

In his autobiography, *Soldiering On*, published in 1954, Gough states that: 'In discussing the various personalities who have crossed my path, I have passed some severely adverse comments, for I have felt how important it is, in writing of matters which are to some extent historical, to speak without fear, favour or affection.' That much is true, but he is far more reticent when writing of the various allegations that were made about himself. Matters like his relations with the Canadian Corps, his actions and decisions at Bullecourt, the process by which – and the reasons why – the leading role at Passchendaele was switched by Haig from Gough to Plumer, are given only the briefest of mentions, or are not mentioned at all.

A general fights his battles according to the orders he is given, but the manner in which he fights them, whether cautiously, boldly or recklessly, stems, at least in part, from his character. Soldiering has a way of exposing a man's character, of calling forth actions that reflect the way he really is, rather than the man he might, on mature reflection, prefer to be, and far less than the man suggested by the image he presents to the world at large. As a horseman and subaltern, Gough hurled himself at obstacles, regardless of the dangers and the consequences. Now he hurled his men forward whatever the risks, and the cost was frequently high.

For two generations, Field Marshal Haig has been roundly criticised, often unjustly, for real or perceived flaws in his character or for his supposed lack of professional ability. In fact, Haig was neither a callous man or a bad general. Like most people, he had the faults of his virtues, and one of these was an excessive loyalty to his subordinates and friends. Loyalty is admirable; excessive loyalty can be dangerous. Being slow to make friends, Haig clung to those he had closely, yet by 1917 certain of his subordinates, whom he counted as friends – General Charteris, his Intelligence chief, and General Kiggell, his Chief of Staff, for example – were not giving him the support and advice he needed – though they may have been giving him the advice he *wanted*, which is not the same thing. The role of Charteris and Kiggell in Third Ypres will be discussed later, but at the opening of the battle Haig's gravest error was the appointment of his friend and fellow cavalryman, Lieutenant-General Sir Hubert Gough, to organise and command the spearhead of the offensive.

There is little need to debate this point, for Gough himself agreed with it: 'It was a mistake not to entrust the operation to Plumer, who had been on that front for more than two years, instead of bringing me over on to a bit of ground with which I had practically no acquaintance.' While that is honest and generous, it is not the whole story, for in fact the greatest problem came when Gough altered Haig's original plan. The objectives of that plan have been listed, but Gough was also supposed to make the main thrust of his attack *on the high ground*, through Gheluvelt, Broodseinde and Moorslede, ground which would then be taken over by Second Army. That army would then, in effect, protect Gough's right flank and rear while Fifth Army pushed north, having also been directed to avoid entanglement in the Houthulst Forest, which lay north-west of Passchendaele.

Gough resolved to change all that, stating that he had decided not to push directly north but to *pivot* his army on its left flank, taking in the Houthulst Forest and letting only his right wing sweep along the Passchendaele Ridge. This, Gough added, removed Roulers as an objective for Fifth Army. It also amounted to a major change in the plan, and was a direct contradiction of Field Marshal Haig's orders.

Haig had the Roulers rail junction, four miles beyond Passchendaele, as a prime target for the Fifth Army, but it was essential to sweep up to the Passchendaele Ridge in force, since otherwise none of the other objectives would be attainable. Haig should have gone at once to Gough's head-quarters and insisted on strict adherence to his plan – or sacked him on the spot. He did not do either. Instead, he displayed, as always, that willingness to let the field commanders have the final decisions about an attack, since it was they who had to fight it. It was, however, a principle that should not have applied when it affected the strategy of the entire offensive.

Haig met Gough on 28 June, 'urging the importance of the right flank. The main battle will be fought for the ridge and our plans must be made accordingly. I impressed on Gough the importance of the ridge in question [the Passchendaele Ridge] and that the advance north should be limited until the right flank has been secured.'

In the event, Gough ignored this urging, but Haig also fell short of his duty. He did not have to 'urge' the Fifth Army commander; Gough was a subordinate, and Haig should have 'ordered' him to place the weight of his attack on the right flank; if that subordinate failed to comply, he should have replaced him. The final result of all this shilly-shallying was that the Passchendaele offensive, instead of being a strong thrust northwards along the ridge to secure vital and obvious objectives, was changed to a wheeling movement to the north and east. Gough was wrong for failing to realise that the Passchendaele Ridge was the vital ground, to the taking of which all his resources – which he was later to claim had been inadequate – should have been directed. Haig was wrong for failing to get a grip of his subordinate at this time, and for accepting a re-casting of his plan. Not until the battle was going seriously awry did Haig intervene.

Another problem, the effects of which will be seen later, was that all this discussion and argument in London or in Belgium was causing further delay, and yet even when the go-ahead was received, Gough was not ready. The attack had been scheduled for 25 July, but Gough asked for a postponement until the 28th – and then General Anthoine, commanding the French First Army on Gough's left flank, requested a delay until the 31st. On that day, seven weeks after the taking of the Messiness-Wyteschaete Ridge, the Third Battle of Ypres finally began.

The attack on the Pilckem Ridge, the opening battle of Third Ypres, was preceded by the most intensive barrage yet seen in this war. It lasted from the 17–30 July, and during that time no fewer than 4,300,000 shells of all calibres were sent into the German lines. This barrage caused a great many casualties and did severe damage to the German trenches. Some 30,000 enemy soldiers were killed or wounded in the days before the infantry assault, and their front-line positions were levelled, but the Germans had got well ahead with their defensive preparations in the weeks since Messines. Their positions around the Salient had always been immensely strong and now the entire front east of Ypres was well provided with reinforced-concrete pillboxes and belts of wire, covered by the interlocking fields of fire from hundreds of machine-guns. In addition, this bombardment was cutting up the ground, breaking the low dikes along the drainage ditches, and creating deep shell holes. At midnight on the 30th the barrage took on a new ferocity and for the next three hours a tornado of shelling swept the German positions. The infantry of Gough's Fifth Army, went over the top a little before dawn, at 0350 hours, and just as they moved out of their trenches it began to rain.

The attack on 31 July was successful. This success has to be seen in Great War terms, but the infantry crossed the German front lines with little opposition, took over 5,000 prisoners, most of them dazed by shellfire, and advanced an average of 2 miles on a front of 15 miles. Yet good though this was, it still fell short of the designated objectives for that day, for the German tactic of defending ground with artillery was emphasised by the terrible bombardment that fell on the attacking troops. Almost worst of all, the rain continued . . . and continued.

Even though it went on raining for several days, the effect of the downpour was almost immediate. At the end of the first day shell holes were filled to the brim, while the open ground was turning into a quagmire under the relentless shelling. The effect of rain on the entire Passchendaele offensive is often mentioned in the histories but rarely stressed, although the effect of prolonged rain was *the* factor that inhibited the offensive and curbed the infantry's assaults. Attacks made in dry weather usually succeeded; those made in the mud generally petered out with loss.

The generals were well aware of this, for at his first evening conference for his divisional commanders on 31 July, General Gough referred to the rain as 'a curse', and on the following day Haig wrote in his diary that it had been 'A terrible day of rain. The ground is like a bog in this low-lying country.' On 4 August, he noted, again in his diary, that 'In view of the bad weather and wet ground General Gough has cancelled the orders he issued for the furtherance of his attack.' Fifth Army was already sinking into the mud, and the advance had stalled.

Brigadier-General Charteris recorded his views in his diary on the same day. 'All my fears about the weather have been realised and it has killed this attack . . . I went up to the front line this morning. Every brook is swollen and the ground is a quagmire.' This entry is interesting, for it has frequently been stated that Haig's staff never went up to the front line and did not know – or care – about the condition of the ground. Charteris's comments clearly refute that notion, and it seems at the very least highly unlikely, since they lived in the same mess, that he would not have passed on his observations to Haig and Kiggell. If that is one unfair charge dismissed, the fact that the rain caused Gough to call off the Pilckem attack also goes some way towards refuting the myth that the Passchendaele offensive was pressed at any and all costs, despite the weather and the state of the ground.

The weather played such a large part in the Third Ypres battles that it has provided a separate controversy. Charteris claimed that the meteorological records indicated that bad weather 'arrived in Flanders every August, with the regularity of the Indian monsoon'. There is plenty of anecdotal evidence that refutes this contention, most obviously that the advance to and retreat from Mons in nearby Hainault in August 1914 was conducted in terribly hot weather that the troops found most trying. GHQ contained a meteorological section and its commander, Lieutenant-Colonel Gold, disputed Charteris's claim, saying that the Flanders weather was quite unpredictable; he added that the Intelligence chief's statement was not worth formal refutation. The truth seems to lie somewhere between the two. Flanders is not blessed with a kindly climate. Rain can and does fall there at any time and especially in the autumn, but the rains that fell in the late summer of 1917 were both heavier and longer-lasting than could normally be expected.

Dry ground was essential, to allow the infantry to move quickly over broken terrain, to move up the artillery, to get reinforcements forward, to support the infantry with tanks, to evacuate the wounded. Tanks had been written into the Pilckem battle plan, with 117 machines committed in support of the attack, but most of these broke down or became bogged. Rain and the mud swiftly drowned the machines, and by 3 August their commanders were petitioning Gough and Haig to call them back from the battlefield. As on the Somme, however, where the tanks were able to move they proved most useful, and they were to stay on the battlefield until early October.

Gough's army attacked three times in August, at Pilckem, at Langemarck, and along the Menin Road. Every time an assault was launched the rain came down with renewed intensity, until men came to believe that the thunder of the guns was causing the clouds to deliver their torrents. Even so, the Fifth Army advanced, slowly, damply and painfully, but without – as always, the term applies to the Great War – significant losses. Casualties of all types by the end of August totalled 68,000, which can be compared to the 57,000 racked up on the first *day* of the Somme. But while losses may have been lighter, they did not seem lighter. The deep mud, the ceaseless rain and the sweeping German machine-gun fire meant that the dead could not be buried or the wounded brought in, a situation which caused the ground along the road to Passchendaele to assume a new dimension of horror – rotting corpses, dead and dying horses and mules, dismembered bodies, scattered limbs and the pitiful wounded, coated in mud and lying unprotected under the relentless, drenching rain.

A month of fighting in terrible conditions took its toll on the generals of Fifth Army, eating into their never-abundant tolerance of General Gough. Brigade and divisional commanders protested long and loud at the condition of their men, and complaints about the staff work at Fifth Army HQ soon reached the ears of Field Marshal Haig. This was a cause for deep concern, for divisional commanders in Third Army had protested about Allenby's Arras offensive, and there were fears that these protests by senior commanders might be a symptom of a deeper disaffection. Gough himself soon came to believe that any advance in these conditions was impossible, and said later that he passed on these views to Haig: 'Tactical success is not possible or would be too costly under these conditions and the attack should now be abandoned.'

The C-in-C did not agree. He thought it far too soon to give up the attack, with none of the original objectives taken, and further believed that the only way to win was to keep on pounding the enemy to his front; for, as he told Gough and Plumer, 'By these means, and only by these means, can we ensure final victory, by wearing out the enemy resistance.'

Haig's enemies were not all to his front. At his back stood the Prime Minister, and after a week of battle at Third Ypres Lloyd George had changed his mind yet again. He was now planning to do something about the situation on the Western Front, and Field Marshal Sir Douglas Haig. The Flanders offensive was bogged down in mud and the time had come for an alternative strategy. On 8 August, a swiftly convened conference in London was asked to approve the alternative plan of sending heavy guns and twelve British divisions to Italy. Robertson managed to stave off this demand for the time being, but it did not go away. Lloyd George was speaking no more than the truth when he pointed out that the go-ahead for the Flanders offensive had been given on the clear understanding that it would lead to swift results, and that it was to be abandoned for an effort in Italy if its aims were seen to be unattainable. Though he was a Haig supporter, the CIGS recognised this argument as valid, and said as much in a letter to Haig: 'The Powers-that-be are beginning to get a little uneasy in regard to the situation. The casualties are mounting up and the Ministers will persist in asking whether a loss of say, 300,000 men will lead to a really great result, because if not, we ought to be content with something less than we are now doing.'

Three hundred thousand men! That is close to the total number of dead lost by the British in all three services during the entire six years of fighting in the Second World War. What gains could possibly be contemplated, let alone formally committed to paper, that could weigh against the death or wounding of 300,000 men? Besides, and lending support to the idea of sending aid to Italy, General Luigi Cadorna, Chief of the Italian General Staff, seemed to be doing well in his offensive, the eleventh Battle of the Isonzo, with the result that fresh pressure was brought to bear on Haig and Robertson, urging them to release more heavy guns to the Italians. On 4 September, Haig agreed to send 100 heavy guns to Italy from the French First Army on the Nieuport front, provided they were returned in time for his planned attack on the Ostend area. Lloyd George was delighted with this gesture, but his glee was not to last long. Before the French guns got to Italy, Cadorna's offensive collapsed and the Italian Army went into winter quarters.

In Flanders, however, the fighting continued, but there were changes. Haig could not bring himself to dismiss General Gough, who was now vastly unpopular with the British forces, but he decided that the overall command at Ypres must now go to Plumer. The change was made on 25 August, and the effect was to reverse the roles of the two armies. From now on Plumer's Second Army would spearhead the advance along the ridges to Passchendaele, while Gough's Fifth Army would protect its flank. This plan was far more sound, but it could not be put into effect straight away. The bulk of the artillery and most of the Engineers' stores – among them those vital duckboards which alone made movement possible over the mud, and road-building materials without which the army could not move at all – had to be transferred from Gough's command to Plumer's army.

The result was another delay. The fighting on the Western Front was not confined to the Salient, however, and between 15–20 August the Canadian Corps of First Army, in the sector south of the Salient, now commanded by the redoubtable Lieutenant-General Arthur Currie, took Hill 70, north of Lens, though with heavy casualties, losing over 8,000 men killed, wounded and missing.

Hill 70 was Currie's first battle as Canadian Corps commander and it was a classic of preparation, careful planning and repeated rehearsals, carried out on ground resembling the battlefield. The objective given to Currie by Horne, the First Army commander, was the town of Lens, but Currie persuaded him to change this to Hill 70, on the northern outskirts of the town. Currie did not want to see his men swallowed up in street fighting in an industrial and urban complex and knew that the Germans would react strongly to the loss of Hill 70, which dominated the city, and would launch determined counter-attacks to retake it. Currie laid his plans accordingly, turning Hill 70 into an artillery killing field, supplemented by the fire of 160 machine-guns.

The attack was launched on 15 August and the Canadians quickly carried Hill 70. Over the next three days the Germans launched no fewer than 21 counter-attacks, each one broken up with appalling casualties to the attackers, over 20,000 compared with 8,000

Canadians. The Germans never retook Hill 70 and Currie noted in his diary that 'It was a great and wonderful victory. GHQ regarded it as one of the finest performances of the war . . .' (Colonel Terry Cave, letter to the author, 1997.)

In early September, the former commander of the Canadian Corps, and now the GOC, Third Army, General Byng, gave Haig details of his plan for an attack towards Cambrai by his army, which held the sector of line south of First Army, but was told that though the Field Marshal liked this idea, any attack must be delayed until the offensive in Flanders had run its course.

In the Salient, meanwhile, Plumer's first attack, on the Menin Road Ridge, went in on 20 September. The object of this battle, a combined attack by Second and Fifth Armies under Plumer's overall command, was to take the Gheluvelt Plateau with Second Army while Gough's Fifth Army on the left took the Ypres ridge from Zonnebeke to Gravenstafel. Plumer was planning a type of massive bite-and-hold operation (or a 'phased advance' as the Official History calls it), an advance in four stages, each of no more than 1,500 yards, amounting in total to 6,000 yards. There would be a pause of six days between each phase in order to bring up the guns, and the first stage of this advance would be the attack on the Menin Road Ridge.

This first assault was to be supported by 1,295 guns, 575 of them heavy, and by 4 regiments of tanks and 26 RFC squadrons. The artillery would concentrate on destroying enemy strongpoints and machine-gun posts, and on counter-battery fire, before providing a creeping barrage for the infantry assault, which would be made by four divisions on a 4,000-yard front. The infantry would also use a new formation, with two lines of skirmishers preceding sections of infantry, each section containing a mixed group of riflemen, Lewis gunners and bombers, tasked to isolate and eliminate the German strongpoints and machine-gun positions, all moving out behind a storm of gas shell and an intense barrage from artillery and medium machine-guns.

A whole month had been wasted since Gough's first attack had been halted and, such is the perverse nature of war, during that month the weather in Flanders had been dry and sunny. The ground around Ypres dried out to such an extent that horses went lame from the hard going, and clouds of dust became a major irritation. As luck would have it, this good weather held during the attack on the Menin Road Ridge between 20 and 25 September. The first attack went well and by midday on the 20th both armies had got on to their objectives. German counter-attacks had been anticipated and duly came in during the afternoon, but visibility was good and the British artillery was therefore able to engage the advancing enemy troops, causing severe casualties among them.

The attacks against both armies were beaten off, and although the Germans continued to attack over the next five days the British were not seriously troubled before the Menin Road Ridge battle officially ended on

25 September. The first of Plumer's phases had succeeded, and at a comparatively low cost, Second Army losing 9,000 men killed, wounded and missing, and Fifth Army around 11,000. The German defences around the Salient had not been able to stop a well-planned attack and, thus encouraged, Haig felt able to proceed.

By now, however, the C-in-C's concept of the battle had changed somewhat. By the end of August he no longer anticipated a breakthrough and would have settled for the capture of the entire Passchendaele Ridge and a further writing-down of the German Army. The Passchendaele offensive had already been scaled down, for the seaborne assault by Rawlinson had been abandoned, and the thrust north by the French First Army and the Belgians never started. The divisions of General Rawlinson's Fourth Army were gradually taken away to reinforce Gough or Plumer, and by the early autumn the former was left without an army and kicking his heels.

Second Army's success on the Menin Road Ridge in September revived all Haig's hopes, and on the 21st, the day after that attack began, he ordered Plumer to proceed with the next phase.

On 26 September, therefore, Plumer struck again, this time with an assault against Polygon Wood. This attack, made by I Anzac with supporting attacks by elements of three British corps, also went well; operations were called off on 3 October, by which time the Second Army had completed the second phase of its advance across the Gheluvelt Plateau in a remarkably short space of time, though the speed of the attack had been paid for with heavy losses. The five British and two Australian divisions engaged in the Battle of Polygon Wood lost 15,375 men killed, wounded and missing.

On 28 September, at a meeting with Plumer and Gough, Haig told them that since the ground had turned firm and recent attacks had gone well he intended to exploit the next assault, the third phase of Plumer's plan, an attack by both I and II Anzac at Broodseinde on 4 October, by sending the cavalry forward. 'I am of the opinion that the enemy is teetering,' he said (according to the *Australian Official History*), 'and a good, vigorous blow might lead to decisive results.'

Exactly where Haig obtained the information to support this statement is unclear, for even Charteris, the usual source of optimistic statements, had doubts about any future attacks, because as autumn drew on the ground would take ever longer to dry out after rain, and more rain was inevitable. In the event, Haig was rewarded with another victory, or at least another advance, when the Anzacs, again supported by British divisions, this time from four corps, attacked and captured the village of Broodseinde on 4 October. Although the Battle of Broodseinde cost another 8,000 casualties, the Second Army now stood within reach of the Passchendaele position. Plumer's phased advances were working, though the cost of making them was starting to mount. The Germans were exacting an increasingly heavy toll from the British troops, and if these attacks were to continue, further heavy losses could be anticipated.

At least the offensive was gaining ground. The Germans were now waiting anxiously for the autumn rains to come to their aid; the commander in Flanders, Field Marshal Crown Prince Rupprecht, called the rain 'Our most effective ally', and he was right. New tactics were introduced in an effort to cope with the British artillery and to curb the attacks of the British and Anzac infantry. The German tactic was now to let their front lines absorb the first attacks, the enemy giving ground to pull the British infantry in before the pillboxes and strongpoints, where they could be raked with machine-gun fire and pounded with artillery then driven back by strong counter-attacks against their flanks. Still the British gained ground, their own artillery and machine-guns often shredding counter-attacks before they could advance a few yards. Then the rains came again.

A thin rain fell during 4 October, the day of the Broodseinde attack, but that night it began to rain harder and by dawn on the 5th it was coming down in torrents. From then on it seemed as if the rain never stopped, and with it the most terrible part of the Passchendaele battle began, on ground that became not just waterlogged and boggy but a dangerous inland sea, where the shell holes became deep pools, and the rain-soaked ground a form of quicksand, affording no support to man, beast or machine. Anyone who strayed from or fell off the network of duckboards that covered the battlefield could be trapped, sucked down and drowned. Men, horses, guns, tanks, transports, all suffered this fate, and it rapidly became clear that in the existing conditions the attack should be halted.

Haig, however, was determined to press ahead. On that decision a great many of the accusations of callousness and incompetence levelled against him have found a foothold, and it is clear now – and should have been clear then – that the best and most obvious decision was to call the attack off. Plumer, Gough and Charteris were all of that opinion, and although they were willing to continue the offensive if ordered, there was no enthusiasm for the task.

There were, however, two factors that militated against a decision to halt the attacks. The first was that if the British Army stopped now, without clearing the ridges around Ypres, all these months of fighting would have been for nothing. They would have no firm, defensive line to hold in the coming winter, and must either remain in their present mud-soaked misery or pull back. If they fell back it must all be done again, against even stiffer German resistance and a renewed and stronger line of defences.

There was also the fact, the overriding fact, that Haig believed he could still take the Passchendaele position. It lay just ahead, in plain sight when the rain lifted; if his troops could get there that would be a great triumph, a final reward for months of sacrifice. After all, the rain might stop, and since Plumer had already won three useful battles in his phased attacks since late September, there was good reason to suppose that he might do equally well in what was left of the autumn. Haig therefore ordered further attacks – and immediately fell foul of Lloyd George, who thought that by pressing on with the offensive the Commander-in-Chief had 'completely lost his balance'.

The Prime Minister was not the only one, either at the time or since, to feel that it was now, in early October 1917, that Douglas Haig forfeited all sympathy or claims to support. The Third Battle of Ypres had been going on for two months, losses had been high, gains modest – and in any case not the ones promised – winter had arrived early and conditions were known to be impossible . . . and now Haig was ordering further attacks. If the man was not mad, runs the argument, then he was certainly wholly indifferent to the sufferings of his men.

Apart from the C-in-C, Lloyd George also singled out Charteris for condemnation, stating later that it was the Intelligence chief's doctoring of reports that fuelled Haig's belief that the enemy was failing and that victory was still attainable. There is some truth in this charge. Charteris was adept in finding silver linings to the blackest clouds; as an old friend who had served with Haig since 1914 and shared his fortunes throughout the war, he had considerable influence with his chief, who tended to heed him.

Good news is always preferable to bad, and Haig himself remarked that 'In war we tend to believe what we wish for.' Here the problems raised by Charteris's selective reporting were compounded by his own incurable optimism, for he would take up some hopeful point from one of the Intelligence reports and interpret it into a policy statement that went far beyond what had been stated in the original report. The effect was to convince Haig that if he kept on pounding and continued the attacks, the seriously weakened German Army would give way. Given that this was a war of few absolutes – except casualties – there is some merit in this view. The Germans *had* suffered terribly in the last year, and their army in Flanders had taken a hammering in recent weeks, but there is no evidence whatsoever that all this had brought that fine and professional army to the point of collapse.

On 9 October, the Germans beat off an attack by Second Army at Poelcapelle, an attack doomed by poor staff work and indifferent artillery preparation, as well as by a lack of co-ordination between the guns and the infantry – and, of course, by the mud. The assault simply could not be got forward, for any movement over such ground was both slow and exhausting. For a Western Front attack to succeed it required both weight and momentum but, thanks to the mud, the attack at Poelcapelle had neither. Plumer's army suffered 9,000 more casualties and gained less than a mile. The sufferings of the wounded were terrible; it took sixteen men to carry a stretcher case through the mud, and many wounded men sank out of sight and drowned before the stretcher-bearers could find them.

It was now clear to almost everyone that the offensive must be halted, but there was still the village of Passchendaele, shattered and wrapped in wire, but just up ahead on the ridge, a distant reward for a summer-long effort. These attacks were now being flung in at short notice, the long-established need for careful artillery preparation and reconnaissance by the infantry sacrificed to the belief that the enemy was on the ropes and that another attack – or perhaps two – would drive him to the floor. The actual result was that the attacks themselves began to come apart.

On 12 October, just three days after Poelcapelle, Haig turned to II Anzac, and sent them thrusting forward against Passchendaele, the last bastion. The First Battle of Passchendaele lasted one day, and that evening an Australian patrol actually entered what remained of the village . . . and found it deserted.

That was the only 'success', however, and the patrol soon withdrew, for the attack had been a shambles. The artillery could not get forward, the guns and ammunition supplies were deep in mud, the infantry, struggling forward as best they could, had no cover and the creeping barrages they had become used to failed to materialise. When the Anzac battalions reached the Bellevue Spur, one of the positions defending Passchendaele, they walked into a hail of fire and died on the German wire in their hundreds. The 3rd Australian Division lost nearly 3,000 men in a few hours. Even the tough and resilient Australians and New Zealanders were weakened by this constant fighting in terrible conditions. The fighting had now lasted for two and a half months and the Second and Fifth Armies had advanced no more than six miles for the loss of some 200,000 men – and Passchendaele remained untaken.

Yet Haig still elected to go on. There was, he calculated, just time, before the weather and conditions became wholly intolerable, for one more attack, and just one unit that could accomplish the task and give him some claim to victory: the redoubtable Canadian Corps under its Canadian commander, General Currie. On 13 October, the day after First Passchendaele, Currie, then with his corps in First Army, away to the south, received orders to take his Canadians up to Flanders.

Currie had come a long way since 1914, rising from brigadier to lieutenant-general, and being awarded a knighthood in June 1917. Now, with the departure of Byng to Third Army in place of Allenby – and on the former's personal recommendation – he had taken charge of the Canadian Corps – in effect the Canadian field army, a force of four divisions totalling some 100,000 men – the first officer from the Empire to rise to a corps command. This was a remarkable feat, especially when it is recalled that three years earlier. Currie had been a civilian and a none-too-successful estate agent.

Arthur Currie was a good – perhaps even a great – soldier, popular with his men, well regarded by his British colleagues and superiors, and quite determined not to let the Canadian Corps go into battle until he was happy that they had every conceivable advantage. He was also equally determined that he would not serve under General Sir Hubert Gough of the Fifth Army. He had made that point abundantly clear to his own First Army commander, General Horne, and Horne had passed the message on to General Kiggell at GHQ. Currie's ultimatum was accepted calmly by Haig, for the two men liked and respected each other. 'The Canadian Corps will go to General Plumer and not to Gough,' the Field Marshal ordered, following a recommendation from Kiggell, 'because they do not work well with the latter. It seems he drove them too much on the Somme last year.'

For his part, Currie later wrote of Haig: 'I met him many times, and although he never had much to say, he always impressed me greatly. Leaving on one side his manner, his bearing and his appearance – all of which fitted so well with his high rank, one felt that here you were dealing with a thoroughly honest, decent, manly man.'

Currie also had the twin advantages of knowing the Salient and of getting on well with Plumer. The Canadian had fought at Second Ypres and commanded the 1st Canadian Division at Mount Sorrel in 1916, before going on to the Somme and Vimy Ridge. Now he was to command in the Second Battle of Passchendaele, a struggle that would last for two long and terrible weeks. He had heard about the fighting, and having made a visit to the front, he went to Plumer and suggested that the attack be cancelled. 'Our casualties will be high – at least 16,000 men –' he said, 'and we have to know if the success would justify the sacrifices.'

Plumer was not sure that they would, but Haig wanted Passchendaele and expected Currie to get it for him. The Field Marshal was well aware of the dangers he was asking them to face; whatever his failings, however, he did not lack moral courage. He paid a visit to the Canadian Corps, and made a speech to the officers that the Canadian troops were to remember down the years:

> Gentlemen, it has become apparent that Passchendaele must be taken and I have come here to ask the Canadian Corps to do it. General Currie is strongly opposed to doing so, but I have succeeded in overcoming his scruples. Some day I hope to be able to tell you why this must be done, but in the meantime I ask you to take my word for it. I may say that General Currie has demanded an unprecedented amount of artillery to protect his Canadians and I have been forced to acquiesce.

Haig may have normally been inarticulate, but this speech was masterly. He did not *order* the Canadians to take Passchendaele, he *asked* them to do so, and freely admitted that their commanding general was opposed to the operation – but had agreed to it if his corps was properly supported. The Canadians could not resist such a plea, to their nation or their honour as soldiers, and they set about planning an attack that would give the Field Marshal what he wanted.

Currie would take Passchendaele, but in his own way, and in his own good time. He began by sending his Intelligence officers out to gather all the information they could about the German positions and to make a careful detailed study of the ground. Observation posts (OPs) for that abundant artillery were established well forward, and a steady and accurate barrage now began to fall on the Passchendaele defences. Nothing could be done about the state of the terrain, or so it seemed, but Currie did not accept that the mud should stifle his attack.

As usual, he went forward to see the ground for himself, and returned worried by the appalling conditions and upset by the large number of unburied dead. One of his next directives was to order canvas bolt-and-magazine covers for every rifle and breech covers for every machine-gun, in an attempt to minimise the number of weapons that would otherwise be clogged by mud. These may have seemed simple devices, but few other units had thought of acquiring them so far, and weapons jammed by mud would not fire. In the coming battle most of the Canadian infantry would at least be able to fire their rifles, and that was some small comfort. Currie also visited every Canadian battalion as they marched in from First Army, told them frankly what they were up against, and assured them that it could be done, that with good judgement and guts, Passchendaele could be taken.

He also entered into a furious dispute with the Second Army MGRA, Major-General Sir Noel Birch, before he got those extra guns he had been promised. The Canadian Corps normally had 320 guns; Currie had that number raised to 587, and a high proportion of these were heavy weapons. These guns began firing on the German positions and soon swept away the wire that had halted the Australians at Bellevue Spur. Currie then ordered the very heavy guns, the 9.2-inch and 12-inch howitzers, to concentrate their fire on the pillboxes. These concrete emplacements could not often be destroyed, but the effect of a heavy shell or shells landing on the roof sent such a concussion though the structure that the men inside were soon reduced to despair.

Currie also sent forward the formidable Canadian machine-gun companies, who began to sweep the area in the rear of the enemy defences with a nightly blizzard of fire, preventing the arrival of food and supplies or the relief of men in the German front-line positions. The Germans were not slow to respond and great artillery duels were soon taking place between the Canadian and German gunners, in which the former did no more than hold their own. Finally, when the British seemed unable to provide what he considered to be an adequate supply of duckboards, Currie found a sawmill, combed his ranks for lumberjacks and had them go to the rear, fell trees, cut planks and provide enough duckboards to create a whole new network of paths through the mud. These plank roads, creeping across the mud at the rate of a quarter of a mile a day, were to be the winning weapon in Currie's ingenious arsenal. Now the front-line troops could be supplied, the guns sent forward, the wounded evacuated, and the dead recovered for decent burial.

This is not to say that all the difficulties grew easier, however. Communications were problematic, as it was impossible to bury the telephone cables in the mud and the signallers had a terrible job finding and repairing breaks. The guns settled deeper in the mud with each discharge and tended to set back and drop rounds short among the Canadian front-line trenches – and there are few things infantry detest more than being shelled by their own guns. Meanwhile, plans went ahead for the infantry attack.

Currie had decided on a three-phase attack, three setpiece engagements to carry the Passchendaele Ridge position, the objectives codenamed, in the order in which they were to be taken, the 'Red', 'Blue' and 'Green' Lines. The 3rd and 4th Canadian Divisions would take the first two positions; the 1st and 2nd were to capture the Green Line and mop up any further opposition. Not having rushed his plans, Currie was determined not to rush his attack. There would be a pause between the first and second stages of two or three days, and a pause of five or six days before the final assault on the Green Line. These attacks would take place on 26 and 30 October and on 6 November, a timetable that caused a row with General Gough. The latter had scheduled an attack by his Fifth Army for 22 October, and asked Plumer to order the Canadians to attack on the same day. The latter passed this message on to Currie, who refused to budge. Plumer then told Gough that Currie would attack when the Canadians were ready and not before, at which Gough stormed out of the meeting, asking 'Who is commanding Second Army?'

On the 22nd, the Canadian Corps moved up to relieve II Anzac, and at 0540 hours on 26 October, after a four-day barrage, the Canadian Corps went over the top. Owing to the mud, the creeping barrage moved even more slowly than usual, at 100 yards every 8 minutes. This was still too fast, for the ground offered no footing and the advance was more like wading than walking. The Canadian guns were dropping rounds short, the German pillboxes were spraying the field with fire, and the rain which had accompanied most of these Third Ypres battles was again sluicing down. The fighting went on in these terrible conditions for two days, the Canadians attacking by day and night, beating off counter-attacks and pressing on again. The fighting gradually concentrated around a position called Decline Copse on the Passchendaele Ridge, south of the village, which the Canadians took with the bayonet on the night of 27 October.

The Red Line had not been completely taken, but at least the Canadians had obtained a jumping-off position for the next phase of their attack, though at considerable cost – 2,481 men killed, wounded or missing, with casualties in some battalions reaching 70 per cent; four VCs were won. Now the next stage of the battle had to be considered. Mules came forward over the plank roads by night, bringing up supplies of food, ammunition and grenades, and when the rain died out on the night of 27–28 October some of the Canadian units were able to edge forward and take up more ground. From these positions they attacked again on the 30th.

The Canadians were not alone in their efforts. On their right, I Anzac were in action and on their left General Maxse's well-trained and hard-fighting XVIII Corps were also pushing forward. On the northern flank of Second Army General Gough was still attempting to make some headway with the

Fifth Army, fighting for the Houthulst Forest. This lower ground was an ocean of knee-deep mud, and the troops fighting through it were soon completely exhausted.

The Canadian attack on the 30th went in at dawn, 0550 hours the infantry advance accompanied by the fire of 420 guns. The aim now was to take those positions untaken on the 26th and the Blue Line positions as well. The chief hindrance, however, was the notorious Bellevue Spur that had defeated the Australians, and it was soon obvious that the Germans were determined to hang on to this position at all costs and they greeted the Canadian advance with torrents of machine-gun fire. Even so, the Canadians got on, finding the ground drier and progress easier as they advanced. A patrol even penetrated to Passchendaele village, just as the Australians had on 12 October, and like them finding it deserted, but withdrew as the fighting intensified.

Fortunes were mixed, but casualties everywhere were heavy. Several battalions lost half their men, and although the Bellevue position and the Crest Farm strongpoint were taken, the attacking battalions were used up in the process. In the 3rd Division sector, the crack Princess Patricia's Canadian Light Infantry (PPCLI) won two VCs that day, but lost 363 men, 80 per cent of the officers and 60 per cent of the men; only 200 of this fine battalion answered the roll call at the end of the day. The 49th (Edmonton) Battalion on the left of the PPCLI lost 75 per cent of the men committed . . . and still the fighting continued.

The fighting for the ruins of Passchendaele had developed into a 'soldier's battle' fought by small groups of men picking their way forward through the mud, attacking whatever enemy position lay in their path, each sub-unit supporting its neighbours with covering fire. At least the Canadians, like the British on the Menin Road Ridge, had now got the measure of the pillboxes: Currie's infantry knocked them out, one after another, by the use of fire-and-movement tactics. One section would spray the pillbox weapon slits with rifle and Lewis-gun fire while another worked its way up, using every scrap of cover, to lob grenades though the entrance or the embrasures.

It was slow, but it was highly effective. By the end of the day, although most of the objectives had not been completely taken, the Canadian Corps had advanced over half a mile and were within reach of Passchendaele. To get this far that day the corps had lost a further 2,321 men, of whom 884 had been killed. Currie decided to hang on to the ground that had been gained, and use it for launching further attacks. He had been less than impressed with the performance of Gough's Fifth Army, which should have been keeping up on his left flank but had failed to do so. Currie did not like Gough and had no faith in his abilities, which may have coloured his views, for the Fifth Army divisions were moving on far worse ground and against equally stubborn opposition; it was hardly surprising, therefore, if they fell behind.

The Canadians had now advanced far enough to be within reach of their

Green Line objectives. Currie now had to get the 1st and 2nd Divisions up and the all-important guns must be hauled forward to re-register and support the attack. This done, he intended to attack again on 6 November. The assault, the last of the Passchendaele battles, was to be an all-Canadian affair; in every other sector only the artillery would be engaged.

The Germans, too, were bringing in fresh troops, and their newly arrived 11th Division had now taken over the positions opposite the Canadian line, These men were watching their front when the two Canadian divisions came in on their positions at 0600 hours on 6 November. Currie had elected for surprise, a short barrage and a swift assault, and after just two minutes of drumfire shelling the barrage began to creep forward and the infantry, who had moved out into no man's land and therefore escaped the German fire that fell on their front-line trenches, came in close behind it. By 0745 two Canadian battalions of the 1st Division were already on the Green Line position, 1,000 yards from their assault trenches.

Meanwhile, the 2nd Division had taken Passchendaele, 'a pile of bricks with the ruin of a church, a mass of slaughtered masonry and nothing else left on this shell-swept height'. The Canadians came in close behind the creeping barrage and took the village so quickly that the defenders among the ruins could make only a token resistance. By 0740 hours Passchendaele was in Canadian hands and from the far side of the village, just 60 yards above sea level, they could see the unmarked country beyond the Salient, a land of tall trees and green fields and undamaged houses, a stunning contrast to the mud, rubble and shattered stumps they had got used to in the last few weeks.

For the next three days the Canadians consolidated their hold on the Passchendaele position. On 10 November they beat off a heavy German counter-attack, and on that day the Second Battle of Passchendaele, and the Third Battle of Ypres, officially ended. By that time General Plumer had departed for Italy, to put fresh heart into the armies there after the defeat at Caporetto, General Rawlinson had taken over Second Army, and General Byng had laid his plans for an attack at Cambrai.

Taking the Passchendaele Ridge had cost the Canadians 12,403 men killed, wounded and missing, though altogether their time in the Salient had cost them 15,654 casualties in all, almost the exact total forecast by Currie when he agreed to undertake the operation. The entire battle had cost the British and their Canadian, Australian and New Zealand allies in Second and Fifth Armies a total of 244,897 casualties of all types. This figure includes what the Official History calls 'normal wastage', and can be compared with the Somme losses which, over four more weeks, came to 419, 654 men killed, wounded and missing.

German losses were never exactly established, but the volume of the British Official History covering Third Ypres, published in 1948, gives a figure of 217,000 casualties of all types for the German Fourth Army alone. This does not include the figures for those divisions that left that army during the battle, or for those fighting in the Rupprecht Army Group; as a result, the Official History calculates the entire German losses as being nearer 400,000, which many historians have dismissed as a vast over-estimate.

The Battle of Passchendaele has gone down in history as another holocaust, a futile battle, badly handled by the generals, who purchased a useless acreage of ground with a great sacrifice of lives. That the gains of Passchendaele were vastly exceeded by the cost is too obvious to deny, but there are some reasons to suggest that the generals were not entirely to blame for all that happened there.

The aims of the offensive, to clear the Belgian coast, maintain the pressure on the German Army, assist the French while their armies were in disarray, regain the outer hills around the Salient and, perhaps, achieve a break-through, were all valid objectives. That only a few of them were achieved is not sufficient reason for not having tried to do so, while the fact that the Passchendaele Ridge was taken, the French given time to recover and the Germans further reduced, may all be chalked up on the credit side.

If Haig had halted his offensive at the end of September, or after the taking of Broodseinde early in October, his soldiers would have been spared the full horrors of the autumn offensive, and his reputation would not have been as badly damaged as it was by the allegation that he pushed his men to fight a pointless battle in intolerable conditions. The conditions were indeed intolerable, but in spite of them, some five weeks later the Canadians took Passchendaele.

By the end of September, Plumer's first two 'steps' or phased attacks had worked well. The British now held more than half the Gheluvelt Plateau, and there was good reason to assume that if they continued like this the Germans would be pushed off the Ypres ridges. The rain fell on the Germans as readily as on the British, their ground was shelled as heavily, their sufferings were as great, their losses at least roughly the same. Haig's character dictated the need to press on until Passchendaele was taken and some definite defensive line achieved, and in early October the ground was firm and the Germans on the defensive. Both Gough and Plumer advised against any idea of a breakthrough to Roulers, but felt that the advance along the ridges was feasible. The Battle of Broodseinde on 4 October took the front-line troops to within 2,000 yards of Passchendaele. And then the rains fell again.

The battles at Passchendaele were not all fought in mud and rain, however, though that is the picture retained in the popular imagination. There were spells of good weather, long enough to dry out the ground until clouds of dust became a trial to the artillery. The phases fought in dry weather succeeded, but when the rains came – and they seemed always to fall at crucial stages in the battle – the ground quickly turned into a quagmire.

Passchendaele is a battle that might almost have been a victory. It was started too late in the year, it suffered from long delays between its component parts, and from the delay instigated by Gough between Plumer's victory at Messines and the start of Third Ypres proper, and the troops were most unlucky with the weather. Knowing all this *now*, it is easy to say that the attack should have been called off after Broodseinde. A glance at the map, however, reveals that such a halt would have left the British armies in an untenable position for the winter, particularly on the Fifth Army front where the ground, seamed by streams or bekes – the Steenbeke, the Lekkerboterbeke, the Zonnebeke and several more – and anyway low-lying, would soon become a morass. When you cannot stay where you are, and do not wish to fall back, the only alternative is to push on – and pushing on would at least kill a lot of Germans.

Whatever the exact total, German losses at Passchendaele can be numbered in the hundreds of thousands. Coming as they did on top of the losses at Verdun, on the Somme, at Arras, in the Nivelle offensive, and from the steady drip of casualties suffered every day of the war, even when no major offensive was in progress, they represent a further draining away of German military strength. This strength was about to be increased, however, at least on the Western Front, for far away in Russia, a revolution had broken out. When the new rulers of Russia concluded a separate peace with the Central Powers, scores of German divisions would be freed for the Western Front.

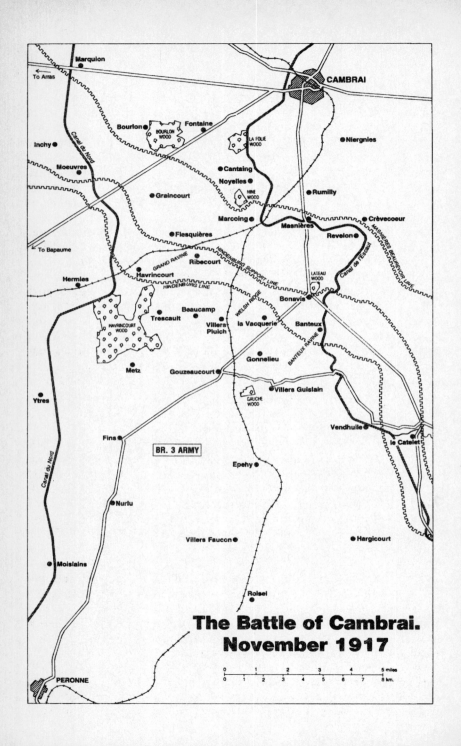

The Battle of Cambrai.
November 1917

CHAPTER 19

CAMBRAI,
NOVEMBER 1917

*'Tomorrow the Tank Corps will have the chance for which it
has been waiting for many months – to operate in good going
in the van of the battle.'*

Brigadier-General Hugh Elles, commanding the Tank Corps, 19 November 1917

The Battle of Cambrai, which began on 20 November 1917, was in the planning stage well before the battle of Passchendaele ended. It was originally planned as a 'raid', a chance to show what the tanks could do if certain factors, notably surprise and dry ground, obtained. Cambrai rapidly grew to much more than that, and is studied today as one of the most complex and interesting battles of the Great War.

The battle began exceptionally well, and rapidly took on the appearance of a stunning victory. The Hindenburg Line was breached on a front of six miles, with a depth of penetration of up to four miles. The German trenches were swiftly overrun, thousands of prisoners were taken and a hundred German guns were trundled back to the British lines. It seemed that the long-awaited breakthrough had finally been achieved, and to celebrate this victory church bells all over Britain rang out a joyous peal on 21 November. Then it all began to go terribly wrong.

Ostensibly, the Battle of Cambrai had everything. It was well planned and superbly executed, new methods were tried, old lessons applied, and the enemy both surprised and overwhelmed . . . and yet, as so often before, the advance soon petered out. The battle ended with a German counter-attack on 30 November that not only recovered all the lost ground, but also took territory that the British had held for years. How could something that had begun so well go so suddenly and terribly awry?

The story of Cambrai begins in June 1917 when Lieutenant-Colonel J.F.C. Fuller, General Staff Officer of the Tank Corps, having discussed the idea with the corps' commanding officer, Brigadier-General Hugh Elles, sent a paper to Haig's headquarters suggesting that the ground between

Cambrai and St Quentin was ideal for a sudden but brief tank attack. This part of the front was held by the Third Army, commanded by Lieutenant-General Sir Julian Byng who had five corps under command and was responsible for a front of some forty miles. The Cambrai sector lay south of the Arras battlefield on ground as yet unravaged by shellfire. The region was one of downland and open fields, interspersed with woods and copses, the ground firm and dry, and only lightly held by the German Second Army, which was snugly in position behind the defences of the Hindenburg Line. Fuller suggested that a mass of tanks could spearhead an attack here, crush the German wire, allow the infantry through to widen the breach, and then let the cavalry exploit east into open country.

This was not envisaged as a major offensive, but at the very least it would distract the Germans and prove useful in reducing their reserves around the Ypres Salient, since some would have to be sent south to defend the Cambrai sector. Fuller's paper was passed around at GHQ, but the proposal was finally vetoed by General Kiggell, Haig's Chief of Staff, who believed that the British Army should focus its attention on the coming Passchendaele attack in the Salient.

Fuller revived the proposal in August, when the tanks attached to Fifth Army were already floundering in the Flanders mud. Both he and Elles were now thinking of a tank 'raid' on Cambrai and this time the proposal had the support of General Byng, who was already considering a major push towards Cambrai and liked the idea of including a large force of tanks in his plan. This was not quite what Elles and Fuller had in mind, however; they wanted to demonstrate that tanks could penetrate the German line, even one as thick as the Hindenburg Line, where the trenches were effectively tank traps 10 feet wide, and the wire was in belts 50 yards thick. Having smashed through these defences, all that the two tank officers had in mind was the spreading of alarm and despondency behind the German lines followed by a swift return to base, the whole operation to take no more than eight hours.

Byng was thinking of something on a much larger scale and proposed that his attack could go in at some time in September. Kiggell again urged Haig to reject this proposal, on the same grounds as before, that the British armies could not cope with two major attacks at the same time. By September, however, it was becoming obvious that the Flanders attack was grinding to a halt and Haig began to consider a thrust on some other part of the front to draw off German reserves and raise spirits at home, not least among the members of the Cabinet. The idea of an attack on Cambrai was therefore re-examined, and its merits recognised. On 13 October Byng was authorised to start planning an attack, with Z-day fixed for 20 November, although the basic concept of the operation had by now changed. This was no longer a tank raid. It was to be a full-scale attack aimed at securing a breakthrough, but on a strictly limited time scale.

Byng and his staff began planning the attack with great enthusiasm but rapidly discovered a few snags, the chief of which was a shortage of reserves to push through any breach the tanks might make. Previous accounts in this book have illustrated the importance of adequate reserves, but those that existed in October 1917 were needed in Flanders. Haig therefore told Byng that he must manage with only the usual reserves available to Third Army, plus the Cavalry Corps, adding that if the attack did not achieve some definite results in forty-eight hours he would call it off.

The cavalry force available to Byng – the Cavalry Corps of five divisions under the command of Lieutenant-General Sir Kavanagh – was not inconsiderable, and since cavalry was still the only arm mobile enough to exploit a breakthrough, this was clearly most useful. Byng was planning an initial breakthrough by seven divisions of infantry and three brigades of tanks, towards and around the town of Cambrai, on a 10,000-yard front between two waterways, the Canal de l'Escaut and the Canal du Nord. The first objective was the village of Flesquières and the ridge of the same name, which overlooked the Hindenburg Line south-west of Cambrai. Then the attack would swing north, across the Bapaume–Cambrai road, to take the Bourlon Ridge. Finally, while the Cavalry Corps exploited south and east of Cambrai, the rest of the force, supported by V Corps, the reserve formation, would push north.

The attack would be in three phases. In the first part, seven divisions drawn from III and IV Corps, supported by tanks, would break through the Hindenburg Line and capture the canal crossings at Masnières and Marcoing. Then the Cavalry Corps would come up, cross the canal and advance to the east of Cambrai, while IV Corps took Bourlon Ridge and Wood, west of the city. Cambrai, and the surrounding country would be captured and all the German divisions in the north and east of the city would be destroyed. The initial attack would be confined by the Canal du Nord, which was dry and empty, and by the Canal de l'Escaut; the latter, however, was full of water and a formidable obstacle, though spanned by bridges which must be seized swiftly if the cavalry advance was to proceed. This first assault would be spearheaded by the tanks, which would advance without a preliminary artillery barrage and be closely followed by a mass of infantry to widen the breach for the cavalry.

Using tanks offered Byng the great advantage of *surprise*, a rare asset for a Western Front commander. In previous battles, days of pre-assault artillery bombardment had been necessary to destroy the enemy's wire and shatter his front-line trenches. These tasks were usually accomplished, but one side result was that the barrage alerted the enemy that an attack was coming – and where. Now, according to Elles and Fuller, the tanks could roll over the enemy wire and tackle the defenders in the German front-line trenches, and thus the days of preliminary bombardment were not necessary. As a result, the main use of artillery would be for counter-battery work against those German guns which might otherwise ravage the advancing infantry and cavalry, but here too technology had come to the assistance of the British gunners.

Before guns can be used effectively they have to be 'ranged' or 'registered' against the enemy positions. The usual ranging routine was for the direction and range of an enemy position to be calculated off the map, using a compass and protractor. One gun in the battery would set this range and direction on its gunsight and fire a series of 'ranging shots' at the required distance on that bearing, the fall of which would be observed and corrected by a forward observation officer. All the other guns in the battery would put the same corrections on their gunsights but would do no firing until the ranging gun was on the target. The other guns would then fire in their turn and their fall of shot would be duly corrected until all the weapons were dropping shells on the right target. These individual sight settings would then be written down, and when set on the gunsights, and the weapons adjusted for elevation and windage, should have put all the guns on that target. The battery would then register another target in the same fashion until all the likely targets within range had been calculated and recorded. The system sounds simple, as it was – if laborious – but it did not always work; it took time and it betrayed the battery's intentions to the enemy, who only had to shift position to negate the whole process. Moreover, the business of ranging was also subject to a number of technical difficulties. Atmospheric conditions, wind speed and direction, changes in the ammunition, wear to the gun's barrel and recoil mechanism, the digging in of the gun trails under the force of the recoil, all combined to vary the fall of shot, so that guns had to be corrected constantly during the actual shoot. This ranging process also enabled the enemy to fix the position of the guns and subject them to counter-battery fire which, with wire-cutting, became the principal occupation of the artillery in the days before an assault.

Now a new method of fixing the range and location of enemy batteries was being developed, after the use of aerial photography had led to the making of more accurate maps. The new system, which consisted of two processes called 'flash spotting' and 'sound ranging', was based on the fact that light travels faster than sound. The position of an enemy gun could be accurately determined from observing the flash, and the range obtained accurately from calculating the difference between the moment the flash was sighted and the moment the sound of the gun being fired was heard. Both the speed of light and the speed of sound are fixed by the laws of physics. The muzzle flash of a gun reached the observers faster than the sound of the weapon's discharge, and by comparing the time between the two it was possible to come up with an extremely accurate range to the target, thus eliminating, or greatly reducing, the time needed for the standard ranging procedure. This process became known as 'silent registration', and by adopting it the bulk of the artillery, having set their guns and calibrated their sights, were able to remain silent, until they opened up as part of the main barrage just before Zero.

In the Cambrai attack, although the main task of cutting the enemy wire was left to the tanks, artillery would still be used in quantity. Byng would have more than 1,000 field guns supporting the seven infantry divisions which would make the assault. He would also have a further two divisions in support and three in reserve from V Corps, as well as the three tank brigades, a total of 474 tanks which would be used right in strength across the front, and not scattered among the assaulting brigades in 'penny packets' of two or three tanks, as formerly at Bullecourt and Flers-Courcelette. Elles and Fuller also went to great lengths to involve the infantry commanders in tank tactics and stressed, from bitter experience in earlier tank engagements, that the tanks and infantry must stay together for mutual support, the former to tackle the wire, trenches and machine-guns that could hold up the infantry, the infantry to protect the tanks against anything the Germans might use as anti-tank weapons, and against any enemy infantry attempting to close with the machines and destroy them with grenades.

Tanks could take ground, but infantry were needed to hold it. Since both the assault tanks and the infantry needed support in these tasks, this time there were also to be a number of tanks adapted for different purposes, starting with 'fighting' tanks to crush the wire and deal with the enemy trenches. The leading tanks would carry 'fascines', great rolled-up bundles of timber which they would release into the enemy trenches to create a bridge over which the machines could cross. Thirty-two tanks were equipped with hooks and chains with which to snag the enemy wire and drag it aside. There would be a number of supply tanks carrying fuel, ammunition, water and food, as well as tanks equipped for signal work, carrying telephone cables and carrier pigeons. There were even three tanks equipped with wireless, in touch with rear headquarters and supporting aircraft; warfare was becoming sophisticated by the end of 1917. The tanks committed to the Cambrai assault were the new Mark IVs, whose front plating would resist armour-piercing bullets. These tanks were also mechanically far more reliable than the Mark Is which had taken part in the battles at Flers and Bullecourt.

The Cambrai attack would also be supported by the Royal Flying Corps, which was now taking a major part in all Western Front operations, making reconnaissance and contact patrols, bombing and machine-gunning enemy positions, bringing back a stream of photographs and information to GHQ and the corps commanders. Being an Army formation the RFC was organised on Army lines, and its 3 Brigade, fourteen squadrons mustering some 270 aircraft and 6 observation balloons (one for each assault division), was tasked with providing air support for Third Army. The Germans were believed to have only seventy-eight aircraft for the Cambrai front, and only twelve of these were the first-line Albatros fighters, so for the opening stages of the battle Byng's forces enjoyed air superiority.

As described above, Byng's plan called for the tanks to make a breakthrough just ahead of the infantry and lead Third Army in the capture of two important physical features, Flesquières Ridge and village in the centre, and Bourlon Wood and Ridge on the left flank, all on high ground which overlooked Cambrai, seven miles behind the Hindenburg Line. When the tanks and infantry had done that, the Cavalry Corps would pass through and surround the town itself. Finally, infantry, tanks and cavalry would then round up the Germans in the Cambrai 'pocket' before pressing on north and east towards Valenciennes.

This cavalry 'exploitation' depended on the taking of the Flesquières Ridge and Flesquierès village. There was a looming snag here, for the division tasked to take Flesquières was the 51st (Highland) Division, and its GOC, Major-General George Harper, though an excellent and much loved divisional commander, had little time for tanks. Haig was also particularly insistent that the attackers must seize the Flesquières positions and Bourlon Ridge on the first day; a study of the map on page 408 will be useful at this point, for these features were to prove crucial in the days which followed the first attack.

Field Marshal Haig and his army commanders have often been accused of bulldozer tactics, of ordering their corps and divisional commanders to make attacks which, in retrospect, stood little or no chance of success. In fact, this was rarely the case for, as was demonstrated on the Somme and elsewhere, their normal practice was to delegate any task to the lowest practicable command level, at division or even brigade, and let that commander decide how the task should be accomplished and draw up the relevant plans. Haig and his army commanders could, and often did, criticise these plans but in the end, if the junior commander wanted to carry out a task in a particular manner, he was usually allowed to proceed. General Harper of the 51st Division is a case in point, for although he was obliged to use tanks, he deployed them in 'penny packets' well ahead of his infantry. The result was that the toughest position on the entire front was tackled without the mutual support that tanks and infantry enjoyed in other parts of the field.

Another problem lay with the command of the 'exploitation' force, the five divisions of the Cavalry Corps, whose commander, General Kavanagh, elected to make his HQ at Fins, six miles behind the front line. Three cavalry divisions, the 1st, 2nd and 5th, were at Fins by 0620 hours on the morning of the battle but the other two, the 3rd and 4th, were kept further back. The cavalry were to be commanded from Corps HQ at Fins and could not move until ordered to do so by Kavanagh, which meant that any request for the deployment of the cavalry – the follow-up force for the entire attack – must go back from the front to the commander of the infantry division, thence to Kavanagh, who would give the order to the waiting cavalry divisions. In retrospect, it is obvious that these divisions should have either been placed under the direct command of the infantry corps commanders making the attack, or that Kavanagh should have taken his first three divisions up and stayed with them, close to the front line. The most vital information a commander can have is knowledge of what is going on at the front. This was always hard to come by, but the problem could be intensified if the commander was not at his headquarters when some news eventually got back. The most reliable information was coming in from the RFC contact patrols, and the custom had therefore arisen of generals staying well back, close to an airfield, in places where their telephone lines could not be cut by shellfire – and from where they, in turn, could maintain contact with their superiors.

In the Great War, it was considered far more important for a divisional commander to be in touch with his corps or army commander than with his brigade or battalion commanders. The favoured line of communication went 'up' rather than 'down', which meant that those commanders who should have been in constant touch with the front-line situation, and able therefore to react to it, were tied to their headquarters. This was a particular problem for an attacking force, since in an assault the situation was sure to be fluid and any breach needed rapid exploitation before the enemy acted to close it. At Cambrai, the siting of the Cavalry Corps HQ was such a fundamental error, such an obvious and inevitable cause of delay – and delay had ruined so many attacks in this war – that Byng or Haig should have ordered Kavanagh to move his headquarters forward, rather than risk the kind of delays that had proved so disastrous at Loos and elsewhere. That they did not do so remains both unexplained and inexplicable.

The enemy defences opposite Third Army were held by troops of the German Second Army, under the command of General G. von der Marwitz. His army was part of the Army Group commanded by Crown Prince Rupprecht of Bavaria, and consisted of six infantry divisions in two corps or 'groups', the 'Arras Group' and the 'Caudry Group'. This part of the front did not have the physical defensive advantages of the Somme or the Salient, so the German prepared positions had been made particularly strong and, being part of the Hindenburg Line, were both intricate and extended to a great depth. First came the main Hindenburg Line, part of which was on a slope overlooking the Grand Ravine, a dry shallow gully before the British front line; there was also a strongly fortified trench system ahead of the Hindenburg Line, on the forward slopes. A mile behind the front line was the Hindenburg Support Line, and three to four miles behind that lay yet another defensive position, the Beaurevoir–Masnières–Marcoing Line. The average depth of the German defences before Cambrai was five miles.

This position had trenches dug in the chalk up to 18 feet deep and dugouts up to 40 feet deep, and all the defending troops had been trained in new defensive tactics. No longer did the Germans occupy their front-line trenches during bombardments. When shells began to fall, the bulk of the troops took cover deep underground, leaving a few sentries in well-protected posts to look out over no man's land and warn when the barrage lifted. There were also pillboxes of reinforced concrete, impervious to anything but a direct hit from a super-heavy gun, each equipped with machine-guns and having a wide field of fire over the belts of wire. The Germans had calculated that to break through this section of the front would take weeks, and that they would therefore have ample time to bring up reserves and seal off any breach. The defenders were also supported by a number of counter-attack divisions, currently resting and training well behind the line, but ready to rush up to the front and drive the attackers out again. There were three elements in this form of defensive position. The first and second were strong defences and resolute defenders. These would take a toll of the attackers and slow down any advance, and then the third element would come into play, the rapid deployment of counter-attack divisions to drive the assaulting infantry back. For the British the crucial element that would undermine this position and thwart the counter-attack divisions was *surprise*, and Byng made great efforts to obtain it. The tanks were brought up by night over 15–18 November, the noise of their engines covered by machine-gun fire, and were carefully hidden in woods or camouflaged to conceal them from enemy aircraft. The staff work was superb – as it needed to be, for the logistical problems were daunting. The tanks alone needed 165,000 gallons of petrol, 75,000 of oil and grease, 500,000 rounds of 6-pounder ammunition and 5 million rounds of .303 for their machine-guns – all this volatile matériel had to be brought up and secreted close to the front in the few days before the battle.

Finally, on the evening of 19 November, all that could be done had been done. Elles, commanding the tanks, decided to finish his preparations by writing an Order of the Day for his corps. His words are worth recalling, as they rebut the statements of those historians who accuse all the generals of staying in châteaux well behind the lines, and of taking no part in the battle.

SPECIAL ORDER NO. 6

1. Tomorrow the Tank Corps will have the chance for which it has been waiting for for many months – to operate on good ground in the van of the battle.
2. All that hard work and ingenuity can achieve has been done in the way of preparation.
3. It remains for unit commanders and tank crews to complete the work by judgement and pluck in the battle itself.
4. In the light of past experience I leave the good name of the Corps with great confidence in their hands.
5. I propose leading the attack of the Centre Division.

Signed
Hugh Elles, Brig.-Gen.
Commanding Tank Corps.

This order was read to all the tank crews that night and its effect might be imagined. At 0600 hours next morning, Tuesday, 20 November, General Elles took his position in the top of *Hilda*, the leading tank of H Battalion in the Centre Division and shook out the brown, red and green* Tank Corps

---

* Symbolising 'Through mud and blood to green fields beyond'.

flag he had brought up for the occasion. Zero hour for the attack was 0630 on the morning of Tuesday 20, November and all the tanks were on the start line an hour before. The British infantry were now sending out parties to cut gaps in their own wire ready for the advance. This activity was observed by the enemy and the German guns began to fire on the British front-line trenches.

Dawn came slowly, bringing with it mist and a thin rain, and at 0620 the artillery began to fire smoke and high-explosive shells on to positions behind the German front line. Ten minutes later, concealed behind this barrage and the dense cloud of smoke, the British infantry began to move forward. Led by the tanks, they had soon crossed the 500 yards of no man's land and were making their way through the gaps made by the tanks in the German wire.

On the whole, defeats provide more stories than victories, and the account of the first day of Cambrai can be quickly told. By 0800 hours the whole of the main Hindenburg Line position, from Havrincourt south to the Canal de l'Escaut, had been taken. The Grand Ravine, which had seemed to be a great obstacle, had proved to be no more than a shallow valley, while the apparently impenetrable Hindenburg Line was now a mass of flattened wire, beyond which the British tanks were ranging east, machine-gunning and shelling the remaining defenders in the German communication trenches, strongpoints and dugouts. Hundreds of prisoners were walking slowly to the rear and the tanks and infantry were now moving on inexorably towards the Hindenburg Support Line. General Elles had stayed in *Hilda* as she forged through the German wire, but the tank had ditched; besides, he could do no real good in the front line anyway. He therefore walked back to his headquarters at Beaucamp, thoroughly delighted with the performance of his corps. All seemed to be going well, and the need now was to keep up the momentum of the attack and get the cavalry forward before the German reserves arrived. The question growing in the minds of the infantry commanders, however, was 'Where is the cavalry?'

The Cambrai attack had come as a terrible surprise to the Germans. Marwitz, dragged from his bed by his anxious staff, rapidly realised that the British had already broken through the Hindenburg Line at Havrincourt. Once appraised of this fact Crown Prince Rupprecht saw his entire southern front collapsing and sent an urgent plea for reinforcements to Ludendorff. The latter promised to send divisions as soon as possible, but added that this would take at least forty-eight hours; meanwhile, he said, Rupprecht should hold on, muster what force he could, and counter-attack if possible.

Such an attack did not seem at all likely, however, for the British were still advancing. By 1130 hours they had taken a large part of the support line, advanced over two miles on a six-mile front, wiped out three German divisions, and taken a number of guns and some 2,000 prisoners. The citizens of Cambrai were waiting for liberation, and the advancing British infantry were looking over their shoulders, waiting for sight of the cavalry. Victory seemed to be within their grasp everywhere but on the Flesquières

Ridge and at Flesquières village, where the 51st(Highland) Division were in trouble.

The village of Flesquières lay on the crest of the ridge, in the centre of the front chosen for the British assault. From Flesquières there was good observation over most of the front of attack, and by advancing through the village the 1st Cavalry Division were to spearhead the move on Cambrai – but first Flesquières must be taken. This was the task of the 51st Division, and it was one that clearly required the support of tanks. As we have seen, though, General Harper did not approve of tanks, and although he had reluctantly accepted the order to use the seventy allotted to his division, he did so without enthusiasm. His attack went in at Zero hour, led by the tanks, but on his divisional front the infantry stayed well behind them, not close in their tracks as elsewhere, and that essential co-operation between infantry and armour, the latter to breach the line and deal with the machine-guns, the former to take the enemy position *and hold it*, was completely lacking. The lesson that tanks and infantry have to work together had yet to be learned by Harper and his division.

The main Hindenburg Line was penetrated by the tanks and fell quickly, long before Harper thought it would. The division should then have pressed on, but its general decided to stick to his original plan and ordered his men to wait for one hour before pressing on to attack Flesquières – village and ridge – and the support line. While the division was waiting, the men rooting about in the enemy dugouts for food and cigars, reinforcements from the German 27th Reserve Infantry Regiment arrived at the Flesquières position. German artillery, drawn up in dead ground behind the ridge, also remained unmolested, and the guns began to engage those tanks – unsupported by infantry – that came probing over the top of the ridge. Eleven were put out of action here before the infantry came forward again.

The Highland Division began to move forward once more at 0930 hours. They again advanced with the tanks well in front of the infantry, utterly unaware that German guns were in ambush on the far side of Flesquières Ridge. As the machines came over the crest, exposing their lightly armoured bellies, these guns opened fire. Within half an hour twenty-seven tanks were on fire or abandoned along the ridge and although the advancing Highlanders soon shot down the gunners and silenced the guns the damage had been done; at just after 1000 hours the British attack at Flesquières had been halted. As has been said, the essence of armoured warfare is that tanks and infantry must work together, for both are vulnerable separately. General Harper's stubborn refusal to accept the disciplines of tank warfare was to cost his division dearly and deny General Byng an outright victory on the first day of Cambrai.

This slaughter of the tanks was later attributed to the gallantry of a single German officer, who allegedly manned and fired a gun on his own after its crew had been killed. This now seems highly unlikely, but whatever was the exact cause, the British attack on Flesquières stalled. Heavy machine-gun fire from the village was sweeping the ridge and the tanks that could have dealt with it had been destroyed. A battalion of German troops was dug in among the ruined houses and shattered walls of Flesquières and they held out all day, fighting off the British infantry and making the useful discovery that a bag of grenades thrown under a tank would usually blow the track off.

The tanks and the 51st Division infantry continued to attack Flesquières, but their attacks were not co-ordinated. Tanks got into the village, but since no infantry came up in support, they withdrew. Then the infantry attacked but, lacking tank support, the platoons were ravaged by German machine-guns. Harper continued to make frontal attacks and the two divisions on his flanks, the 6th and the 62nd (2nd West Riding), which could have put in flank attacks on Flesquières with their own tanks in support, were too busy with their own tasks. The fight for the village went on throughout the day, but it stayed firmly in enemy hands. A battalion of stubborn German infantry and a few guns had succeeded in halting an entire British division and a brigade of tanks.

Elsewhere the attackers fared better. With tanks and infantry working closely together, IV Corps drove ahead relentlessly into the enemy line, with the 12th (Eastern) Division soon taking the Bonavis ridge and commanding the Canal de l'Escaut on the right flank of the advance. Losses had been small, and fifty-five of the seventy-six supporting tanks were still in action when the division regrouped on the Hindenburg Support Line. The 6th Division, attacking to the right of Flesquières, had encountered very little opposition and by 1100 hours had penetrated the main Hindenburg Line and captured their sector of the Support Line. Objectives beyond this line, at Nine Wood and Marcoing, were also taken, and in the early afternoon a squadron of cavalry from the 5th Cavalry Division came galloping up to capture the village of Noyelles.

By the middle of the afternoon, therefore, Third Army had achieved a remarkable success. Their forward positions now ran from Gonnelieu in the south, east to Latteau Wood and then north to Marcoing, Nine Wood, Noyelles, Flesquières, Graincourt and so to the Canal du Nord. This represented an advance of five miles on a six-mile front and most of the credit was justly given to the tanks which, in punching a wide breach in the Hidenburg Line, had done all they had promised to do. Only at Flesquierès were the Germans still holding out, but this position was now untenable since there were British divisions on either flank. A break-through had been achieved and the task now was to exploit it – and that required the cavalry.

At Zero hour that morning three cavalry divisions, the 1st, 2nd and 5th had been waiting at Fins. Two others, the 3rd and 4th, were further west, at Athies and Bray, and the plan was to move these two forward to Fins as the first three divisions were committed to the battle. This commitment would come when the Cavalry Corps commander, General Kavanagh, or General Byng were able to see how the battle was progressing. When news arrived that the offensive was going wonderfully well, however, both generals refused to believe it.

Given the results of previous British assaults on the Western Front, this scepticism is understandable, but the effect was most unfortunate. Kavanagh was not ready to commit his regiments when the first reports came in, and when these reports were finally accepted as giving a true picture of the battle, it took time to issue and distribute orders. The 1st Cavalry Division was not ordered forward until 0825 hours, and it was not until two hours later that the leading files of this division began to move to Flesquières, on the mistaken assumption, based on an RFC report, that the village had been taken by the Highland Division.

The rare sight of masses of horsemen moving up to the front was a wonderful spectacle to the files of infantry plodding forward across the open downland, but the cavalry advance did not last long. When word reached the 1st Cavalry Division that Flesquières was still holding out, the whole force moved into the shelter of the Grand Ravine and waited for further orders to advance. None arrived and the division stayed there, though the country on either side of Flesquières was wide open and ideal for exploitation.

The 5th Cavalry Division was on the move from Fins, trotting out at just after noon and making its way forward towards Masnières and Marcoing, two villages on the Canal de l'Escaut, while the 2nd Cavalry Division, making for Marcoing, did not move out until 1400 hours. These unfortunate delays were entirely the fault of the corps commander, Kavanagh, who was still at Fins, well to the rear of his leading divisions, seemingly unaware of the situation up at the front and unable or unwilling to commit them to the advance.

This was both a tragedy and a grave mistake, for the whole purpose of cavalry in this war was *exploitation*. Now that the RFC had taken over the cavalry's former role of reconnaissance, exploitation – pushing through a breach in the enemy line to spread alarm and confusion and pave the way for a further advance by the infantry – was the sole reason for retaining cavalry forces at all. Now such an opportunity existed, but Kavanagh's divisions were not ordered to exploit it. As Bryan Cooper wrote in his *The Ironclads of Cambrai* (1967): 'In every sector of the Front, where opportunities occurred for exploitation by the cavalry, these were delayed until the necessary orders had been received from Cavalry Corps HQ and by then it was usually too late.'

One position that should have been taken was the village of Cantaing, which occupied an important position just west of Cambrai, between the Canal de l'Escaut and the village of Fontaine. Cantaing was empty at 1340 hours but by the time the 1st Cavalry Division moved up to it at 1600 the Germans had reoccupied the position and greeted the advancing horsemen with machine-gun and rifle fire, forcing the leading regiment, the 4th Dragoon Guards, to pull back. This was November and days were short, and it was not until night had fallen that the cavalry could move forward once more.

A great opportunity had been lost, but worse was to follow. Horses need rest, grain and water, and water was not available in the forward areas. Kavanagh therefore ordered the 2nd and 5th Cavalry Divisions to pull back to Fins. This they duly did, and most of the 1st Cavalry Division, which had been champing at the bit in the Grand Ravine all day, came back with them. Elsewhere, those cavalry regiments that did get ahead were soon forced to stop. To get across the Canal de l'Escaut it was necessary to take the bridges at the village of Masnierès before the Germans could blow them up. The tanks leading the advance on Masnières did not arrive in time to stop them being blown, and one partially destroyed bridge collapsed when a tank attempted to cross it. A number of cavalry regiments then came up, but the only unit to get across was a squadron of the Fort Garry Horse from Alberta, part of the Canadian Cavalry Brigade of the 5th Cavalry Division, which crossed the canal on a footbridge and went rampaging ahead, losing two-thirds of their strength before they withdrew to Masnières. The actions of the Fort Garry Horse apart, the overall contribution of the Cavalry Corps to the first day at Cambrai was almost zero.

The effect of Kavanagh's decision to recall the cavalry to Fins was to see most of the gains made by the tanks and infantry negated on 30 November, but the cavalry were not the only units to fall short of requirements. Flesquières village still held out, and Bourlon Ridge and Wood were still untaken. No general expects complete success in every part of a major attack, and at Cambrai some reverses were inevitable. The fact remains, however, that a major breach had been made in the Hindenburg Line on the 20th, and the only reserves available to exploit it – the cavalry – were now back where they had been before the battle started. That this was allowed to happen is a reflection on both Kavanagh, the corps commander, and Byng, the army commander, who should have taken a closer interest in the actions of his only reserves at this critical juncture in the battle. A great victory had been achieved on 20 November, but unless it could be exploited, it would lead to nothing.

The night of the 20th-21st saw a great deal of activity on both sides of the line. Casualties on the British side had been small, just over 4,000 men killed, wounded and missing, but the troops needed food and water, more ammunition and grenades, and the artillery had to be brought up to support further movement on the next day. The tanks were also in need of maintenance. Of the 374 'fighting' tanks which had rolled out that morning just under half, 179, were already out of action, from enemy action, mechanical breakdown or because they had ditched. Frantic efforts were being made to get as many as possible back into fighting trim, but to fill the gaps those tanks that had been tasked to clear the wire away on the first day were now sent back to the assault battalions. All had to be refuelled, re-armed and serviced. There was no rest for the tank crews, but the knowledge of all they had achieved that day kept the men working hard all night, preparing for fresh successes on the morrow.

At their respective headquarters, Haig and Byng were jubilant, although the former was concerned that the Bourlon Wood position had not been taken and put that forward as a priority task for the following day. By the time Byng issued his orders for the next phase, at 2000 hours on the night of 20 November, the tasks facing Third Army were clear.

The main requirement was to press on before the Germans could muster their reserves and seal the breach. In the light of this, IV Corps were therefore ordered to take Bourlon Wood, an objective Byng listed as 'of paramount importance', and tanks and RFC squadrons were tasked to support the corps in this. Meanwhile III Corps were ordered to capture the Masnières–Beaurevoir–Marcoing Line, and especially to take Masnières so that the cavalry could pass through and cross the Canal de l'Escaut. Since this was considered the easier assignment, 3 Tank Brigade, attached to III Corps, was sent to support IV Corps. This move had an unwelcome side effect, however, for in their move across the rear area the tanks managed to sever most of the telephone lines linking the forward units with their headquarters, with the result that a severe communications problem arose at a critical time.

The Germans spent that night trying to recover from a disastrous day. Three of their divisions had suffered severely and a great many guns had been lost. At one point in the evening, orders were issued to prepare Cambrai for street fighting but as the British attack slowed and no exploitation was made, the Germans, ever resilient, managed to establish a viable defensive line – the Cantaing Line – between Moeuvres, Cantaing and Revelon, into which every spare company and newly arrived battalion was hurriedly flung. They must hold on and gain time, for it was considered unlikely that the divisions ordered up to Cambrai could arrive before 23 November. Nevertheless, as the night wore on the German position grew stronger everywhere as divisions and regiments behind Cambrai were combed for troops, and every spare man and gun was sent forward. There was, too, another factor that the Germans hoped would work to their advantage: as dusk fell on 20 November it began to rain, and it continued to do so heavily for most of the night.

When dawn came it was still raining, as it would all day. The first effect was greatly to hamper flying operations and the movement of tanks – most unfortunately, since the support of armour and aircraft was vital to the success of the main attack on Bourlon Wood. The day began with good news, however, when it was discovered that Flesquières was deserted. The men of the 51st (Highland) Division moved into the village at 0600 hours and pushed on from there over the ridge to Cantaing, where they were greeted by heavy machine-gun fire. Fighting along the Cantaing Line, a position the cavalry should have taken on 20 November, was to go on all day, but it soon became apparent that any success here depended on the eviction of the Germans from Bourlon Wood, which dominated the Cantaing Line and where the enemy had assembled a mass of machine-guns and artillery.

General Harper did not wait for the wood to be taken. Cavalry had now moved up on his flank and with the Queens Bay's (2nd Dragoon Guards) in support he sent his 154 Brigade against Cantaing without the assistance of tanks. The Highlanders were checked by fire from the German trenches and the cavalry were held off by machine-guns and artillery. Then the tanks arrived, thirteen from B Battalion, Tank Corps, and quickly broke into the village with the infantry and dismounted cavalry mopping up behind. By 1300 hours Cantaing had fallen, and 400 prisoners had been taken before the tanks withdrew to refuel.

Tanks from H Battalion also took the village of Fontaine, four miles from the outskirts of Cambrai, bursting through the Cantaing Line and getting into the village half an hour before the infantry came up. The infantry, Seaforth Highlanders and Argyll and Sutherland Highlanders from the 51st Division, duly occupied Fontaine but were out on their own for, unknown to the tank commanders and at least to some of his battalion commanders, Harper had ordered his troops to cease attacks on the Cantaing Line until Bourlon Wood had been taken. Byng and Harper could not know it, but that decision marked the end of the British advance in the Battle of Cambrai. From Fontaine it was no great distance to the outskirts of Cambrai and had the cavalry come up and moved forward much might have been achieved, but Harper's order to wait stopped any further advance.

Bourlon Ridge, with its wood and the village of Bourlon, was a key position in the Cambrai fighting, dominating both the battlefield area and the thoughts of all the senior British commanders, from Haig to Harper. The task of clearing Bourlon Wood on the 21st was given to the 62nd Division and the unit chosen for the attack was 186 Brigade, commanded by Brigadier-General R.B.T. 'Boys' Bradford, VC, just twenty-five years old and the youngest general on the Western Front. Bradford had the support of eighteen tanks from G Battalion and some squadrons from 1 Cavalry Brigade. He had no objections whatsoever to tanks, and therefore held up his attack until the machines had arrived and their commanders had been briefed on their tasks.

Even so, the attack did not go well. Positions that might have fallen easily the previous day were now resisting strongly, the German troops in the Hindenburg Support Line at Bourlon proving particularly stubborn, though the position was finally penetrated at one point. The tanks got into Bourlon Wood but the infantry were raked by machine-gun and artillery fire and were unable to support them. Bradford's brigade battered their way forward but were eventually forced to dig in and hold the gains they had made, with the bulk of the Bourlon position still untaken. The attack would have to be renewed on the following day, when the task would be even harder.

Third Army were attacking everywhere on 21 November, but with mixed fortunes. In their sector, III Corps had concentrated on capturing Masnières as a prelude to a major attack on the entire Masnières–Beaurevoir–Marcoing Line, a position which followed the course of the Canal de l'Escaut. The village fell after a day of street fighting and was in British hands by 1600 hours. While this was being done the main task of the corps began, a push against a mile-wide section of the Masnières–Beaurevoir Line, between the Cambrai road and the village of Crèvecoeur, a combined attack by two brigades, one each from the 20th and 29th Divisions. This attack began well but quickly stalled as the infantry could not get across the canal bridges, which were under heavy fire, and the tank commanders could not cross because it was feared that the bridges would not support the weight of their machines.

The Germans had clearly recovered from the shock of the mass armoured attack on the first day and were starting to stalk the tanks as they roved before their positions, firing armour-piercing bullets into their vulnerable sides and rear, where the armour was less thick. At 1030 hours the enemy also put in their first counter-attack, a regiment of the German 107th Division moving against the village of Noyelles. This position was held by men of the Royal Fusiliers, the Middlesex Regoment, and dismounted troopers of the 18th Hussars, and after a day of close-quarter street fighting the enemy were driven out. German counter-attacks were now being made all along the British front and by nightfall it was apparent that holding on to the ground already taken might not be easy, and that pushing on was becoming ever more difficult. Before the battle started Field Marshal Haig had declared that he was prepared to break it off after forty-eight hours if the attack stalled or no further gains seemed possible. That decision, to hold on or continue the offensive, still had to be made, but in the meantime the troops were told to dig in and hold the ground gained while their commanders made an assessment of the situation.

For Third Army, 21 November had not been a good day. Poor staff work, the delays in getting orders forward after the telephone lines had been cut by the tanks, and the stubborn refusal of General Harper to fight a modern battle, had all contributed to the slowing down of the attack. The infantry had rapidly become used to the comforting presence of the tanks – even in Harper's 51st (Highland) Division – and were increasingly reluctant to move without them. As for the cavalry, they had done very little and had come to be regarded by the infantry as a useless frill cluttering up the battlefield, at least in their mounted role, though cavalry regiments did sterling service when fighting on foot. Very little had been achieved by III Corps, and IV Corps and the Cavalry Corps had only completed the tasks they should have carried out on the previous day. The pattern of Cambrai was beginning to assume an all too familiar, Western Front form: initial success, decline of momentum, stalemate.

The German strength was now steadily increasing. Three fresh divisions had already arrived at the front and six more were promised. Crown Prince

Rupprecht had combed the Fourth Army for guns and men, and if he could hold on one more day, until the morning of the 22nd, he would have enough artillery and men to launch a counter-attack. For a brief while the initiative still rested with Haig and Byng. They now had to decide what to do with that advantage.

Clearly, not much more could be done on the III Corps front, where the advance had come up against the Canal de l'Escaut and the bridges were down and under fire. On the other hand, if the Bourlon Ridge position could be taken, the Hindenburg Line would be compromised along a wide sector of the German front. Haig therefore had a tough decision to make. Should he cut his losses, revert to the 'raid' notion originally proposed by Fuller and Elles, and pull back, or should he carry on attacking at Bourlon and see what could be achieved there?

Given Haig's stubborn character, the decision to press on could not have been long in doubt, but there were almost certainly other factors affecting his decision. Third Ypres had ended and the cost of getting to the Passchendaele Ridge had been high. The church bells of Britain had rung out to celebrate the victory of 20 November, but if it all ended in another costly stalemate Lloyd George would have another weapon to wield against his senior commanders. The conclusion of Haig's deliberations was that III Corps would go over to the defensive and hold the line of the Canal de l'Escaut, while IV Corps would devote all its strength to the capture of the Bourlon position.

Having arrived at this decision by 2100 hours on 21 November, Haig and Byng had to decide how to carry it out. The first requirement was for more men. Third Army still had the three divisions of V Corps in reserve and Haig obtained permission to retain two of his GHQ Reserve divisions currently earmarked for transfer to Italy. He therefore had five infantry divisions and the Cavalry Corps with which to back up the IV Corps attack at Bourlon. With good planning and adequate tank and artillery support, this should be enough to win the day.

Bourlon Ridge is not a major physical feature. It rises from the northern side of the Bapaume–Cambrai road and is nowhere more than 50 yards high. The top of the ridge carries the wood, which extends for several hundred acres, and on the far slope is the small village of Bourlon itself. Taken individually, any one of the three German positions – ridge, wood or village – was no great obstacle, though taking even one of them had so far proved impossible. Taken together, and manned by resolute troops, the Bourlon position was very formidable indeed.

The Germans were well aware of this and were taking steps to reinforce the Bourlon position. Their right-hand sector was in the 'Arras Group' area of Second Army, under the command of General von Moser. He had four divisions holding his right flank of which three, the 107th, 119th and 214th, had units occupying the defences on or close to Bourlon Wood. Two more divisions were being hurried down from Flanders and one of these, the 3rd

Guard Division, already had one regiment in Bourlon Wood and the village. The RFC had greatly assisted the British advance, and in order to curb their bombing and strafing Jagdgeschwader I – Richthofen's Circus – was dispatched to Cambrai, and was ready for operations over the front from dawn on 24 November.

The enemy had also devised fresh stratagems for beating off tank attacks. These tactics were based on the fact that tanks without infantry are vulnerable to field or anti-tank artillery, and to the actions of hostile infantry. The Germans knew that tanks would lead the British attack and now ordered their men to take cover, refrain from firing and let the machines pass. They were then to engage the British assault troops with machine-gun fire, thereby separating the armour from its infantry support. The tanks would then be tackled by special groups equipped with armour-piercing ammunition and a good supply of grenades. This course of action represents another development in tank tactics. Tanks had been developed to support the infantry, but the Battle of Cambrai, in which the tanks were supposed to dominate the battlefield, demonstrated that armour needs infantry support. After Cambrai, the British tanks and infantry operated as mutually supporting arms.

Byng decided on a setpiece attack against Bourlon, a push on a front from Inchy to Fontaine, with the main attack by the fresh 40th Division concentrated on the central Bourlon position. He allowed a full day for preparation, intending to attack in force at 1030 hours on 23 November, following a half-hour hurricane bombardment of the Bourlon position and the laying down of a smokescreen. During the 22nd, while the tanks were mustered, refuelled, repaired and brought forward, and the artillery pounded the Bourlon position, the situation on the British front actually deteriorated. The front-line divisions attempted to consolidate their positions but constant local counter-attacks by fresh German troops prevented them from doing so, and in several places they were driven back. The most serious loss was the village of Fontaine, which the Germans took back on the afternoon of the 22nd, after General Harper had refused to reinforce the defenders on the grounds that the village could be easily retaken after the Bourlon position fell. In the coming attack, therefore, the main task of the 51st (Highland) Division was to retake Fontaine

At dawn on 23 November, Byng prepared to renew the Cambrai battle. The tired 62nd Division had been replaced by the 40th, and a total of eighty-eight tanks had been assembled in support. Three infantry battalions from the 51st Division, with thirty-six tanks in support, had the task of retaking Fontaine, while the rest of IV Corps moved on Bourlon and the German positions astride the Canal du Nord. All was ready just after dawn, and at 1030 hours the attack began.

The crux of the Battle of Cambrai was the fight for Bourlon Ridge. If that could be taken, victory could be claimed and the recent agonies of Passchendaele partly alleviated. Field Marshal Haig was already well aware that, in Britain, the rumblings of discontent over that battle were rising to an all-out roar of disapproval, but victory is a universal panacea. Haig would not send men into a hopeless fight simply to salvage his own reputation, but he would have been less than human if he had not calculated that his own survival as C-in-C partly depended on the outcome of this attack on Bourlon.

Twenty-two tanks and the 6th Gordon Highlanders of the 51st Division made an immediate thrust for Fontaine. Three tanks got into La Folie Wood, but the 'male' tank was swiftly knocked out and without the fire of its six-pounders the other tanks and the infantry were unable to take La Folie Château in the middle of the wood. The rest of the tanks swept on to Fontaine, but there General Harper's insistence that the infantry should stay well back helped the Germans beat off the advance. The tanks were greeted with a blast of armour-piercing bullets and a shower of grenades from German positions all over the village; sixteen were either knocked out or forced to withdraw before the defenders needed to turn their weapons on the advancing infantry. The attack at Fontaine faltered, but another fifteen tanks swept past the village and led the 6th Seaforths up towards Bourlon Wood. Here again, the separation of tanks and infantry brought the attack to a halt, but Harper's men continued to batter away at Fontaine throughout the day – without result, for apart from the lamentable use of tanks, the Highlanders were outnumbered. No more than two battalions were committed to the attack at any time, and yet some ten German battalions were defending the village.

The main attack on Bourlon Wood and Bourlon village was in the hands of the 40th Division. Their assault was preceded by a bombardment on the edge of the wood which turned into a creeping barrage – 100 yards in 5 minutes – as the assault went in. Clearing the wood was the task of 119 Brigade, assisted by sixteen tanks of G Battalion, but these had not been able to refuel and failed to arrive by Zero hour. At the last minute, therefore, four tanks of D Battalion were transferred from the group of thirteen machines which had the task of helping 121 Brigade take Bourlon village.

The attack by 119 Brigade went well. Spearheaded by the 19th Royal Welsh Fusiliers and the 12th South Wales Borderers, within an hour they had advanced halfway through Bourlon Wood, led by the three tanks, which did great execution among the machine-gun posts. As the infantry halted to reorganise in the middle of the wood they had a heartening reinforcement when thirteen of the G Battalion tanks originally tasked to support them came rumbling up the slope. With their assistance the Welsh battalions pressed on and by 1245 hours had taken the northern edge of the wood. However, the South Wales Borderers had been cut up by machine-guns and had not managed to clear the western part of the wood, though they had pushed one company through to the edge of Bourlon village.

The village and the western edge of Bourlon Ridge were the task of 121 Brigade, an assault spearheaded by the 20th Middlesex and the 13th

Yorkshire Regiment (Green Howards). The attack was not a success. The tanks forced their way into the village, rolling over barricades and knocking down garden walls, but the infantry were unable to follow in the face of fierce resistance from the well-dug-in and carefully concealed German infantry, who sent out parties to ambush the tanks. The attack was also compromised by the failure of the 36th (Ulster) Division assault on their left, and the Middlesex and Green Howards were eventually forced to pull back from the village and take up a position running south and west back to their start line. West of the Canal du Nord, 108 Brigade of the 36th Division made better progress, the village of Moeuvres, being taken by the Royal Irish Fusiliers and the Royal Irish Rifles. These battalions had no tank support, but did get help from the air, RFC fighters diving down to strafe enemy positions.

By mid-afternoon, the IV Corps attack had done fairly well, driving a deep salient into the German line, taking most of Bourlon Wood and about half the ridge. However, Bourlon village and the villages of Fontaine and Moeuvres on the right and left flanks of the main attack had not been taken . . . and then, at about 1500 hours, the Germans counter-attacked.

The counter-attack started with a half-hour bombardment of Bourlon Wood, followed by the advance of several German Guard battalions. The two Welsh battalions beat off this attack with rifle and Lewis-gun fire and by dusk had managed not only to push the enemy back, but had also taken the crest of the ridge. When troops of the 51st (Highland) Division came up on their right, a continuous defence line was formed from the top of Bourlon Ridge down to the western outskirts of Fontaine.

At the end of the day the result was inconclusive. The centre had done well and seized most of Bourlon Wood, but the flanks had made no real progress. If Byng and Haig elected to reinforce success and push ahead in the centre tomorrow, the result would only be to increase the depth of the salient which the Germans would surely pinch off with flanking attacks from Fontaine and Moeuvres. The crux of the battle for Bourlon had now switched to the flanks.

There were other problems. Richthofen's squadrons had appeared and were already shooting down British machines, beginning to establish air superiority over this section of the front. The tanks had been in action for several days and needed to be withdrawn for maintenance and to rest the crews. Only twelve tanks, from the hundreds that had attacked on the 20th, would be available on the 24th. It was raining hard, sometimes turning to snow, and if the attack was resumed more troops and more artillery must be found, not least to compensate for the shortage of tanks.

Byng studied the problem and made his dispositions. The Guards Division relieved the 51st (Highland), and dismounted troopers from the 1st and 2nd Cavalry Divisions were put at Byng's disposal for an attack in the centre, against Bourlon village. This was to be made by 121 Brigade of 40th Division, supported by the twelve tanks, and Zero hour was set for noon on

24 November. During the morning of the 24th this was changed to 1500 hours, and then the IV Corps commander, Lieutenant-General Woollcombe, postponed the attack until the following day to allow him time to find more tanks. This decision did not reach 121 Brigade however, and at 1500 hours they went into the attack.

The result was a shambles. The tanks went ahead and, entering Bourlon village, rooted out most of the machine-gun nests on the outskirts, but behind them the Highland Light Infantry (HLI) and the Suffolk Regiment failed to keep up. Some infantry came up later, and part of the HLI got into the village, but the rest of the brigade was held outside. Matters were also deteriorating in Bourlon Wood, where the Germans had put in another counter-attack at 0845 that morning, and had then attacked repeatedly throughout the day. These counter-attacks were supported by intense artillery fire, but cost the Germans heavy casualties. The British managed to hang on and when dusk fell most of the wood and the ridgeline were still in their hands, but no further progress had been made.

The battle was slowly swinging in the Germans' favour. They were bringing up more divisions and were bound to grow stronger, while Third Army had shot its bolt. Haig and Byng did not yet realise this, however. Again we return to one of the greatest delusions of all the Great War generals, on both sides of the line – the belief that one more push could turn defeat into victory, or restore momentum to stalemate. In this instance, the deciding factor was the existence of those five British cavalry divisions, some 40,000 mounted men, waiting at Fins to exploit a breach. The first day at Cambrai had sent hopes of a cavalry breakthrough soaring, and Haig was still in the grip of that euphoria. As a result, having visited Byng's HQ at Albert and talked the situation over, he ordered a renewal of the attack at Bourlon, and told General Kavanagh that he would have command of all operations north of Bourlon when the cavalry broke through. Perhaps such an incentive would inspire Kavanagh and put some drive into his actions, but first the Bourlon position had to be taken.

Attempts to do this continued on 25 and 26 November, but all failed. Even a thrust to rescue those elements of the Highland Light Infantry still holding on in Bourlon village was driven back. By the morning of the 25th the HLI, now out of ammunition, were forced to surrender; only eighty men were still alive. The reason for these repeated failures at Bourlon village is simple: a lack of tanks to suppress the enemy machine-guns and hinder the steady build-up of German resistance. Tanks had made the successes of Cambrai possible; a lack of tanks simply put the battle back to the *status quo ante*, into a murderous contest of attrition, and casualties were mounting. The 40th Division, after two days at Bourlon, had already lost over 4,000 men, and other divisions had suffered in proportion.

Heavy losses were the last thing Haig wanted, and on the evening of the 25th he suggested to Byng that since General Woollcombe was making no progress with his IV Corps, Byng should take personal charge of the fight for Bourlon. He also sent a message to the CIGS, General Robertson, a message which reads like a protective memorandum:

> My orders to Byng are the complete capture of Bourlon position and such tactical points on its flanks as are necessary to secure it. The positions gained are to be held and the troops are to be ready to exploit any local advantage and follow up any retirement of the enemy. Nothing beyond above to be attempted. For purposes stated, 2nd and 47th [1/2nd London] Divisions and cavalry remain at his disposal for the present. Bourlon hill is of great importance because it overlooks Cambrai and the approaches to the town as well as the country northwards to the Sensée marshes.

This note may have staved off any immediate action by Lloyd George or the War Cabinet Committee to halt the attack, but if anything worthwhile was to be achieved it must be achieved quickly. Haig therefore urged Byng to take Fontaine and Bourlon 'not later than the 27th', before consolidating on a line running along the northern crest of Bourlon Ridge, beyond both villages and Bourlon Wood. For this purpose Byng was to attack with the 62nd and Guards Divisions, with all the tanks available, and the Cavalry Corps standing by to exploit any breakthrough.

Monday, 26 November, was spent in bombarding the enemy positions. Byng proposed sending the Guards Division against Fontaine, while the 62nd Division would attack Bourlon village and the northern part of the wood. In support would be thirty-two tanks and three dismounted regiments of the 2nd Cavalry Division. Zero hour was fixed for 0620 on the 27th. As the night wore on, the tank crews and infantrymen prepared for another thrust at the ridge.

Byng and his commanders knew it would be a difficult task, but they did not know just how difficult. On the other side of the ridge General von Moser had also been preparing a counter-attack, but unlike Byng's two-division effort, Moser was making a major assault. He now had *seven* divisions on the Bourlon front, mustered into three groups, and all were being steadily reinforced with fresh men and heavy guns. By the night of the 26th, Moser and Crown Prince Rupprecht calculated that their forces were not only sufficient to beat off any British attack, but were also adequate for a local offensive. This would be the first offensive mounted by the German Army against the British since Second Ypres, more than two and a half years before, but the generals had no doubts that it would succeed. Before that offensive could be launched, however, the Germans had to endure one more day of attack at Bourlon and Fontaine.

The attempt to retake Fontaine was made by the Guards Division, with 2 Guards Brigade leading the attack. They ran into heavy machine-gun fire almost at once as they followed the creeping barrage, but by 0715 hours the

Grenadier Guards were in the village, fighting it out with defenders in cellars and strongpoints. The Scots Guards, fighting along the road to Cantaing, were supposed to link up with the Grenadiers but were badly cut up by machine-gun fire and unable to do so. The Coldstream Guards entered the village at considerable cost while the Irish Guards, attacking with great élan, took the north-eastern corner of Bourlon Wood at the point of the bayonet. These attacks were supported by eight tanks which did useful work in Bourlon Wood, but were of less help in the rubble-strewn streets of Fontaine, where the German machine-gunners were well concealed and equipped with armour-piercing ammunition.

The Guards Division was an elite force, and by 0830 the battalions at Fontaine had moved on through the village, though they had not wiped out all the defenders. They were then faced with an immediate counter-attack by nine German battalions. A terrible street fight began, the Guards beating off infantry assaults on their front and flanks while the unsubdued Germans in Fontaine began to fire into their positions from the rear. The remaining houses were soon on fire, shells were plunging on to the ruins and in the middle of all this the companies, platoons and sections of the Guards fought it out with the Germans, often hand to hand. They were heavily outnumbered and at around 1000 hours, having been ordered to withdraw, they came slowly back, bringing out their wounded and as many German prisoners as they could find. Fewer than 500 men returned to the British lines, for 2 Guards Brigade's losses in this short fight at Fontaine totalled over 1,000 men.

Meanwhile, the 62nd Division had been attacking Bourlon Wood, with two brigades up, supported by nineteen tanks. The advance through the wood went well, and two battalions of the Duke of Wellington's (West Riding) Regiment entered Bourlon village and made some progress there with the aid of tanks, until they were forced to a halt by fire from German batteries outside the village. A supporting attack from the south by two other Yorkshire battalions also penetrated the village but the attackers then came under close-range fire from German field guns hidden in the ruins, as well as from well-concealed machine-gun nests. Ten of the fifteen tanks that rolled into the village were swiftly knocked out, and after two hours of close-quarter fighting the British pulled back.

By midday, the assault had petered out all along the IV Corps line and it was apparent to all the senior British officers concerned that the Battle for Cambrai was over. There had been no breakthrough to open country, and now the only reserves available were the cavalry. To send them up would be to invite more casualties, and Haig therefore had no option but to call the battle off, ordering his men to dig in where they were while a firm defensive line was established along the Flesquières Ridge, to which they would withdraw later. This was a position that commanded the ground before Cambrai and one which Haig and Byng felt sure they could defend. This they would soon have to do, as it turned out, for on 30 November the

German Second Army came against the British line with all the power that it could muster.

The decision to launch a counter-offensive at Cambrai had been reached on the afternoon of 27 November at a conference in Le Cateau called by Crown Prince Rupprecht of Bavaria. Those attending included General von der Marwitz and the commanders of the forces which constituted the Arras, Caudry and Busigny Groups. The meeting was also attended by General Ludendorff; he was not pleased with the reverses Second Army had suffered in the Cambrai battle, and both Prince Rupprecht and Marwitz were anxious to assure him that the situation would soon be put right.

Their plan for the counter-offensive was for the Caudry and Busigny Groups to attack with seven divisions from the south-east and push directly through Flesquières and Havrincourt Wood to Metz. At the same time the Arras Group, with three divisions, would thrust south from Bourlon and link up with the other groups at Flesquières. These thrusts, if successful, would not only destroy a large number of British divisions in the new Cambrai salient, they should also retake much of the Hindenburg Line.

On the following day, 28 November, the Arras Group began a bombardment of the Bourlon line with gas and high-explosive shells. This bombardment caused a large number of casualties among the British troops and disrupted the relief of the Guards Division at Fontaine by the 59th Division, and of the 62nd Division in Bourlon Wood, which was being replaced by the 47th (1/2nd London) Division. With the arrival of the 2nd Division, one of the GHQ Reserve divisions kept back from Italy, this meant that the IV Corps front was held by fresh divisions, supported by the bulk of the Third Army artillery. To the south, however, III Corps was not so well placed. All four of the divisions which had made the attack on the 20th – and had been engaged in heavy fighting ever since – were still in the line. The southern flank of the III Corps front was held by the 12th (Eastern) Division which had the 55th (West Lancashire) Division of General Snow's VII Corps on its right flank.

Snow's corps had not been directly involved in the battle, but its commanding general had been observing the increased amount of activity across the enemy line, and was quite convinced that the Germans were planning a counter-attack in strength. He could not get this point across to Byng or Haig, even after he sent a warning on 25 November that such an attack seemed likely on the 29th or 30th and would probably come in against the Banteux Ravine, a feature which lay across the front of III Corps and his own VII Corps. Reports of the German build-up were also coming in from RFC patrols and from observers on points overlooking the battlefield. Enemy activity – ranging artillery fire, the presence of observation balloons, the sound of transport moving up by night, increased patrolling – all hinted strongly at an attack.

Byng and his staff took no notice. According to the reports coming from

Charteris at GHQ, the Germans were as exhausted as the British and, after their losses at Passchendaele and Cambrai, were in no condition to launch any major offensive. As a result, according to the Official History, 'Third Army issued no warning, ordered no movement of reserves, took no steps to ensure that troops in the rear area should be readily available.'

Fortunately, some of the divisional commanders in Third Army were more alert or more cautious. On the afternoon of the 29th, the commanders of the two divisions in position by the Banteux Ravine, Major-General Jeudwine of the 55th (VII Corps), and Major-General Scott of the 12th (III Corps), met at the village of Villers-Guislain, where their sectors joined, to consider defensive measures. As a result, machine-gun posts were established, field guns positioned and standing patrols established to cover the Banteux Ravine and give early warning of an attack. The two divisional commanders seem to have been well aware of what was pending, but quite unable to get that opinion shared by their superior officers. At 0600 hours next morning, 30 November, all that was to change.

As General Jeudwine had predicted, the German attack began on his front with a pre-dawn bombardment of his divisional positions, which gradually spread down the entire VII Corps line. After an hour of this, three divisions of General von Kathen's Busigny Group launched a fierce attack across the Banteux Ravine, deploying stormtroops and flame-throwers. This attack was supported by aircraft which came swooping down to strafe the British trenches. At the same moment artillery fire from the Arras and Caudry Groups began to fall on the III and IV Corps positions.

The German infantry swept into the 55th Division positions and while some held, the division was thinly spread out and their lines were soon penetrated as far as Villers-Guislain behind the Banteux Ravine, where, in spite of the heavy losses inflicted on the advancing enemy by their machine-guns, the defenders were forced to withdraw, leaving behind a number of heavy guns. By 0800 hours the entire VII Corps position was in danger of being outflanked on its left, and at 0900 General Snow urgently requested aid from Third Army HQ. The only reserves available at the time were the cavalry, and accordingly the 4th and 5th Cavalry Divisions, accompanied by General Kavanagh, moved up to Villers-Faucon.

Snow also requested the help of the Guards Division, so recently relieved from the line, but they had already been committed to help III Corps, which was also in trouble. The Germans were across the Banteux Ravine and now attacking the flank and rear of III Corps, while the Caudry Group attacked it from the front. The crux of the battle began to concentrate to the rear of Villers-Guislain around Gauche Wood, a feature south of the village on the road to Péronne, Gouzeaucourt, which had fallen into German hands at about 0830 hours.

Gouzeaucourt had been well to the west of the British front line and the news that it had fallen, with all that that implied, at last galvanised Byng into action. He summoned up reserves, mustered guns and began to get a grip on the battle. This was barely in time, for the Third Army front was crumbling in several places. Fortunately, having taken Gouzeaucourt with compara- tive ease, the Germans hesitated and waited for further orders before pressing west. They were also waiting for the arrival on their right flank of the Caudry Group divisions, which had put in a frontal attack north of the Banteux Ravine, forcing 35 Brigade of the 12th Division back west of Gauche Wood.

The 20th (Light) Division had been preparing a defence line north of the Canal de l'Escaut, and they were still working on this when German troops appeared in their rear, having broken through at the ravine. The troops of 59 Brigade, holding the right flank, had hardly recovered from that surprise when the Caudry Group came sweeping in against their front. The brigade fought back to back but the Germans were coming in from every direction and in great force, attempting to wipe them out. In what was often hand-to- hand fighting, whole companies were swept away, entire battalions were overrun, and the division were forced back to the slopes of Welsh Ridge, leaving behind almost half their strength killed, wounded or prisoner. They managed to find a defensible position in front of La Vacquerie and there they were able to stem the German advance.

Later reports indicate that halting the enemy's advance at any one point was not hard to do; the problem was that German infantry then appeared from somewhere else and outflanked the British position. The advancing German troops were employing the newfangled but highly effective 'infil- tration tactics', which in practice meant that when they encountered firm opposition they simply veered away to find a gap elsewhere. Another push would probably have levered the 20th Division out of La Vacquerie but instead the Germans turned north to attack the 29th Division, which was holding the line along the Canal de l'Escaut and fighting desperately to retain Masnières. This they managed to do, and thereby prevented the Germans destroying III Corps and falling on the rear of IV Corps, now heavily engaged at Bourlon.

Bourlon was attacked at 0900 hours by General von Moser's Arras Group, their attack preceded by an hour-long artillery bombardment. Then came a massed infantry assault, but with the 29th Division defending their rear, the three divisions of IV Corps at Bourlon were able to hang on to both Cantaing and Bourlon Wood, though the 47th (1/2nd London) Division was driven off the crest of the ridge. At Moeuvres, east of Bourlon Wood, the 56th (1/1st London) Division, holding part of the Hindenburg Line, found this position a disadvantage, for the German storm troopers were able to bomb their way into the heart of their position up the line's communication trenches.

The German counter-offensive had got off to a very good start. After just six hours it had almost cut off the British salient from Havrincourt up to Bourlon, and advanced up to three miles along sections of the line. Their attack from the south had done particularly well, and in the north only desperate fighting had prevented the German push from levering loose the entire British front line. To push them back the defenders needed rapid reinforcement, a counter-attack . . . and some tanks.

Cambrai began as a tank battle, but by 30 November most of the ironclads were out of action, and those that could still run were being pulled out of the line and sent west for maintenance and repair. Even so, when the sound of violent battle to the east reached the ears of the tank commanders, those majors and lieutenant-colonels who commanded the tank companies and brigades, they mustered what machines they could find, refuelled and re-armed them, and sent up a total of sixty-three to provide the hard-pressed infantry with some support.

Other support was also coming, from the Cavalry Corps, the Guards Division and the 62nd Division. The Guards retook Gouzeaucourt by 1430 hours and were joined there by twenty-three tanks, which took up positions around the village and helped to consolidate the defence. They were still holding this position at nightfall when Byng issued his orders for a counter-attack on the following day, with the aim of recapturing at least the old, pre-20 November, British line just east of the village, part of which was now in German hands.

For their part, the Germans intended to renew their attack and push west towards Havrincourt and Metz to complete the task of cutting off the British salient and the seven divisions inside it. They had not done as well as they had hoped, but there was still scope for further success, and their plan for 1 December called for a six-division thrust by the Busigny and Caudry Groups towards the line from Beaucamp to Trécault, taking Gouzeaucourt, La Vacquerie and Villers-Plouich on the way. Zero hour for this attack was 0930, but the British managed to put in their counter-attack two hours earlier with a thrust by thirty-one tanks and a force of cavalry and infantry against Gauche Wood, south of Gouzeaucourt.

Sixteen tanks led the attack by the Guards against Gauche Wood, spraying the trees and stumps with fire as they advanced, the 2nd Grenadiers running close behind their tracks to take the wood at the point of the bayonet. The fight went on all morning with cavalry troopers coming up to help the Guards snuff out the last of the German machine-guns, and by 1130 hours the wood was in British hands. The surviving tanks then pushed on to Villers-Guislain, but heavy machine-gun fire prevented the Lucknow Cavalry Brigade of the 4th Cavalry Division getting up to join them and at nightfall they withdrew. On other parts of the front the British counter-attack was less successful, but by the end of the day their line had been pushed back eastwards and the danger of a German breakthrough to Metz had been averted.

The German attacks that day succeeded in retaking Masnières on the Canal de l'Escaut and in pushing part of the British front back across the Cambrai–Bapaume road from the Hindenburg Line position, but that was all. Like the British attack ten days earlier, the German counter-offensive had run its course, though the battle was not yet over. It continued for another six days, and finally ended on 7th December when snow and rain made further attacks by either side unprofitable.

The honours at Cambrai, as on the Somme the year before, were about even. The British had first taken a piece of the German line and the Germans had retaliated by taking an almost equal amount of the British line. The casualty bill was also similar, British losses coming to just over 44,000, and German losses being estimated at between 45,000 and 55,000. Some 10,000 German soldiers had been taken prisoner on 20 November, while over 6,000 British troops had been captured in the German offensive of 30 November.

The most important lessons learned at Cambrai concerned the use of tanks. The Tank Corps had done splendidly from first to last, and though the price paid was heavy, it had proved its worth as a war-winning element on the Western Front. Casualties in men and matériel were high: 1,153 Tank Corps officers and men were listed as killed, wounded or missing, over 25 per cent of those who took part. Of the 474 tanks that went into the battle, less than a third were fit to be used again after it, but these losses were swiftly made up with new tanks, the Mark V, which had heavier armour and a more reliable engine.

There were, of course, recriminations. A battle like Cambrai which begins with high hopes and large gains, and ends with reverses and considerable losses, could not be allowed to pass away as just another Western Front engagement. Lloyd George saw Cambrai as yet another example of military bungling, and yet another reason to get rid of Field Marshal Haig. On 5 December the War Cabinet demanded an explanation from Haig, insisting on a full and accurate account of the battle.

The main question asked by the War Cabinet was why General Byng had not sent out a warning order to his troops in the days before the German onslaught, when his front-line commanders were reporting an enemy build-up. Byng's reply was quite reasonable; namely, that since the front-line commanders knew an attack was pending, there was little point telling them about it by issuing a warning order. To tell his corps commanders something they had just told him would indeed be a pointless exercise, and the front-line commanders were clearly aware of the pending attack. This point is borne out by the evidence of the Third Army War Diary, which on 29 November notes that 'Special arrangements were made this day by III and VII Corps to meet a possible hostile counter-attack.'

In fact, the generals themselves wanted to analyse what had gone wrong. Having made their enquiries they decided that the blame rested with the junior officers and the men, citing poor command qualities in the officers and a lack of soldiering skills in the men, especially in the handling of machine-guns. In his report to Haig on 17 December, Byng cited instances of machine-gun crews retiring, and some defensive positions being abandoned, before there was any real need to do so, attributing these withdrawals to a lack of discipline and training.

There may have been a certain amount of truth in these allegations but, if so, the fault did not lie with the young officers or the private soldiers. According to the American General John. J. Pershing (of whom we shall hear more later), the troops now coming out to the British Armies in France had had only nine weeks' training, and after nine days in France – one trench tour – were sent into the line as fully trained soldiers. Warfare had become a good deal more technical in the last eighteen months – though no less terrible – and this amount of training was simply not adequate.

As for the more experienced men, most of them had taken part in at least one major offensive in 1917, at Arras or Passchendaele; many had taken part in both. As a result the men were not fully rested or in any real condition to face another battle. However valid Byng's reasons were, his blaming of his troops for the reverses at Cambrai left a bad taste, and his reputation has suffered from what was, and is, seen by many people as an attempt to smear the good name of his men. Yet this accusation against him is no more valid than the accusation against his soldiers which prompted it. Byng was intensely loyal to his troops, and always had been. He did not believe in inquests or recriminations, and had he not been asked for the causes of the Cambrai reverses he would probably have said nothing. When he was asked he gave his honest opinion, and refused to comment further or defend himself from the inevitable, subsequent, allegation that he was shifting the blame on to his troops.

Despite the failures of, notably, Generals Kavanagh and Harper, Byng refused to blame any of his subordinate commanders in his answers to the War Cabinet. Haig concurred in this. The War Cabinet next asked General Smuts to tour Third Army and report on the battle. Smuts duly confirmed Byng's views, but added that some brigade and even battalion commanders might have been partly to blame for the reverse, though he agreed that many of the troops and junior officers had not been up to the task. And there the matter rested, rumbling on until the German offensives in March 1918 turned the attention of the senior politicians and commanders to other, more urgent, concerns.

The Higher Command clearly had a case to answer, however, and for all Byng's reluctance to apportion blame heads began to roll. The cavalry had not been handled well, and Byng decided that some of his infantry corps commanders also lacked zeal, and were either tired or simply too old. Pulteney (III Corps), Snow (VII Corps) and Woollcombe (IV Corps) were all sent home over the next three months, never to command front-line troops again. In March 1918, Haig told Lieutenant-General Kavanagh that he would be replaced, but the German spring offensive intervened and Kavanagh remained in command of the Cavalry Corps until the end of the war. Perhaps surprisingly, Major-General Harper of the 51st (Highland) Division was promoted to command of IV Corps, and led that formation with some distinction in the battles of 1918.

The real reason for the reverse at Cambrai is probably the one given in his memoirs by General Ludendorff: 'The English Commander [Byng] was not able to exploit his great initial success, or we should not have been able to limit the extent of the gap.' The reasons why Byng was not able to exploit the tank breakthrough have already been explained. The Cavalry Corps' failure to push on due to Kavanagh's convoluted command structure and the distance of his headquarters from the front, as well as the failure of Harper to work closely with the tanks at Flesquières, clearly contributed to the problem, and both of these failures should have been anticipated by Byng.

His entire plan had been based on an infantry advance *supported by tanks and exploited by the cavalry*. As a cavalryman, he should have seen that Kavanagh's method of controlling his corps from Fins, and his distance from the front, obviated any chance of rapid exploitation. The facts dictate these conclusions, far more than any explanations in journals, diaries, or subsequent histories. The attack on Flesquières failed, the cavalry failed to exploit the breakthrough at Masnières, and Byng failed to do very much about it.

Cambrai is the great 'might-have-been' of the Great War. Perhaps the underlying reason why the battle went awry was summed up by the tank pioneer, Colonel Swinton, who, on hearing of the breakthrough on 20 November, remarked: 'I bet that GHQ are just as much surprised by our success as the Germans, and quite unready to exploit it.' This seems a sound judgement. Byng made very few errors in this battle, but the ones he did make were fundamental, and should have been foreseen. The same charge can be levelled against Field Marshal Haig, for very little of what happened at Cambrai was actually new. The old problem of a failure to get the reserves up to exploit the breach in the enemy line led to the old problem of statemate. Haig and Byng were lucky that the German counter-offensive did not achieve more than it did, and equally lucky to keep their jobs when the full story of Cambrai came out in January 1918.

CHAPTER 20

HAIG AND LLOYD GEORGE, APRIL 1917–MARCH 1918

'I believe that the War is being deliberately prolonged by those who have the power to end it . . . I am not protesting against the conduct of the War but against the political errors and insincerities for which the fighting men are being sacrificed; also I believe that I may help destroy the callous complacency with which those at home regard the continuance of agonies which they do not share, and which they have not sufficient imagination to realise.'

Captain Siegfried Sassoon, MC, letter to the CO of his battalion
of the Royal Welsh Fusiliers, subsequently read out in the House of Commons, 30
July 1917, and published in *The Times* on the following day

In a book that concentrates on the battles of the Western Front and the men who fought them, it is easy to forget that there was another world in Western Europe between 1914 and 1918, well outside what came to be called 'the Zone of the Armies'. The Western Front extended for some four hundred miles, but was only a few miles wide, and people only a short distance from the front had little notion of what went on there. Close to and at the front the destruction was terrible and total; years of constant shelling and frequent offensives had created a livid scar across the face of Western Europe, a scar littered with the constructions and equipment, and the detritus, of vast modern armies at war. Yet the destruction and loss of life were confined to the territory within the reach of artillery.

Just a mile beyond the range of the guns, normality began to return. For a few more miles the countryside of France and Belgium was a patchwork of camps and ammunition dumps, of engineer field parks, hospitals, and small villages occupied by resting troops, of cavalry picket lines, airfields and railway marshalling yards, all crammed with busy soldiers. Here, in the Zone of the Armies, the prevailing easterly winds brought the constant, door-slamming sound of the guns, but a mile or so further west even that faded away, leaving a world that seemed suddenly and strangely peaceful.

It took less than half a day to get from a front-line trench to Waterloo Station, and there are many accounts of soldiers who breakfasted in a shell hole and dined at the Ritz. This contrast between life at the front and life at home was so absolute that it seemed to the soldiers that the civilians lived not just in another country, but in a different world. Siegfried Sassoon said as much in his famous letter, a bitter missive which, it should be noted, attacks not the generals at the front but the politicians and public at home, the people who had the power to end this war but lacked the will, or perhaps the desire, to do so . . . or so it seemed.

As 1917 dragged its weary way towards another new year, the prospects for ending the war seemed more remote than ever, though the losses of the previous twelve months and the increased suffering and privation inflicted on the populations of all the belligerents, but especially in Germany, made it clear that the war could not go on much longer. The problem of ending the fighting remained constant, but the question was how to do so, and on what terms.

The actions of the politicians have to be seen as forming a background to the fighting at the front, rather than taking place solely in the political arena. The remark attributed to Clemenceau – who became Prime Minister of France in November 1917 – that 'War is much too serious a thing to be left to the military', is no more than the simple truth, especially in a war on the scale of that fought between 1914 and 1918. The politicians wanted a say, not just in the long-term aims and strategy of the war, but in the way that it was being fought tactically and in the deployment of the troops and their commitment to battle. While the British generals were fighting the German Army on the Western Front, another battle, less bloody but no less fierce and vital, was being waged in London between the generals and the politicians, and most fiercely of all between Field Marshal Haig and his ally at the War Office, Wully Robertson, the CIGS, and their sworn enemy, the Prime Minister, David Lloyd George. This conflict can be picked up again at the opening of the Arras offensive on 9 April 1917.

Two factors dominated strategic thinking in 1917. The first was the imminent collapse of Russia, a process which began in March 1917 when a group of workers met in the Duma, the Russian parliament, at Petrograd (St Petersburg), then the capital, and revived the revolutionary Workers', Peasants' and Soldiers' Council – or *Soviet*. The Tsar was forced to abdicate on 15 March, and he and all his family were arrested on the 20th. From that moment the final collapse of Russian will to continue the war with Germany was only a matter of time. Moreover, the situation in Russia throughout 1917 was beyond any help the Western Allies could offer, for the country was sliding remorselessly into civil war.

In May 1917 Alexander Kerensky, the Minister of Justice in the Provisional Government, was appointed Minister of War, but the Germans, sensing the chance to end the war in the east, allowed the Bolshevik activist Vladimir Ilyich Lenin, who had been forced to flee Tsarist Russia years earlier, to cross their border and enter Russia. Lenin was opposed to the continuation of the war and rapidly rose to become the leader of the anti-Kerensky Bolshevik Party. However, before the Bolsheviks could act, Kerensky ordered Marshal Alexei Brusilov to launch another offensive. The attack, which began on 1 July 1917, soon petered out, and by the end of August the Russians were in full retreat. Brusilov was sacked and the position of Kerensky – who became Prime Minister on 25 July – steadily weakened; revolution broke out in October and by 7 November 1917 the Bolsheviks were in power, while Kerensky was eventually driven into exile.

The Bolshevik leaders – Lenin, Leon Trotsky, Josef Stalin – needed a breathing space in order to fasten Communist rule firmly on their country, as well as to end the war's disastrous social and economic effects, and promptly sued for peace with the Central Powers. An armistice was declared on 16 December 1917 and a peace treaty, on terms highly favourable to Germany, was signed on 29 March 1918 at Brest-Litovsk, close to the border with what is now Poland. Between those dates the Germans transferred scores of divisions and thousands of guns to the Western Front; indeed, they were a week into their great March offensive against the British Third and Fifth Armies by the time the treaty was signed.

The second factor, a counter-balance to this disaster, was the entry of the United States into the war on the side of the Entente in April 1917. The Commander-in-Chief of the American Expeditionary Force, Major-General John J. Pershing, reached France on 22 June 1917, but it was to be many more months – in fact a full year – before a sizeable American army was fully trained and able to join in the fighting in France. Considerable arguments among the Allies lay ahead as to how and where these new American divisions were to be employed. Pershing wanted a million men in France, but the French and British generals would have happily settled for a quarter of that number – if these fresh troops were placed under their direct command.

The situation of the United States Army in 1917 was rather worse than that of the BEF in 1914, at least in terms of its ability to fight a large-scale, modern war. The US Army was very small and entirely volunteer. Its role was almost entirely confined to defending the Mexican frontier against bandits and containing the remnants of the Indian nations on their reservations. It had no heavy artillery, almost no aircraft, very little ammunition, was undermanned and badly trained, and altogether in no condition, in terms either of manpower or of equipment, to fight a European war. The great assets the USA offered to the Entente Powers, however, were an almost unlimited supply of fresh men, an instinctive grasp of modern technology and a great deal of American 'get-up-and-go'. One example of the second quality, and of American eagerness to adopt new forms of warfare, comes from the Air Corps. The United States entered the war with just 55 aircraft; by the time the war ended they had 17,000. This swift expansion was reflected in the growth of the US Army, which increased rapidly as the cream of American manhood rushed or were drafted into the service. In June 1917 there were some 175,000 US troops under training in France; at the war's end 17 months later there were nearly 2 million.

The Allied generals, British as well as French, were very anxious to get their hands on these young American soldiers and incorporate them into their own armies by battalions and regiments if not full divisions. General Pershing and the US Government had other ideas. They had no intention of letting another nation use their young fighting men as cannon fodder, and they intended to fight in France as an American army, under American control, or not at all. For their part, the Allied governments recognised that the intervention of the United States could mean eventual victory, but were alarmed to discover that it would take at least a year before the American army – or armies – envisaged by Pershing and his government could take the field in any strength.

In the meantime, the weight of the war on the Western Front rested on the French and British Armies, and the state of the former was still a cause for deep concern. The French Army had now been fighting desperately for three years and was almost at the end of its physical and moral resources. The will to fight of the relentlessly gallant *poilus* had been eroded by the terrible losses at Verdun and on the Somme, and shattered in the shambles created by General Nivelle during his offensive on the Chemin des Dames in April 1917.

After May 1917 mutiny had stalked the French Army for many months. In some cases divisions refused to return to the front, or battalions declared that they would go into the line but only to stand on the defensive; they would fight if attacked, but refused to advance. Leave parties refused to rejoin their regiments, and often beat up the military policemen sent to coerce them. By November, following some draconian measures and the sensible actions of General Pétain, the French Army had largely recovered from this trauma, but for the time being its generals were far from anxious to commit it to another offensive.

The French idea in late 1917, and one endorsed by David Lloyd George after Passchendaele and Cambrai, was to go over to the defensive and wait until the American troops were in the line in strength before attacking again. This may have sounded sensible, but General Ludendorff had no intention of letting the Allies remain at rest until the Americans took the field. Lloyd George's notion, that the Allied armies would be left in peace if they adopted a defensive posture, was a delusion, and a dangerous one at that.

The weight of the fighting in late 1917 and the early months of 1918 fell on the British. If the war was to continue and the Germans held at bay until the Americans arrived there was no alternative, but the great losses inflicted on the German Army and the (very) slight gains made on the Western Front at Passchendaele had been paid for with equally terrible losses among the British and Dominion forces. By the end of Third Ypres the British armies were growing short of men, and were in any case in urgent need of rest as well as reinforcement. True, the Germans had also suffered, and General Birdwood's comment on Passchendaele, 'Haig's offensive, costly and unsuccessful though it had been, was of great value in pinning down and exhausting the enemy,' is no more than the truth. The snag was that the depleted German armies in the west were receiving fresh troops from the east, while Lloyd George declined to provide Haig with any reinforcements at all.

During the winter of 1917–18 Haig felt that his armies should be reinforced with the troops held at home. By the spring of 1918 there were around 450,000 fit and able soldiers in Britain and Haig wanted them in France, to fill out the depleted ranks of his fighting divisions. Lloyd George, however, was dreaming of another way, or another man, someone other than Field Marshal Haig, a man who could find a short cut to victory, a less painful way out of this endless war than a further sacrifice of men.

The stresses of war were not only on the Allied side. The population of Germany was approaching starvation, their food supplies curtailed by the Allied blockade. The daily rations of the civilian population were inadequate, for the bulk of the available supplies went to feed the field armies; in homes all over Germany, but especially in the cities, children could not sleep because they were hungry. The German Army, though still full of fight, had taken terrible losses in three years of war, and every German street contained its mourners. The Austrians were deeply disillusioned with the war they had done so much to start, and the Emperor Carl had already put out peace feelers to the Entente, attempting to make a separate peace with France and Britain behind the back of his German partner.

If the Austrians were failing fully to support the Germans, the Italians were proving a liability to the British and French. In Britain, the losses at Arras and Passchendaele, totalling some 390,000 men killed, wounded and missing, horrified the Prime Minister, his War Policy Committee, Parliament and the country at large. Desperate to avoid further losses on such a scale, Lloyd George's first plan was to step up the war in Italy, where Italian casualties could replace those of Britain. To aid the Italians in their fight, Lloyd George had, as we have seen, ordered the dispatch of hundreds of heavy guns and then of several British divisions. These arrived, over time, on the Italian front where General Cardona was planning a major offensive. Cardona fought two battles in mid-1917, his Tenth and Eleventh Battles of the Izonzo in May and August, with no more success than in the previous nine encounters. Disaster came in October, when an Austro-German force under General Otto von Below smashed the Italian armies at Caporetto and in 10 days drove them back some 80 miles on a 90-mile front, taking 275,000 prisoners – an even greater number deserted – and more than 2,500 guns. Winter staved off a total defeat but, for the moment at least, Italy was no longer an effective combatant, and an Anglo-French force with five British divisions under General Plumer – a general and divisions that Haig could ill spare – was rushed out to shore up a defensive line on the River Piave, well inside Italy's north-eastern frontier.

The secret Austrian peace proposals might have been welcome in this situation, but they came to nothing because the Italians wanted concessions Austria-Hungary could not accept. Another attempt at reconciliation by the Pope, Benedict XV, also failed to make ground, and it became clear that the war must continue until one side or the other was unable to continue. In January 1918 the US President, Woodrow Wilson, made yet another attempt to mediate, proposing peace on the basis of 'Fourteen Points', a list of concessions from both sides and proposals which he hoped would ensure a lasting peace once the guns stopped firing. This effort did not meet with much success, Clemenceau remarking, 'Fourteen Points? *Le bon Dieu* only needed ten.' In truth, the European nations were not yet ready for peace, and besides, at the end of 1917, with the Americans about to reinforce the Entente and the collapse of Russia freeing a host of German troops for deployment on the Western Front, there was good cause for doubt as to where the laurels of victory would eventually fall.

There were other theatres of war apart from the Western Front, and here Allied fortunes varied. In the Balkans, the Franco-British force remained in Salonika, achieving very little, but General Allenby, transferred to the command in Palestine, was soon making great headway against the Turks. Beersheba was encircled at the end of October, and Allenby took Jerusalem on 11 November, the first Christian general to enter the Holy City since the Crusades. In Mesopotamia, British, Indian Army and Dominion troops captured Baghdad on 11 March 1918. Outside of France and Italy – and, though on a much smaller scale, East Africa – the war was going well for the Entente; knowing this, Lloyd George wanted more effort devoted to those fronts, rather than to the fighting in France and Belgium.

All this was very well but, as Haig and Robertson never ceased to point out, the main theatre in this war the Western Front. Any success elsewhere, however good it might look in an official dispatch or in the newspapers, did very little to shorten the war. What was needed, they insisted, was for every man, gun and round of ammunition to be sent to the Western Front. That was where the bulk of the German armies were, that was where they could and must be defeated. This view was strongly supported by the French, and implacably opposed by David Lloyd George.

Lloyd George's opposition to Haig has many roots, but as 1917 went its bloody way the Prime Minister came to one conclusion that overrode the considerable personal animosity he felt towards his dour Scots field commander: he believed that to send more men to France was to send them to be slaughtered. Many people agreed with him – as many continue to do – and thus came to share his opinion of the Great War generals. Yet while he had no faith in Haig as a commander – for reasons already explained – he could not get rid of him.

All other methods having failed, Lloyd George saw that the only way to stop Haig throwing away lives by the tens of thousands in hopeless offensives was to deny him reinforcements. Since the supply of troops to theatres of war was within the remit of the War Cabinet, the Prime Minister was able to starve Haig's command of men. Without reinforcements, the Commander-in-Chief in France would be hard pressed to hold his line and would certainly be unable to build up reserves, the essential requirement for an offensive. To make that even more certain, Lloyd George agreed to French requests that the British should take over more of the front, thus thinning out Haig's available manpower even further.

An understanding of the matter of reserves is crucial to a grasp of one of the main problems affecting the Western Front commanders. Under 'normal' conditions, when no particular offensive was in progress, the British Armies in France could just manage with their normal establishment of corps and divisions. These rotated in and out of the line, and it should not be imagined that under 'normal' conditions the British troops in France occupied the front-line trench shoulder to shoulder, or stayed in that line for weeks. General Monash described in a letter what happened in his 3rd Australian Division in 1917, and the Australians' experience was duplicated by other corps:

> The whole of my sector, 5 out of 92 miles of front held by the British, is held by only one platoon each of four companies, one for each of the four battalions in each brigade, while the other battalions of the division – infantry and engineers – have all sorts of work to do which not only has nothing to do with the trenches but often takes them many miles to the rear. The 'front line' is not really a line at all but a complex and elaborate system of field works extending back several thousand yards . . . a front-line battalion stays in only six days, during which each platoon is changed round so that at the worst a man seldom does more than 48 hours' continuous trench duty every 12 days and every 48 days the whole brigade gets relieved by the reserve brigade and goes out for a complete rest . . . at least that is my system, designed to spread the stress on personnel as widely as possible.

A divisional front might be held by no more than four platoons, with the other units of their brigade stepped back in rear, in support trenches or in reserve, ready to provide help in the event of an attack. The troops rotated through the front, support and reserve lines, and actually spent very little time standing on the firestep of a front-line trench. The reason for this – apart from spreading the stress, as Monash makes clear – was to create a reserve of rested men in case of need.

The idea that the infantry spent all their time in trenches, more often than not in hand-to-hand combat with the Hun, is another Great War myth.

Charles Carrington, an infantry officer and author of *Soldier from the Wars Returning* etc., drew up a chart of his time in France in 1916. Though this included his participation in the Battle of the Somme, during which he fought at Ovillers and Le Sars, he only spent sixty-five days in the front line that year, spread over twelve trench tours. He spent thirty-six days in the support trenches, one hundred and twenty days in reserve, and seventy-three days resting. Of the remainder, twenty-one days were spent at Army or Divisional Schools or on training courses, seventeen on leave and ten in hospital (ill, not wounded). He also spent nine days at base and no fewer than fourteen days 'travelling about' – he moved eighty times that year. Carrington's twelve trench tours in 1916 saw him in action just four times, once in an attack, twice while on bombing raids, and once while his company was holding a front-line trench.

Taken across the armies as a whole, this state of affairs was, however, always in flux. Just to begin with, there was a steady stream of casualties, the British total running in 'normal' times at around 2,000 men a week. Other factors like sickness, a shortfall in recruits, the demands of other theatres, such as Palestine or Italy, a need to extend the line by taking over more of the French sector, all sucked away at the Army's front-line strength. A battalion with a theoretical ration strength of 1,000 men might be hard pressed to put 700 on parade. The 'rifle strength' of many battalions was often even smaller, when those sick (quite apart from casualties), or away on courses, or detached to brigade or division, or sent for pioneer work, were deducted from the total strength; moreover, the rifle strength was in any case smaller than the total, since numbers of men were detailed for stretcher parties and other essential work.

When an offensive was announced all this had to change. The divisions charged with the assault had to be brought up to strength – 'fattened up' was the gruesome phrase commonly employed – then rested and trained for the attack while other divisions not detailed for the attack held the line. Then, on the assumption that the attack would be a success, more divisions were needed to exploit that success. It was recognised quite early on in the war that the formations making an attack would be so exhausted and 'written down' in strength by the first assault that the task of exploiting any successes must be given to others. In practice, the assault divisions were often left in the line to fight on, but in an ideal world they would have been pulled back after the first day or so, and replaced by fresh divisions *from reserve*. In short, reserves were crucial to the planning and mounting of offensives.

Every element in the British Army strove to maintain a reserve, even in the middle of a battle. A brigade of four battalions would attack with two in the lead, one in support, and one in reserve. The divisional commander would keep a brigade in reserve if at all possible. Then there were corps reserves, army reserves and GHQ reserves, these last being divisions or artillery regiments that could only be committed to the battle on the direct orders of the Commander-in-Chief. Without reserves, an army could not attack, so that by cutting off the supply of reinforcements needed to create reserves, Lloyd George was preventing Haig from prosecuting the war through offensive action.

There was, however, a serious flaw in Lloyd George's thinking. Reserves were not only essential for attacks, they were also vital for counter-attacks during enemy offensives, for shoring up a weakened sections of the line, for reinforcing or replacing 'written-down' divisions, or for manning defensive positions in the rear of the front line, as a backstop for any units forced to withdraw. Lloyd George does not appear to have realised that when he held back troops in order to prevent Haig from making an attack, he was reducing the latter's ability to fight off a German offensive.

At first sight it is easy to sympathise with Lloyd George's views, which sprang from humanitarian motives and were fuelled by the casualty figures he read each day at his desk. For the Prime Minister, representing all the people, to refuse his generals a further supply of cannon fodder for more fruitless offensives can be seen in such a light as the right and proper thing to do.

Unfortunately, Lloyd George left one element out of his calculations; the Germans. He may have decided that attacks must be avoided and the British armies put on the defensive, for if the two sides just sat there, glaring through the wire, the stream of casualties should slow to a comparative trickle. The Germans, however, had no intention of remaining quiet on the Western Front. Throughout the winter of 1917–18, as more divisions arrived from Russia, they were preparing for a major offensive in the west that would sweep them to victory over France and Britain. Their arrival was soon known to Allied Intelligence, and a German offensive in the spring was anticipated as a result. Those troops that Lloyd George kept in Britain should have been sent to France, to construct new defences in depth on the British front line, people them against the forthcoming German attack, train for defensive action, and man those defences when the attack came in. Lloyd George did not see it that way. Field Marshal Sir Douglas Haig was the man in his sights, and Haig's command must be cut down, rather than built up. As a step towards that end, the Prime Minister decided to get rid of Haig's stout supporter, General Sir William Robertson, the CIGS.

With trouble brewing for Haig in London, more familiar problems reappeared in France that October, with a demand from the French Prime Minister and Minister for War, Paul Painlevé, who had become Premier in September, but was replaced by Clemenceau in November, that the British should take over more of the front line, a demand that was supported by Lloyd George. Haig was then deeply involved with the Passchendaele offensive and replied, in a memorandum to Robertson on 8 October, that since the French were not attacking 'they should be able to hold their line with the troops they had and not expect the British to relieve them.' Robertson was coming under increasing pressure at this time, and was now dismayed to discover that Lloyd George was inviting military advice from Field Marshal French and General Sir Henry Wilson, rather than from himself, the CIGS, the official adviser to the Prime Minister and government on the conduct of the war.

French and Wilson submitted formal papers on the conduct of the war to Lloyd George, and copies of these were sent to Haig for comment. He did not find them impressive. French's paper came to the conclusion that the British and French Armies should stand on the defensive until the Americans arrived in force, and Wilson put forward the idea of an 'Inter-Allied Council' to oversee the conduct of the war . . . 'presumably with himself as the Head of the British Staff section', as Haig bitterly – and accurately – noted in his diary on 31 October. He had always been wary of the oft-mooted 'Combined Staff' notion, suspecting, correctly, that it was a French ploy to take over his command; the idea did have merit, however, and would not go away.

Clearly, there were advantages in a unified command on the Western Front and a single overall commander, but Haig did not think so at the end of 1917. His view was based on some – indeed, considerable – bitter experience of working with the French over the last two years and can be understood on those grounds alone, although it is in fact likely that he rejected the idea on principle. Haig never suggested that he himself might fill the post of 'Generalissimo' over the French and British (and, ultimately, United States) Armies, though he might well have done so in mid-1917, when France's forces were in desperate trouble.

Haig did not want a foreign commander appointed over his head, and assumed that any French general would feel the same way. In this he was quite correct, but the French idea was that a *French* general should assume the supreme command – and, naturally, they did not find that notion at all unacceptable. Pétain came to Haig's headquarters on 1 November, and showed the Field Marshal a memorandum he had written to the French Prime Minister, Paul Painlevé, which stated that the British and French Armies were now equally powerful and both had competent commanders. Provided he and Haig consulted and co-operated, especially in supporting each other during attacks, a unified command offered no extra advantages.

Pétain's views are debatable, but his memorandum, not surprisingly, overlooked Lloyd George's hidden agenda. So far as the latter was concerned, the object of setting up some form of unified command on the Western Front was not merely in order to co-ordinate the struggle against the Central Powers. Lloyd George also saw it as a way of getting rid of Haig and Robertson, or at the very least of having their actions placed under some form of external control.

The subject came up for further discussion in Paris on 4 November, at a meeting attended by Haig, Lloyd George and Smuts. Lloyd George began by stating the necessity for an 'Inter-Allied Supreme War Council', and then asked Haig for his views. The latter replied that the idea had surfaced at regular intervals since August 1914, and had been rejected each time as unworkable; for good measure, he added that he thought it would be unworkable now. Lloyd George countered this by stating that the two governments had in fact already decided to form such a council, to which Haig responded, typically, that in that case there was no more to be said.

It would have been more straightforward if Lloyd George had simply informed Haig of this decision, rather than telling him in such a deliberately humiliating way, but being straightforward was not one of the Prime Minister's qualities. There was, moreover, worse news to follow. The Supreme War Council was to consist of the two Cabinet War Committees plus a general from each of the Allied commands. The French general was to be Foch – or his deputy, Colonel Weygand, who was Foch's creature – and the British general would be Sir Henry Wilson. The US delegate was General T.H. Bliss, Pershing's Chief of Staff, an officer who, until now, had spent most of his time beating the clutching hands of General Foch away from the troops of the four American divisions now in training in France. This Supreme War Council, which would sit at Versailles, was ostensibly charged with the co-ordination of war strategy as a whole, but was in fact a step towards the creation of a unified Allied command.

If none of this got the meeting off to a happy start, the atmosphere gradually worsened. When discussing the Italian situation, in the light of the defeat at Caporetto, Haig urged that no more men or guns should be sent to that front; Lloyd George replied that he would decide what action to take when the situation became clearer. He then went on to complain that the 'military' – that is, Haig and his cronies – were attacking him behind his back and planting untrue stories in the press, an allegation which Haig vehemently denied. In due course the meeting broke up, but a week later Lloyd George returned to the attack with a speech in Paris during which he openly criticised the army commanders. This speech recoiled on him, however, attracting unfavourable press comment and an open repudiation from Sir Edward Carson, the Ulster leader and, as First Lord of the Admiralty, a member of the War Cabinet.

Four days later, on 16 November, the French Government fell and a new administration was formed with Georges Clemenceau as Prime Minister and Minister for War. Clemenceau, generally known as 'the Tiger', was to bring a new urgency to the prosecution of the war and was instrumental in speeding the recovery of the French armies, a process encouraged on 20 November by the success the British appeared to be having with their Cambrai offensive. When this failed on 30 November, however, Lloyd George returned to the attack.

There was a long discussion in Cabinet yesterday, [wrote Robertson to Haig on 6 December] and Lloyd George was well on the war path . . . His great argument is that you have long said the Germans are on the down grade in morale and that you advised attacking them though some 30 [German] divisions should come from Russia; and yet only a few divisions have arrived and you are hard put to hold your own. He says that the Cambrai events are due to Charteris's error of judgement as to [German] numbers and efficiency. This of course is his way of getting out of the drafts question [i.e. drafts of reinforcements for France]. We have plainly told Cabinet in writing that we shall lose the war unless the armies are brought up to strength and kept at strength until the American divisions arrive.

Battle was now joined between Lloyd George, on the one hand, and Robertson and Haig on the other, and memos and letters flew between the CIGS and the Commander-in-Chief. Haig's view was that if he had indeed lost the Prime Minister's confidence then he should be sacked. If this was not in fact the case, then the carping should cease and he should be supported and given all the reinforcements he needed. Had Haig offered to resign, Lloyd George would have accepted with alacrity, but *sacking* him was out of the question.

Even after Passchendaele and Cambrai, Haig enjoyed the support of the Army, the French, the King, most of the Cabinet and the public. The plain truth was that Haig was irreplaceable. Even the press were broadly in support, though Lloyd George's views on the losses at Passchendaele and Cambrai had made the front pages in recent weeks. Besides, if he went, who would replace him? General Sir Ian Hamilton, once considered one of the Army's brightest stars, had been destroyed by the failure in the Dardanelles, for the Gallipoli disaster had led to his being relieved of his command. Allenby, although forging ahead in Palestine, had only some eight months ago proved less than impressive on the Western Front. Wilson was unpopular and distrusted, and the other army commanders – Byng, Plumer and Horne – were supporters of Haig and believers in his philosophy. Rawlinson, who might have been capable of the task, was not even considered.

A number of historians have alleged that the Australian, Monash, and the Canadian Corps commander, General Currie, were both in line for the overall command of the British Armies in France. Since this would have required a double leap in promotion for both men, from corps to army command, and then to Commander-in-Chief, this pretty tale has no basis in fact, and can in fact be traced to some comments in Lloyd George's memoirs. There was, of course, General Sir Henry Wilson, forever hovering in the wings, but the idea of the volatile and scheming Wilson as Commander-in-Chief of the British Armies in France struck most people – or at least most of those that mattered – as ludicrous.

Lloyd George was therefore stuck with Haig, but if he could not dismiss him he could at least control him, by striking away his supporters, men like Robertson, Kiggell and Charteris. Thus the War Cabinet elected to believe that the information they were getting from Robertson and Haig was not correct, but that the blame lay not with those officers but with Brigadier-General Charteris. Charteris was certainly not the most efficient of Intelligence officers; on 27 November, for instance, three days before the German counter-attack at Cambrai, he told Haig that 'the German troops are very thin on this front except at Bourlon,' from which the latter concluded in his diary that the situation was 'most favourable to us'. Charteris was therefore the first to go, leaving Haig's GHQ on 14 December. The next to go was Haig's Quartermaster-General (QMG), Lieutenant-General R.C. Maxwell, who had also apparently forfeited the confidence of the War Council; he was replaced on 16 December. Then the new year arrived, bringing with it news that German divisions were daily leaving Russia and being shipped to the Western Front, as well as a further request from French GQG for an extension of the British line. Both these items worried Haig, but a greater danger lay in London, where Lloyd George was about to move in on the CIGS, General Sir William Robertson.

On New Year's Day, Lord Derby, the Minister for War, told Haig that Lloyd George intended to get rid of Robertson and replace him with Henry Wilson. Derby insisted that he deplored this suggestion, but added that he himself wanted General Kiggell removed as Haig's Chief of Staff, as he was 'tired'. Since Kiggell did not enjoy good health, this was one move to which Haig reluctantly agreed, and the former left his post on 12 January – the third member of the Commander-in-Chief's personal staff to go in four weeks. It took exactly four more weeks for Lloyd George to get rid of 'Wully' Robertson.

Following the appointment of General Wilson to the Supreme War Council at Versailles, Lloyd George found himself with two military advisers, and found, too, that he much preferred the advice offered by Wilson from Versailles to that contributed by Robertson, his official adviser, in London. On 26 January Wilson advised Lloyd George that the Western Front forces should go over to the defensive while a major effort under Allenby was mounted in Palestine. Robertson's response was to threaten resignation if this course of action was taken. Then, on 31 January, Haig attended a meeting of the Supreme War Council at Versailles, at which Lloyd George produced figures to prove that, contrary to the Field Marshal's information, the British Armies in France already had more than enough men for any coming operation.

This was simply not true. After Cambrai, Haig estimated that his armies were short by some 75,000 men, and that unless something was done to correct it, the shortfall would rise to around 250,000 men in the next twelve months. In addition, if, as seemed probable, the Germans attacked in the spring, the shortage might reach the quarter-million total before that season was out. He had told the War Office at the end of November that unless reinforcements were provided he would have to break up around fifteen divisions to fill up the ranks in the remaining formations; in reply, he had been told to refrain from that step while fresh totals for reserve in Britain were calculated. On 10 January, after taking over more of the French line, the British Armies in France totalled fifty-seven infantry divisions, of which forty-seven were British, five Australian, four Canadian, and one New Zealand. There were also five cavalry divisions, but the rifle strength of each was estimated as being no more than that of a single infantry brigade. The War Cabinet, however, then decided that the number of brigades in each British division should be reduced from four to three, and that no extra reinforcements should be sent to the armies in France other than those necessary to maintain them at their present strengths.

The Ministry of National Service, which directed all the available manpower of the UK, estimated that it would have no more than 100,000 men available for the British Armies in France during the whole of 1918, barely enough to cope with the daily casualties and sickness; the Ministry did not apparently consider diverting some of the 192,000 men who were already earmarked for the armies in the Near East and Middle East and the Balkans. This decision to withhold reinforcements would have a dire effect on the armies attempting to prepare for the anticipated spring German offensive in France. So, while the German strength built up behind the Hindenburg Line, Britain's more than adequate army reserves were kept at home.

The Supreme War Council meeting of 31 January ordered Haig to stay on the defensive on the Western Front at least until the spring. Lloyd George insisted, however, on pressing ahead with an attack in Palestine, although Robertson spoke out against it, much to the Prime Minister's annoyance. Discussions then moved on to the crucial issue of French and British reserves. Lloyd George proposed that an 'Inter-Allied Reserve' should be created from the Anglo-French armies and that Foch should be placed in charge of it. Haig suspected that this was another step towards the appointment of a 'Generalissimo'; once the politicians had approved the idea, therefore, he asked the hard question as to who it was that he, the Commander-in-Chief of the British Armies in France, should appeal to for access to his own reserves – his own CIGS in London, or a French general? It was a good point. A C-in-C must have access to reserves – it followed, therefore, that the only way the proposed system could work would be if the man commanding the reserves was made the overall Allied commander in France.

In spite of Haig's misgivings, a committee was then set up to deal with the issue of reserves, with Foch as its president. Haig was told that orders affecting reserves would be issued by members appointed to the Supreme War Council – a statement which, though vague, seemed to suggest, in the case of reserves for Haig's armies, Henry Wilson, the British Military Representative. The Council also decided, once more in spite of Haig's objections, to increase yet again the British share of the front line, though it was left to Haig and Pétain to work out when this should take effect.

The matter of Robertson's position as CIGS now moved quickly to a conclusion. On 9 February, Haig was summoned to London and told by

Lord Derby that Robertson was to be replaced, whether Haig liked it or not. The new CIGS would continue to be Supreme Military Adviser to the Government, while the Military Representative at Versailles would also serve as the Deputy CIGS. This last officer – Wilson at that time – would direct Haig on the matter of the Inter-Allied Reserve. Haig had already heard from Wilson on this matter, and told Derby that Wilson and Foch seemed to be acting as if they were already the 'Generalissimos' commanding all the Allied armies in France.

Some of these decisions did not survive Haig's subsequent meeting with Lloyd George, at which the former pointed out that the Supreme War Council now had extremely wide-ranging powers, and that the Military Representative had the power to make decisions which ought properly to be taken by the British Government. He also pointed out that only the – British – Army Council or his – British – superiors could legally give him orders. Lloyd George replied that the he had always wanted closer contact with Haig, but had felt that if he had communicated with him directly it might have been thought that he was going behind Robertson's back. The Field Marshal therefore suggested that the best solution was to let Robertson and Foch work together on the matter of reserves, to which Lloyd George answered that he had come to the same conclusion, and as a result had decided to send Robertson to Versailles as Supreme Military Representative, and to bring Wilson back to London as CIGS.

It is possible that Lloyd George have been passing through one of his mood swings at this time, edging towards the benevolent, for he then suggested that it would be a good idea if Haig became Commander-in-Chief of *all* the British land forces, in *all* theatres. A more cynical explanation, however, is that this was a move to 'kick Haig upstairs'. Whatever the Prime Minister's reasons, Haig rejected the proposal on the grounds that with so many changes in the command structure already in hand, no further change should be made to the British command in France.

As might have been predicted with certainty, Robertson refused to accept the position at Versailles, for he felt that the real power would rest with Wilson in London. Since Wully Robertson lacked the latter's talent for 'mischief' – Wilson's own term for his relentless drive for self-advancement and his backstairs manoeuvring – he was probably correct. Two days later Haig heard that Robertson had been offered the choice of either going to Versailles or of remaining as CIGS, but had decided to resign as, in his opinion, the CIGS ought to be the British Representative at Versailles. So, on 16 February 1918, General Sir Henry Wilson became CIGS, while his close friend General Sir Henry Rawlinson became British Military Representative at Versailles.

As has been noted previously, when a general is not otherwise employed he cannot make better use of his time than by spending it in calculating what the enemy is doing, or what he himself would do, were he in the enemy's place. Field Marshal Haig had a lot on his mind in the first months of 1918, but after the collapse of the Russian war effort in October 1917 and news of the resultant transfer of many German divisions to the Western Front, it became clear to him and to most of his military colleagues that the Germans would launch a major offensive in France as soon as the ground dried out in the early spring of 1918, in an attempt to win the war before the American divisions could bring their weight to bear. The most important questions facing Haig were where and when this attack would come, and what forces he would have available with which to defeat it. At a War Cabinet meeting on 7 January, he was asked to state his views as to what the enemy would do in the coming year. Given his notorious inarticulacy, his vague reply – that the Germans had taken a hammering at Passchendaele and Cambrai and were now worn out – left the War Cabinet with the impression that the Field Marshal thought the Germans would not attack at all.

Haig was much more lucid, however, when committing his thoughts to paper. On the following day he sent the War Cabinet a note which stated that 'The crucial period for the Allies is the next few months. During this period the Central Powers may make a determined effort to force a decision on the Western Front . . . provision must be made to meet such an eventuality and to replace losses which would certainly be incurred in withstanding a heavy and sustained attack.' Lloyd George was not the only one to wonder why Haig seemed to have changed his mind completely in just twenty-four hours.

Yet it was thanks to Lloyd George that the forces to meet such an attack were not adequate. The essential element in an infantry division was its rifle strength, the number of fighting men it could put in the line. By January 1918, Haig's front-line infantry strength was some 25 per cent – say, 75,000 men – below establishment. The only exceptions to this dire situation were the Anzac and Canadian divisions, for their home governments had kept them up to strength. As a result the Dominion divisions were able to retain their four-brigades-to-a-division formation. The British Government could have done the same had some of the trained men in Britain been sent to France.

On 1 January 1918, according to a War Office return quoted in the Official History, there were over 30,000 officers and some 600,000 men in the UK, fully trained, fit and ready for 'General Service' – employment in any theatre. Even 10 per cent of these men would have made all the difference to the situation on the Western Front, not simply by being available to stem the German attack in March, but also by being available to work on developing the defences before that attack came in. As it was, the British Army's front-line divisions in France and Belgium were reduced from four to three brigades, and a great deal of unnecessary reorganisation took place, eating away at time and efficiency. The men in these divisions needed rest and training for defensive action, but there was no time for that. The line taken over from the French around St Quentin was in a poor state of repair and needed a great deal of work before it would be of any real use in stemming a German attack. There was too much work to do, and too few Pioneers and Sappers to do it. As a result, infantry battalions that should have been resting or training were obliged to work in bitter winter weather, digging trenches and wiring defence posts, or moving up heavy loads of ammunition. This wore them out and reduced their effectiveness still further. There was, however, no help for it . . . and the blame for this state of affairs rested squarely with Lloyd George and General Wilson.

Neither man was a fool. Had Lloyd George not been obsessed with his fear of another Haig offensive and blinded by his personal detestation of the Field Marshal, he would have realised that the need to strike before the Americans were in the field in force *demanded* a German attack – and that the collapse of Russia ensured that it would be a major and exceptionally powerful one. For his part, Wilson was an intriguer, but he was a soldier and a British officer. His role was to provide Lloyd George with sensible military advice, but here again he was so busy pushing the interests of the French in general, and of Foch in particular, that he became blind to the growing menace of the German armies mustering in strength behind the Hindenburg Line, and concentrating on the British sector of the front.

Realising that Lloyd George was not going to send an adequate supply of men out to France, Haig's first move was to hang on to all the troops he had, resisting every attempt to switch any of his divisions to the Inter-Allied Reserve. At the end of February, seven weeks before the German spring offensive began, the GHQ Reserve for his entire force – four armies – stood at just *eight* divisions. Clearly he could not spare a single one of these if an attack was coming, but this provoked another row on 5 March two weeks before the German attack, when he informed the Supreme War committee at Versailles that he had no divisions to spare for the Inter-Allied Reserve at this time.

The Supreme War Council had now directed its Military Representatives 'to transmit its orders to the Armies of their several countries', and their first order was for the release of divisions to form a General Reserve of thirty divisions. The Executive Committee – Foch and Rawlinson – told their governments that Haig had refused to hand his divisions over to the Inter-Allied Reserve, adding that consequently the role of the committee could not be fulfilled and they must therefore resign. They did not add, however, that General Pétain had also refused to hand over any of his French divisions.

On 14 March, just a week before the German attack, Haig was summoned to Downing Street and harangued by Lloyd George, who first tried to persuade him to deny the likelihood of a German attack, and then alleged that he had previously stated that any German attack would be a minor affair, affecting a small part of the front, an allegation Haig strongly denied. He was then asked whether he would attack if he were in Ludendorff's position, to which he replied that it was impossible to foretell what the enemy might do, but that he had to be fully prepared for an attack on a 50-mile front. In any case, he added, he needed substantial reserves, and more drafts from the UK were therefore urgently required.

Lloyd George then moved on to the matter of the Inter-Allied Reserve, telling Haig that all the other commanders had agreed to contribute troops and that he was the only one to refuse. This was not true, but Haig merely replied that the matter of reserves was a military decision and one of which he must be the best judge. He added that he only had eight divisions under his hand in GHQ Reserve, to which Lloyd George, in a typical volte-face, agreed that it was too late to shift these to the Inter-Allied Reserve in view of the apparent imminence of a large-scale German attack – the attack which he had himself as good as refuted earlier at this same meeting. The final outcome was a face-saving formula, one which acknowledged the need to establish a general reserve, but which delayed actually doing so until sufficient American forces were in the field to permit the removal of British and French divisions from the line.

Haig was undoubtedly right in this matter, as Lloyd George was just as surely wrong, both in insisting on the creation of a general reserve at this time, and in denying Haig reinforcements. It had become a clash of wills between the two men, for in this matter Lloyd George had little support at home, even from members of his own Cabinet. Winston Churchill, Minister of Munitions since July 1917, and a man who had spoken out repeatedly against the senselessness of Western Front offensives, urged the Prime Minister to send out drafts of reinforcements, but Lloyd George remained obdurate. Even articles in the press failed to sway him. When Colonel Repington, now the Military Correspondent of the *Morning Post*, wrote an article criticising Lloyd George and the Supreme War Council in Versailles, using privileged information he could only have received from someone in the War Office, Lloyd George had him prosecuted under the Defence of the Realm Act for revealing military secrets.

Repington and the Editor of the *Morning Post* duly appeared in court, where they were fined £100 and discharged, but the Prime Minister's actions reveal that he was under increasing strain at this time. He wrote later that by bringing an action against Repington and obtaining the resignation of Robertson he had drawn the teeth of the 'military junta aiming to overthrow the civilian government and replace it with a military dictatorship'. This preposterous comment appeared in his *War Memoirs* some years later, but it does indicate his state of mind in February 1918, especially when his thoughts turned to Field Marshal Haig.

Lloyd George was out of his depth in military matters, something which may well have been part of the problem. The difficulties facing the generals in the field were not open to the kind of compromises and secret deals to which a professional politician was used. In the military field there were right and wrong ways to do things, and those who got it wrong paid a high price for their failure . . . as did their men. Haig's calm assurance, his air that he knew best, was infuriating, but Lloyd George had been wrong about Nivelle – a matter in which Haig maintained a saintly but eloquent silence – and he was wrong again over the question of drafts for the front. A large part of the blame for what went wrong on and after 21 March 1918 rests upon the Prime Minister, David Lloyd George, who failed to accept that a general must have soldiers for defence, as well as for attack.

That a German attack was coming was common knowledge. The Kaiser's eldest son Wilhelm, Crown Prince of Germany and Prussia, and an army commander on the Western Front, had assured Berlin newspapers that he would be 'lunching in Calais on 20 March' and in Paris three weeks later, and there was ample intelligence information warning of the coming offensive from sources open to Lloyd George as well as to Haig. On 2 March, more than a week before the two men met at Downing Street. Haig's new Intelligence officer, Brigadier-General Cox, presented his reasons for thinking that the enemy were preparing an attack on the fronts of Third and Fifth Armies, and even Wilson, Lloyd George's chosen adviser as CIGS, believed that a major German attack was in the offing. All the available information implied that the offensive would come on the British front and Haig was already urging his commanders to prepare their positions for an imminent, large-scale attack before he left for the Downing Street meeting with Lloyd George on 14 March. The only real question was where the blow would fall, but Haig and most of his generals believed that it would fall on their forces, rather than the French.

Hindenburg and Ludendorff had surveyed the whole Western Front before deciding on a dual-attack strategy, with the British as the main target. Haig had now taken over the front line from the French as far south as the River Oise, thus further thinning out his divisions, so that the British Army now held 123 miles of front, from the Ypres Salient to beyond the Oise. The German idea was to launch an attack, codenamed 'Michael', which would break through on this front between the Scarpe and the Oise, with the centre of the thrust across the old Somme battlefield towards Amiens. Once this attack was under way, and Haig's slender reserves had been committed to stemming it, a further attack, condenamed 'George', would be launched in Flanders. On Z-day, the German armies in the west could muster no fewer than 194 divisions. Seventy-one of these were to be hurled against the twenty-six British and Empire divisions of the Third and Fifth Armies which lay in the path of their attack.

Quite apart from the disparity in numbers, Haig's divisions were in no state to contain this attack. They were under strength already, and the line was therefore thinly manned and lacked depth for the sort of battle that was about to break over it. Moreover, the British armies were not used to defensive fighting. For the last three years they had been fighting an offensive battle, and when they were forced to go over to the defensive they had little of the enemy's experience, and less of the equipment or the expertise that the German Army had developed over the same period. The reverse was not true, for the German assault divisions had been brought from Russia, where they had been waging an offensive war for the last three years. They were fully familiar with assault tactics, including the use of creeping barrages, smoke and gas concentrations, and infiltration by storm-troops.

The essence of German offensive infantry tactics in 1918 was a continuous advance by a process of infiltration. The new defences developed by both sides to cope with the huge artillery concentrations helped this tactic, for the long line of manned front-line trenches that provides one of the main images of the Great War was no longer common. There were still trenches, but defence now depended on interlocking fields of fire, on concrete strong-points manned by machine-gunners overlooking wide belts of barbed wire, and on the rapid action of counter-attack divisions. The only elements lacking on the German side were tanks, which they had not developed, and cavalry forces, which they had run down, but this was largely compensated for by a skilful use of aircraft.

The British decided to adopt the defensive measures they had themselves found so hard to overcome in Flanders, largely abandoning the 'Front Line-Support Line' method for a system of defensive 'zones'. They therefore transformed the front line into the 'Forward Zone', a narrow trench-and-strongpoint position designed to delay the German advance and warn the 'Battle Zone' that the attack was coming. Battle Zone positions, two or three miles in rear of the Forward Zone, were the bastions of this form of defence and should have had deep dugouts, a network of communicating trenches to let the defenders move about, pillboxes, thick belts of wire covered by machine-guns sited for interlocking fire, field artillery, and direct, deeply dug, telephone links with heavy artillery some distance to the rear but on hand for defensive fire tasks. Prepared for all-round defence, they should also have had a number of counter-attack divisions near by, ready to intervene once the Battle Zone had broken up the enemy attack. In reality, however, very little of this defensive system existed.

The last line of defence should have been a 'Rear Zone', a mile or so behind the Battle Zone, but this had been no more than marked out when the German offensive began. Furthermore, there were two other major problems with the British defensive line. Firstly, Haig did not have the troops to man it, and those he did have were not fully trained. As a result the men did not grasp the concept of 'zone fighting', nor did they like it. Secondly, these zones were not designed to defeat the attacker, but to disrupt the attack, cause casualties, and slow it down. That done, a large force of reserves, kept in the rear until the attack developed, would launch a counter-attack and defeat the enemy in the field. Thanks to Lloyd George denying him reinforcements, however, Haig only had eight divisions, *two per army* in reserve for his entire front of more than 120 miles.

Byng and Gough, commanding the Third and Fifth Armies, on which this attack would fall, put the bulk of their troops into the Forward and

Battle Zones. Given their shortage of men and the unprepared state of the Rear Zone this was sensible. It has been alleged by various historians that Haig miscalculated the distribution of his forces, allocating twelve divisions to cover the 42-mile front of Fifth Army while Byng had fourteen divisions to cover the 28-mile front of Third Army. Why Haig did this can be explained by looking at a map and remembering the past. Throughout the war, the British armies had been obliged to defend the Channel ports, especially Calais and Boulogne. That is why the first two battles were fought at Ypres in 1914 and 1915, and that is why, in 1918, Haig put the bulk of his resources in the north. If the Germans broke through in the north, they could sweep across a narrow band of territory to the coast. If they did that and took Calais, the British Army would be in a terrible plight and the Allied line cut in two. In the south, on Gough's Fifth Army front, a breakthrough, while unpleasant, would not be nearly so disastrous, for Fifth Army had room to retreat.

Haig was prepared for Fifth Army to fall back, to withdraw, if need be. That fact has often been overlooked, but withdrawal is a legitimate military manoeuvre and has the benefit of taking much of the force out of an enemy attack – provided it is a *controlled* withdrawal, to prepared and well-defended positions. Haig, always the optimist, did not think it would come to that, however. On 2 March 1918 he confided to his diary that his 'main fear was that the Germans would find the British defences so strong that they would hesitate to attack for fear of heavy losses'.

Haig need not have worried on that score. Ludendorff had three full armies for his first attack, the Seventeeth, Second and Eighteenth, each full of tough, experienced troops, skilled in infiltration tactics, well provided with artillery, flamethrowers and grenades. At 0440 hours on the foggy morning of 21 March 1918 their guns began to pound the British positions, thereby starting the most critical battle of the war.

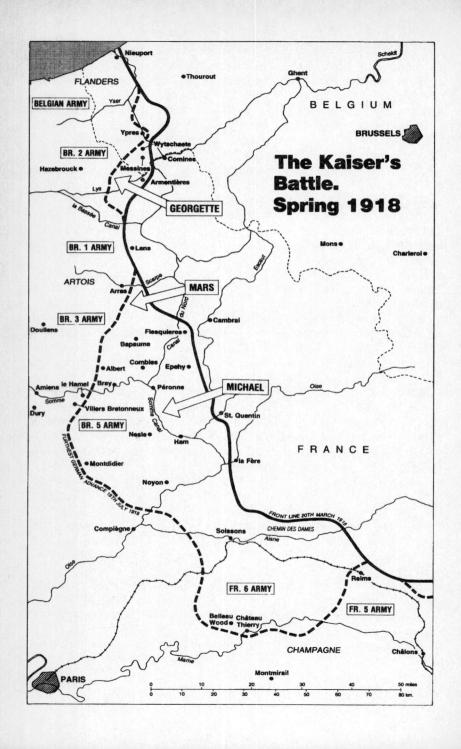

CHAPTER 21

THE KAISER'S BATTLE,
March–May 1918

*'It must be freely admitted that the British Armies of 1918,
after two and a half years of offensive warfare, were not well
trained to stand on the defensive and deal with an attack by
infiltration; they were totally untrained in carrying out a
retreat.'*

Brigadier-General Sir J. E. Edmonds,
Military Operations France and Belgium 1918, Volume I

What happened during the *Kaiserschlacht*, the 'Kaiser's Battle' of 1918, and the events which followed the opening of the German Michael offensive on 21 March, are too well known to need more than a broad outline here. Put simply, the Germans attacked a weakened British line on the sector held by the Third and Fifth Armies, broke through on the Fifth Army front and drove Gough's army back for some forty miles, practically to Amiens. That much is undisputed but, as the Official History points out, 'More legends have been current with regard to the March Offensive and its continuation, the Lys Offensive, than about any other great battle of the War.' This statement, which goes on to analyse some of these 'legends', seems to be an accurate summation of the reasons *why* this great German onslaught has attracted so much attention and critical comment.

The period from the start of the offensive to the end of the war, but particularly from March to July 1918, offers such a variety of action and counter-action, and so many opportunities for debate, that it requires a great deal of study just to discover what exactly was going on at any given time. This chapter therefore seeks to avoid plunging into detail, but attempts instead to explain why these events happened, and how it was that, after three and a half years of stalemate, the Western Front finally returned to open warfare.

The Michael offensive punched a great hole in the British line, led to the dismissal of General Gough, and forced Field Marshal Haig to place himself and his armies under the overall command of General Foch. None of this had been anticipated when the German guns began to flay the Third and Fifth Army positions on the first morning of the spring of 1918.

Ludendorff began his offensive with a five-hour artillery bombardment from nearly 6,500 medium and heavy guns along the 50-mile front of the Third and Fifth Armies between the Somme and Cambrai. This bombardment, of high-explosive, phosgene-gas and lachrymatory-gas shells, fell not only on the Forward Zone but also on positions and road junctions well behind the Battle Zone, and lasted until five minutes before Zero. There was then a final barrage on the front-line positions from more than 3,500 mortars, after which the German infantry advanced 'without Hurrahs' led by stormtroop detachments armed with grenades and flamethrowers.

Ludendorff threw sixty-six German divisions against the Third and Fifth Armies. Omitting the divisions not used in the first assault, nineteen went in against six divisions of Third Army, and forty-three fell on the fourteen infantry and three cavalry divisions – these last together equivalent in rifle strength to one infantry division – of Gough's Fifth Army. Fifth Army actually consisted of just twelve divisions of which eleven divisions were in the line and one, the 50th (Northumbrian), was in army reserve. In addition there were two divisions, the 29th and 30th, held in GHQ Reserve by Haig, but allocated to Fifth Army. The three cavalry divisions were also in reserve two in corps reserve and one, the 3rd Cavalry Division, in GHQ Reserve. It is clear that even without such terrible odds, Gough would have been hard pressed to maintain his front against any forceful attack.

The Fifth Army occupied a front of 42 miles. A large part of this long sector had recently been taken over from the French. When Gough arrived to inspect the line in early January he discovered that the French positions were either inadequate, non-existent or, in the rear areas, actually being dismantled by the local people, who wanted to return the land to cultivation. One of his first actions was to order that French farmers filling in trenches and removing barbed wire east of Amiens should stop this work at once and restore these defences. Much of what Gough then had to do has been covered in an earlier chapter; the existing defences must be improved and new defences constructed, and the men trained in how to fight this new form of defensive battle in the Forward, Battle and Rear Zones. The greatest problem was that these positions did not currently exist; the men had to dig and wire them, and then occupy them, so that time for training in how to fight from them was extremely limited.

Put simply, the task was too much for Gough's limited number of men in the time available. As a result the defences were not adequate. The Forward Zone had been completed, as had most of the Battle Zone although some positions there were in the course of final completion when the attack came in. The Rear Zone, however, had hardly been started, and consisted, at best of knee-deep trenches cut in the grass. These in-depth defences were not designed to cover a small area but to give protection for a depth of some miles, *and over a front of forty-two miles.* Digging hundreds of miles of trenches – for men and telephone cables – would have taken all the resources at Gough's disposal, leaving him with nothing with which to hold the front line. He reported all this to GHQ, asking for more Sappers and Pioneers, pointing out the length of his front, the shortage of labour, the lack of light railways,* the poor state of the roads, all the factors that hindered the work of constructing his defence line. Gough was being honest, not pessimistic, and said that if he could have the men and stores he needed he hoped to have his front in an adequate state of defence by 15 March. The problem was insoluble, however, because the men were simply not there, or likely to be there. War Office estimates of reinforcements available for the four British armies in France for April came to no more than 18,000 men, and Lloyd George was determined that no more troops should be sent.

General Ludendorff had no such worries. Tens of thousands of fresh, trained German soldiers were coming west from Russia and Poland, fleshing out the ranks of the three armies which were now assembling in readiness to fall on the British line. By the end of December 1917 the German armies in west had received more than a dozen divisions and their number continued to grow; by the end of February the Germans had 185 divisions on the Western Front, and this total was increasing at the rate of 10 a month. In the end Ludendorff had seventy-one divisions for his assault in the west, and of these, twenty-five went to the Eighteenth Army, twenty-one to the Second Army and twenty-five to the Seventeenth Army.

Nor was there anything haphazard about the transfer of these divisions, for Ludendorff had been planning this attack for some time. After a conference with his generals in October 1917 his conclusion had been similar to that arrived at by the Allied generals: 'The German Armies must strike at the earliest possible moment in 1918, if possible by the end of February or at the latest by the end of March, before the Americans can throw large forces into the scale.'

At another conference on 21 January 1918, the commanders of the attacking armies were put on the alert; thereafter a series of 'warning orders' were issued detailing preparations for the attack, culminating in the actual operational order, which went out on 10 March. The general intention of the main attack, Operation Michael, was to break through at the southern end of the British line, in the sector recently taken over from the French, with La Fère as the objective, and press on west and north towards Péronne, Arras and beyond. The Seventeenth Army would attack towards Bapaume, the Second Army towards Péronne, the Eighteenth Army south, towards Ham on the Somme. A second attack, 'Mars', by the Seventeenth Army from Arras which would by then be in German hands, would

---

* Narrow-gange track was laid in the rear areas behind the British front line, along which small locomotives hauled stores, ammunition and men from railheads and depots and supply points.

go in some days later, when the artillery deployed for Michael was again available. The preparations for 'George', on the Lys, would be continued with the intention of attacking at some time in April.

Ludendorff's orders conclude:

> The offensive is principally intended to strike the British. They now stand opposite us on the whole front of the Group of Armies which is to make the offensive. It need not be anticipated that the French will run themselves off their legs to hurry at once to the aid of their Entente colleagues. They will first wait and see if their own front is to be attacked and decide to support their Ally only when the situation has been quite cleared up.

This final assumption proved entirely accurate.

Preparations for the assault were meticulous. Great quantities of ammunition were prepared and the German artillery commander, Colonel Georg Bruchmüller, who, in spite of his relatively lowly rank, was regarded as one of the great gunnery experts of the war, laid careful plans for a drenching fire on the British Forward and Battle Zones before and during the infantry advance. This fire would begin two hours before the attack and go on, with intervals to check the ranges and adjust the fall of shot, until 0935 hours, though in the event a thick mist prevented the German artillery observers correcting the fire until later in the day.

The infantry were urged to keep close to this barrage, but above all to *push on*. Ludendorff had taken a good look at the British tactics over the past few years and put his finger accurately on the main problem: 'The success of a breakthrough,' he states in his initial instructions for this offensive, 'is not only a question of tactics and strategy but is essentially one of *reinforcement and supply* [author's italics].' Ludendorff's other points are also worth noting, for they explain how the German infantry were able to penetrate the British line with such relative ease, and thereby start the grim process that came to be called the 'March Retreat':

> The objective on the first day is the enemy's artillery. The objective for the second day depends on what is achieved on the first. There must be no rigid adherence to plans made beforehand.
>
> Infantry which looks to right or left soon comes to a stop. Touch with the enemy is the desideratum. A uniform advance in line must in no case be demanded. The fastest, not the slowest must set the pace. No time must be given to the enemy to surround any troops who have forced their way into a position ahead of their fellows.
>
> The advance of the infantry must be organised in complete combination with that of the artillery, but changes must be made as necessary by means of light signals.

The reserves must be put in where the attack is progressing, not where it is held up.

Continual scouting and patrolling must be kept up ahead of the advance and on the flanks.

The infantry must first see what it can do for itself, and must not call for artillery support directly it is held up.

Anyone who has studied the attacks that had been made in the war so far will see the point of these instructions. The tactics advocated by Ludendorff are still employed by armies today, and are popularly known as 'recce pull', since reserves and follow-up forces are 'pulled in' to support an advance against any part of the enemy line found to be vulnerable by the attacking troops.

The abandoning of the old linear type of position in the face of the penetrations achieved by full-scale attacks backed by ever-heavier artillery fire enabled infiltration tactics to work. The first army to introduce them as a standard battlefield tactic was commanded by Ludendorff, and to him is due the credit for seeing what was needed to penetrate the British line. True, he was also lucky, in that he had at his disposal large armies filled with fresh troops used to open warfare, but a general often makes his own luck. When he does, more luck often follows – and so it was with Ludendorff's offensive of March 1918.

The German infantry assault at 0940 hours enjoyed the inestimable advantage of just such luck, for their advance was cloaked by a thick mist which reduced visibility to a few yards. Although opinions differ as to which side gained the greatest benefit from this, it would appear that the balance of advantage lay with the advancing German infantry. Screened by the mist from aimed fire, they found that Bruchmüller's bombardment had cut many useful gaps in the British wire. Following Ludendorff's instructions, the assault troops were soon inside the defences of the Forward Zone and attacking the defenders from every side. General Maxse, commanding XVIII Corps, had already made a guess at what the German tactics would be, and his prediction turned out to be correct: '*Stormtruppen* and machine-gunners go ahead and do not stop for anything. They are followed 200 yards behind by masses of infantry. The Hun idea is that these Storm troops will make holes and continue their advance past our strong points. They have been training to go 12km, 7 miles on the first day.'

This is exactly what happened, the enemy employing plenty of grenades and flamethrowers, and even a few tanks, for good measure, and the British line was soon penetrated in a hundred different places. The fighting on 21 March was a 'soldiers' battle', fought out by platoons and companies and battalions, by units cut off from support from the flanks and rear, in swirling fog and smoke, without communications. It was a bitter battle and the German infantry had the best of it. Before long the Forward Zone had been overrun, and before the morning had passed the stormtroopers were leading the rest of their infantry into the Battle Zone.

British communications, especially between the infantry and the artillery, were severed by shellfire, and since the British gunners could not see their aiming posts in the fog, such fire as went down was often inaccurate. Neither could the RFC render much assistance, for fog and smoke obscured the ground and the Germans had plenty of fighters up, dominating the air over the battlefield. The fighting on 21 March is best imagined as a confused brawl fought in a dense fog. Before long many of the defending units were falling back, or wandering about in the mist, trying to find some position to defend that the German infiltrators had not already outflanked.

By the end of the day on the Fifth Army front, the German infantry had overrun the Forward Zone and in many places were across, or well inside, the Battle Zone. In the south, from La Fère to the Somme Canal, the Battle Zone was already in German hands, and the British III Corps had put preparations in hand to withdraw overnight to the Rear Zone, although, since this barely existed, the line of the Crozat Canal, about two miles behind the Battle Zone, looked a more suitable place at which to make a stand. North of the Somme Canal, the 30th Division were holding on to the forward edge of their Battle Zone, the canal protecting their right flank, but further north the Germans were inside the Battle Zones of the other divisions to a varying degree all the way to Épéhy, in the 21st Division area.

Yet further to the north, as far as the Flesquières Salient on the Third Army front, the German advance had been held, but there had been penetrations of the Battle Zone east of Bapaume. The enemy now only had to make one major push and they would be through the Battle Zone defences and into open country, with only the Somme to cross. The situation looked desperate, and so it was, but the Fifth Army was still in being and still in action, and only in the south was it preparing to pull back. In other parts of the line some formations had been overrun and a number had gone to the rear, but a majority of the Fifth Army units attacked, and all those of the Third Army, were fighting hard to hold their positions, or at least to slow down the German advance.

Byng's Third Army did not lose so much ground, having better-prepared positions and more men to defend them, but their right-flank divisions had to fall back to keep in touch with those of Gough's left flank as they were forced back. Even so, the stout fight put up by Third Army forced Ludendorff to change his original plan. By the 24th the Fifth Army had been badly damaged but not totally destroyed. The Third Army was holding on in the centre, and the weak spot seemed to be the junction between the two armies, where the Fifth Army was hanging on, if barely, waiting for some of Pétain's forty reserve divisions to come to their aid.

At this point Ludendorff changed his plan. The original task of General Oskar von Hutier's Eighteenth Army was to hold back the French in the south while the two other German armies, the Second and Seventeenth, smashed a breach and then turned northwards and rolled up the British line. Now, said Ludendorff, 'The object is to separate the French and British

Armies.' He therefore ordered all three German armies to press on towards Amiens, with the aim of dividing the two Allied armies and driving them apart.

This advance went rapidly ahead. After just three days the German armies occupied a front astride the Somme, from Bapaume through Combles to Péronne and Nesle. They continued to grind forward, especially in the south, and by the time the tide was stemmed on 5 April they had made an advance on a line between St Quentin and Villers-Bretonneux of some forty miles. Seen on a map (page 460), the ground now occupied by the Germans is pear-shaped, narrow in the north, near Arras on the Scarpe, where they had not yet attacked, widening slowly as the advancing German line is followed south, taking in Bapaume, Albert and Bray-sur-Somme, all of which were now in enemy hands, skirting Villers-Bretonneux, which had been lost and retaken, and passing west of Montdidier, before the line turns east again and sweeps back across the Oise.

The rapid withdrawal of the Fifth Army caused consternation among the Allied commanders and political leaders. On 23 March, two days into the attack, Haig wrote in his diary, 'I cannot make out why the Fifth Army has gone back so far without making some kind of stand.' The short answer is that the Germans had attacked with great skill and in overwhelming strength and were still coming on. The weak and inadequately manned British defences had fallen, and with no reserves available to make a defensive line the Fifth Army were doing the next best thing: trying to stay in being as an army, falling back to avoid annihilation, and attempting to avoid a total rout.

As Haig had pointed out before the battle, the British were desperately short of reserves, and the eight infantry divisions in GHQ Reserve and three cavalry divisions in Fifth Army reserve were soon sucked into the battle. The arrangement agreed with the French before the British took over more of the line in January was that each army would provide mutual support in case of a German attack – and if ever mutual support was needed, this was the time. Some French formations, notably II Cavalry Corps and V Corps, had arrived in the British III Corps area on 22 March, but they had come up without artillery or food. On 23 April, two days after the opening of the Michael offensive, Haig visited Gough's HQ at Villers-Bretonneux, just east of Amiens, and was met there by Pétain, who brought some disquieting news. In January, Haig had agreed to an extension of the British line to La Fére on the Oise, on the clear understanding that Pétain would support him if the former French sector of the line, now occupied by Fifth Army, was attacked. Now that attack had come in, the French C-in-C declined to help.

Pétain believed that he was about to be attacked in Champagne, and while he agreed that it was important for the British and French armies to stay in touch, he could not – or would not – spare troops to bolster the Fifth Army's front. Gough, fighting desperately with two German armies, was receiving the same news from the French generals on his flank. General Humbert, commanding the French Third Army, in reserve behind the right of Fifth Army, told Gough that 'no troops had been placed at his disposal by General Pétain for co-operation with me [Gough] . . . though the particular role of Humbert's Army, as I had been given to understand it, was to move up to our support in case of necessity, and take over its original front, relieving Fifth Army.'

Later on, Humbert arrived at Gough's HQ and when the latter said how glad he was to see him, the French general shrugged and replied, 'Mais je n'ai que mon fanion' ('But I have only my flag'), nodding at the small pennant on his staff car which, Gough wrote later, 'was not exactly the aid we were looking for at that moment'. On the following day, 24 March, Pétain arrived at Haig's Advanced HQ at Dury, four miles south of Amiens, with even worse news, telling Haig that he was in the process of forming a Reserve Army Group under General Émile Fayolle and intended to use this to cover a wholesale withdrawal of the French Army towards Paris. Once again, as so often before in this war, the French were looking after their own interests, and leaving their ally to sink or swim. Pétain was quite frank about it. 'I at once asked Pétain if he meant to abandon my right flank,' Haig recorded. 'He nodded assent and added "It is the only thing to do, if the enemy compel the Allies to fall back still further." '

The problems of a divided command were now fully exposed. The British had to screen their supply routes back to the Channel ports. The French were far more concerned with protecting Paris – and Pétain had *all* the Allied reserves. Some *forty* French divisions were now gathering at Montdidier, while every division of the British Armies in France was either already in the fighting line or in close support. If both Commanders-in-Chief stuck to their plans, the inevitable result would be a parting of the Allied armies. Into the gap thus created the German armies would swiftly flow, to roll up and defeat the British and then to turn their full might against the French. If this were to happen – and on 24 March there was little to prevent it – the war was lost.

Haig therefore sent an urgent telegram to the CIGS, General Sir Henry Wilson, asking him to come out to France immediately and 'arrange that General Foch, or some other determined general who would fight, should be given supreme control of operations in France'. Wilson's rampant francophilia and his close friendship with Foch might at last be used to his country's good.

Haig's telegram was just one of several urgent messages flowing across the Channel as the Fifth Army fell back. Lloyd George had already sent Lord Milner, a member of his War Cabinet, hurrying to Paris for a meeting with Clemenceau. Foch, too, had cabled Wilson, also asking him to come over, and armed with this double invitation the CIGS reached Montreuil just before noon on 25 March. Haig and Wilson then had a discussion in which, according to the latter, Haig agreed that Foch should be asked to 'co-ordinate' the actions of the French and British armies.

Wilson went on to Paris and put this suggestion to Foch. Since this is what both men had been angling for since 1914, it is hardly surprising that Foch agreed. On the following day, 26 March, the various leaders met in the Hôtel de Ville (town hall) at Doullens, HQ of Byng's Third Army. France was represented by President Poincaré, Clemenceau, Pétain, Foch and Weygand, Britain by Milner, Wilson, Haig, and the latter's Chief of General Staff (CGS), Lieutenant-General Sir Herbert Lawrence. Before that conference began, however, Haig had another private meeting with Plumer, Byng and Horne, respectively the commanders of the Second, Third and First Armies in which he told them that Amiens must be held 'at all costs', and that no more ground must be lost. The generals then returned to their commands and Haig went in to meet his allies

The conference began with a discussion of the situation, and of the decision that Amiens must be held at all costs. Then came a declaration by Pétain that the British had evidently been defeated, the Fifth Army destroyed, he was therefore ordering the French armies to withdraw and make a front screening Paris. Haig demurred, pointing out that the Fifth Army was still fighting, with some of its corps actually under French command, and that although it had certainly fallen back, most of the front was intact; in short, Gough's army had bent, but it had *not* broken. The need now, Haig stressed, was to defend Amiens, a vital rail and road centre for the British, and for the French and British armies to stay in touch. Pétain disagreed, claiming that the Fifth army, 'Alas, no longer exists, it is broken,' and compared its performance with that of the Italians at Caporetto, a remark which, as the Official History records, produced a sharp rebuke from Wilson. It then transpired that Pétain had not been informed by his subordinate, General Fayolle, that Maxse's XVIII Corps and Lieutenant-General Sir Herbert Watts's XIX Corps of Fifth Army were still largely intact and that four French divisions of Fayolle's Sixth Army had filled in the gap between Maxse's corps and Lieutenant-General Richard Butler's III Corps of Fifth Army.

Foch then broke in to state that the Allied armies must fight in front of Amiens, that they must fight where they now were – 'Since we have not been able to stop the Germans on the Somme we must not now retire a single inch.' Haig's moment had come. 'If General Foch would consent to give me his advice,' he said, 'I will gladly follow it.'

With that remark, Field Marshal Sir Douglas Haig changed the command structure of the war. It took a few minutes for the politicians understand the import of Haig's statement, and then to seize their opportunity, but Clemenceau swiftly came up with the proposal that 'General Foch is charged by the British and French Governments with the co-ordination of the action of the British and French Armies in front of Amiens. He will arrange to this effect with the two Generals-in-Chief [Haig and Pétain] who are invited to furnish him with the necessary information.'

This proposal was too vague for Haig, however, who pointed out that

Foch must have full authority over all the operations on the Western Front, not just before Amiens. After Pétain had agreed, the proposal was duly amended to that effect and signed by Clemenceau and Milner. The long-dreaded, and long-resisted, moment had passed, and Haig was heard to murmur his relief that now he was to 'deal with a man rather than a Committee'. Lord Milner then asked General Lawrence, Haig's CGS, how the politicians in London could help the generals, and was told, 'By leaving them alone.'

Foch lost no time getting a grip on his new command. His first act, even before leaving Doullens, was to order Pétain to accelerate the movement of the French First Army divisions to the north of the Oise, and to start building up a strong force before Amiens, using some of the French divisions currently in reserve. He then went directly to Gough's HQ at Dury, where he spoke sharply to the Fifth Army commander and ordered him that there must be no more retirements, though he offered no hints as to how this was to be achieved. Gough was somewhat surprised at Foch's att.. .de, for he felt, with some reason, that in the circumstances his army had done well, and believed that the same opinion was held at Haig's HQ – as indeed it was. He had understood that when the German attack came, and if it could not be held, he was to fight a rearguard action and thus buy time while the counter-offensive was organised.

Above all, Gough felt, as he wrote in his book about the March Retreat, 'that the [Fifth] Army had faithfully carried out the terrible and heavy task Haig had set it', and he was therefore more than a little taken aback by Foch's manner and by the questions the latter hurled at his head, since he had not yet been informed that Foch was now effectively the Supreme Commander. Why was Gough at his HQ and not with his troops in the fighting line? was one question; Why could Gough not fight as the British had fought at First Ypres? was another; followed by Why did the army retire? Gough spoke good French, but he was too polite to make the obvious retorts: that generals no longer rode about on white horses in the van of the battle, waving swords and cheering their men on; that First Ypres had been an altogether different kind of shambles – and Foch had not been of great help on that occasion; and, finally, that if Foch did not know the situation that had developed over the previous months, before and behind Gough's line, and in which the various elements had combined to create the current predicament, then he must be woefully ignorant of the facts.

In the same book, however, Gough merely points out, mildly, that he was at his HQ because he had an appointment to meet Foch there, and because that was his proper post anyway. He goes on to say that at First Ypres in 1914 the Germans had had nothing like the men and guns they had deployed on 21 March 1918, and that the Fifth Army had fought a rearguard action since that day because the strategic and tactical situation demanded it, and because such an action, if one proved necessary, was in accordance with the plan of his Commander-in-Chief.

Foch, though, did not wait for the answers to any of these questions. Neither did he enquire into the state of Gough's forces or their current positions. Ordering that 'There must be no more retreat, the line must be held at all costs,' he walked out of the room, got into his car and drove away.

Gough was subsequently informed that his right-hand corps, Maxse's XVIII, would shortly be relieved by French First Army units and could be withdrawn into Fifth Army reserve. Duly encouraged by this, he telephoned General Lawrence to inform him that in his opinion the German attack was petering out, and that if some fresh divisions could be sent to Fifth Army, he would counter-attack towards the Somme. Since no fresh British divisions were available, however, this proposal was not taken up.

Gough was in fact right, for though the Germans captured Bray-sur-Somme, south of Albert, on 26 March, there were growing signs of fatigue and indiscipline in their ranks. The German infantry had been marching and fighting for five days now and were becoming tired, but much of the discontent they were also beginning to display was due to their discouraging discovery of how well-supplied the British troops were. In the trenches and dugouts overrun in their advance the German soldiers found wine and coffee, ample food, including large supplies of meat and cheese, warm clothing and good boots, items that had become rare indeed within the blockaded confines of Germany. As a result, the German infantry, instead of pushing ahead, were stopping to loot. Drunkenness and a reluctance to move on were slowing down the advance of the German Army, adding to the problems caused by lengthening supply lines, battle losses and fatigue. This came too late to save General Gough. On 27 March orders came from the CIGS instructing Haig to remove Gough from the command of Fifth Army. Haig complied with this order, replacing him with Rawlinson, but kept Gough at GHQ, perhaps intending to find him other employment.

Meanwhile, the pressure on the British front lessened. The Germans had no cavalry to exploit their breakthrough, and this was the time and place where mounted troops could have justified their place in the Line of Battle, but the Germans had long since sent most of their cavalry troopers into the line as infantry. Infantry, therefore, must force the pace and keep the British moving back. Eventually, as in 1914, the German infantry could not manage that pace. The 'Mars' offensive, or as the British called it, the 'Battle of Arras, 28 March, 1918', failed to make much ground and was called off on the same day, and attacks on other sections of the Third Army front proved equally ineffective. Only in the south were the Germans still pushing ahead, but even here their advance was slowing.

The orders issued by Foch for the deployment of the Allied armies gradually had an effect, although he found that Pétain was now reluctant to accept his suggestions. As a result, at another inter-Allied conference at Beauvais on 3 April Foch's remit was extended to cover the 'strategic direction of military operations on the Western Front, for all three Armies, American, British and French', while their respective Commanders-in-

Chief, Pershing, Haig and Pétain, retained control of their tactical deployment and were allowed the right of consultation with their national governments if they felt the interests or safety of their armies were threatened. Even this extension of Foch's powers was not found to be enough, however, and on 14 April he asked to be appointed to the new post of 'Commander-in-Chief of the Allied Armies'. His request was granted. Thus, and again with the right of resort to their home governments if they felt the need, the three Allied generals came under Foch's direct and absolute command.

During all this the fighting went on unabated. Then, on 5 April, Ludendorff called a halt to Operation Michael, admitting that the attempt at a breakthrough had failed 'because the enemy resistance was beyond our powers'. By then the German advance between the Oise and the Somme had come to a stop as much from tiredness and a shortage of supplies as from any resistance or counter-attacks put in by the British and French forces. Casualties had been high, the British having lost 163,00 men killed, wounded, missing and captured, the French 77,000, and the Germans something in excess of 70,000. German losses were in the region of 250,000, with especially heavy casualties among the stormtroops.

This halting of the German attack came too late to save the career of General Sir Hubert Gough. Lloyd George was well aware of the part his own failure to supply reinforcements to the armies in France had played in the creation of the March Retreat débâcle, and needed a scapegoat before the bulk of the blame was pinned on him. At the Beauvais conference, therefore, openly worried that he would be attacked in the House of Commons for not having tackled the manpower problem before, he confided to Haig that he held Gough directly responsible for the disaster that had befallen the Fifth Army.

Haig pointed out that at no time had Gough lost his head, and that he had done his best under very difficult circumstances, adding that 'Gough had few reserves, an extended front and increased hostile forces' – facts of which the prime minister was all too well aware – 'and a long front entirely without defensive works and recently taken over from the French where he had to face the brunt of the German attack.' Nevertheless, Lloyd George remained adamant that Gough must go, but Haig refused to send him home without a direct order. This order duly arrived in a telegram from Lord Derby, the Secretary for War, on 4 April. As for his army, that was to be renamed as the Fourth Army, and General Sir Henry Rawlinson was to be brought over from the Supreme War Council at Versailles to command it. Haig was upset by this, to him, unjust action, and told Derby that if his own resignation was desired he was willing to offer it. The Secretary for War declined to take up this suggestion – but Gough still had to go home.

General Sir Herbert Gough was not a great commander. He had not done well on the Somme or at Passchendaele, but even so it is ironic that he was finally sacked for a failure that was certainly not entirely his fault. It is unlikely that anyone faced with the situation in which he found himself on 21 March could have done any better. Gough had probably reached his command peak at corps level, but after studying the dreadful problems in March 1918 it is possible to feel a certain sympathy for him. His sacking was unjust, even though his dismissal was no great loss to the ranks of the High Command.

The effect of Lloyd George's actions over the previous winter were now becoming obvious to all. Haig's armies had been deliberately starved of troops and, since Haig rightly regarded the northern end of his line, from Arras to the Salient, as the most vital section of the Western Front, that was where the bulk of his slender resources were placed, so that Gough, away to the south, had had to make do with whatever could be spared. Added to this was the French requirement, accepted by Lloyd George, that the British Army should take over more of their line in the south; the old French line, poorly fortified, was made Gough's responsibility, and he had neither the men nor the matériel to improve the defences before the Michael attack was launched.

Moreover, Gough had never been charged with holding the St Quentin position against a strong attack. It was accepted that he would have to fall back and Haig was quite prepared for this to happen, provided Amiens could be held. What happened after the initial German attack owed as much to bad luck as bad management. The fog greatly aided the attackers, and no army then in the line, Allied or German, could have withstood the weight of the 6,000 guns and thousands of mortars so skilfully deployed by Colonel Bruchmüller, Ludendorff's artillery commander.

Nor was Gough well served by all of his troops, although the majority fought doggedly, and often with great gallantry in the face of hopeless odds. Even so, some units clearly did fall back before they needed to – some even as far as the Somme – but here again the situation they were faced with has to be taken into account. All armies have a preferred manner of fighting, and the British soldier, though always superb in defence, preferred to fight in line and have his flanks secure. The defensive strongpoints or 'birdcages' he was ordered to defend at St Quentin were not to his taste at all, and he had little training in and no experience of holding them. The time that they might have spent in training to hold these positions had been spent in digging and wiring them. As a result, the men were tired as well as poorly trained; furthermore, in spite of all their efforts the defences were still inadequate.

Defending a position that has been infiltrated, outflanked and surrounded calls for more than barbed wire and dugouts – it requires a certain attitude of mind and resilience of spirit. The British Army did not acquire these until the middle years of another war, when the Guards held the 'Knightsbridge Box' in the Western Desert against Rommel's panzer attacks, and the British and Indian Army garrison of the 'Admin Box' in Burma fought on until relieved despite being completely surrounded and cut off by the Japanese. On the Western Front in 1918, however, 'infiltration' was a comparatively new form of warfare, and during Operation Michael it did what it was intended to do; it made the defenders anxious about their rear and flanks, and thus prone to fall back.

Ordering a unit to fight 'to the last man and the last round' is a command rarely used at least by sensible commanders, because it cannot be taken seriously. When all hope has gone, when the ammunition has run out and the enemy is around or inside the defences, in great force and with a supply of grenades and equipped with flamethrowers, further resistance is pointless, for it only leads to even greater loss of life. The German attack swamped the defences of the Fifth Army and swept them away, and a large part of the blame for that lay in the office of the Prime Minister in Downing Street. When all the circumstances are taken into account, the lack of men and matériel, the extension of the British line, the concealing fog and the overwhelming weight of the German attack and its accompanying bombardment, the retreat of the Fifth Army on 21 March and on the days following is, at the very least, understandable. In the event, the falling back of Gough's army was nowhere near as fatal to the Allied cause as subsequent accounts have alleged. It may, in the long run, even have been advantageous, for it finally brought the German armies out from behind those defences which had served them so well and for so long. When everything is taken into account, it cannot be fairly maintained that the only reason the Fifth Army was defeated in March 1918 was because it had an incompetent commander.

Gough duly gave up his command, and Haig gave him the task of surveying the defences of Amiens, but within a few days a message arrived that Gough must be sent home to face an inquiry. In the event, this never took place, probably because Lloyd George was well aware that some of the facts it would reveal would not be to his credit. The matter of the lack of reinforcements for France could not be hushed up, as was shortly to be proved. In May, Major-General Sir Frederick Maurice, formerly Director of Military Operations (DMO) under Robertson at the War Office, and therefore a man in a position to know the facts, wrote a letter to the press, refuting claims made by Lloyd George in the House of Commons in April to the effect that Haig had had more than enough men in France to stem the German attack in March. Maurice had resigned his post in protest at the Prime Minister's falsification of the true facts.

Lloyd George had told the House that: 'Notwithstanding the heavy casualties in 1917, the Army in France was considerably stronger on the 1st January 1918 than on the 1st January 1917,' and had added that anyway there were no men available in Britain to reinforce him. The 'Maurice letter' calling this statement into question caused a considerable storm when it was published in the newspapers, but Lloyd George was able to ride the furore out by revealing that his declaration in April had been based on figures supplied by General Maurice's department; he did not reveal, however, that these figures had subsequently been corrected.

This letter to the press, and Lloyd George's ostensible ability to refute it, ended Maurice's military career. The true facts did not come out until 1954, when a book by Lord Beaverbrook, *Men and Power*, revealed that the expansion of the Army *in France* between 1917–18 had been entirely due to the increase of labour, transport and non-combatant personnel, totalling just under 400,00 men, but including large contingents of Italians, Chinese, and South African natives. The *fighting* strength of the BEF had indeed fallen, though in fact there had been no fewer than 607,403 soldiers in the UK 'fit for general service' in the early months of 1918. Lloyd George had been well aware of all this when he made his statement to the House of Commons in April 1918. His career, however, unlike General Maurice's, survived the controversy.

Gough duly departed for England, never to hold an active-service command again. He had hardly left when, on 9 April, as the offensive on the Fifth Army front petered out, Ludendorff switched his artillery and his attention to the Lys front. The second German attack, now codenamed 'Georgette', came in against Horne's First Army and Plumer's Second Army along the River Lys, on a 12-mile front between the La Bassée Canal and Ypres.

This attack was well timed, for in the previous ten days both these armies had sent a number of divisions to support the Third and Fifth Armies. The main weight of the German attack, by fourteen divisions, nine in the attack and five in reserve, and supported by a tremendous quantity of artillery, came in against XI and XV Corps of Horne's First Army. These two corps had just four divisions in the line with two in reserve, and one of these front-line formations, a recently arrived Portuguese division in XI Corps, soon collapsed, letting the German stormtroops and infantry into the heart of the British position. As on 21 March, this attack was also assisted by a dense fog, and by nightfall on 9 April the First Army had been driven back some three miles to the line of the River Lys.

On the morning of the 10th, the second phase of Georgette, a powerful assault against Plumer's Second Army to the North, came in between Armentières and the Ypres–Comines Canal. The object of this attack was to seize the Messines–Wytschaete Ridge captured by Second Army in the previous year but, after a fierce defence by three divisions of IX Corps, it was beaten off.

Not so the attack against First Army, which gradually spread to the north and east, its object the taking of the British supply base at Hazebrouck. If this fell, there was nothing to stop the German Sixth Army pressing on to the Channel ports and cutting the British forces in two. The latter, however, were putting up a tremendous fight in what became, in effect, the 'Fourth Battle of Ypres' and gradually the attack was held. During the rest of April the Germans only gained another eight miles; they were finally stopped five miles from Hazebrouck, and there the attack petered out.

Nevertheless, Haig was faced with a critical state of affairs, for this was the situation he had always feared, the reason why he had been obliged to starve Gough's army of men and supplies. Haig's prime task was to defend the Channel ports, and these lay only thirty miles from the Lys position. He also had to maintain contact with the French armies to the south, even though Armentières had fallen and the German Sixth Army was pushing west up the Lys valley. Foch declined to supply any reserves, so yet again the British were on their own. The crux of the battle came on 11 April when, faced with no other option, Haig issued his famous Order of the Day, a message which concluded bleakly:

> There is no other course open to us but to fight it out! Every position must be held to the last man: there must be no retirement. With our backs to the wall and believing in the justice of our cause, each one of us must fight on to the end. The safety of our homes and the freedom of mankind alike depend on the conduct of each one of us at this critical moment.

This situation did, however, concentrate the mind of General Foch, who now realised that the main objective of the German attacks since 21 March had been to destroy the British Army. Once that had been done, Ludendorff would turn the full weight of his armies on the French; self-interest therefore demanded that every effort be made to shore up the British line. This decision came none too soon, for the German offensive in the north had now pressed the British back to the outskirts of Bailleul. Plumer was given permission to withdraw three miles, and three French infantry and three cavalry divisions were placed under his command. The Belgian divisions in the north of the Salient also extended their line, and thus reinforced, the British line held.

On 29 April the Georgette offensive ground to a halt and the great German offensive against the British line ended. The cost to the Germans had been considerable: 240,000 lost men in just under six weeks, an indication to Lloyd George, had he cared to notice it, that German attacks could cause casualties as readily as British attacks, and that there was no easy way to fight and win this war. Villers-Bretonneux had been lost on the 24th, in the first tank-versus-tank battle in history, but the Anzacs recaptured the town on the following day. To even the score, Mount Kemmel, previously a bastion in the British line on the Salient, was lost by the French on the same day. The total losses French and British, came to 348,000 men killed, wounded and missing, almost the same as the German total . . . a figure approaching 700,000 casualties from all sides in less than two months, and still the war went on.*

On 19 April, while the battles along the Lys continued, Foch told Haig that he intended to position a reserve of fifteen French divisions behind the

---

* These figures are taken from the Official History, *1918*, Volume III, p. 490.

British line but that in order to do so, the British must take over yet another section of the French front. This could be done by sending some tired divisions to a quiet sector of the French line and Haig duly agreed, on the understanding that there should be no permanent mingling of French and British divisions. In the end five British divisions, all from IX Corps, were sent south to the Chemin des Dames and took up position in a quiet sector of the front, three in the line and two in reserve. They were still there when the Germans struck here on 27 May, the main attack falling on the section of the French front held by these British divisions.

The German attack, codenamed 'Blücher', was wholly unexpected by the Allies. It began with a tremendous Bruchmüller-style bombardment which obliterated the wire and most of the front-line trenches and dugouts before moving relentlessly back to pound the rear areas. After two and a half hours of this, seventeen divisions of German infantry attacked the Chemin des Dames ridge and swept across it and down into the Aisne valley, getting across the river before the bridges could be blown. In a single day they advanced ten miles, further than they had ever managed against Gough in March, and a week later they were back on the River Marne, where they had last been in 1914, and their heavy guns were shelling the outskirts of Paris. The five British divisions caught up in this onslaught lost 28,000 men killed, wounded and missing, but earned high praise from their French colleagues. More ominously for the Germans, this battle brought a new element into the war when, on 1 June, part of the US 3rd Division took part in the defence of Château-Thierry, the town on the Marne which marked the farthest point of this latest German advance.

Other US divisions were now entering the line, and with their appearance at the front the German High Command knew that they had now lost the war, though it might last a little while longer and cost a further quantity of lives. After 1 June it was only a matter of time, but the American C-in-C, General Pershing had been, and remained, reluctant to commit his men to battle before they were properly trained and equipped, and adamant that US troops would not be used as infantry reinforcements for either the British or French field armies, as Foch, and to a lesser degree Haig, were so anxious to use them.

Like Douglas Haig and his predecessor as Commander-in-Chief, Sir John French, General John J. Pershing was a cavalry officer. Born in Missouri in 1860, he graduated from the US Military Academy, West Point, in 1881, in time to take part in the last stages of the Indian Wars in the South-West, during which he served against the Apache and Comanche tribes in Arizona and Texas, and eventually rose to the command of the 10th Cavalry, a regiment of black troopers known to the Indians as the 'Buffalo Soldiers'. It was this posting as a commander of black troops that earned him the nickname 'Black Jack' Pershing. Pershing fought Apaches along the Mexican border, saw active service in Cuba during the Spanish–American War of 1898, served in the Philippines (then a US dependency) against the Moros in 1903, and with the Japanese Army during the Russo-Japanese War of 1904–5, and in 1916 led the American Punitive Expedition into Mexico in pursuit of the bandit and revolutionary Pancho Villa. By 1917 Pershing was probably the most experienced battlefield commander in the United States Army.

He also had powerful political connections and spoke adequate French, two qualities that combined in his favour when it came to choosing a commander of the American Expeditionary Force (AEF). He had married Frances Warren, daughter of the Governor of Wyoming who was also a US Senator, and had been raised to the rank of Brigadier-General by the personal order of President Theodore ('Teddy') Roosevelt, who himself had fought in Cuba. Pershing was also a notorious womaniser, and had managed to father at least two illegitimate children in the course of his travels; in 1915, however, he suffered personal tragedy when his wife and three daughters were killed in a fire at the San Francisco Presidio, and he was left alone to raise his son, the sole survivor.

Pershing had only lately returned from chasing – and failing to catch – Pancho Villa when, in the spring of 1917, the call came from Washington, offering him the command of the American Expeditionary Force. He and a small staff arrived in France in June to a tumultuous welcome that was only slightly muted by the discovery that the hoped-for, limitless supply of American troops lay some time in the future.

Pershing's situation in some ways mirrored that of Field Marshal French in 1914, while the situation of the BEF at the start of the war was similar to that which confronted the AEF in 1917–18. The United States Army was small, and primarily designed to defend the land frontiers of the United State. It was therefore ill equipped for war of the type and scale of the one now raging on the Western Front in France. Practically everything needed had to be manufactured from scratch or obtained from the French or British, from rifles and steel helmets to field artillery and aircraft, and though great numbers of American men were drafted into the US Army in 1917, they had to be trained, clothed, equipped and transported to France. The old rule for equipping an army, that 'In the first year you got nothing, the second year a little and in the third year as much as you need', could not be applied to the situation affecting the US troops; there simply was not the time. The French and British armies were at the end of their resources, especially of manpower, able to fight on, but unable to do more than that, and much more was needed if the Germans were to be defeated.

Pershing was unwilling to send his troops into action in battalion strength under French or British officers, and although by the middle months of 1918 some American units had seen action, and the first few divisions to complete their training had spent some time in the line with British units in order to learn what the conditions and fighting were like, Pershing was anxious to develop a full-size and properly equipped American Army before he entered the battle. The main struggle against the Germans therefore remained in the hands of the French and British. Plans for the deployment of US divisions were, however, on the agenda at a conference called at Versailles on 2 June, a meeting attended by Clemenceau, Foch, Lord Milner, who had replaced Lord Derby as the British Secretary for War, and Haig.

The latter declared himself to be most unhappy with the performance of the French Army in recent weeks, and deplored Foch's proposal to remove all the American divisions currently training with the British armies and use them to relieve French divisions in the line, in order to free French formations for the battle then raging on the Marne. Haig believed that the French Army had been 'fought out' by the battering it had taken since the beginning of 1917, and that it lacked officers and competent NCOs. Far better, he felt, to press on with the formation and 'blooding' of the American divisions – a force of 100 divisions was mentioned – and have them grouped into armies and into the line as all-American units.

This was not a clear-cut argument, for both Foch and Haig had a point. The crucial factor was time. It takes a certain amount of time to train any soldier and prepare him and his comrades for battle, but it takes a good deal longer to find and train staff officers and field commanders at battalion, brigade and divisional level. As we have seen, trained, efficient staff officers are essential to the planning of attacks and the management of forces, and the US Army was very short of them. That army had expanded rapidly since 1917 and had now run out of senior commanders. The obvious option was to take the US infantry and put them under experienced battlefield commanders from the French or, since there would be fewer language difficulties, the British Armies. This was a logical solution, and would have brought the superb US soldiers into the battle quickly but Pershing would not have it . . . and on balance he was probably right, troops fight better under their own commanders.

Foch was more concerned with shoring up the French line on the Marne and on 3 June he began to move reserves south, formations which included British divisions currently in reserve behind the British front. This action disturbed Field Marshal Haig. He had divined Ludendorff's strategy of striking up and down the Western Front at any point where the Allied line was found to be unsupported, and consequently feared that once his line was depleted of reserves another German attack would come in there. There was a confrontation between Foch and Haig over this movement of reserves but the former stuck to his right, as Allied 'Generalissimo', to move 'his' reserves to any point he wished. The crux of the argument was that Foch had ordered these divisions to move without consulting Haig or sending the order via his GHQ. This was not the agreed chain of command, and was, moreover, yet another example of the French pushing any agreement as far as it would go.

The German Blücher attack on the Noyon-Rheims Salient ended on 4 June, and on the 9th Ludendorff struck again, not at the British, as Haig had feared, but at the French Third Army between Montdidier and Noyon, again thrusting south and west towards Compiègne and Paris. This fourth attack, codenamed 'Gneisenau', was made by General von Hutier's Eighteenth Army, which had proved so successful against Gough, and the Germans advanced ten miles before they were halted outside Compiègne. The French collapse did a great deal to restore Haig's reputation, and rather more to curb the arrogance of the French. Foch began to pay more attention to what Haig had to say, while the usual mutterings from Downing Street became muted. Pétain was now out of favour, and General Charles Mangin, a fierce, fighting general who had taken a leading role at Verdum and in Nivelle's offensive, but who had been removed from command after the failure of the latter, was recalled to service. The American divisions were now arriving in France in quantity, their training was well under way and from mid-June, after three hard and dangerous months, matters were beginning to look up for the Allies.

The Germans, however, were not yet either defeated or dismayed, and they struck again at the French on the Noyon–Montdidier front in the Battle of the Matz. This battle lasted five full days, although by the 11th the German advance had been halted. General Mangin, commanding the French Tenth Army, then struck back hard, with the US 1st and 2nd Divisions leading his attack. From then on the balance of the battles began to turn the Allied way, and slowly they began to push the Germans back.

On 25 June, the US Marines took Belleau Wood. Three days later Vaux, near Soissons, was in American hands and on that day Mangin got his troops back on to the Chemin des Dames near Soissons. On the Somme, on 4 July, the Australians under Monash maintained their reputation as crack troops by taking Le Hamel; four companies of the US 33rd Division (National Guard) took part in the Hamel battle, and celebrated Independence Day in the German trenches. The dust had barely settled after this victory, however, when, on 15 July, another massive German attack came in against the French.

This, the fifth offensive, codenamed 'Reims-Marneschutz', was a double thrust by the German First, Third and Seventh Armies. The Seventh Army attacked on the Marne between Château-Thierry and Rheims while the German Third and Fourth Armies struck east from that city, the combined offensive aiming to eliminate the French salient at Rheims, cut the railway link from there to Châlons and make a decisive move towards Paris. This attack soon petered out, however, for the French were able to avoid the usual shattering effects of Colonel Bruchmüller's artillery bombardment by evacuating their front-line trenches, and counter-attacked vigorously when the German infantry came forward. The assault, the last offensive mounted by the German Army in the Great War, ground to a halt by 17 July. A week later General Plumer sent the Second Army into the attack and recaptured Meteren . . . and so the fighting continued, up and down the line.

The war still had more than three months to run and there was a great deal of fighting still to be done, as well as a great many casualties still to be suffered, but the end was no longer in doubt. That this was so was not simply because Ludendorff's great gamble had failed, although it had, and disastrously. The Germans had fixed their hopes upon a massive assault, but that had meant coming out from behind that deep defensive line from which they had defied and punished the Allies for so long. The German Army, miles from its fortified Hindenburg Line positions, could now be fought in the open and, apart from the wonderful advantage of ever-increasing numbers of American troops, there were other factors that now made an Allied victory certain. The French and British were learning how to fight the German Army, how to strike and strike again at weak points in the line. The days of dogged trench warfare, with all the inherent advantages that gave to the defence, were over. Now the armies were in the open field and victory would go to the generals who handled them best.

The cost had been high. The British, who had borne the brunt of these recent attacks, had lost a great quantity of men, and the French Army was barely hanging on. Haig was still there, as indomitable and as immovable as ever, but Gough had gone, his reputation in tatters. The judgement of history ought to be that both Gough and his Fifth Army had done well, if not very well, in the hard circumstances that befell them on 21 March and in the days thereafter, but that is not how history tells it. Now, however, the Anglo-French line had stabilised, the Americans were in the field, the Germans had been held after three months of fighting, and General Foch was Commander-in-Chief of the Allied Armies. It was time for the Allies to consider what the next step should be.

The Final Offensive. July–Nov 1918

CHAPTER 22

THE TURN OF THE TIDE
AND THE HUNDRED DAYS,
JUNE–NOVEMBER 1918

*'The invader has recoiled. His effectives are falling, his
morale is weakening, whilst on our side our American
comrades have already made our disconcerted enemy feel the
vigour of their blows. Today I say to you, with tenacity,
boldness and vigour, victory must be yours.'*

Marshal Ferdinand Foch, Commander-in-Chief
of the Allied Armies, 7 August 1918

On 24 July 1918, General Foch, Commander-in-Chief of the Allied
Armies in France, summoned his Commanders-in-Chief, Field Marshal Haig, General Pétain and General Pershing, to a meeting at his
headquarters in the Bombon Château near Melun, 25 miles south-east of
Paris. Though the Second Battle of the Marne was still being fought out and
would not end until 6 August, by the end of July the Entente Powers and
their army commanders knew that victory was in sight, even if it was not yet
actually within their grasp. Foch, believing that the time was ripe for a
counter-offensive in which the Germans could be decisively defeated, wished
to consult with his army commanders on the part their various forces might
play. He was particularly anxious that the American Army should now
bring its weight to bear and thus tilt the balance against the German forces.

Foch was right in his first premise. The Germans had been halted or
turned back, the big gamble of the Michael, Mars, Georgette and the other
assaults had failed and the strategic objectives of those engagements, to
destroy the British Army, split the Allied armies in two and then turn in
force upon the French, had not materialised. The three subsequent attacks
upon the French had achieved even less. Moreover, the Allies were at long
last fighting as a united force, and had the prospect of an almost unlimited
supply of fresh troops from the United States, some of whom were already in

the field. The emergencies of the last few weeks had obliged General Pershing, Commander-in-Chief of the American Expeditionary Force, to lend some of his divisions to the French or British Armies, where they had done extremely well. It was now generally accepted, not least by Pershing, that the US troops were now ready to join the battle in strength.

The experiences of General Pershing from the time he reached France in June 1917 are relevant to this story, not least because they point up the fact that the constant pressure brought to bear since 1914 on the British Commanders-in-Chief, French and Haig, to put themselves and their troops directly under French command, was by no means unique to the British. The French, who had a very good opinion of themselves as soldiers and, with rather less validity, as generals, were only interested in US troops up to the rank of, say, captain, and had attempted to absorb American soldiers into their armies from the moment the United States entered the war. This attitude and these constant demands did not go down well with Pershing. 'The constant inclination on the part of certain elements among the French to assume a superiority that did not exist, then or at any later period, added to the attempts of some of them to dictate, had reached the limit of patience,' Pershing records in his memoirs, following a criticism of his staff and organisation by a French politician, adding that 'if his [the politician's] people would cease troubling themselves about our affairs and attend more strictly to their own we should all get along much better.'

Elsewhere in his memoirs he wrote:

> Both the French and British Missions [in Washington] were very keen to have American recruits fill up the ranks of their armies. The French really wanted us to send small untrained units for incorporation into their divisions . . . they proposed voluntary enlistment in the French Armies, using French depots, centres of instruction and instruction units. With this system we could utilise men with the least delay. These volunteers could be withdrawn from the French Army and placed at the disposal of the American Commandant [i.e. C-in-C] when the regularly organised [US] forces arrived.

A similar proposal came from the head of the British Mission, Major-General Tom Bridges, and both were rejected by Pershing, who was 'decidedly against our becoming a recruiting agency for either the French or the British'.

The French thought that the best way to employ this cornucopia of manpower from the United States was to have the men arrive with just rifles and machine-guns and slot them into the ranks of the French Army. The same notion, though suggesting incorporation in larger units and made in a more tactful fashion, was put forward by Field Marshal Haig, mainly on the grounds that while it took a few months to train an infantryman, it took years to train senior commanders and staff officers. It would therefore save time, that always precious time, if the US troops were put under British command, where there would be fewer language problems, and then, once their staff and senior officers had learned the ropes, they could be sent back to Pershing and formed into American divisions, corps and full armies.

Given the situation confronting the Allies in 1917–18, this was not a bad idea, and in some respects Pershing went along with it. He knew that his men needed front-line experience and when the British and French offered training facilities, instructors, field and heavy artillery, and the chance to spend a few days or weeks in the line attached to their units, he was willing to accept, and even grateful. Beyond that point, however, he would not go, and no amount of Anglo-French pressure could budge him. In this Pershing was quite right, not least because American public opinion would not have tolerated a situation that placed their young men under foreign control.

The French would not accept Pershing's refusals, with the result that a great deal of valuable time was spent in committee, presenting and re-presenting a proposal to which Pershing would never agree. Pershing maintained his position in the face of all persuasion, and when some US companies were included in the Australian attack at Le Hamel in July 1918, he expressed his disapproval to Field Marshal Haig in strong terms, and made it clear that it must not happen again. He was going to put an American army in the field.

Creating that army took time, however. Nevertheless, Pershing had some advantages not open to the long-departed Field Marshal French; not the least of which was that he knew from the start what was required, in terms of equipment and manpower. Equipment, especially artillery, could be borrowed or built under licence from the British or French and, thanks to the fact that the American armaments industry had expanded during the course of the war to cope with orders from the British Government, there were plenty of factories in the USA tooled up for the manufacture of weapons and ammunition. Pershing also possessed the energy and go-ahead spirit so typical of the American people and he and his men flung themselves into the task of preparing to meet the Germans in the field with great enthusiasm. Even so, it still took more than a year after the United States had entered the war before any large numbers of US troops became involved in the fighting, though some elements managed to get themselves into combat soon after arriving in France.

Even by the summer of 1918, the question of how the US troops were to be employed remained a controversial one. Having abandoned the idea that they could draft American 'doughboys'* directly into the ranks of their battalions, the French wanted to integrate the new American divisions into the French armies. The British, with the experience

---

* A doughboy was a kind of dough cake; American soldiers were first nicknamed thus in the 1840s, from the supposed resemblance of their large brass uniform buttons to doughboys. The name fell out of use in the Second World War, when it was replaced by 'GI', from 'government issue' or 'general issue'.

they had first gained from integrating the Canadian Corps into the BEF, knew this would not be acceptable. The Canadian and, to a lesser extent, the Australian divisions, preferred to fight as a united corps, eventually under their own national commanders. This kept them happy and produced two of the finest fighting corps of the war. Haig suggested that American divisions should be attached to British corps *only for their initial battlefield experience* before forming their own corps and armies, and this was the method eventually adopted.

Pershing remained determined to resist any attempt by his allies to take over the American troops, but by the summer of 1918 he had seen the need to modify his position slightly. He had few officers with the necessary experience to handle a division in the field – and a US Army division was roughly twice the size of a French or British division. He had also realised that all troops need 'blooding' – an introduction to battlefield realities in the company of more experienced comrades – and that the essential element for winning this war was a co-ordination of effort, not simply around the conference table, but in the field, where the armies and their component parts must support each other. By the late spring of 1918 there was also the stark fact that unless Pershing committed his troops soon, the French and British might collapse.

This fact was raised at a meeting of the Supreme War Council at Abbeville on 1–2 May 1918. Pershing was again asked to let the French or British use his divisions, and he again refused. Foch then asked 'Are you willing to see our forces driven back to the Loire?' Pershing replied that he was prepared to take that risk, since 'the time may come when the American Army may have to stand the brunt of this War and it is not wise to fritter away our resources in this manner.' The Generalissimo retorted that the war might be over before the Americans took the field, and the first day of the meeting broke up in some acrimony. On the following day, Lloyd George made his appeal to Pershing, pointing out that since 21 March the French and British Armies had lost over 600,000 men, and that if America did not come to their aid soon, perhaps Ludendorff's March gamble would pay off and the French and British would lose the war.

It was a valid point. Although it took a few more meetings, Pershing eventually agreed that his divisions *could* be attached to British corps, though under their own officers, who would thereby gain practical field or staff experience. These attachments were not only for familiarisation duties. The US divisions could also provide reserves and support in case of need. Foch did not like this, seeing it as an attempt to create an Anglo-American, anti-French axis, but he eventually agreed, if only to get large bodies of US troops committed to the fight, and American units were soon spread about among the Allied armies. Pershing's soldiers, who had been very anxious to enter the fighting, welcomed his decision, and in the fighting of late June and July proved that the American troops – if not the American staff – were the equal of any in the field. By the end of July these problems and quarrels were at an end, for there were by then enough trained US units in France to allow an American First Army of thirteen divisions to be formed and put in the field.

Ludendorff had now been attacking for four months, striking heavy blows all along the Allied line, from the Ypres Salient to the banks of the Marne. These attacks, if often tactically successful, had not given the Germans any strategic gains and the cost had been appalling on both sides. The casualties caused to the Allies were now less significant than the losses on the German side, for the Allied dead and wounded could be replaced by American troops who were arriving by the tens of thousands every month. By the end of July 1918 there were more than 1 million American soldiers in France, and their supplies were now flooding into French ports at the rate of 20,000 tons a day. The German Army – indeed, Germany herself – had run out of resources, and with the failure of the attacks around Rheims and on the Marne, it was evident that Ludendorff's bid to defeat the British and French before the Americans took the field had failed.

Nevertheless, the German Army was still powerful and still fighting. Unless and until it could be decisively and clearly defeated the war would go on. Germany was starving, there were riots in the cities and murmur of mutinies in the harbour-locked ships of the High Seas Fleet, but the Germany Army in the field was still resolute. It is possible to deplore the Kaiser and his government and, while remembering that Germany plunged Europe into war twice in twenty-five years, in 1914 and 1939, still feel a certain amount of sympathy for the German soldier of the Great War, as well as admiration for the sheer guts and professionalism those soldiers showed in battle even as the war was being lost.

The task of the Allied commanders was to defeat that army, and the first step towards that end was to wrest the initiative back from Ludendorff and force his armies onto the defensive. Foch had been inclined to wait and attack, again in 1919 when the full force of the American armies would be available, but Haig felt that if the war could be pressed now and the initiative wrested from Ludendorff in the next few weeks, victory might still be achieved in 1918. By the end of July Foch was beginning to share that opinion.

At the 24 July meeting at the Bombon Château he proposed a series of co-ordinated attacks with the objective of freeing the three lateral railways so vital to the future operations of the Allied Armies. These rail links – the Paris–Châlons, Paris–Avricourt and Paris–Amiens lines – had either been cut by the March offensive, or were threatened or presently under fire from German guns. The three railways were essential to the rapid movement of Allied reserves up and down the front, either to repel enemy attacks or, more to the current purpose, to establish reserves behind the front-line armies and as a first step in pushing the German Armies back towards the Rhine.

Steps to achieve that end had already begun. At the beginning of July Haig had allowed Rawlinson's Fourth Army to mount an attack against the village of Le Hamel, near Villers-Bretonneux, twelve miles east of Amiens. Rawlinson gave this task to the Australian Corps (formed from I and II Anzac) which was under the command of an Australian officer, Lieutenant-General Sir John Monash, one of the great soldiers of the war. Monash committed the 4th Australian Division to this attack, with elements of the US 33rd Division and sixty tanks under command, and this force set out to take the Hamel position, aiming to advance on a front of about three and a half miles to a depth of some one and a half miles. Le Hamel was occupied by the troops of four German infantry regiments and although their defences were not in good order, driving them out was still a formidable undertaking.

Surprise was the essential element, and was maintained to such an extent that the plan of attack was not revealed to the ten assaulting battalions until three days before Zero. Since the country was open, Monash elected to use the tanks in two waves, one ahead of the first line of infantry, and a support line of tanks ahead of the second line of infantry, with special detachments to clear the well-defended positions in Hamel Wood as well as the villages of Hamel and Vaire, the whole preceded by a heavy artillery bombardment from 628 guns, half of them howitzers. The attack would also be supported by four RAF squadrons – the Royal Flying Corps had amalgamated with the Royal Naval Air Service to become the Royal Air Force on 1 April – which would bomb and strafe the enemy trenches and supply lines. The barrage drenched the German line with fire and the attack went in at 0310 hours on 4 July, US Independence Day. The result was a striking victory for Monash and his men.

Like Arthur Currie of the Canadian Corps, John Monash was not a professional soldier, nor did he come from a military family. Monash was Jewish, born in 1865, and was fifty-three when he took command of the Australian Corps. He had joined the Militia as a private in the University Company of the Victoria Rifles, and had graduated from Melbourne University in 1893 with a degree in engineering before returning to university to read law, qualifying as a lawyer in 1895, although he then worked as engineer. He had remained in the Militia, transferring from the Rifles to the artillery, and by 1903 he was commanding 3rd Company of the Garrison Artillery Regiment in Melbourne with the rank of major. By 1913 he had risen to the rank of colonel and had command of a Militia unit, 13 Infantry Brigade (Militia formations were manned by part-time soldiers). Monash was a well-educated man and a thinking soldier, with service in the Intelligence Corps as well as in the infantry and artillery, to his credit, and a pamphlet he produced during his Militia days, *A Hundred Hints for Company Commanders*, later became a standard Australian Army textbook.

Colonel Monash commanded 4 Australian Infantry Brigade at Gallipoli, where it took part in the Anzac landing on 25–26 April 1915, and was promoted brigadier-general in July. After the evacuation he took his brigade to France, arriving there in June 1916. He was not involved in the Somme fighting, for in July he returned to England to take command, as a major-general, of the newly arrived 3rd Australian Division which he took to France in December. Eighteen months later, on 31 May 1918, and now a lieutenant-general, he replaced Birdwood as commander of the Australian Corps.

The laurels bestowed on the Australian troops included a clutch of honours and awards for General Monash, which has not stopped allegations from Australian writers that the 'British High Command', which presumably means Field Marshal Haig, despised Monash for his Jewish origins and constantly reminded him that he had no professional military experience. There is no evidence for these allegations whatsoever.

According to John Terraine, Haig was a great admirer of Monash, and other senior British officers, including Plumer, Harington and Fuller, also held him in high esteem. Haig's diary for 1 July 1918 records the comment: 'I spent an hour with Monash and went into every detail of an operation he is shortly to carry out with the Australian Corps [the Le Hamel attack]. M. is a most thorough and capable commander who thinks out every detail of any attack and leaves nothing to chance. I was greatly impressed with his arrangements.' In his memoirs, Monash makes no reference to meeting disparagement or prejudice of any kind in Britain. His letters to his wife, to whom he wrote constantly throughout the war, record only the kindness and support he received in Britain and on active service. His short army career during the war saw him rise in four years from colonel to lieutenant-general and corps commander, head of his country's field forces and, knighted by his sovereign, King George V (twice – he was appointed KCB in 1918, and GCMG in 1919), returning home weighed down with honours and awards. This hardly supports the claim that Monash 'suffered prejudice at the hands of his British colleagues', his superior officers, or the British 'Establishment', but this might be a good point at which to examine certain allegations about the British Army spread by some Dominion historians.

The March retreat was a considerable reverse, and the performance of some British units during the Michael offensive and in subsequent engagements in the spring and early summer of 1918 has provided some historians in Canada and Australia with useful ammunition for another extended round of 'Pommie bashing'. There is no smoke without fire, and there can be little doubt that the Dominion divisions did very well, while some British units fell back before they needed to, and others went back too far.

This is not the say that the gleeful comments made in Canberra and Ottawa about the command, courage and fighting ability of British soldiers should be accepted without rebuttal, and a closer examination of the situation tends to indicate that while the Australian, Canadian and New Zealand divisions fought well in the Hundred Days, so did as many – or more – British divisions, in spite of their manpower handicaps and the maulings they had suffered in the earlier 1918 fighting.

All but seven of the fifty British divisions involved in the Hundred Days had been heavily engaged in the Michael offensive or the Georgette attack on the Lys; seventeen had been involved in both, and five had also been embroiled in the Blücher offensive on the Aisne. This level of commitment to battle continued until the very end of the war; fourteen British divisions each suffered casualties of over 2,500 men in the last six weeks of the war alone . . . and yet the British offensive did not grind to a halt. It should also be remembered that the Canadian Corps had hardly been engaged at all in the great battles in the spring of 1918, and its divisions were therefore intact and relatively fresh when the great Allied attack began on 8 August.

Peter Simkins, Senior Historian at the Imperial War Museum in London, said as much in a paper presented at a History Conference held at the Australian Defence Force Academy, Canberra, in September 1993, and parts of his address lay out the situation clearly.

> Many Australian soldiers were critical of the quality of British troops on the Western Front in 1918 and derogatory comments about the morale, the fighting ability or the command of the 'Tommies' are by no means difficult to find . . . even so, the splendid tactical achievements by Australian soldiers have become somewhat distorted, helping to create the myth of the 'colonial superman'. As a consequence the contribution of the British soldier to the ultimate victory has been overshadowed.

Simkins goes on to analyse the fighting during the Hundred Days and compares the performance of Australian, British, Canadian and (the single) New Zealand Divisions in opposed attacks; his detailed investigations throw up some interesting statistics. For example, the successful opposed-attack record of the nine British divisions in Rawlinson's Fourth Army during the Hundred Days was 70.7 per cent – exactly the same as in the five Australian divisions, and only slightly lower than that of the four, much larger, Canadian divisions (72.5 per cent), and well above that of the New Zealand Division (64.5 per cent). Moreover, two British divisions – the 19th (Western) and 66th – had success rates of 100 per cent, and the 9th (Scottish) Division had a success rate of 93 per cent, this last averaged out over fourteen separate attacks. The 24th Division racked up an 85-per-cent success rate, and the 16th (Irish) Division 80 per cent. This evidence hardly accords with the popular Dominion opinion that all the British divisions were useless.

There is more, however. Simkins points out that six Dominion divisions (1st, 2nd and 5th Australian and 1st, 2nd and 3rd Canadian) achieved a success rate of between 70 and 80 per cent in opposed attacks, but so, quite apart from the divisions mentioned above, did five more British divisions (Guards, 18th [Eastern], 24th, 34th and 38th [Welsh]). From this it is possible to infer that *ten* British divisions did as well, or better than the *six* crack Dominion divisions.

Simkins gives many more examples, and continues. 'If one then considers the number of attacks carried out by individual British and Dominion divisions and also the "battle days" on which each division saw meaningful action, the British units again stand up well in comparison with the Dominion divisions.' In fact, a comparison of successful attacks and 'battle days' reveals that during the Hundred Days, most British divisions, 'in spite of the crises they experienced earlier in the year, actually made a very weighty contribution to the Allied victory'. This conclusion would seem to be both accurate and fair, and is reached, not in any attempt to downgrade the reputation of the Dominion divisions, but to point out, yet again, the often-overlooked fact that the British divisions also played a decisive part – whatever is now maintained in Ottawa, Canberra or Wellington.

This view is certain to be challenged and all statistical evidence is subject to the accusation that 'there are lies, damned lies, and statistics'. Before that old *canard* is trotted out to refute Peter Simkins's arguments, it should be pointed out yet again that he presented them, not in the UK, but in a speech to an audience of Australian soldiers and historians in Canberra, where it was received with tolerance and respect.

Quite what is gained by these Dominion allegations is difficult to judge. Another popular, but totally unfounded, Australian story which might be scotched here is that Monash was in line for promotion to the command of all the British Armies in France in 1918. Since a similar tale is also current in Canada, with Lieutenant-General Sir Arthur Currie as the man due to take over from Haig, it seemed wise to investigate this rumour at the Australian War Memorial in Canberra, Australia's national military archive. The Australian researcher's report is as follows:

> There is no truth in this story. Monash was a corps commander in 1918 (so becoming C-in-C would have required two steps in promotion) and at the end of the war and became best known for his efforts to repatriate Australian soldiers home when the war ended. At the end of the war there were two myths prevalent among Australian soldiers on the Western Front. One, that the war would have ended sooner had Monash been in command and, two, that he would have been made C-in-C if the war had continued. These feelings seem to have arisen from the natural pride of the forces in a commander of repute from their own country. This in turn may have arisen from Monash's own consistent efforts to have the work and successes of Australian soldiers recognised.
>
> The other factor which probably had a greater influence on the Monash-as-C-in-C myth was Lloyd George's written remarks in his memoirs. It seems he had a long-standing dislike of Haig and was prepared at any time to do him down. He was also influenced by Liddell Hart, a great admirer of General Monash. This was a potent combination. Lloyd George's writings after the War spoke of a

'Dominion General' being qualified for the C-in-C position, which a Canadian biographer of Currie took to mean him.

So, the myth would seem to be a combination of rumour and grumblings of the type I imagine is natural among troops and a lot of hindsight. (Alison Yamasaki, Canberra, to the author, April 1997.)

Monash was a fine man and a good general but, as one of his biographers, P.A. Pederson, has pointed out, when he took command of the Australian Corps it was 'a magnificent instrument, just when the tide was turning in the Allies' favour and he was never compelled to fight with the odds against him. He also had the first attribute for a great general – he was lucky.'

Lest any Australian historian or critic should take offence at this brief overview of General Monash – and taking offence is something that they can often be all-too-eager to do – let it be noted that not I, nor anyone I consulted in the course of researching and writing this book, has anything but the warmest praise for General Monash and the splendid troops he had the honour to command. The same is true for Currie and the Canadians. The only point I would make, however, is that the British troops from the United Kingdom also performed well, did their fair share of fighting, for longer, and suffered far and away the bulk of the casualties. A small acknowledgement of that fact from time to time might not go amiss.

The Australians scored a great success at Le Hamel. The German line was pushed back by over a mile, and 1,400 German prisoners were taken, for the cost of 775 Australian and 134 American soldiers killed, wounded, and missing. This was the first of a series of attacks Haig was to mount from then on, often with the Canadian and Australian troops in the van.

The French were also about to take the field in force, and Foch selected General Mangin of the Tenth Army and General Jean Degoutte of the Sixth Army to lead the offensive. On 18 July their armies struck the German line on the Aisne on a 25-mile front between Soissons and Château-Thierry. This attack was supported by 200 French light tanks, and by 5 August they had driven the Germans from the salient south of the Aisne and taken nearly 30,000 prisoners and 793 guns.

Haig's forces then resumed the offensive, in line with the directive issued by Foch on 24 July which required the clearing of the Paris–Amiens railway line and pushing the Germans back towards Roye. Haig therefore ordered Rawlinson to prepare an attack on the north-western flank of the German salient east and south of Amiens created by their advances in March and April. According to Rawlinson, it was he who proposed the attack to Haig, suggesting, 'an offensive east of Villers-Bretonneux if he would give me the Canadians. To my delight, DH said he had already decided to do this . . .'

Haig did not trust 'Rawly' fully, not least because the latter was a bosom companion of the devious Wilson, but he did not let that mistrust prevent him using Rawlinson's undoubted abilities in the field. The Fourth Army commander was a general who could learn from his mistakes, and one who was not afraid of innovation. His planning here called for an attack by three corps, two of these being the Australian and Canadian Corps. By now, however, the Australian divisions had been in action for some months, and in consequence were in urgent need of rest and reinforcement. Indeed, the shortage of men was acute, for Australia had declined to vote for conscription; as a result, three Australian battalions had to be disbanded and their men redistributed to bring some of the other units up to strength.

The Canadian Corps, on the other hand, was up to full strength, and much stronger than any British corps, with four full battalions to every brigade. In fact, its fighting strength had actually been increased with the addition of 100 men to every battalion, adding an extra 4,800 bayonets to the formation's fighting strength; a Canadian division now mustered some 20,000 men, compared with the 15,000, at best, in a British division. Currie's staff work was also of a high order. One of his unsung successes was the secret transfer that August of his 100,000-strong corps, by night, from its position near Arras in the First Army area, down to Amiens and Rawlinson's Fourth Army command. This move, which brought the Canadian Corps into the line a few hours before Zero, was accompanied by the first use of wireless deception in this war, when two battalions and some attached units were sent up to the Ypres Salient in order to create the impression that the Canadians were moving there.

These two corps were to attack south of the Somme, with the Canadians on the right of the Australians. On the right of the Canadians was the French First Army, and on the north bank of the Somme, to the left of the Australians, was the British III Corps under General Butler, a corps that had suffered heavy casualties in the March Retreat. This attack was to be supported by 324 Mark V heavy tanks and 184 supply tanks, a creeping barrage and General Kavanagh's Cavalry Corps, which would in turn be supported by 96 of the new light Whippet tanks, significantly faster than the Mark Vs. Haig was going for a breakthrough, and was more than willing to provide Rawlinson with all the necessary elements for success.

The attack, which came to be called the Battle of Amiens, went in at dawn on 8 August, and this time it was the advancing Allied troops who were concealed by a thick mist. The Australians and the Canadians made a gain of 5 miles on an 8-mile front and took 13,000 prisoners and 334 guns. Only one corps of the French Army attacked at all; fortunately, that was the corps on the right of the Canadians, so their advance was covered. Matters did not go well north of the river, however, where the supporting tanks got lost in the fog and Butler's III Corps only advanced a mile, taking their first objective but then coming to a halt, largely because the men had not been sufficiently well trained and the junior leaders lacked experience. The Official History records that 'All the divisions of III Corps had been in the line or in close reserve since March, had suffered heavily in the March Retreat and the 58th Division had taken part in the battle at Villers-

Bretonneux in April, losing 3,530 all ranks.' Butler's corps had been largely reconstituted since 21 March. In the spring it had contained three divisions, the 14th (Light), the 18th (Eastern) and the 58th, but the 14th had been taken out of the line and the 12th (Eastern) and 47th (1/2nd London) Divisions had arrived, so that III Corps, although stronger, had two divisions which had been ravaged in March and topped up with newly arrived reinforcements, and two divisions which had not been under Butler's command before. All four were in need of training for, to quote the OH again, 'There was not only a shortage of experienced officers and NCOs, but the ranks of the infantry units had been filled up with young recruits from home.' These replacements had had less than three months' basic training, and were wholly without experience in the line.

The comparison between what was managed north of the Somme and the achievements of the Australian and Canadian Corps to the south, also underlines the benefits of the Dominion system of control, under which divisions were kept permanently within the same command. British divisions were moved about from corps to corps according to need, and this inevitably led to a certain dislocation.

As for Fourth Army's attack, a breach had been made but the expected exploitation had not followed, for the brigade of Whippet tanks, instead of being turned loose to exploit the breakthrough on the Australian and Canadian fronts, was kept tied to the cavalry. As always, the Germans were quick to respond, and the tank attack was soon halted with the loss of many machines and considerable casualties among the crews. The Battle of Amiens between 8–12 August was a useful victory, though casualties were still high, amounting to some 22,000 men killed, wounded and missing: 9,074 Canadians, 7,137 British and 5,991 Australians.

This battle, and especially the first day of it, was above all a great victory for the Australian and Canadian Corps, and their exploits deserve fuller consideration. They were two of the best-trained and best-led corps in Haig's army, and Rawlinson, knowing their worth, gave them anything they asked for by way of support. The Australians, moreover, had got over that distrust of tanks engendered by their experiences at Bullecourt, and over 400 machines, either fighting or supply tanks, went into action with the assault troops.

The Canadian Corps attacked on a 7,000-yard front, preceded by an artillery and smoke barrage and a mass advance of the tanks. The Canadians had also worked out some refined infantry tactics, the leading battalions advancing in waves, the first wave consisting of skirmishers, the last wave of men carrying extra supplies of grenades and ammunition. The intermediate lines advanced in section – ten-man – groups, in single file or diamond formation with a signal party advancing with the fourth wave, and the follow-up battalions were in diamond formation or in file. Many of these troops had been deployed in no man's land before the attack commenced. The Canadian Corps took all its objectives except on the right flank, and prepared to renew the attack on the following day.

Monash committed four divisions of his Australian Corps on a front of 7,500 yards, supported by the British 5 Tank Brigade, 1 Cavalry Brigade, and an armoured-car battalion. Their first objective lay two miles ahead of their lines at Cerisy, and was to be taken by the 2nd and 3rd Australian Divisions, after which the 4th and 5th would pass through to take the second objective, between two and three miles further on, at Morcourt. The 1st Australian Division, would be in reserve. By 0710 hours the first objective was in Australian hands, the diggers keeping close behind the barrage and supported on to the objective by nineteen tanks, four having been lost in the advance. The second phase, the advance by the 4th and 5th Australian Divisions, began at 0840, the troops pressing forward onto the Santerre plain under heavy German artillery fire. Losses up to this point had been around 1,000 men but casualties now began to increase, though the tanks were doing good work against the German machine-guns. By 1400 hours the second Australian objective had been secured and the troops set about consolidating their line, having made an advance of 5 miles and captured some 8,000 Germans, as well as 173 field guns and a quantity of machine-guns and other equipment. Fourth Army had driven the Germans back from Amiens in less than half a day, the Australians advancing 5 miles and the Canadians 8, and Ludendorff was duly dismayed.

Rawlinson's attack on 8 August shook the German High Command. Ludendorff recorded that 'August 8th was the black day of the German Army in the History of this war. This was the worst experience I had to go through.' This last remark is interesting, for it provides some evidence – and more was to come later – that the situation of Germany and of the German armies was at last beginning to break the iron resolve of this formidable soldier. General von Lossberg, Chief of Staff of one of the German army groups, records that Ludendorff 'gave an impression of very great despondency', when he met him at OHL (Oberkommano der Heeresleitung – Supreme Army Command, equivalent to British GHQ or French GQG) that day. Ludendorff's dejection continued. On 14 August, at a meeting of the German Crown Council at Spa in Belgium, he recommended immediate peace negotiations, a proposal backed up by the Austrian Emperor Carl. On the following day, Crown Prince Rupprecht of Bavaria wrote from his Army HQ in Flanders to Prince Max of Baden, a leading political figure and a second cousin of the Kaiser, telling him that 'Our military situation has deteriorated, I no longer believe we can hold out over the winter and catastrophe may come earlier. The Americans are multiplying in a way we never dreamed of and have 33 divisions in France.'

Rawlinson kept up his attack on the following day, 9 August, though only 145 of the tanks committed on the first day of the battle were still in action. On the 10th Foch, recently created a Marshal of France, visited Haig at his Advanced HQ and ordered him to keep Rawlinson pressing forward in the general direction of Ham on the Somme, while the French First and Third Armies further south finally cleared the Germans from the salient between

Montdidier and Noyon. Foch also suggested that the British Third Army under Byng should also enter the fray with an attack towards Bapaume and Péronne.

Haig demurred. German resistance was stiffening on Rawlinson's front and Haig had finally learned that to press an attack too far was to throw away the gains already made. He therefore proposed halting Rawlinson's offensive within the next few days, but agreed to keep up the pressure by sending Byng's Third Army into the attack against the right of the German forces opposing Rawlinson's army, meanwhile committing Horne's First Army at Monchy-le-Preux. Foch was happy with this latter proposal, but wanted Rawlinson to continue attacking as well. On 12 August, at a conference with Horne and Byng, Haig directed that the Third Army should press on towards Bapaume and First Army should attack and capture Monchy, these operations to begin on 15 September. Foch accepted this, but ordered that Fourth Army should carry on attacking on the Somme, since the Allied Generalissimo was convinced that the German troops had been demoralised by the Amiens battle. Haig passed on this order to Rawlinson by telephone and then went to meet him at Canadian Corps HQ, where the latter showed him a message from Currie stating that pushing on as ordered would be 'very costly'. Haig pointed out that Foch wanted the Fourth Army to continue attacking, at which Rawlinson stated that his men had already done enough, and concluded by asking Haig 'Are you commanding the British Army, or is Marshal Foch?'

Haig went on to visit the British 32nd Division at Le Quesnel, where he was told that the German opposition on the Fourth Army front had indeed stiffened, and that they were encountering an increasing number of machine-guns in well-wired defensive positions. Thus informed – or reminded – Haig reverted to his original plan, and ordered Rawlinson to halt his attacks. He then wrote to Foch to tell him that while the Fourth Army would maintain pressure south of the Somme, the fight would now be taken up by the Third Army north of that river and by the First Army east of Arras. This decision, as well as Haig's defiance of his orders, infuriated Marshal Foch. At a meeting at the latter's HQ on 14 August, Haig found it necessary to remind the Marshal that his powers of command over an Allied army, if wide, were not infinite: 'I spoke to Foch quite straightly and let him understand that I was responsible to my Government and fellow citizens for the handling of the British forces.' As always with the French, a firm response paid dividends. Foch now declared that all he wanted was to know what was happening, so that he could co-ordinate the British attacks with those of his other armies, adding that he thought Haig was perfectly right not to assault a German prepared position. The battle was going well, which may have helped Foch reach this conclusion. Four days later Prime Minister Clemenceau arrived unexpectedly at GHQ and presented Haig with the Médaille Militaire, medals being the usual French panacea for ruffled feathers among their allies.

In the event, these disagreements over strategy between Foch and his generals did no particular harm, and had one advantage in that they provided those generals with a chance to consider their plans in the context of what was happening on other parts of the front. There can be little doubt that Foch was beginning to understand the management of an international force, and was handling his role as Generalissimo with increasing skill and tact. For his part, Haig's reputation with the French and with the British Government had recovered from the reverses of March and April, and he had learned, moreover, that the appointment of a Supreme Commander had the distinct advantage of keeping Lloyd George off his back.

The Prime Minister was still dabbling in military affairs, however. On 12 August General Pershing arrived at Haig's HQ with a complaint. It appeared that Lloyd George had been attempting, through 'political channels' – in other words by using the British Ambassador in New York to make direct contact with the US War Department, via the US Secretary of State – to arrange that the five American divisions currently in training with the British armies should remain there for operations. Quite apart from the fact that Pershing needed these divisions for his forthcoming attack on the St Mihiel Salient, this sort of backstairs dealing, a regular ploy of both the French and British Governments, drove him to fury. Moreover, and rather more to the point, it did not work.

In contrast to the strained relations existing between Lloyd George and Field Marshal Haig, the US Government backed Pershing to the hilt and simply relayed these requests to him for action or comment, leaving any decision to him. Even so, behaviour such as Lloyd George's, so common with politicians, might easily have damaged the good relations between the generals but Haig and Pershing got on well and always spoke openly to each other. In this instance Haig told the American general plainly that since the British had trained and equipped these divisions, they expected to have some return on their investment, to which Pershing promptly agreed, asking only that they should be returned to him when the current fighting was over. At this Haig relented and said, 'Pershing, of course you shall have them, there can never be any difference between us.' As a result, the US 33rd, 78th and 80th Divisions were sent to the American First Army; however, the US 27th and 30th Divisions fought on with the British Army until the end of the war.

The situation at the end of the Battle of Amiens on 12 August was that the French First Army and the British Fourth Army now faced strongly entrenched enemy positions and had therefore halted. Foch now wanted to extend the attack on both wings of these two armies, with the French Tenth and Third Armies attacking on the right while the British Third and First Armies attacked on the left, in a south-easterly direction, to turn the line of the Somme and outflank the defences now holding up the British Fourth and French First Army. This was a sound plan, and on 19 August Haig visited Byng at his Arras HQ and directed him to break the German front with Third Army and press on towards Bapaume. Horne would then strike east from Arras with his First Army while, up in the Salient, Plumer's Second Army was to push on and retake Mount Kemmel. These plans were in line with Haig's previous orders and his overall intention; the German armies were to have no rest, no time to regroup, no opportunity to switch reserves.

On 20 August, Mangin's Tenth Army struck at the Germans south of the Oise. On the 21st, keeping up this relentless round of Anglo-French attacks, Byng's Third Army, consisting of three corps mustering thirteen divisions and two cavalry divisions, thrust towards Baupaume supported by five battalions of tanks – 156 machines – and some armoured cars. Byng attacked on a front of 14 miles, a wide front for such a force, but the Germans of Below's Seventeenth Army had only ten divisions with which to oppose them. Within two days Third Army had advanced 4 miles and taken 5,000 prisoners. This was open warfare, and the young soldiers brought out from Britain to fill the ranks of Third Army did well at it, keeping close behind the creeping barrages, working with the tanks, pushing on steadily across the old Somme battlefield and the higher ground towards the Scarpe.

The benefits of a unified command were now becoming apparent. Foch and Haig and their subordinate generals were repeating Ludendorff's spring tactics by making a series of co-ordinated attacks at points all along the German line. Even with the advantage of interior lines of communication, Ludendorff could not switch his reserves up and down the line on a daily basis, and in the face of these constant attacks by the Allied armies his front began to crumble.

Haig sensed this. On 22 August he sent a message to his army and corps commanders, urging them to press home their advantage:

> I request that Army Commanders will, without delay, bring to the notice of all subordinate leaders the changed conditions under which operations are now being carried on and the consequent necessity for all ranks to act with the utmost boldness and resolution in order to get full advantage from the present favourable situation.
>
> The methods which we have employed hitherto, when the enemy was strong, are no longer suited to his present condition. The enemy no longer has the means to deliver counter-attacks on an extended scale, nor has he the numbers to hold a continuous position against the very extended advance which is now being directed upon him . . . risks which a month ago would have been criminal to incur must now be incurred as a duty. Reinforcements must be directed on the points where our troops are gaining ground, not where they are checked; let each of us act energetically and without hesitation push forward to our objective.

The army commanders responded to this encouragement. The Battle of Albert which began on August 21 petered out on 29 August, but there was no rest for the Germans. On 26 August, Horne's First Army had struck on a 6-mile front east of Arras, making an advance of 4 miles during which the 3rd Canadian Division retook Monchy-le-Preux. Haig was now using his four armies superbly, making a series of limited attacks that kept the Germans constantly off balance and slowly shifting back. As the First Army attacked Monchy, Haig ordered the Third Army to press on, with the Fourth Army keeping up on its right flank and First Army pushing up on its left to pierce the Drocourt-Quéant Switch Line north of Bullecourt closing up on the Hindenburg Line.

The effect on the German forces facing this pressure was like a dam moving under the weight of floodwater; the wall shifts, almost imperceptibly at first, then a small breach appears, and then, if the pressure is maintained, the whole edifice – in this case the entire German line – is in danger of being swept away. These gains were not without loss, however. The British armies suffered some 80,000 casualties in August alone, but now there was a difference; there was a return on this expenditure, in ground gained and prisoners and material taken. Over 70,000 German troops and nearly 800 guns had been captured in the past four weeks and army morale was high; moreover, Lloyd George was silent.

Foch appreciated what Haig was doing, and said so in a letter to the Field Marshal on 26 August:

> I can only admire the resolute manner in which you press the business forward, giving no respite to the enemy and constantly increasing the scope of your action. It is the persistent widening and intensifying of the offensive – this pushing forward vigorously on carefully chosen objectives without over-preoccupation as to alignment or close liaison – that will give us the best results with the smallest losses, as you have so perfectly understood. No need to tell you that the armies of General Pétain are about to recommence their attacks using similar methods.

All the evidence suggests that Foch meant every word of this encouraging letter. The crucial question now, therefore, is why were these successful methods not tried before? The answer probably lies with the situation on the ground in the summer of 1918, and with the growing skill of the Allied armies. From the end of 1914 to the third week of March 1918, with the arguable exceptions of the counter-attack at Neuve Chapelle in March 1915 and the gas attack at Ypres in April of that year, the Germans had mounted just two offensives on the Western Front between First Ypres in 1914 and the March Offensive in 1918; the first was their major onslaught at Verdun in February 1916, the second when they counter-attacked Byng's Third Army at Cambrai on 30 November 1917. In all the other engagements on the Western Front (apart from the exceptions already cited) they had fought on the defensive, using their prepared positions to great advantage.

Ludendorff's Michael attack in March 1918 changed the entire nature of the war. While it gave the Allies a terrible shock, caused them horrendous casualties and drove a 40-mile-deep bulge in their line, it brought the German Army out from behind their fortifications and restored open warfare to the Western Front.

From April 1918 until well into July, the Germans were attacking, taking heavy casualties but driving the Allies back. Then their advance faltered, fresh US troops entered the fray, the American First Army was formed in August, and the British and French Armies recovered their balance and began to fight superbly. The elements of fighting a modern battle had been learned on the Somme and at Passchendaele. The French and British had spent a great deal of time, and hundreds of thousands of lives, beating their soldiers' heads against the German defences but now all that experience was at least proving useful, in better infantry tactics, in the mounting of all-arms attacks, and in the use of artillery, tanks and aircraft in skilful combination, and in support of the infantry. New equipment, such as better radios to improve communications and light tanks to speed up the exploitation of any breach, also had their part to play.

The conclusion has to be drawn that in 1918 all the suffering paid off. Once out from behind their fortifications the Germans were open to defeat and they were now being steadily beaten . . . and by the same generals – Byng, Rawlinson, Plumer, Horne – who had fought on the Somme and at Ypres and Arras and Cambrai, and have since been roundly condemned for 'incompetence'. (The main absentee was Gough, who *was* incompetent and had already lost his command.) As for Field Marshal Haig, he was by this time, without any doubt, the finest commander on the Western Front.

The Germans came out to fight for two reasons. Firstly, the time seemed ripe for them to do so, for the dangers of fighting on two fronts had been eliminated when Russia fell out of the war. Secondly, with the imminent arrival of millions of American troops, fighting to a stalemate, and thus to an end of a kind, was no longer possible. The British, French and Americans now had the force, in men, guns and tanks, to break the German line and having done so, to exploit that victory. The only answer, therefore, was to gamble, to leave the trenches behind and beat the British and French before the Americans could intervene.

The Great War has few absolutes, and there were, naturally, many other factors affecting the German decision to fight an open war, among them starvation at home, unrest in the German Navy, reverses among her allies in the Balkans and the Near East and Middle East, the terrible casualties at Verdun, on the Somme, at Passchendaele and on the Chemin des Dames, and the constant daily losses all along the front. The war had to be ended, and since Germany (like the Allies) wanted to end it with a victory, this last gamble seemed not only worthwhile, but imperative.

Haig replied to Foch's letter on the following day, suggesting that since the British armies were pushing the Germans back between Cambrai and St

Quentin, it would be a sound move if the American Army were to strike up from the south between the Meuse and the Aisne, in the direction of Mézières. Such an attack would not only threaten the flank of the German forces in the north, where their attention was focused on Haig's advance, it might also outflank the Hindenburg Line, towards which the enemy were gradually retreating. If this position could be outflanked before the Germans reached it, the task of reducing it would be simplified. Even if that aim was not achieved, a thrust from the south would threaten those vital lines of communication at Mézières on which the German 'interior-lines' strategy depended.

Foch was much taken with this idea and went at once to Pershing's HQ to lay the scheme before him. Unfortunately however, he also suggested that since the US Army was 'inexperienced' it would be as well to place it under the control of a French commander, at least for the coming thrust. Pershing, unsurprisingly, flatly rejected this proposal, and the American attack, in the Meuse-Argonne sector was only launched on 26 September. Since Pershing's forces did indeed lack experience the attack at first proved a failure. During the first four days of fighting the US First Army made a maximum gain of eight miles, and found, as Pershing records in his memoirs, that:

> The difficulties encountered by our inexperienced divisions during this phase of the fighting were not easily overcome . . . liaison between the various echelons was hard to maintain, and perfect teamwork between the artillery and the infantry was not at once attained. The tanks gave valuable assistance at the start but they became especial targets for the enemy's artillery and their numbers were rapidly diminished . . . it is one thing to fight a battle with well-trained, well-organised and experienced troops and quite another to take green troops, and organise, train, and fight them, all at the same time.

This last point is crucial to an understanding of Pershing's – and his troops' – problems. At the end of September 1918, nearly a year and a half after America entered the war, the US Army's strength in France stood at 71,000 officers and 1,634,220 enlisted men. This was a vast force but since it lacked training and battlefield experience, it could not be fully effective in the field; as a result, the First US Army was not finally formed until 10 August 1918, with Army HQ at La Ferté-sous-Jouarre, on the Marne a little west of Château-Thierry.

The Meuse-Argonne attack lasted forty-seven days, at that time the longest battle in American history. It started on a front of 24 miles but as more troops, French as well as American, were sucked into the fray, the front expanded to a width of 90 miles, and in the end involved more than 1,200,000 men. The Americans eventually succeeded in advancing 32 miles, but the fighting here was only terminated by the Armistice. When the war ended, the US armies had lost 130,000 men killed or missing, and a further 200,000 wounded, figures which, although small in Great War terms, give some indication of the fierceness of the fighting in the last months of 1918.

While the US troops were battering their way across the Argonne, Haig's armies and most of the French forces not engaged alongside the Americans – the American Second Army was formed in early October – had moved up to the Hindenburg Line. This had always been a formidable position but had become even more so in recent weeks as the Germans worked frantically to improve and extend it in depth, preparing to resume that defensive trench warfare which had served them so well in the past. The British were recovering all the ground lost in the Michael offensive; the Somme was recrossed and Péronne retaken, Monash's Australians sweeping down on the town from the north to outflank the German line. The advance only halted when the British armies drew up along the line they had occupied before the great attack of 21 March.

The German positions were, if anything, more daunting than they had been in 1917, consisting as they did of the Hindenburg Line or Siegfried Stellung, the Wotan Stellung or Drocourt–Quéant Switch Line, which extended the system to the north, and finally the Flandern Line. As has been said, these 'lines' were all deeply dug, extended fortifications, some miles in depth, a maze of strongpoints, wire, trenches, dugouts, and pillboxes with interlocking fields of fire, and overlooked by supporting artillery, the sort of positions that would make any attacker quail. Behind all this, some ten miles to the rear, lay a further line, the Hermann Stellung, which ran south from Le Cateau, near the Belgian frontier, through Valenciennes to Tournai. Haig was now mustering his men for the attack on these lines, and for this he needed more troops. These the British Government were unwilling to send, for the War Secretary, Lord Milner, again thought that Haig was being over-optimistic in his aim of piercing the Hindenburg Line, and feared that if more troops were sent out they would be used for 'another Passchendaele'.

On 15 September Haig called Horne, Byng and Rawlinson to a conference at Montreuil, in the course of which he laid out his plans for the forthcoming attack. These called for an attack all along the line, but the first requirement was total co-operation between the armies in order to establish themselves within striking distance of the enemy's main defences on the general line St Quentin–Cambrai. The Third Army (Byng) was to co-ordinate its actions with the other two armies; the First Army (Horne) was to extend its line to cover and attack Bourlon Wood; and the Fourth Army (Rawlinson) was to strike at the enemy line between Le Verguier and Épéhy, in co-operation with the French First Army. This attack, the Battle of Épéhy, was launched on 18 September, when the Fourth Army and V Corps of Third Army swiftly overran the outworks of the Hindenburg Line, driving the Germans back into their main defences. One result of this victory was the dismissal of

General von der Marwitz, commander of the German Second Army, 'due to the failure of his left wing on September 18,' as the Official History puts it. With that much achieved – and with 9,000 prisoners taken – Haig halted his offensive. He now began to prepare for a major assault on the Hindenburg Line, in conjunction with his allies and under the direction of Marshal Foch.

A new Allied strategy was at work along the Western Front. Since 8 August the British armies had advanced 25 miles on a front of 40 miles and most of this ground had been covered in the last three weeks. On the Somme in 1916 the British had advanced 8 miles on an eighteen-mile front in *four and a half months*. Casualties had also fallen. That Somme advance had cost Haig's armies 420,000 men; losses in the advances since 8 August, in the Battles of Amiens, Albert (1918), the Scarpe, Bapaume and Épéhy, and half a hundred other engagements in the last five weeks, amounted to 190,000 men killed, wounded and missing; 40 per cent of these casualties were in Fourth Army. More than 100,000 German prisoners had been taken, and the enemy was no longer fighting with his former dogged skill.

Attitudes had changed as well. A year before, Haig would have pressed on with the Épéhy attack, driven by the need to achieve some definite objective, or would have been obliged to press on by the requirement to support the French. Now matters were different. The co-ordination provided by Foch as Supreme Commander gave support to each attack and created a balanced offensive, in which no one army had to carry the whole burden. Haig's men now had the German Army hanging on to the Hindenburg Line by its fingertips. To prise those fingers loose the whole weight of the Allied armies in France could now be employed, and Haig could afford to wait until the other armies, especially the French First Army on the British right, were ready to enter the battle.

In the event, he did not have to wait long. Foch ordered Haig, Pétain and Pershing to launch simultaneous attacks on the Hindenburg Line between 26 and 29 September. To increase the pressure on the Germans still further, Foch ordered the Northern Group of Armies in Belgium – Plumer's Second Army and the Belgian Army, both now under the overall command of Albert, King of the Belgians – to launch an attack around the Ypres Salient.

The opening moves came from Pershing's Americans, with their attack in the Argonne on 26 September. On the same day the French Fourth Army attacked on the right of the US advance. Neither attack gained much ground, but this twin offensive rocked the German line. When the British First and Third Armies attacked the Hindenburg Line at Cambrai on the following day, they broke through with comparative ease, spearheaded by Currie's Canadian Corps, which had been transferred to First Army at the end of August. Supported by fifteen tanks, the Canadians took Bourlon Wood and swept across the Canal du Nord. Meanwhile, Byng's Third Army, with thirty-eight tanks in support, tore through the first and second Hindenburg Line positions and took Cambrai on 30 September. Finally, the Northern Group of Armies launched their attack in the Salient on 28

September, taking the whole of the Gheluvelt Ridge and sweeping on up the Lys valley towards Roulers, one of the unattained objectives of the Passchendaele offensive in 1917.

Then came the knock-out punch. On 29 September Rawlinson sent five corps, including the Australians and two American divisions he had under command, to attack the Hindenburg Line between St Quentin and Cambrai. The assault was supported by 175 tanks and by the end of the day the Fourth Army had captured the first and second lines of the Hindenburg position on a front of 5 miles. Rawlinson poured men and artillery into this gap and, after five days of fighting, captured the third line, for the loss of around 15,000 men killed, wounded and missing – a far cry from the casualties incurred on the first day of his Somme attack in July 1916. 'Today,' he wrote in his diary on 5 October, 'the 2nd Australian and the [British] 25th Division broke through the Hindenburg Line and my leading troops are out in the open so my victory is won.'

Final victory would take a little longer, but otherwise Rawlinson was right. The Central Powers were falling apart, for Bulgaria had capitulated on 30 September, had asked for terms and had begun to evacuate her troops from Greek and Serbian territory. This action drove Ludendorff into another fit of depression and was, he said later, the moment when the war was lost. On the following day, 1 October, Allenby's army entered Damascus, driving the Turkish Army back in full retreat.

On the Western Front the German Army fought on grimly, but it too was forced to fall back. The Central Powers were finished if the German Army in France could be defeated in the field, and now that army, driven from its best-prepared and most defensible stronghold, was in full retreat. On 6 October, a 'Note' arrived in Paris from the German, Turkish and Austrian Governments, asking for an immediate armistice. Foch, the Commander-in-Chief of the Allied Armies, was generous in acknowledging the architect of that submission. 'Here,' he told Haig, showing him a newspaper report of the Central Powers' Note, 'here is the immediate result of the British piercing the Hindenburg Line . . . the enemy has asked for an armistice.'

It took another five weeks to end the war, and men died on every day of that interval, even in the last hours before the Armistice; just two minutes before the ceasefire a Canadian soldier, Private George Price, was killed by a sniper a mile outside Mons. Turkey capitulated on 30 October. On the following day the Serbian Army, marching from Salonika, re-entered their country's capital, Belgrade. The Habsburg Empire was already disintegrating. Hungary and Bosnia declared their independence, the latter as the State of the South Slavs, on 31 October, the day after Austrain delegates arrived at Padua to discuss peace terms with the Italians. All fighting on the Italian front ended on 4 November and with their victory at Vittorio Veneto the Italians at last avenged Caporetto.

It remains a matter of wonder that while whole libraries could be stocked with books on the disasters and defeats suffered by the British and French Armies from 1914 to the spring of 1918, the sweeping victories on the Western Front during the rest of 1918 have gone largely unrecorded. Yet victories they were, and an armistice – and ultimately peace – was the soldiers' eventual reward for what had been earned by the skilful handling of the generals and the courage and tactical ability of the officers and men. Their battles and triumphs in 1918, in 'the Hundred Days' from August to November, have been all too often forgotten in works about the Great War, but accounts do exist and it is surprising that more historians do not consult them. Vilifying the generals and revelling in defeat may be more satisfying, or even enjoyable, but it does not tell either the whole story of the Great War, or the true one.

On 31 October the Kaiser left Berlin for the Belgian town of Spa, where OHL was sited, and there announced his willingness to abdicate in favour of his son. Then, inevitably, he changed his mind and refused to go, although the German Navy had already mutinied and there were mobs in the streets of Cologne, Hamburg, and Berlin, calling for an end to the war. Inspired by Russia's example, red flags were flying in many German cities, Communist agitators were everywhere, and revolution was in the air, but still the Kaiser hung on, hoping for some solution that would keep his dynasty in power. He even suggested that he should remain in Spa while his generals and ministers negotiated the Armistice, and then lead his army back to Berlin, where he would use it to suppress the mobs and restore order.

It was, of course, much too late for that. The German negotiators were already discussing terms with the principal Allied representatives. Marshal Foch and the British Admiral Sir Rosslyn Wemyss, in a railway carriage in a siding in the Forest of Compiègne. At Spa, the Army Chief of Staff General Wilhelm Gröner, destroyed the Kaiser's last delusion with a few blunt words: 'The Army will march home to peace and order under its generals but not under the command of Your Majesty, for it no longer stands behind Your Majesty.' On the following morning, 10 November 1918, Kaiser Wilhelm II, Emperor of Germany and King of Prussia, abdicated and left for Holland and exile. He never saw Germany again.

The Great War ended at 11 o'clock on the morning of 11 November 1918, 'the eleventh hour of the eleventh day of the eleventh month'. When the guns finally stopped firing on the Western Front the leading – Canadian – elements of the British Army pushing the Germans back to their own frontier had reached a Belgian town called Mons, the place where British troops had first engaged the German Army in 1914. For a price of half a million lives lost and another one and a half million men wounded – in the British armies on the Western Front alone – the war brought these soldiers back to the town where it had all begun four years before. That fact, that completion of the circle of havoc which had started here in 1914, may have brought a brief, ironic smile to the grim face of War.

CHAPTER 23

A VERDICT
ON THE GENERALS

*'My research has convinced me that between 1914 and 1918,
Britain, fought a just and necessary war to defeat an
aggressive, expansionist militaristic power.'*

Dr Gary Sheffield, Department of War Studies, RMA, Sandhurst

The Great War did not end on 11 November 1918. That was the day of the Armistice, the day the guns stopped firing, but it was another eight months before the protagonists assembled in the Hall of Mirrors at Versailles and signed the notorious treaty that brought a brief peace to Western Europe, but which led inexorably to the Second World War – and thereby changed 'the Great War' into 'the First World War'. The Allied victory was celebrated in London on 19 July 1919, when a great procession of troops marched through the city to Buckingham Palace, where King George V took the salute. By then, most of the soldiers who had fought in the war – and survived – had been demobilised.

The events that took place in Western Europe after the Treaty of Versailles was signed – the rise and fall of the Weimar Republic, the growth of fascism, the effects of the Wall Street Crash in the United States, the slump of the 1930s, the development of the strange belief in post-war Germany that her army had not been defeated in the field, but 'stabbed in the back' by the politicians and people at home, especially the Jews, German rearmament – these took time to develop. These and other matters, like the advent of Adolf Hitler, the rise of the dictators, Mussolini, Hitler, Franco, and the coming of the Spanish Civil War, would all figure in a study of the inter-war years. Most of what happened after the Great War was due to that war, but that story has no place here. The purpose of this book is to examine a number of allegations made against certain generals who fought on the Western Front during the Great War. With that war now over, the case against them can be summarised.

The mass condemnation of the generals as a *group* is easily dismissed. Even the most fervent, present-day detractor of the generals concedes that some were a good deal better than others. Byng, Plumer, Rawlinson (at least in his 1918 reincarnation), Dominion generals like Monash and Currie, foreign generals like Foch, Joffre and Ludendorff, have escaped the sweeping condemnation of incompetence, for the broad thrust of the accusation is made against the British generals, and especially against Field Marshal Haig. The case for Sir Douglas Haig will be summarised presently, when the case against the rest has been considered.

On the basis of the evidence, presented in earlier chapters, it is surely not possible for any reasonable, fair-minded person to sustain the accusation that the British generals, as a group, were *entirely* to blame for the tragic losses on the Western Front, or that any one general can be held solely to account for the particular disasters of any one battle . . . which is not to say that some of the generals were not at least partly to blame. There were mistakes, certainly, and a whole generation of historians, endowed with the precious gift of hindsight, has gleefully pointed them out.

Making mistakes, however, is not the charge brought against the generals. The allegation levelled at these officers by certain historians and by the general public in Great Britain and certain countries of the old Empire is that the generals – apart from those exceptions noted above, although they too are sometimes included – were *all* useless, and *entirely* responsible for the losses on the Western Front. Since there is no evidence to support that heavy charge, the verdict must surely be 'not guilty'.

And yet the problem with reaching such a verdict is that while a man may be acquitted of a charge on the basis of the evidence, he may yet leave court to discover that most people remain convinced of his guilt. In such circumstances, at best, the Scots verdict of 'not proven' would be muttered behind his back, even by fair-minded people. So it is with the Great War generals, for the allegation that they were incompetent has become a myth, something that people believe without really thinking about it, or knowing exactly why. It therefore seems necessary to make a short summary of the evidence and set before the reader all the reasons why the generals cannot, as a group, be guilty as charged.

Two courses were open to the British Government in the years before 1914: either to increase the Army to a viable size for a Continental struggle, or to break off those 'conversations' with the French and make it very clear that Britain would not take part in such a war at all. In the event, Britain opted for a third course, and sent the BEF to France as it was, small and ill equipped for a major war of the kind that rapidly developed. Her generals then had three years of agony and frustration before the British armies were sufficiently and suitably equipped, supplied with trained soldiers and able to take a proper part in the struggle at all.

There was plenty of evidence prior to 1914 that a great Continental war was coming, but successive governments chose to ignore it, and the British public were not interested. French and Haig had attended German Army manoeuvres, and all Europe had heard the threats of the Kaiser. Henry Wilson was in constant touch with Foch and laying plans for Britain's involvement when war came – and then there were those 'conversations' between the French and British staffs. By 1914 the British Government knew what was going on in Continental Europe, and failed to take suitable action. The British are always unready for war – as was proved most recently in the Falklands – and have a tendency to trust their Regular forces to see them through in the early days of a conflict. This places a heavy burden on the military, but is the price that has to be paid – and is perhaps well worth paying – for living in a democratic, liberal and generally agreeable country.

The Great War was different from all previous wars. This was the first truly technological war, introducing – among a host of other, less obtrusive, innovations – tanks, submarines, aircraft, artillery of tremendous power, and automatic weapons of great reliability and very high rates of fire. And yet, though it was a technological war some elements of technology were missing, most notably a dependable means of battlefield communication.

It was also a war quite outside the experience of the generals – especially of the British generals, whose previous major war had been an open campaign against the Boers, much of it fought with mobile columns. Both the nature of the Great War and the way in which it would be fought had in fact been spelt out in the Russo-Japanese War of 1904–5, a conflict which involved heavy artillery, machine-guns and trench systems. The British Government chose to neglect all this and similar portents; that, however, was not the fault of the generals.

The 'whys' of the principal Great War battles and offensives on the Western Front have already been covered in some detail in this book, but it may still be necessary to summarise what caused the war to develop in the way it did. When the generals are seen in the context of their times, when the full situation is understood, their actions become easier to understand and their problems may even attract a little long-overdue sympathy.

1. When the Great War broke out in 1914 it took all of Western Europe by surprise. Even those nations which had been preparing for war were surprised by the suddenness with which it arrived and the speed with which it spread. No nation expected the war to last very long or to develop into such a bloody struggle. No nation was more surprised than Britain, a country totally unprepared for the kind of war – both in style and scale – that developed on the Continent. There is some blame to be laid here, but it cannot be fairly laid on the generals. The British Government had permitted senior staff officers to indulge in 'conversations' with the French General Staff, and to draw up outline plans for the dispatch of an Expeditionary Force, but the British Army remained small, even for the discharge of its Empire responsibilities. The Continental armies could muster millions; the ration strength of the entire British Army in 1914 was 247,500.

From at least 1906, when General von Schlieffen finished polishing his famous Plan, what was developing on the Continent must have been obvious. Why else did France have a vast army and a three-year conscription period, if not for war . . . or for *revanche* for the loss of Alsace and Lorraine, which must just as certainly mean war?

Germany had an even bigger army, amounting to 1 per cent of her population, more than 600,000 men under arms at any one time, even in peacetime as well as a growing number of reserves and a vast quantity of modern artillery – for what purpose but war? She was building warships and had widened and deepened the Kiel Canal, for no other purpose than to dominate the oceans and thereby challenge the supremacy of the Royal Navy. Of all the nations of Europe, however, Germany should have avoided war for, as Marshal Foch pointed out in his memoirs,

> The Germany of 1914 would never have resorted to war if she had properly estimated her own interests. No appeal to arms was necessary. She had only to continue an economic development that already was penetrating every country of the world. Who would have dared oppose her? . . . Her trade and commerce were moving forward with steady strides that left other nations behind. There was no need for Germany to resort to war in order to conquer the world.

Common sense might have kept Germany from war, but that quality is never very common, especially in autocratic states dominated by a military caste, which was the state of Germany under the second Kaiser in the years before 1914. Germany went to war because the leaders of that country saw the trouble in the Balkans not as the seeds of tragedy, but as an opportunity, a chance to smash their enemies in France and Russia and to break out of their 'encirclement.'

For her part in this coming contest Britain had prepared an Expeditionary Force of just six infantry divisions and a single cavalry division, plus various supporting arms and services – in all amounting to some 160,000 men – and had no plans to introduce conscription at all. The British Government had made no *political* commitment to a war in Europe, and the public would not in any case have supported such a commitment prior to 1914. As a result, no resources were devoted to developing a suitable army and the blame for that – if blame is due – rests with the politicians of the day and, since Britain is a democracy, with the British electorate. Certainly it was not the fault of the generals. The British are not a warlike nation, but the price of failing to prepare for war was paid in 1914 – and again in 1940 – by the soldiers of the British Army, and of the Empire.

2. Much of the tragedy of the Great War stems from this lack of preparedness. If Britain had to go to war at all, then the country – and especially the Army – should have been ready for it. There was the War Book, which set out the way to war in the smallest detail, but the British Army it dispatched to France was small and short of the means to fight a Continental war, especially heavy artillery. Because the Army was small, the British munitions industry was

small, so that when it became necessary to raise large armies to fight a Continental war the industry to arm and support the soldiers simply did not exist. Arms cannot be designed, tested and manufactured and munitions plants cannot be built overnight, and those factories that existed were prevented from immediately increasing production by the trade unions. It takes *time* to build more plant, *time* to place contracts, *time* to introduce new working practices, *time* to design and install new machine tools, *time* to train the workers, test the arms and create adequate stocks of weapons and shells. During that time the war had to be fought with the means available, and the soldiers suffered terribly in consequence. This, too, was not the fault of the generals. Perhaps, somewhere under all that public condemnation that has fallen upon the generals, lurks a sneaking sense of national guilt at the way these soldiers were sacrificed so that a pre-war generation might pay low taxes.

3. Nor was equipping the front-line forces the only problem. During 1914–1916 the British Army was expanding rapidly, as hundreds of thousands of civilians flocked to the Colours, in Britain and her Empire. These recruits had to be clothed, equipped, armed and trained, yet the instructors to train them and the arms and kit with which to equip them were not available. This was not the fault of the generals either; the war to which the nation and its government had committed the Army was on an unimagined scale, and the means to cope with its demands did not exist and could not be quickly created.

4. The men – the private soldiers – could be trained in months, but the senior NCOs, the officers and, above all, the *staff* officers needed to control and command these armies, had to be selected, trained and given time to gain practical experience. In a rapidly expanding army, which grew from a small expeditionary force to five full armies in just two years, time to gain that experience was not available. This was not the fault of the generals.

5. The Great War was a technological war, dominated on land by new and powerful forms of weaponry, in artillery, machine-guns, aircraft, and tanks. These changed the entire face of warfare and forced the generals to fight a conflict which was completely different in style and scale from anything that had gone before. Moreover – and this point needs to be stressed constantly, for it is crucial – some of the means to fight such a war effectively, notably voice communications on the battlefield, did not exist in any suitable form between 1914 and 1918. Had good radio communications been available the outcome of many battles would have been very different. The absence of good, reliable, battlefield communications – also not the fault of the generals – was *the* major factor in the tactical disasters that overtook the armies after battle had been joined.

6. The two British Commanders-in-Chief, Field Marshal Sir John French and Field Marshal Sir Douglas Haig, were instructed by the British

Government to *co-operate closely with the French*. As a result, their actions, certainly until the summer of 1917, nearly three years into a four-year war, were inhibited by the need to conform to the wishes of their allies. Vital matters for any general, such as the timing, location and duration of his battles, were subjugated repeatedly to the wishes of the French, and depended on French co-operation. The results of that co-operation – and the lack of it – were felt at Neuve Chapelle, Second Ypres, Aubers Ridge, the Somme and half a dozen other battles on the Western Front.

Since the BEF was at first small, dependent on French logistical support and fighting on French soil, some of this was inevitable, at least until after the Battle of the Somme, but the French commanders were not always the great generals they considered themselves to be, and rarely gave their British allies an adequate measure of support. A lot of British lives were lost as a consequence of that instruction from the British Government.

7. Political decisions on strategy also inhibited the generals. To hang on to Ypres for emotional and political reasons when the Salient was clearly indefensible, or could only be held at great cost – as at First and Second Ypres – was another cause of loss. The losses at Neuve Chapelle were due to a desire to demonstrate Britain's wartime commitment to the French, and the same is true of the disaster at Loos. The strategy of the 'Easterners', which soaked up over a million British soldiers, was another drain on the resources needed for a decisive victory. Such a victory could only be won where eventually it was won – by defeating the German Army *on the Western Front* – a fact that Lloyd George and his cronies refused to accept.

8. The development of the trench system caused a costly stalemate for the best part of three and a half years. The trench system on the Western Front arose almost by accident, certainly not as part of a deliberate policy or intention of the generals, but the result was that all the armies, British, French and German, had to fight a war for which the officers and men lacked both the equipment and the experience.

9. The old British Regular Army – what its opponent, General von Moltke, called 'that perfect thing apart' – was destroyed in 1914–15.* After that Britain had an amateur, poorly trained army, because there was no one left to train it properly, and because 'on-the-job training' in battle was costly in casualties and took time. It was a mistake not to raise the new armies on the basis of the Territorial Force, which at least had a structure on which a more professional army could have been built. This error was made by Lord Kitchener and endorsed by the British Government.

* As was said much earlier, in the first four months of the war – that is, from Mons to the end of First Ypres – the BEF suffered casualties (all types) of just under 90,000 men. That is equivalent to its *entire* original strength.

Here as elsewhere, however, there are few absolutes, and Colonel Terry Cave of the Western Front Association points out that Kitchener had some sound reasons for rejecting the Territorial system:

> Apart from his dislike of part-time or weekend soldiers – as he regarded them – Kitchener had to consider that the Territorials were intended for home defence; they could not be sent overseas unless they volunteered and he had no means of knowing what percentage of the force would volunteer; the first calls for volunteers met with a mixed reception. The Territorial units were under the command of their County Associations who were often anxious to retain such control and the men had joined for specific engagements. As a result they could, and often did, claim discharge when their time was up – even if they were actually in the trenches at that time. Kitchener felt that the Territorial system would not be able to cope with the tremendous expansion of the Army he was planning (to 70 divisions) when it was not up to strength itself and needed several months' training to do the job for which it was intended. (Letter to the author, 1998.)

10. The 'learning curve' for the British and French generals remained fairly flat and only starting to rise significantly during the Somme battles of 1916. Some of this was due to the factors described above, a shortage of equipment and men, especially well-trained men, but it is also possible that the Entente generals were too old. In 1917–18 Haig and Foch were constantly urging Pershing to appoint young men to command posts in the new American armies, since the demands and rigours of this new Western Front warfare wore out older men rapidly.

This was good advice, but in 1914–15 the British and French had to use the general officers they had, the ones with some experience of warfare, staff work and logistics. Only later in the war, as the armies expanded, could younger, fresher men be found and brought up to command positions. Nevertheless, as Haig's battles in 1915 make clear, the generals and professional soldiers were constantly trying to learn from their mistakes and develop new tactics to cope with a changing situation. So too, alas, were the Germans.

These ten points cover just some of the factors which inhibited the generals in the Great War. Some were overcome, others disappeared as the war changed, but the word which appears constantly in that summary is *'time'*. It took time to put all these matters right, and the British armies suffered during that time, but in due course – in 1918, to be exact – it all came good. The British armies that fought on the Western Front from June to November 1918 were superb – as were their commanding generals.

Some of the other minor charges have weight. The cavalry ethos in the British Army was certainly strong, a fact confirmed by what happened to the tank and cavalry units after the war ended. It then became popular in cavalry circles to claim that trench warfare on the Western Front had been a singular occurrence which would not arise again, since the tank was increasingly vulnerable to armour-piercing shells and bullets. This opposition had a detrimental effect on the tank units and in the years immediately after the war while the number of horsed cavalry regiments fell from thirty-one to twenty-two, the number of tank battalions fell from twenty-five to two. In 1925, seven years after the war ended, Field Marshal the Earl Haig (as he had become) could remark, 'Some enthusiasts . . . prophesy that the aeroplane, the tank and the motor car will supersede the horse in future wars. I am all for tanks and aeroplanes but they are only accessories to the man and the horse.' It should be noted, however, that this was addressed to an enthusiastic audience at the Cavalry Club, and that Haig may well have tailored his opinions to his listeners. Yet as late as 1936, long after Haig's death, the British Army was spending £400,000 a year on horse fodder and just £121,000 on petrol (Army Estimates, 1935–6). Haig's old regiment, the 7th Hussars, only gave up its horses for the Mark VI Vickers tank in 1937, when the regiment was stationed in Egypt.

If this book has destroyed the ingrained notion that all the generals were incompetent, what of the accusation of callousness, of indifference to casualties? There seems to be little evidence to support that charge, and plenty of examples of generals making every effort to take care of their men, minimise the losses, and especially to arrange for the recovery and care of the wounded. The idea that they were indifferent to the sufferings of their men is constantly refuted by the facts, and only endures because some commentators wish to perpetuate the myth that these generals, representing the upper classes, did not give a damn what happened to the lower orders. In fact, as we have seen, incompetent generals who threw away the lives of their men in badly handled attacks were swiftly sacked, very often never to hold active command again.

The man most often accused today of incompetence and callousness, Field Marshal Haig, is also the man most often referred to in the memoirs and books of the time as someone the soldiers greatly admired. Charles Carrington, who served throughout both world wars, writes that 'Above the Corps commanders we [Carrington was an infantry subaltern in the Great War] condemned on insufficient evidence and the Army Commanders of whom we knew nothing, was the C-in-C. I wish to place it on record that never once during the war did I hear such criticisms of Sir Douglas Haig as are now current when his name is mentioned . . . He was trusted and that put an end to discussion.'

What of the generals who have featured in this book? What judgement can fairly be made of their performance during it, and what happened to them after the war was over? A brief look at their subsequent careers might not go amiss before they fade from view.

Field Marshal Lord Kitchener did not survive the war and has no grave but the sea. He was an old man in 1914 and the two years he served as Secretary of State for War before his death took their toll, but Kitchener served his country well in the Great War. He saw that it would be a long war, a war that would require an army of millions, and he took immediate steps to create just such a force. It might have been better if he had used the existing structure of the Territorial Force as the basis for such a formation, but no one else could have brought so many civilians to the Colours in the years before conscription, while his reasons for rejecting the Territorial option have already been aired. He should be credited with prevailing on Sir John French to keep the BEF in the line on the Marne in 1914, and for resisting French demands for the immediate dispatch of troops to the front on the grounds that to send half-trained men into battle 'was little short of murder'. That the generals were only interested in their soldiers as cannon fodder is another Great War myth.

Field Marshal Sir John French did not have a good war. He was out of his depth from the start, and the Army lost a good man through his vendetta against General Smith-Dorrien. That alone might not condemn him, but his volatility, his tendency to heed the last person he had spoken to, his lack of grip in handling his command and his willingness to rewrite the record of his actions to show them in a favourable light, all speak against him. He was not the right man to command the BEF in 1914, and they were well rid of him after the Loos débâcle of 1915. In spite of all that, honours descended on him; he became a Knight of St Patrick, a member of the Order of Merit, received a grant of £50,000 for his war services and eventually an earldom (he had been given a viscountcy in 1916). He died in 1925, and a bust and tablet to his memory stand in the church of St George at Ypres, a town his army defended for so long and so well; the title he took was Earl of Ypres.

General Sir Horace Smith-Dorrien went to take command in East Africa after his dismissal from Second Army but soon became ill and had to come home, his military career effectively over. Smith-Dorrien was an outstanding general at both corps and army level, and as he was senior to Haig it is more than likely that, had he not been recalled, he would have been given command of the BEF when French was sacked. How he would have performed in that more demanding role can only be guessed at. Smith-Dorrien died from injuries sustained in a road accident in 1930.

General Sir William Robertson became GOC, Eastern Command, after resigning as CIGS. He then succeeded Sir John French as C-in-C Home Forces and after the war commanded British occupation troops in Germany. For his wartime service he was awarded a baronetcy, £10,000, and promotion to field marshal. It is hard to see anyone doing any better than Robertson did during his period as CIGS, and his stout-hearted support of Haig and the 'Westerner' position, in spite of all the pressure brought to bear on him by Lloyd George, stands to his credit. He died in 1933, and is remembered as one of the most popular officers in the Army and – apart from General Sir William Slim (later Field Marshal the Viscount Slim) in the Second World War – the only private soldier in the British Army to rise to to the rank of field marshal.

General Sir Henry Wilson came to an untimely end in 1922, shot to death outside his home in London by two IRA gunmen. After the war he was raised to the rank of field marshal and rewarded with £10,000 and a baronetcy. He retired from the Army shortly before he was murdered; his killers were caught, tried and hanged. Wilson's reputation has not gained much lustre with the years. He was an inveterate intriguer, and much of his not inconsiderable military talent went into making 'mischief', as he himself would have freely admitted. Henry Wilson was an intelligent man, but his career was blighted by his passion for intrigue and his love of France, which went some way beyond the limit of reason and caused problems for his brother officers in the British Army, the men he should have supported. In the end, though, Wilson's obvious lightness of character prevented him from doing too much harm. Everyone found him amusing, but nobody trusted him. He kept dabbling in politics on leaving the Army, and it was his meddling in Irish affairs that led to his death.

General Sir Henry Rawlinson can be fairly regarded as one of the great soldiers of the Great War, although the casualties of 1 July 1916 will always count against him. He rose on ability, for his first Commander-in-Chief in France, Sir John French, did not like him, and his second, Sir Douglas Haig, did not trust him. Rawlinson was a good soldier who served in every rank from divisional general to army commander during the Great War, and who performed at least adequately well in every post. Certainly he was wily, but he was also clear-headed. He possessed a good sense of humour and was a stout admirer and supporter of Douglas Haig, whatever reservations Haig may have cherished in return. In the end, however, they developed a mutual esteem and became good friends.

After the war Rawlinson was granted £30,000 for his wartime services and given a barony, taking the title Rawlinson of Trent. In 1919 he went to Russia in command of the Murmansk expedition, an attempt to aid the 'White' Russians in the civil war against the Bolshevik but returned a few months later to take up the Aldershot Command before becoming C-in-C, India, his ultimate goal. He was not to enjoy that post for long, however, for he died suddenly after a medical operation in 1925.

General Sir Herbert Plumer led his beloved Second Army into Germany at the end of hostilities, where he commanded the Army of Occupation. In 1919, as a reward for his wartime services he was promoted to the rank of field marshal and made first a baron and later a viscount, taking the title Viscount Plumer of Messines after his most famous victory. In spite of his unlikely, Colonel-Blimpish appearance, Plumer was an outstanding general, a man who inspired confidence in his colleagues, superiors and subordinates, an officer who took good care of this men. His handling of the attack at Messines and the later stages at Passchendaele were outstanding, and the outcome of

Third Ypres might have been very different if Plumer had been in command from the start. He received a grant of £30,000 for his war services and in 1919 became Governor and Commander-in-Chief, Malta, and from 1925–8 was High Commissioner in Palestine. The latter was not an easy posting, but Plumer handled what were at times extremely volatile situations with firmness, matched by sympathy, tact, and a marked absence of bias. He died in 1932 and lies buried in Westminster Abbey.

General the Hon. Sir Julian Byng was another excellent commander. He fought in some hard campaigns and enjoyed great success, but also at least one reverse – at Cambrai – which might have ended his career. Byng's greatest triumph was in planning and executing the attack on Vimy Ridge in 1917 but he did almost equally well while in command of Third Army during the March Retreat in 1918 and in the fighting that followed. He did not believe in inquests into his successes or failures, but kept his attention firmly fixed on the next battle. He was also lucky in that much of his Western Front experience was gained while in command of the superb Canadian Corps. After the war he was awarded £30,000 and a barony, which was later raised to a viscountcy; he took the title Viscount Byng of Vimy. Between 1921 and 1926 he was an extremely popular Governor-General of Canada, during which time he never missed a Canadian Corps reunion, and was Chief Commissioner of the Metropolitan Police from 1928–31. He was raised to the rank of field marshal in 1932 and died in 1935.

General Sir Edmund Allenby made his name in Palestine in 1917–18, fighting against the Turks. He captured Jerusalem and then Damascus, and between those two events fought the Battle of Megiddo (September 1918), a brilliantly handled action and a crushing victory which drove the Turks out of the war; far from being hidebound, he became a patron and supporter of Lawrence of Arabia and, in this open campaign, proved a skilful commander of his disparate force of British, Dominion and Indian Army troops, and Arab irregulars. As a reward for his victories he was promoted to the rank of field marshal and created Viscount Allenby of Megiddo, with the grant of £50,000. He stayed on in Egypt after the war as High Commissioner, remaining in that post until 1925; during that time he ended the British protectorate and re-established Egypt as an independent kingdom. He died in 1936 and is widely regarded in many quarters as the best general of the Great War, although a good number of those who served under his command, especially in France, held a contrary opinion. By contrast, General Sir Archibald Wavell (later Field Marshal the Earl Wavell), who commanded the British forces in the Western Desert (as C-in-C Middle East) in the Second World War and became C-in-C, India, and then Viceroy, claimed Allenby, with whom he had served in Palestine, as his hero. Allenby seems to have performed no more than adequately on the Western Front, but he flourished later and earned his high place in British military history.

General Sir Henry Horne, stout soldier and commander of the First Army from 1916–18, faded from the scene, leaving few traces behind, no memoirs, no private papers, no diaries. He has become the 'unknown general' of the Great War, but what evidence there is states that he was a good one. He received a barony and a grant of £30,000 for his war services and was C-in-C, Eastern Command from 1919–23, retiring three years later; he died in 1929.

General Sir Hubert Gough outlived his critics, for he died in 1963 at the age of ninety-three. Lloyd George refused to grant him an inquiry into the events leading to his dismissal from the command of Fifth Army, and although he was sent on missions to the Caucasus and the Baltic after the war, his military career was effectively at an end when he was recalled in 1918, although he was, perhaps as a consolation, appointed GCMG (to add to his KCB and KCVO from 1916 and 1917) in 1919. He left the Army in 1922 and went into business, first as a farmer and later as a partner in a successful public company. He was one of the pallbearers at Haig's funeral in 1928, and in 1937 was appointed GCB in the King's Birthday Honours list, an award which he took, rightly, as belated recognition of his services in command of Fifth Army in 1918. He commanded a unit of the Home Guard in London in the Second World War, and devoted the later years of his life to a resolute defence of his own reputation, writing two studies of the campaigns he fought during the Great War, as well as a volume of memoirs. History has tended to modify the harsh views it once held about Hubert Gough, and has come to recognise that he had an impossible task in 1918 and did as well as anyone could have done in the circumstances. Even Lloyd George made some amends in his memoirs, published in the 1930s.

Birdwood was the last of the British officers considered in this book to rise to army command, leaving his beloved Australian Corps for the reconstituted Fifth Army in May 1918. He was granted a baronetcy and £10,000 for his war services, and in 1920 he toured Australia and New Zealand, meeting enthusiastic welcomes from his former diggers wherever he went. Later that year he sailed for India to take over the Northern Command, a post he retained until 1924. In 1925 he was appointed field marshal and returned to India as Commander-in-Chief, a post he held until his retirement in 1930. King George V was anxious to appoint him Governor-General of Australia but that country's Labour Prime Minister, James Scullin, told the King that the time had come for an Australian to receive that appointment, which went to Sir Isaac Jacobs, the Australian Chief Justice. Birdwood was then offered the post of Master of Peterhouse College, Cambridge, a position he held until 1938. He entered the House of Lords as a baron, taking the title Lord Birdwood of Anzac and Totnes, became Colonel of the Royal Horse Guards (The Blues) after the death of their previous Colonel, 'Wully' Robertson, served in the Home Guard in the Second World War and died in 1951.

Birdwood's career in the Great War gives the lie – as does Byng's – to those who allege that Dominion troops resented having to serve under British officers. Few British officers can have come from a more typical, even pukka, background than this officer of the Indian Army, but his fondness for his diggers was fully reciprocated by the men themselves, as was evident from the tremendous welcome Birdwood received during his post-war visits to Australia. This would not have been the case had he been either incompetent or callous. He served with the Australians in almost all their great battles, in Gallipoli, on the Somme and at Bullecourt, and the mutual regard that developed between them is one of the warmest tributes a general and his soldiers can share.

Loaded with honours, Lieutenant-General Sir Arthur Currie returned to Canada after the war. He attempted to rebuild his civilian career, but controversy – and the enmity of Canada's former War Minister, Lieutenant-General Sir Sam Hughes, who had been sacked in 1916 – was to dog him for the rest of his life. After retiring from the Army in 1920 (having been promoted to full general a year earlier) he became Principal and Vice-Chancellor of McGill University in Montreal, a post he held until his death. Currie was a successful Vice-Chancellor, well respected in the university and in Canadian society, and was a great personal friend of the Governor-General (from 1921–6), Julian Byng. Nevertheless, controversies from the war surfaced from time to time.

Although Currie had always taken great care of his men, it was alleged that he had volunteered them for the hardest missions in 1917 and 1918, and Hughes, his bitter enemy, frequently accused him of deliberately sacrificing his troops in the pursuit of personal glory. Hughes was a Member of Parliament and invariably sheltered behind parliamentary privilege when making these slanders. He died in 1921, but seven years later an Ontario newspaper repeated his accusations and Currie issued a writ for libel. The trial lasted two weeks, during which the defence dragged out Currie's pre-war peculations for another airing, but he won the case. The strain cost him what remained of his health, however, and he died in 1933, aged fifty-seven.

General Sir Arthur Currie was a great soldier, perhaps the best corps commander of the war, a man who planned his attacks with great care and took the time afterwards to analyse the battle and see what had gone wrong. Truly successful generals also have to be lucky, and Currie had more than his share of luck. He was never to command an army, however, and his ability at a higher and much more difficult level of command therefore remains untested. Although the myth that he was in line to take over the BEF in 1919 has surfaced from time to time to the present day, this story is without foundation, except in the memoirs of David Lloyd George.

Currie was also lucky to serve in, and then to command, the superb Canadian Corps, a formation that remained at full strength throughout the war, and which did not suffer from the constant chopping and changing of divisions that so inhibited the British corps. He was lucky in his immediate superiors, the British generals Alderson and Byng, men who admired Currie and promoted his interests. He possessed the strength of character to take chances, but his greatest strength lay in his innate soldiering ability, something that few men have, something that cannot be taught, but a quality that Arthur Currie, despite an unmilitary background and an unsoldierly appearance, possessed in great measure.

After the Armistice, Lieutenant-General Sir John Monash accepted the post of Director-General of Australian Repatriation and Demobilisation in London. Responsible for sending his soldiers home, he did not return to Australia himself until December 1919, arriving to face a personal tragedy. His wife had developed cancer while he was overseas, but had decided to keep this fact from him, knowing that he had problems enough in France. She was very ill by the time her husband got home, and died shortly afterwards. Monash retired in 1930 with the rank of full general, became Vice-Chancellor of Melbourne University, and died in 1931. Monash University, near Melbourne, founded in 1958, honours his memory. Today he is regarded by most Australians and many historians as the best general of the Great War.

Like Currie, Monash was a superb soldier; like Currie, Monash's name had been mooted as commander of the British Armies in France in succession to Haig; and, again like Currie, his reputation has come under attack from military historians. The proposal that Monash or Currie should become C-in-C can be traced to Lloyd George, who, according to Pederson's biography, was using Monash's reputation to 'bludgeon Haig'. This myth grew, and it has even been alleged that Monash was 'in line for the post of Generalissimo of the Allied Forces in France, which went to General Foch' (Major-General Sir Kingsley Norris, quoted in Pederson's *John Monash*), which seems a flight of fancy.

Monash was a good soldier, but the highest command he held was at corps level. How he would have handled an army, let alone the entire British force of *five* armies, remains a matter of speculation. It is a happy general whose career peaks when he has reached that level of command at which his abilities can flower and his limitations are minimised; many a fine major-general has been found wholly unsuited to higher command. Monash was lucky to learn his trade slowly and to take up command of the Australian Army Corps when the tide of the war was turning in the Allies' favour. He was also lucky to serve in, and have command of, such a fine corps, but when all that is said, he was a good, efficient and intelligent officer, and a brilliant planner, a soldier who fully deserved the respect he earned from his superiors and subordinates.

It has been alleged that Monash's command during the crossing of the Hindenburg Line in 1918 was 'erratic' and that his performance in that campaign 'showed that he was not infallible' (Pederson, *The Commanders*) – but few commanders are. He was also accused of arrogance and ambition and of 'attempting to perform functions properly discharged by his staff', but these charges cannot detract from his overall reputation, or from the high regard felt for Monash by his officers and men, and by his allies.

Many of the generals wrote their memoirs after the war, the notable exception being Field Marshal Haig, but few accounts of the Great War were as successful as General John Pershing's book, *My Experiences in the World War*, which won the Pulitzer Prize in 1932, and has been continuously in print ever since.

The American armies did not play a major part in the fighting during the Great War, but their presence in France was crucial to the Allied victory, the guarantee that Germany would eventually be defeated. Those US divisions that were committed to battle did extremely well, but the state and size of the their army in 1917 meant that by the time the Americans were ready to commit large forces to the struggle the war was virtually over.

Among the reasons for this delay – the others included a lack of men, staff officers, equipment, heavy guns, and shipping to transport the troops to France – was Pershing's determination that his men would fight only in formed US units as part of a US army. This decision, though decried at the time by the French and the British, was almost certainly right. Many American divisions did fight with the French or British Armies, and at least two stayed with the British Fourth Army until the end of the war. Although Pershing's insistence on creating an American army kept many of his divisions from the field, the creation of such a powerful army was crucial to the final outcome . . . and probably kept thousands of doughboys from participation in fruitless French and British attacks. Pershing was not a great battlefield general, but as Commander-in-Chief of the American Expeditionary Force he served his men and his country well.

After the war Pershing was awarded the rank of General of the Armies, one of only two people ever to hold that rank, the other being George Washington. By an overwhelming vote of Congress he was named. Presidential Chief of Staff, a vote that President Wilson chose to ignore. When Pershing arrived home he led victory parades in New York and Washington, and then went about the country making speeches. He also took a leading role in founding the American Legion for ex-servicemen, and found himself involved in the race for the presidency in the elections of 1920, standing against two later Presidents, Calvin Coolidge and Herbert Hoover. Pershing came from Nebraska, and entered the campaign by standing as a 'favourite son' candidate in the Nebraska primary. His appearance on the political scene brought out some enemies, who alleged, among other things, that he had never visited a battle front in France, and that he had, 'systematically eliminated any officer who ranked him or showed ability' (Richard Goldhurst, *Pipeclay and Drill*). In the event, Pershing came last in the primary poll and withdrew from the presidential race.

The Republican Warren Harding won the presidency, and in July 1921 he appointed Pershing his Chief of Staff, a post he held until he retired from the Army in 1924. Leaving the service, he then became director of the US Battlefields Monuments Commission, and spent several months each year in France, organising the building of American cemeteries and controlling the growing number of US Army memorials in the Argonne and other American sectors of the old front line. He also used his influence to promote the interests and career of one of his former officers, Colonel George C. Marshall, who would rise to be Chief of Staff of the US Army in the Second World War, and, as Secretary of State after it, would be the inspiration behind the Marshall Plan that rebuilt Continental Europe after the war. In 1941 Pershing's health began to fail and he entered the Walter Reed Hospital, Washington, where he spent the last seven years of his life, much of it in charting the course of the Second World War on maps pinned about the walls of his room.

'Black Jack' Pershing died in his sleep in July 1949, aged eighty-eight. He was buried in Arlington National Cemetery, Virginia, among the graves of other soldiers from the American Expeditionary Force. Declining the offer of help from his father, Pershing's son entered the US Army as a private soldier in 1941 and finished the war as a major. The General's grandson, Second Lieutenant Richard Pershing, was killed in action in Vietnam in February 1968 and lies buried beside his grandfather at Arlington.

Marshal Joffre the man who, in 1914, saved France, and thus Europe, faded into obscurity after his dismissal in December 1916. He was given an office in the École de Guerre but rarely went there, and was never known to return to his desk after lunch. When he rode through Paris, in the Victory Parade in 1919 few among the cheering thousands knew who he was. He showed no interest in the inquests into the Great War that took place after its end, and refused to discuss his battles, although he prepared a thick volume of memoirs for eventual publication in 1932. By then he had been dead for a year.

Marshal Foch remained in command of the French armies after the war, and was loaded with awards and decorations, including the rank of field marshal in the British Army; a statue of him stands outside Victoria Station in London. He died in 1929, aged seventy-nine. His funeral in Paris was attended by dignitaries from all over the world, and a huge crowd jammed the streets to watch as his coffin passed; his *Memoirs* appeared two years later. His protégé, General Weygand, as he became, held high command after the Great War; as Commander-in-Chief of the Allied armies in France, he presided over his country's humiliating surrender in June 1940.

General Pétain's life ended in tragedy. He became the leader of France after her defeat by Hitler's armies in 1940 and elected to collaborate with the conquerors. Pétain's regime, established in the spa town of Vichy, adopted many of the policies of Nazi Germany, notably in the persecution of the Jews, but was by no means unpopular with large sections of the French population or at least not until a German defeat became probable. He was taken off to Germany in 1945 but returned to France to face trial in 1946. Found guilty of high treason, he was sentenced to death; no one, however, wished to execute the hero of Verdun. The sentence was commuted, but he spent the rest of his life as a prisoner on the Île d'Yeu, off the Vendée coast of

Western France. He was released in 1951 and died a month later, aged ninety-five. His name was expunged from the memorial to those who saved Verdun, and despite occasional efforts to have it reinstated, has never been re-inscribed.

Colonel-General von Moltke, Chief of the German General Staff, did not long survive his dismissal by the Kaiser in September 1914, just five weeks into the war. He was utterly shattered, both as a man and a soldier, by the collapse of the Schlieffen Plan and the reverses on the Marne. There is an account of him sitting before the map table at OHL, 'broken down completely, pale and pathetic'. Moltke ruined Germany's best hope of winning the war when he tinkered with the Schlieffen Plan and allowed Kluck to march his army north of Paris. In truth, he was a pale shadow of his mighty uncle, and there are doubts as to whether his heart was ever in this war. Strangely, Moltke himself was the first to see the error of his action and the inevitability of the defeat that must follow. He retired to his estates and died in 1916, aged sixty-eight.

General von Falkenhayn lived until 1922 but never recovered from the strain of the battles he had fought on the Somme and at Verdun. When he left the High Command in 1916 it was noted that his hair had turned completely white. The Kaiser offered him the post of Ambassador to the Sublime Porte – Turkey – but he preferred to accept the command of the Ninth Army in Romania, and led it successfully in a number of offensives in 1917 and 1918. He left the army after the Armistice and spent the last years of his life lecturing on military strategy at Berlin University.

Field Marshal Paul von Hindenburg remained a power in German affairs, even after the war. Though Ludendorff resigned his post before the war ended, Hindenburg stayed on as head of the German Army until after the Paris Peace Conference of 1919 and the signing of the Treaty of Versailles. He then entered politics as a candidate for President of the Weimar Republic in 1925, and was duly elected. Winning the election was one thing; leading this new democratic state when saddled with a vast bill for reparations and a looming world slump was quite another. In 1933 he made way for the man who would be his successor, nominating a former German Army corporal, Adolf Hitler, as Chancellor of Germany. He died a year later, aged eighty-seven, before the full extent of that mistake had become visible. It might be said in Hindenburg's defence that his influence was so great in Germany that Hitler and Nazism were only able to flourish after the old Field Marshal's death.

Erich Ludendorff left the German Army before the end of the war, resigning on 26 October 1918, by which time he was on the verge of a nervous breakdown. He entered politics in 1920 and stood as the National Socialist (Nazi) candidate in the Weimar elections of 1924, and served in the Reichstag until 1928. During this period he met Adolf Hitler and soon had his measure, telling Hindenburg in 1933 that 'This accursed man will take our Reich into the abyss.' This was something of a volte-face, for in 1923 Ludendorff had taken part in the abortive putsch organised by Hitler and the Nazis in Munich, although he was acquitted at the subsequent trials at which Hitler and others were gaoled. Retiring from politics, he died in 1937, by which time the balance of his mind was at best questionable. Ludendorff and his wife became fanatical followers of a pagan cult that worshipped ancient gods, something which alienated him from Hitler and the Nazi Party; moreover, haunted by Germany's massive war debts, the General paid a large sum of money to a con man for a 'magic box' that supposedly produced endless supplies of paper money. Perhaps his experiences during the war helped to strip Ludendorff of his sanity, but whatever the case, it was a sad end to one of the Great War's finest commanders.

And so, finally, to Field Marshal Sir Douglas Haig, the man around whom so many of the Great War disputes have centred. It has to be admitted that even now, two years into a detailed study of the generals of that war, Haig remains an enigma to this writer, as he does to many others.

Perhaps this is partly due to the fact that over the decades since the Great War, or at least since Lloyd George's six volumes of memoirs appeared in the 1930s, Haig's reputation has acquired a great deal of baggage. When an accusation is constantly repeated, it begins to take effect, whatever evidence is produced to prove it false. A large number of people still *hate* Douglas Haig – many of them born years after his death – blaming him for the disasters of the Great War and the deaths of their ancestors, writing abusive letters to the newspapers – and to authors whose views do not chime in with their own. Seventy years after his death, Haig is still a controversial figure.

The charges of incompetence and callousness can be dismissed as easily for Haig as for any of the other generals, either on the grounds that they are wholly without foundation, or because the actions for which he stands accused were fully justified by the circumstances of the time. Certainly he made mistakes, *but he also won the war*. Everyone in authority makes mistakes, but when a commanding general makes them, men die. Men also die, and die in large numbers, when a general makes no mistakes at all. The best way to save men's lives in battle is to stay away from war.

Haig was the Commander-in-Chief of the British Armies in France for much of the war, and most of the men from the British, Dominion and Imperial forces who died on the Western Front were killed while serving under his command. This should not be taken to mean that their deaths were his fault. All the problems inherent in that command bore most heavily on Douglas Haig, and the weight was crushing. No other British general could have withstood the pressure, and most of those generals knew it. If Haig is judged by the same standards as the other commanders, he must be acquitted of both charges, simply because the men he commanded will not condemn him, and the facts do not substantiate the charges levelled by outsiders. 'Haig was not a cold-blooded butcher, as history has tended to portray him,' writes the Canadian historian, Daniel Dancocks, in his *Legacy of Valour*. 'Indeed, he was devoted to the men under his command.'

Haig's enemies have trawled the accounts of the time – diaries, memoirs, articles, letters – to find evidence against him, carefully ignoring the other side of the story. Dancocks relates two incidents that show another facet of his admittedly dour and undemonstrative character. When the artist William Orpen arrived at GHQ in 1917 to paint Haig's portrait, he was told, 'Go and paint the men. They are the fellows who are saving the world, and they are getting killed every day.' Then again, after the war, when he was congratulated on the victory, he said 'You must not congratulate me,' and pointing to a soldier close by added, 'It is fellows like him who deserve congratulations.'

There is plenty of other evidence to refute the old lies, not the least of which is the fact that great crowds lined the streets to cheer Haig and his fellow generals when they returned to London in December 1918, and that in 1920 a national subscription raised enough money from the British public for Haig to purchase and rebuild his family home at Bemersyde on the River Tweed. The allegations that he was callous, or careless of the lives of his soldiers, are refuted by this evidence of his popularity, evidence which many historians have chosen to ignore.

Nor was Haig an incompetent soldier. He constantly sought innovation, varied his tactics to cope with the problems encountered in previous battles, and was among the first to see the advantages of aircraft and tanks in the infantry-support role. More than that, he was also, quite literally, irreplaceable, something to which even his bitterest enemy, Lloyd George, bears reluctant witness. If the Prime Minister could have found a better man to command the British Armies in France, then their Commander-in-Chief would undoubtedly have been sacked, but there *was* no one better. Haig's abilities have been illustrated time and again in this book, and since that record will stand inspection, it need not be recycled here.

The heaviest charge that can be laid against Field Marshal Sir Douglas Haig is that he kept up his attacks for too long, and pressed them home when any further gains could only be achieved at the cost of heavy casualties. There is weight in this charge, but the fault, if fault it is, lies not in Haig's competence but in his character. He did not pursue his attacks blindly or unthinkingly, but because he believed that if they could be pushed on and made to succeed, then weeks or months of effort – and their concomitant casualties – might to some extent be justified. Besides, giving up the fight was not in his nature.

Much of the criticism Haig has attracted stems not from his nature or his ability, however, but from certain of his personal characteristics. He was reserved, inarticulate and remote, in many ways a typical Lowland Scot, but behind that dour façade he was also a considerable optimist. Those two apparently conflicting facets of his character combined to make him a tough and resolute general, the dourness making him press on, the optimism convincing him that the end result would be favourable – sometimes in spite of considerable evidence to the contrary.

It is not hard to see why Haig has attracted enmity, even years after his death. He did not go out of his way to court popularity and modern writers do not like that; a public figure, even a historical figure, is likely to be judged today on the basis of his popularity, not his competence. Haig was not interested in public relations or glad-handing. He did his job, and he did it to the best of his ability; that had to be enough. It was certainly enough for his soldiers. They may not have loved Haig, but they trusted him. Few soldiers love their generals; all they ask is that he should be competent and careful of their lives, and the soldiers Haig commanded thought him sound on both counts.

Lloyd George, who remained Prime Minister until the Coalition Government fell apart in 1922, continued to disparage Haig, even when the war was over and his *bête noire* had retired from the active list. But while the former's memoirs drove the first nail into Haig's reputation, the attempts to belittle or discredit the former C-in-C had begun a good deal earlier. No high office was offered when Haig's Army career ended, and it was well into 1919 before he was given the peerage that most thought he deserved – and that a lowly barony, although this was raised to an earldom in 1922. Parliament also voted him the sum of £100,000 for his services during the war, but Haig refused to accept any reward until his soldiers received their gratuities and pensions. He became Commander-in-Chief, Home Forces in 1919, but held that command for only a few months, for the post was abolished in January 1920.

In 1920 he used his influence to weld two of the main ex-servicemen's associations into the British Legion, and set up what is now called the Poppy Appeal, although it was better known for many years as the Earl Haig Fund, to care for old soldiers and their dependants; he was also active in setting up similar funds and associations in South Africa and Canada. When the restoration of Bemersyde was complete he moved there with his family, but he was not to enjoy his ancestral home for long.

In January 1928, Field Marshal the Earl Haig of Bemersyde died suddenly in London of a heart attack, aged sixty-six. He was accorded a state funeral, at which tens of thousands of his old soldiers turned out to see his coffin pass, and more than 30,000 veterans followed it to its final resting place in the ruined cloister of Dryburgh Abbey by the Tweed. There, under a simple soldier's headstone, the Field Marshal lies, far from the battlefields of France and the vast, silent army of the Great War dead. Let him lie in peace, and let his memory be respected. Douglas Haig did this state some service, and he deserves a kinder and a fairer judgement than posterity has granted him till now.

SELECT BIBLIOGRAPHY

T his list is by no means one of all the books I have consulted, but those which readers might find most immediately useful in pursuing their Great War studies. Certain magazines, notably *Stand To: The Journal of the Western Front Association*, the *Imperial War Museum Review*, A.J. Peacock's *Gunfire*, the *Army Quarterly and Defence Journal*, the *British Army Review*, and the *Poppy and the Owl* from the Liddle Collection at the University of Leeds, have also proved most useful.

Ballard, Brigadier-General C., *Smith-Dorrien*, London, Constable, 1931

Barnett, Correlli, *The Swordbearers*, London, Eyre & Spottiswoode, 1963

Barnett, Correlli, *Britain and her Army, 1509–1970: A Military, Political and Social Survey*, London, Allen Lane, 1970

Baynes, Lieutenant-Colonel Sir John, Bt, *Far from a Donkey – The Life of Sir Ivor Maxse*, London, Brassey's, 1995

Bean, C. E. W., *The Official History of Australia in the War of 1914–1918*, Sydney, University of Queensland Press (in association with the Australian War Memorial, Canberra), 1933

Beaverbrook, Lord, *Canada in Flanders* (2 volumes), Toronto, Hodder & Stoughton, 1927

Beaverbrook, Lord, *Men and Power, 1917–18*, London, Hutchinson, 1956

Berton, Pierre, *Vimy*, Toronto, Penguin Books, 1987

Birdwood, Field Marshal Lord, *Khaki and Gown: An Autobiography*, London, Ward Lock, 1941

Blake, Robert (ed.), *The Private Papers of Douglas Haig, 1914–1919*, London, Eyre & Spottiswoode, 1952

Blaxland, Gregory, *Amiens 1918*, London, Frederick Muller, 1968

Buchan, John, *The South African Forces in France*, Cape Town, Thomas Nelson, 1920

Buchan, John, *A History of the Great War* (4 volumes), London, Thomas Nelson, 1922

Callwell, Major-General Sir C. E., *Field Marshal Sir Henry Wilson: His Life and Diaries* (2 volumes), London, Cassell, 1927

Carew, Tim, *The Vanished Army*, London, Corgi Books, 1964

Carrington, Charles (as 'Charles Edmonds'), *A Subaltern's War*, London, 1929

Carrington, Charles, *Soldier from the Wars Returning*, London, Arrow Books, 1965

Carver, Field Marshal Lord, *The War Lords*, London, Weidenfeld & Nicolson, 1976

Chandler, David (ed.), *Battlefields of Europe*, London, Hugh Evelyn, 1965

Charteris, Brigadier-General John, *Field Marshal Earl Haig*, London, Cassell, 1929

Charteris, Brigadier-General John, *At GHQ*, London, Cassell, 1931

Christie, Norm, *'For King and Empire': The Canadians at Vimy*, Winnipeg, Bunker to Bunker Books, 1992.

Cooper, Bryan, *The Ironclads of Cambrai*, London, Souvenir Press, 1967

Crozier, Brigadier-General F.P., *A Brass Hat in No Man's Land*, London, Cape, 1930

Cutlack, F. M. (ed.), *War Letters of General Monash*, Sydney, Angus & Robertson, 1935

Dancocks, Daniel G., *Welcome to Flanders Fields: The Canadians at Ypres, 1915*, Toronto, McClelland & Stewart, 1988

Dancocks, Daniel G., *Legacy of Valour: The Canadians at Passchendaele*, Edmonton, Hurtig Publishers, 1989

Davidson, Major-General Sir John, *Haig, Master of the Field*, London, Peter Nevill, 1953

Davies, Frank and Graham Maddocks, *Bloody Red Tabs: General Officer Casualties in the Great War*, London, Leo Cooper, 1995

Digby, Peter, *Pyramids and Poppies: The South African Brigade 1915–1919*, South Africa, Ashanti Publishing, 1993

Dunlop, Colonel John K., *The Development of the British Army, 1899–1914*, London, Methuen, 1938

'Edmonds, Charles', *see* Carrington, Charles

Edmonds, Brigadier-General Sir J. E. (ed.), *History of the Great War: Military Operations, France and Belgium* (14 volumes), London, Macmillan and HMSO, 1922–49

Ewing, John, *The History of the 9th (Scottish) Division, 1914–1919*, London, Murray, 1921

Falkenhayn, General Erich von, *General Headquarters, 1914–1916*, London, Hutchinson, 1919

Falls, Cyril, *Marshal Foch*, Edinburgh, Blackie, 1939

Falls, Cyril, *The First World War*, London, Longman, Green, 1960

Farrar-Hockley, A. H., *The Somme*, London, Batsford, 1964

Farwell, Byron, *The Great Anglo-Boer War*, New York, Norton, 1976

Farwell, Byron, *The Great War in Africa*, New York, Norton, 1986

Ferrero, Professor Guglielmo, *Documents Relating to the Great War*, London, Fisher Unwin, 1915

French, Major the Hon. Gerald, *The Life of Field Marshal Sir John French, First Earl of Ypres*, KP, GCB, OM, GCVO, KCMG, London, Cassell, 1931

French of Ypres, Field Marshal the Viscount, *1914*, London, Constable, 1919

Foch, Marshal Ferdinand (trans. Colonel T. Bentley Mott), *The Memoirs of Marshal Foch*, London, Heinemann, 1931

Fox, Frank, *The Battles of the Ridges: Arras and Messines, March-June 1917*, London, Arthur Pearson, 1918

Gardiner, A.G, *The War Lords*, Toronto, Dent, 1915

Gardner, Brian, *The Big Push: The Somme, 1916*, London, Sphere Books, 1968

Goldhurst, Richard, *Pipeclay and Drill: J.J. Pershing, the Classic American Soldier*, New York, Reader's Digest Press, 1977

Griffiths, Paddy, *Battle Tactics of the Western Front, 1916–1918*, New Haven, Conn., Yale University Press, 1994

Gilbert, Martin, *First World War*, London, Weidenfeld & Nicolson, 1994

Gough, General Sir Hubert, *The Fifth Army*, London, Hodder & Stoughton, 1931

Gough, General Sir Hubert, *The March Retreat*, London, Cassell, 1934

Gough, General Sir Hubert, *Soldiering On*, London, Arthur Barker, 1954

Hankey, Lord, *The Supreme Command, 1914–1918* (2 volumes), London, Allen & Unwin, 1961

Harington, General Sir Charles, *Plumer of Messines*, London, Murray, 1935

Harris, J.P., *Men, Ideas and Tanks, 1903–1939*, Manchester, Manchester University Press, 1995

Henig, Ruth, *The Origins of The First World War*, London, Routledge, 1989

Hindenburg, Field Marshal Paul von, *Out of My Life*, London, Hutchinson, 1920

Holmes, Professor Richard, *War Walks*, London, BBC Publications, 1996

Holt, Toni and Valmai, *Battlefield Guide to the Somme*, London, Leo Cooper, 1996

Horne, Alistair, *The Price of Glory: Verdun, 1916*, London, Penguin Books, 1975

Jackson, Bill and Edwin Bramall, *The Chiefs: The Story of the UK Chiefs of Staff*, London, Brassey's, 1992

James, Lawrence, *Imperial Warrior: The Life and Times of E. M. Allenby*, London, Weidenfeld & Nicolson, 1993

Kruger, Rayne, *Good Bye, Dolly Gray*, London, Cassell, 1959

Keegan, John, *The Face of Battle*, London, Cape, 1976

Kennedy, Paul M. (ed.), *The War Plans of the Great Powers, 1880–1914*, London, Allen & Unwin, 1979

Laffin, John, *British Butchers and Bunglers of World War One*, Gloucester, Alan Sutton, 1992

Lewis, Cecil, *Sagittarius Rising*, London, Peter Davies, 1966

Liddell Hart, B. H., *A History of the First World War* (2 volumes), London, Cassell, 1970

Liddell Hart, B. H., *The Tanks* (2 volumes), London, Cassell, 1959

Lloyd George, David, *War Memoirs* (6 volumes), London, Ivor Nicholson & Watson, 1933–6

Ludendorff, General Erich, *My War Memories*, London, Hutchinson, 1919

McCarthy, Chris, *The Somme: The Day-by-Day Account*, London, Arms & Armour Press, 1993

McCarthy, Chris, *The Third Ypres, Passchendaele: The Day-by-Day Account*, London, Arms & Armour Press, 1995

Macdonald, Lyn, *1915: The Death of Innocence*, London, Headline Books, 1993

Marshall-Cornwall, General Sir James, *Haig as Military Commander*, London, Batsford, 1973

Masefield, John, *The Old Front Line, or The Beginning of the Battle of the Somme*, London, Heinemann, 1917; London, Spurbooks, 1976

Maurice, Major-General Sir Frederick, *The Life of General Lord Rawlinson of Trent*, London, Cassell, 1923

Middlebrook, Martin, *The First Day on the Somme: 1 July 1916*, London, Allen Lane, 1971

Middlebrook, Martin, *The Kaiser's Battle: 21 March 1918*, London, Penguin Books, 1983

O'Shea, Stephen, *Back to the Front*, Vancouver, Douglas & MacIntyre, 1996

Parsons, I. M. (ed.), *Men Who March Away: Poems of the First World War*, London, Chatto & Windus, 1965

Pederson, P. A., *John Monash*, London, Allen & Unwin, 1984

Pederson, P. A., *The Commanders: Australian Military Leadership in the Twentieth Century*, London, Allen & Unwin, 1984

Pershing, General John J., *My Experiences in the World War*, New York, Frederick A. Stokes, 1931; New York, Da Capo Press, 1995

Prior, Robin and Trevor Wilson, *Command on the Western Front*, Oxford, Blackwell, 1992

Prior, Robin and Trevor Wilson, *Passchendaele: The Untold Story*, London, Yale University Press, 1996

Richards, Frank, *Old Soldiers Never Die*, London, Faber & Faber, 1933

Robbins, Keith, *The First World War*, Oxford, Oxford University Press, 1985

Simkins, Peter, *Kitchener's Army: The Raising of the New Armies, 1914–16*, Manchester, Manchester University Press, 1988

Simkins, Peter, *World War I 1914–1918: The Western Front*, Godalming, CLB Publishing, 1991

Sixsmith, Major-General E. K. G., *British Generalship in the Twentieth Century*, London, Arms & Armour Press, 1970

Smith-Dorrien, General Sir Horace, *Memories of Forty-Eight Years' Service*, London, John Murray, 1925

Terraine, John, *Mons: The Retreat to Victory*, London, Batsford, 1960

Terraine, John, *The First World War, 1914–1918*, London, Arrow Books, 1965

Terraine, John, *The Western Front, 1914–1918*, London, Arrow Books, 1970

Terraine, John, *The Smoke and the Fire: Myths and Anti-Myths of War 1861–1945*, London, Sidgwick & Jackson, 1980

Terraine, John, *White Heat: The New Warfare, 1914–1918*, London, Sidgwick & Jackson, 1982

Tuchman, Barbara, *The Proud Tower*, New York, Bantam Books, 1967

Tuchman, Barbara, *August 1914*, London, Papermac, 1980

Travers, Tim, *The Killing Ground*, London, Allen and Unwin, 1987

Uys, Ian, *Delville Wood*, South Africa, Uys Publishing, 1983

Wavell, Field Marshal Sir Archibald P., *Allenby: Soldier and Statesman*, London, Harrap, 1946

Winter, Denis, *Haig's Command*, London, Penguin Books, 1992

Williams, Jeffery, *Byng of Vimy*, London, Leo Cooper/Secker & Warburg, 1983

Woodward, David (ed.), *The Military Correspondence of Field Marshal Sir William Robertson, CIGS, December 1915-February 1918*, London, Army Records Society and The Bodley Head, 1989

INDEX